1996

FROMMER'S

COMPREHENSIVE
TRAVEL GUIDE

Belgium, Holland
& Luxembourg

4th Edition

by Susan Poole

MACMILLAN • USA

ABOUT THE AUTHOR

Raised in a Southern newspaper family, **Susan Poole** is author of several other Frommer Guides, including *Frommer's The Carolinas & Georgia* and *Frommer's Ireland on $45 a Day*. When she is not traveling, Ms. Poole divides her time between her home in Ireland and New York.

MACMILLAN TRAVEL

A Simon & Schuster Macmillan Company
15 Columbus Circle
New York, NY 10023

ISBN 0-02-860461-X

ISSN 1044-2413

Design by Michele Laseau

Maps by Geografix Inc. and Ortelius Design

SPECIAL SALES

Bulk purchases (10+ copies) of Frommer's Travel Guides are available to corporations at special discounts. The Special Sales Department can produce custom editions to be used as premiums and/or sales promotion to suit individual needs. Existing editions can be produced with custom cover imprints such as corporate logos. For more information write to: Special Sales, Macmillan, 15 Columbus Circle, 15th Floor, New York, NY 10023.

Manufactured in the United States of America

Contents

Around the Grand Duchy   425

SPECIAL FEATURE

Appendix   437

Index   441

List of Maps

About This Frommer Guide

What Is a Frommer Guide?   It's a comprehensive, easy-to-use guide to the best travel values in all price ranges—from very expensive to budget. The one guidebook to take along on any trip.

What the Symbols Mean

★ **Frommer's Favorites**   Hotels, restaurants, attractions, and entertainments you should not miss

$ **Super-Special Values**   Really exceptional values

In Hotel and Other Listings

The following symbols refer to the standard amenities available in all rooms:

A/C   air conditioning
TEL   telephone
TV   television
MINIBAR   refrigerator stocked with beverages and snacks

The following abbreviations are used for credit cards:

AE   American Express   ER   enRoute
CB   Carte Blanche   EU   Eurocard
DC   Diners Club   MC   MasterCard
DISC   Discover   V   VISA

Trip Planning with This Guide

USE THE FOLLOWING FEATURES

What Things Cost in   To help you plan your daily budget

Calendar of Events   To plan for or avoid

Suggested Itineraries   For seeing the countries and regions

What's Special About Checklist   A summary of each city's or region's highlights—which lets you check off those that appeal most to you

Easy-to-Read Maps   Walking tours, city sights, hotel and restaurant locations—all referring to or keyed to the text

Fast Facts   All the essentials at a glance: climate, currency, embassies, emergencies, safety, taxes, tipping, and more

OTHER SPECIAL FROMMER FEATURES

Cool for Kids   Hotels, restaurants, and attractions

Did You Know?   Offbeat, fun facts

Famous People   The nations' greats

Impressions   What others have said

An Invitation to the Reader

In researching this book, I have come across many wonderful establishments, the best of which I have included here. I am sure that many of you will also come across appealing hotels, inns, restaurants, guesthouses, shops, and attractions. Please don't keep them to yourself. Share your experiences, especially if you want to comment on places that have been included in this edition that have changed for the worse. You can address your letters to:

Susan Poole
Frommer's Belgium, Holland & Luxembourg, 4th ed.
c/o Macmillan Travel
15 Columbus Circle
New York, NY 10023

A Disclaimer

Readers are advised that prices fluctuate in the course of time, and travel information changes under the impact of the varied and volatile factors that affect the travel industry. Neither the author nor the publisher can be held responsible for the experiences of readers while traveling. Readers are invited to write to the publisher with ideas, comments, and suggestions for future editions.

Safety Advisory

Whenever you're traveling in an unfamiliar city or country, stay alert. Be aware of your immediate surroundings. Wear a moneybelt and keep a close eye on your possessions. Be particularly careful with cameras, purses, and wallets, all favorite targets of thieves and pickpockets.

Planning a Trip to the Benelux Countries

1

Perhaps nowhere else in all of Europe are there so many points of interest compressed into such a small area as the three countries of Belgium, Holland, and Luxembourg. Topping the list are such purely aesthetic attractions as lyrically beautiful landscapes, artistic masterpieces, cultural events, and intriguing reminder of a long and colorful history. There are also the more mundane (but essential) advantages of convenience, economy, and friendly populations, not to mention a host of travel delights—the exquisite food and drink of Brussels, the exuberant sociability of Amsterdam, and Luxembourg's sidewalk cafés; each country is unique, yet situated within a stone's throw (or a couple of hours) of each other. The diversity of attractions in the Benelux countries (the name comes from a Customs Union agreement signed in 1944 by all three governments while in exile) is enormous indeed.

1 Information, Entry Requirements, and Money

Sources of Information

The official tourist agency for each country maintains overseas branches that provide excellent in-depth information on a vast array of subjects, including special interests, hobbies, and attractions that are available in each country. You'll find national tourist office addresses given in the appropriate chapters; useful overseas addresses for all three countries are given below:

BELGIAN TOURIST OFFICE: **U.S.:** 780 Third Ave., New York, NY (☎ 212/758-8130); **Canada:** P.O. Box 760 Montréal PQ H4A 3S3 (☎ 514/484-3594); **U.K.:** 29 Princes St., London W1R 7R9 (☎ 0171/629-0230); **Belgium:** Rue du Marché aux Herbes 63, 1000 Brussels (☎ 02/504-03-90).

NETHERLANDS BOARD OF TOURISM: 225 N. Michigan Ave., Suite 326, Chicago, IL 60601 (☎ 312/819-0300; fax 312/819-1740); 25 Adelaide St. E., Suite 710, Toronto, ON M5C 1Y2, Canada (☎ 416/363-1577; fax 416/363-1470); 25–28 Buckingham Gate, London SW1E 6LD, England (☎ 0171/630-0451; fax 0171/828-7941).

LUXEMBOURG NATIONAL TOURIST OFFICE: 17 Beekman Place, New York, NY 10022 (☎ 212/935-8888); 36–37 Piccadilly, London W1V 9PA, England (☎ 0171/434-2800); or the **National Tourist Office (ONT),** rue d'Anvers 77, 1130 Luxembourg (☎ 48-79-99).

Entry Requirements

DOCUMENTS

If you're a citizen of the United States, United Kingdom, Canada, or most European countries, the only document you'll need to enter Belgium, Holland, or Luxembourg is a valid passport. If you're a citizen of another country, be sure to check on your country's status before you leave. None of the three Benelux countries requires a visa unless you plan to stay longer than three months within its borders. Nor are health or vaccination certificates required. Drivers need only produce a valid driver's license from their home country.

CUSTOMS

When Entering . . .

BELGIUM & LUXEMBOURG   Travelers over the age of 17 with passports from overseas or non-EU countries may bring in free of duty 200 cigarettes or 50 cigars or 250 grams of tobacco; 2 liters of still wine and 1 liter of spirits; and 1.75 ounces of perfume. Other goods must not exceed a value of BF 2,000 ($57). Citizens of EU countries are allowed to bring in 800 cigarettes, 400 cigarillos, 200 cigars, 1 kilogram of tobacco, 10 liters of spirits, 90 liters of wine (with a maximum of 60 liters of champagne), and 110 liters of beer. Other products and amounts of currency are not limited.

HOLLAND   Visitors 17 years and older from non-European countries may bring in 400 cigarettes or 100 cigars or 500 grams of tobacco; 1 liter of alcohol over 22 proof or 2 liters of alcohol under 22 proof or 2 liters of liqueur plus 2 liters of wine; and 50 grams of perfume. Other goods must not exceed a value of Dfl. 500 ($263). Those from an EU country may import the same as mentioned above for Belgium and Luxembourg.

When Returning to . . .

THE UNITED STATES   One inviolate rule for travelers: To avoid incurring unwarranted duty charges, *always* carry receipts for any articles you take along that were bought on previous trips abroad. Also, keep receipts for current foreign purchases together and accessible to show Customs officials when returning to the United States. U.S. citizens, regardless of age, may bring in foreign goods up to the value of $400 duty-free if they have been out of the country more than 48 hours and have not claimed these exemptions within a 30-day period. There is a 10% duty on the next $1,000 and 12% for all over the next $1,400. Restrictions within those allowances are 200 cigarettes, 100 non-Cuban cigars, and one bottle of perfume that is also trademarked in the United States. No meat, fruit, plants, soil, or other agricultural items may be imported. Special restrictions apply for military personnel and to the importation of antiques, automobiles, and motorcycles; the U.S. Customs Service will furnish details if you write them at Box 1301, Constitution Avenue, Washington, DC 20044.

Goods valued up to $50 may be mailed to the United States duty-free provided they don't exceed one a day to any one addressee. Be sure that all such packages are labeled "Gift—Under $50."

CANADA   Duty-free allowances are limited to $300 a year and a maximum of 200 cigarettes, 50 cigars, 2.2 pounds of tobacco, and 40 ounces of liquor. Gifts mailed from abroad should be plainly marked "Unsolicited Gift, Value Under $40."

UNITED KINGDOM   Duty-free allowances depend on whether your goods were bought in a duty-free shop within these three EU countries or in other non-duty-free shops. If you live in the United Kingdom, your duty-free purchases may include 800 cigarettes, 400 cigarillos, 200 cigars, 1 kilogram of tobacco, 10 liters of spirits, 90 liters of wine (with a maximum of 60 liters of champagne), and 110 liters beer. Other products and amounts of currency are not limited. The Customs regulation most rigidly enforced is the prohibition on importing animals or pets of any kind, and any violation incurs stiff penalties.

Money

TRAVELER'S CHECKS   For safety's sake, you'll want to carry most of your money in traveler's checks instead of cash. Arm yourself with about $100 worth of the currency of your entry country for those first few days' expenses; then cash traveler's checks as you need them—you'll usually get a better exchange rate with these than with cash. Try to avoid having to cash them on weekends or holidays when banks are closed: Exchange rates in hotels or shops are never as favorable. Needless to say, you should keep your traveler's checks separate from the record of their numbers so that if you should be so unlucky as to lose them, replacement is a simple matter.

CREDIT & CHARGE CARDS   Major credit and charge cards are widely accepted throughout the Benelux countries and can be a real convenience when you're traveling. Be aware, however, that you may be billed at an exchange rate that differs from the one in effect when you made the charge, and this may prove to be to your advantage or disadvantage.

If you have an ATM bank card, there are many places where you can use it in the Benelux countries. Check with your local bank for a directory of international services, or call CIRRUS (☎ toll free **800/424-7787**).

2   Health and Insurance

HEALTH

Before leaving home, be sure to pack any medical prescriptions or eyeglass specifications you may need when traveling. Medical facilities in Belgium, Holland, and Luxembourg are excellent. If you need a doctor, dentist, or hospital service, your hotel should be able to help you. Pertinent medical addresses are listed for each country.

INSURANCE

ON DEPARTURE   Before leaving home, check to be sure that your property insurance is up-to-date, with premium payments paid, and that you have full coverage for fire, theft, etc.

HEALTH/ACCIDENTS   If your present policy does not provide travel/accident and medical coverage when you're out of the country, check with your insurance carrier about temporary coverage for the duration of your trip. Most travel agents can arrange this, along with travel delay or cancellation and lost luggage insurance. When renting a car, the small premiums for both collision damage and personal accident insurance are a good investment. Although your credit- or charge-card company may offer such coverage when you use your card for car rentals, there may be difficulties in settling claims through such companies—the premiums are a small price to pay for peace of mind.

3   Tips for the Disabled, Seniors, Singles, Families, and Students

FOR THE DISABLED   Many hotels and restaurants now provide easy access for the handicapped, and some display the international wheelchair symbol in their brochures and advertising. It's always a good idea to call ahead to find out just what the situation is before you book. Holland's Schiphol Arrivals Hall (North) has a service to help the disabled through the airport, and the Netherlands Board of Tourism issues a "Holland for the Handicapped" brochure. There's also comprehensive assistance for the handicapped throughout the Netherlands Railway system. Inquire at the national tourist board offices in Belgium and Luxembourg for specific details on the limited resources in those countries.

An organization helpful to handicapped travelers is **Mobility International USA,** P.O. Box 10767, Eugene, OR 97440 (☎ **503/343-1284**; fax 503/343-6812) which charges a small annual fee and provides travel information for those with disabilities. A useful book for handicapped travelers is *Access to the World: A Travel Guide for the Handicapped,* by Louise Weiss, which can be ordered from Henry Holt & Co. (☎ toll free **800/247-3912**).

An organized tour package can make life on the road much easier. One well-established firm that specializes in travel for the disabled is **Evergreen Travel Service/Wings on Wheels Tours,** 4114 198th St. SW, Suite 13, West Lynnwood, WA 98036 (☎ **206/776-1184**).

FOR SENIORS   Nearly all major hotel and motel chains now offer a **senior citizen's discount,** and you should be sure to ask for the reduction *when you make the reservation*—there may be restrictions during peak days—then be sure to carry proof of your age when you check in (driver's license, passport, etc.). If you fancy organized tours, **AARP Travel Service** (see below) puts together terrific packages at moderate rates.

Membership in the following senior organizations also offers a wide variety of travel benefits: The **American Association of Retired Persons (AARP),** 601 E St. NW, Washington, DC 20049 (☎ **202/434-2277**) and the **National Council of Senior Citizens,** 925 15th St. NW, Washington, DC 20005 (☎ **202/347-8800**).

Major sightseeing attractions and entertainments also often offer senior discounts— *be sure to ask when you buy your ticket.*

FOR SINGLES   If you're traveling on your own you'll have to pay a single supplement for accommodations. One solution to the problem is to team up with another single to share a room at the doubles rate. One organization that can help with that problem is the **Travel Companion Exchange,** P.O. Box 833, Amityville, NY 11701 (☎ **516/454-0880**). Another alternative is to book an organized tour and have the tour operator team you with another single traveler. **Globus-Gateway**—whose tours to Belgium, Holland, and Luxembourg can be booked through travel agents—have been very successful in matching singles.

FOR FAMILIES   One of the most economical travel choices for families is to stay in self-catering cottages or flats, which cost less per person than hotels and B&Bs, and they have the added advantage of retaining a sense of family for children, who often feel a bit uneasy in a hotel setting.

An increasingly popular choice is a farmhouse holiday. Children and parents alike usually enjoy walking the fields and, more often than not, helping with farm chores. Although opportunities for farm stays are not as numerous in the Benelux countries as in some others, the national tourist offices for all three can help you locate possibilities.

As for keeping the children amused, what child wouldn't be happy exploring the castles that are scattered across the Benelux landscapes? Give your youngsters a head start with a short run-down on the people who built these fascinating structures and what happened within their walls, and you'll soon find their imaginations running wild. In the cities, small towns, and villages, the colorful pageantry of past centuries as depicted in numerous festivals will surely delight the younger set. In Holland, watch faces light up at the lilliputian "Holland in a Nutshell" miniatures at Madurodam, while Belgium's *Manneken Pis* will bring giggles and a sense of comradeship. Luxembourg's miniature train is a sure winner, too. Around all three countries, there are wildlife centers, and virtually every sightseeing attraction admits children at half price, while many offer family ticket discounts.

Remember, also, that your trip will be a happier one if the youngsters are involved in the planning—a map and travel brochures will do wonders for a restless child! Bring along a few simple games or books to relieve boredom during long stretches of travel.

FOR STUDENTS Before setting out, use your high school or college ID to obtain an International Student Identity Card from the **Council on International Educational Exchange (CIEE),** 205 E. 42nd St., New York, NY 10017 (☎ 212/661-1414), or 312 Sutter St., Room 407, San Francisco, CA 94108 (☎ 415/421-3473). It will entitle you to several student discounts. For inexpensive accommodations, as well as a great way to meet other traveling students, join **American Youth Hostels,** P.O. Box 37613, Washington, DC 20013-7613 (☎ 202/783-6161), which will, for a fee of $13.95, send a directory of hostels worldwide. They also issue Youth Hostel cards priced at $25 for ages 18 to 54, $10 for those under 18, and $15 for those over 55.

In Holland, the student travel organization NBBS is an invaluable source for cost-cutting assistance, with branches in main cities. Remember to *always* ask about student discount tickets for attractions and public transportation.

4 Alternative/Adventure Travel

EDUCATIONAL/STUDY TRAVEL There are few more exciting or satisfying travel experiences than a period spent abroad pursuing cultural studies while totally immersed in the day-to-day lifestyle of that culture. To help you decide among the many study programs offered in Belgium, Holland, and Luxembourg, contact the **Institute of International Education,** 809 United Nations Plaza, New York, NY 10017 (☎ 212/883-8200). If you're interested in summer study only, ask for their *Vacation Study Abroad* guide that costs about $25. More serious study, which carries academic credit, is covered in their *Academic Year Abroad,* with a price of about $30. In Holland, the **Foreign Student Service,** Oranje Nassaulaan 5, 1075 AH Amsterdam (☎ 020/715915), can furnish general information about study in that country.

WORK CAMPS A vacation spent as a work-camp volunteer can be a rewarding experience. In most cases, you pay your own transportation costs, but are furnished accommodations and meals in exchange for labor. A leading recruitment agency for American volunteers is **Volunteers for Peace,** Tiffany Road, Belmont, VT 05730 (☎ 802/259-2759). Your $10 annual contribution will bring you their newsletter and the *International Work Camp Directory.* There's another $150 charge for arranging a western European work-camp stay.

CYCLING Belgium, Holland, and Luxembourg are all ideal cycling country, and whenever you choose you can take your bicycle on a train. Rental bikes are available at virtually every railway station, and all three national tourist boards can help you plan an itinerary best suited to your personal stamina and time restraints. Holland's excellent *Cycling in Holland* is especially useful in that country, and organized bike tours can be arranged through **International Bicycle Tours,** 7 Champlin Sq. (P.O. Box 754) Essex, CT 06426 (☎ 203/767-7005); and **Cycletours,** Keizersgracht 181, 1016 DR Amsterdam, The Netherlands (☎ 20/627-4098; fax 20/627-9032).

5 Getting There

By Plane from North America

To select the best-priced tickets, you should know about fare structures, seasons, and other general rules of air travel. First, always shop around by calling all the airlines that fly to your destination. The lowest fares in all categories are offered during the off-season, which is generally November through March excluding the Christmas and New Year's holidays and during midweek (Monday through Thursday).

REGULAR & APEX FARES   The lowest fare category for all airlines is usually the **APEX** (Advance Purchase Excursion) rate, which carries restrictions: advance booking (anywhere from 7 to 30 days) and purchase of your round-trip ticket, minimum and maximum stays (usually a minimum stay of 7 days and a maximum stay of 21 days), and penalties for changing travel dates or for cancellation. The rates apply to weekdays only (Monday through Thursday). Tickets may be booked with an open return and are good for a maximum of a year.

Excursion fares are higher than APEX, but there's no advance-purchase requirement (although most do require a specified minimum stay). Regular fares include, in order of increasing expense, coach, business class, and first class. These tickets cost more, but they carry no restrictions. In coach you usually pay for drinks and the seats are not spacious, in business the drinks are free and the seats are wider, while in first class the amenities and services are the best with no additional charges.

In addition to structured fares, airlines often introduce special promotional discounted fares and attractive fly-drive packages. Always check the travel sections of your local newspapers for advertisements about these.

OTHER GOOD-VALUE CHOICES • Bucket Shops   More politely referred to as consolidators, these companies purchase large blocks of unsold seats from the airlines and sell them to the public at deep discounts (20% to 35% off regular fares). Terms of payment may vary from the last minute to 45 days in advance. Check your local newspaper's travel sections for their ads.

• Charter Flights   A charter is a one-time flight between two predetermined points, for which the aircraft is reserved months in advance. Charter flights, booked through a reliable travel agent, often offer the best value for the dollar. Many now come with discount car rentals and accommodations that let you freewheel around the Benelux countries on your own. However, before paying for a charter, check the restrictions on your ticket or contract. You may be asked to purchase a tour package and pay far in advance, and you'll pay a stiff penalty (or forfeit the ticket entirely) if you cancel. Some charter-ticket sellers offer an insurance policy for a legitimate cancellation (like hospitalization or a death in the family). Be aware that a charter might be canceled if the plane is not full. Most travel agents can arrange charter flights.

• Promotional Fares   All airlines offer promotional fares from time to time. Most have days-of-the-week or other restrictions; but no matter when you plan to fly or by whatever airline, it pays to keep a sharp eye out for newspaper, television, or radio advertising in order to take advantage of the considerable savings offered by these fares.

• **Package Tours**   For those travelers who feel more secure if everything is prearranged—hotels, transportation, sightseeing excursions, luggage handling, tips, taxes, and even meals—a package tour is the obvious choice, and it may even help save money.

A good travel agent can tell you about the many excellent conducted coach tours offered in the Benelux region, with all-inclusive rates well below any you could manage on your own. Three leading, reliable operators that include these countries in many of their reasonably priced European tours are: **Globus-Gateway/Cosmos Tours,** 150 S. Roblos Ave., Suite 860, Pasadena, CA 91101 (☎ **818/339-0919,** or toll free **800/556-5454**); **American Express Travel Service,** P.O. Box 5014, Atlanta, GA 30302 (☎ toll free **800/241-7000**); and **Maupintour,** P.O. Box 807, Lawrence, KS 66046 (☎ toll free **800/255-4266**).

TO BELGIUM

Belgium is easily accessible from almost any point around the globe through its excellent **Zaventem Airport,** a free port with excellent duty-free shopping.

AIRLINES   No fewer than 35 international airlines fly into Brussels's Zaventem Airport; but all other things being equal, my personal preference is the national airline, **Sabena.** Their cabin crews seem to be imbued with a very special quality—Sabena calls it *savoir faire*—and take pride in perfection that's so characteristic of the Belgian people. Flying Sabena, in fact, means that my Belgium experience begins when I board the plane. For schedules and reservations, contact your travel agent or Sabena Belgium World Airlines, 720 Fifth Ave., New York, NY 10019 (☎ toll free **800/955-2000**); 401 N. Michigan Ave, Suite 1860, Chicago, IL 60611 (☎ **312/670-1900**); or 1001 De Maisonneuve Blvd. W., Suite 730, Montréal, PQ H3A 3C8 (☎ **514/845-2165**).

FARES   Airfares are one of the most volatile of all travel expenses, and the following are meant purely as a guide—be sure to check all available flights when you book. As we go to press, Sabena and U.S. airlines round-trip fares—New York/Brussels— were averaging $538 and up for APEX, $1,100 in coach, $2,072 in business class, and $3,446 in first class. Tax and Customs fees run just under $30. These fares, of course, all have seasonal variations.

TO HOLLAND

Amsterdam's **Schiphol Airport** is served by airlines from around the globe and is the home base of KLM, Holland's national airline. Opened in 1968, Schiphol is consistently rated the best in the world when international travelers are polled (it certainly gets my vote as the most efficient!). The terminal itself is a wonder of good organization, with signs in English and an automated baggage system that actually manages, 9 times out of 10, to have your luggage waiting by the time you've deplaned and made your way through a streamlined Customs desk and a well-planned escalator/moving-sidewalk network. There are even free luggage trolleys to eliminate the hassle of trying to find a porter (although they seem to be in abundant supply). There's also good bus service and a fast rail link to Amsterdam, as well as a taxi stand just outside the terminal. When it comes to duty-free shops, again Schiphol outdoes almost every other airport; there are more than 50 shops filled with more than 40,000 different items.

There is excellent, frequent train service from the arrivals lounge at Schiphol to Amsterdam, Rotterdam, and The Hague.

AIRLINES   Although most major airlines fly from North America to Amsterdam, my personal choice is Holland's national airline, **KLM.** Since its 1920 flight from Amsterdam to London (the first regularly scheduled air service anywhere in the world), KLM has grown to flights to 129 cities in 79 countries on six continents. From North America, there are flights to Holland from New York, Atlanta, Chicago, Houston, Los Angeles, Vancouver, Montréal, and Toronto. For information and booking, contact your travel agent or KLM, 437 Madison Ave., New York, NY 10022 (☎ **212/223-2860,** or toll free **800/777-5553**).

FARES   As we go to press, round-trip New York/Amsterdam fares were averaging $550 and up for APEX, $1,200 in coach, and $2,705 in business class. Add tax and Customs fees of about $30. All fares are subject to seasonal variations.

TO LUXEMBOURG

Luxembourg's modern **airport** is $3^1/2$ miles outside Luxembourg City, with a Luxair bus service into the central station for LF 150 ($4.30). City bus service from the city center, the youth hostel, and the central station costs LF 35 ($1) plus LF 35 ($1) per piece of luggage—but you should know that this service can be refused during peak hours (around noon) to those carrying a mountain of luggage. Taxi fare from the airport into the city is LF 700 ($20).

AIRLINES   For years, **Icelandair** has led all other airlines in providing the most direct and inexpensive way to reach Luxembourg from the United States. With departures from New York, Orlando, and Baltimore-Washington, and only one stop in Iceland—schedules from U.S. gateways are for various days of the week, daily from New York only in summer. Stopovers in Iceland of up to 21 days are allowed for no additional airfare.

Icelandair also has excellent connecting service from Luxembourg with **Luxair Airline** to London, Munich, Geneva, Amsterdam, Frankfurt, Nice, Paris, Rome, Zurich, Cyprus, and Copenhagen, as well as to other important European and Middle Eastern destinations by major carriers. Luxair is your best bet if you're travelling to Luxembourg from the United Kingdom or another European country, and **British Airways** has regularly scheduled service from London.

FARES   At press time, round-trip fares between New York and Luxembourg were in the following ranges, depending on season: $538 and up for APEX, $1,010 for regular coach fare. Attractive package rates—including accommodations at top hotels, all transfers, and breakfasts—are available, and car rentals can be arranged through Icelandair.

By Cruise Liner from North America

From my perspective there's no more romantic and relaxing way to travel to or from Europe than by ship. And, of course, Cunard's *Queen Elizabeth 2* provides the ultimate in luxury. It is currently the only liner offering regular transatlantic service between New York and Europe, and since it docks in Southampton, you can reach the Benelux countries via train, car-ferry, or airline from London. The transatlantic crossing takes five days, and Cunard offers terrific package fares that let you travel one-way by air, the other by ship at moneysaving prices.

"Luxury" hardly begins to describe your surroundings (a moneysaving tip—some of the B-grade staterooms are even more spacious than the A-grade line). There are four outstanding restaurants, a midnight buffet, morning and afternoon tea service, and 24-hour room service. If five days of leisure sound like a drag, consider just some of the activity options: deck sports, a Golden Door Spa with daily fitness classes, a jogging track, four swimming pools, a youth center with disco and video games, an adult center with games, a children's playroom, and a 530-seat theater showing first-run films. Those of a more studious nature might enjoy the celebrity lecturers, the library, or the computer learning center.

For current schedules and fares (including various packages that include land tours, hotel discounts, etc.), contact your travel agent or **Cunard Line Limited,** 555 Fifth Ave., New York, NY 10017 (☎ **212/880-7500,** or toll free **800/221-4770**).

From Europe

BY TRAIN

Rail service to the Benelux countries from major European cities is frequent, fast, and inexpensive. A first-class **Eurailpass** allows unlimited travel on the rail systems of 15 countries at a cost of $498 for 15 days, $648 for 21 days, $798 for one month, $1,098 for two months, and $1,398 for three months. The **Eurail Youth Pass** is available to those under 26 years of age at a cost of $578 for one month and $768 for two months. Both the Eurailpass and the Eurail Youth Pass must be purchased *before leaving the United States* and are available through travel agents.

The Channel tunnel was completed in 1994, and the first passenger trains began service in November. Trains from London (Waterloo Station) go to either Paris (Gare du Nord) or Brussels (Central Station); the trip between London and the two continental destinations takes just over three hours. At year end, there were two trips a day in each direction between London and both Paris and Brussels. The one-way fares varied from $154 for a first-class unrestricted ticket to $75 for a restricted, nonrefundable ticket. For reservations, call British Rail (toll-free **800/677-8585** in the U.S.).

For those with cars who want to use the Chunnel (a 35-minute trip), contact the Keith Prowse Company (☎ toll free **800/669-8687** in the U.S.).

TO BELGIUM   With the opening of the Chunnel, there will probably be a decline in the traditional rail service to Belgium (train to Dover, then jetfoil to Ostend, and continuation by train to Brussels or Antwerp). For up-to-date information, call British Rail (toll free **800/677-8585** in the U.S. or **0171/834-2345** in the U.K.).

TO HOLLAND   There are rail connections to Amsterdam from France, Germany, Spain, Switzerland, Italy, and Austria, and you can book in advance through any of the Netherlands Board of Tourism offices in the United States and Canada (see "Information, Entry Requirements, and Money," earlier in this chapter). International trains include the *Amsterdam/Brussels/Paris Express,* and connections in Brussels with the *North Express,* the *Ostend-Vienna Express,* the *Ostend-Moscow Express,* and the *Trans-Europe Express.*

TO LUXEMBOURG   The Luxembourg National Railways network has excellent connections with most major European destination cities; and if you're coming from either Holland or Belgium, the Benelux Tourrail Ticket (see "Getting Around," later in this chapter) is your best bet.

BY BUS

TO BELGIUM   There's good coach service to Belgium from most European centers, as well as between London and Brussels or Antwerp. From London's Victoria Station, the **City Sprint** service has several departures daily. Traveling time is just over six hours. For full details, contact **Hoverspeed Ltd.** (☎ **0171/730-0202** or **0181/554-7061** in the U.K.). From other major European cities, inquire at bus stations in your city of departure.

TO HOLLAND   There's good coach service to Holland from most European centers, as well as between London and Amsterdam (via Hovercraft), with two departures daily in the summer. Travel time is just over 10 hours. For full details, contact **Hoverspeed Ltd.** (see "To Belgium," above). Inquire at bus stations in your city of departure for schedules and booking. Connections through Brussels may be necessary.

TO LUXEMBOURG   There's very good motorcoach transportation between Luxembourg City and most major European cities, with the most direct connections generally from Brussels or major cities in Germany. Details can be obtained from coach companies in cities of departure.

BY CAR

The Benelux countries are crisscrossed by a dense, excellent network of major highways connecting them with other European countries, and distances are relatively short. Road conditions are excellent throughout all three Benelux countries, service stations are plentiful, and highways are plainly signposted. Traffic congestion in both Brussels and Amsterdam, however, can cause monumental tie-ups—in these two cities, it's best to park your car at your hotel garage and walk or use local transportation (the best way, incidentally, to see either city).

To drive in Belgium, Holland, or Luxembourg, you need only a valid passport, your U.S. driver's license, and a valid registration for your car.

BY BOAT FROM THE U.K.

TO BELGIUM   There's excellent boat and jetfoil service for foot passengers as well as cars and drivers between Dover/Folkestone in England and Ostend on the Belgian coast, with a minimum of eight sailings daily and sometimes as many as 18 per day during the peak tourist season. Channel crossings take about $3^{1}/_{2}$ hours by boat and just under 2 hours by jetfoil. It will pay for you to inquire about any midweek or weekend specials offered when you plan to travel. Schedules and exact fare information are available from British railway stations in the U.K.

TO HOLLAND   There's excellent Sealink car-ferry service for foot passengers as well as cars between London (via train to Harwich) and the Hook of Holland, where trains carry you on to Rotterdam, The Hague, or Amsterdam, with both day and night crossings. North Sea Ferries also operates a rail/sea service between Hull and Rotterdam (Europort). The crossing by ferry or jetfoil from Dover to Ostend, in Belgium, is slightly shorter, but entails more changes between rail and ship (rail to Brussels, change for Amsterdam, etc.). Details on schedules and prices can be obtained from British railway stations; in the United States, detailed information is available from Brit Rail Travel International, Inc. (☎ **212/575-2667**).

6 Getting Around

BY PLANE   The Benelux cities are so close together that air travel is really not worth the added expense unless time is a factor. Air service among these three countries is largely provided by **NLM City Hopper,** a subsidiary of Royal Dutch Airlines, which has frequent scheduled service to both Brussels and Luxembourg, as well as to Maastricht, Rotterdam, London, and Paris; from Maastricht to Eindhoven and London; from Eindhoven to Rotterdam, Hamburg, Paris, Zurich, and London. For current schedules, fares, and booking, call **020/674-7747** or **020/649-2781** in Amsterdam or toll free **800/777-5553** in the U.S.

BY TRAIN   Nondrivers will find one of the best railway systems in the world operating in these small countries. There is virtually no spot so remote that it cannot be easily and inexpensively reached by trains that are fast, clean, and always on time. As a frequent user of both trains and buses, I can tell you that this is a marvelous way to meet the people who live here, because the people of the Benelux countries spend as much time riding public transportation as they do behind the wheel of an automobile. My one caution also stems from personal experience: Schedules are exact—if departure is set for 12:01pm, that means 12:01pm precisely, not 12:03pm—and station stops are sometimes as short as three or four minutes, which means you must be fleet of foot in getting on and off. There have been times when I fully expected to see half my luggage go chugging off to my next destination, leaving the other half and me on the station platform because I didn't get aboard fast enough!

The five-day **Benelux Tourrail Ticket** is good for unlimited travel in all three countries (for any five days in a one-month period). It's a good buy at BF 6,050 ($172) for first class and BF 4,040 ($115) for second class.

Both Belgium and Holland have discount rail and bus passes for travel within their borders, and Luxembourg has good connections with both countries as well as discounted weekend and public-holiday passes. All three provide good service to other European countries. Bicycles are permitted on trains throughout the region, and in Belgium they can be rented at discount rates at many railway stations. You'll find details in the appropriate chapters.

BY BUS   Intercity coach service is frequent and reliable throughout the Benelux countries, and tourist offices, travel agents, and bus stations can furnish schedule and fare information.

In major cities, there is good bus and/or tram service, which means you can easily deposit the car at your hotel and enjoy the freedom from city driving woes.

BY TAXI   Taxi service is readily available and moderately expensive in major Benelux cities (see the appropriate chapters).

BY CAR   Without question, there's no better way to get around Belgium, Holland, and Luxembourg than by car. No other transportation gives you so much freedom to ramble at your own pace, either on or off the beaten path. You'll find specific requirements, rules of the road, gasoline information, automobile clubs and other driving assistance, and map recommendations in the appropriate chapters for each country.

Rentals   Virtually all major car-rental companies have offices in the three capital cities and some other large cities, although arranging a rental away from a metropolitan area can present problems. Names and locations are listed in the appropriate chapters for each country.

HITCHHIKING Hitchhiking is permitted (*not* encouraged!) in Belgium and Luxembourg, although prohibited on highways (however, you *can* stand on the approach road). It's officially forbidden in Holland, but many a blind eye is turned by officialdom to those standing in a safe spot to hitchhike.

Suggested Itineraries

The sheer diversity of historical, cultural, and entertainment attractions in Belgium, Holland, and Luxembourg is a strong argument for spending your entire holiday in the Benelux region, no matter how much or how little time you have available. Let's look at the possibilities of dividing your time among the three countries if your plans call for stays of one, two, and three weeks.

As you'll see, planning is simplified because distances are short and one-day excursions simple. My recommendation that you base yourself in the capital of each country is made in light of two basic considerations: You just won't be ready to leave any one of the three after just one or two days, and additional evenings will permit you to explore them further as well as feel the pulse of these fascinating cities. And—of prime importance to me, personally—you won't have to pack and juggle the luggage every day.

If You Have One Week

This time span allows only a brief introduction to the Benelux countries, so plan on two days in each capital city, with one day for excursions. Distances are so short between Brussels, Amsterdam, and Luxembourg, and train schedules so convenient, that your travel time will be no more than a few hours. Also, it's a simple matter to book ongoing European travel by air or by train from any of the three cities.

If You Have Two Weeks

This amount of time will allow you to experience the Benelux countries in surprising depth by allotting five days each to Belgium and Holland and three to Luxembourg, with a total of one full day for travel from one capital to another. You'll have to make some hard choices from the suggestions listed below.

BELGIUM Most of your sightseeing can be done in easy day trips from a Brussels base. After devoting your first two days to the city's sightseeing attractions, reserve the remaining three for day trips to your choice of the following destinations: medieval Bruges; historic Ghent; Ostend, Knokke, and other resorts along a 40-mile-long stretch of Belgian coast; Tournai, with its historic churches and museums; Mons and its nearby ruined castles and abbeys; Waterloo battlefield and the picturesque ruins of Villers-la-Ville abbey; Antwerp and its diamond cutters (via Mechelen, with its famous bell ringers); and Liège (home of Europe's oldest street market, held every Sunday).

HOLLAND No fewer than two full days should be allotted to the attractions and charms of Amsterdam. During the next three days, take your pick of day trips to: Aalsmeer, The Hague, Rotterdam, and Delft; the bulb fields and famous Keukenhof Gardens; the fishing villages of Volendam and Marken, with their traditionally garbed populace; the medieval town of Edam and the nearby concentration of windmills; a fascinating (eight-hour) tour of the enclosing dike and the Zuiderzee.

LUXEMBOURG Spend your first day exploring Luxembourg City, with its unique network of cliffside casements, impressive cathedral, Grand Ducal Palace, fortress remains, and European Center (a very good half-day coach excursion will give you a quick look at all these plus the nearby countryside). On one of the remaining days, take a day-long coach tour of the Ardennes region, to see Wiltz (site of the Battle of the Bulge in the winter of 1944–45), and the feudal castles at Esch-sur-Sûre, Clervaux, Vianden, and the Sûre Valley. On your second day, a half-day tour will take you to the Moselle Valley and the famous Bernard Massard Wine Cellars at Grevenmacher.

If You Have Three Weeks

With three weeks at your disposal, you can add two more days to your stay in both Belgium and Holland, and more in Luxembourg. You can then add several overnight destinations in each country, with ample time to travel between points.

BELGIUM Explore the lovely Belgian Ardennes from a base in Spa (which gave its name to a whole new concept of resort) and include a pilgrimage to Bastogne to tip your hat to Brigadier General MacAuliffe and his 101st Airborne Division troops who made such a valiant stand here in 1944. Stop in at tiny Durbuy ("the world's smallest town"), then ramble through wooded hills and charming villages set on the banks of rushing rivers. Move on to the Meuse Valley (a good base is Dinant, where its ancient citadel sits on a rocky perch high above the town) to visit historic Namur and some of the many castles and abbeys that dot the countryside hereabouts.

HOLLAND In Holland, it comes down to an "either/or" choice of how to spend your additional two days. Head north to unique Friesland, Holland's ancient province that preserves its own language and lifestyle, and to Groningen and Drenthe, both so individualistic that you may well feel you've added another distinct European culture to your Benelux stay.

LUXEMBOURG From your day-trip overview of the Grand Duchy's lovely countryside, select a favorite rural town or village and hie yourself off for a serene overnight in one of the many comfortable inns that abound outside the city—it's the perfect end to your Benelux holiday.

7 Where to Stay

Belgium, Holland, and Luxembourg established the Benelux Hotel Classification System back in 1978, then updated the standards in 1994. Each establishment that accepts guests must publicly display a sign indicating its classification (from "1" for those with minimum amenities to "5" for deluxe, full-service hotels). The national tourist boards do an excellent job of providing full accommodations listings and advance booking for their visitors. The Belgian and the Netherlands Tourist Offices will reserve accommodations for you at no charge before you leave home—contact them well in advance at the addresses given in "Information, Entry Requirements, and Money," earlier in this chapter. The Luxembourg Tourist Office will furnish a complete list of accommodations in the Grand Duchy, and bookings can be made directly with hotels or through travel agents.

Hotels

In all three countries, you can choose between luxury (expensive) hotels in city or rural locations, smaller urban hotels with moderate rates and somewhat limited facilities, and charming, family-run country inns. All will be spotlessly clean, and whatever your choice, you can count on a staff dedicated to personal attention and excellent service, from one end of the price scale to the other. The rates quoted always include service charge (usually 15%) and tax, and, in most cases, breakfast.

Prices for double occupancy begin at $250 or up at deluxe hotels, $85 to $250 for the next category down, $60 to $85 in the moderate range, and $45 to $60 for the least expensive. Rates for singles will be slightly lower. You should know, however, that many hotels have a variety of room rates, regardless of classification, and it's sometimes possible to pay less if you'll settle for a shower instead of full bath facilities. Also, weekend or midweek rates are often available. Be sure to inquire about any special rates in effect when you book.

IN BELGIUM   Brussels, often called the "capital of Europe," has some of the most sophisticated luxury hotels in the world; although their prices are in the deluxe category, they represent good value for the dollar. In style and decor, these hotels range from old world to art nouveau to streamlined modern. Amenities may include such extras as swimming pools, tennis courts, health-club facilities, and/or a fine dining room. In most cases, there will be a concierge to arrange almost any service you might need, from theater tickets to restaurant and travel reservations. Outside the city are several outstanding hotels housed in elegant old mansions with magnificent lawns and gardens that also rate the "deluxe" classification. Nearly all these top-grade establishments include a continental breakfast in their rates.

In the moderate price range, Brussels boasts outstanding values in clean, comfortable, and well-run hostelries, with counterparts around the country. Most have rooms both with and without private bath, and the rate nearly always includes a continental breakfast. Motels are not as common as in the United States, but the list is growing, and most offer standard, modern rooms and conveniences. Budget travelers will have to search a bit to find accommodations below the moderate range, but with a little effort (and help from local tourist boards), they can find some in most parts of the country.

IN HOLLAND   Rates at all of Holland's hotels, regardless of price category, generally include a continental breakfast (in Holland this means lots of cheese, fresh breads, sliced meats, etc.), a 15% service charge, and VAT. The Netherlands tourist offices listed earlier in this chapter can furnish a current hotel directory for the entire country that lists hotels by town, showing facilities and prices, as well as their "Benelux classification" based on degree of comfort.

It's a good idea to book your first few nights in advance; this can be done through your travel agent, directly with the hotel of your choice, or through the **Netherlands Reservation Centre,** P.O. Box 404, 2360 AK Leidschendam, The Netherlands (☎ **070/20-25-00**). If you use this latter service, for which there is no fee, allow enough time for them to confirm your reservation before you leave home.

Once you're traveling around Holland, local VVV (tourist information) offices will gladly make hotel reservations to meet your requirements; there may be a small charge for this service.

Amsterdam, as you might expect, has the widest choice of hotels, some of which are luxury establishments, with prices to match, but when it comes to value received, your dollars will be well spent. In style and decor, they range from old world to ultramodern to canalside charm. In most cases there will be a concierge to arrange almost any service you need.

In the moderate price range, there are outstanding values in clean, comfortable, and well-run hostelries around the country as well as in the larger cities. Many have rooms both with and without private bath, priced accordingly. Budget travelers may have to search a bit to find accommodations below the moderate range, but a little effort combined with help from local VVV offices will locate them.

IN LUXEMBOURG   You can expect to pay LF 6,500 ($185) and up double for luxury hotel accommodations in Luxembourg City; city hotels in the moderate range charge about 2,400 to 2,800 ($68 to $80), while budget hotels charge LF 1,500 ($43). In the provinces, small hotels and inns run about LF 1,800 ($51) or less.

Bed-and-Breakfasts

In Holland, it's possible to stay with private families in virtually every region. Because there's no national listing of such homes, however, you'll have to check with local tourist offices for names, addresses, and prices (inexpensive in most cases). One word of warning: If you plan to travel in July or August and would like this kind of accommodation, you'd better make arrangements several months in advance. The Netherlands tourist offices in the United States, listed in "Information, Entry Requirements, and Money," earlier in this chapter, can help with addresses of local VVV offices.

In Belgium and Luxembourg, B&B means a small hotel or pension.

Youth Hostels

The Benelux countries are literally filled with high-grade hostels, in both urban and rural settings. Prices for a dormitory bed run around $9; with breakfast, about $11.

The first thing to be said about hostels is that, although they're called "youth hostels," you'll be welcomed if you're 6 or 60. The second thing is that in order to use them you must have an **International Youth Hostel Card,** which must be purchased before you leave home. It's available from **American Youth Hostels, Inc.,** P.O. Box 37613, Washington, DC 20013, and costs $10 for those under 18, $25 for those ages 18 to 54, and $15 for those over 55. For an additional $13.95 you can purchase their *International Youth Hostel Handbook* (Vol. I, *Europe and the Mediterranean*).

IN BELGIUM   If you'd like a list of the hostels in Belgium, write directly to **Infor-Jeunes,** rue du Marché-aux-Herbes 27, 1000 Brussels; or **Info-Jeugd,** Gretrystraat 28, 1000 Brussels.

IN HOLLAND   For details on the more than 45 hostels in Holland, contact **Stichting Nederlandse Jeugdherberg Centrale (NJHC),** Prof. Tulpplein 4, 1018 GX Amsterdam, The Netherlands (☎ **020/55-131-55**).

IN LUXEMBOURG   Hostels are located in Beaufort, Bourglinster, Echternach, Ettelbruck, Grevenmacher, Hollenfels, Lultzhausen, Luxembourg City, Troisvierges, Vianden, and Wiltz. Standards are exceptionally high in all. For complete details, including extra services available, get the "Youth Hostels Guide" from the **Luxembourg Youth Hostels Association,** place d'Armes 18, Luxembourg (☎ **2-55-88**).

Camping

Recreational vehicles are increasingly popular with touring families, and there are outstanding camping grounds throughout Belgium, Holland, and Luxembourg. Prices run between $8 and $15 per night, depending on location and facilities. Each country can furnish a directory of its campgrounds.

IN BELGIUM   The Belgian Tourist Office can supply a brochure listing camping facilities, or you may write for a directory and other information to: **Royal Camping and Caravanning de Belgique,** rue de la Madeleine 31, 1000 Brussels (☎ **02/513-12-87**).

IN HOLLAND   The Netherlands tourist offices can supply a directory of all camping facilities, but all bookings must be made directly. Bikers should inquire about the special eight-day "Hospitable Bike Camping" package available during spring and summer: Contact **"Gastvrije Fietscampings" Foundation,** P.O. Box 93200, 2509 BA Den Haag, The Netherlands (☎ **070/14-71-47**). Again, summer reservations must be made well in advance.

IN LUXEMBOURG   Luxembourg's camping grounds are numerous and well equipped. The government rates each one and requires that the rate be shown at the entrance. Be advised that it's illegal to park a vehicle used for lodging on public roads or in public places. For a free guide listing all camping facilities in Luxembourg, contact the tourist offices listed in "Information, Entry Requirements, and Money," earlier in this chapter.

Farm Holidays

Although this is a fairly new trend in Benelux countries, more and more farm families are offering home stays to tourists. This is a marvelous way to experience life inside those farm complexes that still retain their medieval, farmyard-centered architecture and/or Belgium's more modern farmhouses. Breakfast will always be provided, and it's often possible to arrange for a home-cooked evening meal. Arrangements (including prices) must be made directly with farm families; for detailed information, contact individual tourist offices at addresses given in "Information, Entry Requirements, and Money," earlier in this chapter.

8   Where to Dine

If I were asked to give one unconditional guarantee for your Benelux visit, it would be this: You will eat well, and you'll never be far from a good place to eat. Standards of ingredients, preparation, presentation, and service are extraordinarily high throughout Belgium, Holland, and Luxembourg—and the number and diversity of restaurants is nothing short of staggering. This is perhaps the one single area in which you'll get the best value for your dollar in every price range from budget to deluxe.

To some degree, dining out in the Benelux countries takes on the aspect of entertainment. Whereas many Americans view dinner as a prelude to an evening, for people here dinner *is* the evening. They would no more tolerate rudeness or being rushed through their meal than they would bad food poorly prepared. And therein lies a caution—be sure you allow enough time for each meal. That impeccable service may not be indifferent, but to Americans it can sometimes seem slow. My advice is to do as the natives do and give yourself over to the occasion. Relax, enjoy your surroundings and your companions, and you may even find that the wait between courses enhances your appreciation of each new dish.

In all three Benelux countries, sidewalk cafés are as numerous as blooms in a Dutch tulip field—and it's a safe bet that you will quickly become as fond of them as are the locals. What may come as a surprise is the fact that these charming eateries lining city streets and village squares have the same high standards as the upscale restaurants.

There's a very good reason for this: People in the Benelux countries like to eat. And they like to eat well.

Food

BELGIUM'S CUISINE

For the most part, the food you eat in Belgium will be based on French cuisine; however, Belgian chefs add their own special touches, incorporating such native specialties as *jambon d'Ardenne* (ham from the hills and valleys of the Ardennes) or savory *boudin de Liège* (a succulent sausage mixed with herbs). Almost every menu lists *tomates aux crevettes* (tomatoes stuffed with tiny, delicately sweet North Sea shrimp and light, homemade mayonnaise)—filling enough for a light lunch and delicious as an appetizer. A very special treat awaits visitors in May and June in the form of Belgian asparagus, and from October to March there's endive, which is known in Belgium as *witloof* (white leaf).

If you're basically a steak-and-potatoes person, you're in good company, for Belgians dote on their *bifteck et frites,* which is available at virtually every restaurant—even when not listed on the menu. Lest you think that *frites* in Belgium are the same as french fries at home, let me hasten to enlighten you. These are twice-fried potatoes, as light as the proverbial feather. They're sold in paper cones on many street corners and (in my opinion) are best when topped with homemade mayonnaise, though you may prefer curry or even your usual catsup. Frites will also accompany almost anything you order in a restaurant.

Seafood anywhere in Belgium is fresh and delicious. *Moules* (mussels) are absolutely addictive and are a specialty in Brussels, where you'll find a concentration of restaurants along the Petite rue des Bouchers that feature them in just about every guise that can be imagined. *Homard* (lobster) also comes in a range of dishes, and a heavenly Belgian creation is *écrevisses à la liègeoise* (crayfish in a rich butter, cream, and white-wine sauce).

HOLLAND'S CUISINE

Dutch national dishes tend to be of the ungarnished, hearty, wholesome variety—solid, stick-to-your-ribs stuff. A perfect example is *erwtensoep,* a thick pea soup cooked with ham or sausage that provides inner warmth against cold Dutch winters and is filling enough to be a meal by itself. Similarly, *hutspot,* a potato-based "hotchpotch," or stew, is no-nonsense nourishment that becomes even more so with the addition of *klapstuk* (lean beef). Hutspot also has an interesting intangible ingredient—a story behind its name that's based on historical fact.

Seafood, as you might imagine in this traditionally seafaring country, is always fresh and simply—but very well—prepared. Fried sole, oysters from Zeeland, mussels, and herring (fresh in May, pickled other months) are most common. In fact, if you happen to be in Holland for the beginning of the herring season, it's an absolute obligation—at least once—to interrupt your sidewalk strolls for a "green" herring from a pushcart; prices run the gamut from dirt-cheap to astronomical. The Dutch are also uncommonly fond of eel.

At lunchtime, you're likely to find yourself munching on *broodjes,* small buttered rolls usually filled with ham and cheese or beef. Not to be missed are the delicious, crêpelike pancakes called *pannekoeken* or *poffertjes,* which are especially good topped with apples, jam, or syrup. Desserts at any meal lean toward fruit with lots of fresh cream, ice cream, or *appel gebak,* a lovely and light apple pastry.

So much for native dishes. Holland, however, has imported so many international dishes that one—the Indonesian *rijsttafel,* a feast that brings small portions of anywhere from 15 up to as many as 30 different dishes to table to eat on a base of plain rice—has become such a favorite it can almost be considered "national." Be assured that should you develop a yearning for some other national cuisine while in Holland, it will probably be available.

LUXEMBOURG'S CUISINE

Luxembourg, like Belgium, leans toward French cuisine but appropriates bits and pieces from neighboring Germany. Smoked pork and sauerkraut (*jud mat gardebo'nen*) is a favorite. A Luxembourg specialty is roast thrush (*grives*), and if you're there during the game season, try wild boar. The pastries are outstanding, and the ubiquitous pastry shops are a constant temptation.

Drink

In a word, *beer.* It's Belgium's national drink; it's practically an institution at any Dutch lunch and after work; and Luxembourg's breweries compare favorably with any in the world. Imported beers are freely available, but you won't want to miss sampling at least a few of the more than 300 brews produced in Belgium alone. Most are lagers, but local breweries have been extremely inventive in adding such unexpected ingredients as cherries.

Wine lovers will find the best vintages from France widely available, and there are some remarkably good table wines at quite low prices. Luxembourg's Moselle Valley wineries produce outstanding riesling, rivaner, auxerrois, and several sparkling wines that rival champagne but are less expensive.

Holland's native *jenever,* a deceptively smooth, mild-tasting gin, rivals beer in the affections of the Dutch. It comes in a colorless *jonge* (young) form or the amber-colored *oude* (old) version—either can be lethal if not sipped slowly, or if sipped in extravagant quantities.

9 What to Buy

While the Benelux countries are not known for bargain prices, they do constitute one of the best marketplaces in the world when it comes to the variety of goods for sale. After all, it was trade that has built and sustained these nations from earliest times. Consequently, there is within their boundaries a vast supermarket of goods produced at home and abroad.

IN BELGIUM   Look especially for antique lace—a bit pricey, but good value. European antiques may be found in Brussels shops and street markets. Excellent galleries in Brussels offer paintings by recognized masters of the past as well as budding masters of the future. As the diamond-cutting center of Europe, Antwerp offers excellent shopping for these precious stones. "Chocoholics" will be in heaven here. Other gustatory delights to take home include thin, spicy biscuits known as speculoos.

IN HOLLAND   Serious shoppers in Holland will be attracted to delftware from Delft and Makkum, the antiques shops of Amsterdam and The Hague, and diamonds from master cutters in Amsterdam. Others will look for charming, old-fashioned clocks, crystal, and pewter. Farther down the "serious" (and also "expensive") list come chocolates, cheeses, liqueurs, flower bulbs, and wooden shoes.

IN LUXEMBOURG Paintings by artists from the Grand Duchy, as well as the rest of Europe, are featured at many fine galleries in the city of Luxembourg. Porcelain plates decorated with painted landscapes of the duchy, as well as cast-iron wall plaques produced by Fonderie de Mersch depicting castles, coats-of-arms, and local scenes are excellent souvenirs of a Luxembourg visit.

Getting to Know Belgium

2

ACROSS THE CENTURIES, ALL THE GREAT POWERS OF EUROPE HAVE FOUGHT FOR, WON, lost, and won again domination over the territory that now goes by the name of Belgium and the adjoining lands once known collectively as the "Low Countries." The attraction? A network of waterways—the Scheldt and Meuse Rivers among the most prominent—connecting far-flung inland points to strategic North Sea ports.

The story of those great struggles across the landscapes of fragmented holdings of the counts (counties) and dukes (duchies) of Flanders, Liège, Brabant, and Hainaut is a fascinating one. Played out sometimes on the fields of battle, again in the marriage bed, and occasionally around the treaty table, its convoluted plot touches every phase of European history. As the tale unfolds, the stage is set for the entrance of today's Belgium, an independent nation at last, with a population vividly reflecting its heritage from a host of alien conquerors.

1 Geography, History, and Politics

Geography

It's a small, compact country—11,800 square miles (about the size of Maryland) and only 150 miles across from the sea to the Ardennes—yet Belgium holds within its borders astounding scenic diversity. Water is a crucial part of the landscape. Rivers that run from south to north carve out the great Meuse and Scheldt basins, then hurry to empty into the North Sea in estuaries that serve as the natural harbors that have, from the beginning, attracted the covetous attention of the great European powers. Major highways trace river routes. In the Ardennes, heavy rain swells rushing mountain streams most years. Annual rainfall in Belgium, in fact, is almost double that in Holland.

THE REGIONS IN BRIEF For a graphic picture of the two ethnic regions, Flanders and Wallonia, draw an imaginary east-west line across the country just south of Brussels. The northern provinces of East and West Flanders, Antwerp, Limburg, and part of Brabant are Flemish. This is where you'll find the medieval cities of Ghent, Mechelen, Ypres, and Bruges; the port and diamond industry of Antwerp (home of the great Flemish painter, Rubens); and some 40 miles of gorgeous beaches along the coast of West Flanders. It is also home to approximately one million more inhabitants than Wallonia.

South of that imaginary line, Wallonia consists of the provinces of southern Brabant, Hainaut, Namur, Liège, and Luxembourg. The art cities of Tournai and Mons, historic castles by the score, and scenic resort towns of the Ardennes are the tourist attractions of this beautiful region.

History

Dateline

- 58 B.C. Julius Caesar marches against Belgae tribes.
- A.D. 800 Charlemagne named Emperor of the West and introduces agricultural reform, creating the title of count.

➤

BEFORE THE 12TH CENTURY Julius Caesar marched his Roman legions against the ancient Belgae tribes in 58 B.C., and for nearly five centuries thereafter, great roads were built to carry a procession of goods from all over the Continent to these all-important ports. Thus it was that this corner of Europe early on began its tradition of commerce and trade.

From the beginning of the 5th century, Roman rule gave way to the Franks, who held sway for nearly 200 years. In the year 800 the great Charlemagne was named Emperor of the West; he instituted an era of agricultural reform, setting up underling local rulers known as counts. In 814 Charlemagne's death resulted in the bold usurping of absolute power by the very counts on whom he had relied for allegiance to his Carolingian throne. By 843 his son had acceded to the Treaty of Verdun, which split French-allied (but Dutch-speaking) Flanders in the north from the southern (French-speaking) Walloon provinces.

Then came Viking invaders, who attacked the northern provinces, and a Flemish defender known as Baldwin Iron-Arm became the first Count of Flanders in 862; his royal house eventually ruled over a domain that included the Netherlands and lands as far south as the Scheldt in France. Meanwhile, to the south, powerful prince-bishops controlled most of Wallonia from their seat in Liège.

As Flanders grew larger and stronger, its cities thrived and its citizens wrested more and more self-governing powers. Bruges (Brugge) emerged as the leading center of European trade as its monopoly on English cloth attracted bankers and financiers from Germany and Lombardy—with nary an inkling that its fine link to the sea, the River Zwinn, would eventually choke with silt and leave it high and dry, forever landlocked. Ghent (Gent) and Ypres (Ieper) locked into the wool trade and prospered. Powerful trade and manufacturing guilds emerged and erected splendid edifices as their headquarters. In Liège, great fortunes were made from iron foundries and the manufacture of arms.

THE 12TH TO THE 15TH CENTURY The era from the 12th through the 15th century was one of immense wealth, much of which was poured into fine public buildings and soaring Gothic cathedrals that survive to this day. During the 14th century, wealthy patrons made possible the brilliant works of such Flemish artists as Van Eyck, Bosch, van der Weyden, and Memling.

As cities took on city-state status, the mighty Count of Flanders, with close ties to France, grew less and less mighty; in 1302, France's Philip the Fair made a bid to annex Flanders. In his bold grab for such a rich prize, however, he reckoned without the stubborn resistance of Flemish common folk. Led by the likes of Jan Breydel, a lowly weaver, and Pieter de Coninck, a butcher—and armed with little more than spiked iron

Dateline

- **843** Treaty of Verdun splits Flanders from the Walloon provinces.
- **1302** Philip the Fair of France defeated at "Battle of the Golden Spurs" in Flanders.
- **1328** Beginning of Hundred Years' War in Flanders.
- **Mid-1400s** Philip the Good, Duke of Burgundy, gains control of Low Countries.
- **1400s–1600s** Era of rule by Franks.
- **1500s** Era of Flemish artists—Van Eyck, Bosch, van der Weyden, and Memling.
- **1555** Philip II of Spain introduces Inquisition persecution against Protestants.
- **1568–1648** William the Silent leads Protestants' rebellion to regain control of seven northern provinces.
- **1713** Spanish Netherlands (including Belgium) comes under rule of Hapsburgs of Austria.
- **1795** French rule of Belgium begins.
- **1831** Belgium becomes a constitutional monarchy headed by King Leopold.
- **1914** German forces invade Belgium.
- **1918** End of World War I.
- **1940** King Leopold III surrenders Belgium to Germany at outset of World War II.
- **1944** Benelux Union with Holland and Luxembourg signed in London by governments in exile.
- **1945** World War II ends.

➤

- 1950 Leopold III returns to throne.
- 1951 Leopold III abdicates in favor of his eldest son, Baudouin.
- 1971 Moderate constitutional reforms are introduced granting some regional autonomy.
- 1992 Both branches of the legislature vote to ratify the Treaty on European Union.
- 1993 King Baudouin dies. He is succeeded by his brother, Albert II (born 1934).
- 1993 Constitution is amended to create a federal state composed of the autonomous regions of Flanders and Wallonia, the bilingual city of Brussels, and autonomous German-speaking communities.

balls attached to chains that could be twirled overhead and aimed at the enemy with deadly accuracy—they rallied to face a heavily armored French military. A confrontation arose on July 11, 1302, in the fields surrounding Kortrijk, and when it was over, victorious artisans and craftsmen scoured the bloody battlefield, triumphantly gathering hundreds of golden spurs from slain French knights. Their victory at the "Battle of the Golden Spurs" is celebrated to this day by the Flemish.

Sadly, that valiant resistance had been crushed by 1328 and Flanders suffered under both the French and the English during the course of the ensuing Hundred Years' War, eventually building strong ties with England. When Philip the Good—Duke of Burgundy in the mid-1400s and ally of England's King Henry V—gained control of virtually all the Low Countries, he was able to quell political troubles in Ghent and Bruges, but unable to prevent extensive looting in Dinant or the almost total destruction of Liège. His progeny, through a series of advantageous marriages, managed to consolidate their holdings into a single Burgundian "Netherlands." Brussels, Antwerp, Mechelen, and Louvain attained new prominence as centers of trade, commerce, and the arts.

By the end of the 1400s, however, Charles the Bold, last of the dukes of Burgundy, had lost the Duchy of Burgundy to the French king on the field of battle, and once more French royalty turned a covetous eye on the Netherlands. Marriage to Mary of Burgundy, the duke's heir, appeared a sure route to bring the Netherlands under French rule, and a proposal (in reality an ultimatum) was issued to Mary to accept the hand of the French king's eldest son. To the French prince's consternation, Mary promptly wrote a proposal of marriage to Maximilian of Austria. The Austrian's acceptance meant that the provinces became part of the extensive Austrian Hapsburg empire.

THE 16TH & 17TH CENTURIES It was a grandson of that union, Charles V—born in Ghent and reared in Mechelen—who for 40 years presided over most of Europe, including Spain and its New World possessions; he was beset by the Protestant Reformation, which created dissension among the formerly solid Catholic populace. It all proved too much for the great monarch, and so he decided to abdicate in favor of his son, Philip II of Spain.

Philip took control in an impressive ceremony in the Palace of the Coudenberg in Brussels in 1555. An ardent Catholic who spoke neither Dutch nor French, he brought the infamous instruments of the Inquisition to bear on an increasingly Protestant — and increasingly rebellious—Netherlands population. The response from his Protestant subjects was violent: They went on a rampage of destruction that in a single month of 1556 saw churches pillaged, religious statues smashed, and religious works of art burned.

An angry Philip commissioned the zealous Duke of Alba, his most able general, to lead some 10,000 Spanish troops in a wave of retaliatory strikes that should have brought the rebels to their knees. The atrocities committed by order of the Duke of Alba as he swept through the "Spanish Netherlands" constitute a tale of horror virtually unparalleled in the annals of European history. He was merciless—when the Catholic counts of Egmont and Hornes tried to intercede with Philip, he put them under arrest for six months, then had them publicly decapitated in the Grand' Place in Brussels as an example meant to intimidate other "softies."

Instead of submission, however, this sort of intimidation led to a brutal conflict that lasted from 1568 to 1648. Led by William the Silent and other nobles who raised private armies, the Protestants fought on doggedly until finally independence was achieved for the seven undefeated provinces to the north, which became the fledgling country of Holland. Those in the south remained under the thumb of Spain and gradually returned to the Catholic church. As an act of revenge, Holland closed the River Scheldt to all shipping, and Antwerp, along with other Flemish cities, withered away to a shadow of its former prosperity.

THE 18TH & 19TH CENTURIES   At the beginning of the 18th century the grandson of Louis XIV ascended the Spanish throne, thereby bringing French domination to Spain's possessions in the Low Countries. That domination was short-lived, however; in 1713 the Spanish Netherlands was returned to the Hapsburgs of Austria. A series of revolts against reforms instituted by Joseph II, Emperor of Austria, helped to consolidate a sense of nationalism among the Low Country natives, who—for the first

Did You Know?

- Belgium's 15-mile track from Brussels to Mechelen, opened in 1835, was the first railway on the European continent.

- The St. Hubert Arcades, opened to the public in 1847, were the first covered shopping arcades in Europe.

- The oldest private houses still in existence in Europe are nos. 10 and 12, rue Barre Saint-Brice in Tournai, dating from 1175.

- The world's first diamond engagement ring was bestowed on Mary of Burgundy by Archduke Maximilian in Bruges in 1477.

- The bobbin-lacemaking technique, as differentiated from needle lacemaking, originated in Bruges.

- The *Lion of Waterloo* mound was created by Liège women (*botteresses*) who carried soil from the battlefield in wicker baskets on their backs.

- The manufacture of playing cards has been a Belgian specialty for over 100 years, with the largest factory in Turnhout exporting between five and seven million packs a year.

- The "Little Blue People" known as Smurfs were the creation of Belgian artist Pierre Cuilliford, who named them *Schtroumpf,* which translates—loosely— as "whatchamacallit."

- For several centuries, the citizens of the town of Geel have taken mentally disturbed persons into their homes, nourishing them and caring for them, earning the town the title "Town of Charity."

time—began to call themselves Belgians. Austrian-Belgian conflicts raged fiercely until 1789, when all of Europe was caught up in the French Revolution.

In 1795, Belgium wound up once more under the rule of France; it was not until Napoléon Bonaparte's crushing defeat at Waterloo—just miles from Brussels—that Belgians began to think of national independence as a real possibility. Its time had not yet come, however, for the Congress of Vienna decreed that Belgium once more unite with the Netherland provinces of Holland. It didn't take long for the Dutch to learn that governing the unruly Belgians was more than they had bargained for, and by 1830 rioting in Brussels was the last straw. A provisional Belgian government was formed with an elected National Congress. On July 21, 1831, Belgium officially became a constitutional monarchy when a relative of Queen Victoria's, Prince Leopold of Saxe-Coburg, became king, swearing allegiance to the constitution.

The new nation set about its own version of the industrial revolution with a vengeance: developing its coal and iron natural resources, and rebuilding its textile, manufacturing, and shipbuilding industries. The country was hardly unified by this process, however, for most of the natural resources were to be found in the French-speaking Walloon regions in the south, where prosperity returned much more rapidly than in Flanders.

The Flemish—many of whom felt more closely allied to the Dutch nation across their border—felt they were being shunted into a secondary position and bitterly resented the greater influence of their French-speaking compatriots. The acquisition of a French-speaking Belgian colony in the African Congo region was viewed by many as further evidence of domination by an oppressive enclave, and there were increasing signs of trouble within the boundaries of their own country.

THE 20TH CENTURY It took yet another invasion to bring a semblance of unity. When German forces swept over the country in 1914, the Belgians mounted a defense that made them heroes of World War I—even though parts of the Flemish population openly collaborated with the enemy, hailing them as "liberators" from Walloon domination. Still, tattered remnants of their national army—led by their "soldier-king," Albert I—held a tiny strip of land between De Panne and France for the entire four years of the war.

With the coming of peace, Belgium found its southern coal, iron, and manufacturing industries reeling, while the northern Flemish regions were moving steadily ahead developing light industry, especially around Antwerp. Advanced agricultural methods yielded greater productivity and higher profits for Flemish farmers. By the end of the 1930s the Flemish population outnumbered the Walloons by a large enough majority to install their beloved language as the official voice of education, justice, and civil administration in Flanders.

With the outbreak of World War II, Belgium was once more overrun by German forces. In the face of overwhelming military superiority, King Leopold III decided to surrender to the invaders, remain in Belgium, and try to soften the harsh effects of occupation. By the war's end he was imprisoned in Germany, and a regent was appointed as head of state. His controversial decision to surrender led to bitter debate when he returned to the throne in 1950, and in 1951 he stepped down in favor of his son, Baudouin.

During Baudouin's 42 years as king, much progress was made in achieving harmony among Belgium's linguistically and culturally diverse population. During the 1970s efforts were made to grant increasing autonomy to the Flemish and Walloons

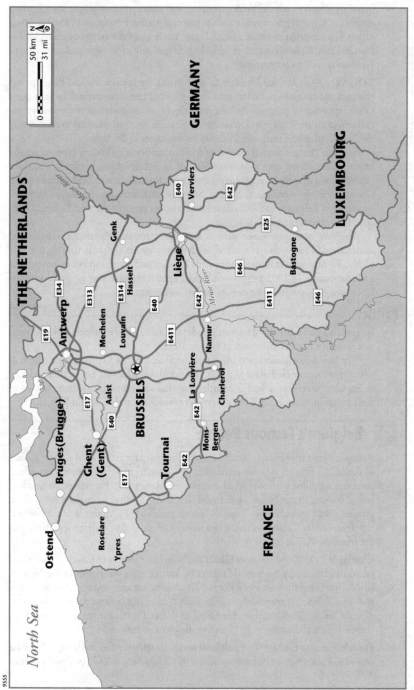

North Sea

THE NETHERLANDS

GERMANY

LUXEMBOURG

FRANCE

Ostend
Bruges (Brugge)
Roselare
Ypres
Ghent (Gent)
Aalst
Tournai
Mons-Bergen
BRUSSELS
Antwerp
Mechelen
Louvain
La Louvière
Charleroi
Namur
Hasselt
Genk
Liège
Verviers
Bastogne

Meuse River
Meuse River

E19
E34
E313
E314
E40
E17
E40
E17
E42
E411
E42
E411
E42
E40
E42
E46
E411
E46
E25
E40
E42

0   50 km
0   31 mi

N

9555

Belgium

in the areas where each was predominant, as well as to apportion power to each group within the national government and the political parties. Finally, in 1993, the constitution was amended to create a federal state, made up of the autonomous regions of Flanders and Wallonia, together with the bilingual city of Brussels and autonomous German-speaking communities.

TODAY Against a long history of occupation by foreign troops, Belgium has emerged as a natural site for the coming together of European nations in their quest to achieve unity of purpose. Its long centuries of accommodation make it a sympathetic host for the European Union and its strategic location was vital in establishing the North Atlantic Treaty Organization headquarters in Brussels.

Belgium's long history as a center of trade continues; it's a leading exporter among industrial countries, with more than 50% of its industrial production destined for export. Along with high-technology industry, traditional crafts—like lacemaking and tapestry weaving—continue to flourish. Scores of international organizations are headquartered in Belgium, and Brussels is home base for possibly the world's largest concentration of international diplomats.

Together with most other western European nations, Belgium has experienced something of a recession and relatively high unemployment (almost 10%) in the early 1990s. To deal with this, the government has imposed certain spending restrictions and raised taxes. In 1993 Belgium embarked upon a multiple-year program to transfer certain state-owned businesses to private ownership.

Politics

Belgium is a parliamentary democracy under a constitutional monarch, Albert II, who succeeded his brother Baudouin as king in 1993.

The legislature is composed of a Senate and Chamber of Representatives, both of whose members are elected for four years. Difficulties in achieving a consensus on issues of linguistic diversity, as well as on other political and economic matters, has led to the formation of many coalition governments since the end of World War II.

2   Belgium's Famous People

Bruegel, Pieter (the Elder) (ca. 1525–69) Dismissed for centuries as a mere "painter of peasants," Bruegel is today recognized as a giant of mid-16th-century art whose paintings are filled with allegorical and proverbial meaning. He trained in Antwerp before moving to rue Haute 1132 in Brussels in 1563 where he painted some of his greatest works including his "Seasons" paintings, *Peasant Wedding*, and the brilliant *The Procession to Calvary*—the first in a series of religio-political allegories referring to the rebellion against Spain.

Charles V (1500–58) Born in Ghent to Philip I and Joanna of Castile, Charles was raised in Flanders by his aunt, Margaret of Austria, who was regent in the Netherlands. Inheriting the vast Holy Roman Empire, he became embroiled in the many wars of religion that erupted during the Reformation and became the standardbearer of the Counter Reformation. He failed to defeat Protestantism. He divided his empire before abdicating in 1558 and retiring to a monastery.

Franck, César (1822–90) A Belgian-French composer. After studying at Liège he moved to Paris where he became organist at St. Clotilde and in 1872 professor of organ at the Paris Conservatory. Among his famous works are the Symphony in D minor, the *Variations Symphoniques* for piano and orchestra, and the *Trois Chorals* for organ.

Hergé   (1907–83) Cartoonist and creator of Tintin, the boy reporter, and his dog, Snowy.

Maeterlinck, Maurice   (1862–1949) Symbolist author who wrote in French. His works influenced the pre–World War I generation with their mysticism, ennui, and sense of impending doom. He won the Nobel Prize for literature in 1911. Among his famous works is *Pelléas et Mélisande* (1892), which inspired Debussy's opera.

Magritte, René   (1898–1967) Surrealist painter whose works contain startling juxtapositions of realistic images. Magritte is practically synonymous with surrealism.

Rubens, Peter Paul   (1577–1640) Influential baroque painter. Born in Westphalia, Rubens and his family returned to Antwerp where he trained as a painter. In 1600 he went to Italy where he spent eight years in the service of the Duke of Mantua before returning to Antwerp in 1608. More than 2,000 paintings have been attributed to his studio. Among his most famous monumental works are *Raising of the Cross* (1610), *Descent from the Cross* (1611), and *The Assumption,* all painted for the cathedral at Antwerp. He also worked for the French, Spanish, and English courts. His works are filled with dynamic, exuberant figures—especially voluptuous, buxom females.

Simenon, Georges   (1903–89) Prolific Belgian-born author of novels and short stories, Simenon is most famous for his creation of Inspector Maigret in his series of crime novels.

Vesalius, Andreas   (1514–64) Flemish anatomist. He became professor of anatomy at the University of Padua where he produced his *De Humani Corporis Fabrica,* based on his dissections of human cadavers. He was criticized because his work overthrew many previously held superstitions and traditional religious tenets.

Yourcenar, Marguerite   (1903–87) Brussels-born author and the first woman to be elected to the Académie Francaise. *Hadrian's Memories* and many of her other works have been translated into dozens of languages.

3   Art and Architecture

Art

Despite its small geographic size, Belgium has exerted a significant influence on the Western art world. The works of Hieronymus Bosch, Bruegel, Rubens, van Dyck, the brothers Van Eyck, and Magritte represent only a fraction of the treasures you'll see gracing the walls of Brussels's Musée Communal and Musée d'Art Ancien, the Museum of Fine Arts in Tournai, the Groeninge Museum in Bruges, and Ghent's Museum of Fine Arts.

The Golden Age of Flemish painting occurred in the 1400s, a century dominated by the so-called "primitive" artists, whose work was almost always religious in theme, usually commissioned for churches and chapels, and was largely lacking in perspective. As the medieval cities of Flanders flourished, so did the Flemish school of painting, as princes, wealthy merchants, and prosperous guilds became patrons of the arts.

In the 15th century, the function of art was still to praise God and illustrate religious allegory, but **Jan Van Eyck** (ca. 1390–1441), one of the earliest Flemish masters, brought a sharp new perspective to bear on traditional subject matter. His *Adoration of the Mystic Lamb,* created with his brother Hubert for St. Bavo's Cathedral in Ghent, incorporates a realistic landscape into its biblical theme.

The "primitives" sought to mirror reality, to portray both people and nature exactly as they appeared to the human eye, down to the tiniest detail, without classical distortions or embellishments. These artists would work meticulously for months—even years—on a single commission, often painting with a single-haired paintbrush to achieve a painstakingly "lifelike" quality.

One extraordinary artist of the late 15th century and early 16th century was Hieronymus Bosch, who was born and worked in Hertogenbosch. Little is known about his life and training, but his works stand today as seeming forerunners of surrealism, filled as they are with fabulous beasts, bizarre plants, and monstrous figures that supposedly were inspired by folk tales, allegories, and religious literature. Among the most famous of these grotesqueries are *The Garden of Earthly Delights, The Last Judgment,* and *The Temptation of St. Anthony.*

Bosch probably influenced an even greater Flemish artist of the 16th century who lived and worked for many years in Antwerp. From 1520 to 1580 Antwerp was at its height. It was one of the world's busiest ports and banking centers; as such it eclipsed Bruges as a center for the arts. Many of the artists working here looked to the Italian Renaissance masters for their models of perfection. Although he studied in Italy, **Pieter Bruegel the Elder** (ca. 1525–69) integrated Renaissance influences with the traditional style of his native land. He frequently painted rural and peasant life, as in his *Wedding Procession,* on view at the Musée Communal in Brussels.

Although Bruegel painted fewer than 50 oils, and finished another 250-plus drawings and etchings, he is considered a great 16th-century artist whose works are filled with allusions and allegorical references to the politics and culture of the period. He pioneered in painting scenes of snow and ice as in *The Hunters in the Snow;* his marine engravings are magnificent and exact in their detail; he transferred many biblical dramas to the Low Countries, as in *The Tower of Babel,* which also graphically portrays the most advanced construction methods of the century. In fact, all his paintings seem to provide more visual excitement because of the many actual, plausible, and explicit period details.

There is also another side to Bruegel—the fabulist, the creator of bizarre, dreamlike symbols reminiscent of Bosch. Many of these works, depicting the Dutch rebellion against the Spanish, are filled with death, destruction, machines of war, fire, conflict, decay, and corruption. Much of the symbolism is obscure to us today, but it would have been clear to the contemporary Flemish audience full of hatred toward their Spanish masters. Among these paintings is *The Temptation of Saint Anthony.* Others comment on the morality of contemporary society and the rampant profiteering and greed exemplified by *Big Fish Eat Little Fish, Avarice,* and the rest of the "Seven Deadly Sins" series. All of Bruegel's pictures and engravings warrant close examination of the details which reveal the depth of the satire. Some of his most famous paintings were completed between 1559 and 1568 when he painted *The Battle Between Carnival and Lent, The Netherlandish Proverbs,* and *Children's Games,* all satirical studies of society; and *Mad Meg* and *The Fall of the Rebel Angels,* both of which seem to deal with the political situation of the time. In 1563 Bruegel moved to Brussels where he lived at rue Haute 132. Here Pieter and Jan, his two sons, also artists, were born, and here he produced such works as the wonderful "Seasons" landscapes—*Hunters in the*

Snow, The Corn Harvest, The Return of the Herd, The Storm, Hay-Making, The Peasant Wedding, and *Peasant Dance.* Among Bruegel's final works were those that related to current events although they were ostensibly based on New Testament themes like *The Procession to Calvary* and *The Numbering of the People at Bethlehem.* In both cases, Bruegel transfers the events to a wintery Flemish village. They culminate in *The Massacre of the Innocents,* which experts feel refers to the crushing repression by the Duke of Alba and his rule of terror. Again, the biblical story is transferred to a Flemish landscape so that even the soldiers are wearing the red cuirasses of the Spanish infantry and the cavalry wears the black cuirasses of the German mercenaries. Bruegel's legacy survived in his sons—Jan, who specialized in decorative paintings of flowers and fruits, and Pieter the Younger, whose reputation has suffered until modern times.

Peter Paul Rubens (1577–1640) was the most influential baroque painter of the early 17th century. The drama in his works, such as *The Raising of the Cross,* housed in the Antwerp cathedral, comes from the dynamic, writhing figures who people his canvases. His renditions of the female form gave rise to the term "Rubenesque" to describe voluptuous, buxom women who appear in his masterpieces.

Portraitist **Antony van Dyck** (1599–1641), one of the most important talents to emerge from Rubens's studio, served as court painter to Charles I of England, though some of his best religious work remains in Belgium. Look for the *Lamentation* in the Museum voor Schone Kunstenthe in Antwerp, and the *Crucifixion* in Mechelen cathedral.

Belgium's influence on the art world is by no means limited to the old masters. **James Ensor** (1860–1949) was a late 19th-century pioneer of modern art, producing such works as the *Entry of Christ into Brussels.* Ensor developed a broadly expressionistic technique, liberating his use of color from the demands of realism, and took as his subject disturbing, fantastic visions and images.

Surrealism easily broke ground in Belgium, perhaps because of the earlier Flemish artists with a penchant for the bizarre and grotesque, and attracted such artists as **Paul Delvaux** (1897–1989). The best known of the Belgian surrealists, however, was unquestionably **René Magritte** (1898–1967). His neatly dressed man in the bowler hat, whose face is always hidden from view, became one of the most famous images of the surrealist movement.

Architecture

Little remains from the early centuries after the collapse of the Roman Empire and it is not until after A.D. 1000 when the Romanesque style appears that we can really begin to discuss Belgian architecture per se. Even then it's difficult to talk about a Belgian style because the history of the area that was Belgium—that is, Flanders (East Flanders, West Flanders, Antwerp, Limburg, and part of Brabant) and Wallonia (Hainaut, Liège, Luxembourg, Namur, and the remainder of Brabant)—lends itself to no easy architectural definition or history. If a general statement can be made about Belgian-Dutch architecture (as distinct from that of Holland) it is that it drew its inspiration from the south and was more often directly influenced by France, whereas Holland was influenced by Germany.

To return to architectural history for a moment: The greatest example of the Romanesque in Belgium is Tournai's magnificent black marble cathedral in which the nave (dating from 1110) retains the original Romanesque fenestration. The east end of the cathedral is Gothic and the transepts are in a transitional style. Belgium also has a number of castles that exhibit Romanesque traces, such as the one in Antwerp's port, the Steen, and Ghent's Gravensteen Castle, which was the seat of the counts of Flanders.

During the Gothic period Belgian architecture was greatly influenced by French Gothic, especially in the 14th century. The basic floor plan of a Gothic cathedral is like a cross, with the long beam running from west to east. It's divided into the nave, where worshipers would sit, and the choir. Behind the choir there's generally a rounded apse, and an aisle called the ambulatory. The "crossbeam" of the cross is called the transept.

The entire structure is punctuated with pointed arches and spires, pointed Gothic vaults in place of rounded ceilings—everywhere points stretching upward to the heavens. The exteriors are covered by a filigree of stone and statuary.

The great ecclesiastical Belgian examples are St. Michael's Cathedral, in which the choir is in fact the earliest Gothic work in Belgium, and the churches of Notre Dame in Mechelen, St-Pierre in Louvain, and St. Bavo's in Ghent. Antwerp Cathedral is perhaps the most imposing example of late Gothic; it was begun in 1352 at the east end and the nave was completed in 1474.

Examples of great Gothic civic architecture also abound. In the 15th century Bruges became a center for the Hanseatic League, while other important commercial centers emerged in Ghent, Antwerp, Louvain, and Ypres. Each has a rich heritage of civic buildings from the period—guild halls, exchanges, warehouses, and wealthy merchant residences. Among the finer examples of this richly ornate architecture is the Cloth Hall at Ypres (built 1200–1304), the Cloth Hall in Mechelen, the Grande Boucherie in Ghent, and the Vieille Boucherie in Antwerp. Gothic style continued until the early 16th century when Renaissance decorative elements began to appear. The outstanding example of this Flemish mannerism is the Antwerp Town Hall built in 1561–65 by Cornelius Floris. The 17th century favored a more classical style.

During the 18th century Belgium developed a baroque style that is best exemplified in Brussels's Grand' Place where the buildings are richly decorated. After 1750 neoclassicism took over, influencing such urban designs as place Royale in Brussels, which was laid out by the French architect Barre.

Much Belgian civic architecture in the 19th century was classical, for example, the Théâtre de la Monnaie (1819). Again, architecture and urban planning were influenced by France, specifically by the Second Empire. A stroll along boulevard Anspach will reveal iron grillework and mansard roofs and other elements of this style. Two buildings remain from the period, the Palace of Justice and the Stock Exchange. The second is neobaroque, while the first, by Joseph Poelaert, is equally heavy although some believe it's more original.

Another style appeared briefly at the turn of the 20th century. Decorative in essence, it was called "art nouveau" in England and the United States but Jugendstil (coup de jouet) in Belgium and Holland. Glass and iron were art nouveau's prime materials, worked with decorative curved lines and floral and geometric motifs. Belgium produced one of its greatest exponents in Victor Horta (1861–1947); his work can be seen in Brussels where the Tassel House (1893) and the Hôtel Solvay (1895) are forerunners of the ambitious Maison du Peuple (1896–99) with its concave, curved facades and location within an irregularly shaped square. His most famous building, though, is the Innovation department store (1901) which, unfortunately, was destroyed by fire.

Modern architecture was largely introduced to Belgium by Henry van der Velde (1863–1957); he was interested in functionalism and had studied in Weimar at the school that eventually developed Bauhaus under Gropius.

4   Religion, Myth, and Folklore

RELIGION   The vast majority of Belgians are Catholic, although there is a sizable Jewish community and a smattering of Protestants. Throughout the centuries, Belgians—nobles and peasants alike—have proclaimed their faith by way of impressive cathedrals, churches, paintings, and holy processions. One of the most practical applications of that faith is attributed to a Liège priest, who established the first community of lay sisterhoods known as *begijnhois* (Beguine in English, *béguinage* in French) about 1189. These communities of widows and disadvantaged women enjoy a pious community life that is both a refuge and a source of companionship without being bound by religious vows. You'll find these charming clusters of quiet streets, small houses, a church, and a community hall right in the center of such cities as Bruges and Ghent, where they form a sort of village in the heart of the city.

MYTH & FOLKLORE   Folklore plays a large part in Belgium's national daily life, with local myths giving rise to some of the country's most colorful pageants and festivals, such as Ypres's Festival of the Cats. Bruges's pageants of the Golden Tree, and the stately Ommegang in Brussels. Antwerp owes its very name to the myth of a gallant Roman centurion who slew a despotic giant and cut off his hand, giving the city its "Red Hand of Antwerp" symbol. In Belgium's renowned puppet theaters, marionettes based on folkloric characters identify their native cities—Woltje (Little Walloon) belongs to Brussels, Schele to Antwerp, Pierke to Ghent, and Tchantchès to Liège.

5   Cultural and Social Life

In the northern provinces, some 5 ¹/₂ million inhabitants speak a derivation of German that evolved into Dutch and its Flemish variation, a legacy of the Franks. To the south, about 4 ¹/₂ million Walloons speak the language of France. In Brussels the two languages mingle. So strong is the feeling for each language in its own region, however, that along the geographic line where they meet it's not unusual for French to be the daily language on one side of a street while neighbors on the opposite side chatter away in Flemish. And throughout the country, road signs acknowledge both languages by giving multiple versions of the same place name—Brussel/Brussels/Bruxelles or Brugge/Bruges, for example. There is even one small area in eastern Belgium where German is the spoken tongue! Belgium, then, is left with not one, but three, official languages: Dutch, French, and German.

History has left its stamp on more than just language. In both Flanders and Wallonia people cling as tightly to their traditions and customs as they do to their speech. Religious lines are sharply drawn as well, with little mingling of Catholics,

IMPRESSIONS

Belgium suffers severely from linguistic indigestion.
—R. W. G. Penn, *Geographical Magazine*, March 1980

Protestants, and anticlericalists. In the area of public life that will most affect you as a visitor, you'll find three separate national tourism agencies offering assistance: one for Flanders, another for Wallonia, and yet another for that special case, Brussels. If that sounds complicated, it's not, for there's little overlapping and they work together with a smoothness that seldom reveals just which agency may be helping you.

In short, far from being a homogeneous, harmonious people with one strong national identity, Belgians take considerable pride in their strongly individualistic attributes. Do they get along with one another? Well, in a manner of speaking. After all, for hundreds of years both the Flemish and the Walloons were forced to adopt an outward appearance of compatibility with all sorts of alien rulers, yet time and again events revealed their strong inner devotion to independence: Thus the thoroughly in-dependent Flemish accept the fact that Brussels (located in their geographic territory) conducts the country's business in French, and Walloons head for the beaches of Flanders without a second thought. Virtually every Belgian is bilingual, with English thrown in for good measure. So they not only get on fairly well with each other, but they also make it easy for the visitor. With centuries of practice behind them, they are quite willing to adapt their language to the occasion, all the while fiercely protecting and preserving the heritage that is uniquely their own.

Courtesy based on mutual acceptance of differences is the prevailing rule among Belgians, and it's the thing you'll notice most on your first encounters, whether with salespeople in the shops, restaurant personnel, taxi drivers, or railway station porters. It is, however, a courtesy dispensed with a healthy dollop of reserve. Now, that sort of cautious courtesy could appear to be a cool aloofness that is rather off-putting. But don't be misled. If there is one characteristic all Belgians have in common, it's the passion with which they pursue any special interest—be it art, music, sports, or that greatest of all Belgian passions, food. Show your own interest in the subject at hand and coolness evaporates as you're welcomed into an affectionate fraternity.

Undoubtedly, the Belgian's appreciation for the good things of life springs from this passionate nature. Indeed, appreciation is at the bottom of a national insistence on only the best. Standards are high in every area of daily life, and woe betide the chef who tries to hoodwink patrons with less-than-fresh ingredients, the shopkeeper who stocks shoddy merchandise, or any service person who is rude—their days are surely numbered. Belgians—Flemish or Walloon—are eminently practical, and none will spend hard-earned money for anything that doesn't measure up.

Ah, but when standards are met, to watch Belgian eyes light up with intense enthusiasm is nothing less than sheer joy. Appreciation then moves very close to reverence, and it can be generated by perfection (or near perfection) in just about anything: from a great artistic masterpiece to a homemade mayonnaise of just the right lightness to one of Belgium's 300 or more native beers. If you have shared that experience with a Belgian companion, chances are you'll find your own sense of appreciation taking on a finer edge.

6   Performing Arts and Evening Entertainment

Nighttime in Brussels can be just about anything you want it to be. Cocktail bars vary from the old, established, almost "clubby" type to the avant-garde to the bizarre; and there are café theaters, a traditional puppet theater, café cabarets, dinner shows, night-clubs, concerts, ballet and opera and legitimate theater in season (September to May), jazz clubs, and discothèques. Elsewhere, major cities have good theater, concerts, and musical variety houses—but there are few sophisticated dinner shows or nightclubs, except for Antwerp, Liège, and resort areas along the coast and in some Ardennes locations.

Gambling casinos featuring roulette and baccarat can be found in Ostend, Blankenberge, Chaudfontaine, Knokke-Heist, Middelkerke, Namur, and Spa. To gain admittance, you must be over 21, present your passport and driver's license, and pay a small admission fee. Minimum bets are quite low, and you'll pay a 6% tax on your winnings. Never mind that the croupiers speak French—they're all expert linguists and will be quite happy to take your money in English.

For current information on after-dark entertainment during your visit, pick up a copy of **"BBB Agenda"** for a small charge at the Tourist Information Brussels office in the Town Hall, Grand' Place, Brussels (☎ 02/513-89-40).

MUSIC   Brussels is home to the Opéra National and the Belgium National Orchestra. They both tour other major cities, with performing seasons that are becoming more and more extended over the year. Check local venues to see what's on when you're there.

THEATER   Most theatrical performances are in French, and preopening "out of town" trial runs for plays destined for Paris are performed in Brussels. See Chapter 4 for more details on the Brussels theater. Outside Brussels, you'll frequently encounter local theatrical troupes, often quite good, although the performances will probably be in French or Flemish.

PUPPET THEATERS   A special word is in order about a rather special sort of theater—the wooden marionettes that have entertained Belgians for centuries. In times past, puppet theaters numbered in the hundreds nationwide (Brussels alone had 15), and the plays were much like our modern-day soap operas. The story lines went on and on, sometimes for generations, and working-class audiences returned night after night to keep up with the "Dallas" of the times. Performances centered around folklore, legends, or political satire.

Specific marionette characters came to personify their home cities: in Brussels, it was a cheeky ragamuffin named Woltje (Little Walloon); Antwerp had the cross-eyed, earthy ne'er-do-well, Schele; in Ghent, Pierke was modeled on the traditional Italian clown; and Liège's Tchantchès stood only 16 inches high and always appeared with patched trousers, a tasseled floppy hat, and his constant companion, the sharp-tongued Nanesse (Agnes).

Today a few Belgian puppet theaters still survive, and their popularity has increased in recent years after a decline following World War II, when bombing raids severely damaged many theaters and destroyed many marionettes.

7   Sports and Recreation

The sports-minded will find a wide variety of facilities available in Belgium. There are bowling alleys in most major cities, riding stables around the country (including many in the immediate vicinity of Brussels), racecourses in Ostend and Waregem, ice-skating rinks in Brussels, public swimming pools galore, tennis courts in every major location, canoeing clubs in several cities, a host of golf courses open to visitors, and there's good skiing around Liège in winter months.

For names and addresses of sports federations that can furnish details of what's on when you're in Belgium and how you can participate, contact the Belgian Tourist

Office in New York or at rue du Marché-aux-Herbes 63, 1000 Brussels
(☎ **02/504-03-90**), or the Brussels Tourist Information (T.I.B.) office in Town Hall,
Grand' Place, 1000 Brussels (☎ **02/513-89-40**). Local tourist offices also have this
kind of information.

There's also excellent fishing throughout the country. You'll need a license, which
is available at any post office; its cost will depend on the number of days you plan to
fish and the number of lines to be used. Any Belgian Tourist Office can furnish more
detailed information on where to fish for what, seasons, etc.

8 Food and Drink

Fortunately, Brussels's 1,500-plus restaurants come in all styles, sizes, cuisines, and
price ranges. French cooking prevails but there are some exquisite Belgian specialties
you shouldn't miss. If budgetary considerations are important, this is one place you
can dine well with a slim purse. However, it's my firm conviction that even those on
a tight budget should set aside the wherewithal for at least one big splurge in one of
Brussels's fine restaurants—expensive, but food for the soul as well as the stomach.

All your Belgian meals will not, however, be taken in city restaurants. I'll venture
a guess that you'll fall quite happily into the very Belgian habit of lunching at sidewalk cafés or simply munching on waffles or *frites* (french fries with a Belgian difference) from street vendors. Tiny village bistros and roadside cafés set out light or hearty
meals with as much pride and professionalism as their city cousins.

No matter where you eat, you should know that service will be professional but is
invariably slower than what you're probably accustomed to. Belgians don't just dine;
they savor each course—if you're in a hurry, you're better off heading for a street
vendor or an imported fast-food establishment.

Note: Most Belgian restaurants are open seven days a week from noon to 2:30pm
for lunch and from 7 to 10pm for dinner. These hours may vary, however.

THE CUISINE

Aside from virtually any of your own favorite French dishes, you'll find Belgian specialties on every menu. Seafood is always fresh, the Belgians swear they have the best
beef in the world, any vegetable becomes a delicacy, pastries and sweets are an art form,
and each course is presented with a flourish worthy of its ingredients. The following
are especially noteworthy:

Asperges à la Flamande   Lovely local white asparagus served with sliced or crumbled
egg and melted butter for dipping.

Bifteck   Steak, which comes in many forms: sautéed, served with butter or béarnaise
sauce; with marrow (entrecôte à la moelle); with cracked black pepper (steak au poivre).

Chicorée-Witloof   Belgian endive, wonderful when served wrapped in thin slices
of ham with a topping of cheese sauce.

Crevettes   Tiny shrimp from the cold waters of the North Sea, served in a variety of
ways: Look for *tomate aux crevettes* (tomato stuffed with shrimp and mayonnaise) and
croquettes de crevettes (crusty, deep-fried cakes).

Frites   Twice-fried french fries, lighter than any you've ever encountered, served
with bifteck or moules or in paper cones and topped with homemade mayonnaise or
catsup.

Gaufres   Those wonderful Belgian waffles; try them with sugar, fruit, and/or whipped cream.

Gaufres aux Fruits   Small, thin waffles filled with a prune or apricot mixture.

Gaufres de Liège   A heavy waffle topped with caramelized sugar.

Jambon d'Ardenne   Smoked ham from the Ardennes—positively addictive.

Lapin à Bière   Rabbit cooked in beer—inexpensive, hearty, and delicious.

Marcassin   Wild boar from the Ardennes, usually served roasted.

Moules   Mussels, a Belgian national dish.

Oie à l'Instar de Vise   Goose that has been boiled, then sautéed.

BEER & WINE

What to drink with all those tasty dishes? Why, beer—of course! Belgium is justly famous for its brewing tradition, and there are more than 300 brands produced within its borders (some believe it's probably 1,000). Needless to say, with such a choice it may take quite a bit of sampling to find a favorite (my own turned out to be Chimay, a dark, rich brew). Among names to look for that you won't find outside Belgium are those still brewed by Trappist monks, Orval and Westmalle; Faro, Krieklambiek, and Lambiek from the area around Brussels; and Leuven.

If, by chance, you're not a beer drinker, or want a change, the finest wines from France, Italy, Spain, Portugal, Luxembourg, and Germany are always available at prices way below what you'd pay at home.

9 Recommended Books

History

Fitzmaurice, John. *The Politics of Belgium: Crisis and Compromise in a Plural Society.* St. Martin's Press, 1983.
Gilliat-Smith, Ernest. *The Story of Bruges.* Gordon Press, 1983.
Kossman, E. H. *Low Countries: Seventeen Eighty to Nineteen Forty.* Oxford University Press, 1978.
Polasky, Janet L. *Revolution in Brussels, 1787 to 1793.* University Press of New England, 1987.

Art

Friedlander, Max J. *From Van Eyck to Bruegel.* Cornell University Press, 1981.
Klein, H. Arthur, and Mina C. Klein. *Peter Bruegel the Elder.* Macmillan, 1968.
Roberts, Keith. *Bruegel.* Salem House (Phaidon Color Library), 1983.

3

Planning a Trip to Belgium

PLANNING A VISIT TO BELGIUM IS EASY. GOOD TRANSPORTATION BY ALMOST ANY means is plentiful; getting around is a simple matter, whether you prefer to drive or use the excellent public transportation system; accommodations to suit every taste and pocketbook are plentiful throughout the country; sightseeing and nightlife provide an exciting combination of the old and the new; and you can look forward to some of the best dining you're likely to experience in a lifetime.

1   Currency and Costs

The **Belgian franc** (BF) is made up of 100 centimes, and notes are issued in 50-, 100-, 500-, 1,000-, 5,000-, and 10,000-franc denominations. Coins come in 1, 5, 10, and 20 francs, and it's a good idea to keep a small supply of these on hand for tips, telephone calls, and the like.

The Belgian Franc

For American Readers   At this writing $1 = approximately 35 francs (or 1 franc = 2.8¢), and this was the rate of exchange used to calculate the dollar values given in this book (rounded off).

For British Readers   At this writing £1 = approximately 53 francs (or 1 franc = 1.9p), and this was the rate of exchange used to calculate the pound values in the table below.

Note   The rates given here fluctuate from time to time and may not be the same when you travel to Belgium. Therefore this table should be used only as a guide:

BF	U.S.$	U.K.£	BF	U.S.$	U.K.£
1	.03	.02	500	14.29	9.43
5	.14	.09	750	21.43	14.15
10	.29	.19	1,000	28.57	18.87
20	.57	.38	1,250	35.71	23.58
25	.71	.47	1,500	42.86	28.30
30	.86	.57	1,750	50.00	33.02
40	1.14	.75	2,000	57.14	37.74
50	1.43	.94	2,500	71.43	47.17
75	2.14	1.42	3,000	85.71	56.60
100	2.86	1.89	3,500	100.00	66.04
125	3.57	2.36	4,000	114.29	75.47
150	4.29	2.83	4,500	128.57	84.91
200	5.71	3.77	5,000	142.86	94.34
250	7.14	4.72	6,000	171.43	113.21

What Things Cost in Brussels	U.S.$
Taxi from the airport to the city center	34.00
Métro from the airport to the city center	2.42
Local telephone call	.30
Double room at the Royal Windsor Hotel (deluxe)	341.00
Double room at the Hotel Arlequin (moderate)	84.00
Double room at the Sabina (budget)	54.00
Lunch for one at Falstaff (moderate)	24.00
Lunch for one at 'T Kelderke (budget)	14.00
Dinner for one, without wine, at Maison du Cygne (deluxe)	71.00
Dinner for one, without wine, at Falstaff (moderate)	32.00
Dinner for one, without wine, at the 'T Kelderke (budget)	17.00
Glass of beer	2.00
Coca-Cola	1.00
Cup of coffee	1.80
Roll of ASA 100 color film, 36 exposures	4.80
Admission to the Musée Communal	Free
Movie ticket	7.10
Theater ticket to the Opéra National	10.00–85.00

2 When to Go—Climate, Holidays, and Events

"In-season" in Belgium means mid-April through mid-October. The peak of the tourist season is July and August, and in all honesty, that's when the weather is at its finest. The weather, however, is never really extreme at any time of year; if you're one of the growing numbers who favor shoulder- or off-season travel, you'll find Belgium every bit as attractive during those months. Not only are airlines, hotels, and restaurants cheaper and less crowded during this time (with more relaxed service which means you get more personal attention), but there are also some very appealing things going on. For example, Brussels swings into its rich music season in April, and Tournai turns out for the colorful thousand-year-old Plague Procession the second Sunday in September.

CLIMATE   Belgium's climate is moderate, with few extremes in temperature either in summer or winter. It does, however, rain a lot, although there are more showers than downpours. Temperatures are lowest in December and January, when they average around 42°F, and highest in July and August, when 73°F is the average temperature.

HOLIDAYS   Legal holidays are: January 1 (New Year's Day), Easter Monday, May 1 (Labor Day), Ascension Day, Whitmonday, July 21 (Independence Day), August 15 (Assumption Day), November 1 (All Saints' Day), November 11 (Armistice Day), November 15 (Dynasty Day), and December 25 (Christmas).

Belgium Calendar of Events

February

- **Annual Carnival,** Hasselt. Street festivities and election of Carnival Prince. Five days preceding Shrove Tuesday.
- **Carnival Procession,** Tournai. Shrove Tuesday.
- **Carnival,** Binche. Shrove Tuesday.
- **Traditional Religious Procession,** Aalst. Shrove Sunday.

March

- **Rat Mort masked ball,** Ostend. Early Mar.
- **Blancs Mousis carnival parade,** Stavelot. Mid-Lent.

April

- **Courses du Côte,** La Roche, Ardennes. International auto-and-motorcycle road race over difficult terrain. Mid-Apr.
- **International Folklore Festival,** Leuven. Easter weekend.
- **Flower Market,** Koksijde. Easter Sun.
- **Flower Show,** Ghent. Late Apr.

May

- **Procession of the Holy Blood,** Bruges. Ascension Day.
- **Street performance (St. George slays the dragon),** Mons. First Sun after Whitsun.
- **Handswijk Procession,** Mechelen. Late May.
- **Regatta,** Ghent. Held at Aquatic Stadium. Late May.
- **International Fair,** Liège. Late May.

June

- **Day of the Four Processions,** Tournai. Second Sun.
- **Carillon concerts at St. Rumbout's tower,** Mechelen. Mid-June through August, Sat to Mon evenings.
- **Cartoon Festival,** Knokke-Heist. June to Sept.

July

- **Summer Festivals,** Ostend/Knokke. July to Aug.
- **Carnival processions,** Tournai. Led by Chevaliers de la Tour. Second Sun.

August

- **Festival of Flanders,** Ghent. Aug to Sept.
- **Seafarers Day,** Ostend. Early Aug.
- **Flemish Painting Pageant,** Koksijde. First Sun.
- **Marktrock rock festival,** Leuven. Mid-Aug.
- **Outremeuse Folklore Festival,** Liège. Mid-Aug.
- **Blessing of the Sea,** Knokke-Heist. Mid-Aug.
- **Sanguis Christi** (Modern passion play) Bruges. Late Aug in years ending in 2 or 7.

September

- **Knights of Flamiche,** Dinant. Mid to late Sept.
- **Procession of the Plague,** Tournai. Commemorating 1090 epidemic. Second Sun.
- **Horticultural and Floral Pageant,** Mechelen. Second Sun.

November
- **International Film Festival,** Ghent. Mid to late Nov.

December
- **Nut Fair,** Bastogne. Ancient matchmaking market. Mid to late Dec.
- **Feast of the Nativity,** Liège. Dec 25.

Brussels Calendar of Events

January
- **International Motor Show.** Late Jan or early Feb.
- **Festival de Cinéma,** at Palais des Congrès. Late Jan.

February
- **Antiques Fair,** Palais des Beaux-Arts. Early to mid-Feb.

March
- **Sport Exhibition,** Parc des Expositions. Early to mid-Mar.
- **International Book Fair,** Palais des Congrès. Mid-Mar.
- **International Festival of Fantasy Films,** Auditorium 44. Late Mar.

April
- **Music season opens.** Early Apr.

May
- **Queen Elizabeth International Musical Competition.** For young musicians. Early May.

June
- **Cinquantenaire.** 20km race. Early to mid-June.

July
- **Ommegang,** Grand' Place. Historic pageant and procession. Early July.
- **Brosella Folk and Jazz,** Théâtre de Verdure. Early July.
- **Entertainment,** Grand' Place. Entire month.
- **National Festivities.** Celebrating Belgian National Day. July 21.

August
- **Planting of the Meiboom (Mayboom) tree,** Grand' Place. Early Aug in even-numbered years.
- **Carpet of Flowers,** Grand' Place. Early Aug in even-numbered years.

September
- **Brussels Marathon.** Early Sept.
- **Eddy Marckx Grand Prix,** Bois de la Cambre. Mid-Sept.
- **Open Carriage fashion display,** Bois de la Cambre. Mid to late Sept.
- **Liberation parade.** With *Manneken Pis* dressed in the uniform of the Welsh Guards in honor of city's 1944 liberation. Sept 3.

October
- **Food Fair,** Parc des Expositions. Early to mid-Oct.

November
- **St. Verhaegen Day.** Students honor their patron saint by taking over the city for the day.

December
- **Christmas Market,** Sablon. Entire month.
- **Nativity scene and Christmas tree,** Grand' Place. Entire month.

---

3 Getting Around

Its compactness makes Belgium a tourist's delight for sightseeing. Drivers will find excellent roadways, and nondrivers are catered to with one of Europe's densest railway systems.

BY TRAIN   All major tourist destinations in Belgium are within easy reach by rail from Brussels. What's more, trains are so fast and so frequent (every half hour during peak travel hours, about every hour at midday) and distances so short that day trips from a Brussels base are easily managed. For example, Antwerp is only 29 minutes away; Ghent, 32 minutes; Namur, 40 minutes; Bruges, 55 minutes; and Liège, 75 minutes.

If all or most of your travel will be by rail, your best investment is the **Benelux Tourrail Ticket**, which covers unlimited travel for any five days (travel does not have to be on consecutive days) within any one-month period and costs BF 6,050 ($172) for five days of first-class travel, BF 4,040 ($115) in second class.

Even if you make only one or two day trips by rail, be sure to inquire about Belgian Railways' **Minitrips**—one-day excursion tickets to major sightseeing destinations at discount prices. There are also bicycles for rent at major destinations.

For those traveling in all three Benelux countries, the five-day Benelux Tourrail Ticket is a good buy, and for rail travel throughout Europe, the best value is the Eurailpass (see "Getting There" in Chapter 1).

BY BUS   In Brussels, Antwerp, Ghent, and other major cities, there is good local bus service. Regional buses serve virtually every region of the country, with fares and schedules available from local bus or railway stations. Travel agents can furnish details of the excellent network of coach tours (some for as long as 10 days) operated by **Europabus** in conjunction with Belgian State Railways.

BY CAR   Driving conditions are excellent in Belgium, with lighted highways at night, roadside telephones connected to the 900 emergency number, and "TS" (Touring Secours) yellow cars that patrol major highways to render emergency service at minimal cost. If you have car trouble, simply pull off the road and lift the hood and wait for the TS.

Rentals   Rental cars with U.S. specifications are available from **Hertz** (☎ toll free **800/654-3001** in the U.S.), with offices at bd. Maurice Lemonnier 8 in Brussels and at Brussels Airport; and **Avis** (☎ toll free **800/331-2112** in the U.S.), with offices at the airport and rue Américaine 145 in Brussels (☎ **537-12-80; 02/724-06-25** from outside the country). Rates begin at about BF 1,650 ($47) per day for a small car, and there's a small charge for each kilometer traveled. If you plan to arrive by train, you can book a rental car through Belgian Railways to meet you at most major stations.

Automobile Clubs   With headquarters in Brussels, both the **Royal Automobile Club de Belgique,** rue d'Arlon 53 (☎ **230-08-10**), and the **Touring Club de Belgique,** rue de la Loi 44 (☎ **233-22-11**), have working arrangements with international Automobile Association clubs. Get information from your local club before leaving home.

Gasoline   Super-grade petrol will cost around BF 35 ($1) per liter, or BF 140 ($4) per gallon.

Driving Rules   To drive in Belgium, U.S. citizens need only a valid passport, a U.S. driver's license, and a valid auto registration. Minimum age for drivers is 18. On highways, speed limits are 70kmph (43 m.p.h.) minimum, 120kmph (74 m.p.h.) maximum; in all cities and urban areas, the maximum speed limit is 60kmph (37 m.p.h.). One important driving rule is the *priorité à droite* (priority of the right), which makes it perfectly legal to pull out from a side road if it's to the right of the flow of traffic. That means, of course, that you must keep a sharp eye on the side roads to your right.

Road Maps   Tourist offices can furnish excellent city, regional, and countrywide maps. The Michelin map, to the scale of 1:350,000, is also reliable and detailed.

Breakdowns/Assistance   If you have car trouble, simply pull off the road, lift the hood, and wait for the "TS" (Touring Secours)—yellow cars that patrol major highways to render emergency service at minimal cost.

HITCHHIKING   It is generally an easy matter to hitch a ride on Belgium's main roads, which connect all major cities around the country. Remember, however, that *hitchhiking is illegal on motorways,* although authorities are pretty lenient about access roads.

Suggested Itineraries

Belgium is so crammed full of places to go and things to see and do that you'll be hard-pressed to decide just how to spend your time. The itineraries below are merely suggestions for a stay of a week or two—they may be juggled to suit your personal interests and style of travel.

With only one week in Belgium, my strong recommendation is to base yourself in Brussels and make day-long forays to historic cities that are at most a little more than an hour away by train. That way, you'll have time to get a real feel for this intriguing capital as well as the highlights of the great centers of art and history nearby. If you're driving, you may choose to stay overnight in, say, Bruges, Antwerp, or Liège rather than return to Brussels. Drivers can pick up an excellent and very detailed "Itineraries for Motorists" booklet from the Belgian Tourist Office that sets out driving routes in every region.

CITY HIGHLIGHTS

Among the Belgian cities you won't want to miss are: **Bruges,** one of Belgium's most romantic, perfectly preserved medieval towns; **Ghent,** whose narrow streets and gabled buildings hold traces of an exciting history and bold deeds of the past; **Ostend** and its neighboring coastal towns, each with its own distinctive seaside resort personality; **Tournai,** the country's second-oldest city, with its awe-inspiring cathedral; **Liège,** the rebel city with its colorful street market and engaging puppetry; and **Dinant** as well as other charming towns in the picturesque Ardennes.

PLANNING YOUR ITINERARY

If You Have One Week

Days 1 and 2   Don't budge from Brussels without a minimum of two days to explore its sightseeing splendors.

Day 3   Travel to Antwerp via Mechelen (with a stop to visit its medieval town square and carillon museum). In Antwerp, visit the house that was home to Rubens and St. James's Church to see examples of works by Rubens and other master painters. Return to Brussels for dinner and evening entertainment.

Day 4   Spend the day in Ghent, ancient seat of the counts of Flanders. Visit St. Bavo's Cathedral and view *The Adoration of the Mystic Lamb,* masterpiece of the Van Eyck brothers. Take time for a boat trip on the canals or the River Leie. Return to Brussels.

Day 5   Get an early start to allow a full day in Bruges, a fairytale medieval city that has been called the most romantic in the world. Start with a boat ride through the canals, then go shanks' mare to see Michelangelo's *Madonna and Child* in marble at the Church of Our Lady, the Memling Museum, and the busy, colorful Grote Markt at the city's center. Return to Brussels.

Day 6   Get another early start for the long drive or 75-minute train ride to Liège, one of Belgium's oldest and liveliest cities. Take a look at the 11th-century Palace of the Prince-Bishops, the Cathedral of St. Paul, the fascinating Museum of Walloon Life, and the Museum of Walloon Art. If this is a Sunday, don't miss the colorful street market.

Day 7   Unless you decide to devote this last day to further exploration of Brussels, travel to Tournai, where you'll want to visit the awe-inspiring Cathedral of Notre-Dame that dates from the 11th century, the Museum of Fine Arts that houses masterpieces by the likes of van der Weyden (a native son of Tournai), Rubens, van Gogh, Brueghel, and a host of others. Return to Brussels.

If You Have Two Weeks

If you have two weeks in Belgium, add the following excursions. While a car is not absolutely essential, it will give you total freedom to ramble through areas that invite more loitering than quick travel by public transport. The suggested order may be reversed to suit your travel plans—save the coastal resorts for last if you're flying out of Brussels, the Ardennes if you're traveling on in Europe.

Days 8–10   Travel the 75 miles from Brussels to Ostend on Belgium's 40-mile coastline. Choose an accommodations base from Knokke (with its casino and golf course), Ostend (busy, good shopping center), or the quieter resorts of Blankenberge, Den Haan, and De Panne. The primary attraction is the wide white-sand beach that stretches the entire length without interruption.

Day 11   Travel leisurely across the country to the Ardennes, Belgium's hilly, heavily wooded beauty spot, and settle into a sightseeing base at Durbuy (a charming old castle town), Dinant, La Roche, Malmédy, Saint-Hubert, or Bouillon.

Days 12–14   You're within easy driving distance of Spa (which gave its name to a whole resort concept) and Bastogne, as well as magnificent scenery and some of the best dining in the country (this is the region renowned for its smoked ham—and not recognized enough for its freshwater trout).

Fast Facts: Belgium

American Express   You'll find American Express International, Inc., at place Louise 2, 1000 Brussels (☎ **02/512-17-40**).

Business Hours   Banks are usually open Monday through Friday from 9:15am to 3:30pm, and some branches are also open on Saturday morning. Shops generally stay open from 10am to 6pm Monday through Saturday, although more and more are also open on Sunday. Most department stores have late hours on Friday, remaining open until 8 or 9pm.

Climate See "When to Go," earlier in this chapter.

Clothing First and foremost, bring along a raincoat. Showers are frequent and often unexpected. Otherwise, casual clothes for daytime activities, comfortable walking shoes (cobblestones abound and can be murder on shoes), and at least one nice outfit for after-dark Brussels.

Crime See "Safety," below.

Currency See "Currency and Costs," earlier in this chapter.

Customs See "Information, Entry Requirements, and Money" in Chapter 1. Note that upon your arrival in Belgium by either air or sea, you may leave luggage containing dutiable items with Customs officials for safekeeping while you travel around the country.

Documents Required See "Information, Entry Requirements, and Money" in Chapter 1.

Driving Rules See "Getting Around," earlier in this chapter.

Drug Laws Belgium has rigid prohibitions against the possession and/or use of drugs, and a strict enforcement policy virtually guarantees stiff fines and/or jail sentence for offenders.

Electricity If you plan to bring a hairdryer, radio (other than battery-operated), travel iron, or any other small appliance with you, pack a transformer and European-style adapter plug, since the electricity in Belgium is almost always 220 or 130 volts AC, 50 cycles.

Embassies/Consulates Embassies are located in Brussels, the national capital. The Embassy of **Australia** is in the Guimard Center, rue Guimard 6–8, 1040 Brussels (☎ 02/231-05-00). The Embassy of **Canada** is located at av. de Tervuren 2, 1040 Brussels (☎ 02/735-60-40). The Embassy of the **Republic of Ireland** is at rue du Luxembourg 19, 1040 Brussels (☎ 02/513-66-33). The Embassy of **New Zealand** is located at bd. du Regent 47–48, 1000 Brussels (☎ 02/512-10-40). The Embassy of the **United Kingdom** is in Britannia House, rue Joseph-II, 1040 Brussels (☎ 02/217-90-00). The Embassy of the **United States** is located at bd. du Regent 25–27, 1000 Brussels (☎ 02/513-38-30), and there's a consulate in Antwerp at Nationalestraat 5 (☎ 03/225-00-71).

Locations of diplomatic representatives of other countries can be obtained from the Ministère des Affaires Etrangères, rue des Quatre Bras 2, 1000 Brussels (☎ 02/516-81-11).

Emergencies In case of an accident, dial **900.** For emergency medical service in the Greater Brussels area (around the clock), dial **479-18-18** or **648-80-00.** Emergency dental service is available by phoning **426-10-26** or **428-58-88** in Brussels. Should you need police assistance, the number to call is **101.**

Gasoline See "Getting Around," earlier in this chapter.

Hitchhiking See "Getting Around," earlier in this chapter.

Holidays   See "When to Go," earlier in this chapter.

Information   In the United States, advance information for your trip is available through the Belgian Tourist Office, 780 Third Ave., New York, NY (☎ 212/758-8130). In Belgium, the main office is at rue du Marché-aux-Herbes 63, Brussels (☎ 02/504-03-90). There are more than 40 local tourist offices throughout Belgium, and a complete list of addresses and telephone numbers is available from the main office in Brussels.

Legal Aid   With offices in most major cities (check local telephone directories for addresses and telephone numbers), the **MAIC** organization specializes in legal help for foreign nationals.

Mail   Airmail postage to North America is BF 38 ($1.10) for postcards, BF 42 ($1.20) for letters up to 10 grams (about 0.4 oz.). The local letter rate for Belgium and Europe is BF 30 (85¢) for letters up to 20 grams, BF 16 (45¢) for postcards.

Passports   U.S. and Canadian citizens who plan to be in the country 90 days or less need bring only a valid passport—no visa is required. Citizens of other countries should consult the nearest Belgian consulate.

Pets   Pets entering the country must have a veterinarian's certificate attesting to good general health and rabies vaccination in the prior 12 months. The certificate must be dated no less than 30 days or more than one year from the date of entry.

Police   For police assistance, dial **101.**

Safety   When you're traveling in any unfamiliar city or country, stay alert. Be aware of your immediate surroundings. Wear a moneybelt and keep a close eye on your possessions. Be particularly careful with cameras, purses, and wallets, all favorite targets of thieves and pickpockets. Every society has its criminals. It's your responsibility to be aware and alert even in the most heavily touristed areas.

Telephone/Telegraph/Telex/Fax   Direct dialing to other European countries as well as overseas (including the United States and Canada) is available in most hotel rooms in Brussels. Coin **telephone** boxes that display stickers showing flags of different countries can be used to make international calls with operator assistance. Holders of AT&T credit cards may obtain details of the moneysaving USA Direct Service by calling toll free **800/242-1013,** ext. 6191, in the U.S.

   Coin telephones accept BF 5 (14¢) and BF 20 (55¢) coins, and it's advisable to have a good supply of these coins when you place a call. Most local calls cost BF 10 (28¢). Many public telephones now accept Telecards rather than, or in addition to, coins. Cards can be purchased at newsagents and some shops.

   To send a **telegram** by telephone, dial 1325. Telegrams can also be sent through the reception desk at most hotels; the Régie des Télégraphes et Téléphones (RTT), bd. de l'Impératrice 17, Brussels (☎ 513-44-90).

   Major hotels will have **telex** and **fax** facilities, as does the Régie des Télégraphes et Téléphones (RTT), listed above.

Time   Belgium is six hours ahead of eastern standard time in the United States (9am in New York is 3pm in Belgium). Clocks are moved ahead one hour each year at the end of March and back one hour at the end of September.

Tipping Restaurants and hotels will almost always include a 16% service charge and the 19% value-added tax (VAT)! No more quick math in your head—unless, that is, you've had really exceptional service and want to add a little more. Taxis include the tip in the meter reading.

As a general guide, these are the usual tips for other services: in theaters, BF10 (30¢) to the usher; hairdresser, 20% of the bill (leave it with the cashier when you pay up); porters, BF 30 (85¢) per piece of luggage.

Tourist Offices See "Information," above.

Visas Visas are not required for U.S. and Canadian citizens who plan to be in the country 90 days or less.

Brussels

4

"**B**RUSSELS IS THE PARIS OF THE BELGIANS," A 19TH-CENTURY VISITOR WROTE. THESE days, Belgians will tell you—with at least a modicum of justification—that Brussels has outstripped Paris by a long shot. After all, isn't this the city that's known universally as the "capital of Europe"? And isn't it true that Parisians many times come by train for the sole purpose of a night at the opera and a fine meal in a restaurant even better than one at home?

Of course, comparisons, at best, should be avoided, and Brussels has no need of Paris as a measuring stick—she stands quite firmly on her own as a leading city of Europe and the world.

BY WAY OF BACKGROUND

No one knows when trading first began at this point on the River Senne, but archeologists tell us that Neolithic man was here, and Romans once built their opulent villas in the vicinity. It's fairly certain that the bishop of Cambrai found a Merovingian settlement here in A.D. 695. It has been confirmed that by 966 a village was in existence, for it was mentioned by the name "Bruocsells" (brook dwelling) in a document signed by Emperor Otto I the Great.

BRUSSELS BECOMES A TOWN It wasn't until 977, however, that Brussels began to take on the form of a proper town. That's when Charles of Lorraine, Duke of Lower Lotharingia (the first duke of the Brabant line), built a castle on the island of Saint Géry in the Senne that became a gathering point for traders and artisans. Two years later he took up residence there, thus giving Brussels a firm date (979) on which to hang her 1,000 years, celebrated with much ceremony in 1979.

By the year 1100, fortifications surrounded the settlement—by then expanded to include some 5,000 inhabitants and the new Coudenberg castle to which the duke had repaired. In 1379 a second line of fortified ramparts enclosed what is now the heart of Brussels; today a modern boulevard traces their course (changing names several times along the way, but nearly always called *petite ceinture*—"small belt"—by residents).

FOREIGN RULERS COME & GO Those fortifications failed to prevent the tugs of war, political intrigues, and marriages that saw Brussels first under one foreign banner, then another, through the next few centuries. Civil unrest, usually led by members of the crafts guilds, waxed and waned, as citizens chaffed under yokes that were sometimes harsh, sometimes benign.

Flemish, Austrian, Burgundian, and Spanish rulers came and went, leaving behind Belgian heroes still revered today, among them Everard 't Serclaes, who led a mere 100 men against Flemish troops in the 1300s, and the beloved counts of Egmont and Hornes, who paid with their heads in 1568 for leading the opposition to the Inquisition horrors imported from Spain. The latter were publicly decapitated on the Grand' Place, where in 1402 the Luxembourg Duchess Jeanne and Wenceslas, her husband, had overseen the initial stages of construction of the Town Hall, which became the centerpiece of a magnificent array of buildings housing the trade and craft guilds.

The Hapsburgs of Spain held Brussels in thrall during most of the 17th century; but when Charles II of Spain died without an heir, Louis XIV of France sent his armies, with Maréchal de Villeroi at their head, to wrest control. In two of the most destructive days in its long history, the city sustained a bombardment from August 13 to 15, 1695, that demolished nearly 4,000 buildings, damaged half a thousand more, and reduced the Grand' Place to utter ruin, with only the Town Hall left standing amid

What's Special About Brussels

Public Spaces
- Grand' Place, a splendid esplanade enclosed by gabled medieval buildings—at its most beautiful at night in the golden glow of floodlights.
- Place du Grand-Sablon, lined with houses of master artisans, with a marvelous antiques flea market on weekend mornings.
- Place du Petit-Sablon, a statuary garden surrounded by a wrought-iron fence adorned with 48 bronze statuettes.

Museums
- Musée d'Art Ancien, featuring masterpieces from the 14th to the 17th century.
- Musée Horta, displaying prime examples of the art nouveau architect's genius.
- Musées Royaux d'Art et d'Histoire, world famous for its fabulous artifacts collections.

Churches
- Cathedral of St. Michel, from the 13th century, with impressive towers and beautiful stained-glass windows.
- Church of Notre-Dame-du-Sablon, flamboyantly Gothic, with a celebrated statue of St. Hubert.

Parks
- Parc de Bruxelles, with the Palais Royal and the Palais de la Nation at opposite ends.
- "The Bois," filled with beech trees, with a small lake as its centerpiece.

Monuments
- *Manneken Pis,* Belgium's "oldest citizen," the irreverent little bronze statue of a small boy caught in an act of nature.
- The Atomium, a striking replica of an iron molecule built for the 1958 World's Fair, with exhibits and panoramic views of the city, plus a leisure park at its foot featuring "Mini-Europe" and water sports.

the rubble. In an amazing show of determination and building skill, carpenters, stonemasons, and other artisans set to work to rebuild the vanished Guild Houses, and by 1698 the gloriously ornate conglomerate of baroque buildings you'll see today was complete in all its splendor.

In 1716 Brussels fell into the hands of the Hapsburgs of Austria, and once more the crafts guilds rumbled with discontent. In 1719 yet another hero entered Brussels folklore when François Anneessens, a respected craftsman and outspoken advocate of municipal rights, was decapitated. He lies buried in Notre-Dame de la Chapelle, on rue des Ursulines.

IMPRESSIONS

It is a white sparkling, cheerful, wicked little place, which however one finds rather good for one's spirits.
—Matthew Arnold, 1854

THE STIRRING OF INDEPENDENCE   The city was in a state of shock from which it did not begin to recover until the arrival of Charles of Lorraine in 1744, but by 1789—despite factional riots in the streets—Brussels followed the example of revolutionary France and joined the people of Brabant in proclaiming (in January 1790) the United Belgian States. Divisions between factions deepened, however, and after one or two Austrian attempts to assume control, the revolutionary French government moved in to put Brussels once more under French domination.

There it remained until Napoléon was ignominiously defeated on the battlefield of Waterloo not far from the city. Independence eluded Belgium once more, however, since the Congress of Vienna awarded control of Belgium to the Dutch in 1815. Brussels became a second capital of the Kingdom of the Low Countries, owing allegiance to Holland's William I of Orange.

INDEPENDENCE AT LAST   William's rule was destined to be another in the line of very short reigns, for the citizens of Brussels agitated more and more for Belgian self-rule. Finally, on a warm night in August 1830, it was an audience attending the opera *La Muette de Portici* at Théâtre de la Monnaie not far from the Grand' Place who responded enthusiastically to an aria that spoke of "Sacred Love of Country" and lit the fuse that was to kindle a strong, steady flame to burn away forever the yoke of foreign rule.

Their applause and lusty shouts of patriotism were picked up by passing pedestrians outside, who took up the cry and carried it throughout the city. Before long a Belgian national flag appeared on the scene and crowds were singing a new national anthem. The fervor grew until the end of September, when the Dutch ruler sent 14,000 troops to quell this disturbance. Patriots from Liège rushed to join the ranks of Brussels soldier-citizens; and when open battle broke out in the Park of Brussels, it took just four days to rout the Dutch. On September 27, 1830, the Kingdom of Belgium came into being, and Brussels—with its 100,000 inhabitants—was declared its capital. Belgium was, at long last, its own ruler.

AFTER INDEPENDENCE   In the years since independence, Brussels has stepped out with spirit and verve to take its proper place on the world stage. By 1834 a university was founded; in 1835 Europe's first railway line ran from Brussels to Mechelen; another European "first," the covered pedestrian thoroughfare, Galeries Saint-Hubert, appeared in 1846, a mecca for fashionable gatherings and shopping; in 1871 the unsightly River Senne was covered by one of the beautiful wide boulevards constructed along the line of the city's ancient fortifications; great public buildings were erected; Brussels hosted three World Expositions (in 1880, 1888, and 1897), for which it constructed the Park of the Cinquantenaire; Brussels architect Victor Horta inaugurated the ornate "art nouveau" era; a 20th-century Brussels hero emerged when Burgomaster Adolphe Max led the defiance of German invaders in 1914, and his example inspired Van der Meulebroeck to do the same in 1940; the 1958 World's Fair left a soaring model of the atom as a permanent reminder of peaceful uses for atomic power; the European Economic Community chose Brussels as its headquarters in 1959; NATO followed suit in 1967; and a multitude of international corporations flocked to Brussels as it gained increasing prominence and world stature. Brussels's population has mushroomed to one million, of whom more than one-fourth are of foreign origin.

It's small wonder that Brussels is now widely recognized as the "capital of Europe"!

1 Orientation

Arriving

BY PLANE   There is direct train service between 5:30am and 10:55pm from **Zaventern Airport,** some $8^1/_2$ miles from the city center, to all three of the city's principal railway stations (Gare du Nord, Gare Centrale, and Gare du Midi), with a fare of BF 125 ($3.55) in first class, BF 85 ($2.40) second class. Tickets are available at the tourist office in the luggage hall and at all railway stations—there's a supplementary charge if you buy your ticket on the train. Taxis that display an orange sticker depicting a white airplane offer reduced fares from the airport to the city center; others will charge about BF 1,200 ($34).

BY TRAIN   For schedule and fare information on travel in Belgium and abroad, call **219-26-40** in Belgium. Tickets are sold at all stations and through travel agents, and timetables are available at railway stations.

There are five large railway stations in the Greater Brussels area, but travelers arriving from other European countries will probably want to get off at one of the three major stations: **Gare Centrale,** carrefour de l'Europe 2; **Gare du Midi,** rue de France 2; and **Gare du Nord (C.C.N.),** rue du Progrès 86. Trains traveling within Belgium also use **Gare du Quartier Léopold,** place du Luxembourg, and **Gare de Schaerbeek,** place Princesse Elisabeth 5.

BY BUS   Most buses from continental destinations arrive at **Gare du Midi** (see above); schedules and fares are available at that station's booking hall.

BY CAR   Those driving into Brussels would be well advised to proceed directly to their hotel, park the car in any available facilities (see "Getting Around," below), and leave it there for the duration of their visit.

Tourist Information

In Brussels, the **Belgian Tourist Office** is located at rue du Marché-aux-Herbes 63 (☎ 02/504-03-90) and the **Tourist Information Brussels (T.I.B.)** office is in the Town Hall, Grand' Place (☎ 02/513-89-40). Besides providing tourist information, including a comprehensive guidebook that includes an excellent map showing the main monuments and sightseeing attractions, the T.I.B. sells 24-hour tourist tickets for the métro, trams, and buses; makes hotel reservations; and has well-trained, multilingual tourist guides who may be engaged by the hour or day.

The Brussels offices are open in the summer daily from 9am to 6pm; in the winter Monday through Saturday 9am to 6pm; Sunday hours vary.

City Layout

Although the heart-shaped inner city of Brussels—roughly $1^1/_2$ miles in diameter—is filled with sightseeing treasures, the 19 separate, self-governing municipalities comprising the $62^1/_2$ square miles of Greater Brussels offer many attractions of their own. And nearly 14% of this densely populated city—comprising the neighborhoods of Saint-Josse-ten-Noode, Saint-Gilles, Koekelberg, Etterbeek, Schaerbeek, Molenbeek-Saint-Jean, Ixelles, Ganshoren, Forest, Jette, Woluwe-Saint-Lambert, Berchem-Sainte-Agathe, Evere, Anderlecht, Wolowe-Saint-Pierre, Bruxelles,

Auderghem, Uccle, and Watermael-Boitsfort—consists of parks, woods, and forests, making this one of the greenest urban centers in Europe.

The center city, once ringed by fortified ramparts, is now encircled by broad boulevards known collectively as the **Petite Ceinture.** Flat in its center and western areas, to the east it climbs the hills that comprise upper Brussels and are crowned by the Royal Palace and some of the city's most affluent residential areas and prestigious office buildings. The **Grand' Place** (Grote Markt) is at the very center of the heart and serves as a handy point of reference for most visitors. Brussels's excellent railway system runs almost directly through the middle, with the **Gare du Nord** (Noord Station) just across the northern rim of the Petite Ceinture, the **Gare Centrale** (Central Station) in the center city not far from the Grand' Place, and **Gare du Midi** (Zuidstation) near the southern rim. The street signs are in both French and Dutch.

STREET MAPS   Go by the tourist office and pick up their **Brussels Guide and Map;** it's the most comprehensive street map of the city, and provides a wealth of other visitor information.

2   Getting Around

BY METRO   Brussels has an excellent network of métro (subway) lines that cover 28 miles through the city. Métro entrances are clearly marked by signs bearing a white M on a blue background. In this city, a descent underground takes you into an art center, with excellent paintings especially commissioned by contemporary Belgian artists. Maps of the métro network are free at tourist offices, and service is continuous from 6am to midnight, with timetables displayed at each stop.

BY BUS & TRAM   Above ground, yellow trams and buses run from 6am to midnight, and timetables are posted at stops. Tram and bus stops are marked by red-and-white or blue-and-white signs, and all are marked SUR DEMANDE, which simply means you lift your hand to signal the tram or bus as it approaches. Prices are BF 150 ($1.40) for a single ("direct") ticket, BF 230 ($6.55) for a five-trip card, BF 120 ($3.40) for a 24-hour unlimited-rides card, and BF 305 ($8.70) for a 10-trip card.

BY TAXI   The minimum rate for taxis is BF 100 ($2.85), and charges per kilometer vary from BF 40 to 58 ($1.15 to $1.65), depending on location. Tip and taxes are included in the meter price, and you need not add another tip unless there has been exceptional service (help with heavy luggage, etc.). Taxis cannot be hailed on the street, but there are taxi stands on all principal streets. To telephone, call **511-22-44** or **513-62-00.**

BY CAR   My best advice is to park your car either at your hotel or one of the many public parking areas—the tourist office or your hotel can furnish the address of the nearest one—and not set foot in it until you're ready to leave the city. Traffic is fast-moving and more than a little daunting for those unfamiliar with the city. Good public transportation and/or the occasional taxi ride will get you anywhere you want to go inexpensively and hassle-free. If you must resort to on-street parking, meters have varying hours of operation and charges, and you should always have a supply of BF-5 and BF-20 coins.

Rentals   See "Getting Around" in Chapter 3.

BY FOOT   This is really the way to get around Brussels, and the trick to that is to take the city one area at a time. The city center is pure delight for walkers, and outlying regions are easily reached by public transport. Be warned, however, that ancient cobbled streets are no place for high heels, and a full day's sightseeing calls for your most comfortable walking shoes.

Fast Facts: Brussels

American Express   American Express International, Inc., is located at place Louise 2, 1000 Brussels (☎ **02/512-17-40**).

Area Code   Brussels's telephone area code is **02.**

Babysitters   Many hotels can provide reliable babysitting service. A student babysitting roster is maintained by U.L.B. Service, "Jobs," CP 185, av. F. D. Roosevelt 50 (☎ **650-26-46**).

Bookstores   At W. H. Smith & Son, bd. Adolphe-Max 71–75 (☎ **219-50-34** or **219-27-08**), you'll find the best and most comprehensive selection of English-language books. Books in English can also be found at the Strathmore Bookshop, rue St-Lambert 110, in Woluwe-Saint-Lambert (☎ **771-92-00**), and the House of Paperbacks, 813 chaussée de Waterloo (☎ **343-11-22**).

Business Hours   Banks are open Monday through Friday from 9:15am to 3:30pm, and some branches are also open on Saturday morning. Shopping hours are 10am to 6pm or 7pm Monday through Saturday, with shops in some districts also open the same hours on Sunday. Most department stores stay open until 8 or 9pm on Friday.

Car Rentals   See "Getting Around," earlier in this chapter.

Climate   See "When to Go" in Chapter 3.

Currency   See "Information, Entry Requirements, and Money" in Chapter 1.

Currency Exchange   Major banks and major railway stations have currency-exchange services. Also **Paul Loy Foreign Currency,** rue de la Montagne 6 (☎ **511-72-17**), is open Monday through Friday from 9am to 6pm, Saturday from 10am to 6pm, and on Sunday from 11am to 1pm. Most hotels will also exchange currency, but the rate is generally much less favorable than at banks.

Dentists   For emergency dental service, phone **426-10-26** or **428-58-88.** They can locate an English-speaking dentist.

Doctors   For emergency medical service in the Greater Brussels area (around the clock), dial **479-18-18** or **648-80-00.** Be sure to explain that you want an English-speaking doctor.

Embassies/Consulates   See "Fast Facts: Belgium" in Chapter 3.

Emergencies   In case of accident, dial **100.** For day or night emergency medical service, call **479-18-18** or **648-80-00:** for police assistance, **101;** for fire, **100.**

Information   See "Tourist Information" in "Orientation," above in this chapter.

Language   Shops, restaurants, and hotels are usually staffed by at least one or two fluent English-speakers.

Lost Property The Belgian National Airport office in the arrival hall can help if you've lost any luggage or other property aboard an aircraft (☎ **723-60-11**); for property lost within the airport itself, go to the Airways Management (R.V.A.) office in the first-floor visitors hall (☎ **722-39-40**), which is open only on weekdays.

Newspapers/Magazines For English-speaking visitors, the most useful publication is the weekly magazine, *The Bulletin,* published each Thursday.

Police In an emergency, call **906** or **101.**

Post Office The post office at Gare du Midi, av. Fonsny 48A, is open 24 hours every day; all others are open weekdays from 9am to 5pm, and are closed weekends and public holidays. Conveniently located post offices are at Centre Monnaie, Gare Centrale, Gare du Nord, rue du Progrès 80, the Bourse, and the Palais de Justice.

Radio/Television You'll hear French, Dutch, and German on television and radio, with an occasional imported English-speaking program. Some American-produced television shows are dubbed into another language, which can be quite entertaining. BBC World News is broadcast on medium-wave radio several times a day, with varying wavelengths and times of broadcast: Inquire at your hotel or consult local newspaper listings.

Religious Services For information on hours of religious services—including Catholic, Protestant, Jewish, Eastern Orthodox, and Anglican—contact Bruxelles-Accueil-Ponte Ouvente ASBL, rue de Tabora 6 (☎ **511-27-15** or **511-81-78**), Monday through Saturday between 10am and 6pm. They also serve as a social information center for foreigners.

Safety When you're traveling in an unfamiliar city or country, stay alert. Be aware of your immediate surroundings. Wear a moneybelt. Every society has its criminals; it's your responsibility to be aware and alert even in the most heavily touristed areas.

Taxes Restaurants and hotels usually include a 16% service charge as well as the 19% value-added tax (VAT).

Taxis See "Getting Around," earlier in this chapter.

Telegrams/Telex/Telephone See "Fast Facts: Belgium" in Chapter 3.

3 Accommodations

Brussels has good accommodations in every price range. The flood of high-level diplomats and business executives has brought with it deluxe hotels of just about every international chain, as well as new or remodeled Belgian establishments—all catering to affluent and expense-account budgets. With typical Belgian practicality, however, the city also offers a good supply of accommodations in the moderate and inexpensive ranges. All rates include VAT, a service charge, and usually a complimentary continental breakfast.

Both the **T.I.B.** office in Grand' Place (☎ **513-89-40**) and the **Belgian Tourist Office** at rue du Marché-aux-Herbes 63 (☎ **504-03-90**) will make reservations for a small fee, and the T.I.B. publishes an annual **"Hotel Guide"** with listings by price range. They can also provide complete information on the **hostels** of Brussels.

When booking, if at all possible you should confirm your reservation in writing to the hotel, stating the number of rooms desired, single- or double-bed preference, private bath or shower requirements, any room-location preferences (with view of garden, river, etc.), length of time you expect to stay, and the exact date and approximate time of your arrival.

The **Hotel Reservation Service** (☎ and fax **02/534-70-40**), located in a tiny booth in the Central Station, near the Meeting Point (and the steps leading to the restrooms), can make room reservations in Brussels (and throughout Europe) in one- to five-star hotels for a flat fee of BF 85 ($2.40) per group (that is, it will charge BF 85 even if you reserve three or more rooms) in Brussels and BF 185 ($5.40) for other European location. It's open seven days a week, from 9am to 9pm in summer, from 10am to 8pm in winter. This is a private firm staffed with English-speaking personnel. The métro station is around the corner (you don't have to leave the building to reach it), and I was told that they can find you a room even on days when Brussels is "sold out."

Notes: Because Brussels's population fluctuates on weekends, when many businesspeople and diplomats are away, many of the higher-priced hotels offer special Friday-through-Sunday prices at substantial savings. If you plan your Brussels visit for the weekend, be sure to ask your hotel about reduced rates.

All my recommended accommodations come with bath unless otherwise noted.

Very Expensive

Hilton Brussels, bd. de Waterloo 38, 1000 Brussels.
   ☎ **02/504-11-11,** or toll free **800/445-8667** in the U.S. Fax 02/504-21-11.
   450 rms, 21 suites. A/C MINIBAR TV TEL
   Rates: BF 11,900 ($340) single; BF 12,900 ($368) double; BF 23,000–55,000 ($657–$1,571) executive floor and suites. AE, MC, V.

Located away from the city center in ultrasmart "upper Brussels," this 27-story hotel (with wheelchair access) offers large and beautifully furnished rooms, with plush, modern decor and every amenity you can think of. For those to whom money is truly no object, the Hilton offers four floors of executive rooms and suites. Some of the city's best shopping is just steps away.

   Dining/Entertainment: Both its rooftop En Plein Ciel restaurant and the elegant dining room, Maison du Boeuf, have won local acclaim, with prices in the BF-1,100 to -1,800 ($31 to $51) range.

   Services: Wheelchair access, babysitting.

   Facilities: Conference rooms, banqueting rooms, car parking.

★ **Hôtel Président,** bd. Emile-Jacqumain 180, 1210 Brussels. ☎ **02/217-20-20.**
   Fax 02/218-84-02. 310 rms, 16 suites. MINIBAR TV TEL
   Rates (including breakfast): BF 7,500 ($214) single; BF 8,000 ($228) double; BF 14,000–40,000 ($400–$1,140) suite. Weekend rates available. AE, DC, MC, V.

Near the World Trade Center and within walking distance of the Gare du Nord, the Président is a bit out from the city center, but there is a shuttle service (also to the airport) and the location offers welcome quiet, a relief from the usual inner-city noise. Its lobby and public rooms glitter with marble, mirrors, and elegant chandeliers. All guest rooms are furnished in a modern decor, and the private baths have heated towel rails and hairdryers. The suites are spacious, and the Presidential Suite has its own kitchen, large sitting room and dining area, two bedrooms, and a seashell-shaped Jacuzzi.

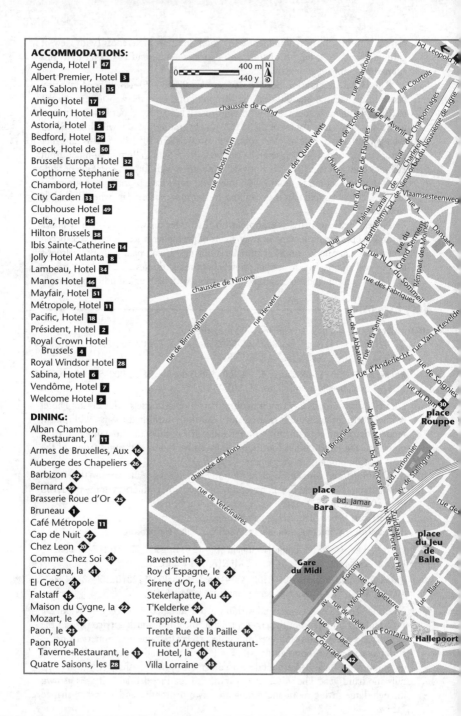

ACCOMMODATIONS:
Agenda, Hotel l' **47**
Albert Premier, Hotel **3**
Alfa Sablon Hotel **35**
Amigo Hotel **17**
Arlequin, Hotel **19**
Astoria, Hotel **5**
Bedford, Hotel **29**
Boeck, Hotel de **50**
Brussels Europa Hotel **32**
Copthorne Stephanie **48**
Chambord, Hotel **37**
City Garden **33**
Clubhouse Hotel **49**
Delta, Hotel **45**
Hilton Brussels **38**
Ibis Sainte-Catherine **14**
Jolly Hotel Atlanta **8**
Lambeau, Hotel **34**
Manos Hotel **46**
Mayfair, Hotel **51**
Métropole, Hotel **11**
Pacific, Hotel **18**
Président, Hotel **2**
Royal Crown Hotel
 Brussels **4**
Royal Windsor Hotel **28**
Sabina, Hotel **6**
Vendôme, Hotel **7**
Welcome Hotel **9**

DINING:
Alban Chambon
 Restaurant, l' **11**
Armes de Bruxelles, Aux **16**
Auberge des Chapeliers **26**
Barbizon **52**
Bernard **39**
Brasserie Roue d'Or **25**
Bruneau **1**
Café Métropole **11**
Cap de Nuit **27**
Chez Leon **20**
Comme Chez Soi **30**
Cuccagna, la **41**
El Greco **21**
Falstaff **15**
Maison du Cygne, la **22**
Mozart, le **42**
Paon, le **23**
Paon Royal
 Taverne-Restaurant, le **13**
Quatre Saisons, les **28**
Ravenstein **31**
Roy d'Espagne, le **21**
Sirene d'Or, la **12**
Stekerlapatte, Au **44**
T'Kelderke **24**
Trappiste, Au **40**
Trente Rue de la Paille **36**
Truite d'Argent Restaurant-
 Hotel, la **10**
Villa Lorraine **43**

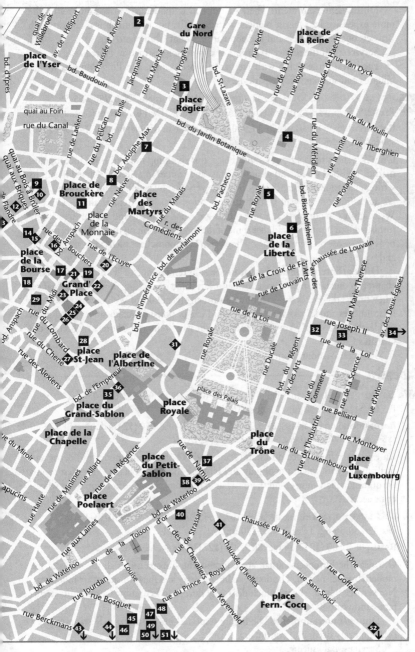

Brussels Accommodations & Dining

Dining/Entertainment: There's a quite nice, moderately priced grill room, the more expensive La Maison Blanche restaurant (its business lunch is a favorite with Brussels businesspeople), and the popular President Club piano bar.

Services: Shuttle service to airport or city center destination on request.

Facilities: Fitness club with Jacuzzi, sun bed, sauna, and Ping-Pong, as well as billiards and snooker; ample parking.

★ **Royal Windsor Hotel,** rue Duquesnoy 5, 1000 Brussels. ☎ **02/505-55-55.** Fax 02/505-55-00. 275 rms, 30 suites. A/C MINIBAR TV TEL **Métro:** Central Station.

Rates (including breakfast): BF 11,950 ($341) single or double; from BF 14,000 ($400) suite. AE, DC, MC, V.

Only 2¹/₂ short blocks from Grand' Place, this sparkling modern hotel incorporates marble, polished wood, and gleaming brass and copper in a decor designed to suit its setting. The tone of elegance is set from the very first by its lobby and the huge circular medallion on the wall behind the reception desk that depicts all the Duke of Wellington's major battles. Some rooms are wood paneled and all are luxuriously furnished, but it must be said that some of the rooms are a bit on the small side, though none has a sense of cramped space. The elegant bathrooms have such extras as hairdryers and scales.

Dining/Entertainment: Les Quatre Saisons restaurant (see "Dining," later in this chapter) is outstanding, where gourmet meals come in a setting of intimate elegance. Then there's the wonderfully clubby Edwardian-style Duke of Wellington pub, where light lunches and snacks are available amid lots of polished mahogany, etched glass, and leather upholstery. You can dance into the wee hours at the hotel's nightclub, the Griffin's Club.

Services: 24-hour room service.

Expensive

Alfa Sablon Hotel, rue de la Paille 2–8, 1000 Brussels. ☎ **02/513-60-40.** Fax 02/511-81-41. 30 rms, 2 suites. A/C TV TEL

Rates (including breakfast): BF 6,950 ($198) single; BF 8,650 ($247) double; BF 12,000 ($342) suite. Weekend discounts available. AE, DC, V.

An easy walk from place du Grand-Sablon, this hotel is ultramodern in decor and furnishings, with much use of gray and black in the color scheme. The guest rooms are quite adequate in size, and there's a bar in the hotel also. The hotel provides wheelchair access.

Brussels Europa Hotel, rue de la Loi 107, 1040 Brussels. ☎ **02/230-13-33.** Fax 02/230-36-82. Telex 25121. 240 rms. A/C TV TEL

Rates: BF 8,500 ($242) single; BF 9,500 ($271) double. AE, MC, V.

Out near the European Parliament building, the Europa meets all the needs of the modern businessperson. The decor is contemporary and the furnishings are functional. Not surprisingly, its clientele includes many European Economic Community dignitaries and visitors.

Dining/Entertainment: The highly respected Les Continents Restaurant has a contemporary decor and continental cuisine.

Services: Babysitting.

Facilities: Sauna, garage for guests, solarium.

Copthorne Stephanie, av. Louise 91–93, 1050 Brussels. ☎ **02/539-02-40.**
Fax 02/538-03-07. 142 rms, 1 suite. A/C MINIBAR TV TEL
Rates (including breakfast): BF 8,950 ($255) single; BF 9,950 ($284) double. AE, MC, V.

This sleekly modern hotel looks as if it were designed for the 21st century. Every feature, from lobby design and fittings to furnishings in the kitchenette suites, is streamlined, functional, and representative of the very best in avant-garde planning. It's located in a pretty section of avenue Louise, one of the city's most select shopping streets. The rooms include a lovely roof garden suite, the luxurious Connoisseur Rooms, as well as the spacious Classic Rooms, some of which feature kitchenettes.

Dining/Entertainment: The Gourmet Restaurant has both a French and an international menu.

Services: Babysitting.

Facilities: Indoor swimming pool, garage, wheelchair access.

★ **Hôtel Amigo,** rue de l'Amigo 1, 1000 Brussels. ☎ **02/547-47-47.**
Fax 02/513-52-77. 181 rms. 5 suites. A/C MINIBAR TV TEL **Métro:** Bourse.
Rates: BF 5,950–6,950 ($170–$198) single; BF 6,750–11,950 ($192–$341) double; BF 16,500–27,500 ($47–$785) suite. AE, MC, V.

This superb hotel has the most convenient location on the accommodations scene— just one block off Grand' Place. Although the Spanish Renaissance architecture is right at home with its ancient neighborhood, the hotel only dates back to 1958. Its flagstone lobby, clubby bar, small restaurant, and other public rooms are the epitome of understated good taste, with lots of Oriental rugs, antiques, wall tapestries, and wood accents. The rooms are fairly spacious and elegantly appointed, and service from the friendly, efficient staff is as deluxe as the hotel itself.

Dining/Entertainment: There are a bar and a small restaurant on the premises.

Services: 24-hour room service, babysitting.

Facilities: Safe-deposit boxes, wheelchair access.

Hôtel Astoria, rue Royale 103, 1000 Brussels. ☎ **02/217-62-90.** Fax 02/217-11-50.
113 rms, 12 suites. A/C MINIBAR TV TEL
Rates: BF 6,500 ($185) single; BF 6,500 ($185) double; BF 12,500 ($357) suite. AE, DC, MC, V.

A reader wrote to tell me about this grand old hotel that dates from 1909, with all the belle époque and art nouveau panache of that era. My own inspection bears out that reader's raves, and I found the Corinthian columns, antique furnishings, and textured marble of its lobby quite charming, as was the ornately decorated Pullman Bar just off the lobby. The guest rooms are attractive and nicely furnished, and some are equipped for the physically handicapped.

Hôtel Mayfair, av. Louise 381–383, 1050 Brussels. ☎ **02/649-98-00.**
Fax 02/649-22-49. 95 rms. 4 suites. MINIBAR TV TEL
Rates: BF 8,200 ($234) single or double; BF 11,000–13,000 ($314–$371) suite. AE, V.

This small hotel south of the city center is tastefully decorated, and its rooms are comfortable and pleasantly furnished.

Dining/Entertainment: There's a nice bar and a small restaurant serving moderately priced meals.

Services: Babysitting.

★ **Hôtel Métropole**, place de Brouckère 31, 1000 Brussels. ☎ **02/217-23-00.**
$ Fax 02/218-02-20. 400 rms, 10 suites. TV TEL **Métro:** De Brouckere.

Rates (including breakfast): BF 7,900 ($225) single; BF 9,400 ($268) double; BF 12,000–31,000 ($342–$885) suite. AE, DC, MC, V.

This classic old-world hotel dates from the late 1800s, and its splendidly ornate interior is a turn-of-the-century showcase of marble, gilt, soaring ceilings, potted palms, and lavishly decorated public rooms. What's more, it's right in the middle of the city center, with excellent shopping just out the back door and Grand' Place only a few blocks away. The spacious rooms with classic furnishings and the corridors leading to them also hark back to former days.

Dining/Entertainment: The elegant L'Alban Chambon restaurant caters to the sophisticated gourmet (see "Dining," later in this chapter) and the richly Victorian Café Métropole, with its unique gas lamps and heated sidewalk terrace, is utterly charming. Both are worth a visit even if you don't stay here.

Services: 24-hour room service, babysitting.

Facilities: Relaxation center with a sauna, Turkish bath, Jacuzzi, solarium, and a flotation tank; wheelchair access.

★ **Jolly Hotel Atlanta**, bd. Adolphe-Max 7, 1000 Brussels. ☎ **02/217-01-20.**
$ Fax 02/217-37-58. 238 rms, 3 suites. MINIBAR TV TEL **Métro:** De Brouckere.

Rates (including breakfast): BF 7,700 ($220) single; BF 8,500 ($242) double; BF 12,000–16,000 ($342–$457) suite. Children under 12 stay free in parents' room. Weekend discounts available. AE, EU, V.

The prestigious Jolly hotel chain based in Italy has transformed this Brussels landmark into a model of modern comfort and sophisticated decor they dub "Italian modern." Its location couldn't be better for shopping, and Grand' Place is only a few minutes' walk away. Room amenities include an extra telephone in the bathroom and hairdryers.

Dining/Entertainment: An outstanding breakfast is served in the window-walled rooftop dining room overlooking the city, and the cozy lounge off the lobby features piano music as well as light snacks.

Services: 24-hour room service.

Royal Crown Hotel Brussels, rue Royale 250, 1210 Brussels. ☎ **02/220-66-11.**
Fax 02/217-84-44. 307 rms, 8 suites. A/C MINIBAR TV TEL

Rates: BF 8,500 ($242) single; BF 9,300 ($265) double; BF 11,900–31,800 ($340–$908) suite. AE, DC, EU, MC, V.

This fine luxury hotel, formerly the Hyatt Regency Brussels, has an ideal location for exploring both the "old Brussels" of the city center and the newer "upper city," and is adjacent to the Botanical Gardens. The public rooms are elegantly modern, with lots of mirrors, marble, and crystal chandeliers. The guest rooms are somewhat smaller than in some other hotels of this category, but all are attractively and comfortably furnished.

Dining/Entertainment: Hugo's, its gourmet restaurant, features French cuisine, and there's Chee Nang for Chinese specialties. Hugo's Cocktail Lounge serves drinks.

Services: Babysitting.

Facilities: Solarium, wheelchair access.

Moderate

City Garden, rue Joseph-II 59, 1040 Brussels. ☎ **02/230-09-45.** Fax 02/230-64-37. 94 apartments, 2 suites. A/C MINIBAR TV TEL **Métro:** Arts/Loi or Maelbeek.

Rates: BF 2,500 ($71) apartment for one; BF 3,000 ($85) apartment for two; BF 7,500–9,600 ($214–$274) suite. AE, DC, EU, MC, V.

Situated in the business district near the European Parliament building—only four minutes by subway from the city center—this very modern hotel offers all apartments, varying in size from studios to one or two bedrooms. All have complete kitchen units, and there's a coffee shop serving breakfast, as well as a restaurant and winter garden.

Clubhouse Hotel, rue Blanche 4, 1050 Brussels. ☎ **02/537-92-10.** Fax 02/537-00-18. 80 rms, 3 suites. A/C MINIBAR TV TEL

Rates (including breakfast): BF 6,100 ($174) single; BF 7,100 ($202) double; BF 11,500 ($328) suite. AE, DC, V.

In the "upper Brussels" district, not far from fashionable avenue Louise, this small gem offers rooms with bright modern furnishings, and some have kitchenettes. A breakfast buffet is served in a pleasant and intimate dining room.

Hôtel Albert Ier, place Rogier 20, 1210 Brussels. ☎ **02/217-21-25.** Fax 02/217-93-31. 285 rms. MINIBAR TV TEL

Rates (including breakfast): BF 3,000–4,000 ($85–$114) single; BF 3,500–4,500 ($100–$128) double. AE, EU, MC, V.

The rooms here are rather basic, but comfortable and attractive. All rooms have a bath and a color TV. There's also a restaurant on the premises.

★ **Hôtel Arlequin,** rue de la Fourche 17–19, 1000 Brussels. ☎ **02/514-16-15.** Fax 02/514-22-02. 60 rms. TV TEL **Métro:** Bourse.

$ **Rates** (including breakfast): BF 2,200 ($62) single; BF 2,950 ($84) double. AE, DC, MC, V.

Among moderately priced hotels, the Arlequin takes first place on several counts. First, it's in the very heart of the city, just steps away from Grand' Place, with the restaurant-lined Petite rue des Bouchers right outside its back entrance. (That entrance is inside a shopping arcade, but there's easy access from both rue de la Fourche and Petite rue des Bouchers.) Then there are the terrific views of the towering Town Hall spire (spectacular when lit at night), overlooking rooftops and narrow medieval streets. I must add my compliments to the obliging staff, from whom I enjoyed nothing but friendly courtesy during my stay. The guest rooms are rather plain, with color schemes of light gray and beige; the furnishings are modern and comfortable. Highly recommended.

Hôtel Bedford, rue du Midi 135, 1000 Brussels. ☎ **02/512-78-40.** Fax 02/514-17-59. 285 rms, 11 suites. MINIBAR TV TEL **Métro:** Bourse.

Rates (including buffet breakfast): BF 5,900–7,500 ($168–$214) single; BF 7,100–8,450 ($202–$241) double; BF 15,000 ($428) suite. AE, DC, MC, V.

This modern hotel is an easy walk from Grand' Place. Its public areas, which include a bar and a restaurant, are tastefully decorated, and each of the attractive guest rooms has modern, comfortable furnishings.

Hôtel Chambord, rue de Namur 82, 1000 Brussels. ☎ **02/513-41-19.**
Fax 02/514-08-47. 69 rms. A/C MINIBAR TV TEL

Rates (including breakfast): BF 4,195 ($119) single; BF 4,795 ($137) double.
AE, DC, MC.

Located in a posh shopping area, this hotel is under the same ownership and management as the Vendôme (below) and offers modern comfort at moderate rates in this expensive neighborhood. The rooms are nicely appointed, and there's an attractive bar that also serves as a breakfast room.

Hôtel Delta, chaussée de Charleroi, 1060 Brussels. ☎ **02/539-01-60.** Fax 02/537-90-11.
246 rms. MINIBAR TV TEL

Rates (including English or American breakfast): BF 5,500 ($157) single; BF 6,500 ($185) double. AE, DC, MC.

This large modern hotel in "upper Brussels" has comfortably furnished and attractively decorated rooms that have recently undergone renovation. The Bambou Restaurant serves a continental menu at moderate to inexpensive prices. It's 5 minutes by car from the Central Station and airport, 10 minutes from the North and South stations.

Hôtel l'Agenda, rue de Florence 6, 1050 Brussels. ☎ **02/539-00-31.**
Fax 02/539-00-63. 36 rms, 2 suites. MINIBAR TV TEL

Rates: BF 3,300 ($44) single; BF 3,600 ($102) double; BF 4,100 ($117) suite.
AE, DC, MC.

This exquisite little hotel is just steps away from avenue Louise, and its very modern, recently refurbished rooms come with complete kitchens. Try for the room that overlooks the inner courtyard.

Hôtel Lambeau, av. Lambeau 150, 1200 Brussels. ☎ **02/732-51-70.**
Fax 02/732-54-90. 24 rms. TV TEL **Métro:** Georges-Henri.

Rates (including buffet breakfast) BF 2,000–2,500 ($57–$71) single; BF 2,800–3,100 ($80–$89) double or twin. AE, MC, V.

Only 15 minutes by métro from the Central Station, this hotel opened in 1994 and offers excellent value for money. The rooms are attractively decorated and contain such additional features as pants presses and hairdryers. The friendly owners speak English.

★ **Hôtel Vendôme,** bd. Adolphe-Max 98, 1000 Brussels. ☎ **02/218-00-70.**
Fax 02/218-06-83. 118 rms. TV TEL

$ **Rates** (including continental breakfast): BF 3,950 ($112) single; BF 4,550 ($130) double.
AE, DC, MC, V.

This small hotel is one of Brussels's most conveniently located moderately priced hotels, a short walk from good shopping, slightly farther to Grand' Place. The rooms are rather plain but comfortably furnished, and some have minibars. Breakfast is served in the cheerful, greenery-filled winter garden, with a skylight to shed natural light. "Business Club" rooms are newer and larger.

Ibis Sainte-Catherine, rue Joseph-Plateau 2, 1000 Brussels. ☎ **02/513-76-20.**
Fax 02/514-22-14. 235 rms. TV TEL

Rates: BF 3,200 ($91) single; BF 3,550 ($101) double. AE, MC, V.

Located in the fascinating (and central) "fish market" district, this is a large, modern member of one of Europe's leading budget-priced hotel chains. The rooms are brightly furnished, the bathrooms have stall showers, and there's a children's play area.

 Manos Hotel, chaussée de Charleroi 100–104, 1060 Brussels. ☎ **02/537-96-82.** Fax 02/539-36-55. 38 rms and suites. TV TEL

 Rates: BF 3,975 ($113) single; BF 4,875 ($139) double; BF 5,680–6,580 ($162–$188) suite. AE, DC, MC, V.

From the time you step into the lovely reception hall lined with classical wall murals, there's a warm, welcoming ambience that spills over throughout this small hotel. The guest rooms and suites (which sleep four to six) are bright and cheerful with furnishings of blond-toned woods. The bar has a pleasant aspect and opens into a small garden, and the tearoom has the inviting look of a living room, with comfortable seating arranged in companionable groups. The hotel is located off avenue Louise.

Inexpensive

Hôtel de Boeck, rue Veydt 40, 1050 Brussels. ☎ **02/537-40-33.** Fax 02/534-40-37. 35 rms. **Métro:** Louise.

Rates (including buffet breakfast): BF 1,400–2,500 ($40–$71) single; BF 1,600–2,500 ($46–$80) double. Additional person BF 675 ($19) extra. AE, DC, MC, V.

A 10-minute walk from place Louise, this hotel has extra-spacious rooms that are adequately furnished. Some rooms have color TV and phone. About half the rooms can accommodate four or five, making it ideal for small groups and families.

Hôtel Pacific, rue Antoine-Dansaert 57, 1000 Brussels. ☎ **02/511-84-59.** 18 rms (some with shower only). **Métro:** Bourse.

Rates (including breakfast): BF 1,050 ($30) single without shower; BF 1,650–1,750 ($47–$50) double without shower, BF 2,150 ($61) double with shower. Showers BF 100 ($2.85) extra for those in rooms without shower. No credit cards.

A good value in an unbeatable location, just a five-minute walk from Grand' Place and two blocks from the Bourse, the Pacific has a friendly soft-spoken owner, Paul Pauwels. Most rooms are large, with plumbing fixtures dating from 80 years ago. Breakfast is served at street level in a fin-de-siècle room decorated with a zebra skin, a Canadian World War II steel helmet, railway signal lamps, copper pots, and a Buddhist prayer wheel.

Hôtel Sabina, rue du Nord 78, 1000 Brussels. ☎ **02/218-26-37.** Fax 02/219-32-39. 24 rms. TV TEL

Rates: BF 1,900 ($54) single or double without bath, BF 2,200 ($62) single or double with bath. V.

This small hostelry is like a private residence, presided over by the friendly and hospitable Renée and Jean Boulvin. The gracious living room has a warm, homey atmosphere, and although rooms vary in size, all are quite comfortable and nicely furnished.

 Welcome Hotel, quai au Bois à Brûler 23 (side entrance at Brandhoutkaal 23), 1000 Brussels. ☎ **02/219-95-46.** Fax 02/217-18-87. 6 rms. MINIBAR TV TEL **Métro:** Ste-Catherine.

Rates: BF 2,100 ($60) single; BF 2,900 ($82) double. Continental breakfast BF 250 ($7) extra. AE, DC, MC, V.

This cozy little hotel, the smallest in Brussels, is high on my personal list of favorites. Michel and Sophie Smeesters are the friendly and helpful owners, who have created bright, cheerful guest rooms, each equipped with table and chairs for comfortable seating. On the two floors above—no elevator, you'll have to walk up—is their superb restaurant (see "Dining," later in this chapter). A small tiled dining room with colorful wall mosaics and a tiny marble-topped bar is the setting for breakfast and, in the evening, dinner for guests who prefer not to dine in the main restaurant. A walk through the kitchen to the restaurant reveals hanging copper pots and pans whose high shine is indicative of the degree of cleanliness and personal pride in this rather special little hotel. Amenities include room safe, trouser press, and hairdryer.

Private Homes

Brussels has an excellent bed-and-breakfast organization, **The New Windrose,** av. Paul-Dejaer 21a, 1060 Brussels (☎ **02/534-71-91;** fax 02/534-71-92), which will send you a complete list of host families, personal profiles of the families, and the rates charged. It can make reservations and assist in all types of other arrangements. There's a booking fee of BF 350 ($10), and three categories of rates, ranging from $28 single to $97 double. Phone or fax them for more details (if you phone, ask for Madame Nadine Fierens, who speaks fluent English).

4 Dining

Brussels offers no fewer than 1,500 top-quality restaurants for your dining pleasure. Spend as much as $70 for dinner in one of the culinary giants or as little as $10 for one prepared with as much loving care—and often with as much expertise—in a smaller, more intimate and informal place.

Quite simply, the people of this city regard dining as a fine art and their own favorite chef as a grand master. They demand near perfection from the kitchen—and quite often they get it—and grade restaurants in the city by awarding irises, the flower of Brussels, instead of traditional stars. Each year the tourist office issues a comprehensive dining directory entitled "Gourmet" that includes each establishment's rating. It's a very good idea to pick up a copy at the beginning of your stay in the city. A warning, however: You're very likely to discover your own "best kitchen" early on and find yourself returning to the same eatery time after time.

The Brussels restaurant scene literally covers the entire city, but there are one or two culinary pockets you should know about. It has been said that you cannot have truly visited this city if you have not dined at least once along either **rue des Bouchers** or its offshoot, **Petite rue des Bouchers.** Near Grand' Place, both are lined with an extraordinary array of small, ethnic (everything from French to Spanish, Italian, Greek, etc.) restaurants, most with a proudly proclaimed specialty, and all with prices that are unbelievably modest (under $12). Reservations are not usually necessary in these colorful, and often crowded, restaurants—if you cannot be seated at one, you simply stroll on to the next one. Food preparation in virtually every one will meet those high Brussels standards.

Then there is the **Marché aux Poissons** (fish market) section with its cluster of small restaurants boasting truly excellent kitchens. Only a short walk from Grand' Place, in the Ste-Catherine area, this is where fishermen once unloaded their daily catches from a now-covered canal. Seafood, as you'd expect, is highlighted here (to my knowledge, there is only one place that features steak) and you must book ahead—a delightful afternoon's occupation is a stroll through the area to examine the bills of fare exhibited in windows and make your reservation for the evening meal (the everyday fruit and vegetable outdoor market in place Ste-Catherine is also a sightseeing attraction in itself).

Warning: Many restaurants close on Sunday, so it pays to plan ahead for weekend meals.

Expensive

 L'Alban Chambon Restaurant, in the Hôtel Métropole, place de Brouckère 31. ☎ 217-23-00.

Cuisine: FRENCH. **Reservations:** Recommended for dinner. **Métro:** De Brouckere.
Prices: Lunch BF 1,350 ($38); dinner BF 2,500 ($71); AE, DC, MC, V.
Open: Lunch Mon–Fri noon–2:30pm; dinner Mon–Fri 7–9pm. **Closed:** Public holidays.

In this wonderfully romantic old-world dining room, you dine by candlelight. The cuisine definitely falls into the gourmet category, and service is of the pampering style. Not surprisingly, there's a very good wine list. A special treat if your timing is right is Opera Night, celebrated six times during the year, when a gourmet dinner, including wine, and an opera concert will set you back BF 3,500 ($100)—worth writing ahead for dates. Highly recommended.

Barbizon, Welriekenweg 95. ☎ 657-04-62.

Cuisine: SEAFOOD. **Reservations:** Required.
Prices: Appetizers BF 600–1,300 ($17–$37); à la carte meals BF 3,000–4,200 ($85–$120); fixed-price meal BF 3,800 ($108). AE, MC, V.
Open: Dinner only, Thurs–Mon 6:30–10:30pm.

Gourmet seafood delights are specialties at this timbered farmhouse about 3 miles to the southeast of the city. The decor is rustic of course, and there's a small outside garden for good-weather dining. La fantaisie de coquilles St-Jacques poêlées, salmon steamed with chervil, a lobster-based waterzooï (thick, creamy soup), and shrimp mousse are just a few of the outstanding creations on the menu.

Bernard, rue de Namur 93. ☎ 512-88-21.

Cuisine: SEAFOOD. **Reservations:** Required.
Prices: A la carte dinner BF 3,000 ($85); plat du jour under BF 1,000 ($28). AE, DC, MC, V.
Open: Dinner only, Tues–Sat 6:30pm–midnight.**Closed:** July.

This is another very good seafood restaurant, and also a local after-theater favorite. The traditional menu presents a continental cuisine, and classy late-night "snacks" might include caviar or foie gras.

Bruneau, av. Broustin 73–75. ☎ 427-69-78.

Cuisine: CONTINENTAL. **Reservations:** Required.
Prices: Fixed-price dinner BF 3,500 ($100). AE, DC, MC, V.
Open: Dinner only, Fri–Mon 6–10pm. **Closed:** Public holidays.

This small, elegant restaurant that rates three stars from Michelin serves classic dishes built around choice ingredients available each day. No matter what your choice, you just can't go wrong here, and one highly recommended specialty is the unusual ravioli of celery with truffles and aromatic extracts. It's near the basilica in Koekelberg.

★ **Comme Chez Soi,** place Rouppe 23. ☎ **512-29-21** or 512-36-74.

Cuisine: FRENCH. **Reservations:** Required, as far in advance as possible.
Prices: Lunch BF 2,000 ($62); dinner BF 3,200 ($91); fixed-price dinner BF 2,800 ($80).
AE, DC.
Open: Lunch Tues–Sat noon–2pm; dinner Tues–Sat 6:30–10pm. **Closed:** July.

Tiny in size (it seats only 45), this elegant restaurant is in an old town house just a
short six blocks from Grand' Place. In a setting of newly decorated belle époque
ambience, owner Pierre Wynants—one of the most revered chefs in Europe—
masterminds meals that can only be called perfection. Two specialties for which he is
known are chicken of Provence with a crayfish sauce (le poussin des marchés de
Provence et sauce béarnaise d'écrivisses) and a luscious concoction of veal sweetbreads
and kidneys in a cream sauce flavored with Ghent mustard (la cassolette de ris de rognon
de veau à la moutarde gantoise). Lunch is not so often booked and is a good alternative to dinner.

★ **La Maison du Cygne,** rue Charles-Buls 2. ☎ **511-82-44.**

Cuisine: FRENCH. **Reservations:** Required, as far in advance as possible. **Métro:** Cen-
tral Station–Bourse.
Prices: Lunch BF 1,500–BF 2,500 ($42–$71); dinner BF 2,000–4,000 ($57–$114).
AE, DC, MC, V.
Open: Lunch Mon–Fri noon–3pm; dinner Mon–Sat 7pm–midnight. **Closed:** Dec 25–
Jan 1 and three weeks in Aug.

This grande dame of Brussels's internationally recognized restaurants has been awarded
one Michelin star. Overlooking Grand' Place from the second floor of one of the few
private residences among those splendid guildhalls, the "House of the Swan" features
polished walnut walls, bronze wall sconces, and lots of green velvet. To the
management's credit, the caring, stylish service is as elegant as the decor. The menu
offers haute-cuisine French classics, such as waterzooï de homard, veal sautéed with
fresh cèpes, and excellent tournedos with green peppercorns. There are also fine chicken
and fish dishes, and specialties such as huftnes au champagne, goujonnette de sole
mousseline, and dos d'agneau façon du Cygne. Because of its location, the Swan is
usually crowded at lunchtime, but dinner reservations are somewhat more available.
In my book, every dollar buys double value.

★ **Les Quatre Saisons (The Four Seasons),** in the Royal Windsor Hotel, rue
Duquesnoy 5. ☎ **511-42-15.**

Cuisine: FRENCH. **Reservations:** Recommended. **Métro:** Central Station or Bourse.
Prices: Lunch BF 2,000 ($57); à la carte dinner BF 3,000–4,000 ($85–$114); plat du
jour BF 900 ($25). AE, DC, MC, V.
Open: Lunch Mon–Fri noon–2:30pm; dinner Mon–Sat 7:30–10:30pm. **Closed:** Three
weeks in July–Aug.

This quietly elegant and popular restaurant is done up in soft shades of pink and cream
and has an air of romantic intimacy. It was named the best hotel restaurant in
Brussels in 1987 by a leading Belgian restaurant guide, and its head chef, Jan Raven,
has won several prestigious culinary awards. Menus are seasonal, with different specialties each month. Among the favorites are crépinette de pigeon (pigeon in spinach
leaves), rose de saumon au fumet de seiches (salmon with squid sauce), and terrine de
lotte marinée à sel marin (terrine of monkfish). There's an excellent and comprehensive wine list. Highly recommended.

Villa Lorraine, chaussée de la Hulpa 28. ☎ **374-31-63.**
Cuisine: FRENCH. **Reservations:** Recommended.
Prices: Five-course à la carte dinner BF 3,500 ($100). AE, DC, MC, V.
Open: Dinner only, Mon–Sat 6:30–10pm. **Closed:** Aug.

Classic French creations are featured by one of the city's top kitchens in this renovated château on the fringes of the lovely forest park, Bois de la Cambre. The dining rooms are spacious, with wicker furnishings, flower arrangements everywhere, and a skylight. In good weather you may elect to have drinks outside under the trees. Among the classic French offerings are saddle of lamb in a delicate red-wine and herb sauce, cold salmon with a herb sauce, partridge cooked with apples and baked lobster with butter rose.

Moderate

Aux Armes de Bruxelles, rue des Bouchers 13. ☎ **511-21-18.**
Cuisine: BELGIAN/FRENCH. **Reservations:** Recommended. **Métro:** Central Station or Bourse.
Prices: Lunch or dinner BF 1,200–2,000 ($34–$57). AE, DC, MC, V.
Open: Tues–Sun noon–11:15pm.

This one is a Brussels tradition, with gracious, rather formal service, but a casual, relaxed ambience. It's an excellent place for your introduction to Belgian/French cooking, since it offers just about every regional specialty you can think of (including mussels in every conceivable guise) from a menu that will let you sample anything from their excellent beef stewed in beer to a delicious waterzooï to a steak with pepper-and-cream sauce, all at quite reasonable prices. It's just off Grand' Place.

Chez Leon, rue des Bouchers 18. ☎ **511-14-15.**
Cuisine: BELGIAN. **Reservations:** Required. **Métro:** Central Station or Bourse.
Prices: Average lunch or dinner BF 835–1,000 ($24–$28). AE, DC, MC, V.
Open: Daily noon–midnight.

This bistro on Brussels's "street of restaurants" is the domain of Guy Deberghes, the sixth generation of his family to run the long-standing favorite of Brussels natives. His mother, affectionately known as Madame Jo and now retired, still comes in regularly to welcome diners. Just off Grand' Place, the large place stays busy and can be noisy, but is worth seeking out among its 80 or so neighboring eateries. Belgian specialties are featured, and it is well known for its seafood.

★ **Falstaff,** rue Henri-Maus 23–25. ☎ **511-98-77.**
Cuisine: BELGIAN. **Reservations:** Not required. **Métro:** Bourse.
Prices: Dinner BF 850–1,400 ($24–$40). AE, DC, MC, V.
Open: Daily 7am–2am.

This colorful art nouveau–style tavern and restaurant across from the Bourse in what were originally private mansions of the late 1800s is a tribute to the Shakespearean hero of *The Merry Wives of Windsor.* Huge stained-glass scenes in the style of Pieter Brueghel the Elder memorialize the Falstaff legend, and the Brueghelian style is carried out in table settings and in the period dress of waiters and waitresses. There's even a Brueghelian Menu, featuring Belgian specialties like melle Beulemans (chicken with chicory) or rabbit casserole in Gueuze. The à la carte menu is extensive. The prices are so reasonable that Falstaff can be considered either moderate or inexpensive, depending on your appetite.

Le Mozart, chaussée d'Alsemberg 541. ☎ **344-08-09.**
> **Cuisine:** STEAK/SEAFOOD. **Reservations:** Not required.
> **Prices:** Lunch or dinner about BF 1,700 ($48); salads and sandwiches under BF 600 ($17). No credit cards.
> **Open:** Tues–Thurs noon–3 or 4am, Fri–Sat noon–5 or 6am.

There's more than a little bit of whimsy in the decor of this café and restaurant in the southern suburbs, with its kleig lights, big-band musician puppets suspended from the ceiling (along with a vintage Chevy adorned with steer's horns!), and photos of jazz greats on the ceiling—not surprising, perhaps, since the proprietors of this lively place are Remo and Linda Gozzi, who also own the Brussels Jazz Club. Specialties are excellent steaks, chops, and seafood dishes, and lighter fare such as salads and sandwiches. As you might expect, this place attracts professional musicians.

Ravenstein, rue Ravenstein 1. ☎ **512-77-68.**
> **Cuisine:** SEAFOOD/CONTINENTAL. **Reservations:** Recommended. **Métro:** Central Station.
> **Prices:** Lunch BF 1,400 ($40); dinner BF 2,000–3,500 ($57–$100). AE, DC, MC, V.
> **Open:** Lunch Mon–Fri noon–2:30pm; dinner Mon–Fri 6:30–9:30pm. **Closed:** Aug.

Dining at the Ravenstein is an aesthetic as well as a culinary experience, just a short walk from Grand' Place. This was the home of a Brussels nobleman back in the 16th century, and it retains its Flemish character with copper-hooded fireplaces and lots of polished wood paneling.

★ **La Sirène d'Or**, place Ste-Catherine 1A. ☎ **513-51-98.**
> **Cuisine:** SEAFOOD. **Reservations:** Required. **Métro:** Ste-Catherine.
$ **Prices:** Lunch "le menu du chef" about BF 1,800 ($51); dinner BF 2,400–3,000 ($68–$85). AE, DC, MC, V.
> **Open:** Lunch Tues–Sat noon–3pm; dinner Tues–Sat 6:30–10:30pm. **Closed:** Jan 1, July, Dec 25.

In the fish-market area, this small, casually elegant restaurant is another gem that has won my heart. The chef, Robert Van Duuren, once cooked for a very demanding Prince Albert of Liège! I love the setting here: dark wood walls, overhead beams, velvet-seated chairs, and Belgian lace curtains at the windows. But it's the cuisine that sets this place apart. There's a lovely grilled turbot with ginger, and an absolutely magnificent bouillabaisse Grand Marius (a luscious fish concoction properly redolent of garlic).

Au Stekerlapatte, rue des Prêtres 4. ☎ **512-86-81.**
> **Cuisine:** TRADITIONAL. **Reservations:** Recommended.
> **Prices:** Average dinner BF 1,200 ($34); house specials less. No credit cards.
> **Open:** Dinner only, Tues–Sun 7pm–1am.

For hearty food in a convivial atmosphere, you can't do much better than this brasserie in the old working-class district of Les Marolles. The rambling old building has the comfortable feel of a place that has picked up its furnishings, mirrors, and wall paneling over the years and left them as they fell. Oilcloth-covered tables are packed virtually one against the other, and there's the rise and fall of conversation between regulars who come here for the ample servings of waterzooï, eels cooked with herbs, smoked ribs, sausages, and duck.

★ **Trente Rue de la Paille,** rue de la Paille 30. ☎ **512-07-15.**

    Cuisine: SEAFOOD/NOUVELLE CUISINE. **Reservations:** Recommended.
    Prices: Lunch BF 1,200 ($34); dinner BF 2,400 ($68). AE, DC, MC, V.
    Open: Lunch Mon–Fri noon–2:30pm; dinner Mon–Sat 6:30–11:30pm. **Closed:** July,
    public holidays.

Owner/chef André Martiny has created a lovely country look in this small, cozy restaurant right around the corner from place du Grand-Sablon. Lots of plants and flowers, and candlelight in the evening. The menu includes innovative seafood dishes as well as traditional favorites. The marvelous mille-feuille of salmon and asparagus is a personal favorite. A real charmer.

La Truit d'Argent Restaurant-Hôtel, quai au Bois à Brûler 23. ☎ **219-95-46.**

    Cuisine: FRENCH. **Reservations:** Recommended. **Métro:** Ste-Catherine.
    Prices: Three-course lunch BF 2,000 ($57); dinner BF 2,800 ($80) for four courses,
    BF 3,400 ($97) for six courses. AE, DC, MC, V.
    Open: Lunch Mon–Fri noon–2:30pm; dinner Mon–Sat 7–11:30pm.

This small, elegant restaurant in the fish-market area is the creation of Michel and Sophie Smeesters (see "Accommodations," earlier in this chapter). Superb is the way to describe the food that comes to table. Fish, meat, and fowl dishes are imaginative and prepared from choice ingredients, and the presentation is nothing less than exquisite—so pleasing to the eye you might well hesitate to destroy the image by tucking in. A personal favorite is homard de St-Jacques aux champignons des bois (lobster with mushrooms in a delicate cream sauce). Service is professional and friendly.

"FISH MARKET" GEMS IN THE MODERATE RANGE

Space is too limited to list all the good restaurants in the Marché aux Poissons area, but in addition to the very special La Sirène d'Or (see above), you should know about the following. Most serve lunch from noon to 2:30pm and dinner from 6:30 to 10pm on weekdays (call ahead to check), MasterCard and Visa are accepted at most, and reservations are suggested at all. Prices will average about BF 1,000 ($35) and up at lunch, BF 1,600 ($45) and up at dinner.

At quai aux Briques 44 ★ **Jacques** (☎ **513-27-62**) is a small, rather plain brasserie that is a favorite of most Brussels residents who eat regularly in the fish-market district. Seafood is the thing to order here, although three versions of steak appear on the menu. There's a good list of reasonably priced wines. Other recommendations are: **La Belle Maraichère,** place Ste-Catherine 11A (☎ **512-97-59**); **Le Quai,** quai aux Briques 14 (☎ **512-37-36**), which specializes in lobster; **La Villette,** rue du Vieux-Marché-aux-Grains 3 (☎ **512-75-50**), a real charmer, with a good wine cellar, and the only one in the fish market area (as far as I could ascertain) that specializes in steak—especially in Aberdeen Angus beef—as well as seafood; and **Cochon d'Or,** quai aux Bois à Brûler 15 (☎ **218-07-71**).

Inexpensive

Auberge des Chapeliers, rue des Chapeliers 1–3. ☎ **513-73-38.**

    Cuisine: BELGIAN. **Reservations:** Not required. **Métro:** Central Station.
    Prices: Lunch or dinner BF 500–1,200 ($14–$34). AE, DC, MC, V.
    Open: Lunch daily noon–2:30pm; dinner daily 6pm–midnight.

This 150-year-old building, just off Grand' Place, has been serving up bistro food for more than a quarter of a century in a setting of dark wood, exposed beams, and checkered tablecloths. Popular with locals who live and work in the area, as well as with tourists who are fortunate enough to find it, it can be chock-a-block at the height of lunch hour, so it's a good idea to come just after noon or just after 2pm. The menu features traditional Belgian pork, chicken, beef, and seafood dishes, and an excellent waterzooï. Servings are more than ample.

Au Trappiste, av. de la Toison-d'Or 7. ☎ **511-78-39.**

Cuisine: BELGIAN. **Métro:** Namur.
Prices: Main courses BF 180–600 ($5–$17). AE, DC, MC, V.
Open: Daily noon–midnight.

If you're in the pricey avenue Louise–chausée de Wavre area, this is the one—and perhaps the only—inexpensive dining option. A brasserie-style spot with mirrors, chandeliers, and brass railings, it offers a good plat du jour which might be vegetable soup followed by dishes like gulash, fried fish, breaded veal cutlet, or pasta of some sort.

★ $ **Brasserie Roue d'Or,** rue des Chapeliers 26. ☎ **514-25-54.**

Cuisine: BELGIAN/GRILLS/SEAFOOD. **Reservations:** Not required. **Métro:** Central Station.
Prices: Main courses BF 250–360 ($7–$10); full meal BF 650–900 ($18–$25). AE, MC, V.
Open: Lunch Mon–Fri noon–3pm; dinner Mon–Fri 6pm–12:30am.

This large, high-ceilinged brasserie, off Grand' Place, is under the same ownership as 'T Kelderke (see below). The decor is one of dark wood, lots of mirrors, and marble-topped tables, and the extensive menu caters to just about any appetite, from grills and hamburgers to a good selection of salmon and other seafoods. It's a convivial place, with an extensive wine, beer, and spirits list, and a loyal local following.

★ $ **Cafe Metropole,** in the Hôtel Métropole, place de Brouckère 31. ☎ **217-23-00.**

Cuisine: LIGHT MEALS/SANDWICHES/SNACKS/AFTERNOON TEA. **Reservations:** Not accepted. **Métro:** De Brouckere.
Prices: Plat du jour BF 350 ($9.80); light meal BF 300–420 ($8.40–$11.75). AE, MC, V.
Open: Daily 9am–2am.

Many Brussels visitors never get beyond the pleasant heated sidewalk section of this massive, Victorian-style café. Do have a bit both outdoors *and* inside. Inside you'll find a casually elegant decor, highlighted by a marble fireplace and colorful wooden puppets hung from the high ceilings, and comfortable leather seating arranged in cozy groupings. The menu is wide-ranging—sandwiches, soups, quiches and other light meals, and snacks (a personal favorite is the plateau de Fekauokis, a tray of toast rounds topped with marvelous cheeses, fish, beef, pâté, and caviar, a meal in itself!)—and the bar menu fills no fewer than six pages, including some rather special specialties from the head barman.

Cap de Nuit, place de la Vieille-Halle-aux-Blés 28. ☎ **512-93-42.**

Cuisine: ITALIAN/BELGIAN. **Reservations:** Not required.
Prices: Main courses BF 240–610 ($7–$17); plat du jour BF 330 ($9). AE, DC, EU, MC, V.
Open: Daily 6pm–7am.

Near Grand' Place, this place stays open all night. The modern decor, the late hours, and the 28 varieties of beer attract a crowd between the ages of 20 and 40. The plat du jour, served all night, is the best deal and is reliably tasty.

El Greco, Grand' Place 36. ☎ **511-89-82.**

> **Cuisine:** GREEK. **Reservations:** Not required. **Métro:** Central Station or Bourse.
> **Prices:** Dinner under BF 1,000 ($28). AE, DC, MC, V.
> **Open:** Daily noon–3am.

Singing waiters turn inexpensive dining into real fun here on Grand' Place. Moussaka and other traditional Greek dishes are featured.

La Cuccagna, chaussée de Wavre 39. ☎ **513-31-10.**

> **Cuisine:** ITALIAN. **Reservations:** Recommended at dinner.
> **Prices:** Pizza and pasta BF 170–660 ($5–$19); meat and fish courses BF 350–440 ($10–$12.50). AE, EU, MC, V.
> **Open:** Lunch Mon–Sat noon–2:30pm; dinner Mon–Sat 6–11pm.

This is an atmospheric spot for a well-priced meal. The rigatoni that I enjoyed could easily have made a meal in itself and cost under $7. The decor is antiqued-pastel colors and faux classical columns.

Le Paon, Grand' Place 35. ☎ **513-35-82.**

> **Cuisine:** BELGIAN. **Reservations:** Recommended. **Métro:** Central Station or Bourse.
> **Prices:** Dinner under BF 1,000 ($28). MC, V.
> **Open:** Dinner only, daily 6–11pm.

You'll dine by candlelight in this 17th-century house on Grand' Place, where the menu features regional specialties like waterzooï, rabbit cooked in beer, and other traditional dishes.

★ **Le Paon Royal Taverne-Restaurant,** rue du Vieux-Marché-aux-Grains 6. ☎ **513-08-68.**

> $ **Cuisine:** BELGIAN. **Reservations:** Not required. **Métro:** Ste-Catherine.
> **Prices:** Lunch or dinner BF 850 ($24); plat du jour BF 450 ($13). AE, DC, MC, V.
> **Open:** Tues–Sat noon–9:30pm. (Tavern, Tues–Sat 8am–10pm.)

In the fish-market district, this is one of my favorite small, inexpensive cafés, with a rustic wood-and-exposed-brick interior and beamed ceiling. You can choose one of the 65 brands of beer behind the tiny bar and a snack, and at lunchtime there's a hearty plat du jour consisting of a traditional Belgian dish. In fine weather, chairs are sometimes set out under the trees in the little park just across the street.

Le Roy d'Espagne, Grand' Place.

> **Cuisine:** SANDWICHES/SNACKS. **Reservations:** Not required. **Métro:** Central Station or Bourse.
> **Prices:** Sandwiches under BF 375 ($10.50). MC, V.
> **Open:** Daily noon–1am.

This is one of the many "drop-in" inexpensive drinking establishments serving food that line the square. It's a large, rustic-style place, with wooden puppets hanging from the ceiling, puppets serving as newel posts for the center stairs, and a full-size stuffed horse right in the center of things (I never did get the story on how or why it's here— you might ask!). There's a menu consisting primarily of sandwiches (including one of smoked ham of the Ardennes), cheese, and other snacks. It's a good place for a light lunch accompanied by Belgian beer.

'T Kelderke (The Cellar), Grand' Place 15. ☎ **513-73-44.**

Cuisine: BELGIAN. **Reservations:** Not required. **Métro:** Central Station or Bourse.
Prices: A la carte dishes BF 500 ($14) plat du jour BF 360 ($10). AE, MC, V.
Open: Daily noon–2am.

Despite the plethora of good restaurants around Grand' Place, I find myself returning again and again to this rustic downstairs establishment. It serves up the classic *hearty*
dishes of Belgian cuisine, and you'll eat in the company of Brussels's natives, who often
bring the family. I always order lapin à la bière (rabbit cooked in beer), but eventually
I hope to get through a number of other appealing dishes, including côtes de mouton
provençale (mutton chops), hoche-pot (a tasty beef stew), moules (mussels) in season
in many different versions, and a large menu of other selections. Even with wine or
beer, your bill won't top $25.

5 Attractions

Brussels is a sightseer's paradise, with such an incredible variety of things to see and
do that it can sometimes be overwhelming. History is just around every corner, there
are more than 75 museums dedicated to just about every special interest under the
sun, impressive public buildings beckon for inspection, leafy parks and interesting
squares lined with sidewalk cafés offer respite for weary feet, and there's good public
transport to those attractions beyond walking distance of the compact, heart-shaped
city center. That city center could, in fact, quite easily consume your entire sightseeing
time, for this is where you'll find many of Brussels's most popular attractions.

Your very first stop should be at the **Tourist Information Brussels (T.I.B.)**
office in the Town Hall in Grand' Place to pick up their comprehensive guidebook
and city map. The helpful guide does not confine itself to sightseeing, but is a gold
mine of information on the practicalities of your stay in the city. If your stay is a short
one, you may want to engage one of their multilingual guides (a full dozen languages
are spoken), available at very reasonable rates, to make the best use of your time.

The Top Attractions

PUBLIC SPACES

⭐ **Grand' Place**

Grand' Place (*Grote Markt* in Flemish) is today, as it has been since the 12th century,
the very heart of Brussels. This large cobblestone square has served as the stage for
Belgium's great pageant of history—monarchs traipsing through en route to victory
or defeat; and patriots shouting rebellion, then losing their heads in front of
the 15th-century Town Hall (Hôtel de Ville). From that civic building's lofty
spire, the patron saint of Brussels, Saint Michael, keeps watch over it all as he perches
above the city crushing the devil beneath his feet.

Your first sight of Grand' Place will be a memorable one. In fact, I challenge you
to enter the square from any one of the narrow streets that converge there without an
audible gasp at the pure splendor of it all. Impressive as it is by day, it's most beautiful
in the golden glow of floodlights after dark. Completely enclosed by tall, gabled buildings literally dripping with ornamentation and statuary, the huge space is alive with
the hubbub of daily commerce exactly as it has been from the beginning. Daily, there's
a colorful flower market; Sunday mornings are given over to a bird market; and on
weekend evenings in summer, frequently there are band concerts.

Back in 1695 only the venerable Town Hall (begun in 1404 and completed in 1480) was left standing after a savage 48-hour bombardment from forces of the French king, Louis XIV. In less than four years, Belgian craftspeople erected the magnificent group of edifices you see today. Built to house the craft guilds that sponsored their construction, their curvy baroque facades are similar yet distinctively individual.

Look for the Neo-Gothic and misnamed King's House (it has been used for any number of civic purposes, but has never housed a monarch!), the repository of the municipal museum since the late 1800s. Victor Hugo spent part of his anguished exile at no. 26 (The Pigeon). The six connected houses at the upper end of the square are known collectively as the House of the Dukes of Brabant, and those nobles are represented by 19 busts prominently displayed at the top of the ground floor—see if you can identify the guilds that set up residence here by the emblems on display higher up (cabinetmakers, millers, masons, wine and vegetable merchants, tanners, and the "Four Crowned Crafts" of stone cutters, roofers, masons, and sculptors). Be sure to save time for a visit to both the Town Hall and the Museum of the City of Brussels in the King's House (see "Museums," below). Métro: Central Station or Bourse.

Place du Grand-Sablon

Place du Grand-Sablon, just off rue de la Régence, is also lined with houses of master artisans, and the square boasts a lovely statue of the goddess Minerva, given to the city in 1751 by one Lord Bruce, Count of Ailesbury, as a token of appreciation for his hospitable reception. At the top of the square sits the flamboyantly Gothic Notre-Dame-du-Sablon, built by the crossbowmen of the city in the 15th century to replace an earlier chapel that was destroyed. Antiquing is especially good in this neighborhood, and on Saturday and Sunday mornings a marvelous antiques flea market sets up shop.

Place du Petit-Sablon

Just across rue de la Régence, place du Petit-Sablon is a statuary garden, with figures of great 16th-century humanists at one end, some 48 bronze statuettes adorning the surrounding wrought-iron fence (symbolizing the Brussels Corporations), and statues of two of Brussels's favorite heroes, the patriotic counts of Egmont and Hornes, who were beheaded in Grand' Place during the 16th century for actively resisting Spanish oppression.

Place Royale

Place Royale is the dividing point between rue de la Régence (which leads to the Palais de Justice) and rue Royale, and is just opposite the Royal Palace. Of interest here is the notable collection of sculptures at St-Jacques-sur-Coudenberg.

Parc de Bruxelles

Brussels Park is bordered on one side by rue Royale, on the other by rue Ducale. At one end, across rue de la Loi, is the massive Palais de la Nation, and across place des Palais at the other end is the Palais Royal. This beautiful park was once the private domain of the dukes of Brabant, and in 1830 it was where Belgian patriots confronted Dutch troops in a conflict that resulted in independence for their country.

The Bois de la Cambre and Forêt de Soignes

Known affectionately as simply "the bois," the Bois de la Cambre lies at the top of avenue Louise. Its centerpiece is a small lake centered by a small café. Back in the 1800s, beech trees of the huge adjoining Forest of Soignes covered a full 30,000 acres, dwarfing its present size, even though it's still monumental by modern standards.

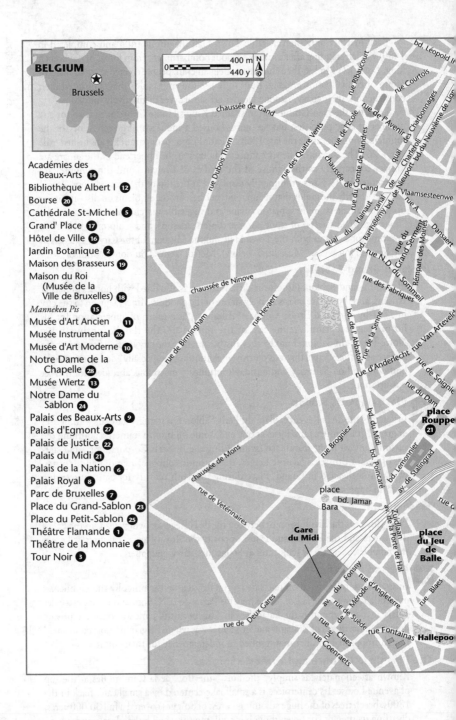

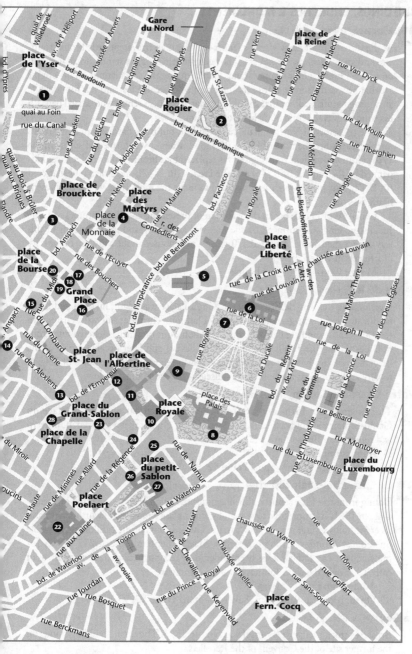

Brussels Attractions

BUILDINGS, CHURCHES & MONUMENTS

 Manneken Pis, rue de l'Etuve.

At the top of almost every visitor's "must-see" list is an irreverent little bronze statuette known as *Manneken Pis.* A small boy caught urinating, he stands atop a fountain on rue de l'Etuve, not far from Grand' Place. Among the speculations on his origins are that he was the son of a Brussels nobleman who became lost and was found while answering nature's call, or that sprinkling a hated Spanish sentry who passed beneath his window was the little boy's form of rebellion.

The true story of "Little Julian" has been lost, but there has been an effigy in his form at least since the time of Philip the Good, when it was formed of sugar. In the 17th century an ancient stone figure was replaced by a bronze replica, which was kidnapped by the English (in 1745) and the French (in 1747), and stolen and shattered (in 1817). The pieces were carefully fitted to make the mold from which the present figure was cast.

Louis XV of France began the tradition of presenting colorful costumes to Little Julian (the king was outraged by the French kidnapping and made amends in this way). Since then, he has acquired 570 outfits, now housed in the Museum of the City of Brussels in Grand' Place.

Metro: Central Station or Bourse.

Palais du Roi, Grand' Place.

Overlooking the Parc de Bruxelles, the King's Palace was begun in 1820 and had a facelift in 1904 in the grandiose Louis XVI fashion. The older side wings date from the 18th century and are flanked by two pavilions, one of which sheltered numerous notables during the 1800s (the Hôtel de Bellevue) and later became a part of the Belgian royal family residence. Bellevue is now a repository for treasures of Belgian royalty and is open to the public as a museum (see "Museums," below).

Notre-Dame-du-Sablon, rue de la Régence.

This magnificent 15th- and 16th-century marvel sits at one end of place du Grand-Sablon and holds a celebrated statue of Saint Hubert that was seized in Antwerp and returned to Brussels in 1348.

Admission: Free.
Open: Mon–Sat 9am–6pm. **Tram:** 92, 93, or 94.

 La Cathédrale Saint-Michel, parvis Ste-Gudule.

Dating from the 13th century, this magnificent church acquired the title of "cathedral" in 1961. Its impressive towers and stained-glass windows are worth a visit, and its crypt holds several members of royalty. Guided tours of the carillon are available on request Monday through Saturday May to September; call **217-83-45** for information. The cathedral has been undergoing reconstruction in recent years; as of early 1995 only the choir loft has not been completed.

Admission: Free.
Open: Mon–Sat 9am–6pm, Sun 1:30–5pm. **Tram:** 92, 93, or 94.

La Bourse, rue Henri-Maus 2.

Brussels's stock exchange (Bourse) was built in 1873. The ornate building stands on the former site of the Convent of the Récollets.

Admission: Free.
Open: Mon–Fri 7am–6:30pm. Must telephone **509-12-11** in advance to arrange visit. **Métro:** Bourse.

Church of St. Nicholas, rue au Beurre.

At the back of the Bourse, this lovely little church is almost hidden by the fine old houses surrounding it. Traditionally the spiritual home of hopeful dancers, it holds a small painting by Rubens (*Virgin and Child*) and the beautiful *Milkmaid* by Marc Devos.

Admission: Free

Open: Mon–Fri 7:30am–6:30pm, Sat 9am–5:30pm, Sun 7:30am–7:30pm.
Métro: Bourse.

MUSEUMS

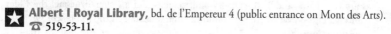

Albert I Royal Library, bd. de l'Empereur 4 (public entrance on Mont des Arts). ☎ **519-53-11.**

This is an astounding tribute to the written word down through the centuries, with manuscripts and ancient books, as well as up-to-date, high-level books in all disciplines in the Book Museum; and typographical, binding, and lithographical exhibits in the Printing Museum. This is also the National Library of Belgium.

Admission: Free.

Open: Mon–Sat 9am–noon and 2–5pm. **Closed:** Last week in Aug, public holidays.

Brewery Museum, Maison des Brasseurs, Grand' Place 10. ☎ **511-49-87.**

In the beautiful Guild House of the Brewers, you'll find numerous paintings, stained-glass windows, and collections of pitchers, pint pots, and old china beer pumps. The lovely old house, with its arched cellars, is a veritable beer museum, where you can admire an authentic 18th-century brewery with its wooden fermentation and brewing vats and all the tools of the time.

Admission: BF 100 ($2.85).

Open: Mon–Fri 10am–noon and 2–5pm, Sat 10am–noon. **Closed:** Nov–Mar.
Métro: Central Station or Bourse.

Hôtel de Ville (Town Hall), Grand' Place. ☎ **512-75-54.**

Although technically not a museum, this should top any sightseer's list, not only for a fascinating glimpse into Brussels's tempestuous past, but for a firsthand look at offices of functioning aldermen and impressive chambers in which the City Council convenes. Walls are hung with 16th-, 17th-, and 18th-century tapestries, and huge paintings depict many of the strong foreign leaders who have influenced the city's past. One look, for example, at the Duke of Alba's cruel features brings instant insight into the brutal oppression he imposed on Belgium.

Admission: Free.

Open: Tues–Fri 9:30am–5pm. **Closed:** During official receptions and when the council is in session. **Métro:** Central Station or Bourse.

Musée d'Art Ancien, rue de la Régence 3. ☎ **508-32-11.**

Masterpieces from the 14th to the 17th century are featured here. The Flemish Primitive section includes works by van der Weyden, Bouts, and Memling;

IMPRESSIONS

If any person wants to be happy I should advise the Parc. You sit drinking iced drinks and smoking penny cigars under great old trees.
— Robert Louis Stevenson, 1872

Renaissance masters represented include Brueghel and Bosch; and Rubens and Van Dyck are prominent in the baroque collection. Guided tours are available by request.
Admission: Free.
Open: Tues–Sun 10am–noon and 1–5pm. **Tram:** 92, 93, or 94. **Bus:** 20, 34, 38, 71, 95, or 96.

Musée Communal (Museum of the City of Brussels), Maison du Roi (King's House), Grand' Place. ☎ 511-27-42.

Exhibitions in this historic building trace the city's development both in historical and archeological relics. Porcelain and ceramic collections are especially noteworthy, as are two 15th- and 16th-century altar screens and a Pieter Brueghel the Elder painting. This is also where you'll find the fine wardrobe of the *Mannekin Pis.*
Admission: Free.
Open: Mon–Fri 10am–12:30pm and 1:30–5pm, Sat–Sun 10am–1pm. **Métro:** Central Station or Bourse.

Musée Bellevue, place des Palais 7. ☎ 511-44-25.

In this former royal residence, salons have been restored with 18th- and 19th-century furnishings to frame memorabilia collections of lace, costumes, silver, china, hunting guns, jewelry, fans, and earthenware birds. Guided tours are available for a small charge.
Admission: Free.
Open: Sat–Thurs 10am–4:45pm. **Closed:** Public holidays. **Métro:** Parc.

★ Musée Horta, rue Américaine 25, Saint-Gilles. ☎ 537-16-92.

Brussels owes its rich collection of art nouveau to Victor Horta, a resident architect who led development of the style. His home and adjoining studio are now open as a museum. Restored to their original condition, the large, airy rooms hold prime examples of Horta's genius, and there's a marvelous stained-glass skylight.
Admission: BF 100 ($2.85).
Open: Tues–Sun 2–5:30pm. **Closed:** Public holidays. **Tram:** 81 or 92. **Bus:** 54 or 60.

Musées Royaux d'Art et d'Histoire, Parc du Cinquantenaire 10, Etterbeek. ☎ 741-72-11.

Famed throughout the world, the Royal Museum of Art and History holds fabulous artifact collections from ancient Egyptian, Near Eastern, Greek, Roman, and South American civilizations. Other sections include lace, tapestry, Far Eastern furniture, toys, stained glass, ceramics, jewels, folklore, and old vehicles that include 18th-century coupes, sedan chairs, sleighs, and royal coaches. There's also an Exhibition for the Blind set up by the Education Department.
Admission: Free.
Open: Tues–Fri 9:15am–5pm, Sat–Sun 10 am–5pm. **Closed:** Monday. **Métro:** Mérode.

Royal Museum of Central Africa, Leuvensesteenweg 13, Tervuren. ☎ 769-52-11.

This museum has excellent exhibits dealing with both human and natural sciences in Africa.
Admission: Free.
Open: Tues–Sun 10am–4:30pm. **Closed:** Monday. **Tram:** 44.

Cool for Kids

Atomium, bd. du Centenaire, Laeken. ☎ **477-09-77.**

From the moment you arrive in Brussels, you'll be aware of this striking replica of a molecule of iron—it's visible against the skyline from any vantage point in the city. Built for the 1958 World's Fair, it has now become a museum, with permanent exhibitions on the peaceful uses of atomic energy. It's well worth a visit for both the exhibits and the panoramic views of the city (there's also an inexpensive restaurant on the premises).

At the foot of the Atomium, **Bruparck!,** a 12-acre leisure park, features a "Mini-Europe" exhibit, with some 400 models of buildings, landscapes, roads, and railways. You can visit a re-creation of Brussels as a medieval village. If water sports appeal, head for one of the pools at the **Oceadium Water Leisure Center.** For more information call 477-03-77.

Admission: Atomium, BF 160 ($4.50); general admission to Bruparck, Oceadium Water Leisure Center, and Atomium, BF 850 ($24).

Open: Daily 9:30am–6pm. **Métro:** Heysel. **Tram:** 81.

Musée des Enfants, rue du Bourgmestre 15, Ixelles. ☎ **640-01-07.**

This excellent children's museum offers hands-on experience with a wide range of everyday-life objects.

Admission: BF 180 ($5).

Open: Wed and Sat–Sun 2:30–5pm. **Tram:** 23 or 90. **Bus:** 71.

More Attractions

Notre-Dame de la Chapelle, place de la Chapelle. ☎ **519-26-56.**

This Romanesque-Gothic church is interesting both historically and architecturally. François Anneessens, a Brussels hero who lost his head for civil rights, is buried here (you'll find a commemorative plaque in the Chapel of the Holy Sacrament), and the epitaph to Pieter Brueghel the Elder and his wife is also in one of the chapels. The church is currently closed for restoration; inquire at the tourist office to see if it's open at the time of your visit.

Tram: 92, 93, or 94.

Palais de Justice, place Poelaert.

The Palace of Justice sits rather ironically on the spot where the city's criminals once swung from the gibbet. The massive building, built in the 1800s, holds 245 offices and consulting rooms, plus 27 courtrooms.

Admission: Free.

Open: Guided tours Mon–Fri 9am–3pm, Sat–Sun by request (call **508-61-11** for information). **Métro:** Louise.

Palais de la Nation, at the rue de la Loi end of the Parc de Bruxelles (public entrance at rue de Louvain 13).

The Palace of the Nation is the seat of the Senate and Chamber of Representatives. When Parliament is in session, visitors are not allowed, but you can request a free guided tour; call **513-38-40** for information.

SPECIAL-INTEREST SIGHTSEEING

ARAU (Workshop for Urban Research and Action), rue Henri-Maus 37 (☎ **513-47-61** or **512-56-90**), conducts Saturday-morning tours at BF 500 ($14) of art nouveau architecture; art deco architecture of the 1930s; or the squares, parks, and gardens of the city (offered on a rotating basis, with only one of the three offered each Saturday). Tour reservations must be made through their office, and pickup is at designated points in the city center. Tours operate from March to November, but private tours may be arranged all year.

ORGANIZED TOURS

Coach tours, approximately three hours in duration, are available from **Panorama Tours,** rue du Marché-aux-Herbes 105 (☎ **513-61-54**), and **De Boeck Sightseeing Tours,** rue de la Colline 8, Grand' Place (☎ **513-77-44**). Each tour costs BF 750 ($21). Bookings may be made through most hotels, and arrangements can be made for hotel pickup. Tours operate from March to November, but private tours may be arranged all year.

From mid-May to the end of September, the **Chatterbus Tour,** rue des Thuyas 12 (☎ **673-18-35**), operates a daily three-hour tour starting at 10am (also at 2pm during July) from the Galeries Saint-Hubert, a shopping mall next to rue du Marché-aux-Herbes 90, a few steps off Grand' Place. It's a walking tour covering the historic center, followed by a bus ride through areas the average tourist will never see. You'll hear about life in Belgium and get a real feel for the city. The price is BF 320 ($9).

Walking Tour 1
Ilôt Sacré to the Marolles

Start   Town Hall, Grand' Place.

Finish   Town center.

Time   About three hours.

Best Times   Saturday or Sunday morning, when you can shop the books-and-antiques market in place du Grand-Sablon.

This walk winds its way through and around the splendid Grand' Place and will have the benefit of orienting you to the heart of the old city. Conveniently, this walking tour begins at the Town Hall, in which you'll find the tourist office; so after you've picked up some brochures and asked the staff whatever questions you may have, proceed down Petite rue des Bouchers. This district, called the Ilôt Sacré, is a jumble of streets and passages where street musicians and vendors of souvenirs provide a noisy and colorful atmosphere. On Schuddeveld, a tiny cul-de-sac off Petite rue des Bouchers, is the:

1. **Théâtre Toone,** the famous folk puppet theater. A performance at Toone should not be missed. This is a good opportunity to see when tickets are available.

    Walk along rue des Dominicans and rue de l'Ecuyer to the:

2. **Galeries St-Hubert** (St. Hubert Arcades), built in 1847 and the first covered shopping arcade in Europe. Rue de la Colline continues the mall and leads back to:

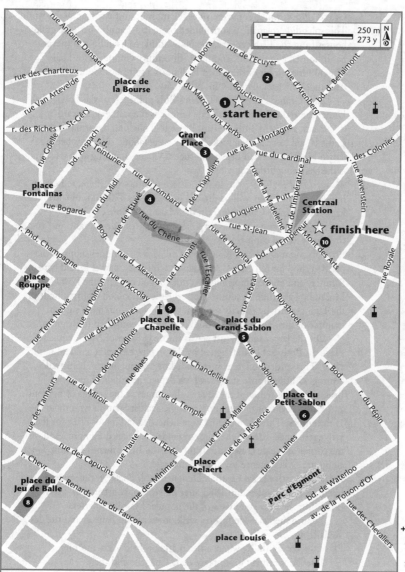

Walking Tour—Ilôt Sacré to the Marolles

0 | 250 m
0 | 273 y

N

rue Antoine Dansaert
rue des Chartreux
rue Van Artevelde
place de la Bourse
rue des Riches r. St-Géry
r. Cdelle
bd. Anspach
r. d. Teinturiers
place Fontainas
rue Bogards
r. Phd. Champagne
place Rouppe
rue Terre Neuve
rue du Midi
r. Bog.
rue du Lombard
rue de l'Etuve
rue du Chêne
rue d'Alexiens
rue du Poinçon
rue d'Accolay
rue des Ursulines
rue des Tanneurs
rue du Miroir
rue des Vystandines
rue Blaes
rue d. Chandeliers
rue d. Temple
rue des Capucins
rue Haute
r. d. l'Epée
rue des Minimes
rue du Faucon
r. Chevr.
r. Renards
rue du Faucon
place du Jeu de Balle
place de la Chapelle
place du Grand-Sablon
rue d. Sablons
rue Lebeau
rue d'Or
rue de l'Hôpital
rue l'Escalier
rue d. Dinant
rue d'Arenberg
bd. d. Berlaimont
r. de l'Ecuyer
rue des Bouchers
r. d. Tabora
rue du Marché aux Herbs
start here
Grand' Place
rue de la Montagne
rue du Cardinal
rue de la Madeleine
rue Duquesn.
rue St-Jean
Putt.
bd. de l'Impératrice
bd. de l'Empereur
Mont des Arts
Centraal Station
finish here
r. des Colonies
rue Ravenstein
rue Royale
rue d. Ruysbroek
place du Grand-Sablon
place du Petit-Sablon
r. Bod.
r. du Pépin
rue Ernest Alard
rue de la Régence
rue aux Laines
place Poelaert
Parc d'Egmont
bd. de Waterloo
av. de la Toison-d'Or
rue des Chevaliers
place Louise

Church ✝■

1 Théâtre Toone
2 Galeries St-Hubert
3 Grand' Place
4 *Manneken Pis*
5 Place du Grand-Sablon
6 Place du Petit-Sablon
7 Palais de Justice
8 Place du Jeu de Balle
9 Notre-Dame de la Chapelle Church
10 Mont des Arts

3. **Grand' Place,** which some consider the most beautiful square in the world. This splendid esplanade is surrounded by Italian-Flemish baroque guild houses from the 17th century, the Neo-Gothic Maison du Roi (never has it housed a monarch), and the 15th-century Gothic Town Hall. The 300-foot tower of the Town Hall bears a spire surmounted by the Archangel Michael, patron saint of the city.

Leave Grand' Place by rue Charles-Buls to the left of the Town Hall. Under the arches of the Maison de l'Etoile is the statue of Everard 't Serclaes, a hero of 14th-century Brussels. Touching the arm of the statue is said to bring you luck. Not far away (about 100 yards behind Town Hall) on rue de l'Etuve and rue du Chêne, standing atop a fountain is the charming little statue of:

4. *Manneken Pis* (1619), the "oldest citizen of Brussels." If you're here on a holiday, the little boy will be dressed in one of his 570 colorful costumes kept at the Musée Communal (in the Maison du Roi).

To your left, go up rue du Chêne; along rue de Dinant and rue de Rollebeek you'll come to:

5. **Place du Grand-Sablon.** This square, filled with antiques shops, is the place to shop for old curios. A books-and-antiques market is held here on Saturday and Sunday mornings. At no. 40, you can visit the Post Office Museum. Take time to admire Notre-Dame-du-Sablon Church, built in the 15th century by the city's crossbowmen. The church is a superb example of the flamboyant Gothic style, which flourished in Belgium.

Off the larger square, just across rue de la Régence, you'll come to:

6. **Place du Petit-Sablon,** designed by the architect Beyaert and laid out in 1890. This garden square is surrounded by a wrought-iron balustrade bearing 48 little bronze statues, which depict the guilds of medieval Brussels. In the center of the square, the statues of the counts of Egmont and Hornes symbolize Belgium's struggle against Spanish tyranny in the 16th century. These two counts were beheaded in Grand' Place for their active resistance. Behind the garden stands the Palais d'Egmont. And on the corner of rue de la Régence is the Musical Instrument Museum. Go along rue de la Régence toward the majestic:

7. **Palais de Justice** (Law Courts). Designed by J. Poelaert, this massive building was completed in 1883 after 20 years of construction. From this point, there's a good view of the popular Marolles quarter.

Behind the Palais de Justice, walk down rue du Faucon and rue des Renards to:

8. **Place du Jeu de Balle,** where a flea market is held every morning.

Rue Blaes brings you to place de la Chapelle and the:

9. **Notre-Dame de la Chapelle Church,** with its remarkable Romanesque-Gothic architecture. This church has always been frequented by famous people—some of whom are commemorated in bas-reliefs and frescoes. Should its restoration permit, inside you'll find the tomb of painter Pieter Brueghel the Elder. The memorial "The Velvet Brueghel" was done by the artist's son Jan. Tradition has it that the artist lived and died near here at no. 132 rue Haute. Along the boulevard de l'Empereur, on your right you'll come to:

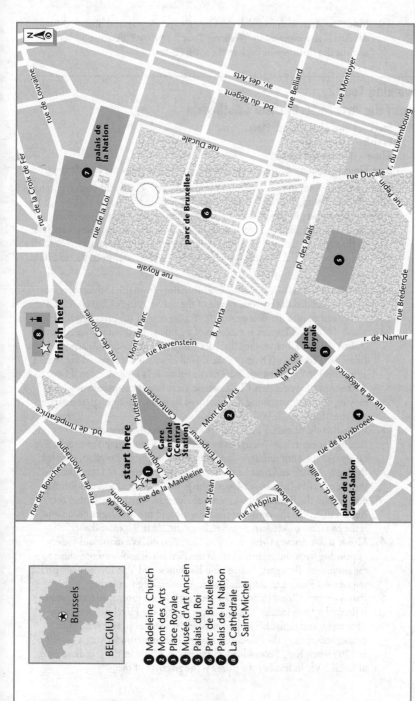

Walking Tour—Mont des Arts to St. Michael's Cathedral

BELGIUM

★ Brussels

1. Madeleine Church
2. Mont des Arts
3. Place Royale
4. Musée d'Art Ancien
5. Palais du Roi
6. Parc de Bruxelles
7. Palais de la Nation
8. La Cathédrale Saint-Michel

✝ ◼ Church

start here

finish here

10. **Mont des Arts,** with its Palais des Congrès and the national library. (Mont des Arts is also explored in "Walking Tour 2," below.) Take rue St. Jean and rue des Eperonniers back to the town center.

Walking Tour 2
Mont des Arts to St. Michael's Cathedral

Start Town Hall, Grand' Place.
Finish Town center.
Time About three hours.
Best Times A sunny morning or afternoon, so you can enjoy the Parc de Bruxelles.

We begin again from in front of the Town Hall, Grand' Place. Although it's technically not a museum, you should take a glimpse inside the Town Hall to see the impressive chambers in which the City Council convenes. The walls are hung with impressive tapestries and you'll get a sense of the city's tempestuous past. Once outside, go through rue Chair et Pain and walk up rue du Marché-aux-Herbes in the direction of the Central Station, which was designed by architect Victor Horta. You'll see the:

1. **Madeleine Church,** a charming Gothic oratory from the 15th century, to which was added the baroque facade of the old St. Anne's Chapel. A little farther on, go into the Bortier Arcade. You're now in the precinct called:

2. **Mont des Arts.** This area is made up of a garden, the Bibliothèque Albert I (Albert I Royal Library), the Palais des Congrès (Convention Palace), and Palais de la Dynastie (Dynasty Palace)—all of which were erected between 1954 and 1965. On the left, next to the Palais de la Dynastie, you'll find the famous Mont des Arts Clock, whose giant face is decorated with 12 moving figures representing the history of Belgium. Go through the park and rue Montagne de la Cour to:

3. **Place Royale.** Standing in the center of this perfectly symmetrical rectangular esplanade—designed by architect B. Guimard in the neoclassical style of the 18th century—is a statue of Godefroy de Bouillon, who led the First Crusade and became the first king of Jerusalem. On the square is the church of St-Jacques-sur-Coudenberg, reminiscent of a Greco-Roman temple, and the Palace of the Counts of Flanders, which now houses the Audit Office. On the corner of place Royale and rue Montagne de la Cour is the Museum of Modern Art. Nearby on rue de la Régence, the:

4. **Musée d'Art Ancien** (Museum of Ancient Art) offers a marvelous variety of painting from the great masters of the Flemish School—among them the primitives, Brueghel, Rubens and his pupils, and Van Dyck. Walk back to place des Palais and the grandiose structure facing you is the:

5. **Palais du Roi** (Royal Palace). Overlooking a broad promenade, the palace is flanked by two lodges: The one to the right is the Hôtel Bellevue, now a museum; and to the left is the Palais des Académies (Royal Academies), former residence of the Prince of Orange. The palace underwent a facelift in 1909 when King Leopold II had the facade rebuilt in the grandiose style of Louis XVI. In front of the palace is the greenery of the:

6. **Parc de Bruxelles.** Originally, this *warande* (pleasure garden) belonged to the dukes of Brabant and served as their hunting grounds. The park became property of the city in 1776 and was laid out as a French garden in 1787. It was here in this park that the fight for Belgian independence began in 1830 between Dutch troops and Belgian nationalists.

Crossing the park (directly opposite the Royal Palace), you'll come to the:

7. **Palais de la Nation** (House of Parliament), built in the neoclassical style. Walk along rue Royale (on the perimeter of the park) toward the Congress Column, erected in 1859 and commemorating the National Congress of 1830. At the foot of the monument burns the eternal flame in homage to the unknown soldiers of the two world wars. On the left, rue de Ligne will lead you down to place Ste-Gudule and:

8. **La Cathédrale Saint-Michel** (St. Michael's Cathedral). Flanked by two square towers, this beautiful church was begun in 1266 and finished in the 17th century and finally attained cathedral status in 1961. Step inside and bathe in the magnificent light of St. Michael's stained-glass windows from the 16th century created by painter Bernaert van Orley.

Stroll down toward rue du Marché-aux-Herbes and you'll find yourself back in the city center.

---

6 Special and Free Events

I sometimes feel that simply strolling the streets of Brussels is one of the world's best free attractions. But during July, you won't pay a penny to enjoy the festive ✪ **Ommegang** celebration in Grand' Place (see "Brussels Calendar of Events" in Chapter 3) and the street entertainment around this area during the entire month. In August, there's the **Planting of the Meiboom** ("Mayboom" or May Tree), another joyous public occasion. And every two years, Grand' Place is covered by a spectacular Carpet of Flowers for all to see at no charge.

---

7 Sports and Recreation

SPECTATOR SPORTS

★ **HORSE RACING** There are three tracks in the Brussels area: **Boitsfort,** chaussée de la Hulpa 51 (☎ **660-28-39** or **672-14-84** for dates and fees), reached by tram no. 94 or bus no. 42; **Groenendaal,** Sint-Jansberglaan 4, in Hoeilaart (☎ **673-67-92**); and **Sterrebeek,** du Roy de Blicquylaan 43, in Sterrebeek (☎ **767-54-75**), reached by tram no. 39 or bus no. 30.

SOCCER The **Maison du Football,** av. Houba de Strooper 145 (☎ **477-12-11**), can arrange tickets for international football (soccer) matches if you phone Monday through Friday between 9am and 4:15pm.

RECREATION

There's a wide variety of facilities—tennis and squash courts, Olympic swimming pool, gymnasium, and martial arts instruction—at the **Complex Sportif de Woluwe-Saint-Pierre,** av. Salome 2 (☎ **762-12-75**).

BOWLING   Leading bowling alleys are **Bowling Crosly Brunswick,** quai du Foin 43 (☎ **217-28-01**); and **Bowling Crosly Empereur,** bd. de l'Empereur 36 (☎ **512-08-74**).

HORSEBACK RIDING   For information on riding stables, contact the **Fédération Royale Belge des Sports Equestres,** av. Amoir 38 (☎ **374-47-34**).

ICE SKATING   There's ice skating from September to May at **Forest National,** av. du Globe 36 (☎ **345-16-11** for hours and fees), reached by bus no. 48 or 54; and at **Poseidon,** av. des Vaillants 4, in Woluwe-Saint-Lambert (☎ **762-16-33**), reached by métro to Tomberg or bus no. 28.

8 Savvy Shopping

Brussels is not the place to come in search of bargains—on the whole it's rather expensive—but it *is* the place to look for those Belgian specialties that are either unavailable or even more expensive elsewhere, such as lace, of both antique and recent manufacture; leather goods; and edibles like chocolates (some of the world's best), pralines, and the thin, spicy biscuits called speculoos.

Shopping hours are generally 10am to 6pm Monday through Saturday, and you'll find many stores observing the same hours on Sunday. Department stores stay open later on Friday, until 8 or 9pm.

Note: An excellent magazine devoted almost entirely to Belgian shopping, *Belgian Promenade,* is published by the Chamber of Commerce for Art, Quality Goods, and Services. Your hotel may provide free copies—if not, look for it at newsstands.

The Shopping Scene

SHOPPING PROMENADES

Many of Brussels's most interesting shops are clustered along certain streets, which comprise a promenade or arcade. The **rue Neuve,** which starts at place de la Monnaie and extends north to place Rogier constitutes a pedestrian shopping mall; this busy and popular area is home to many boutiques and department stores, including City 2—a modern shopping complex. **Boulevard Anspach** from the Stock Exchange up to place de Brouckère houses a number of fashion boutiques, chocolate shops, and electric appliance stores. The **Anspach Center** (near place de la Monnaie) is a shopping mall.

The elegant **Galeries Saint-Hubert** (off rue du Marché-aux-Herbes) attracts many visitors since it was Europe's first covered shopping arcade (built in the mid-19th century) and offers exceptional quality merchandise such as Brussels lace and jewelry. **Avenue Louise** also attracts those in search of world-renowned, high-quality goods from such stores as Cartier, Burberry's, Louis Vuitton, and Valentino.

The **Galerie Agora** (off the Grand' Place) offers a wide variety of modestly priced merchandise, for example: leather goods, clothing, souvenirs, records, and jewelry.

OUTDOOR MARKETS

Flea Market, on place du Jeu-de-Balle, a large square near the Gare du Midi. If you have time and enjoy looking through lots of old items, you may be rewarded with some exceptional decorative items, as well as unusual postcards, clothing, and household goods. The market is held daily from 7am to 2pm.

Antiques Market, in the area near place du Grand-Sablon, is held every weekend. Because Belgium sets standards for items that can be called "antique" (they must be authentic), they command relatively high prices. In the same area are regular antique stores that are open during the week. The market is open Saturday from 9am to 6pm, Sunday from 9am to 2pm.

Bird Market, near the Grand' Place, on Sunday offers countless varieties of birds. Although *not* practical for the traveler to buy, the birds can be admired for their beauty. The market is open on Sunday from 7am to 2pm.

Flower market—many varieties of flowers are sold every day in the Grand' Place.

Sunday Bazaar, situated along both sides of the railroad tracks from place de la Constitution to the Gare du Midi. This market, which takes place every Sunday from 6am–1pm, entails a large number of Middle Eastern and South European merchant who offer food products and household goods, as well as unusual items from the Mediterranean area.

Shopping A to Z

Here's a short list of my personal recommendations, which are only a small sampling of Brussels's best shopping. However, they do provide a little something extra in the way of shopping ambience, as well as value for the dollar.

BOOKS

City Press Center, bd. Anspach 67. ☎ **511-11-22.**

There are large selections of English-language periodicals and paperback books in this international press shop. It's open Monday through Saturday from 8am to 8pm and on Sunday from 9am to 8pm.

★ **W. H. Smith & Son,** bd. Adolphe-Max 71–75. ☎ **219-50-34** or **219-27-08.**

This is the place to visit for the best and most comprehensive selection of English-language books, magazines, and newspapers.

FOOD & WINES

★ **Dandoy,** rue au Beurre 31. ☎ **511-03-26.**

This is a tiny little shop where buying crisp butter cookies, molded gingerbread cakes, or cinnamon cookies becomes a very special Brussels shopping treat; and whether you carry them home or yield to the temptation of instant munching, they're an extraordinary taste treat.

★ **De Boe,** rue de Flandre 36. ☎ **511-13-73.**

In the food and drink department, my first "don't miss" is a small shop in the fish-market area. It's a place of heavenly smells (they roast and blend coffee beans), a fantastic selection of wines that cover the price range from $7 to $500 (an excellent place to pick up wines for hotel-room consumption or to carry home), and a marvelous array of specialty crackers, nuts, spices, teas, and gourmet snacks, many of which come in tins that make them suitable to bring back home. Closed Monday.

Wittamer, place du Grand-Sablon 12–13. ☎ **512-37-42.**

For candies to take home or mouth-watering rolls, breads, pastries, and cakes for on-the-spot consumption, go by Wittamer. They've been turning out sinfully indulgent goodies since 1910, and I absolutely defy you to walk out empty-handed.

LACE

Maison Antoine Old Brussels Lace Shop, Grand' Place 26.

Among the many lace shops in Brussels, I especially like this establishment.

Rose's Lace Boutique, rue des Brasseurs 1.

This shop is on a tiny street just off Grand' Place and along with the above establishment offers wide selections and a good price range.

LEATHER GOODS

 Delvaux, galerie de la Reine 31. ☎ **512-71-98.**

Some of the most beautiful handmade leather items to be found in all of Europe come from this establishment. The quality and beauty of each piece make it a good buy, even if expensive.

SCULPTURE

 Gallery Dieleman, Sablon Shopping Gardens, place du Grand-Sablon 36.

This is a wonderland of exquisite bronze sculptures that range from pieces small enough to carry in a handbag to monumental works of art that would demand a special setting. It carries only signed originals, and each comes with a folder that has information on its creator and a photo and description of the piece. Any one of the large selection would make a lasting travel souvenir that could only appreciate in value.

---

9   Evening Entertainment

Brussels offers a wide array of evening activities, including dance, opera, classical music, jazz, film, theater, and discos. For a complete listing of events, it's best to consult the weekly English-language *What's On* magazine; it's available without charge from T.I.B. (Tourist Information Brussels) in the Town Hall at Grand' Place.

The Performing Arts ——————————————————

OPERA & BALLET

Théâtre Royal de la Monnaie/Opéra National, place de la Monnaie (☎ 218-12-11), the historic theater founded in the 17th century, is home to the Opéra National and L'Orchestre Symphonique de la Monnaie. Ballet performances are also presented here.

CLASSICAL MUSIC

The ✪ **Palais des Beaux-Arts,** rue Ravenstein 23 (☎ 507-82-00), is home to the Belgium National Orchestra. Also, check locally for any periodic concerts scheduled in **Cirque Royal,** rue de l'Enseignement 81 (☎ 218-20-15), and free Sunday-morning concerts in the city's churches and cathedral.

THEATERS

Brussels theater is quite important among French-speaking countries, with more than 30 theaters presenting performances in French, Flemish, and (occasionally) English. Among the most important are: **Théâtre Royal du Parc,** rue de la Loi 3 (☎ 511-41-49), for classic and contemporary drama and comedies; **Théâtre Royal des Galeries,** galerie du Roi 32 (☎ 512-04-07), with a wide variety of offerings, including drama, comedy, and musicals; and the art deco–style **Théâtre du Résidence Palace,** rue de la Loi 155 (☎ 231-03-05).

PUPPET THEATER

⭐ **Théâtre Toone,** impasse Schuddeveld, just off Petite rue des Bouchers 21.
☎ **513-54-80.**

Look for the small wooden sign in the tiny alleyway—impasse Schuddeveld—to reach this theater. It comprises an upstairs room in a bistro by the same name. Because Belgium has a long tradition of puppet theaters (see Chapter 2, Section 6), this may be the most popular theater in Brussels. It's the last in the Toone line that dates back to the early 1800s—the title being passed from one puppet master to the next. They present such classic tales as *The Three Musketeers, Faust,* and *Hamlet.* Although the dialog is usually in French, that should present no difficulties since it is easy to follow the action on stage.

Admission: Ticket, 400F ($11.40).
Open: Performances Tues–Sat at 8:30pm.

The Club and Music Scene

CABARET & DINNER DANCING

Wednesday through Sunday, there's a transvestite dinner show at **Chez Flo,** rue au Beurre 25 (☎ **512-94-96**). At **Le Slave,** rue Scailquin 22 (☎ **217-66-56**), a gypsy orchestra plays Russian music during dinner. There's marvelous Hungarian and gypsy music, as well as jazz and just about any type of music you request, into the wee hours at **Le Huchier,** place du Grand-Sablon (☎ **512-27-11**), where you can also order light snacks along with your libations. **Le Pavillon,** in the Brussels Sheraton Hotel, place Rogier 3 (☎ **224-31-11**), provides live music for dinner dancing on Friday and Saturday. And burlesque takes center stage at dinner on Saturday at **Moustache,** quai au Bois à Brûler 61 (☎ **218-58-77**). Night owls can book into **Show Point,** place Stephanie 14 (☎ **217-01-67**), in the avenue Louise area for nonstop "big show" entertainment from 10pm until dawn Monday through Saturday.

JAZZ & BLUES

At last count, no fewer than 26 cafés and restaurants were advertising periodic jazz sessions, so it will pay for you to check with the tourist board and local newspapers during your visit. There are a dozen or so small taverns and bistros where jazz is played in a much more intimate fashion—and unless you're nightclub oriented, it's lots more fun! ⊡ The **Brussels Jazz Club,** Grand' Place 13 (☎ **512-40-93**), is a long-standing mecca for outstanding jazz performers, and you'll find a headliner scheduled most nights (closed Wednesday and Sunday). Call early for reservations and be prepared to

The Major Concert and Performance Halls

Cirque Royal, rue de l'Enseignement 81 (☎ **218-20-15**).

Palais des Beaux Arts, rue Ravenstein 23 (☎ **507-82-00**).

Théâtre du Résidence Palace, rue de la Loi 155 (☎ **231-03-05**).

Théâtre Royal de la Monnaie, place de la Monnaie (☎ **218-12-11**).

Théâtre Royal des Galleries, galerie du Roi 32 (☎ **512-04-07**).

Théâtre Royal du Parc, rue de la Loi 3 (☎ **511-41-49**).

Théâtre Toone, impasse Schuddeveld (☎ **513-54-80**).

pay a cover charge and high prices for drinks. In direct contrast, ✪ **Pops Hall,** rue Lincoln 53, in the Uccle district (☎ **345-95-81**), is a small corner bistro owned by a jazz musician who often takes the stand himself. Since music is not scheduled every night, best call ahead to see if it's on—although this place is so much fun I'd recommend an evening here even without the music. Prices are as small as Pops Hall itself, and they cover an enormous amount of nighttime entertainment, whether it be music or just lively conversation.

DISCOS

Perhaps the fastest-changing entertainment scene in Brussels is that of discothèques. Need I say it: Be sure to check locally to see if the following are still in operation. The most sophisticated disco in Brussels is ✪ **Griffin's Club** in the Royal Windsor Hotel, rue Duquesnoy 5 (☎ **505-55-55**), which is in full swing every night except Sunday. **Les Enfants du Golf Drouot,** place de la Chapelle 6 (☎ **502-68-17**), is open nightly. **Le Garage,** rue Duquesnoy 16 (☎ **512-66-22**), just off Grand' Place, caters to a mostly younger set. At **Le Machado,** rue des Chapeliers 14 (☎ **513-36-91**), salsa and samba are featured.

The Bar Scene

A favorite Brussels night out is one spent in one of the small bistros where drinking and conversation fill the entertainment bill.

Unique, to say the least, is a Brussels favorite, **A la Morte Subite,** rue Montagne-aux-Herbes-Potagères 7 (☎ **513-13-18**), a bistro of rather special character whose name translates to "sudden death." That strange name stems from an ancient "double or nothing" game once played here. The place is now in its third generation of ownership by the same family, and is famous for its wide variety of Belgian beers: *gueuze* (a unique taste which takes some getting used to), *Faro, kriek* (cherry), *framboise* (raspberry), *cassis* (black currant), and on and on. They also offer a great *tartine beurre* (a long slice of homemade bread slathered with butter), which goes down well with the beer. Always crowded, this is a friendly place to meet and mingle with Belgians of all ages and stations in life.

In a quite different vein, ✪ **La Fleur en Papier Doré,** rue des Alexiens 55 (☎ **511-16-59**), is located in a 16th-century house. This has been a bistro and pub since 1846, and from the beginning it has been a mecca for poets and writers. Even now, about once a month young Brussels poets gather there informally for poetry readings—the date varies, but you might inquire by phone, or better yet, just drop by and ask in person. This is a wonderfully atmospheric old pub, much like a social club, where patrons gather for good conversation and welcome any and all newcomers. They also serve what is possibly the best onion soup in Brussels, a great late-night snack.

The following are only a few of Brussels's pubs and bistros that can be recommended. **'T Spinnekopke,** place du Jardin-aux-Fleurs 1 (☎ **511-86-95**), is located in an 18th-century house and is good for conversation. **A l'Image de Notre-Dame,** impasse, rue du Marché-aux-Herbes 6 (☎ **219-42-49**) is also rather quiet. **Cirio,** rue de la Bourse 18 (☎ **512-13-95**), is worth a visit for the fine decor as well as good conversation. And **Toone VII,** impasse Schuddeveld, Petite rue des Bouchers 21 (☎ **511-71-37**), is the home of the puppet theater and an artistic hangout.

Movies

Since most movies are shown in the language in which they were filmed, you'll find many English-language films at any time. Major cinemas in the city center are: **Aventure,** Galerie du Centre 57 (☎ **219-17-48**), which has three cinemas; **City 2,** rue Neuve 235 (☎ **34-97-30**), with eight cinemas; and **USG Brouckere,** place de la Brouckere 38 (☎ **34-97-30**), which also has eight cinemas (the last two have the same phone number).

10   Networks and Resources

FOR STUDENTS

SOS Jeunes 24/24 (☎ **512-90-20**) is a useful contact hotline, and the following colleges have English-speaking staffs and can furnish details of student clubs and associations.

The Open University, chaussée de Bruxelles 233, 1410 Waterloo (☎ **354-90-93**), offers various academic degrees via correspondence courses and tutorials.

Vesalius College, 2 Pleinlaan, 1050 Brussels (☎ **641-28-21**), offers undergraduate degrees in 10 majors.

FOR GAY MEN & LESBIANS

The age of consent for gays in Belgium is 16, and the national gay and lesbian organization is headquartered in Antwerp. For countrywide information, contact **FWH,** Dambruggestraat 204, Antwerp (☎ **03/233-25-02**), or **Info Homo,** av. de Roodebeek 57 (☎ **02/733-10-24**). The Brussels section of the *Best Guide to Amsterdam & the Benelux for Gay Men and Lesbians* lists accommodations, bars, and nightclubs, and there's an annual free updating service for the listings.

For health information, contact **Help Info AIDS,** rue Duquesnoy 45 (☎ **514-29-65**); or **CETIM** (Hospital Universitaire Saint-Pierre), rue Haute 322 (☎ **538-00-00,** ext. 1177).

FOR WOMEN

Contact **WOE, The Women's Organization for Equality,** rue Blanche 29, off avenue Louise (☎ **538-47-73**); or **International Inner Wheel,** rue Royale 33 (☎ **219-30-60**), for information on weekly public meetings and other information of interest to women.

FOR SENIORS

For **urgent social assistance,** call **425-57-25.** See "Fast Facts: Brussels," earlier in this chapter, for medical and safety emergency numbers.

11   Easy Excursions

The lovely Brabant countryside around Brussels is one of scenic beauty, as well as one dotted with sightseeing attractions well worth the short trip.

BEERSEL

Only 5¹/₂ miles to the south of Brussels—a little off the Mons road, watch for the signpost—the only example of a ★ **fortified medieval castle** still intact is at Beersel.

Set in a wooded domain and surrounded by a moat, the three-towered 13th-century castle is reached by a drawbridge. Pick up the excellent English-language guidebook at the entrance for a detailed history of the castle and its inhabitants, then wander through its rooms for a trip back through time. End your visit with a stop at the magnificent mausoleum that holds the recumbent alabaster effigies of Henry II of Witthem and his wife, Jacqueline de Glimes, who lived here during the early 1400s. Visiting hours can vary, so it would be best to check with the T.I.B., Grand' Place, when you're on the spot.

Leafy pathways through the grounds invite leisurely walks, and this is a favorite rural retreat for Brussels residents, especially during the summer months. At the entrance to the park, you'll find **Auberge Kasteel Beersel,** Lotstraat 65, 1650 Beersel (☎ 331-00-24), a charming rustic restaurant with decor of dark wood, exposed brick, and accents of copper and brass. In good weather there's service on the shaded outside terrace. Light meals (omelets, salads, soups, sandwiches, etc.) are available, as well as complete hot meals for both lunch and dinner, and prices are in the moderate range. Booking is not usually necessary, and you're very welcome to stop in just for a relaxing draft of Belgian beer.

GAASBEEK

The ancestral château of the counts of Egmont is at Gaasbeek, some 8 miles from Brussels on the Mons highway. Its furnishings are nothing less than magnificent, as is the castle itself. All the rooms are splendid, and far from presenting a dead "museum" appearance, they create an eerie impression that the counts and their families may still be in residence and will come walking through the door any moment. Before each guided tour, there's a slide show that will increase your appreciation for the countless works of art, silver items, religious artifacts, and priceless tapestries. Check with the Brussels tourist office for opening hours and entrance fees.

WATERLOO

European history—indeed, the history of the entire world—was changed by the fierce conflict that took place on the battlefield at Waterloo in 1815 when Napoléon Bonaparte was defeated by England's Duke of Wellington. Today it has reverted to a landscape of peaceful, rolling farmland broken by the 100-foot-high memorial mound, **La Butte du Lion** (Lion's Mount), which was built through the efforts of Belgian housewives, who brought earth by the bucketful to the spot where Holland's Prince of Orange was wounded in the battle. Some 226 steps lead to its top, where there's an observation platform. A building at the foot of the mount houses *Panorama*, a 360° painting of the battle.

Nearby, 3 miles north of the town center, is an old inn, now the **Wellington Museum,** in which the Duke of Wellington headquartered the night before the battle was joined (open from April to mid-November, daily from 9:30am to 6:30pm; other months, daily except Christmas and New Year's Days from 10am to 5pm). **Napoléon's headquarters,** on the Charleroi road, is named the **Musée du Caillou** and is open April through October, Tuesday through Sunday from 10:30am to 6pm, 1:30 to 5pm in other months.

MECHELEN

Situated on the De Dije River and the Leuven Canal, Mechelen is just 10 miles from Brussels and the same distance from Antwerp—a perfect stop when traveling between those two cities on the E10 motorway. It's a city that wears its long history well (the Gauls and Romans were here as early as 500 B.C.), and its medieval town square evokes the late 1400s and 1500s, when this was a religious, cultural, and artistic center of Europe.

The **Tourist Office,** located in the Town Hall on the square (☎ **015/21-18-73**), offers conducted tours, including one to **St. Rombold's Cathedral** and a climb up the tower to see its famous carillon—at noon, you can hear a brief recital of the bells ringing out over the city. The ✪ **Royal Carillon School** here is the most famous in Europe and possibly in the world, attracting students from around the globe. Visit the **City Museum,** which includes a carillon section, as well as classic and modern paintings and sculpture. In Tivoli Park there's a **Children's Farm,** as well as a **Bee-Keeping Museum** inside the castle. Children of all ages will love the fairytale **Toy Museum,** at Nekkerspoelstraat 21. The Grote Markt reverts to its original purpose on Saturday mornings, when a ✪ **street market** is held just as in medieval times. The tourist office can furnish opening times and fees (which vary) for the above.

Mechelen has been an important center of tapestry weaving since medieval times, and Belgium's magnificent tapestry presented to the United Nations headquarters in New York was woven here. There's a **tapestry factory** still in operation; inquire at the tourist office for arrangements to visit and view their beautiful collection of ancient tapestries as well as those of more recent vintage.

5

Antwerp

Antwerp owes its life to the River Scheldt, its soul to the artist Rubens, and its name to a giant of ancient days called Druon Antigon. Legend has it that Druon levied exorbitant tolls on every Scheldt boatman who passed his castle; and if anyone would not or could not pay up, the big man gleefully cut off the miscreant's hand and threw it into the river. Druon's comeuppance, however, came in the form of a Roman centurion named Silvius Brabo, who slew the cruel giant and promptly cut off his hand and threw it into the river, thus avenging the poor, wronged boatmen. The Flemish *hand-werpen* (throwing of the hand) eventually became Antwerpen, the city's Flemish name.

Of course, historians who deal only in dry, dull facts tell a different story. They hold that seamen on ships sailing up that broad pathway bringing the commerce of the world to the city's wharves described its location as *aan-de-werpen* (on the wharves). But to the people who live here, the severed, bleeding "Red Hand of Antwerp" is the very symbol of their city. Today you'll find two statues in the town commemorating the Roman's act of revenge, and replicas of the giant's hand appear in everything from chocolate to brass.

But when you come right down to it, if there were no River Scheldt, there would be no Antwerp by any name. It is the natural, deep-water harbor that made it a Gallo-Roman port in the 2nd century B.C. and over the centuries attracted a bevy of covetous invaders.

As for Rubens, that master is only one of several artists who left their baroque mark on the face of this city and a great love of beauty in the hearts of its inhabitants. You'll see that love expressed in their buildings, in works of art publicly displayed, and in the contents of some 20 museums.

Despite fluctuations in its economy marked by a period of international recession during the late 1970s, Belgium has built Antwerp into the world's fifth-largest port, as well as perhaps its most important diamond center. It is the acknowledged "Diamond Center of the World," the leading market for cut diamonds and behind only London as an outlet for raw and industrial diamonds.

BY WAY OF BACKGROUND

From the beginning of Antwerp's recorded history in the 7th century until the 14th century, the city and its port suffered invasion by the Norse, followed by a parade of rulers that included the Salic Franks of Germany, the dukes of Brabant, the counts of Flanders, the dukes of Burgundy, and in the 1500s, the Hapsburgs, whose Charles V brought welcome prosperity. Antwerp outstripped its rival, Bruges, an important port on the River Zwinn; set up a commercial exchange that was a model for the Royal Exchange in London; and attracted a number of banking princes who brought their counting houses with them.

By the late 1500s, it was thoroughly Protestant and the headquarters of William the Silent. That religious persuasion brought down upon its head the wrath of the Duke of Alba during his sweep through the Low Countries to quell the revolt against Philip II of Spain. In November of 1576, his soldiers slaughtered some 8,000 Antwerp citizens and destroyed 1,000 buildings in a single night.

Thus conquered and occupied by Catholic Spain, Antwerp was fair game for the victorious Protestant Dutch to the north, whose territory held the Scheldt's estuary. In retribution against Catholic rule in Antwerp, they closed the river in 1648, cutting off Antwerp from the sea and ushering in two full centuries of economic decline,

What's Special About Antwerp

Public Spaces
- Grote Markt, not as dramatic as Brussels's Grand' Place, but still the center of everyday activity.

Museums
- Royal Museum of Fine Arts, featuring the world's finest collection of Flemish masterpieces.
- Rubens House, the artist's impressive home and studio, with a fine collection of his works.
- The Steen, a medieval fortress now housing the National Maritime Museum.

Churches
- Cathedral of Our Lady, from the 12th century, with seven naves, 125 pillars, and three Rubens masterpieces.
- St. Jacobskerk, flamboyantly Gothic, with the tomb of Peter Paul Rubens.

Specialty Sights
- Diamondland, where more than 12,000 expert cutters and polishers transform undistinguished stones into glittering gems.
- Antwerp Zoo, 25 acres where animals roam freely, bounded only by artificial reproductions of natural barriers.

although it continued to be a commercial center and a rising cultural force as Peter Paul Rubens and Anthony Van Dyck came to the fore.

It wasn't until the French Revolutionary Convention reopened the Scheldt in 1795 and Napoléon built a naval depot in 1800 as a base for operations against the English that Antwerp's port again came into its own. Then, in 1815, it fell under Dutch rule once more when Belgium was ceded to the Netherlands by treaty.

With the coming of Belgian independence in 1830, the Dutch held onto Antwerp until 1832; and from then until the 1860s, they continued to exact a toll on ships sailing through the Dutch stretch of the Scheldt to reach Antwerp. Free navigation on the river brought with it a rapid expansion of the port, and since then Antwerp has never looked back, although it suffered in both World Wars I and II and was the target of German V-1 and V-2 rocket attacks long after the city had been liberated by Allied troops in World War II.

Today it's one of the major European gateways, with its port relocated some 8 miles downstream from the city proper. Its thriving diamond-cutting industry includes 4 of the world's 18 diamond exchanges, and its petrochemical and banking industries add new luster to its commercial enterprise, and with it all, Antwerp protects and cherishes its cultural heritage.

IMPRESSIONS

This goodly ancient City methinks looks like a disconsolate Widow, or rather some super-annuated Virgin that hath lost her Lover. . . .
—James Howell, 1619

1 Orientation

Arriving

BY PLANE   Antwerp's nearest airport is about $3^{1}/_{2}$ miles to the east at **Deurne,** with city bus service between the main road outside the airport and Pelikaanstraat in the city proper. Taxi fare is about BF 550 ($15) to or from the city center.

BY TRAIN   Antwerp's two train stations are at **Berchem,** $2^{1}/_{2}$ miles south of the city center, and **Central Station,** 1 mile east of Grote Markt, on the edge of the city center. For schedule and fare information, call **03/204-20-40.**

BY BUS   Long-distance buses arrive and depart from bus depot on Franklin Rooseveltplaats, a short distance northwest of Central Station. Timetables and fare information are available from a kiosk in Central Station.

BY CAR   Major highways connecting to Antwerp's inner-city Ring Expressway are the A14-E17, from Ghent; the N49 from Knokke, Bruges, and Zeebrugge, bypassing Ghent; the A1-E19 from Brussels via Mechelen; and the A12-N277 from Brussels via Laeken.

Tourist Information

The **Tourist Office,** Grote Markt 15 (☎ **03/232-01-03**), is open daily from 9am to 5pm.

City Layout

The Central Rail Station serves as a focal point. When you're standing in front of the station, the large square opposite you is Koningin Astridplein; to the east is the 25-acre Antwerp zoo; and to your left is Pelikaanstraat, a major diamond center street. De Keyserlei runs toward the river and joins the Meir, Antwerp's main shopping street that leads into Schoenmarkt, a short street that curves around the 24-story Torengebouw to reach a large square known as Groenplaats, where there's a statue of Rubens and the Cathedral of Our Lady. One short block beyond Groenplaats (toward the river) puts you right into the large Grote Markt (Market Square), bordered by its Renaissance Town Hall and 16th-century guild houses. This is also where you'll find one of those statues of the Roman soldier Brabo. Follow the quaint little street named Suikerrui (it means "sugar quay") right down to the river, where you'll see the medieval fortified castle, Steen, that now houses the maritime museum.

The best **city map** is that supplied by the tourist office.

2 Getting Around

BY PUBLIC TRANSPORTATION (BUS/TRAM)   Trams are the best way to get around the city; a single fare is BF 40 ($1.15). The most useful tourist line is the one that runs all the way from the cathedral to the Central Station. There's also a long-distance bus from the Sabena Airlines office in De Keyserlei to Brussels airport.

BY BICYCLE   You can rent bicycles at Central Station; but be warned, traffic can be heavy and hard to negotiate.

BY TAXI   The numbers to call for taxis are **216-01-60** and **238-38-38.** Taxis cannot be hailed on the street but can be found at stands.

ON FOOT Antwerp is a good walking city, with its major sightseeing attractions easily reached from one major street, which changes its name as it goes along.

Fast Facts: Antwerp

American Express There's an office at Frankrijklei 21, 2000 Antwerp (☎ 03/232-59-20).

Area Code Antwerp's telephone area code is **03** (**3** if calling from outside the country).

Bookstores English-language books are available at FNAC Bookshop, Groenplaats 31, and Standaard, Huidevetterstraat 57.

Car Rental There are two Avis offices; one at Plantin en Moretuslei 62 (☎ **218-94-96**) and a second at the airport (same telephone). Hertz is located at Mechelsesteenweg 43 (☎ **233-29-92**) and at the airport (☎ **230-16-41**).

Embassies/Consulates See "Fast Facts: Belgium" in Chapter 3.

Emergencies For police and fire, dial **101;** for an ambulance, **100.**

Hospital For medical problems, go to St. Elizabeth Hospital, Leopoldstraat 26 (☎ **223-56-11** or 223-56-20).

Information See "Tourist Information," in "Orientation," earlier in this chapter.

Luggage Storage/Lockers There are coin-operated lockers at Central Station.

Post Office The main post office is at Groenplaats 42, open Monday through Friday from 9am to 6pm and on Saturday from 9am to noon.

Taxis See "Getting Around," earlier in this chapter.

3 Accommodations

There are good hotels right in the city, and rates are a little lower than those in Brussels. However, many of the top hotels are on the city's outskirts.

The tourist office has a free, same-day reservation service—you make a small deposit, which is then deducted from your hotel bill. They also publish a booklet listing all Antwerp accommodations and rates.

A word of warning to budget travelers: The "tourist rooms" that usually mean accommodation bargains in private homes are rather different in Antwerp—it's a discreet way of advertising very personal services that have nothing to do with a room for the night.

Expensive

 Alfa de Keyser Hotel, De Keyserlei 66–70, 2018 Antwerp. ☎ **03/234-01-35.** Fax 03/232-39-70. 260 rms. A/C MINIBAR TV TEL **Tram:** Central Station.

Rates: BF 6,500 ($185) single; BF 8,500 ($242) double. Weekend discounts available. AE, DC, MC, V.

Just one block from the Central Station, this seven-story, modern hotel boasts a striking marble lobby and rooms that are nicely furnished. There's good parking nearby, important for drivers who want to stay in the city.

Dining/Entertainment: A good restaurant and popular bar complete the amenities.

Services: Full attentive round-the-clock service, in-room trouser press, one-day laundry and dry cleaning.

Facilities: Health and relaxation center, swimming pool, solarium, whirlpool.

★ **Sofitel Hotel,** Desguinlei 94, 2018 Antwerp. ☎ **03/216-48-00.** Fax 03/216-47-12. 221 rms. MINIBAR TV TEL **Directions:** Drive south of the city on the ring road, motorway, and Singel; it's 10 minutes from the city center and 15 minutes from the port and the industrial zone.

Rates: BF 6,500 ($185) single; BF 7,000 ($200) double. Substantial weekend discounts available. Children 12 and under stay free in parents' room. AE, DC, MC, V.

This ultramodern luxury hotel gives you the best of Antwerp's two worlds—the scenic beauty of the park in which it is set, with the city's attractions about five minutes away. Each room is superbly furnished, with such extras as tea and coffee maker, trouser press, and morning newspaper.

Dining/Entertainment: Tiffany's is a superb gourmet restaurant. Breakfast and the Pullman Lunch Buffet are served in the Park Relais, the Lobby Terras serves snacks, and the Pullman Bar is a cozy, congenial meeting place.

Services: Express laundry and dry cleaning service; flight, rail, and restaurant reservations at the reception desk; babysitting; hotel doctor.

Facilities: Fitness club and sauna, lobby shop, underground parking for 50 cars.

Moderate

Alfa Empire Hotel, Appelmansstraat 31, 2018 Antwerp. ☎ **03/231-47-55.** Fax 03/233-40-60. 70 rms. MINIBAR A/C TV TEL **Tram:** Central Station.

Rates: BF 5,800 ($165) single; BF 7,500 ($214) double. Weekend discounts available. AE, DC, MC, V.

In the heart of the diamond quarter, not far from the Central Station, this modern hotel equips each room with a kitchenette, radio, and other amenities. Nearby, there is good shopping, as well as several theaters and restaurants.

Alfa Theater Hotel, Arenbergstraat 30, 2000 Antwerp. ☎ **03/231-17-20.** Fax 03/233-88-58. Telex 33-910. 127 rms. MINIBAR TV TEL

Rates: BF 5,750 ($164) single; BF 7,650 ($218) double. Weekend discounts available. AE, DC, MC, V.

Kitchenettes also come with the rooms here, and the location is convenient to the Rubens House and the theater district. Furnishings are modern and attractive. The restaurant is open weekdays only, but there are several quite good eateries nearby.

Ibis Hotel, Meistraat 39, 2000 Antwerp. ☎ **03/231-88-30.** Fax 03/234-29-21. 150 rms. TV TEL

Rates: BF 2,850 ($81) single; BF 3,150 ($90) double. Weekend rates available. MC, V.

The Ibis is a modern hotel right in the city center, convenient for sightseeing and just across from the weekend bird and flower market (Vogelmarkt). The guest rooms are nicely furnished with a bright decor. There's no restaurant, but several good ones are in the area.

★ **Novotel,** Luithagen-haven 6, 2030 Antwerp. ☎ **03/542-03-20.** Fax 03/541-70-93. 119 rms. A/C TV TEL

$ **Rates:** BF 3,700 ($105) single; BF 4,500 ($128) double. Weekend discounts available. AE, DC, MC, V.

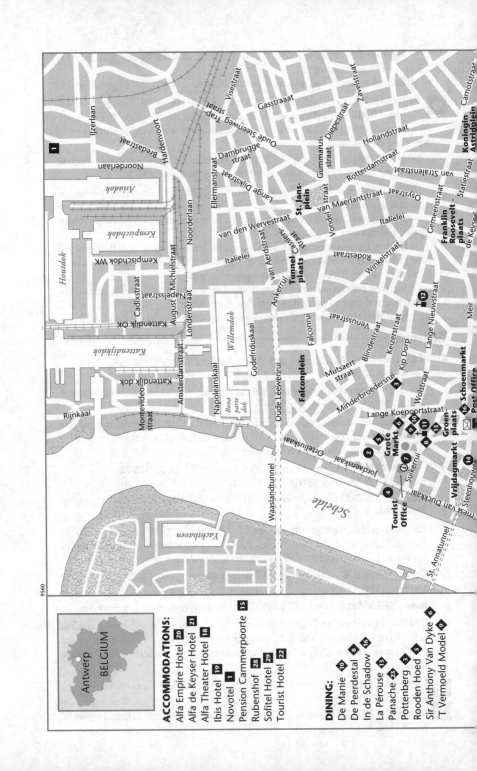

ACCOMMODATIONS:

Alfa Empire Hotel **20**
Alfa de Keyser Hotel **21**
Alfa Theater Hotel **18**
Ibis Hotel **19**
Novotel **1**
Pension Cammerpoorte **15**
Rubenshof **28**
Sofitel Hotel **29**
Tourist Hotel **22**

DINING:

De Manie **10**
De Peerdestal **8**
In de Schadow **16**
La Pérouse **13**
Panache **23**
Pottenberg **3**
Rooden Hoed **5**
Sir Anthony Van Dyke **6**
'T Vermoedel Model **9**

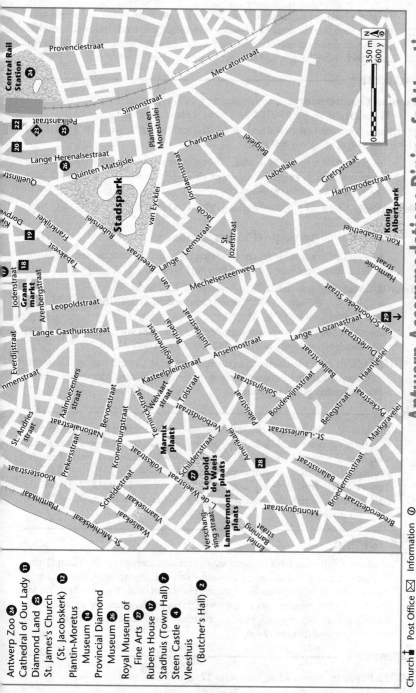

Antwerp Accommodations Dining & Attractions

Antwerp Zoo **24**
Cathedral of Our Lady **11**
Diamond Land **25**
St. James's Church
(St. Jacobskerk) **12**
Plantin-Moretus
Museum **14**
Provincial Diamond
Museum **26**
Royal Museum of
Fine Arts **27**
Rubens House **17**
Stadhuis (Town Hall) **7**
Steen Castle **4**
Vleeshuis
(Butcher's Hall) **2**

Church ✝   Post Office ⊠   Information ℹ

Located a little out from the city—in the docks area, north of the city center—this modern hotel is set in gardenlike landscaped grounds, and has bright, well-furnished rooms, wheelchair access, good parking, a garden terrace, a restaurant, a golf practice range, three tennis courts, and a heated swimming pool.

Inexpensive

Pension Cammerpoorte, Steenhouwersvest 55, 2000 Antwerp. ☎ **03/231-28-36.** Fax 03/226-29-68. 9 rms. **Tram:** Groenmarkt.

Rates (including buffet breakfast): BF 1,950–2,650 ($55–$75) single; BF 2,450–3,150 ($70–$90) double. No credit cards.

This pension is very centrally located. The rooms are clean and comfortable, and some face the cathedral. It's a good, inexpensive choice—but note that there is no elevator to rooms that are spread over three floors.

Rubenshof, Amerikalei 115, 2000 Antwerp. ☎ **03/237-07-89.** Fax 03/248-25-94. 20 rms. TV TEL

Rates: BF 1,700 ($48) single; BF 2,750 ($78) double. MC, V.

The rooms in this small hotel are somewhat plain, but comfortable and adequately furnished. It's located near the Royal Fine Arts Museum.

Tourist Hotel, Pelikaanstraat 22, 2018 Antwerp. ☎ **03/232-58-70.** Fax 03/231-67-07. Telex 33-612. 138 rms (some with bath). MINIBAR TV TEL **Tram:** Central Station.

Rates: BF 1,500 ($42) single without bath, BF 2,050 ($58) single with bath; BF 1,900 ($54) double without bath, BF 2,800 ($80) double with bath. AE, MC, V.

This reliable hotel's location is conveniently beside the Central Station. The rooms aren't fancy, but quite adequate and comfortable, with private bath or shower. There's also a moderately priced restaurant.

Hostels

In addition to the conventional youth hostels (see the tourist office for a complete list), there are two reliable hostel-type accommodations (no membership required) with rates of BF 500 to BF 900 ($14 to $25): **New International Youth Pension,** Provinciestraat 256, 2018 Antwerp (☎ **03/218-94-30;** fax 03/281-09-33); and **Square Sleep-Inn,** Bolivarplaats 1, 2000 Antwerp (☎ **03/237-37-48;** fax 03/248-02-48), which also rents studios with kitchenettes for an amazing BF 600 ($17) per person.

4 Dining

With some 300 restaurants scattered around the city, you can opt for a casual, inexpensive lunch and elegant, gourmet—and costly—dining at night; pub eating for pennies; and moderate prices for all meals. The tourist office has a handy restaurant booklet that lists most eateries in town with prices and an ethnic-foods breakdown, including long lists of snack bars, pizza parlors, waffle and pancake houses, and tearooms for rock-bottom eating.

Expensive

 La Pérouse, Ponton Steen, Steenplein. ☎ **231-73-58.**
Cuisine: FRENCH. **Reservations:** Required.

Prices: Lunch BF 1,650 ($47); dinner about BF 2,900 ($82). AE, MC, V.
Open: Tues–Sat noon–midnight. **Closed:** Aug.

This floating restaurant is moored at the foot of the Suikkerui (during August it abandons its fine cuisine to take on full-time sightseeing voyages). The waterzooï de poussin is a prime example of how this thick, creamy stew should be prepared, and other specialties include lobster salad and monkfish with noodles.

★ **Sir Anthony Van Dyck,** Oude Koornmarkt 16. ☎ **233-19-25.**
Cuisine: SEAFOOD/BELGIAN. **Reservations:** Required.
Prices: Dinner about BF 2,800 ($80). MC, V.
Open: Dinner only, Mon–Fri 6:30–11pm. **Closed:** Most of Aug.

In a charming Renaissance setting (down a small alley practically beneath the cathedral tower) that reflects the best of Antwerp's "good living" flair, the Sir Anthony Van Dyck provides exquisite, lightly sauced meals in complete harmony with the surrounding tapestries, oil paintings, and overhead beams. Seafoods are outstanding, and the goose liver is not to be missed. Prices are high but you can eat for less from the à la carte menu if you choose with care. My best advice here, however, is to "go for broke"—it's an experience that doesn't come along every day!

★ **'T Vermoeid Model,** Lijnwaadmarkt 2. ☎ **233-52-61.**
Cuisine: SEAFOOD. **Reservations:** Recommended.
Prices: Dinner BF 2,000–2,600 ($57–$74). MC, V.
Open: Dinner only, Mon–Fri 6:30–11pm.

This rustic Flemish restaurant is a delight, both aesthetically and gastronomically. Built right into the walls of the cathedral, it specializes in seafood, with smoked trout a local favorite.

Moderate

De Manie, H. Conscienceplein 3. ☎ **232-64-38.**
Cuisine: CONTINENTAL. **Reservations:** Required.
Prices: Appetizers BF 600–900 ($17–$24); main courses BF 1,000 ($35); fixed-price dinner, including wines, BF 3,000 ($85). AE, DC, MC, V.
Open: Lunch Mon–Tues and Thurs–Sat noon–2:30pm; dinner Mon–Tues and Thurs–Sat 6:30–9:30pm.

This bright, modern restaurant comes up with such originals as an appetizer of quail salad with goat cheese and artichoke, and baked goose liver with bilberries and honey, as well as innovative main dishes—filet of hare with cranberries, chicory, and juniper sauce and grilled wood pigeon with gratinéed brussels sprouts are typical of menu specialties, which change every six months. The food is excellent, and the setting is exceptionally relaxing. It's located near St. Katelijnevest.

★ **De Peerdestal,** Wijngaardstraat 8. ☎ **231-95-03.**
Cuisine: FRENCH.
Prices: Fixed-price lunch BF 1,000 ($35); fixed-price dinner BF 1,800 ($51). AE, DC, MC, V.
Open: Lunch Mon–Sat noon–2:30pm; dinner Mon–Sat 6–11pm.

In this large, rustic restaurant near the cathedral, you can enjoy a light meal of omelets, salads, stuffed tomato, and the like, or indulge in heartier fare such as fish or steak. Despite its size, there's something almost cozy about the place, where patrons frequently read newspapers as they eat at the long bar.

Rooden Hoed, Oude Koornmarkt 25. ☎ **233-28-44.**

Cuisine: FRENCH. **Reservations:** Required.
Prices: Average meal about BF 1,200–1,450 ($34–$41). AE, DC, MC, V.
Open: Lunch Fri–Tues noon–2:30pm; dinner Fri–Tues 6–10:30pm.

Near the cathedral, this pleasant, rather old-fashioned restaurant with a rustic decor serves good, hearty food at very moderate prices. Mussels, sausages (which come with sauerkraut and mashed potatoes in a delicious "choucroute d'Alsace"), waterzooï, and fish are featured on the menu.

Inexpensive

⭐ **In de Schaduw van de Kathedraal,** Hansschoenmarkt 17–21. ☎ **232-40-14.**

Cuisine: FRENCH. **Reservations:** Recommended.
Prices: Meals BF 500–1,800 ($25–$51). AE, DC, MC, V.
Open: Lunch Wed–Mon noon–3pm; dinner Wed–Mon 6–10pm.

Traditional Belgian cuisine gussied up a bit is featured in this attractive restaurant in the city center. Mussels and eel are featured in several guises, and beef is well represented on the menu. The specialty of the house is bouillabaisse (for two), which is enough to feed a family of five.

💲 **Panache,** Statiestraat 17. ☎ **232-69-05.**

Cuisine: CONTINENTAL. **Reservations:** Not required. **Tram:** Central Station.
Prices: Average meal BF 750–900 ($21–$25). AE, DC, MC, V.
Open: Daily noon–midnight. **Closed:** Aug.

You pass through a sandwich, snack, delicatessen (charcuterie) section to reach the large, busy restaurant here near Central Station. The large menu features such widely diversified choices as spaghetti, chicken croquettes, veal, chicken, steaks . . . if your appetite calls for it, you're sure to find it!

For the most control over your food costs, make your selections from the long counter that includes sandwiches, herring, cheese, pastries, and other goodies, all with low price tags, that can be combined to make up a satisfying, inexpensive meal.

⭐ 💲 **Pottenbrug,** Minderbroedersrui 38. ☎ **231-51-47.**

Cuisine: FLEMISH/BELGIAN. **Reservations:** Required.
Prices: Steak BF 1,000 ($28); leg of lamb BF 400 ($25); fish BF 800 ($23). AE, DC, MC, V.
Open: Lunch Mon–Fri noon–2pm; dinner Mon–Fri 7pm–midnight, Sat 6:30–11pm.

There's a casual, relaxed atmosphere in this place that goes with the sand on the floor and the stove in full view. The menu is mainly traditional Flemish dishes, with French additions. The same owners run **The Hippodroom,** Leopold de Waelplaats 10 (☎ **238-89-36**), in an ancient town house opposite the Royal Museum of Fine Arts, with similar hours, prices, and menu.

5 Attractions

Antwerp is a good walking city, with its major sightseeing attractions easily reached from one major street that changes its name as it goes along: Italielei, Frankrijklie, Britselei, Amerikalei.

The sightseeing treasures are best seen at a leisurely pace—after all, who would want to gallop through Rubens's home at a fast clip. But if time is a factor or if you'd like a good overview before striking out on your own, the city makes it easy by providing guides for walking tours, regularly scheduled coach tours, and a series of boat trips to view Antwerp from the water, as so many of her visitors have first seen her down through the centuries.

If you're a dedicated do-it-yourselfer, you can get maps and sightseeing booklets from the tourist office to guide you. Walking trails have been marked within the city that will lead you through typical streets and squares to find the main points of interest. There's even a free ferryboat ride across the Scheldt if you decide against one of the boat excursions.

Many of Antwerp's museums and churches are open to the public at no charge, and where there is an entrance fee, it's minimal.

Around Grote Markt

Grote Markt, while not nearly so dramatic as Brussels's Grand' Place, is no less the center of everyday activity. In the center of this large square is a huge fountain showing Brabo in the act of throwing Druon's severed hand into the Scheldt.

Stadhuis (Town Hall), Grote Markt.

The Renaissance Stadhuis (Town Hall) was built in the mid-1500s, burned out by the Spanish in 1576, and rebuilt as you see it now. Look for the frescoes by Leys, an important 19th-century painter, some interesting murals, and in the burgomaster's room, an impressive 16th-century fireplace.

Admission (including guided tour): BF 30 (85¢).

Open: Mon–Sat 9am–3pm.

Vleeshuis (Butcher's Hall), Vleeshouwersstraat 38–40.

Around the square and in the surrounding streets you'll see excellent examples of 16th-century guild houses. One worth a visit is the Vleeshuis, a short walk from the Stadhuis. A magnificent Gothic structure, it now functions as a museum of archeology, ceramics, arms, religious art, sculpture, musical instruments, coins, and medieval furnishings. The collections give a good general idea of the daily life in Antwerp during the 16th century as do the historical paintings (look for the striking *The Spanish Fury,* picturing Antwerp's darkest hour). There's also an Egyptian section.

Admission: BF 75 ($2.15) adults; BF 30 (85¢) children 12–18, unemployed persons, students, and pensioners, free for children under 12, soldiers, and inhabitants of Antwerp.

Open: Tues–Sun 10am–5pm. **Closed:** Major holidays.

The Top Attractions

 Cathedral of Our Lady, Hansschoenmarkt.

You'll want to see this towering Gothic edifice (in the city center, at Hansschoen Markt) for several reasons. Its architecture is simply stunning—there are seven naves and 125 pillars—and it's the largest church in both Belgium and Holland. Begun in 1352, the cathedral's original design included five towers, but only one was completed. Its history includes devastation by religious iconoclasts, deconsecration in 1794 that resulted in the removal of its Rubens masterpieces, and slow rebirth beginning after Napoléon's defeat in 1815. Today, three Rubens masterpieces on view are *Elevation of the Cross,* his *Deposition,* and *Assumption.* Rombouts's *Last Supper,* an impressive stained-glass window dating from 1503, is also outstanding.

Admission: BF 60 ($1.70).

Open: Mon–Fri 10am–5pm, Sat 1–4pm, Sun 1–9pm.

Royal Museum of Fine Arts, Leopold de Waelplaats. ☎ 238-78-09.

Housed in this impressive neoclassic building is a collection of paintings by Flemish masters that is second to none in the world. To see them, pass through the ground-floor exhibitions of more modern artists' canvases and ascend to the second floor, where you'll find more Rubens masterpieces in one place than in any other. They're in good company—Jan Van Eyck, Roger van der Weyden, Dirck Bouts, Hans Memling, the Brueghel family, Rembrandt, and Hals are all represented. All told, these walls hold paintings spanning five centuries. To view them is a moving experience.

Admission: BF 100 ($2.85).

Open: Tues–Sun 10am–5pm. **Closed:** Major holidays. **Tram:** 8 from Groenplaats.

★ Rubens House, Wapper 9–11.

Peter Paul Rubens, whose father was an Antwerp attorney who went into exile in Germany and died there, was brought back to this city at an early age by his mother. By the time he was 32, his artistic reputation was firmly established, and he had a profound effect on the city. In 1610, when he was only 33, his great wealth enabled him to build this impressive home and studio along what was once a canal, the Wapper (it's about midway down the Meir). Today you can wander through its rooms, with the decor and furnishings of Rubens's time, and come away with a pretty good idea of the lifestyle of patrician Flemish gentlemen of that era. There are examples of his work scattered throughout, as well as others by master painters who were his contemporaries. In the dining room, look for his self-portrait, painted when he was 47 years old. Rubens was a lover and collector of Roman sculpture, and some of the pieces in his sculpture gallery appear—reproduced in amazing detail—in his paintings. A visit here—a short walk east of the city center—is pretty much essential if you are to fully appreciate most of what you'll see elsewhere in Antwerp.

Admission: BF 75 ($2.15) adults, BF 30 (85¢) students.

Open: Daily 10am–5pm.

★ Steen Castle, Steenplein 1. ☎ 232-08-50.

Always referred to simply as "The Steen," this medieval fortress's oldest stones date from the early 13th century—it's Antwerp's oldest building. Built on the banks of the River Scheldt (at Steenplein), it has served a number of purposes over the centuries, and today it houses the National Maritime Museum. There's an extensive library on river navigation and almost every nautical subject, as well as interesting exhibits about the development of the port and maritime history in general. The most eye-catching of all are models of old-time sailing ships, in particular, East India Company clippers.

Next to the museum there's an interesting industrial archeological division with the remains of the old Antwerp port, open Easter to November 1.

Admission: BF 75 ($2.15) adults, BF 30 (85¢) students.

Open: Daily 10am–5pm. **Closed:** Major holidays.

More Attractions

★ Antwerp Zoo, Koningin Astridplein 26. ☎ 231-16-40.

This amazing 25-acre zoo is just east of Antwerp's Central Station. Its large collection of animals from around the world roam freely through spaces bounded for the most part by artificial reproductions of natural barriers; for example, bright lights instead of closed cage doors keep the aviary bird population at home. There's also an aquarium, winter garden, Egyptian temple, anthropoid house, museum of natural history, deer parks, Kongo-peacock habitat, and a planetarium. The zoo is a real standout among Antwerp's treasures.

Admission: BF 390 ($11) adults, BF 240 ($7) students.

Open: Summer, daily 9am–6:30pm; winter, daily 9am–4:45pm. **Tram:** Central Station; then walk east.

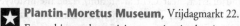 **Plantin-Moretus Museum,** Vrijdagmarkt 22.

From this stately patrician mansion in the city center, Christoffle Plantin established a printing workshop in the late 1500s whose output set print and publishing standards that have had worldwide influence. An astonishing multilanguage (Hebrew, Greek, Syriac, Latin, and Aramaic) edition of the Bible and translations of great works of literature came from these presses. Plantin's name survives in today's publishing world as a widely used typeface. His grandson, Balthasar Moretus, was a contemporary and close friend of Rubens—who painted the family portraits you'll see displayed here, and illustrated many of the books published by the Plantin-Moretus workshop.

Admission: BF 75 ($2.15) adults, BF 30 (85¢) students.

Open: Tues–Sun 10am–5pm. **Closed:** Major holidays.

St. Jacobskerk (St. James's Church), Lange Nieuwstraat 73.

This flamboyant Gothic church with its baroque interior is the final resting place of Peter Paul Rubens, Antwerp's most illustrious resident from the world of art. Several of his works are here, as well as some by Van Dyck and other prominent artists. There's also a glittering collection of gold and silver and religious objects. It's a short walk east of city center, north of Rubens House.

Admission: BF 50 ($1.40).

Open: Summer, Mon–Sat 2–5pm; winter, Mon–Sat 9am–noon.

ANTWERP'S PORT

Although it has now been shifted to Zandvliet, some 8 miles downstream from the city proper, Antwerp's port is the very reason for its existence, and is well worth a visit if only to appreciate its vast size. There is no less than 60 miles of quays, and the entire harbor/dock complex covers 40 square miles. The Flandria boat cruises and coach tours (see "Organized Tours," below) offer the best view for tourists, but the tourist office can furnish detailed information for those who wish to drive the plainly marked "Havenroute" (if this includes you, keep a sharp eye out for hazards of this busy workplace—open bridges, rail tracks, moving cranes, etc.).

DIAMONDS

If anyone knows for certain exactly when Antwerp began to develop as an important facet of the diamond industry, he or she isn't talking. It probably began so gradually that no one at the time took note of what was happening. However, today the city is acknowledged to be the world's leading diamond center. Some 70% of the world's diamonds are traded here annually—valued at more than $6 billion!

★ **Diamondland,** Appelmansstraat 33A. ☎ **234-36-12.**

More than 12,000 expert cutters and polishers are at work here, and it's fascinating to watch as undistinguished stones are transformed into gems of glittering beauty.

Located just a few steps from the Central Station, Diamondland provides a first-hand look at the whole process. This luxurious showplace provides a guided tour of its workrooms, and you can take home a souvenir of lasting value for a price tag considerably lower than you'd pay elsewhere.

Admission: BF 30 (85¢).

Open: Mon–Sat 9am–6pm. **Tram:** Central Station.

Provincial Diamond Museum, Lange Herentalsestraat 31–33.

Exhibits here (in the diamond district, near Central Station) trace the history, geology, mining, and cutting of diamonds. There are periodic diamond-cutting demonstrations on Saturday afternoon.

Admission: Free.

Open: Tues–Sun 10am–5pm. **Closed:** Major holidays. **Tram:** Central Station.

WALKING TOURS

The tourist office can arrange for a highly qualified guide to accompany you on walking tours around the city at a set rate of BF 10,200 ($34) for the first two hours, BF 600 ($17) for each additional hour. There are also clearly marked self-guided walks, with brochures available from the tourist office.

ORGANIZED TOURS

BY BOAT The ✪ **Flandria boat line** offers two cruise options. There's a 50-minute excursion on the river, with half-hourly departures during summer months, at a cost of BF 240 ($6.85), and an extensive trip around the harbor that lasts 2$\frac{1}{2}$ hours and costs BF 375 ($11). In July and August, there's a delightful harbor dinner cruise with a BF-1,500 ($43) fare. For departure points (most leave from the Steen) and exact sailing schedules, contact Flandria Boat Excursions, Steenplein (☎ 231-31-00).

BY BUS The tourist office can furnish details of coach tours of Antwerp and its environs as well as those that include such destinations as Ghent and Bruges.

6 Savvy Shopping

SHOPPING DISTRICTS Expensive, upmarket **shops, boutiques, and department stores** populate De Keyserlei and the Meir. For **haute couture** it's Leopoldstraat; for **lace,** the streets surrounding the cathedral; for **books,** Hoogstraat; for **electronics and antiques,** Minderbroedersrui; and for **diamonds,** Appelmansstraat and nearby streets, all near Central Station.

SHOPPING HOURS Most shops are open Monday to Saturday, 9am to 5pm.

MARKETS Antwerp's famed street markets are fun as well as good bargain-hunting territory. Outstanding among them are the **Bird Market,** on Sunday mornings in Oude Vaartplaats near the City Theater; this general market includes live animals, plants, textiles, and foodstuffs. The **Antiques Market,** at Lijnwaadmarkt (north gate of the cathedral), takes place all day on Saturday from Easter to October. At the **Friday Market,** on Wednesday and Friday mornings on Vrijdagmarkt facing the Plantin-Moretus Museum, household goods and secondhand furniture are auctioned.

7   Evening Entertainment

Antwerp is as lively after dark as it is busy during daylight hours. Be your tastes purely classical or more attuned to lighter amusements of more recent vintage, you'll find entertainment aplenty. To check on what's doing while you're in the city, pick up a copy of *Antwerpen,* a monthly publication available at the tourist office.

Main **entertainment areas** are Grote Markt and Groenplaats, both of which contain concentrations of bars, cafés, and theaters; **High Town** (Hoogstraat, Pelgrimstraat, Pieter Potstraat and vicinity) for jazz clubs and bistros; **Stadswaag** for jazz and punk; and the **Central Station area** for discos, nightclubs, and gay bars. The **red-light district** is concentrated in Riverside Quarter.

The Performing Arts

OPERA & CLASSICAL MUSIC

Schedules, prices (some are free), and bookings are available from the tourist office for such concert series as "Midday Concerts," "Concerts of Early Music," "Organ Cycles," and other cultural performances. Antwerp's **De Vlaamse Opera (Flanders Opera)** performs from October to July at Van Erbornstraat 8 (☎ **233-66-85**); there are frequent performances by the **Flanders Ballet** and symphony and other musical concerts in **Queen Elisabeth Concert Hall,** at Koningin Astridplein (☎ **233-84-44**), **deSingel** (with three halls), and **Hof ter Lo,** a virtual rock temple.

THEATERS

Antwerp has more theaters than any other Flanders city, as well as two excellent theater companies, **Jeugdtheater** and **KNS, the Royal Flemish Theater.** You should be aware that plays will be presented in Dutch or the Flemish dialect. More often than not, however, you'll be able to follow the plot line, regardless of language difficulties, and the quality of the shows merits attendance. For details and bookings of current performances, contact **Theatercentrum,** Theaterplein (☎ **232-66-77**).

You will also have little or no trouble following plots at the delightful ✪ **Vancampens Puppet Theater,** Lange Nieuwstraat (☎ **651-99-11** for schedules).

FILMS

In a lighter vein, Antwerp may well lead all of Belgium in the number of movie theaters and foreign films shown. All movies are shown in their original languages, with Dutch and French subtitles, and you'll find most of the theaters along De Keyserlei and its side streets. As for the films, they might be anything from the latest award winner to porn—Antwerp is sophisticated enough to take each at face value. The largest concentration of cinemas is in the Central Station area, and lists of current film showings are published in daily newspapers.

The Club and Music Scene

Along De Keyserlei and its side streets, there's a conglomeration of disco and strip bars—some very high class, others (obvious at a glance) frankly low class or vulgar. If you're looking for a respectable disco, check the area between Groenplaats and Grote Markt.

The Bar Scene

When the sun goes down, the people who live here head for their favorite café or bar for an evening of Belgian beer and good conversation—and you'll be very welcome to join their circle. If you miss an evening so occupied, it's safe to say that you haven't really seen Antwerp!

Bars and pubs, of course, all have personalities of their own, and the following is a general guide for those you may fancy: **street cafés** are found in Groenplaats and Grote Markt; **"brown cafés" and bistros** are clustered on Hoogstraat, Pelgrimstraat, Pieter Potstraat, and surroundings; **beer cellars** are on Stadswaag; **taverns and boulevard cafés** are strewn along De Keyserlei; **artists' cafés and bars** are in Quartier Latin near the City Theater; and **gay bars** are mostly in the Central Station area.

The following are just a few among the hundreds of pubs you might enjoy: **Groote Witte Arend** (The Great White Eagle), on Reyndersstraat; **Pelgrom,** on Pelgrimstraat; **Engel,** in Grote Markt; **Elfde Gebod,** on Torfbrug; and **Kulminator,** Vleminckveld 32, which displays a huge selection of beers behind glass, with virtually every Belgian beer made on hand.

8 Easy Excursions

From an Antwerp base, both **Brussels** and **Mechelen** are an easy drive or train ride for day trips (see Chapter 4).

LIER

Just 10 miles southeast of Antwerp, Lier is worth a drive, or bus or train trip, if only to see the **Municipal Museum Wuyts,** Florent van Cauwenberghstraat 14, just off Grote Markt in the town center, with hours of 10am to noon and 1:30 to 5:30pm April through October, Saturday through Tuesday and Thursday. Its quite good art collection includes paintings by Rubens, Jan and Pieter Brueghel, David Teniers the Younger, and local artist Isidore Opsomer.

Stop by the **Tourist Office** in the Stadhuis in Grote Markt (☎ 03/489-11-11) for **town maps** and other **sightseeing attractions.**

HASSELT

Approximately 48 miles southwest of Antwerp, Hasselt is easily reached by rail or bus and a leisurely drive. Its chief attraction is the not-to-be-missed **Open-Air Museum of Bokrijk** (Openluchtmuseum) and **Bokrijk Estate Park,** 5 miles east of town. The **Tourist Office,** Lombaardstraat 3 (☎ 011/23-95-40; fax 011/22-57-42), can furnish free maps and detailed information; and there is regular bus and train service from Hasselt to Bokrijk.

The Major Concert and Performance Halls

Queen Elisabeth Concert Hall, Koningin Astridplein (☎ 233-84-44).

Theatercentrum, Theaterplein (☎ 232-66-77).

Vancampens Puppet Theater, Lange Nieuwstraat (☎ 651-99-11).

De Vlaamse Opera (Flanders Opera), Van Erbornstraat 8 (☎ 233-66-85).

On the grounds of the huge wooded Bokrijk estate, the museum consists of villages typical of the provinces of Anvers, Flanders, and Limbourg that have been reconstructed with a degree of accuracy in their representation of Flemish-Belgian everyday life that is unequaled anywhere else. Hours for the museum are 10am to 6pm daily April through September and 9am to 5pm in October, and admission is BF 250 ($7.15). Although all buildings and village sites are clearly marked, I strongly suggest the purchase of the detailed English-language guidebook (BF 300/$8.50), which is an education in itself.

6

In Flanders Fields

EVERYDAY LIFE IN MEDIEVAL EUROPE IS AS VIVID AS IMAGES ON TODAY'S TELEVISION screen when you walk the streets of Bruges or Ghent—not medieval Europe *restored*, but medieval Europe *preserved*. Ypres (pronounce it "Ee-pre") has another story to tell: Having suffered centuries of intermittent warfare and almost total destruction during World War I, it has picked itself up in the years since and restored its legacies from a colorful past. In these three towns of Flanders, the spirit of the Flemish people becomes a tangible substance, walking by your side, whispering in your ear, "This is how it was; this is how we lived; this is what has made us what we are today."

A BIT OF HISTORY

Outside the towns, the famous fields of Flanders—immortalized in the famed World War I poem—along the alluvial plains of the River Scheldt are actually polders, much like those in Holland, which consist of land reclaimed after disastrous floods that began a few centuries before the birth of Christ and occurred time and again right up to the 10th century A.D. Extending some 6 to 10 miles inland from the sea, the polders create a landscape of rich farmland crisscrossed by canals and ditches lined with poplars and fields dotted with solitary farmhouses surrounded by their outbuildings. In medieval times these were the large land holdings of feudal lords and wealthy abbeys, and few have been broken into smaller plots in the intervening years—farm boundaries today remain much as they were then.

It is the enduring Flemish spirit that inspired Flemish poet Emile Verhaeren to write:

> *I am a son of this race*
> *With their heads*
> *More solid*
> *More passionate,*
> *More voracious*
> *Than their teeth.*

It is a spirit that has prevailed through centuries of armed conflict, commercial strife, and religious controversy.

Always a buffer between warring political factions, the region nevertheless provided a ready market for England's wool, which its weavers transformed into the Flemish cloth so highly prized in Europe and much of the medieval world—it's the cloth you see draping the figures depicted in the great paintings of the Middle Ages. In the process, the access of Bruges's River Zwinn to the sea made it the busiest port in northern Europe, and the cloth mills of Ghent set an industrial pattern still obvious today.

When the Zwinn inexplicably dried up, its disappearing waters took with them a prosperity that had seemed destined to last forever. But it was to Bruges that Catholic priests and nuns fled for safety during the religious persecutions of the late 1500s. Their housing quarters and places of refuge are there to this day; and when Bruges's perfectly preserved medieval beauty was brought to the attention of the rest of the world in this century, it became a mecca for tourists anxious to touch the past.

IMPRESSIONS

I resolved to journey along with Quiet and Contentment for my companions. These two comfortable deities have, I believe, taken Flanders under their special protection; every step one advances discovering some new proof of their influence.
—William Beckford, 1783

What's Special About Flanders Fields

Bruges
- Gabled houses, meandering canals, and narrow cobblestone streets, producing one of the most romantic towns in Europe.
- Church of Our Lady, with a marble *Madonna and Child* by Michelangelo among its art treasures.
- Memling Museum, in what was a hospital in the Middle Ages, with a magnificent collection of Hans Memling's paintings.
- The Lace Center, where the ancient art of lacemaking is passed on to the next generation.
- Groeninge Museum, with its famed Gallery of Flemish Primitives.
- Procession of the Holy Blood, held on Ascension Day, displaying a relic soaked with the blood of Christ while residents act out biblical episodes.

Ghent
- Medieval Europe preserved.
- St. Bavo's Cathedral, filled with priceless paintings, sculptures, screens, and carved tombs.
- The Graslei, a solid row of towering guild houses.
- Castle of the Counts, with relics of its torture chamber and fine views of the rooftops and towers of the city.

Ypres
- Rebuilt brick by brick following medieval plans, after the devastation of World War I.
- The Menen Gate of the British war cemetery, with the names of the 55,000 British soldiers who died here in World War I.
- Festival of the Cats, when the town jester throws hundreds of velvet cats from the Belfry.

Ghent fought one ruler after another, with mixed results, always holding onto a fierce sense of the working man's independence, a sensibility that has brought it into modern-day industrial importance in a setting that quite happily blends reminders of the past with commercial requirements of today. And Ypres suffered through sieges and open warfare that left it impoverished, but with its indomitable spirit intact—a spirit that shines in the perseverance underlying its incredible 20th-century rebuilding of 13th-century buildings.

Each of the three towns in this chapter is easily visited on day trips from Brussels, and for drivers it's a compact circular travel route. Despite their proximity to the capital city, however, it's highly probable you'll lose your heart to either Bruges or Ghent and hanker for a longer visit (Ypres is an ideal half-day visit from either). For that reason, accommodation recommendations are included in the sections of this chapter, as well as some of Belgium's finest restaurants.

1 Bruges (Brugge)

89km (55 miles) NW of Brussels, 92km (57 miles) W of Antwerp, 46km (28 miles) NW of Ghent, 60km (37 miles) NE of Ypres

GETTING THERE • By Train   Bruges is only 55 minutes from Brussels by train. The **railway station** is about 1 mile south of town, a 20-minute walk to the town center or a short bus or taxi ride. For train and public transportation information, call **078/11-36-63** between 6:30am and 10:30pm.

• **By Bus**   The **bus station** adjoins the train station (see above). Schedule and fare information can be obtained by calling **078/11-36-63** from 6am to 9pm.

• **By Car**   Bruges is reached via E40 from Brussels and Ghent; E17 and E40 from Antwerp; and a signposted, unclassified road north with a signposted turn west at Exit 4 onto E40 from Ypres. For a hassle-free visit to Bruges, drive directly to the large underground car park near the train station at 't Zand and leave your car there until you're headed out of town (see "Getting Around," below).

ESSENTIALS   The **telephone area code** for Bruges is 050.

Orientation   The heart of Bruges is encircled by a broad ring canal that opens at its southern end to become the Lac d'Amour (Lake of Love). In your mind's eye, see the lake as the busy port of the Middle Ages, before the demise of the Zwinn; and save time for at least one walk through the green park along its shores. To one side of the lake is the railway station. Bruges's narrow streets fan out from Grote Markt, and the network of canals threads its way to every section of this small town.

Information   The **Tourist Office,** at Burg 11, 8000 Bruges (☎ **050/44-86-86;** fax 050/44-86-00), is open every day: April to September, Monday through Friday from 9:30am to 6:30pm and on Saturday, Sunday, and holidays from 10am to noon and 2 to 6:30pm; other months, Monday through Saturday from 10am to 12:45pm and 2 to 5:45pm. Ask for the complimentary *Agenda Brugge,* an excellent directory of current goings on, as well as other helpful sightseeing brochures.

GETTING AROUND • By Bus   Most city buses depart from Kuiperstraat near Grote Markt and the train station, with schedules prominently posted.

• **By Bicycle**   If you arrive in Bruges by train, you can rent a bicycle (you must present a valid rail ticket) at the railway station for BF 130 ($3.70) per day (discount for three days or more). Biking is a terrific way to get around or even get to nearby Damme (see below) by way of beautiful canalside, tree-lined roads.

• **By Car**   My best advice on driving in Bruges is "*Don't!*" If you're driving, stash your car at one of the several underground car parks and forget it—not only is this walking territory, but driving the narrow streets can be murder! Taxis are available to get you to your hotel if you plan an overnight stay; otherwise, it's a short walk into the heart of the old city from any of the car parks.

• **On Foot**   The best—and in my judgment the *only*—way to see Bruges properly is on foot. My only word of caution is to be sure to wear sturdy shoes; those charming little cobblestone streets can play hob with lesser gear.

Surely one of the most romantic towns in Europe, Bruges is a fairytale mixture of gabled houses, meandering canals, narrow cobblestone streets, a busy market square, and a populace intent on providing a gracious and warm welcome to its visitors.

What to See and Do

The friendly and extremely efficient tourist office has brochures that outline walking, coach, canal, and horse-drawn cab tours, as well as detailed information on many sightseeing attractions.

Grote Markt (Market Square) is, as it was in the beginning, the heart of the heart and the focal point of your sightseeing. Major points of interest are no more than 5 or 10 minutes' walk away.

GROTE MARKT

Grote Markt, the vast Market Square at the heart of Bruges, is where you'll find the renowned 13th-century **Belfry** of Bruges. An octagonal tower atop **the Halles** (the "Halls" in which much of the commerce of the city was conducted in centuries past) holds a magnificent 47-bell carillon that peals out over the city every quarter hour and in longer concerts several times a day in summer months. If you climb the 366 steps to the Belfry's summit, you will have a breathtaking panoramic view of the city and its surrounding countryside all the way to the sea. Just outside the Halles, the Kiwanis Club of Bruges has erected a bronze replica of the Belfry and Halles with descriptions in Dutch, French, German, and English inscribed in braille for unsighted visitors. Admission to the belfry is BF 100 ($2.85) and it's open daily from 9:30am to 12:30pm and 1:30 to 5pm.

That **statue** in the center of Grote Markt depicts two Belgian heroes, butcher Jan Breydel and weaver Pieter de Coninck, who led the 1302 uprising against wealthy merchants and nobles who dominated the guilds, and went on to victory against French knights later that same year in the Battle of the Golden Spurs. On the corner of Sint Amandstraat at Grote Markt, the small, castlelike building—the **Cranenburg**—was used to imprison Maximilian of Austria, an act for which he later exacted a penalty from the citizens of Bruges that added a note of pure beauty to the city: They were obliged to keep swans in the canals forever. The large Neo-Gothic Government Palace dates from the 1800s and houses the administrative offices of West Flanders.

THE BURG

Several points of interest are located in the Burg, a public square just steps away from Grote Markt, where Baldwin of the Iron Arm once built a fortified castle, around which a village (or "burg") developed.

Town Hall, The Burg.

The Town Hall is a beautiful Gothic structure built in the late 1300s, making it the oldest town hall in Belgium. Be sure to see the upstairs Gothic Room (Gotische Zaal) with its ornate decor and wall murals depicting highlights of Bruges's history.

Admission: BF 60 ($1.70).

Open: Daily 9:30am–noon and 2–6pm.

Basilica of the Holy Blood, The Burg.

Since 1149 this basilica has been a repository of a fragment of cloth soaked with the blood of Christ, which was brought to Bruges during the Second Crusade by the Count of Flanders. Every Ascension Day a colorful Procession of the Holy Blood displays the relic (carried by the bishop of the church) through Bruges's streets, accompanied by beautifully costumed residents acting out biblical episodes. The 12th-century basilica is worth a visit for the richness of its design and the other treasures it holds, even if you have no interest in the relic.

Admission: BF 40 ($1.15).

Open: Basilica, daily 9:30am–noon and 2–6pm; relic, Fri 8:30–11:45am and 3–4pm.

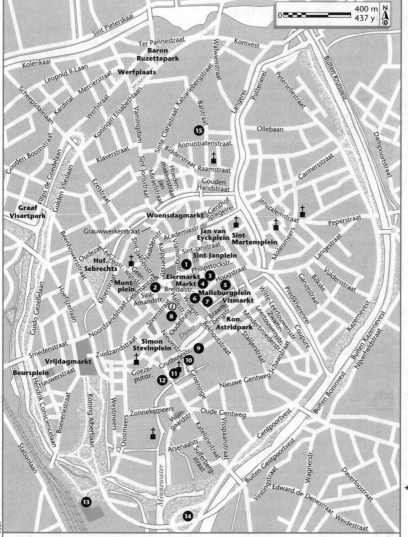

Bruges (Brugge)

0 ___ 400 m / 437 y

N

Basilica of the Holy Blood ❻
Bus Station ⓮
The Burg ❹
Church of Our Lady ⓫
The Cranenburg ❷
Groeninge Museum ❾
Grote Markt ❺
Gruuthuse Museum ❿

The Halles ❽
Hospital of St. John (Memling Museum) ⓬
Lace Center ⓯
Railway Station ⓭
Statue of Breydel and de Coninck ❶
Town Hall ❼
Tourist Information Office ❸

Church ✝   Information ⓘ

OTHER MAIN SIGHTS

 Church of Our Lady, Mariastraat.

It took two centuries (13th to 15th) to build this church, and its soaring 396-foot-high spire is a Bruges point of reference. Among its many art treasures are the marble *Madonna and Child* by Michelangelo; a painting by Anthony Van Dyck; and the impressive bronze figure of Mary of Burgundy, who died in 1482, and that of Charles the Bold, who died in 1477. Under their tombs (finished in the 16th century) a windowpane allows you to view the 13th- and 14th-century graves of priests.

Admission: BF 60 ($1.70).

Open: Mon–Sat 10am–11:30am and 2:30–5pm, Sun 2:30–4:30pm.

 Groeninge Museum, Dijver 12.

The Groeninge ranks among the leading traditional museums of fine arts, and the collection contains a survey of painting in the southern Netherlands and Belgium from the 15th to the 20th century. The famed Gallery of Flemish Primitives holds some 30 works of painters such as Jan Van Eyck, Roger van der Weyden, Hieronymus Bosch, and Hans Memling. Works of Magritte and Delvaux are also on display.

Admission: BF 130 ($3.70).

Open: Apr–Sept, Wed–Mon 9:30am–5pm; Oct–Mar, Wed–Mon 9:30am–noon and 2–5pm.

Gruuthuse Museum, Dijver 17.

This ornate mansion where Flemish nobleman Louis de Gruuthuse lived in the 1400s is now an integral part of the Groeninge Museum (see above). Among the 2,500 numbered antiquities in the house are paintings, sculptures, tapestries, laces, weapons, glassware, and richly carved furniture.

Admission: BF 130 ($3.70).

Open: Apr–Sept, daily 9:30–noon and 2–5pm; Oct–Mar, Wed–Mon 9:30am–noon and 2–5pm.

 The Lace Center, Balstraat 14. ☎ **33-00-72.**

This is a fascinating place—the lace of Bruges is, after all, famous the world over, and you'll be hard-put to resist taking some away as your most lasting memento of Bruges. This is where the ancient art of lacemaking is passed on to the next generation, and you get a firsthand look at the artisans who will be making many of the items for future sale in all those lace shops. Incidentally, the most famous laces to look for are *bloemenwek, rozenkant,* and *toveresseteek.*

Admission: BF 40 ($1.14) adults; BF 25 (70¢) children.

Open: Mon–Sat 10am–noon, 2–6 pm. **Closed:** Sun.

 Memling Museum, Mariastraat.

The building holding the Memling Museum, the Hospital of St. John, dates from the Middle Ages. To see the vastness of the wards when this was a functioning hospital, take a look at the old painting near the entrance that shows small, efficient bed units

IMPRESSIONS

Not a sound rose from the city at the early morning hour, But I heard a heart of iron beating in that ancient tower. . . .
—Henry Wadsworth Longfellow, *The Belfry of Bruges,* 1845

set into cubicles around the walls. The old Apothecary Room is furnished exactly as it was when this building's main function was the care of the sick.

Nowadays visitors come to see the typical medieval hospital buildings filled with furniture and other objects that illustrate their history, as well as the magnificent collection of paintings by Hans Memling. The artist came to Bruges after the death of Roger van der Weyden, and became one of the city's most prominent residents. Roger van der Weyden actually had his workshop in Brussels, and Memling worked in his own atelier in Brussels. Here you'll find such masterpieces as the altarpiece of St. John the Baptist and St. John the Evangelist, also called *The Mystic Marriage of St. Catherine;* the *Ursula Shrine;* and *Virgin with Child and Apple.*

Admission: BF 100 ($2.85) adults; BF 50 ($1.40) children.

Open: Sun–Tues, Thurs –Sat 9:30am–7:30pm. **Closed:** Wed.

SIGHTSEEING TOURS

If you'd like a trained, knowledgeable **guide** to accompany your walks around the town, the tourist office can provide that service at a charge of about BF 1,200 ($34) for the first two hours, BF 600 ($17) for each additional hour.

An absolute "must" for every visitor is a ✪ **boat trip** on the city canals. Year-round, there are several departure points (all plainly marked on city maps available at the tourist office), and the half-hour cruise costs BF 150 ($4.25) for adults, BF 75 ($2.15) for children.

Another lovely way to tour Bruges is by ✪ **horse-drawn cab,** and from March to November they are stationed at the Burg (on Wednesday in Grote Markt). A 35-minute ride costs BF 800 ($23) per cab, BF 400 ($11.50) for each additional 15 minutes.

Three-hour coach tours depart year-round from Market Square, opposite the Belfry Tower, several times a day on selected days of the week (check with the tourist office, since days are subject to change), with fares of BF 330 ($9.40) for adults, BF 200 ($5.70) for children. Book at the tourist office.

NEARBY ATTRACTIONS

Just 4 miles away is the tiny town of **Damme,** once the outer harbor of Bruges. The marriage of Charles the Bold and Margaret of York was celebrated here in 1468, an indication of the importance of Damme during that era. Today visitors come to see the picturesque **Marktplein,** which holds a statue of native Jacob van Maerlant, the "father of Flemish poetry," and for the beautiful scenery en route from Bruges.

One of the nicest ways to get from Bruges to Damme is by canal boat. In summer, departures in Bruges are from the Noorweegse Kaai several times a day (check with the tourist office for schedules and fares), and the half-hour ride is a delight to the senses as you glide through a landscape straight out of the Flemish paintings you've seen in museums. Sailings are frequent enough in both directions to make possible a day trip to Damme, with lunch at one of the many restaurants lining its Marktplein and plenty of time for a sightseeing stroll. The **Damme Tourist Office** is at the Town Hall, Markt 1, 8340 Damme (☎ **050/35-33-19**).

EVENING ENTERTAINMENT

Bruges is one of the best places in Belgium to see the fascinating puppet theater that has been a favorite entertainment in the country for centuries. There's a marvelous collection of puppets and plays at the **Marionettentheater Brugge,** St. Jakobsstraat 36. Call **34-47-60** for performance schedules.

Where to Stay

If a high-rise luxury hotel is your cup of tea, then my best advice is that you stay in Brussels and commute to Bruges. But if the idea of a small, atmospheric hostelry (perhaps right on the banks of a picturesque canal) with modern (if not luxurious) facilities appeals, then you'll find that accommodations here will enhance your visit by enabling you to sink into the timelessness of Bruges.

There are several very good budget hotels in Bruges, most with rooms above restaurants on the ground floor. Some come with baths, but a moneysaving device is to share a bath down the hall—no real hardship in these establishments.

Let me add that *you should not arrive without a reservation!* Bruges is one of Belgium's premier tourist cities, and it's a good idea to make reservations at least two weeks before you plan to come. If by some quirk of fate you come into town and have no place to stay, head immediately to the tourist office—they have a very good reservation service, and can also book in advance for you, as can tourist offices throughout the country. Accommodations are much less heavily booked during the week than on weekends, so come Monday through Thursday if you can. Rates listed here include service and VAT.

EXPENSIVE

Duc de Bourgogne, Huidenvettersplein 12, 8000 Bruges. ☎ **050/33-20-38.** Fax 050/34-40-37. 10 rms. A/C TV TEL

Rates (including breakfast): BF 3,700 ($105) single; BF 5,250 ($150) double. AE, DC, MC, V.

Perhaps the most elegant of the small hotels, the Duc de Bourgogne is located in a 17th-century building on a canal. The fairly large guest rooms here are luxuriously furnished and decorated, with antiques scattered all through the hotel.

Dining/Entertainment: There's a very good restaurant on the ground floor, overlooking the canal (see "Where to Dine," below).

Hotel Sofitel Brugge, Boeveriestraat 2, 8000 Bruges. ☎ **050/34-09-71.** Fax 050/34-40-53. 155 rms. A/C MINIBAR TV TEL

Rates (including breakfast): BF 4,950 ($141) single; BF 5,400 ($154) double. AE, DC, MC, V.

In a unique setting (a 17th-century monastery), this thoroughly up-to-date hotel is located at 't Zand, not far from the railway station in the town center. Its interior is pretty standard "modern," but touches like exposed brick walls and open fireplaces soften the effect considerably. The guest rooms are large and light, with two queen-size beds.

Dining/Entertainment: The restaurant is open all year, daily from 11:30am to 10:30pm. There's also the atmospheric Jan Breydel Bar.

Services: Will arrange boat trips, horse-and-carriage rides through the old center, visits to the museums, excursions to the bird sanctuary.

Facilities: Five conference rooms in the old chapel, heated indoor pool, sauna.

 Oud Huis Amsterdam, Spiegelrei 3, 8000 Bruges. ☎ **050/34-18-10.** Fax 050/33-88-91. 17 rms, 2 suites. A/C MINIBAR TV TEL

Rates (including breakfast): BF 3,850 ($110) single; BF 4,500–6,000 ($128–$171) double; BF 7,000 ($200) suite. AE, DC, MC, V.

Philip and Caroline Traen have transformed this large canalfront building—parts of which date back to the 1300s, most from the 1500s—into a hotel with large and sumptuously furnished rooms. Some of the baths even feature a Jacuzzi, and the colors and decorative accents hark back to the building's origin, based on meticulous research and restoration. The elegant guest rooms in the front overlook the canal; those in back, the garden and picturesque rooftops. The entrance hall, the small salon off the reception area, and the popular "The Meeting" bar are all atmospheric; and there's a charming little courtyard at the rear with umbrella tables and a garden just to one side—the setting for Sunday concerts during June. It must be added that the famed Traen hospitality makes a stay here in the town center very special.

★ **De Snippe,** Nieuwe Gentweg 53, 8000 Bruges. ☎ **050/33-70-70.**
Fax 050 33-76-62. 7 rms, 6 suites. MINIBAR TV TEL

Rates (including breakfast): BF 4,500–6,000 ($128–$171) single; BF 6,000–7,500 ($171–$214) double. AE, DC, MC, V.

Set in an early 18th-century building in the town center and long known as one of Bruges's leading restaurants, De Snippe also offers truly luxurious rooms. Many of the spacious rooms have fireplaces, and all have furnishings of restrained elegance.
  Dining/Entertainment: See "Where to Dine," below.
  Services: 24-hour room service.

MODERATE

★ **Alfa Dante Hotel,** Coupure 29, 8000 Bruges. ☎ **050/34-01-94.**
Fax 050/34-35-39. 22 rms, 2 suites. MINIBAR TV TEL

Rates (including breakfast): BF 2,875–5,850 ($82–$162) single; BF 4,500–6,000 ($128–$171) double; BF 8,000 ($228) suite. AE, DC, MC, V.

This ultramodern brick hotel is set alongside a lovely canal, a short walk from the center of Bruges. The guest rooms are nicely furnished, and there are a good vegetarian restaurant for guests and a bar, and private parking is a real bonus.

★ **'T Bourgoensche Cruyce,** Wollestraat 41, 8000 Bruges. ☎ **050/33-79-26.**
Fax 34-19-68. 8 rms. A/C MINIBAR TV TEL
$ **Rates** (including breakfast): BF 3,200–3,800 ($91–$108) single or double. AE, MC, V.

Opening onto a lovely little inner courtyard right in the middle of things (the Belfry in the town center is just 100 yards away), this tiny family-run hotel provides the very epitome of a Bruges experience. Let me say right up front that the small rooms are not for everyone, but their simple, comfortable furnishings and canal view will utterly charm those not bent on luxurious accommodations. Best of all, however, is the hospitality of Mr. and Mrs. Roger Traen, the proprietors who also oversee their noted restaurant—one of the best in Bruges—which occupies the ground floor.

★ **Hotel Erasmus,** Wollestraat 35, 8000 Bruges. ☎ **050/33-57-81.**
Fax 050/34-36-30. 9 rms. MINIBAR TV TEL

Rates (including breakfast): BF 2,750 ($78) single; BF 3,250 ($93) double. AE, DC, MC, V.

Just steps away from the Belfry, this modern hotel is set in a picturesque little square alongside a canal in the town center. All rooms have writing desks and attractive, modern furnishings. There's a safe available to guests, and each guest receives one free drink in the bar.

Hotel ter Duinen, Langerei 52, 8000 Bruges. ☎ **050/33-42-16.** Fax 050/34-42-16. 18 rms. TV TEL

Rates (including breakfast): BF 2,300–4,000 ($65–$114) single; BF 2,800–4,000 ($80–$114) double. MC, V.

This charming hotel is an ideal marriage between classical style and modern conveniences. Guest rooms are ample in size, nicely appointed, and equipped with hairdryers, and some overlook the ring canal, just north of the town center.

★ **Navarra,** St. Jakobsstraat 41, 8000 Bruges. ☎ **050/34-05-61.** Fax 050/33-76-90. 95 rms. TV TEL

Rates (including breakfast): BF 2,800–3,900 ($80–$111) single; BF 3,300–4,700 ($94–$134) double. AE, DC, MC, V.

In a very central location not far from the Belfry, this was the home of the Prince of Navarre during the 16th century. Its guest rooms have recently been renovated and are nicely furnished, and there are a jazz bar and a private garden. There's a health club, an indoor pool, and a sauna.

Pandhotel, Pandreitje 16, 8000 Bruges. ☎ **050/34-10-64.** Fax 050/340-556. 24 rms. MINIBAR TV TEL

Rates (including breakfast): BF 2,800 ($80) single; BF 5,200 ($148) double; BF 6,500 ($185) family room (sleeps four). Package rates available. MC, V.

The Pandhotel is situated in a very quiet and central area close to the canals, Grote Markt, and museums. This lovely old 18th-century mansion—in its setting among plane trees—is right in the center of town, yet is a virtual oasis of quiet and tranquillity. Its exquisite, old-fashioned furnishings (but modern conveniences, such as hairdryers) lend a special grace to the comfortable rooms, and readers have given Mrs. Chris Dewaele their highest praise for her attention to detail and gracious hospitality.

★ $ **De Swaene,** Steenhouwersdijk 1, 8000 Bruges. ☎ **050/34-27-98.** Fax 050/33-66-74. 22 rms, 3 suites. MINIBAR TV TEL

Rates (including breakfast): BF 4,150 ($118) single; BF 5,100 ($145) double; BF 10,400 ($297) suite. AE, DC, MC, V.

Owned by the charming Hessels family, this small hotel overlooking a canal in the town center has rightly been called one of the most romantic hotels in Europe. All guest rooms are elegantly furnished and very comfortable, each with an individual decor. The lovely lounge is actually the Guild Hall of the Tailors that dates back to 1779. Its restaurant, whose specialty is fish, has also won honors from guests as well as critics, and there's a sauna and an indoor swimming pool.

INEXPENSIVE

Central, Markt 30, 8000 Bruges. ☎ **050/33-18-05.** Fax 050/33-17-91. 7 rms (1 with bath).

Rates (including breakfast): BF 1,365 ($39) single or double without bath; BF 1,625–2,360 ($46–$67) single or double with bath. AE, DC, MC, V.

You couldn't find a more central location than this small hotel on Grote Markt. The rooms are basic (no telephone or TV), but comfortable and quite adequately furnished. You should know that this three-story hotel has no elevator.

★ **Fevery,** Collaert Mansionstraat 3, 8000 Bruges. ☎ **050/33-12-69.** 11 rms. TV TEL
Rates (including breakfast): BF 2,000–2,250 ($57–$64) single or double.
AE, DC, MC, V.

Centrally located near Grote Markt, the upstairs rooms in this small hotel are comfortable and nicely furnished, with a small table and adequate seating in bedrooms. There's a downstairs bar and dining room, and babysitting can be arranged.

Graaf van Vlaanderen, 't Zand 19, 8000 Bruges. ☎ **050/33-31-50.**
Fax 050/34-59-79. 14 rms (7 with bath).

Rates (including breakfast): BF 1,030 ($294) single without bath; BF 1,625–2,465 ($46–$70) single or double with bath. AE, DC, MC, V.

Along the east side of 't Zand near the railway station, this small hotel provides basic but comfortable accommodations and has a budget-priced restaurant. There's no elevator in this three-story hotel.

Hotel 't Keizershof, Oostmeers 126, 8000 Bruges. ☎ **050/33-87-28.**
7 rms (none with bath).

Rates (including breakfast): BF 900 ($25) single; BF 1,250 ($35) double. No credit cards.

Despite being one of the least expensive hostelries in Brugge, the 't Keizershof gets high marks for clean, comfortable accommodations in a quiet, peaceful location. Several languages are spoken by the young couple who own and operate the hotel near the railway station, and they are most helpful to guests in planning their Bruges stay.

★ **Hotel St. Christophe,** Nieuwe Gentweg 76, 8000 Bruges. ☎ **050/33-11-76.**
23 rms (12 with bath).

Rates: BF 1,800 ($51) single with bath; BF 1,800 ($51) double without bath, BF 2,520 ($78) double with bath. MC, V.

This three-story hotel, located between the town center and the railway station, offers a range of price options for comfortable accommodations. Some guest rooms overlook a lovely garden; there's a small bar; and the Vermeersch family, owner/operators, have won high praise from our readers.

Leopold, 't Zand 26, 8000 Bruges. ☎ **050/33-51-29.** 9 rms (5 with bath), 4 family rms. A/C TEL

Rates: BF 1,200 ($34) single without bath; BF 1,600 ($45) single with bath; BF 1,200–1,400 ($34–$40) double without bath. BF 2,000 ($57) double with bath; BF 2,500–3,300 ($71–$94) family room (sleeps four). AE, MC, V.

Another hotel along the east side of 't Zand near the railway station, the Leopold is a well-run establishment. The furnishings are rather basic but quite comfortable, and there's a bar.

READERS RECOMMEND

Pension Het Geestelijk Hof, Heilige Geeststraat 2, 8000 Bruges (☎ **050/34-25-94**).
"*We found this fabulous place in a convenient location, where the innkeeper was a delight, providing us with wonderful breakfasts and mosquito-zapping plug-ins. Our room overlooked a garden, picturesque rooftops, and several church steeples.*"
—Joan Clark, Washington, D.C. [**Author's Note:** Prices in 1995 are BF 1,490 ($42) for a double without bath, BF 1,990 ($56) for a double with bath, and BF 1,890 ($54) for a triple without bath.]

HOSTELS

Bruges has excellent hostel facilities, with rates that average BF 800 ($22) or under. Most do not accept credit cards, and many provide only dormitory accommodations. The tourist office can supply a complete list, and the following can be recommended: **Bauhaus International Youth Hotel,** Langestraat 135–137, 8000 Bruges (☎ 050/34-10-93); **Bruno's Passage,** Dweersstraat 26, 8000 Bruges (☎ 050/34-02-32); and **International Youth Hostel Europa,** Baron Ruzettelaan 143 (☎ 050/35-26-79).

Where to Dine

EXPENSIVE

⭐ **'T Bourgoensche Cruyce,** Wollestraat 41. ☎ 33-79-26.
$ **Cuisine:** CONTINENTAL. **Reservations:** Required.
Prices: Three-course fixed-price meal BF 1,350 ($38) at lunch, BF 2,190 ($62) at dinner. AE, DC, MC, V.
Open: Lunch Thurs–Mon noon–2:30pm; dinner Thurs–Mon 7–9:30pm. **Closed:** Nov.

The rustic charm of this small dining room overlooking a canal in the town center is just one intimation of the culinary delights in store. From the kitchen, the experienced chef sends forth regional specialties that are just simply perfection itself. The menu reflects the very best ingredients that are available in any season, and there's a six-course "gastronomic sampling menu" if you just can't make a decision. Also, regardless of season, a dish not to be missed is the marvelous mosaïque de poissons or any of the other superb seafood dishes.

Duc de Bourgogne, Huidenvettersplein 12. ☎ **33-20-38.**
Cuisine: FRENCH. **Reservations:** Required.
Prices: Fixed-price meal BF 1,300 ($37) at lunch, BF 2,150 ($61) at dinner. AE, MC, DC, V.
Open: Daily 10am–11pm. **Closed:** July.

This large dining room overlooking a canal (it's illuminated at night) is elegant and just this side of "formal" in decor, although in summer there's no rigid dress code enforced. The classic menu is a lengthy one; the fixed-price lunch menu changes daily, and the fixed-price dinner changes every two weeks. Specialties include noisettes of veal au Porto. It's located in the town center near Burg.

⭐ **'T Pandreitje,** Pandreitje 6. ☎ **33-11-90.**
$ **Cuisine:** FRENCH/BELGIAN. **Reservations:** Required.
Prices: Fixed-price meal BF 1,950–2,700 ($55–$77) for five courses, BF 2,300–3,500 ($65–$100) for a seven course feast. AE, DC, MC, V.
Open: Lunch Mon–Tues and Thurs–Sat noon–2:30pm; dinner Mon–Sat 7–9:30pm. **Closed:** Two weeks in Mar, first two weeks in July.

Located in the very heart of Bruges, in the shade of the medieval market hall's bell tower and just off the "Rozenhoedkaai," 't Pandreitje is one of the nicest spots in town. The interior of this Renaissance-era private home has been turned into an elegant Louis XVI setting for a menu of classic dishes. A four-course à la carte meal is superb, and the "menu" of preselected choices is excellent. Try one of their marvelous creative seafood dishes.

De Snippe, Nieuwe Gentweg 53. ☎ **33-70-70.**
Cuisine: BELGIAN/FRENCH. **Reservations:** Required.
Prices: Meals BF 2,500–3,500 ($71–$100). AE, DC, MC, V.
Open: Lunch Tues–Sat noon–2:30pm; dinner daily 7–10pm.

Set in a gabled private house that dates back to the 16th century in the town center, De Snippe enjoys a reputation as one of Brugge's finest restaurants. It's a reputation well earned, especially for its native dishes. Try the crayfish creations, scampi, or sliced wild duck. Nine rooms are also for rent (see "Where to Stay," above).

MODERATE

 De Visscherie, Vismarkt 8. ☎ **33-02-12.**
Cuisine: SEAFOOD. **Reservations:** Recommended.
Prices: Average meal BF 1,600–2,400 ($45–$68). AE, DC, MC, V.
Open: Lunch Wed–Mon noon–2:30pm; dinner Wed–Mon 8:30–10pm. **Closed:** Mid-Nov to mid-Dec.

This attractive restaurant faces the old fish market in the town center, and as you might expect, "fruits of the sea" take top billing on the menu. Freshness is virtually a fetish here, and specialties include shellfish in many guises (try the spotted scallops with roe) and Channel sole.

INEXPENSIVE

Brasserie Erasmus, Wollestraat 35. ☎ **33-57-81.**
Cuisine: FLEMISH. **Reservations:** Not required.
Prices: Snacks and one-plate dishes BF 250–500 ($7–$14). AE, DC, MC, V.
Open: Wed–Mon 11am–midnight.

This small, popular restaurant is one of the most conveniently located "drop-in" places in Bruges—a great stop after viewing the cathedral and museums. It serves a large variety of Flemish dishes, all prepared with beer. About 100 different brands of beer are available. If you need help making a selection, ask owner Tom for advice.

 Den Gouden Meermin/La Sirene d'Or, Markt 31. ☎ **33-37-76.**
Cuisine: FLEMISH. **Reservations:** Not required.
Prices: Main courses BF 280–400 ($7.80–$11.20); full meal BF 1,075 ($30). AE, DC, MC, V.
Open: Daily 10am–10pm.

This is my personal favorite of the many brasseries, tearooms, and cafés that line Grote Markt. There's outdoor dining or a glassed-in room that also overlooks the square. The Flemish dishes are made with fresh local ingredients, and a bowl of homemade soup is delicious. Sandwiches, snacks, and crêpes (a large variety, and all good) are available, a hearty meal comes cheap, and service is continuous.

READERS RECOMMEND

Breydel–De Coninck, Breidelstraat 24 (☎ **33-97-46**). "*This place was great. We ate a pail full of mussels, then came back for another lunch of mussels provençal (mussels in a light red sauce with mushrooms, peppers, and onions), also first-rate. And the homemade ice cream with caramel sauce, oh, was that good!*"—Joyce Siniscalco, Cheshire, Conn. [**Author's Note:** The average price for a meal is BF 1,300 ($37).]

Graaf van Vlaanderen, 't Zand 19. ☎ **33-31-50.**

Cuisine: STEAK/SALADS. **Reservations:** Not required.
Prices: Light meal about BF 750 ($21); salad plates up to BF 480 ($13). AE, DC, MC, V.
Open: Lunch daily noon–2pm; dinner daily 6–9pm.

The budget-priced restaurant in this small hotel near the railroad station has a rather extensive menu, with minute steak, spaghetti, and salads featured.

★ **'T Dreveken,** Huidenvettersplein 10–11. ☎ **33-95-06.**

Cuisine: FLEMISH/SEAFOOD. **Reservations:** Not required.
Prices: Average meal BF 800 ($23). AE, DC, MC, V.
Open: Lunch Wed–Mon noon–2:30pm; dinner Wed–Mon 6:30–10pm.

This charmer, right on a canal in the town center, is a stone house with flowers blooming at diamond-paned windows. There's a cozy, intimate room downstairs and a pleasant, larger one upstairs. Seafood and regional dishes are the specialties here.

NEARBY PLACES TO DINE

Nearby **Damme** has two excellent restaurants that are worth the short drive (or work in a meal between canal-boat excursions).

★ **Bruegel,** Damse Vaart Zuid 26, Oostkerke–Damme. ☎ **50-03-46.**

Cuisine: SEAFOOD. **Reservations:** Required.
Prices: Fixed-price meal BF 1,100 ($31) at lunch, BF 1,600 ($45) at dinner. AE, DC, MC, V.
Open: Lunch Thurs–Mon noon–2:30pm; dinner Thurs–Mon 6–9:30pm.

A little outside the town of Damme, in a farmhouse on the canal is one of the best fish restaurants in the region. Coquilles St-Jacques is one of my personal favorites, but you really can't go wrong with any choice from the extensive menu.

Drie Zilveren Kannen, Markt 9, Damme. ☎ **35-56-77.**

Cuisine: SEAFOOD/CONTINENTAL. **Reservations:** Recommended.
Prices: Average meal BF 1,850 ($52). AE, MC, V.
Open: Lunch Tues–Sat noon–2:30pm; dinner Tues–Sat 6:30–9:30pm.

Located in a 16th-century building in the town center, this lovely restaurant provides an authentic Flemish decor and extraordinary food to match, with a menu that features fish fresh from the waters off nearby Zeebrugge. It's also known for its roast duck.

2 Ghent (Gent)

48km (30 miles) NW of Brussels, 51 km (31 miles) SW of Antwerp, 46km (28 miles) SE of Bruges, 62km (38 miles) NE of Ypres

GETTING THERE • By Train Ghent is only a 32-minute train ride from Brussels. The main railway station, St. Pieters, is a mile south of the city center, and there is good tram service into town.

• By Bus The bus station adjoins St. Pieters railway station (see above).

• By Car Take E40 from Brussels, E17 from Antwerp, E40 from Bruges.

ESSENTIALS The **telephone area code** is 09.

Information The **Tourist Office** is located in the crypt of the Town Hall, Botermarkt, 9000 Ghent (☎ **09/224-15-55;** fax 09/225-62-88), with hours from 9:30am to 6:30pm daily from April to November, 9:30am to 4:30pm daily in other months.

GETTING AROUND • By Tram   Ghent has an excellent tram system, and most lines travel along Nederkouter and continue to Korenmarkt.

• **On Foot**   Without doubt, this is the best way to see Ghent and experience its medieval atmosphere.

SPECIAL EVENTS   If you're here in September and October, you really should plan extra days in Ghent, since international concerts are presented in about 20 settings of medieval splendor during the famed **Festival of Flanders.** For full details before you come, contact Festival of Flanders Secretariat, B.R.T., Eugeen Flageyplein 18, 1050 Brussels (☎ **02/640-15-25;** fax 02/643-75-37).

The colorful **Begonia Festival** takes place the last weekend in August.

If you were to draw an oval from Brussels to Antwerp to Bruges to Ypres and back to Brussels, Ghent would be almost exactly in the center, and that's rather fitting, because this magnificent old city has always been a sort of pivot point for this part of Flanders. Standing at the confluence of the Rivers Leie and Scheldt, Ghent was the seat of the counts of Flanders, and its importance long before they came to power is underscored by the fact that the great castle those counts built in 1180 was actually raised on foundations of even earlier fortifications, some dating to the 900s. Hands-on rule began very early on here, and the plain people—skilled weavers and craftsmen—never learned to live with it.

During the Middle Ages, Ghent became as great a manufacturing center as Bruges was a trading center, and the artisans rebelled not only against an exploitive nobility but even among themselves, guild against guild. Over the centuries the people of Ghent fought the counts of Flanders, the counts of Burgundy, the king of France, the king of Spain, their rivals in Bruges, and . . . well, whenever *anyone* turned up with plans to implement absolute rule, they took up arms. The fact that they so seldom prevailed for any length of time did not deter them in the least: With each new conquest, they'd settle down for a spell, begin to seethe with indignation, finally reach a boiling point, then take to the warpath all over again. Small wonder, then, that in 1815 it was Maurice de Broglie, a bishop of Ghent, who stirred the pot of religion and lit a fire under the rule of Dutch Protestants, a fire that in 1830 would burst into the flame of national independence for Belgium.

With a long history of economic ups and downs that has kept Ghent on a seesaw of growth and decline, the city today has emerged once more as a major industrial center. Her medieval treasures are preserved, not as dry, showcase relics, but as living parts of her present. And to lighten what could be the overpowering grayness of an industrial city, there are the flowers—flowers everywhere create oases of color as a constant reminder that this is also the center of a prosperous horticultural center. Ghent's flower growers are centered around nearby Lochristi. In short, Ghent is a busy, lively city, whose reminders of the past are as comfortable as a pair of well-broken-in shoes.

Orientation

The **Korenmarkt square** is known as the "Centrum" (if you arrive by rail; take tram no. 1, which will take you directly to the Centrum)—this name is a little misleading when you consider that it's not at all "central" to the town hall, cathedral, etc., as is true in most Belgian towns with a central Grote Markt. However, most of the sights you'll want to see lie within half a mile or less of Korenmarkt. The River Leie twists through the city to meet the Scheldt, with major offshoots at the Lieve and Ketelvest canals, as well as several minor waterways. The Citadel Park, location of the Museum of Fine Arts, is near St. Pieter's Railway Station, which lies about 1³/₄ miles south of Korenmarkt.

What to See and Do

Ghent is a city to be seen on foot. Indeed, it's only by walking its streets, gazing at its gabled guild houses and private mansions, looking up at its massive and forbidding Castle of the Counts, and stopping on one of its bridges to ponder the canal beneath that you can begin to get a sense of the extraordinary vigor of the people who have lived here over the centuries. But before setting off, stop in at the tourist office and arm yourself with literature that will bring the city to life.

TOP ATTRACTIONS

First of all, just so you'll know: the "Three Towers of Ghent" you'll hear referred to often are those of St. Bavo's Cathedral, the Belfry, and St. Nicholas Church, which form a virtually straight line in the direction of St. Michael's Bridge.

★ **St. Bavo's Cathedral**, Sint-Baafsplein.

If you see nothing else in Ghent, you should visit this massive cathedral on Sint-Baafsplein in the city center. Don't be put off by its rather unimpressive exterior, an uncertain mixture of Romanesque, Gothic, and baroque architecture. Although it was built in the 14th and 15th centuries, its crypt contains traces of the 12th-century Church of St. John. The interior filled with priceless paintings, sculptures, screens, memorials, and carved tombs, will literally make you catch your breath in awe. About midway along the vaulted nave is one of the most striking pulpits you're ever likely to see. Of white marble entwined with oak, its base is covered with remarkable carvings.

The showpiece of St. Bavo's, however, is the 24-panel *The Adoration of the Mystic Lamb,* in the Vijd Chapel. A stunning work rich in color and detail, it was a commission to the artist Hubert van Eyck in 1420 from a wealthy alderman for this very chapel, where it has remained since its completion in 1432—possibly by the artist's brother, Jan Van Eyck, after his brother's death in 1426.

There are other art treasures in the cathedral, one of which is *The Conversion of St. Bavo* by Rubens, painted in 1624. It's in the Rubens Chapel, one of the many that form a semicircular ambulatory behind the high altar, and to walk through them is much like visiting an exquisite art gallery.

The Romanesque Crypt holds a wealth of religious antiquities, vestments, sculptures, and paintings. Look for the faint traces of frescoes still to be seen on some of the arches (if, that is, they have not been cleaned away—several have disappeared in the wake of restorative "progress").

Admission: Cathedral, free; Vijd Chapel and Romanesque Crypt, BF 80 ($2.30).

Open: Mon–Sat 9:30am–noon and 2–8pm, Sun 1–6pm.

The Belfry and Cloth Hall, Sint-Baafsplein.

Just across the square from the cathedral is the 14th-century Belfry and the Cloth Hall over which it towers. From the **Belfry,** bells sounded the call to arms down through the centuries (a rather frequent occurrence in this rebellious city). The most beloved of the bells was a 1315 giant known as "Roeland," destroyed by Charles V in 1540. Some 37 of the 51 small bells that now make up the huge carillon are from the remains of "Roeland"; and the massive "Triomphante"—which was cast in 1660 to replace the favorite—now rests in a small park at the foot of the Belfry, still bearing

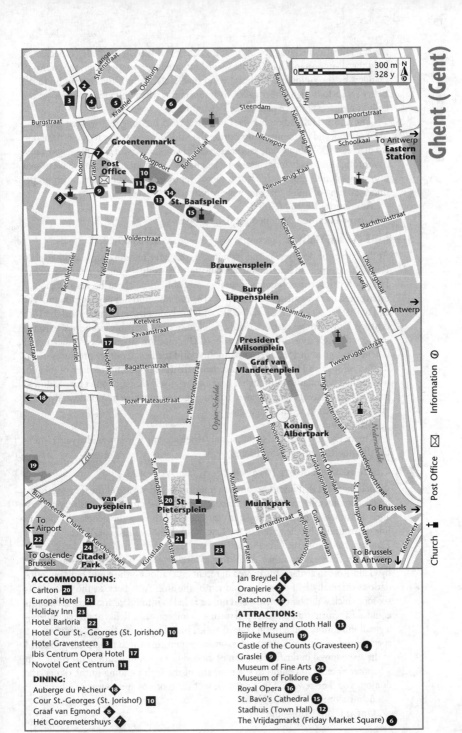

Ghent (Gent)

300 m
328 y
N

Information ⊙
Post Office ⊠
Church ✝■

ACCOMMODATIONS:
Carlton **20**
Europa Hotel **21**
Holiday Inn **23**
Hotel Barloria **22**
Hotel Cour St.- Georges (St. Jorishof) **10**
Hotel Gravensteen **3**
Ibis Centrum Opera Hotel **17**
Novotel Gent Centrum **11**

DINING:
Auberge du Pêcheur **18**
Cour St.-Georges (St. Jorishof) **10**
Graaf van Egmond **8**
Het Cooremetershuys **7**

Jan Breydel **1**
Oranjerie **2**
Patachon **14**

ATTRACTIONS:
The Belfry and Cloth Hall **13**
Bijloke Museum **19**
Castle of the Counts (Gravesteen) **4**
Graslei **9**
Museum of Fine Arts **24**
Museum of Folklore **5**
Royal Opera **16**
St. Bavo's Cathedral **15**
Stadhuis (Town Hall) **12**
The Vrijdagmarkt (Friday Market Square) **6**

the crack it sustained in 1914. A great iron chest was kept in the Belfry's "Secret" to hold the all-important charters that spelled out privileges wrested from the counts of Flanders by the guilds and the burghers of medieval Ghent. If the elevator up to the Belfry's 215-foot-high upper gallery is in operation when you visit, you can see the bells as well as a fantastic panoramic view of the city.

The Cloth Hall, adjoining the Belfry, is a 1425 building that was the gathering place of wool and cloth merchants during the Middle Ages. Today its main attraction is a marvelous 35-minute slide production called *Ghent in Multivision,* presented Tuesday through Sunday in four alternating languages, which means you may have to wait until English rolls around. It's worth the wait, however, for you gain a much deeper understanding of much that you will encounter.

Admission: BF 100 ($2.85).
Open: Tues–Sun 9am–noon and 1:30–5pm.

Stadhuis (Town Hall), at Botermarkt and Hoogpoort. ☎ 23-99-22.

At the corner of Botermarkt and Hoogpoort, this large building turns a rather plain Renaissance profile to Botermarkt, and an almost garishly ornamented Gothic face to Hoogpoort. Its schizophrenic appearance probably came about because Charles V interrupted its construction, started in 1518, and work did not begin again until the end of that century and the early 1600s, with final completion delayed until the 18th century. During those years, changing public tastes and available monies are reflected in the building's style. In its Pacificatiezaal (Pacification Room) the Pacification of Ghent was signed in 1567, declaring to the world the Low Country provinces' repudiation of Spanish Hapsburg rule and their intention to permit freedom of religion within their boundaries. Although it held for a relatively short period, it foreshadowed future declarations of independence. You must be accompanied by a guide, and guided visits are offered in several languages.

Admission: Free.
Open: Easter–Oct, open to public only when accompanied by guided tours Mon–Fri afternoons. **Closed:** Nov–Easter.

 ### Castle of the Counts (Gravensteen), Sint-Veereplein.

Grim is the word that instantly comes to mind at one's first view of the fortress stronghold maintained by the counts of Flanders, and it is safe to say that its very appearance did much to instill the awe and fear necessary to keep the people of Ghent in line. Surrounded by the waters of the Leie, it was built by Philip of Alsace, Count of Flanders, fresh from the Crusades in 1180 with images of a similar crusaders castle in Syria fixed firmly in his mind. According to local legend—supported to some degree by Gallo-Roman artifacts uncovered in recent excavations—the count built on foundations originally laid down by Baldwin of the Iron Arm back in the 800s. If its six-foot-thick walls, battlements, and turrets failed to intimidate attackers, the counts could always turn to a well-equipped torture chamber inside. Relics of that chamber— a small guillotine, spiked iron collars, racks, branding irons, thumb screws, and a special kind of pitchfork designed to make certain that those people being burned at the stake stayed in the flames—can be viewed in a small museum in the castle. On a happier note, if you climb to the ramparts of the high building in the center, the donjon, you'll be rewarded by a great view of the rooftops and towers of Ghent.

Admission: BF 80 ($2.30).
Open: Daily 10am–5pm.

MUSEUMS

Bijloke Museum, Godshuizenlaan 2. ☎ **25-11-06**.

Incorporated in an ancient abbey that dates from the 14th century is an outstanding collection of weapons, uniforms, clothing, and household items from the everyday life of years past. Authentic works of art of Ghent and Flanders are exhibited inside the "House of the Abbess." It's located south of city center.

Admission: BF 100 ($2.85), free for children 12 and under.

Open: Tues–Sun 9am–12:30pm and 1:30–5:30pm.

★ **Museum of Fine Arts**, Nicolaas de Liemaeckereplein 3. ☎ **22-17-03** or **21-54-63**.

Located in the Citadel Park, not far from the railway station, this fine museum houses both ancient and modern art masterpieces, highlights of which are works by Peter Paul Rubens, Anthony Van Dyck, Jeroen Bosch, and Théodore Géricault, along with such moderns as James Ensor, Theo Van Ryssselberghe, George Minne, and Constant Permeke.

Admission: BF 80 ($2.30), free for children 12 and under.

Open: Tues–Sun 9am–12:30pm and 1:30–5:30pm.

★ **Museum of Folklore**, Kraanlei 65. ☎ **23-13-36**.

This fascinating museum in the city center is set in almshouses dating from the 1300s and later, and instead of glass-case exhibits there are authentic replicas of actual rooms in which crafts and skills were practiced. There's also a marionette theater which presents performances on specified days of the week (check with the tourist office for current schedules).

Admission: BF 50 ($1.40).

Open: Nov–Mar, Tues–Sun 10am–noon and 1:30–5pm; Apr–Oct, daily 9am–12:30pm and 1:30–5:30pm.

SIGHTS

★ **GRASLEI**   Not one historic building, but a solid row of towering, gabled guild houses was built along this quay between the 1200s and 1600s, when the waterway formed the harbor of Ghent. To fully appreciate their majesty, walk across the bridge over the Leie to the Korenlei on the opposite bank and view them as a whole, then return to saunter past each, conjuring up in your imagination the craftsmen, tradespeople, and merchants for whom these buildings were the very core of their commercial (and civil liberties) existence. To identify them briefly: no. 1 was the House of the Free Boatmen, dating from the 1500s; no. 2, the Annex House of the Grain Measurers, from the 1600s; no. 3, the House of the Receiver of the Staple (Customs), from the 1600s; no. 4, the Staple Warehouse, from the 1200s; no. 5, the Main House of the Grain Measurers, from the 1500s; no. 6, the House of the Free Masons, from the 1500s; and no. 7, the House of the Un-Free Boatmen. Within the walls of each, enough drama was acted out to fill a library of books based on Ghent's independence of spirit. This is not a street to pass by quickly!

★ **THE VRIJDAGMARKT (FRIDAY MARKET SQUARE)**   During the city's long history, when trouble erupted in Ghent as it so often did, this huge square was nearly always the rallying point. The statue of Jacob Van Arteveld that stands in the square is a tribute to a leader of revolt in the 1300s, and its base is adorned by the shields of some 52 guilds. The square also houses the building in which Belgium's Socialist Party was born under the direction of Ghent's native son, Edward Anseele. Today this is a major shopping area and the scene of lively street markets every Friday morning and Saturday afternoon. A short distance away, the smaller Kanonplein square is guarded by a gigantic cannon known as Mad Meg (Dulle Griet), which thundered away in the 1400s in the service of Burgundian armies.

SIGHTSEEING TOURS

The tourist office can arrange qualified guides for private **walking tours** at a charge of BF 1,200 ($34) for the first two hours, BF 500 ($14) for each additional hour. Ask them also about organized group walking tours sometimes conducted during summer months at a fee of BF 250 ($7) for adults, children free (admission to *Mystic Lamb* included).

Also, ★ **horse-drawn carriages** sometimes depart from Sint-Baafsplein and Korenlei for half-hour rides at a cost of BF 700 ($20)—details at the tourist office.

A tour that should be a part of every visitor's itinerary is a ★ **boat ride** along the canals. Covered boats leave every 30 minutes from 10am to 6pm from the Graslei during the summer, with an interesting narrative given in several languages. The trip lasts about 35 minutes, with fares of BF 130 ($3.70) for adults, BF 110 ($3.15) for children. Open boats leave from the Korenlei (Grasbrug) every 10 minutes, with the same fares but no narrative.

On specified days during the summer (ask at the tourist office) you can also take a **boat trip from Ghent to Bruges** and back, at an adult fare of BF 450 ($13), BF 350 ($10) for children.

Where to Stay

The tourist office provides an up-to-date "Hotels and Restaurants" booklet at no cost and will also make hotel reservations at no charge.

Because of its proximity to both Brussels and Bruges, Ghent is often regarded by tourists as a day-trip destination, but several very good hotels, both in the city center and on its perimeter, make it a convenient sightseeing base.

TWO REAL GEMS

★ **Hotel Cour St-Georges (St. Jorishof)**, Botermarkt 2, 9000 Ghent.
☎ **09/224-24-24.** Fax 09/224-26-40. 28 rms. MINIBAR TV TEL

$ **Rates:** BF 2,600–2,900 ($74–$82) single. BF 3,300–3,900 ($94–$111) double. AE, DC, MC, V.

In the city center opposite the town hall, the Cour Saint-Georges is a historical treasure dating back to 1228 that has been an inn of quality from the very beginning. It has counted among its patrons Mary of Burgundy, Charles V, and Napoléon Bonaparte. You'll dine in the large Gothic Hall with its mammoth fireplace at one end, and even the "modern" annex that houses most guest rooms has foundations that date back to the 9th century. The decor is traditional in the pleasant and comfortable rooms, and the rates are amazingly low for such a prime location (one of the most convenient in town for sightseeing) and all that atmosphere. Needless to say, you should reserve as far in advance as possible.

Dining/Entertainment: The Gothic Hall is about as atmospheric as you can get, and the food is terrific.

⭐ 💲 **Hotel Gravensteen,** Jan Breydelstraat 35, 9000 Ghent. ☎ **09/225-11-50.**
Fax 09/225-18-50. 17 rms, 2 suites. MINIBAR TV TEL

Rates: BF 3,700 ($105) single; BF 4,500 ($128) double; BF 5,900 ($168) suite. Weekend discounts available. AE, DC, MC, V.

On Jan Breydelstraat, a short walk from Graslei, opposite Castle Gravensteen, this lovely mansion was built in 1865 as the home of a Ghent textile baron. You enter through the old carriageway (made up of ornamented pillars and an impressive wall niche occupied by a marble statue), which sets the tone for what you'll find inside. The elegant, high-ceilinged parlor is a sophisticated blend of pastels, gracious modern furnishings, and antiques, with a small bar tucked into one corner. The attractive rooms are comfortably furnished. Those in front look out on the moated Castle of the Counts, while those to the back have city views. There's a top-floor "Belvedere" with windows offering magnificent views of the city. Afternoon tea is also available. There's no dining room, but good restaurants are within easy walking distance.

EXPENSIVE

Holiday Inn, Ottergemsesteenweg 600, 9000 Ghent. ☎ **09/222-58-85.**
Fax 09/220-12-22. 167 rms. A/C MINIBAR TV TEL **Transportation:** Free bus to and from the city center.

Rates: BF 5,700 ($162) single; BF 6,300 ($180) double. AE, DC, MC, V.

Drivers who don't want to drive into the city center will find this hostelry conveniently situated; it's at the intersection of E17 and E40, only 3 miles from the city center and about half an hour from Brussels, Antwerp, and the Belgian coast. The guest rooms are modern and typical of this chain (two double beds).

Dining/Entertainment: The Floralia room is for lunches, dinners, and parties up to 220 people. The restaurant is open daily all year for all three meals, and there's a nicely appointed bar.

Services: Free bus to and from the city center.

Facilities: Swimming pool, tennis court, children's garden, sauna.

⭐ **Novotel Gent Centrum,** Goudenieuwplein 5, 9000 Ghent. ☎ **09/224-22-30.**
Fax 09/224-32-95. 117 rms. A/C MINIBAR TV TEL

Rates: BF 4,100 ($117) single; BF 4,700 ($134) double. AE, DC, MC, V.

The location of this modern hotel couldn't be more convenient for sightseeing—it's very near the Town Hall in the city center, within easy walking distance of all major sights. To this chain's credit, the modern edifice has been designed to fit into its ancient surroundings. The guest rooms are nicely furnished and have individual heating controls. The facilities are all you'd expect from a top hotel, with light, airy public rooms and a garden terrace.

Dining/Entertainment: The restaurant is open daily from 6am to midnight, and the attractive bar has become a meeting place for local businesspeople.

Facilities: Outdoor heating swimming pool.

MODERATE

Carlton, Koningin Astridlaan 138, 9000 Ghent. ☎ **09/222-88-36.** Fax 09/220-49-92.
22 rms. MINIBAR TV TEL

Rates: BF 2,600 ($74) single; BF 3,150 ($92) double. Weekend and midweek packages available. AE, DC, MC, V.

Close to the E17/E40 interchange near the railway station, this modern-style hotel features rooms with pretty standard decor and furnishings. There's no restaurant or bar, but several are in the neighborhood. There's convenient parking in a garage next door.

Europahotel, Gordunakaai 59, 9000 Ghent. ☎ **09/220-60-71.** Fax 09/220-06-09. 37 rms. TV TEL

Rates: BF 2,800 ($80) single; BF 3,200 ($94) double. AE, MC, V.

This is a modern hotel set in the greenery of the Blaarmeersen suburb on Ghent's outskirts. The rooms are large, with bright, attractive furnishings. There's an attractive bar, a good restaurant, and easy parking.

Hotel Barloria, Baarleveldestraat 2, 9034 Ghent. ☎ **09/226-74-32.** Fax 09/226-66-65. 10 rms. TV TEL

Rates: BF 1,850–2,150 ($53–$61) single; BF 2,400–2,700 ($68–$77) double. AE, DC, MC, V.

At Exit 13 ("Ghent West") of the E40 Brussels–Ostend highway, and only a few minutes away from the Flanders Expo Halls, this modern, well-run hotel has a good restaurant and a bar, and the guest rooms are attractive with comfortable furnishings.

Ibis Centrum Opera Hotel, Nederkouter 26, 9000 Ghent. ☎ **09/225-07-07.** Fax 09/223-59-07. 134 rms. TV TEL

Rates (including breakfast): BF 2,850 ($81) single; BF 3,100 ($88) double. No charge for crib. AE, DC, MC, V.

The rooms in this modern hotel are bright and comfortably furnished. There's a nice bar, and although there's no restaurant on the premises, several good eateries are nearby. Here are good accommodations at moderate rates, between the city center and the railway station.

INEXPENSIVE

The most inexpensive accommodations in Ghent are those upstairs rooms (perfectly respectable and comfortable, but without bath or "extras") above the cafés and restaurants along Korenmarkt, near St. Nicholas Church. The tourist office can supply a list of those with satisfactory standards, as well as hostels in the area. Also, inquire at the tourist office about availability of rooms in the University of Ghent residence halls from mid-July to mid-September at very low rates.

Where to Dine

One of the nicest things about Ghent's restaurants is that almost all serve generous portions of traditional Flemish dishes—dishes like the thick, creamy waterzooï (a soup that borders on being a stew, it's so thick); and lapin à la flamande (rabbit with beer, vinegar, and currant juice); or if it's the right season, the delicate asparagus that comes from the Mechelen area. What's more, even the most expensive restaurant sports prices well below those in the gourmet establishments in Brussels. The helpful "Hotels and Restaurants" booklet published by the tourist board (free) lists eateries by cuisine as well as by price.

EXPENSIVE

 Auberge du Pêcheur, Ponstraat 44, Latem/Deurle. ☎ **282-31-44.**

Cuisine: SEAFOOD/FRENCH. **Reservations:** Required. **Directions:** From the city, take A14 (the highway to Deinze) for about 25 minutes and follow the signs for Deurle.
Prices: Fixed-price meal BF 990–1,290 ($28–$36) for a business lunch, BF 2,100–2,950 ($60–$84) for dinner; light meal in the Tavern Grill BF 390–725 ($11–$20). AE, MC, V.
Open: Daily 10am–10pm.

No listing of Ghent restaurants would be complete without mention of this excellent restaurant in a country inn about a 25-minute ride outside the city. The six-course fixed-price dinner features seafood, lamb, and the freshest local specialties available each day. The daily "business lunch" is a good buy and a fine way to combine good eating with a sightseeing foray into the countryside. If you'd like to linger overnight, there are 17 very comfortable rooms, with TVs, minibars, and radios.

Patachon, Korenlei 24. ☎ **225-89-02.**

Cuisine: FLEMISH/BELGIAN. **Reservations:** Recommended.
Prices: À la carte meals BF 1,000–3,000 ($28–$85). AE, DC, MC.
Open: Lunch Thurs–Tues noon–3pm; dinner Thurs–Tues 6:30–10:30pm.

Housed in Belgium's allegedly oldest crypt, dating back to the 12th century, this restaurant radiates an authentic Flemish atmosphere and serves some superbly prepared food to match. The favorite dish is roast goose—every second table orders it. Other dishes range from T-bone steak to grilled pike. The wine list is extensive too.

MODERATE

Cour St-Georges (St. Jorishof), Botermarkt 2. ☎ **224-24-24.**

Cuisine: FLEMISH. **Reservations:** Required.
Prices: Main courses BF 900 ($25); special menu BF 2,000 ($57). AE, MC, V.
Open: Lunch Tues–Sun noon–2:30pm; dinner Tues–Sun 7–10pm. **Closed:** Public holidays; second half of July and first week of August.

The Gothic Hall in this ancient inn is a marvel of dark woodwork, massive fireplace, and stained glass, surrounded by an upstairs balcony. One of the Flemish dishes in which it specializes is eel with green sauce, and the chicken waterzooï enjoys a good local reputation. It's located in the city center, opposite the town hall.

 Graaf van Egmond, St. Michielsplein 21. ☎ **225-07-27.**

Cuisine: FRENCH/FLEMISH. **Reservations:** Required.
Prices: Fixed-price meals BF 520–1,800 ($15–$51) for French menu, BF 450–950 ($13–$27) for Flemish menu in the upstairs grill room. AE, DC, MC, V.
Open: Lunch daily noon–2:30pm, dinner daily 6–11pm.

In a marvelous old Ghent town house of the 1200s on the River Leie in the city center, the Graaf van Egmond serves Flemish specialties like carbonnade flamande (beef stew) and asparagus à la flamande, along with French creations. If you can get a window seat, there's a spectacular view of the towers of Ghent.

Het Cooremetershuys, Graslei 12. ☎ **223-49-71.**

Cuisine: FLEMISH/FRENCH NOUVELLE. **Reservations:** Required.
Prices: Lunch BF 980 ($28); dinner BF 1,490 ($42). AE, DC, MC, V.
Open: Lunch Tues–Sat noon–2pm; dinner Tues–Sat 7–9pm. **Closed:** July 15–Oct 15.

To reach this special little restaurant, mount the stairs in one of the gorgeous 14th-century gabled houses lining the canal. Your entrance into a rather plain room whose walls are hung with musical instruments is greeted by the strains of taped classical music. Don't miss the wonderful waterzooï.

★ **Jan Breydel,** Jan Breydelstraat 10. ☎ **225-62-87.**
$ **Cuisine:** SEAFOOD/FLEMISH. **Reservations:** Recommended.
Prices: Average lunch BF 1,250 ($35); average dinner BF 1,850 ($52). MC, V.
Open: Lunch Mon–Fri noon–2pm; dinner Mon–Sat 7–10pm.

Top honors go to this exquisite restaurant on a quaint street near the Castle of the Counts. Its interior is a gardenlike delight of greenery, white napery, and light woods. Proprietors Louis and Pat Hellebaut see to it that dishes issuing from their kitchen are as light and airy as their setting, with delicate sauces and seasonings making the most of incredibly fresh ingredients. Seafoods or regional specialties are all superb. Highly recommended.

★ **Oranjerie,** Corduwaniersstraat 8, Patershof. ☎ **224-10-08.**
$ **Cuisine:** FLEMISH/FRENCH. **Reservations:** Recommended.
Prices: Fixed-price menu BF 1,400 ($40). MC, V.
Open: Lunch Mon–Sat noon–2:30pm; dinner Mon–Sat 7–11pm.

Petershol (which means "cave" or "hole" in which monks lived a hermit's existence) is an ancient enclave not far from the Castle of the Counts that is fast becoming a gastronomic center as more and more small restaurants move into renovated old buildings. Oranjerie is one of the most delightful of these and—as you might guess from its name—has the bright, cheerful aspect of a garden. The dining rooms are light and airy, there's a skylight, a fountain, a lovely small garden, and lots of lush greenery. The dishes here are beautifully prepared and presented.

INEXPENSIVE

For the least expensive eating, all more or less the same and costing about BF 350 ($10), stop at any of the small restaurants around Saint Bavo's Square. Most have sidewalk tables, which is pleasant in good weather, and all offer very adequate renderings of Flemish dishes.

Evening Entertainment

THE PERFORMING ARTS

From October through mid-June, international opera is performed in the 19th-century **Royal Opera,** Schouwburgstraat 3 (☎ **223-06-81** or **225-24-25**). Ghent venues for those marvelous Belgian ✪ **puppet shows** are: the **Museum of Folklore,** Kraanlei 65 (☎ **223-13-36**); the **Taptoe Teater,** Forelstraat 91C (☎ **223-67-58**); and **Magie,** Haspelstraat 39 (☎ **226-42-18**). Check with the tourist board to find performance schedules during your visit.

BARS & TAVERNS

In typical Flemish fashion, the favorite after-dark entertainment in Ghent is frequenting its atmospheric bars and taverns. You'll have a memorable evening in any one you choose, but **Oud Middelhuis,** Graslei 6, provides a 17th-century setting plus more than 300 varieties of beer—well worth searching out. Near the Castle of the Counts, the **Het Waterhuis,** Groentenmarkt 9, also has a wide selection of Belgian beers (including the locally made *Stopken*).

3 Ypres (Ieper)

110km (68 miles) W of Brussels, 93km (57 miles) SW of Antwerp, 62km (38 miles) SW of Ghent, 60km (37 miles) SW of Bruges

GETTING THERE • By Train and Bus   There is rail and bus service from Brussels, Ghent, Bruges, and the Belgian coast.

• By Car   From Bruges, take E40 and turn south on a signposted, unclassified road at Exit 4. From Ghent, take E40 to Bruges and proceed as above. The drive from Bruges or Ghent is well worthwhile for its scenic beauty, and either is easily accomplished in half a day or less.

ESSENTIALS   The **telephone area code** is 057.

Information   The Ypres **Tourist Office** is in the Town Hall, Grote Markt 34 (☎ **057/20-07-24;** fax 057/21-85-89), with hours of 9am to 5:30pm weekdays, till 5pm on Saturday, Sunday, and holidays; shorter hours October through March.

SPECIAL EVENTS   On the second Sunday in May during even-numbered years (1996, 1998, for example), Ypres celebrates one of Europe's most colorful pageants, the ✪ **Festival of the Cats.** That's when hundreds of velvet cats are thrown by the town jester from the Belfry to crowds below. The custom originated centuries ago when the great Cloth Hall, where cloth was stored until sold, attracted thousands of mice, and cats by the hundreds were imported to eliminate them. Once the cloth was sold, however, the cats themselves became a problem, and the eventual solution was to fling them from the Belfry to get rid of them. How the tradition evolved into today's lively carnival I have no idea, but that seems to matter little when you're caught up in the general revelry that begins with the spectacular Procession of the Cats!

Ypres, set in the flat polder plains of Flanders, owed its early prosperity to a flourishing textile industry, which reached its pinnacle in the 13th century. Sadly, over the centuries, however, the town—victimized by one war after another—has become a mere ghost of its former self.

By far the most devastating of all her wars was World War I, when hardly a brick was left standing after fierce fighting between German and British forces. Many visitors, in fact, come to pay homage to those who fell on the surrounding battlefields and who lie buried in the extensive military cemeteries here. Ypres pays its respects at 8pm every day of the year, when traffic beneath the Menen Gate is halted and members of the local fire brigade sound the Last Post on silver bugles that were gifts of the British Legion. But perhaps the most poignant tribute of all came from poet John McCrae, whose lament began, "In Flanders fields the poppies blow / Between the crosses, row on row. . . ."

Homage could well be paid also to the determined citizens of Ypres who have rebuilt, brick by brick, the most important of its medieval buildings exactly as they were, carefully following original plans still in existence. It's impossible to walk or ride through Ypres without a mental tip of the hat to those who managed this incredible feat.

What to See and Do

In your walks around Ypres, you'll want to look for one or two special sights. One of the few fortifications not demolished during World War I are the **ramparts** that once surrounded the town. You can reach them via stairs at the Menen Gate, and if you walk around to the **Rijselpoort (Lille Gate),** there's one of the most beautiful of the **British war cemeteries** with a grass coverlet that many local people will tell you is greener than any other in Europe. Notice, too, the many streets lined with reconstructed 17th-century facades.

Ypres's medieval glory is reflected in its beautiful Gothic ✪ **Cloth Hall,** the original of which stood from 1260 to 1304. From its center rises a 210-foot-square **Belfry tower,** and also in the hall is the moving **Ypres Salient Museum,** filled with mementos of the horrendous 1914–18 fighting.

On panels set in the **Menen Gate (Menenpoort),** a 130-foot memorial arch, you'll find the names of some 54,896 British soldiers who fell in World War I fighting around Ypres and who have no known grave—a memorial famed throughout Britain and the Continent as the "Missing Memorial."

The graceful spire of **St. Martin's Cathedral** is a landmark in the town, and St. Martin's holds the tomb of a bishop of Ypres named Jansen, whose heretical theories played such havoc in the 17th century.

The **Merghelynck Museum,** Merghelynckstraat 2 (☎ **20-20-42** or **20-06-05**), is a wonderfully lavish manor house furnished with Louis XV and XVI antiques. It's closed on Sunday and holidays and the last two weeks in July; open other days from 10am to noon and 2 to 5pm, with an admission fee of BF 30 (85¢).

The **Bellegodshuis Museum,** Rijselsestraat 38, counts among its treasures the *Virgin and Child,* a 1420 painting of Ypres's own artist, Melchior Broederlam. Open April to October, Tuesday through Sunday from 10am to 1pm and 3 to 6pm, November to March, Monday through Friday from 10am to noon and 3 to 5pm. Admission is BF 50 ($1.40).

Where to Stay

Most visitors prefer to explore Ypres on day trips from a Bruges base, since accommodations are scarce in the town itself. For those who wish to stop overnight, there's the **Hotel-Restaurant Regina,** Grote Markt 45 (☎ **057/21-88-88;** fax 057/21-90-20) a small (17 rooms with private facilities) hotel in the town center with rates in the BF-2,700 to -3,300 ($77 to $94) range. They accept American Express, MasterCard, and Visa.

Where to Dine

There are a number of quite adequate, moderately priced restaurants for lunch or dinner, including the one in the **Regina** (see above). For dining a cut above adequate, look to either of these: **Yperley,** St. Jacobsstraat 1 (☎ **29-98-00**), an elegant restaurant opposite the Lakenhalle, specializing in seafood and French cuisine for BF 1,700 to 2,060 ($48 to $58) at dinner, less at lunch. It's closed for lunch on Saturday and dinner on Sunday; they accept MasterCard and Visa. **Dikkebus Vijver,** Vijverdreef 31 (☎ **20-00-85**), is about 3 miles southwest of town on Lake Dikkebus; this is a pleasant eatery featuring local dishes and seafood specialties at about BF 900 to 1,600 ($25 to $45); they accept MasterCard and Visa.

Belgium's Beaches

7

BELGIUM'S BEACHES ARE WITHOUT DOUBT SOME OF THE BEST IN NORTHERN EUROPE. Strung along a 43-mile North Sea coastline, the beaches are one continuous vista of fine white sand backed by countless dunes and dotted with lovely seaside resorts. There are, in fact, 13 resort towns, each as individual as shells that wash in from the sea. While the unattractive density of accommodations and other commercial developments detracts somewhat from this region's natural beauty, once over the dunes and onto the beaches, Mother Nature comes into her own.

For the visitor, the Belgian coastline presents a happy dilemma—whether to opt for an *au naturel* holiday of sea, sand, and sun, or one of high-flying casino and night-club action, or a "bust out" of sheer gustatory gluttony, or seaside sightseeing expeditions. They're all here awaiting your choice, and with judicious planning, it's quite possible to get around to them all in an incredibly short amount of time.

The dedicated beach bum will find wonderfully wide beaches that stretch back as much as 500 yards at low tide, and a gently sloping decline into the sea that makes for some of the safest swimming in Europe (although authorities constantly warn against swimming along isolated stretches of beach, a warning I hasten to echo). You can skim along the sand on wind-blown sail carts, pedal beach buggies, or join the sun worshippers stretched full length in search of the perfect tan.

When the sun goes down, there are nightclubs that attract top performers during the summer months and four casinos (at Knokke-Heist, Ostend, Blankenberge, and Middelkerke) to tempt the gambler in your soul year-round. Without a lot of time to spare, the gourmand will surely leave frustrated at not being able to gorge at every single one of the excellent restaurants in this small area. Sightseers will be kept busy discovering a unique fishing museum, one dedicated solely to surrealistic paintings, another that houses an important post–impressionist-era art collection, as well as tramping through nature reserves tinged with the hue of sea lavender and alive with the whir of bird wings in a protected environment.

How to plan the holiday that will exactly suit you? First you must take a close look at the personality of the individual resorts and choose the one with the most personal appeal. The four major points of reference are discussed in this chapter, with comments on the smaller communities that can help you decide which location is best for you.

Hotels, holiday flats, and even boardinghouses are plentiful; and the rates are usually less than what you'd expect to pay in such popular vacation spots. Which is not to say, however, that you should just drop in—Europeans come here in droves, and the English think nothing of hopping across the Channel for annual outings. The smart thing to do is book directly or through one of the local tourist offices before you arrive, and it's absolutely essential to book ahead if you're coming on a weekend, since that's when Belgians from inner cities flock to the sea for brief work breaks.

SEEING BELGIUM'S BEACHES

It's an easy matter to dabble in a variety of sightseeing options, and you won't even need a car! There's a marvelous **Kusttram** (Coast Tram) that runs the entire length of the coast, with 15-minute departures during summer months. Charges vary from point to point, but if you decide to go the distance—from Knokke-Heist to De Panne (a two-hour ride)—you'll pay only BF 200 ($5.70), and there are special one- and three-day unlimited travel tickets costing BF 305 ($7) and BF 520 ($15), respectively.

What's Special About Belgium's Beaches

Beaches and Spas
- Some of the best beaches in northern Europe, fine white sand stretching for miles—perfect for a holiday of sea, sand, and sun.
- Thalassa Zeecentrum, in Knokke-Heist, a spa, fitness center, and gymnasium where the hot sea-mud baths may be the cure for what ails you.

Museums
- Fine Arts Museum, in Ostend, displaying the paintings of native sons Ensor, De Clerck, Permeke, and Spilliaert.
- Folklore Museum, in Ostend, depicting native dress and life, with a re-created fisherman's pub and home.
- North Sea Aquarium, Ostend, with displays of fish, molluscs, and crustaceans.
- National Fishery Museum, in Oostduinkerke, with a wonderful collection of fishing-boat models from A.D. 800 to the present.
- Paul Delvauxmuseum, in St. Idesbald, with exhibits of the works of the famous surrealist.

Nature Reserve
- Het Zwin Nature Reserve and Aviary, near Het Zoute, with sea lavender and amazingly rich vegetation, plus hundreds of nesting birds.

Evening Entertainment
- Nightclubs all along the coast, with top performers during the summer months.
- Four year-round casinos, including those in Knokke-Heist and Ostend.

---

1   Knokke-Heist/Het Zoute

24km (14 miles) NE of Bruges, 35km (21 miles) NE of Ostend, 60 km (37 miles) NE of De Panne

GETTING THERE • By Train or Bus   There is frequent train and bus service from Bruges. The train and bus station are located at the south end of Lippenslaan, the main street.

• By Tram   There is frequent tram service from Ostend and other seafront resorts, and the tram station is combined with the train/bus station (see above).

• By Car   From Bruges, take Highway 31 due north; Highway 34 runs the entire length of the coast; from Brussels, take E40.

ESSENTIALS   The **telephone area code** is 050.

Information   The **Tourist Office** is at Zeedijk Knokke 660, Lichttorenplein (☎ **050/60-16-16;** fax 050/62-08-13).

Snuggled up close to the Dutch border, this is the classiest of the Belgian beach areas. Sometimes called "the garden of the North Sea coast," this area actually consists of five beaches: **Heist, Duinbergen, Albertstrand, Knokke,** and **Het Zoute.** Heist attracts average-income (*classy* average-income) families; Duinbergen is chiefly residential and caters to families; Albertstrand is more sporty. And then things begin to reach the upper levels of "class":

Knokke is fashionable—not as exclusive as it once was, but still fashionable. Het Zoute is ultra-fashionable. You can tell by the very look of it; on its main shopping street, Kustlaan, sporting shops are adorned with internationally famous designer names (some designer collections have actually been shown here before Paris!), jewelers, and art galleries. The winding residential streets of Het Zoute fairly shriek "money," and it's big money—the lovely villas proclaim owners of both wealth and exquisite taste. Whether or not you fit easily into this monied environment, a drive, cycle, or walk through Het Zoute provides an interesting glimpse of the wealthy, gracious lifestyle of its inhabitants.

What to See and Do

Top on the list of attractions, it goes without saying, are the five fine beaches, where all manner of seaside sports are available. From time to time there are half-hour sea trips in an amphibious vessel launched right from the beach, sand-castle competitions flourish, and kite flying is a favorite pastime.

In town, take a 30-minute ride through the streets in the ★ **miniature train** that departs from Van Bunnenplein at the promenade. Bikers and/or drivers will enjoy the 30-mile "Riante Polderroute" that begins in Knokke and guides you through wooded parks, gardens, past the Zwin reserve, into polder farm country, past canals and ditches, and on to Damme and Oosterkerke.

It was along this stretch of coast that the River Zwin estuary met the sea and gave Bruges its greatness as a leading European port. Since fickle fate silted up the river and Bruges has settled into a land-locked prominence of quite another sort, the old riverbed (just east of Het Zoute) has turned into a salty, sandy marshland: the ★ **Het Zwin Nature Reserve and Aviary** (☎ 60-70-86). The spongy soil nurtures an amazingly rich vegetation, and it's a lovely sight in summer to see it covered with sea lavender. Hundreds of nesting birds—geese, plovers, white storks among them—find a refuge here both in the aviary near the entrance and flying free as you tramp through a landscape that has been returned to nature. There's also a nice restaurant, Chalet du Zwin, near the entrance and a well-stocked bookshop. Entrance to the refuge is BF 140 ($4) for adults and BF 80 ($2.25) for children up to 12. There's a two-hour guided tour every Sunday and Thursday morning (Sunday only during winter months) starting at 10am.

Located across from the Albertstrand beach at Zeedijk 509, the **Casino of Knokke,** dating from the 1920s, is the epitome of elegance with plush gaming rooms, nostalgic bits of art deco, and glittering chandeliers illuminating a glittering, dressed-to-the-nines clientele. There are two nightclubs, in addition to a ballroom that features leading European entertainers. Its magnificent Salle Magritte dining room is a tribute to surrealist painter René Magritte, whose paintings have been transformed into gigantic murals that adorn the walls. Despite all the glitter—or more accurately, because of it—there's a cosmopolitan relaxation about the casino that makes it fun, and it's well worth taking along dressy attire to have a night here. You'll also need to bring your passport, and you'll pay an entrance fee of BF 100 ($2.85).

Belgium's Beaches

De Panne 5
Het Zoute 2
Knokke-Heist 1
Oostduinkerke 4
Ostend 3

North Sea

0   5 km
     3.2 mi

N

Het Zoute
Het Zwin
Nature Reserve
2
1
KNOKKE-HEIST
St. Kruis
Assebroek
Oostkamp
E40
Lissewege
Zeebrugge
BRUGES (BRUGGE)
Blankenberge
34
Zuienkerke
St. Andries
Zedelgem
Eernegem
De Haan
Bredene
Oudenberg
Gistel
Ichtegem
Stene
3
OSTEND
34
Middelkerke
Westende
E40
Schore
OOSTDUINKERKE
4
34
DE PANNE
5

A cure for all your ills may just be waiting for you at ★ **Thalassa Zeecentrum,** a combination spa, fitness center, and gymnasium. In the "thermal institute," indulge in hot sea-mud baths and a number of other seawater treatments, work out on a wide variety of exercise equipment, or simply swim in the seawater pool or laze in the sauna. You'll find the Zeecentrum in the Hotel La Reserve, Elizabetlaan 158 (☎ **60-06-12**), and if you're a guest there, admission to the fitness club comes with your room rate—others pay BF 300 ($8.50) plus charges based on any additional treatments chosen.

Where to Stay

Some of the most luxurious (and expensive) coastal hotels are located in this area, but there are also many accommodation choices in a wide price range. As in resort areas the world over, rates fluctuate according to the season and there are periodic mid-week reductions, so be sure to ask. You'll also find several good budget hotels located along Lippenslaan in Knokke that offer no-frills double rooms without private bath for under BF 2,000 ($57).

Note: All rates cited below include service and VAT.

EXPENSIVE

★ **Hotel la Reserve,** Elizabetlaan 160, 8300 Knokke-Albertstrand.
   ☎ **050/61-06-06.** Fax 050/60-37-06. 110 rms. MINIBAR TV TEL

Rates (including breakfast): BF 6,000 ($171) single; BF 8,000 ($228) double. AE, DC, MC, V. **Parking:** Private car park.

Although this hotel is quite large, it manages to maintain a comfortable, almost country, air. Located in the town center across from the casino, it's a short walk from the beachfront and is the home of Knokke's important health spa, the Thalassa Center. The guest rooms, all with balconies, are spacious and come with such extras as color TVs that receive a full dozen channels—in addition, of course, to modern furnishings and the comforts of a luxury hotel.

Dining/Entertainment: There's a good restaurant and lounge.

Facilities: Thalassa Center health spa (see "What to See and Do," above), tennis courts.

Pauwels, Kustlaan 353, 8300 Knokke-Heist-Zoute. ☎ **050/61-16-17.**
   Fax 050/62-04-05. 28 rms. MINIBAR TV TEL

Rates (including breakfast): BF 4,250 ($121) single; BF 5,300 ($151) double. AE, DC, MC, V.

This elegant small hotel one block from the beach rubs elbows with upper-stratosphere shops in Het Zoute, and its guest rooms are exceptionally well furnished. There's garage parking. Pets are welcome.

Dining/Entertainment: There's a moderately priced restaurant and an attractive bar.

MODERATE

Lido, Zwaluwenlaan 18, 8300 Knokke-Heist. ☎ **050/60-19-25.** Fax 050/61-04-57.
   40 rms. TV TEL

Rates (including breakfast): BF 1,750–2,200 ($50–$62) single; BF 3,300–3,600 ($94–$102) double. AE, MC, V.

Modern to the *n*th degree in both decor and furnishings, the Lido has well-done-up, bright guest rooms. There's a bar and a good restaurant. It's in the town center.

Parkhotel, Elizabetlaan 204, 8300 Knokke-Heist-Duinbergen. ☎ **050/60-09-01.** 12 rms. TV TEL

Rates (including breakfast): BF 2,900 ($82) single; BF 3,300 ($96) double. Weekend rates available. AE, DC, MC, V.

Some two blocks from the beach, the Parkhotel has nicely appointed rooms that have recently been renovated. There's also an excellent restaurant with moderate prices and a quietly elegant decor, as well as an attractive bar.

INEXPENSIVE

Corner House, Hazegrasstraat 1, 8300 Knokke-Heist. ☎ **050/60-76-19.** 27 rms. TV TEL

Rates (including breakfast): BF 900 ($25) single; BF 1,800 ($51) double. AE, DC, MC, V.

Located not far from the Zwin nature reserve, and quite a distance from the beach, the Corner House offers modest but quite adequate and comfortable accommodations.

Where to Dine

Limited space permits a listing of only the highlights of good restaurants along this part of the Belgian coast—you'll find dozens of fine eateries to supplement the ones below.

★ **Aquilon,** Bayauxlaan 70. ☎ **60-12-74.**
Cuisine: SEAFOOD. **Reservations:** Required, especially on weekends.
Prices: Lunch BF 950 ($27); dinner BF 1,500–2,500 ($42–$71). MC, V.
Open: Lunch Thurs–Tues noon–2:30pm; dinner Thurs–Mon 6:30–10pm.

This ground-floor restaurant just in front of the casino is the most outstanding and most elegant in the area. Allow plenty of time to savor such specialties as veal with mushrooms and truffles or lobster Marguerite.

★ **Casa Borghese (also called Chez Ciccio),** Bayauxlaan 27. ☎ **60-37-39.**
Cuisine: SEAFOOD/ITALIAN/FRENCH. **Reservations:** Required.
Prices: Average meal BF 900 ($25). AE, DC, MC, V.
Open: Dinner only, Fri–Wed 6:30pm–midnight. **Closed:** Oct.

Excellent Italian and French dishes come at surprisingly modest prices here. Ideal for that late-night meal, it's in the town center.

Panier d'Or, Zeedijk 659. ☎ **60-31-89.**
Cuisine: SEAFOOD. **Reservations:** Required.
Prices: Average four-course meal BF 1,400 ($40). MC, V.
Open: Lunch Wed–Mon noon–2:30pm; dinner Wed–Mon 6:30–9:30pm.

Seafood, especially their renowned fish soup, stars at this seaside restaurant. It's a medium-sized place with traditional decor.

2 Ostend

31km (19 miles) W of Bruges, 35km (21 miles) SW of Knokke-Heist, 26km (16 miles) NE of De Panne

GETTING THERE • By Ferry   Ostend is the main ferry terminal for boats to and from Ramsgate. The terminal is located very near the town center at Montgomerydok.

• By Train or Bus   There's good train and bus service from Bruges and Brussels. The train station is located next to the ferry terminal (see above).

• By Tram   Ostend can be reached by tram from any of the other seaside resorts.

• By Car   From Brussels and Bruges, take E40; from any of the seaside resorts, Highway 34.

ESSENTIALS   The **telephone area code** is 059.

Information   The **Tourist Office** is at Monacoplein 2, 8400 Ostend (☎ **059/70-11-99;** fax 059/70-34-77).

Ostend's place as "Queen of the Coast" is quite secure—she has, after all, been in residence here since the 10th century, seen crusaders embark for the Holy Land, been hostess to pirates who found her a convenient base, resisted Spanish rule from the end of the 16th century into the 17th, been the terminal for sea service to England since 1846, seen her harbor blocked to thwart German submarines in World War I, been bombed during World War II—and emerged from that long, eventful history as a busy port and lively recreational haven with Belgium's largest casino, a racetrack, an outstanding art museum, a spa, and no fewer than five excellent sandy beaches.

Though "queenly," Ostend is very much a "queen of the people," welcoming all income levels, with very little of the posh exterior that's so much a part of Knokke-Heist and Het Zoute. Located at almost the exact midpoint of the Belgian coastline, Ostend divides the Oostkust (to the northeast) from the Westkust (to the southwest), and is the ideal touring base for coastal exploration. That fact, coupled with a mass of entertainment facilities that operate around the calendar, draws visitors by the thousands, and Ostend welcomes everyone, with more than 60 hotels, and over 250 restaurants that cater to their comfort.

The elevated Albert I Promenade runs the entire length of Ostend's 3½-mile beachfront and was, before World War II, lined with elegant private seaside villas, many the holiday homes of European royalty. From the debris of bombings during that war that destroyed so many of these fine old houses have sprung hotels and apartment buildings of a purely modern form. There is also a very good shopping district and an Olympic-size indoor swimming pool at the seafront. Outdoor pools are filled with heated sea water.

What to See and Do

While Ostend is the best base from which to explore the entire coast, there's plenty to keep you occupied at this one resort location. Carillon concerts ring from the Festival Hall tower periodically through the summer, and there are bandstand concerts on the Market Square from June to September. For late-night dance clubs, cabarets, and bars, hie yourself off to Langestraat near the eastern end of the beach.

⭐ **James Ensor House,** Vlaanderenstraat 27. ☎ **80-53-35.**

The post-impressionist painter James Ensor (1860–1949) lived most of his life in Ostend, and his home has been restored as it was when his aunt and uncle kept a

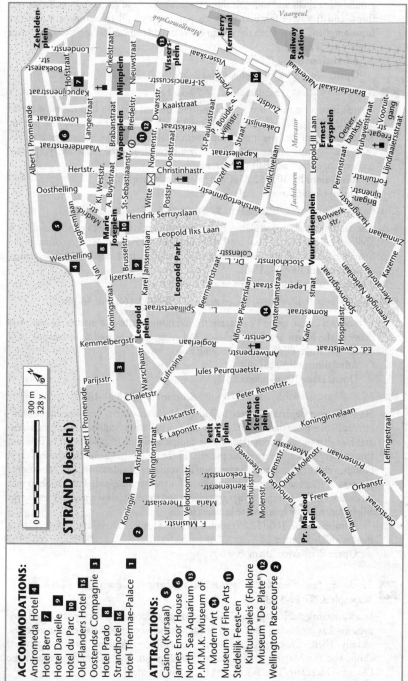

Ostend

STRAND (beach)

ACCOMMODATIONS:
- Andromeda Hotel **4**
- Hotel Bero **7**
- Hotel Danielle **9**
- Hotel du Parc **10**
- Old Flanders Hotel **15**
- Oostendse Compagnie **3**
- Hotel Prado **8**
- Strandhotel **16**
- Hotel Thermae-Palace **1**

ATTRACTIONS:
- Casino (Kursaal) **5**
- James Ensor House **6**
- North Sea Aquarium **13**
- P.M.M.K. Museum of Modern Art **14**
- Museum of Fine Arts **11**
- Stedelijk Feest-en Kultuurpaleis (Folklore Museum "De Plate") **12**
- Wellington Racecourse **2**

Church ✝   Post Office ⊠   Information 𝟎

ground-floor shells and souvenir shop. Ensor's studio and lounge are on the second floor, and if you're familiar with his paintings you'll recognize some of the furnishings and views from the windows. Vlaanderenstraat, leading to the sea, runs directly off Wapenplein.

Admission: BF 50 ($1.40).

Open: Wed–Mon 10am–noon and 2–5pm.

★ Kursaal (Casino), Monacoplein. ☎ 70-51-11.

There's been a casino at this spot since 1852, but the one you find there today was built after World War II, when bombings left the beachfront in ruins. The present Kursaal is one of the largest in Europe, with a concert hall, restaurant, disco, and—of course—gaming rooms. The concert hall is frequently the venue for symphonic concerts, operettas, and ballet performances.

Admission: BF 100 ($2.85) (bring along your passport).

Open: Gaming rooms, daily 3pm–2am.

Museum of Fine Arts, Wapenplein. ☎ 80-53-35.

The paintings of native sons James Ensor, Jan De Clerck, Constant Permeke, and Leon Spilliaert are featured in this second-floor museum (the Folklore Museum occupies the first floor; see below), along with Belgian impressionists. It's located in the town center.

Admission: BF 50 ($1.40).

Open: Wed–Mon 10am–noon and 2–5pm.

★ North Sea Aquarium, Visserskaai 4. ☎ 059/32-16-69 or 50-08-76.

In the town center, along Visserskaai (the old fishing harbor), a marvelous display of many of the North Sea fish, molluscs, and crustaceans, as well as interesting shell collections, make this a good sightseeing stop.

Admission: BF 50 ($1.40).

Open: Daily 10am–noon and 2–5pm.

P.M.M.K. Museum of Modern Art, Romestraat 11. ☎ 50-81-18.

Set in a former department-store building in the town center, the Museum of Modern Art houses more than 1,500 items, including paintings, sculpture, graphics, video, and film that together comprise a rather complete picture of modern art in Belgium from its very beginnings up to the present. There are also frequent international exhibitions, a children's museum, a workshop for youngsters, slide shows, and educational projects. A nice feature here is the facilities for the handicapped. The Art Shop sells art catalogs and functional design art objects, and the Art Café is a pleasant setting for a light lunch or the four-course business lunch.

Admission: BF 100 ($2.85) adults, BF 50 ($1.40) students and senior citizens, free for children under 14.

Open: Wed–Mon 10am–6pm.

★ Stedelijk Feest-en Kultuurpaleis (Folklore Museum "De Plate"), Wapenplein. ☎ 80-53-35.

In addition to exhibits depicting the native dress, folklore, and history of Ostend, this museum has interesting displays of Neolithic and Roman artifacts excavated in the vicinity. There's a re-created fisherman's pub, a fisherman's home, and an old tobacco shop, and the Marine section deals with shipbuilding, fishing boats, and the Ostend–Dover ferry line. It's located in the town center.

Admission: BF 50 ($1.40).

Open: Mon and Wed–Sat 10am–noon and 3–5pm.

Wellington Racecourse, Prinses Stefanieplein 41. ☎ **80-60-65.**

You'll find the only racetrack on the coast here, just across from the seafront at the end of the Royal Arcades. There's a grass track for flat and hurdle racing and a lava track for the trotters. The tourist office can furnish a detailed schedule of races.

Admission: Grandstand seats, BF 300 ($8.50) Mon–Fri, BF 350 ($10) Sat–Sun, BF 450 ($13) public holidays. Free to the field opposite the grandstand.

Open: May–Sept; call for race times.

Where to Stay

Ostend doesn't lack for accommodations, and they're available in every price range, from luxurious hotels right on the beachfront to budget rooms several blocks away from the water. You should *not,* however, leave your reservations until the last minute; book several weeks ahead during the summer, either directly with your choice of hotel or through any Belgian tourist office. Most hotels have special package rates available: summer midweek stays, winter weekends, etc.

Note: The tourist office can also book you into inexpensive boardinghouses.

EXPENSIVE

 Andromeda Hotel, Kursaal Westhelling 5, 8400 Ostend. ☎ **059/80-66-11.** Fax 059/80-66-29. 90 rms. TV TEL

Rates: Oceanfront rooms, BF 5,650 ($161) single; BF 6,650 ($190) double. Rooms facing inland, BF 2,950 ($43) single; BF 4,300 ($122) double. Reductions for children. AE, DC, MC, V.

One of the best luxury hotels in Ostend, this modern hotel also has a choice location—right on the beachfront and just next door to the casino. The marble lobby is an indication of the quality rooms upstairs: The guest rooms are the latest word in comfort and decor, with armchairs to relax in and view the sea through glass sliding doors that open to balconies.

Dining/Entertainment: The Gloria restaurant serves excellent meals in an attractive room overlooking the sea (see "Where to Dine," below), and the cocktail bar opens to the sea, with terrace tables for sunny days.

Services: Babysitting arranged.

Facilities: The Pyramid Relax Pool is a unique work of art by two well-known local artists, and the fitness center features a Jacuzzi, sauna, and solarium; wheelchair access.

Hotel Thermae-Palace, Koningin Astridlaan 7, 8400 Ostend. ☎ **059/80-66-44.** Fax 059/80-52-74. 100 rms. TV TEL

Rates: BF 3,950 ($112) single; BF 5,950 ($171) double. Reductions for children. AE, DC, EU, MC, V.

An integral part of the sprawling thermal-baths complex, this slightly old-fashioned hotel just off the beachfront (built in the '30s) has comfortable, attractive, fairly standard guest rooms, many with a sea view. The hotel provides wheelchair access.

Dining/Entertainment: The Périgord restaurant, built in art deco style, serves high-standard meals at moderate prices.

Services: Babysitting arranged.

★ **Oostendse Compagnie,** Koningstraat 79, 8400 Ostend. ☎ **059/70-48-16.**
Fax 059/80-53-16. 13 rms, 2 suites. MINIBAR TV TEL

$ **Rates:** BF 3,000–3,500 ($85–$100) single; BF 4,000–5,200 ($114–$148) double;
BF 5,700–9,200 ($162–$262) suite. AE, MC, V. **Closed:** Oct.

This small four-star luxury hotel—a former royal villa in a quiet seaside location beyond the busy town center—retains an atmosphere of "home," though admittedly
it's home on a grand scale. A pretty terrace and garden face the sea, floor-length windows with the same view line the drawing room, and the dining room is known for its
kitchen. The guest rooms are beautifully furnished, much like those in a private home,
and the two suites provide such perfect comfort and beauty that they'll tempt you to
settle in for a long spell. This is a rather special place and highly recommended, and
it's also very popular, so book as far in advance as possible.

Dining/Entertainment: See "Where to Dine," below.

Services: Babysitting arranged.

MODERATE

Hotel Bero, Hofstraat 1a, 8400 Ostend. ☎ **059/70-23-35.** Fax 059/70-25-91.
73 rms. TV TEL

Rates: BF 1,900 ($54) single; BF 2,000 ($57) double. Reduction for children. MC, V.

A short distance back from the beachfront, this modern hotel has nicely appointed
rooms at quite modest rates. There's a swimming pool, fitness sauna, solarium, and
whirlpool.

Hotel Danielle, Ijzerstraat 5, 8400 Ostend. ☎ **059/70-63-49.** Fax 059/80-16-95.
24 rms. TEL TV

Rates: BF 2,400 ($68) single; BF 3,100 ($88) double. Reduction for children. MC, V.

The Danielle is an attractive modern hotel in a very convenient location, near the beach
and casino, with well-appointed rooms. They can arrange babysitting, and there's a
good restaurant with moderate prices.

Hotel Prado, Leopold II Laan 22, 8400 Ostend. ☎ **059/70-53-06.** Fax 059/80-87-35.
28 rms. TV TEL

Rates: BF 1,750 ($50) single; BF 2,850 ($81) double. MC, V.

Located on a major midtown street a few blocks from the seafront, this modern hotel
with wheelchair access has comfortable rooms, nicely furnished in the modern mode.
A babysitting service is available.

Strandhotel, Visserskaai 1, 8400 Ostend. ☎ **059/70-33-83.** Fax 059/80-36-78.
21 rms. TV TEL

Rates: BF 2,750 ($78) single; BF 3,300 ($94) double. AE, DC, MC, V. **Closed:** Dec–Jan.

This pleasant, three-star hotel—situated near the yacht harbor and car-ferry terminal—has attractive, comfortably furnished guest rooms. There is a nice restaurant.

INEXPENSIVE

Hotel du Parc, Marie-Joseplein 3, 8400 Ostend. ☎ **059/70-16-80.** Fax 059/80-08-79.
47 rms. TEL TV

Rates: BF 1,600–2,050 ($45–$58) single; BF 2,900–3,100 ($82–$88) double. Reduction
for children. AE, DC, MC, V.

Conveniently located to the casino, the beach, and shopping, this hotel a few blocks from the beach has quite nice guest rooms, recently renovated in functional modern style. There's a nice bar and lounge, and they can arrange babysitting.

⭐ **Old Flanders Hotel,** Jozef II Straat 49, 8400 Ostend. ☎ **059/80-66-03.** Fax 059/80-16-95. 15 rms. TV TEL

Rates: BF 1,450–1,800 ($41–$51) single; BF 2,300–2,800 ($65–$80) double. Reduction for children. AE, MC, V.

This nice, centrally located hotel has a cozy, country-house atmosphere and guest rooms that are plainly, but quite comfortably, furnished. It's a few blocks from the beach.

Where to Dine

Most Ostend restaurants, not surprisingly, specialize in seafood. Not surprising, either, is the freshness of the seafood and the expertise with which these seacoast chefs prepare it: Fishing boats deliver daily catches to the Visserskaai (fisherman's quay), and the cooks are backed by a tradition of treating the fruits of the sea with respect. With some 250 restaurants at hand, you'll seldom be disappointed in any, and Ostend is the ideal place for "window shopping" each day for the setting and menu that has the most momentary appeal. Those listed below are a very personal, subjective list and meant only as an indication of what you'll find on your own. Most serve both a specialty of the day, based on the freshest ingredients available, and a three-course tourist menu, at a set price. And if you're attacked by hunger pangs late at night, many snack bars are open until the wee hours.

Very special indeed are the festive balls and Christmas and New Year's Eve dinners served at the casino. Many Ostend restaurants also feature special dinners and dance music on these occasions.

EXPENSIVE

⭐ **Au Vigneron,** in the Hotel Oostendse Compagnie, Koningstraat 79. ☎ **70-48-16.** 💲 **Cuisine:** FRENCH. **Reservations:** Recommended. **Prices:** Appetizers BF 520–750 ($15–$21); main courses BF 1,000–2,400 ($28–$68); special menu BF 3,000 ($85). AE, DC, MC, V. **Open:** Lunch Tues–Sun noon–2:30pm; dinner Tues–Sat 6:30–11pm.

This restaurant in the Oostendse Compagnie hotel (see "Where to Stay," above)— one of the finest along the entire coast—features classic French haute cuisine. The menu changes according to the best available ingredients, but you can always depend on their menu de dégustation for a memorable meal at a set price. Also of good value are the special dinners for two at BF 3,800 ($111). It's located on the beachfront near the casino.

⭐ **Gloria Restaurant,** in the Andromeda Hotel, Kursaal Westhelling 5. ☎ **80-66-11.** **Cuisine:** SEAFOOD/CONTINENTAL. **Reservations:** Recommended. **Prices:** Average lunch BF 1,200 ($34); average dinner BF 2,400 ($68). AE, DC, MC, V. **Open:** Lunch daily noon–2:30pm; dinner daily 6:30–10:30pm.

This gracious restaurant looking out on the sea is a favorite with locals as well as visitors. Among their specialties are lobster and a variety of North Sea fish, all prepared in mouth-watering creations. Service is as elegant, professional, and polished as are the menu and setting. It's next to the casino.

★ $ **Villa Maritza,** Albert I Promenade 76. ☎ **50-88-08.**

Cuisine: SEAFOOD. **Reservations:** Recommended.
Prices: Four-course dinner BF 2,600 ($74); fixed-price meal BF 2,400 ($68). AE, DC, MC, V.
Open: Lunch Tues–Sat noon–2:30pm; dinner Tues–Sun 6:30–9:30pm.

This exquisite restaurant is housed in a seaside villa that was once the holiday home of a Hungarian baroness. Built in 1885, it's one of the few remaining ornate old buildings that once lined the shore, most of which were destroyed by World War II bombings. Inside, Ostend native Jacques Ghaye has created a sophisticated restaurant with an elegant cuisine. Seafood specialties vary with the season; any one is a culinary delight. Wheelchair access.

MODERATE

Chopin, Alfons Buylstraat 1A. ☎ **70-08-37.**

Cuisine: SEAFOOD/STEAK/FLEMISH. **Reservations:** Not required.
Prices: Average meal BF 1,200 ($34); special lunch menu BF 800 ($22). Reductions for children's half-portions. AE, MC, V.
Open: Lunch Fri–Wed noon–2:30pm; dinner Fri–Wed 6:30–9:30pm.

Monkfish with leeks and grilled lobster are standouts on the menu here, but you really shouldn't miss their terrific waterzooï. It's located in the town center.

INEXPENSIVE

There are several attractive restaurants along the Albert I Promenade—the place to window-shop for your budget eatery—where it's possible to enjoy a good meal for BF 300 ($8.40) and under.

★ **Le Basque,** Albert I Promenade 62. ☎ **70-54-44.**

Cuisine: SEAFOOD. **Reservations:** Not required.
Prices: Average meal BF 570 ($17). AE, DC, MC, V.
Open: Daily noon–11pm.

Ostend sole and seafood on the skewer are featured in this pleasant seaside restaurant, which has an outdoor terrace for fine weather dining.

Old Fisher Restaurant, Visserskaai 34. ☎ **50-17-68.**

Cuisine: SEAFOOD. **Reservations:** Recommended.
Prices: Average meal BF 900 ($25). AE, DC, MC, V.
Open: Lunch Fri–Tues noon–2:30pm; dinner Fri–Tues 6–10pm.

This small eatery on the fishing quays—set about as close to fresh seafood as you can get—features the catches of the day in a wide variety of preparations. Not posh, but atmospheric.

★ **Villa Borghese,** Van Iseghemlaan 65B. ☎ **80-08-76.**

Cuisine: ITALIAN. **Reservations:** Recommended Sat–Sun.
Prices: A la carte meals BF 660–860 ($19–$25). AE, MC, V.
Open: Lunch Tues–Thurs and Sat–Sun noon–2:30pm; dinner Tues–Thurs and Sat–Sun 7–10:30pm. **Closed:** Mar.

There's a real touch of Italy in this restaurant where the manager personally prepares the lasagnes that are their specialty. It's in the town center.

3 Oostduinkerke

20km (12 miles) SW of Ostend

GETTING THERE • By Tram   There is frequent tram service from any of the other coastal resorts.

• By Car   Take Highway 34 from other coastal resorts.

ESSENTIALS   The **telephone area code** is 058.

Information   The **Tourist Office** is in the Town Hall, Leopold II Laan 2, 8458 Oostduinkerke (☎ **058/51-11-89**), open mid-June through mid-September, Monday through Friday from 8am to noon and 1:30 to 5pm. There's also a tourist office in Astridplein (☎ **058/51-13-89**), which stays open daily during summer months from 10am to noon and 2 to 6pm.

Oostduinkerke is one of the coast's small, family-oriented resort towns, yet it holds much of interest to art and nature lovers—whether based here or in Ostend or De Panne, both within easy reach by auto, bike, or tram. Its 5 miles of beachfront encompasses the neighboring small towns of Koksijde and Sint-Idesbald.

What to See and Do

Oostduinkerke's chief attraction is its beautiful, wide ☒ **beach,** the site of a very special activity you'll find nowhere else along the coast. Each day seven stalwart (and aging), yellow-slickered, and oilskin-clad gentlemen mount sturdy horses and wade into the surf at low tide to drag large nets behind them, ensnaring large quantities of delicious crevettes—those tiny, gray shrimp that thrive in the waters of the North Sea. They are following a tradition that dates back several centuries, and it's uncertain if there will be anyone to succeed them. Much of the catch will go into the kitchens of cafés owned by those same horseback fishermen, but if you go to the National Fishery Museum's next-door neighbor, the De Peerdevisser pub, soon after the fishermen return, you can purchase the just-caught, just-boiled delicacies by the sackful.

Sand-yachting is a popular sport at Oostduinkerke, and there are several places on the beach where you can rent the colorful vehicles and participate in the fun. Other beach activities include various festivals throughout the summer (ask the tourist office for a complete list to see what's on during your visit), **sand-castle competitions,** and **horseback riding** on the strand. Horses can be rented from **Hacienda,** Weststraat 3 (☎ **51-69-50**) and Pylyserlaan 50 (☎ **51-20-00**).

Oostduinkerke's beach is backed by impressive sand dunes, one of which, De Hoge Blekker, rises over 100 feet—the highest in the country. **Dune hiking** and **climbing** are very popular with visitors. Free guided **walking tours** are conducted from mid-June to mid-September, leaving at 9am at the foot of the Hoge Blekker and at 2:30pm from the Hotel La Peniche.

Dunenabdij (Abbey of the Dunes), Koninklijke Prinslaan 8. ☎ 51-19-33.

During much of the 12th century this Cistercian abbey was a center of culture for the region. The abbey lay in ruins for several centuries, but in 1949 excavations were begun that have revealed archeological artifacts that shed considerable light on coastal history and the development of this settlement. A small museum on the site presents interesting exhibits.

Near the abbey, the large **abbey farmstead (Ten Bogaerde)** includes a 12th-century barn that is now an agricultural school. It's typical of the large farm holdings of the ancient abbeys.

Admission: BF 80 ($2.30) adults, BF 30 (85¢) children.

Open: Easter holidays and July–Aug, daily 10am–6pm; other months, shorter hours. **Closed:** Jan.

★ **National Fishery Museum**, Pastoor Schmitzstraat 5. ☎ **51-24-68.**

Located in a small park at the rear of the Town Hall, this museum traces on maps the sea routes followed by local fishing fleets and exhibits the implements they have used through the centuries, sea paintings, a fishing-harbor model, North Sea aquarium, and a wonderful collection of fishing-boat models from A.D. 800 to the present. The interior of a typical fisherman's tavern is another highlight.

Admission: BF 80 ($2.30) adults, BF 50 ($1.40) students, BF 30 (85¢) children 6–12.

Open: Daily 10am–noon and 2–6pm.

★ **Paul Delvauxmuseum**, Kabouterweg 42. ☎ **51-29-71.**

In the little town of St. Idesbald, the nephew of internationally famous surrealist artist Paul Delvaux has turned a Flemish farmhouse into this modernized museum for works of his uncle. Delvaux's adulation of the female form is conveyed in many of the paintings, as is his love of trains and train stations.

Admission: BF 150 ($4.30) adults, BF 90 ($2.50) children.

Open: Tues–Sun 10:30am–6:30pm.

Where to Stay and Dine

WHERE TO STAY Hotel accommodations are quite limited, and most visitors come from an Ostend or De Panne base. The tourist office can, however, assist with hotel accommodations and also furnish names of agents for holiday cottages or flats, most of which are available on a weekly basis.

WHERE TO DINE Fresh-caught shrimp are the center of most culinary specialties here, and although few of the moderately priced restaurants can lay claim to being posh or gourmet, their kitchens turn out seafood creations that come very close to that gourmet label, with price tags that are unbelievably affordable. Your best bet is to window-shop the eateries and base your choice on size, decor, and menu.

4 De Panne

26km (16 miles) SW of Ostend, 7km (4 miles) SW of Oostduinkerke

GETTING THERE • By Tram De Panne is the southern terminus of the coastal tram that extends north to Knokke-Heist.

• By Car Take Highway 34 from any of the coastal resorts, and Highway 8 from Ypres to join Highway 34.

ESSENTIALS The **telephone area code** is 058.

Information You'll find the **Tourist Office** in the Town Hall, Zeelaan 21, 8660 De Panne (☎ **058/42-18-18;** Fax 058/42-16-17). During summer months there's also an **information desk** on the Zeedijk promenade (☎ **058/42-18-19**).

De Panne is Belgium's closest coastal point to France and England. Its sandy beaches have been the scene of several significant historical high points: In 1830 Leopold I set foot on newly independent Belgian soil to become the first of the country's own kings (though, Lord knows, it had seen its share of foreign royalty!); during World War I it was here that King Albert I and his queen clung to Belgian resistance against German occupying forces; and in 1940, there was the evacuation of ill-fated troops of the British Expeditionary Forces.

From the wide beach at De Panne, you can see the tall port cranes of Dunkirk: the scene of England's heroic rescue mission that brought some 338,000 beleaguered troops to safety in a makeshift armada of small craft gathered from boat owners around the country in late May and early June of 1940, while under almost continuous bombing attacks from German planes. When it was over, the $7^{1}/_{2}$-mile stretch of beach between Dunkirk and De Panne was a mass of military-equipment litter. It's a little-recognized fact that the British commander, Lord Gort, headquartered not in Dunkirk but here in De Panne.

But it's the wide beach (500 yards at low tide) and spectacular dunes (about one-third of all unspoiled duneland along the Belgian coast) that today bring hordes of tourists to De Panne each year, especially in July and August, when accommodations can be hard to come by despite the presence of thousands of holiday homes and flats. Those dunes are made all the more spectacular by vast wooded areas that turn them into a wonderland of greenery banding the creamy sands of the beach and azure sea beyond.

What to See and Do

Outdoor recreation is what people come to De Panne for, and with all those dunes to explore and the beach for sunning, swimming, and sand-yachting, time will never hang heavy.

A walk through De Panne's tree-lined residential streets, with rows of villas left over from another era, is a delight. Old fishermen's cottages still in use are on Veurnestraat.

The tourist office can furnish a series of beautifully illustrated informative brochures on the dune areas, and they organize special **guided tours** periodically during summer months.

The 850-acre ✪ **Westhoek Nature Reserve** encloses a fascinating dune landscape, with vegetation that varies from full-grown trees to scrubby shrubs. It's a unique opportunity to observe the formation of sand dunes, some in their beginning stages and others formed years ago that are constantly but almost imperceptibly changing. Signposted footpaths guide you all the way.

Straddling the Belgian/French border, the 230-acre **Domein Cabour** is another area that provides interesting walks, and there are frequent guided walks during summer months (ask at the tourist office about schedules).

Calmeynbos (Calmeyn Wood) covers only 110 acres, but is the loving legacy of one man, Maurice Calmeyn, who in 1903 began to plant trees in this area in order to preserve the dunes. Some 25 varieties of his plantings are thriving today.

It's instant enchantment for children at ✪ **Meli-Park,** Adinkerke (☎ **42-02-02**), the famous honeybee-theme and leisure park. A multitude of delightful attractions will appeal to virtually every member of the family. There's Apirama (exploring the bees' kingdom by boat), Elfira (a fairytale wonderland), the animal park, jungle fantasy parrot show, water symphony, Carioca (all sorts of playground activities), and

Phantom Guild, with three different fun fairs filled with rides. Open April through September, daily from 9am to 9pm, Meli-Park is a real treat, and the admission ticket of BF 575 ($16.50) covers all attractions, while children less than 1 meter (3¼ft.) tall or under age 6 go in free.

Where to Stay

Holiday homes, some built as replicas of traditional fishermen's cottages, are the most popular form of accommodation in this largely family-oriented resort. The tourist office can furnish a complete list of rental agents, but you should know that most places are booked months in advance and for periods of no less than a week. One of the largest of the so-called holiday villages is **Duinhoek,** Duinhoekstraat 123, 8660 De Panne (☎ **058/41-52-08**). The tourist office can also direct you to private homes, where a double room and breakfast runs about BF 1,800 ($51). No matter which type of accommodation you choose, to avoid disappointment your best bet is to contact the tourist office, specify the type of accommodation, price range, exact dates of arrival and departure, and a degree of flexibility. If still unsuccessful, consider an Ostend base for day trips.

Where to Dine

There are nearly 100 restaurants in De Panne, covering a wide range of specialties and prices—with a heavy emphasis on seafood, especially shrimp from local waters—and none in the really high-price range. For the least expensive, look to those along the Zeedijk, the beachfront promenade—it's half-tiled, with café terraces right on the sand. On Nieuwpoortlaan there's a row of chip shops selling mussels and frites for next to nothing. The upmarket restaurant below, though pricey, is widely acknowledged to be the best in town.

 Le Fox, Walckierstraat 2. ☎ **41-28-55.**
Cuisine: SEAFOOD. **Reservations:** Recommended.
Prices: Fixed-price meal BF 1,550–3,200 ($44–$91); special menu BF 1,895 ($54). AE, DC, MC, V.
Open: Lunch Wed–Mon noon–2:30pm; dinner Wed–Mon 6:30–10pm.

Just off the beachfront, this leading restaurant offers exceptional seafood dinners, with such specialties as turbot and salmon-and-asparagus fondue.

Art of the Walloons

8

HAINAUT, THE LARGE WALLONIAN PROVINCE THAT STRETCHES ACROSS MOST OF the Belgian/French border, has been the setting for countless conflicts between French nobility who coveted the rich Low Countries and fractious Flemish who were just as determined to resist French domination. Each called on the resources of allies, confiscated vast regions through political marriages, engaged in pitched battles, and struggled to keep the local populations properly subdued.

Later, as coal mining grew in importance, industrialization threatened to overrun the traditional agricultural way of life. Charleroi, the largest city in the province, sits in the central coal basin; and even today, though there is no longer any coal mining in Belgium, great slagheaps dot the Borinage countryside around Mons. Today industrialization takes the form of engineering and manufacturing, and peaceful farmlands still exist as they have for centuries. As you drive through a lush, verdant landscape, it's difficult to picture the days when this was dubbed Belgium's "black country."

The province has a rich, colorful history and is the repository of great art treasures from the past. Charleroi is of little interest to visitors outside the engineering field. It is Tournai, undisputed art center of Hainaut, and Mons, its administrative center and site of many antiquities and museums, that draw us like powerful magnets.

1 Tournai

80km (49 miles) SW of Brussels; 44km (27 miles) NW of Mons

GETTING THERE • By Train or Bus   There is good train and bus service between Tournai and Brussels, about a two-hour ride. The railway station is on the northern edge of town.

• By Car   Tournai is less than an hour's drive from Brussels via A8.

ESSENTIALS   The **telephone area code** is 069.

Information   The large **Tourist Office** (Centre de Tourisme) is located opposite the Belfry at Vieux Marché aux Poteries 14, 7500 Tournai (☎ **069/22-20-45**). The friendly and efficient staff can furnish excellent brochures outlining self-guided tours in and around the town, as well as a host of other information, including a beautifully photographed "Guide to Tournai" that details major religious and artistic attractions, public monuments, and museums.

When you talk about Tournai, you must speak of survival. This second-oldest city in Belgium (Tongeren is the oldest) has, since the century before the birth of Christ, survived a multitude of political, military, and economic disasters that would have swamped many another. For centuries it maintained a position of prominence in Europe as an ecclesiastical center. Its importance for even more ancient centuries was not revealed, however, until an accidental discovery brought to light the fact that the early Roman settlement known as Tornacum at this point on the River Scheldt, a major trade route crossroad, was also the first capital of the Frankish empire.

When a workman, quite by chance, opened the tomb of Childeric, king of the Franks—whose son, Clovis, founded the Merovingian dynasty that ruled for nearly three centuries—it was firmly established that in A.D. 482 Tournai had been the seat of royalty. The tomb also yielded breathtaking royal treasures that the city proudly displays.

In the years since Childeric and Clovis, Tournai has endured a veritable yo-yo existence of foreign rule, with successive domination by the French, the English (it was

What's Special About Tournai and Mons

Museums

- Museum of Fine Arts, in Tournai, with 700 major works of art in an impressive building designed by Victor Horta.
- Museum of History and Archeology, in a 17th-century pawnshop in Tournai, featuring relics, paintings, tapestries, and exquisite 18th-century porcelain.
- Museum of Folklore, in Tournai, displaying re-created rooms that might have been found in a blacksmith's forge, a weaver's workroom, and more.
- Centenaire Museum, in Mons, a cluster of four museums occupying a 16th-century Mont-de-piété (municipal pawnshop).

Churches

- Cathedral of Our Lady of Tournai, a Romanesque-Gothic hybrid from the 12th century, with five towers and magnificent relics in its treasury.

Castles

- Beloeil Castle, near Mons, the "Versailles of Belgium."
- Le Roeuix Castle, near Mons, with a French garden that holds more than 100,000 roses.

Festivals

- Procession of Tournai, a splendid pageant in Notre-Dame Cathedral, held since 1090 to commemorate the lifting of the Black Plague.
- Ducasse de la Trinité Festival, in Mons, beginning with the Procession of the Golden Chariot, including a mock battle between St. George and the dragon, and concluding with the Pageant of Mons, performances by some 2,000 musicians, singers, and actors.

the only Belgian city King Henry VIII managed to conquer, in 1513), the Spanish, the Dutch, the French again, the Austrians, French Empire revolutionary forces, and for a time before Belgium became a kingdom in its own right in 1830, the Dutch once more.

Throughout it all Tournai retained its magnificent works of art and architecture that were the legacy of its platoons of painters, sculptors, goldsmiths, tapestry weavers, and porcelain craftsmen who persistently kept at their labors during all those eventful years. And then came the devastation of World War II, when a full 60% of its buildings were destroyed. It can only be deemed a miracle that the great cathedral emerged with little damage; but if that fact was due to the intervention of Divine Providence, it is surely to the very human perseverance and richness of spirit that we must attribute the fact that Tournai today greets us with its glorious monuments once more intact and its past recaptured so completely that the scars of conflict are scarcely visible.

Talk about survival!

What to See and Do

For some idea of how Tournai looked back in medieval times, take a stroll along **rue Barre Saint-Brice** on the opposite side of the Scheldt from the city center. There, nos. 10 and 12 date from the late 1100s and are the oldest private houses in all of Europe. In the same neighborhood, **rue des Jésuites** holds Gothic-style 13th-century houses.

From April to September, ✪ **hansom cabs** are available to take you through the cobblestone streets of Tournai. The tourist office can give details on departure points, and charges will be around BF 500 ($14) for a 30-minute ride.

The ✪ **"Tournai Seen from the River" boat cruise** on the Scheldt lasts about an hour, departing from the landing stage at pont des Tros Tuesday through Sunday from May to August, at a fare of BF 100 ($2.85). Check with the tourist office for exact sailing times.

All **museums** in Tournai are open Wednesday through Monday from 10am to noon and 2 to 5:30pm, and there is never an admission charge—a lovely gift from the city to its residents and visitors. For more detail on museums and other attractions, call or visit the tourist office.

The Belfry, Grand-Place.

The Belfry of Tournai dates from the late 1100s, making it the oldest in Belgium. The 44-bell carillon plays Saturday-morning concerts, and if you're fit for it, you can climb the 265 steps to its top for a glorious view of the town and surrounding countryside.

Admission: BF 50 ($1.40).
Open: Wed–Mon 10am–noon and 2–5:30pm.

Cathédrale Notre-Dame (Cathedral of Our Lady of Tournai), place P-E-Janson.

This magnificent five-towered cathedral in the city center just off Grand-Place was completed in the late 1100s, but it's not the first place of worship to stand on this spot. As early as A.D. 761, there was a church here, and it is thought the site had once held a pagan temple before that. The 8th-century church was replaced by an 850 structure, which was burned to the ground in 881 by invading Norsemen, only to be quickly replaced. When fire once again destroyed the church in 1060, it was rebuilt by 1089 and became a place of refuge for a plague-stricken population. On September 14, 1090, when the dread disease finally lifted, a grateful bishop led a great procession through the cathedral to honor Our Lady, who was credited with several miraculous cures after hordes of the stricken had poured into the cathedral to pray before her statue. In the years since, the Procession of Tournai has taken place every year, except in 1559 when Calvinists broke into the cathedral in a destructive orgy and were not subdued until after the traditional procession date. Anyone planning a September visit to Europe should reserve the second Sunday of that month for Tournai in order to view its splendid pageantry.

Historians disagree about the exact date the present cathedral—one of the most striking examples of Romanesque architecture in Europe—was completed, but concur that it was sometime between 1140 and 1171. The thickness of its walls and its tiny windows were classical Romanesque, which, in the eyes of a 13th-century bishop, made it hopelessly old-fashioned compared to the Gothic buildings that were then appearing all over Europe. He promptly had the Romanesque choir replaced by one in the Gothic style, ordered stained-glass windows, and before the money ran out entirely, had managed to create a soaring, graceful choir adjoining the long, low Romanesque nave, which never did get its Gothic facelift. Amazingly, when you visit this schizophrenic building today, there is no sense of disharmony, but rather a strange sort of compatible marriage of the two styles.

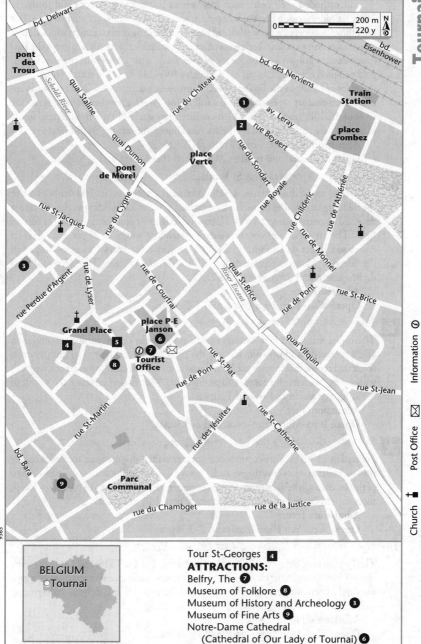

Tournai

pont des Trous
bd. Delwart
bd. des Nerviens
bd. Eisenhower
Train Station
place Crombez
quai Staline
Schelde River
quai Dumon
rue du Château
av. Leray
rue Beyaert
place Verte
rue du Sondart
rue Royale
rue Childeric
rue de l'Athénée
pont de Morel
rue St-Jacques
rue du Cygne
rue de Lyser
rue de Monnel
rue de Pont
rue St-Brice
quai St-Brice
River Escaut
rue de Courtrai
place P-E Janson
Grand Place
Tourist Office
quai Vifquin
rue St-Jean
rue St-Plat
rue de Pont
rue St-Catherine
rue St-Martin
rue des Jésuites
bd. Bara
Parc Communal
rue du Chambget
rue de la Justice

200 m
220 y

BELGIUM
○Tournai

Information ℹ

Post Office ✉

Church ✝ ■

9565

The cathedral itself holds such treasures as paintings by Rubens and Jordaens, 700-year-old murals, a Renaissance pulpit, and a "rose window" of stained glass. But even these wonders pale before those to be seen in the cathedral's treasury, which houses a vast collection of priceless religious relics and antiquities. The centerpiece is the reliquary casque known as *The Shrine of Our Lady,* with its astonishingly beautiful gold-sculpted covering created by Nicholas of Verdun in 1205, which always takes the place of honor in the Procession of Tournai each September. Other treasures include 15th-century tapestries (one is a full 72 feet long!), a jewel-encrusted Byzantine cross of the 10th century, and a 14th-century ivory statue of the Virgin. For all information on the cathedral and the Belfry (see above), contact the tourist office.

Admission: Cathedral, free; Treasury, BF 25 (70¢).

Open: Cathedral and treasury, Wed–Mon 10am–noon and 2–5:30pm.

★ **Museum of Fine Arts,** rue St-Martin.

It's hard to say of this museum which is the more impressive: its 700 works of art or the building that houses them. It's a marvelous white stone building in the city center designed by noted architect Victor Horta, and its interior illumination is that of natural light. The art collection contains such outstanding works as *Virgin and Child* by native son Roger de La Pasture, the 15th-century artist known to us as Roger van der Weyden. Manet is represented, as is Brueghel the Younger, James Ensor, Henri de Braekeleer, and Sir Anthony Van Dyck.

Admission: Free.

Open: Wed–Mon 10am–noon and 2–5:30pm.

★ **Museum of Folklore,** Réduit des Sions.

Two rather marvelous 17th-century buildings in the city center, complete with gables and mullioned windows, provide just the right setting for a series of authentically re-created rooms that might have been found in an ancient farmhouse, tavern, weaver's workroom, blacksmith's forge, and many more. Wax figures enhance the reality of life as it once was in and around Tournai.

Admission: Free.

Open: Wed–Mon 10am–noon and 2–5:30pm.

★ **Museum of History and Archeology,** rue des Carmes.

Located in a 17th-century pawnshop in the city center, this museum features a collection of Tournai relics covering virtually every period, starting with the Gallo-Roman of the 1st through 4th centuries. Art takes center stage in the form of paintings, sculptures, tapestries, and exquisite 18th-century porcelain and china.

Admission: Free.

Open: Wed–Sun 10am–noon and 2–5:30pm.

Tower of Henry VIII (Musée d'Armes), place Verte.

The English king held Tournai for five years, from 1512 to 1518, and left in his wake this 80-foot tower in the city center that now houses an impressive museum of weaponry and a fascinating exhibit centered around the World War II Belgian underground resistance.

Admission: Free.

Open: Wed–Mon 10am–noon and 2–5:30pm.

Where to Stay

If you elect to stay in the Tournai/Mons area rather than making easy day trips from Brussels, you'll find the hotel supply in Tournai rather limited. A wider selection is available in Mons.

IN TOURNAI

 Aux Armes de Tournai, place de Lille 24, 7500 Tournai. ☎ **069/22-67-23** or **22-57-89.** 13 rms. TV TEL

Rates: BF 940 ($27) single; BF 1,600 ($45) double. AE, MC, V.

Conveniently located in the center of town, this small hotel offers comfortable rooms with attractive decor and furnishings. There's a good restaurant in the same building.

L'Europe, Grand-Place 36, 7500 Tournai. ☎ **069/22-40-67.** 8 rms (5 with bath). TV

Rates: BF 1,300 ($37) single (without bath). BF 1,820 ($52) single with bath; BF 1,620 ($46) double without bath, BF 2,100 ($60) double with bath. AE, DC, MC.

The guest rooms of this hotel right on the central square are above a pleasant, moderately priced restaurant. The rooms are plainly furnished, but quite comfortable.

Tour St-Georges, rue St-Georges 2, 7500 Tournai. ☎ **069/22-53-00** or **22-50-35.** 10 rms. MINIBAR TV TEL

Rates: BF 1,050–1,580 ($30–$45) single or double. No credit cards.

The guest rooms at this quiet, conveniently located hotel in the city center are comfortable and attractive. There's a good restaurant on the premises with moderate prices.

EN ROUTE TO MONS

 Hostellerie le Vert Gazon, 7980 Stambruges-Grandglise. ☎ **069/57-59-84.** 6 rms. TV TEL

Rates: BF 2,200–3,600 ($62–$102) single or double. AE, MC, V.

A bit out from a charming little village, just off Highway A16 that runs from Tournai to Mons, this turreted château is set in green, flower-bordered lawns. Its guest rooms are beautifully furnished, as are the reception rooms and dining room, where excellent meals are served for about BF 1,900 ($54), without wine. This restful place is an ideal base for sightseeing forays into both Mons and Tournai. Be sure to reserve as far in advance as possible.

Where to Dine

Almost any of the sidewalk cafés lining Grand-Place will provide excellent meals at moderate prices. Listed below are those exceptional eateries worth seeking out. For inexpensive meals that will average under BF 800 ($23), try the restaurants on place Crombez near the railway station.

The following two recommendations are a step up in decor, service, and cuisine, although prices are still within the moderate range.

Charles Quint, Grand-Place 3. ☎ **22-14-41.**

Cuisine: CONTINENTAL. **Reservations:** Required.
Prices: Average lunch BF 800 ($23); average dinner BF 1,600 ($45). AE, DC, MC, V.
Open: Lunch Fri–Wed noon–2pm; dinner Fri–Tues 6:30–10pm.

This popular, elegant restaurant is nearly always crowded at lunch, and deservedly so. Its kitchen produces excellent fish, fowl, and meat dishes. The restaurant is located in the city center overlooking the Belfry.

 Le Pressoir, Marché aux Poteries 2. ☎ **22-35-13.**

Cuisine: CONTINENTAL. **Reservations:** Required for lunch, recommended for dinner.
Prices: Average lunch BF 1,000 ($28); average dinner BF 1,300 ($37); fixed-price six-course meal BF 1,700 ($48). AE, DC, MC, V.
Open: Lunch Tues and Fri–Sat noon–2:30pm; dinner Tues and Fri–Sat 6:30–9:30pm.

Top recommendation goes to this elegant restaurant just across from the cathedral entrance. In a setting of subdued sophistication are mouth-watering specialties of duck, with turbot featured among the fish specialties.

2 Mons

55km (34 miles) SW of Brussels; 44km (27 miles) SE of Tournai

GETTING THERE • By Train   There is frequent train service from Brussels and via Brussels–Paris express trains. The railway station is on place Léopold, a short walk west from the town center.

• By Car   From Brussels, take Highway 6; from Tournai, E42.

ESSENTIALS   The **telephone area code** is 065.

Information   The **Tourist Office** is at Grand' Place 22, 7000 Mons (☎ **065/ 33-55-80**).

SPECIAL EVENTS   Each spring on Trinity Sunday (the first Sunday after Whitsunday) Mons erupts in a burst of pageantry of vivid color, mock drama, and general revelry when it celebrates the ■ **Ducasse de la Trinité Festival.** It begins with the **Procession of the Golden Chariot,** when that gorgeous vehicle (see below) is drawn through the streets by a team of white horses, followed by richly dressed girls and clerics bearing the silver reliquary that holds the skull of St. Waudru. When the procession has returned to the church, there follows a mock battle between St. George and the Dragon (known here as the "Lumecon"), hilariously enjoyed by the throngs who continue to celebrate until the evening performance by some 2,000 musicians, singers, and actors of the Pageant of Mons brings the day to a close.

Mons, the administrative capital of the Province of Hainaut, began life as a fortified Roman camp, and today it's home to the Supreme Headquarters Allied Powers (NATO). In between those military bookends of history, it has lived a history that would rival many a novel.

The Roman camp became a town, set in this landscape of rolling hills (*Mons,* in fact, means "mount" in Latin), when St. Waudru, daughter of one of the counts of Hainaut, founded a convent here in the 600s. It was fortified by Baldwin of Mons in the 12th century, and again by the Dutch in the early 1800s. But its modern character was formed during the period when it was the center of Belgian coal mining, a development that saw it become an industrial city and cast a grimy pall over its collection of ancient buildings. Today its Grand' Place (Main Square) remains little changed, surrounded by fine buildings of the past, while its outskirts holds suburbs much like those of any modern city.

What to See and Do

Mons is a sightseer's dream: Almost everything you'll want to see is no more than a short walk from Grand' Place.

THE BELFRY TOWER & NEARBY ATTRACTIONS

The first thing you're likely to notice about Mons is its **Belfry Tower.** It sits at the highest point in the town, and don't worry if you feel an irresistible urge to giggle at your first sight of it—its appearance *is* a bit comical, and as Victor Hugo remarked, it does look a bit like "an enormous coffee pot, flanked below the belly-level by four medium-sized teapots." And don't be perplexed if you hear it referred to as "le château"—it sits near the site of an old castle of the counts of Hainaut, and even though the castle was demolished in 1866, people hereabouts have never broken the habit of using the old designation. Actually, the 285-foot-high tower is of 17th-century baroque design, the only one in Belgium, and the view from its top gives you a perfect orientation, with the inner city of Mons below, its industrial suburbs a little farther out, and the countryside beyond. Nothing is left of the castle except interesting subterranean passages.

Just a short distance from the Belfry Tower, the **Chapel of Saint Calixt** (☎ 34-95-55) is the oldest structure in Mons (1051). It is primarily interesting because of three sleeping tomb figures that go back to the 9th century.

The remarkable Gothic ✪ **Collegiate Church of St. Waudru** (1450) honors that daughter of the count of Hainaut whose 7th-century convent marked the beginning of Mons. It stands below the Belfry-Tower Hill, a little to the west. Inside its vast, vaulted room are sculptures and wall carvings of Mons-born Jacques du Broeck that date from the 16th century. Around the choir, a series of 16th-century stained-glass windows depict biblical scenes. At the entrance of the church, the "Car d'Or" (Golden Chariot) waits for its annual spring outing (see "Special Events," above).

MUSEUMS

Canon Puissant Museum, rue Notre-Dame-Debonnaire 22.

This 16th-century lodging house near the railway station holds a rich collection of Gothic and Renaissance furnishings, and nearby is the restored 13th-century Chapel of St. Margaret, with its beautiful examples of religious art.

Admission: BF 50 ($1.40).

Open: Tues–Sun 10am–noon and 2–6pm.

★ **Centenaire Museum,** Grand' Place.

The main quadrangle of the Town Hall leads to the Jardin du Mayeur (Mayor's Garden), a courtyard that leads to a cluster of four museums, collectively known as the Centenaire Museum, all occupying the 1625 *Mont-de-piété* (municipal pawnshop). Outside, there's a prehistoric standing stone and an American tank from World War II, both indicative of what's inside.

Inside **Le Musée de Guerre** are a very complete and sobering World Wars I and II collection, as well as exhibits to illustrate Mon's position of importance in both wars. Then there are the **Ceramics Museum,** with more than 3,000 pieces from the 17th through the 19th centuries; the **Museum of Medals and Coins** (more than 13,000); and the **Museum of Prehistory,** based on local prehistory of the Gallo-Roman and Frankish periods.

Admission: BF 60 ($1.70).
Open: Tues–Sun 10am–12:30pm and 2–6pm.

Maison Jean Lescarts, Musée du Folklore, rue Neuve. ☎ 31-43-57.

Interesting collections of furnishings, as well as folk and craft objects, are located in this 17th-century building in the center of town.
Admission: Free.
Open: Summer, Tues–Sun 10am–12:30pm and 2–6pm; winter, Tues–Thurs and Sat 10am–12:30pm and 2–6pm, Fri and Sun 10am–12:30pm and 2–5pm.

Musée des Beaux-Arts, rue Neuve.

To one side of the Jardin du Mayeur, you'll find the Museum of Fine Arts, with an emphasis on 19th- and 20th-century paintings and sculpture. It's located in the center of town.
Admission: BF 60 ($1.70).
Open: Tues–Sun 10am–noon and 2–6pm.

The Town Hall, Grand' Place.

Grand' Place is where you'll find the 15th-century Gothic Town Hall, which dates from 1458. As you go through its main entrance, look to the left and perhaps stop to rub the head of "the monkey of the Grand-Garde," an iron monkey that's been here since the 15th century granting good luck to all those who make that gesture. Needless to say, by this time he has a very shiny pate. Inside the Town Hall are interesting tapestries and paintings.

NEARBY CASTLES

If you're a romantic, the Province of Hainaut has castles to suit your every fancy, three of them within easy reach of Mons. The one you really shouldn't miss is Beloeil.

Some 13¹/₂ miles from Mons, ✪ **Beloeil Castle,** 7970 Beloeil (☎ **069/68-96-55** or **68-94-26**) has been called the "Versailles of Belgium," and I, for one, would never dispute that title. It is, quite simply, magnificent. The ancestral home of the Prince de Ligne, it sits in its own park, on the shores of a huge ornamental lake amid French-style gardens. For more than a thousand years the de Ligne family has been intimately involved with virtually every significant historical happening in Europe. They have lived in grand style that pervades the vast rooms filled with priceless antiques, paintings by the masters, historical mementos (there's a lock of Marie Antoinette's hair!), and more than 20,000 books, many of them quite rare.

If you can get together a party of 20 or more, it's possible to arrange a private candlelight dinner in the palatial dining room, attended by liveried servants—a once in a lifetime experience for most of us!

The castle itself is reason enough to visit, but a bonus is the Minibel, a 10-acre site that holds reproductions on a ¹/₂₅ᵗʰ scale of some of Belgium's most beautiful and interesting structures. There's the Brussels Town Hall and Grand' Place, the Belfry in Bruges, and many others you'll recognize from your travels. A mini-train takes you to the site from the castle. There's a self-service restaurant for full meals at prices under BF 800 ($23) or light snacks, and hours are 10am to 6pm daily from April through September and on weekends in October. An all-inclusive admission for castle, grounds, and Minibel is BF 500 ($14) for adults, with discounts for groups, students, and seniors.

The home of the princes of Croy, ✪ **Le Roeuix Castle** is 17¹/₂ miles from Mons, 4 ¹/₂ miles northwest of La Louvière. Surrounded by a lovely park and a French garden that holds more than 100,000 roses, it is luxuriously furnished with antiques and works of art. Open Thursday through Tuesday from 10am to noon and 1:30 to 6pm during summer months, with an entrance fee of BF 100 ($2.85).

Mariemont Castle, 16 miles from Mons, is primarily of interest because of its superb park grounds and its museum of antiques, jade, and porcelain. Open year-round, Tuesday through Sunday from 10am to 6pm.

Where to Stay

The best hotels lie outside the city center, but are within easy driving distance. Those in the city are small, with moderate prices.

EXPENSIVE

Casteau Moat House, chaussée de Bruxelles 38, 7061 Casteau (Soignies). ☎ **065/72-87-41.** Fax 065/72-87-44. 71 rms. TV TEL

Rates (including breakfast): BF 2,800 ($80) single; BF 3,900 ($111) double. AE, DC, MC, V.

This large hotel is some 4 miles northeast of Mons. The recently renovated guest rooms are well furnished and attractive, and there's a good restaurant with moderate prices, tennis courts, and bicycle rentals. A sauna and fitness center are in the planning stage.

★ **Hôtel la Forêt,** chaussée Brunehault 3, 7000 Mons. ☎ **065/72-36-85.** Fax 065/72-41-44. 46 rms. TV TEL

Rates: BF 3,900 ($111) single; BF 4,500 ($128) double. AE, DC, MC, V.

This is one of the city's larger hotels, although a little out of town in quiet, rural surroundings off Highway 56. The guest rooms are nicely appointed, with peaceful views of woodlands and fields. There's a warm, inviting look to the lobby and other public spaces, as well as a nice bar, a good restaurant with moderate prices, and a pool.

MODERATE

Hôtel Résidence, rue André-Masquelier 4, 7000 Mons. ☎ **065/31-14-03.** 6 rms. TV TEL

Rates (including breakfast): BF 2,200 ($62) single; BF 2,600 ($74) double. MC.

This small hotel conveniently located in the town center has quite nice, comfortable guest rooms.

Hôtel Saint-Georges, rue des Clercs 15, 7000 Mons. ☎ **065/31-16-29.** Fax 065/31-86-71. 9 rms. TEL

Rates: BF 1,880 ($53) single; BF 2,680 ($74) double. AE, DC, MC, V.

This is a small, well-run hotel, whose comfortable guest rooms, although rather plainly furnished, represent good value for money.

★ **Infotel,** rue d'Havré 32, 7000 Mons. ☎ **065/35-62-21.** Fax 065/35-62-24. 17 rms, 2 suites. MINIBAR TV TEL

Prices: BF 1,950 ($55) single; BF 2,900 ($82) double; BF 4,500 ($128) suite. AE, DC, MC, V.

Centrally located, Infotel is a new hotel, with pretty guest rooms that come with the little extra comfort touches that make it a welcome addition to Mons's hotel scene.

Where to Dine

 Alter Ego, rue de Nimy 6. ☎ **35-52-60.**

Cuisine: FLEMISH/PASTA. **Reservations:** Not required.
Prices: Fixed-price menu BF 700 ($20); à la carte meal BF 1,200–1,800 ($34–$51). AE, MC, V.
Open: Lunch Tues–Sun noon–2pm; dinner Tues–Sat 7–10pm.

Located in the center of town, this is the place to sample that Belgian favorite, rabbit hotpot. And for a change in seafood dishes, go for the ravioli with crab.

 Devos, rue de la Coupe 7. ☎ **35-13-35.**

Cuisine: SEAFOOD. **Reservations:** Recommended.
Prices: Average à la carte meal BF 950–2,400 ($27–$68); five-course fixed-price menu BF 2,800 ($80). AE, DC, MC, V.
Open: Lunch daily noon–2pm; dinner Mon–Tues and Thurs–Sat 7–9:30pm. **Closed:** One week in Feb, three weeks from mid-July.

This is one of Mons's best restaurants, where seafood dishes are a specialty, with Angus beef and veal other menu stars. They also do a delicious roast duckling with black cherries if you request it when booking. It's located in the center of town.

Liège and the
Meuse Valley

9

ONE OF BELGIUM'S MOST IMPORTANT WATERWAYS, THE RIVER MEUSE RISES in France, crosses Belgium, and empties into the sea in Holland. Along its Belgian banks are some of the country's most striking scenery, historic towns and cities, and industrial plants whose commercial livelihood is linked closely to the river.

With so much to see in such a small area, you can base yourself in Liège or Namur and return to comfortable lodgings after day-long rambles. Also, both cities are gateways to the lovely Ardennes region, and if you have only limited time for that beautiful countryside, it's quite possible to pop over for a quick look from either base along the Meuse.

1 Liège

112km (69 miles) SE of Brussels, 33km (20 miles) NW of Huy, 66km (41 miles) NE of Namur

GETTING THERE • By Train or Bus   There is train and bus service to Liège from Brussels, Tournai, and Mons, as well as Maastricht in Holland and Luxembourg. The **main railway/bus station,** which serves all trains, is Gare de Guillemins, a little over a mile south of the city center. Two **smaller stations,** more centrally located (Palais, on rue de Bruxelles, and Jontosse, on rue Stefany), are used by some local and connecting trains.

• By Car   From Brussels, take E40 west; from Namur, Highway 90.

ESSENTIALS   The **telephone area code** is 041.

Information   There are **tourist offices** located at En Féronstrée 92 (☎ 041/21-92-21), and Gare des Guillemins, 4000 Liège (☎ 041/52-44-19). Hours are 10am to 5pm weekdays, 10am to 4pm on Saturday, and 10am to 2pm on Sunday. They can provide brochures outlining self-guided walking tours and during the summer can furnish a qualified guide to accompany you at very modest fees. There's an **Office of Tourism for the Province of Liège** (Fédération Provinciale du Tourisme) at bd. de la Sauvenière 77, 4000 Liège (☎ 041/22-42-10).

CITY LAYOUT   Liège straddles the Meuse, with a backdrop of Ardennes foothills. Using the Meuse as a focal point, you'll find the **Old City** on its west bank, the **Outremeuse** (really a large island) on the other. You'll do your major sightseeing in the Old City, while you'll cross one of several bridges to Outremeuse for lively bars, discothèques, and cabarets at night—unless, it must be added, you decide there's enough nighttime entertainment in the small **"carré district"** of the Old City, circled by rue de l'Université, boulevard de la Sauvenière, and rue Pont-d'Avroy. Several small streets off place St-Lambert are good shopping streets that are reserved for pedestrians only. Tree-lined walks follow the river's banks. For the best views of the city, take to one of the three hills on the periphery.

GETTING AROUND • By Bus   City buses charge BF 38 ($1.10), and there are discounted 8-ride and 24-hour tickets, which can be purchased from bus drivers, ticket booths at major route stops, and the railway station.

• By Foot   Unless you're going from one end of the town to the other, you'll find the city easy walking, with sightseeing highlights close together. As in most cities, this is really the *only* way to see and appreciate Liège.

What's Special About Liège and the Meuse Valley

Museums
- Curtius Museum, in Liège, one of the city's most beautiful houses, with archeological and crafts collections.
- Museum Tchantchès, in Liège, with a marvelous collection of the city's favorite puppet, along with his cohorts and their costumes.
- Museum of Walloon Life, in Liège, with exhibits bringing to life the rich Walloon traditions.

Churches
- Cathedral of St. Paul, in Liège, with the 13th-century polychrome *Madonna and Child* and the white marble and oak pulpit, among other treasures.
- Church of St. Jacques, in Liège, a happy mixture of architectural styles with an intricately designed vaulted ceiling.
- Notre-Dame Collegiate Church, in Huy, famed for its mammoth *Li Rondia,* a beautiful rose window 35 feet in diameter.

Castles and Fortresses
- Castle of Jehay, in Jehay-Bodegnee, a moated castle filled with treasures from the private collections of the prince-bishops.
- Citadel of Namur, fortified since Celtic times, with breathtaking views from the approaching cable car.

First and foremost, Liège is a city of rebels. It has, in fact, well earned its nickname, "La Cité Ardente" (the hot-blooded city). Its most beloved symbol is Tchantchès, a puppet dressed in blue smock, patched trousers, tasseled floppy hat, and red scarf who has since the 1850s been the spokesman of the streets, grumbling at just about everything in sight while espousing every noble cause in sight—the personification of your average, everyday Liègeois.

The powerful prince-bishop of Liège, who held sway over both secular and religious matters, rebelled against every foreign would-be ruler (so angering Charles the Bold of Burgundy that in 1468 he ordered the complete destruction of the city, a task that continued for several weeks and became one of history's most awesome feats of utter devastation, leaving only the churches intact), and the citizens rebelled against the prince-bishops. Not really surprising, since a 12th-century charter guaranteed that "pauvre homme en sa maison est roi" (the poor man in his home is king), and the citizens were not about to forget it—an attitude that is vividly alive in 20th-century Liège.

Not surprising, either, that fiery rebellious Liègeois were ardent supporters of the French Revolution. When that war ended, so did the rule of the prince-bishops. Then, when Napoléon was defeated, it was the Dutch who moved in, but not for long; volunteers left Liège in droves to participate in the Brussels uprising in 1830 that firmly established Belgium as a nation in its own right. Invading German troops, upon reaching Liège in 1914, met that same fiercely independent spirit.

Through it all the city nurtured an impressive list of musicians whose names are legendary: César Franck was a native son, and violinists Ysaye, Beriot, and Vieuxtemps studied here.

Today Liège is one of Belgium's most important crossroads, with a railroad network and three major motorways linking it to the rest of Europe, and—as it has been for centuries—the Meuse serving as a principal commercial trade route.

What to See and Do

Most of the places you'll want to see lie along a 2-mile route, easily covered on foot; and from May to September, there are **boat cruises** on the Meuse (sailing schedules and points of departure are available from the tourist office).

St. Lambert Square and neighboring **Market Square** are the hub of Liège's throbbing daily life. This is where you'll find the 1698 **Perron fountain,** the symbol of freedom to these freedom-loving people, and the 18th-century **Town Hall,** with its lobby sculptures by Delcour.

Note: Financial difficulties have forced the closing of some of Liège's museums, although they are beginning to reopen. The hours listed below are normal opening times, but *be sure to check with the tourist office* for possible changes.

★ **Cathedral of St. Paul,** rue St-Paul 2A.

Except during church services, to see the cathedral's priceless treasures, you may apply to the sacristan (not to worry, you'll be expected). It's a sight not to be missed, if only because of the 13th-century polychrome *Madonna and Child* by the high altar and the white marble and oak pulpit. In the cloisters, the **treasury** holds a small but exquisite collection that includes the gold reliquary that was Charles the Bold's gift of penance after wiping out the city and every able-bodied man in it. The work of Charles's personal court jeweler, the small masterpiece shows a repentant Charles kneeling as St. George looks on. Nearby, a bas-relief depicting the Crucifixion is believed to contain a piece of the True Cross. Also impressive is the bust reliquary of St. Lambert that dates from the early 1500s. Scenes from the saint's life are depicted, and it holds his skull.

Admission: Treasury, BF 50 ($1.40) adults, BF 30 (85¢) children.

Open: Daily 10am–noon and 2–5pm.

Church of St. Bartholomew, place Paul-Janson.

This twin-towered Romanesque church in the city center dates back to 1108, and its baptismal font is the creation of master metalsmith Renier de Huy. Cast in copper and brass in the early 1100s, it is counted among "Belgium's Magnificent Seven." The huge font rests on the backs of 10 small oxen and is surrounded by five beautifully sculpted biblical scenes—truly magnificent.

Open: Tues–Fri 10am–noon and 2–5pm, Sat 2–5pm.

★ **Church of St. Jacques,** place St-Jacques 8. ☎ **22-35-36.**

A happy mixture of architectural styles that are the result of some 400 years of reconstruction and renovation gives this church a Gothic Flamboyant exterior, Romanesque narthex, and Renaissance porch. But it is its intricately designed vaulted ceiling inside that makes it one of the most beautiful interiors in Liège. Call for guided-tour information. It's in the city center, south of the Cathedral of St. Paul.

Open: Sun–Fri 8am–noon, Sat 8am–noon and 4–6pm.

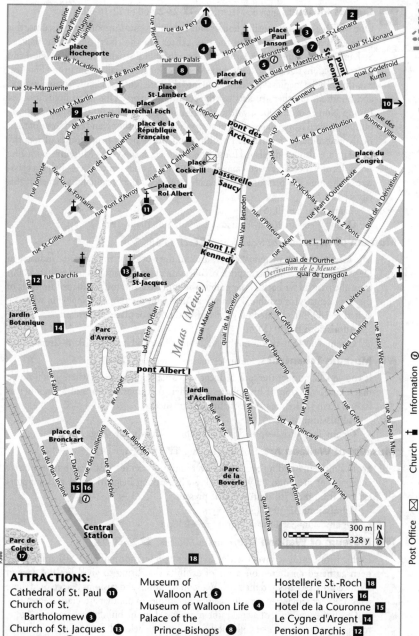

Liège

ATTRACTIONS:

Cathedral of St. Paul ⑪
Church of St. Bartholomew ③
Church of St. Jacques ⑬
The Citadel ①
Curtius Museum ⑦
Museum of Arms ⑥

Museum of Walloon Art ⑤
Museum of Walloon Life ④
Palace of the Prince-Bishops ⑧
Park of Birds ⑰

ACCOMMODATIONS:

Holiday Inn Liège ⑩

Hostellerie St.-Roch ⑱
Hotel de l'Univers ⑯
Hotel de la Couronne ⑮
Le Cygne d'Argent ⑭
Pension Darchis ⑫
Post House Hotel ②
Ramada Liège ⑨

Post Office ⊠   Information ⓘ   Church ✝■

9566

★ **Curtius Museum,** quai de Maestricht. ☎ **23-20-68** or **22-16-00**.

One of Liège's most beautiful houses and Belgium's most important museums, this turreted red-brick mansion in the city center, on the riverfront north of place St-Lambert, was built in the early 1600s by a local industrialist. Its archeological and crafts collections trace the history of the Meuse region from Gallo-Roman and Frankish eras through the medieval period and on into the 18th century. Coins, jewelry, swords, and hundreds of other artifacts tell the continuing story. One room holds relics of Bishop Notger of the 900s, whose "Evangeliary" (prayer book) is covered with exquisitely carved ivory. There are portraits of the prince-bishops, and even some of their richly embroidered vestments. Furniture and works of art from homes of wealthy Liègeois are also on display. Housed here as well is the Glass Museum, with fine examples of Venetian, Phoenician, Roman, Chinese, and—of course!—Belgian glassware. The museum presents a remarkable glimpse of the breathtaking riches of this city's past.

Admission: BF 50 ($1.40).

Open: Wed–Fri 10am–1pm and 2–5pm, Sun 10am–1pm.

Museum of Arms, quai de Maestricht 8. ☎ **21-94-16**.

The manufacture of weapons for sale around the world has been a major industry in Liège for centuries, and this impressive collection of prime examples (more than 3,000) from the past (as far back as the prehistoric stone axe and muzzle-loaded firearms of the 15th century) is exhibited in a private mansion that housed Napoléon when he visited in 1803. It's located on the riverfront, north of place St-Lambert.

Admission: BF 50 ($1.40).

Open: Tues–Sat 10am–noon and 2–5pm, Sun and holidays 10am–2pm.

★ **Museum Tchantchès,** rue Surlet 56, in Outremeuse. ☎ **42-75-75**.

If you've fallen under the spell of Liège's favorite puppet, this is where you'll find a marvelous collection of his cohorts and their costumes. From mid-September to Easter, there are frequent marionette performances.

Admission: BF 20 (55¢).

Open: Tues–Fri 2–4pm, Sun noon–2pm. **Closed:** July–Aug.

Museum of Walloon Art, En Féronstrée 86. ☎ **21-92-31**.

Set in a modern building over by the river in the city center, this small but impressive collection of the works of Walloon (French-speaking Belgian) artists and sculptors extends from the 17th century to the present.

Admission: BF 50 ($1.40).

Open: Mon–Sat 1–6pm, Sun 11am–4:30pm.

★ **Museum of Walloon Life,** cour des Mineurs. ☎ **23-60-94**.

In this 17th-century convent setting in the city center, north of place St-Lambert, has been gathered an incredible array of exhibits that bring to vivid life the days of 19th-century Liègeois and their rich Walloon traditions and customs that colored those days. It's very moving to view in one place examples of popular art, crafts, recreation, and even the workings of a coal mine reproduced in the building's basement. Here, too, is a marvelous puppet collection, including the beloved Tchantchès.

Admission: BF 80 ($2.80).

Open: Tues–Sat 10am–12:30pm and 2–5pm, Sun 10am–4pm.

Palace of the Prince-Bishops, place St-Lambert.

It's easy to feel the immense power of Liège's longtime rulers in the city center as you approach this massive Gothic structure, which took the form you see today from a 16th-century reconstruction. Of primary interest are the two inner courtyards, one lined with 60 carved columns depicting the follies of human nature, the other a quiet, beautiful space that held the gardens of the prince-bishops when they were in residence. The council chambers of the palace are hung with gorgeous Brussels tapestries, and it is sometimes possible to arrange a guided tour through the tourist office. Now the Palace of Justice, this historic building houses courtrooms and administrative offices.

Admission: Free.

Open: Mon–Fri 10am–5pm.

WALKING HIGHLIGHTS

For a feel of **Old Liège,** stroll through the narrow, twisting streets and stairways on Mont St-Martin, all lined with fine old houses.

For superb **views of the city** and the broad, curving Meuse, climb the 353 steps of **de Beuren staircase** off rue Hors-Château. They lead to the hill of **Sainte Walburge,** which has been the setting of more than its share of the bloodier side of Liège's history. It was here, in 1468, that 600 citizens made a heroic attempt to assassinate Charles the Bold, who was encamped with his Burgundian troops. They failed and were massacred to the man. In 1830 a decisive battle in Belgium's fight for independence took place here; in 1914 locals held German forces at bay here long enough for the French to regroup and go on to the vitally important Battle of the Marne; and in 1940 invading German troops met with that same stubborn resistance from the city's defenders.

On the hill of Cointe, the wooded **Park of Birds** is a pleasant, relaxing vantage point for panoramic views of the city. The third hill overlooking Liège is Robermont, where 50 local patriots were executed en masse in 1914.

Where to Stay

What may surprise you about Liège is that its two leading hotels bear the names of American chains. There is, however, an exceptional country inn just 18 miles away, one that offers a much more regional experience yet is within easy driving distance of the city.

EXPENSIVE

Holiday Inn Liège, esplanade de l'Europe 2, 4000 Liège. ☎ **041/42-60-20,** or toll free **800/HOLIDAY** in the U.S. Fax 041/43-48-10. 219 rms. MINIBAR TV TEL

Rates: BF 5,250 ($150) single; BF 5,620 ($160) double. AE, DC, MC, V.

On the Outremeuse side of the Meuse, this giant modern hotel offers all you'd expect of this chain, with exceptionally large, nicely decorated rooms that have queen-size beds in addition to all the usual amenities, a pool, and wheelchair access.

Dining/Entertainment: There's a good restaurant and a pleasant bar popular with locals as well as guests.

Services: Babysitting.

 Post House Hotel, rue Hurbise 160, 4400 Herstal. ☎ **041/64-64-00.** Fax 041/48-06-90. 96 rms. TV TEL

Rates (including breakfast): BF 4,125 ($118) single; BF 5,370 ($153) double. AE, DC, MC, V.

This deluxe modern hotel is 7 miles outside Liège, off the E40 motorway. If it's comfortable accommodations you're after, this is the place to make your base while in the area. The guest rooms are all nicely furnished and decorated. The hotel provides a pool and wheelchair access.

Dining/Entertainment: The restaurant is highly recommended (see "Where to Dine," below).

★ **Hôtel Ramada Liège,** bd. de la Sauvenière 100, 4000 Liège. ☎ **041/21-77-11.** Fax 041/21-77-01. 105 rms, 3 suites. MINIBAR TV TEL

Rates: BF 5,500 ($157) single or double; BF 8,000–10,000 ($228–$285) suite. AE, DC, MC, V. **Parking:** Garage.

In a top location—in the center of Liège, on the edge of the Old City—the Ramada is thoroughly modern, with wheelchair access and recently refurbished, attractive guest rooms with modern decor and furnishings. It's a favorite with European business visitors as well as travelers.

Dining/Entertainment: Its award-winning restaurant is highly recommended, and the bar becomes a "boulevard café" in spring and summer.

Services: Babysitting.

MODERATE

★ **Le Cygne d'Argent,** rue Beeckman 49, 4000 Liège. ☎ **041/23-70-01.** Fax 041/22-49-66. 23 rms. MINIBAR TV TEL

Rates: BF 1,800 ($51) single; BF 2,500 ($71) double. AE, DC, MC, V.

There's a nice homey atmosphere at this small hotel. The guest rooms vary in size, and furnishings are in traditional style. They can provide photocopying for guests, as well as limousine service and car rental. The hotel is located near the train station and the commercial and administrative center.

Hôtel de la Couronne, place des Guillemins 11, 4000 Liège. ☎ **041/52-21-68.** Fax 041/54-16-69. 76 rms, 1 suite. TV TEL

Rates: BF 1,285 ($37) single; BF 1,767 ($50) double; BF 10,000 ($285) suite. AE, DC, MC, V.

The guest rooms here come in a variety of styles. All are comfortable, with modern furnishings, but rather plain in decor. It's near the railway station.

Hôtel de l'Univers, rue des Guillemins 116, 4000 Liège. ☎ **041/52-26-50.** Fax 041/52-16-53. Telex 42-424. 53 rms (49 with bath). TV TEL

Rates (including breakfast): BF 1,400 ($40) single without bath, BF 1,750 ($50) single with bath; BF 1,800 ($51) double without bath. BF 2,100 ($60) double with bath. AE, DC, MC, V.

There's good value for the dollar in this medium-size hotel near the railway station, where the guest rooms are modest in decor, but quite comfortable. There's no restaurant, but several are within walking distance.

INEXPENSIVE

Some of the least expensive accommodations in Liège are in the vicinity of the main railway station. Most are small establishments, clean and comfortable, that offer the moneysaving option of forgoing a private bath. Rates without bath will range from BF 800 to 1,000 ($23 to $28) single without bath, BF 1,000 to 1,300 ($28 to $37) single with bath, BF 1,000 to 1,400 ($28 to $40) double without bath, BF 1,400 to 1,900 ($40 to $54) double with bath.

Especially recommended are: **Pension Darchis,** rue Darchis 18, 4000 Liège (☎ **041/23-42-18**); and **Hôtel du Midi,** place des Guillemins 1, 4000 Liège (☎ **041/52-20-04**).

AN INN NEARBY

 Hostellerie Saint-Roch, rue du Parc 1, 4180 Comblain-la-Tour.
☎ **041/69-13-33.** Fax 041/69-31-31. 12 rms, 5 suites. MINIBAR TV TEL

$ **Rates** (including breakfast): BF 2,900 ($83) single; BF 3,600 ($102) double; BF 5,800 ($65) suite. AE, DC, MC, V.

Although it entails an 18-mile drive to and from the city—south of Liège on the Durbuy road—this country inn is so loaded with charm that it merits my personal top recommendation. It also makes an ideal base for Ardennes day trips. Its gourmet restaurant makes the drive worthwhile for a meal, even if you elect to stay elsewhere. The elegant dining room looks out onto well-tended lawns and gardens dotted with comfortable seating, and there's a riverside terrace for drinks on a summer evening. Each of the luxurious guest rooms is done up in a refined country style. I suspect it is the warm friendliness of owners Frances and Nicole Dernouchamps that prompts so many Americans to extend an overnight stay into several days. Although usually fully booked out for summer weekends, weekdays are often pretty quiet, but advance reservations are strongly recommended.

Where to Dine

The Liègeois are especially proud of their local white sausage (boudin blanc de Liège), and are also fond of thrushes (grives) and goose.

EXPENSIVE

 Au Vieux Liège, quai de la Goffe 41. ☎ **23-77-48.**
Cuisine: SEAFOOD/CONTINENTAL. **Reservations:** Required.
Prices: Fixed-price meal BF 1,100 ($31) at lunch, BF 2,000 ($57) at dinner. AE, DC, MC, V.
Open: Lunch Mon–Sat noon–2:45pm; dinner Mon–Sat 6:30–9:45pm. **Closed:** Mid-July to mid-Aug.

This marvelous restaurant is located in the city center in a four-story 16th-century town house furnished in antiques of that era. Dinner is by candlelight, the waiters are in formal attire, and the food outshines even the setting. Try almost any fish dish (canneloni de poisson au fenouil is a good choice).

 La Diligence, in the Post House, rue Hurbise 160, Herstal. ☎ **64-64-00.**
Cuisine: BELGIAN/CONTINENTAL. **Reservations:** Required.
Prices: Fixed-price meal BF 1,000 ($28) at lunch, BF 1,900 ($54) at dinner. AE, DC, MC, V.
Open: Lunch daily noon–2pm; dinner daily 6:30–10pm.

Just on the outskirts of Liège off E40 in the large modern hotel listed above, this fine restaurant is worth the drive. Prominent on the menu are several traditional Ardennes dishes, as well as steak, roast beef, and veal.

Rôtisserie de la Sauvenière, in the Hôtel Ramada Liège, bd. de la Sauvenière 100. ☎ **21-77-11.**

Cuisine: NOUVELLE/FRENCH. **Reservations:** Required.
Prices: Fixed-price lunch or dinner BF 1,150–1,950 ($32–$55); buffet lunch BF 1,100–1,400 ($31–$40). AE, MC, V.
Open: Lunch daily noon–2:30pm; dinner daily 7–10:30pm.

Nouvelle cuisine adaptations of classic French cuisine are featured at this elegant hotel restaurant on the edge of the Old City. While the set menus offer a host of mouth-watering specialties, don't miss out on the succulent leg of lamb.

MODERATE

$ **Brasserie as Ouhès,** place du Marché 21 ☎ **23-32-25.**

Cuisine: BELGIAN. **Reservations:** Not required.
Prices: Average three-course meal BF 750–2,000 ($21–57). AE, MC, V.
Open: Lunch Mon–Fri noon–2:30pm; dinner Mon–Sat 6pm–midnight.

Liège specialties are served with a flair in this tastefully decorated, rather large restaurant across from Town Hall and set on a narrow oblong public plaza that also holds a number of quite adequate, moderately priced eateries. Ouhès, however, is the best in its price range, and its menu is large enough to suit everyone's taste. Duck appears in more than one guise, and I am partial to the homard grillé, sauce béarnaise. It's extremely popular with local businesspeople at lunch, so go early or late.

Brasserie du Midi, place des Guillemins 1. ☎ **52-20-04.**

Cuisine: BELGIAN/FRENCH. **Reservations:** Not required.
Prices: Plat du jour BF 500 ($14); three-course meal BF 900 ($25). MC, V.
Open: Daily 7am–midnight.

This eatery directly in front of the train station is part of the Hôtel du Midi which occupies a three-story red-brick house. The favorites here are the pizzas, averaging $10 each, and sandwiches, which are available for about $4.

Chez François, rue des Bégards 2. ☎ **22-92-34.**

Cuisine: FRENCH. **Reservations:** Not required.
Prices: Lunch BF 1,000 ($28); dinner BF 2,000 ($56). AE, DC, MC, V.
Open: Lunch Tues–Fri noon–2pm; dinner daily 6–10pm.

In an intimate, 16th-century setting amid a magnificent garden, you dine in the open air at the foot of Mont St-Martin on the edge of the Old City. The menu is rather extensive, and I am especially partial to the way they prepare duck.

Rôtisserie l'Empereur, place du 20-Août 15. ☎ **23-53-73.**

Cuisine: SEAFOOD/GRILLS. **Reservations:** Not required.
Prices: Average three-course meal BF 1,400 ($40). AE, MC, V.
Open: Lunch Wed–Sun noon–2:30pm; dinner Wed–Sun 6–10pm. **Closed:** Aug.

Convenience makes this a good stop on your sightseeing itinerary in the Old City. Near the university, this popular eatery will draw you back time and again for the food alone. Seafood comes in many forms, and the grills are excellent.

INEXPENSIVE

A concentration of quite good, inexpensive restaurants (along with a few costlier eateries that have moved across the river) can be found along rue Roture in Outremeuse (there's a convenient footbridge to reach it from the Old City). Meals in most can be selected from à la carte menus with main courses at about BF 600 ($17). Don't be guided by outward appearance, for many of these present a near-shabby face to the street, yet along with the plain exteriors (and interiors, as well) comes very good food, with pleasant service and the company of locals who know good value when they see it.

A NEARBY RESTAURANT

⭐ **Hostellerie Saint-Roch**, rue du Parc 1, Comblain-la-Tour. ☎ **69-13-33.**

Cuisine: BELGIAN/CONTINENTAL. **Reservations:** Required.

💲 **Prices:** Fixed-price meals BF 1,600–2,600 ($74). AE, DC, MC, V.

Open: Sept–June, lunch Wed–Sun noon–2:20pm; dinner Wed–Sun 6–9pm. July–Aug, lunch daily noon–2:20pm; dinner daily 6–9pm.

Meals in this delightful inn just 18 miles from Liège (see "Where to Stay," above) deserve the designation "gourmet." The setting alone is worth the trip out from town— but when pike or trout fresh from the river outside arrives at table accompanied by vegetables from the inn's own garden, well, all else fades into insignificance. In season, venison from the Ardennes region also makes an appearance.

Shopping

Liège makes shopping a joy by the simple expedient of closing principal streets to all but pedestrian traffic. Those to seek out (all lined with some 5,000 shops and boutiques carrying merchandise of every description and price range) are: rue du Pont-d'Avroy, Vinave d'Ile, rue des Dominicains, rue St-Paul, boulevard d'Avroy, boulevard de la Sauvenière, rue de la Cathédrale, rue Charles-Magnette, rue de la Régence, rue de l'Université, place du Marché, Neuvice et Féronstrée, rue Puits-en-Sock, and rue Jean-d'Outremeuse.

LA BATTE MARKET On Sunday morning, the oldest ✪ **street market** in Europe—and surely one of the most colorful—is strung out along the quai de la Batte on the city side of the Meuse. If there is anything not sold in this mile-long bazaar of stalls, it doesn't come to mind as you stroll past items of brass, clothes, flowers, foodstuffs, jewelry, birds, animals, books, radios, and . . . the list is simply endless. Shoppers from as far away as Holland and Germany join sightseers like you and me, as well as what seems to be at least half the population of Liège. If you're anywhere near Liège on a Sunday, plan to pop in on this marvelous shopping hodgepodge, even if only for the people-watching.

Evening Entertainment

When the sun goes down (and even when it's up), the native Liègeois head for their pick of the city's hundreds of **cafés** and **taverns** to quaff Belgium's famous beers and engage in their favorite entertainment, good conversation. If a quiet evening of the same appeals to you, you'll have no problem finding a locale. Two that can be recommended are the **British Pub,** rue Tête-de-Boeuf 14, and **Tchantchès,** En Grande-Bêche 35 in Outremeuse.

For livelier nighttime fun, there are numerous nightspots in the Old City's "carré" (bounded by rue du Pot-d'Or, rue St-Jean, and rue Tête-de-Boeuf) and along rue Roture in Outremeuse.

The **Théâtre Royal de LAC,** near the Church of St. Jacques, presents concerts by the city's excellent philharmonic orchestra, as well as operas, operettas, and ballets. Concerts are also performed at the **Conservatory of Music.** For schedules and prices of current performances, contact **Infor-Spectacles,** rue en Feronstrée 92 (☎ **22-11-11**), between 11am and 6pm Monday through Friday.

Theaters staging puppet shows performed by the ◼ **Théâtre des Marionnettes** (in dialect, but easy to follow) are in the Museum of Walloon Life, the Tchantchès Museum, and the Al Botroule Museum. Liègeois wit is especially visible as the puppets appear, each sized according to his historical importance—for example, a huge Charles the Bold is attended by midget archers (although just how important Charles would have been without those archers may be debatable!).

Easy Excursions

TONGEREN Within easy day-tripping is Tongeren, Belgium's oldest town. Founded in the 1st century A.D., it has the imposing **Basilica of Our Lady,** a Gothic church with a Brabantine tower and a Romanesque cloister. Its rich treasury has rare religious objets d'art from the Merovingian era up to the 18th century, and it's open from 9am to 5pm daily, with admission of BF 60 ($1.70). Also worth a visit is the **Provincial Gallo-Roman Museum,** with some 18,000 artifacts dating from prehistory through the Roman and Merovingian periods. The Roman period is very important because of the huge collection from Atuatuca Tungrurum, the capital of the Civitas Tungrorum, its cemetery, and the surrounding countryside. Indeed, from the entire province of Limburg, there are collections of pottery, glassware, bronze articles, terra-cotta, and sculptures. They're organized by theme to illustrate everyday life in the countryside and the city, religious practices, etc. Adjacent to the museum is a library and the **Provincial Cabinet of Coins,** open Tuesday through Saturday from 9am to noon and 2 to 5pm, and on Sunday from 2 to 5pm. Admission is BF 60 ($1.70).

For more information, call the Tongeren tourist office (☎ **012/23-29-61**).

OTHER NEARBY EXCURSION TOWNS An interesting Ardennes day trip is to nearby **Spa,** the town whose name has come to mean any health and fitness center. See Chapter 10 for details on Spa, or contact the Spa tourist office (☎ **087/77-25-10**). Both **Huy** and **Namur** (see below) are also close enough for comfortable day-trips.

2 Along the River Meuse

The drive from Liège to Namur traces the River Meuse; and once beyond the industrial outskirts of Liège, the scenery along the river evolves into small towns every few miles, with one of the many castles of the Meuse Valley never far away.

Jehay-Bodegnée

To visit one of the most beautiful castles in the Meuse Valley, take a short detour off the Liège–Huy road (N17) to the small village of Jehay-Bodegnée (look for the turnoff to Amay, then turn left at Amay toward Tongres).

★ **Castle of Jehay,** 4540 Amay. ☎ **085/31-17-16** or **51-28-49**.

This wondrous moated castle is now presided over by the talented and charming Comte Guy van den Steen de Jehay, whose personal history is as fascinating as that of his home. Artist, sculptor, and ironwright, with a keen interest in archeology, he is often on hand as visitors roam through the castle that has belonged to his family since the late 1600s. Moats reflect the castle's striking construction of light and dark stone arranged in checkerboard fashion, with round towers at each end of a central rectangular block. Inside, the rooms are filled with paintings, tapestries, lace from the private collections of the prince-bishops of Liège, silver and gold pieces, jewels, porcelain and glass, antique furniture, and family heirlooms.

Not the least of the castle's treasures, however, are the works of the present count. Be sure to look especially for the bronze *Pythagoras* and a stunning *Marsyas Tortured by the Nymph,* a three-dimensional progressive relief in an innovative technique pioneered by the count. The magnificent ironwork you see in the form of gates and railings is also his work.

Before leaving the castle for the grounds (in which the count has restored and redesigned lawns and gardens beautified with many sculptures and Italian fountains), anyone with even a smidgen of historical curiosity will want to inspect the Celtic foundations that have been unearthed by the present owner. His archeological findings on the estate have revealed clear evidence that this site was inhabited more than 30,000 years ago, and there's a fascinating museum in the vaulted cellars where you can view the leavings of the Mesolithic age, Romans, Gauls, Carolingian Franks, and their successors into the Middle Ages. No visitor should leave without seeing this remarkable private collection of humankind's past in the Meuse Valley. Nor should you miss the castle's chapel on a small islet, which has always served as the parish church, as it does today.

The castle is open only in July and August, on Saturday, Sunday, and public holidays from 2 to 6pm, but phone first (☎ **085/31-17-16**). Admission is BF 200 ($5.70).

Huy

This charming little town on the Meuse began as a thriving center for tin, copper, and wine merchants (its charter was granted in 1066), and has a long tradition of local metalwork. Its most famous native son, Renier de Huy, was the 12th-century goldsmith who designed the baptismal font in Liège's Church of St. Bartholomew. Today pewter holds center stage and Huy's shops are filled with lovely pewter bowls, goblets, pitchers, and other items. The **Town Museum (Musée Communal),** at rue Van Keerberghen 20 (☎ **085/23-24-35**), displays local metalwork, as well as glass objects.

In Grand' Place, the beautiful copper fountain dates back to the 1400s and is known locally as **Li Bassinia.** Also in Grand' Place—not a work of art perhaps, but certainly a haven for a weary sightseer—the Whitbread Pub makes a good stop to refresh body and soul as you contemplate the daily life of this little medieval town. Better yet, you're in luck if you're there when the carillon in the elegant 18th-century Town Hall rings out "Brave Liègeois," as it does every hour.

Huy is an enchanting place in which to stroll through quaint little streets that contrast so dramatically with today's busy thoroughfares. From Grand' Place, walk down rue des Rôtisseurs, rue des Augustins, and rue Vierset-Godin.

The 14th-century Gothic ✪ **Notre-Dame Collegiate Church** is famed for its mammoth *Li Rondia,* a beautiful rose window, as well as stained-glass windows in the choir. In its treasury, the star is an impressive Romanesque shrine of St. Mengold and many items in chiseled copper. Take notice, too, of the stone bas-reliefs along tiny arcaded rue des Cloitres that runs along the side of the church.

High atop a hill overlooking the town, the **Citadel** is almost modern as Belgium measures time—it was built in 1818. It sits where a castle rose in ancient times, and it affords a marvelous view of the town and river below. Take the cable car over, May 1 to mid-September, daily from 10am to 6:30pm.

For more information about Huy, call the tourist office (☎ **085/21-29-15**).

Namur

It is at Namur that the Meuse is joined by the River Sambre, and it is dominated by the awesome Citadel atop a cliff above the town, which hugs the riverbanks. It's considered by many to be the true "Gateway to the Ardennes," and many choose to make this their touring base. Hotel accommodations are limited, however, and you may want to look a little farther into the Ardennes, where several rather special hostelries await (see Chapter 10).

WHAT TO SEE & DO

The presence of that great, brooding Citadel is evidence of the strategic importance attached to Namur in centuries past. Today, however, you will find it a quiet, peaceful town with interesting churches and rows of 17th-century brick homes.

The **tourist office** is in square Europe near the railway station (☎ **081/22-28-59**), open Monday through Friday from 9am to 12:30pm and 1:30 to 6pm. Also, a **tourist office** for the **Province of Namur** is at place St-Aubain 3 (☎ **081/22-29-98**).

Cathedral of St. Aubain, rue de l'Evéché. ☎ **22-03-20.**

The 18th-century Renaissance Italian Cathedral of St. Aubain is built on the site of a 1047 collegiate church of the same name that became the cathedral of the diocese of Namur in 1559. The tower of that earlier building, restored in 1388, remains, with an arrow dated 1648 imbedded on its summit. While not an exact replica of the original building, the present cathedral is indeed impressive, with its columns, pilasters, cornices, vessels, and balustrades. In its **Diocesan Museum** (on the left as you leave the cathedral) is an interesting collection of ecclesiastical relics, gold plate, and sculptures.

Admission: BF 50 ($1.40) adults, BF 25 (70¢) children.

Open: Tues–Sat 10am–noon and 2:30–6pm, Sun 2:30–6pm. **Closed:** Holidays.

★ **Citadel of Namur**, route Merveilleuse 8. ☎ **22-68-29.**

The Citadel is a sightseeing "must." There has been a fortification atop this bluff since Celtic times, after which came the earls of Namur, and then the Dutch, who are responsible for its present shape. Visitors are shown a film on the history of the Citadel and given a tour of the fortifications themselves. The intriguing underground caverns can be explored (by torchlight) with a guide on a 45-minute tour. There's an interesting museum of the forest. A small excursion train runs through the extensive grounds on a 30-minute round-trip.

It's possible to reach the Citadel by car via a narrow, winding road, but I strongly advise using the comfortable cable car—the view during the trip is breathtaking. There's a coffee shop at the top.

Admission: Citadel and museums (includes a 20-minute film), BF 195 ($5.50) adults, BF 100 ($2.85) children.

Open: Daily 11am–7pm. **Cable Car:** Departs from Pied-du-Château Square Easter–Oct, daily 9am–7pm.

Convent of the Sisters of Notre-Dame, rue Julie-Billiart 17.

The convent in the center of town holds Namur's richest prize, the treasures of the Oignies Priory that feature the work of 13th-century master goldsmith Brother Hugo of Oignies. The jewel-studded crosses and reliquaries are decorated with forest motifs and hunting scenes.

Admission: BF 50 ($1.40).

Open: Daily 2–5pm. **Closed:** Last two weeks of Dec.

Félicien Rops Museum, rue Fumal 12. ☎ **22-01-10.**

The work of native son Félicien Rops, a 19th-century engraver and painter, is displayed in this museum near the artist's birthplace in the old quarter of town. The perfection of his soft-ground etchings and drypoint work is internationally recognized, and he is indisputably one of the most outstanding engravers of the late 19th century.

Admission: BF 100 ($2.85).

Open: Daily 10am–5pm. **Closed:** Tues Sept–June.

Nearby Attractions

⭐ Ten miles south of Namur, ✪ **Les Jardins d'Annevoie,** 5537 Annevoie (☎ **082/61-15-55**), the gardens and manor house at Annevoie, should top every sightseeing list for this part of Belgium. The present owner, Jean de Montpellier, lives here with his family and presides over what is sometimes called the "Versailles of Belgium."

While there are indeed similarities to such French classics, those at Annevoie are also reminiscent of Italian and English gardens, yet they possess a unique quality that gives them special character not found elsewhere—the fountains, waterfalls, lagoons, and peaceful canals that are their centerpiece are all engineered without the use of any artificial power. No throbbing pump or other machinery intrudes on their sylvan tranquillity. By an ingenious use of canals to channel natural streams through an uneven terrain, the designer created an entirely *natural* landscape of exquisite beauty. Originally laid out in the mid-1700s by a member of the de Montpellier family, these grounds have been carefully tended and added to by successive generations.

The 18th-century **château** and its outbuildings are laid out in a harmonious design reflected in the lagoon alongside, and inside there are fine architectural details in the woodwork, stuccos, fireplaces, and family chapel.

The Annevoie gardens are open from March 31 to November 3 daily from 9am to 7pm; the château, daily from 9:30am to 6:30pm in July and August, on weekends and holidays only from mid-April through June and the month of September. Visits are limited to 45-minute guided tours at a cost of BF 300 ($8.50) for both, BF 200 ($5.70) for the gardens only, BF 150 ($4.25) for the château only. In addition to a gift shop, there's a rustic pub, decorated with ancient farming implements, that serves snacks, and a full-service restaurant.

WHERE TO STAY

As stated above, accommodations are a bit limited in Namur. The tourist office can help, and there is the option of staying outside town at nearby hostelries.

⭐ **Hôtel Excelsior,** av. de la Gare 4, 5000 Namur. ☎ **081/23-18-13.**
Fax 081/23-09-29. 14 rms. TV TEL

Rates: BF 1,500 ($42) single; BF 2,000 ($56) double; BF 2,700 ($76) triple. AE, DC, MC, V.

This comfortable small hotel with wheelchair access is conveniently located in the town center; the per-room rate may vary a little depending on whether you have a shower or full bath. There's a bar and restaurant on premises.

 Novotel Namur, chaussée de Dinant 1149, 5100 Wépion. ☎ **081/46-08-11.**
Fax 081/46-19-90. 97 rms. MINIBAR TV TEL **Directions:** Take the E411 Brussels–Luxembourg motorway to Exit 14.

Rates (including breakfast): BF 3,400 ($97) single; BF 4,200 ($120) double. AE, DC, MC, V.

Not quite 3 miles from Namur, this is an excellent hotel in a garden setting. The guest rooms are nicely appointed, and facilities include a children's playground, Ping-Pong table, and pool. Close by are golf, tennis, and squash facilities. There's a cozy bar and good restaurant (see "Where to Dine," below).

 Queen Victoria, av. de la Gare 12, 5000 Namur. ☎ **081/22-29-71.**
Fax 081/24-11-00. 21 rms. TV TEL

Rates (including breakfast): BF 1,650 ($47) single; BF 2,050 ($85) double. AE, DC, MC, V.

Although small, this is one of the best of the in-town hotels, with comfortable, nicely furnished guest rooms. There's a bar and good, moderately priced restaurant (see "Where to Dine," below).

WHERE TO DINE

The best meals in and near Namur are in the hotel restaurants listed below and the small bistros (many with sidewalk café service in good weather) around place Marché-aux-Legumes, rue des Frippiers, and rue de la Croix, with prices in the moderate range. For inexpensive meals, look to the cluster of restaurants near the Citadel.

Novotel Namur, chaussée de Dinant 1149, Wépion. ☎ **46-08-11. Directions:** Take the E411 Brussels–Luxembourg motorway to Exit 14.

Cuisine: BELGIAN.
Prices: Average lunch BF 650 ($18); average dinner BF 1,000 ($28). AE, DC, MC.

The quietly elegant restaurant in this hotel specializes in dishes based on local ingredients prepared in traditional methods of this area. Look for fresh trout, Ardennes ham, and lamb. It's located about 3 miles from the town center.

 Le Queen, in the Queen Victoria Hotel, av. de la Gare 12. ☎ **22-29-71.**
Cuisine: SEAFOOD/FRENCH. **Reservations:** Not required.
Prices: Menu of the day BF 600 ($17); fixed-price meal BF 1,200 ($34); average á la carte meal BF 800 ($23). AE, DC, MC, V.
Open: Lunch daily noon–2:30pm; dinner daily 6–11:30pm.

This pleasant hotel restaurant in the town center offers an extensive menu, with such specialties as sole meunière and an excellent bouillabaisse of the North Sea.

The Ardennes

10

THE ARDENNES IS BELGIUM'S WILDEST, MOST HEAVILY FORESTED REGION—AND ITS least heavily populated. The country's landscape slides easily from Flanders's flatness into rolling countryside along the Meuse Valley, then almost abruptly begins to climb into the dense greenery of this mountain range, an extension of the Eifel Massif that stretches from Germany across Luxembourg and this part of Belgium, then on into France.

Villages become farther apart and take on a more uniformly medieval look. To the northeast, German is the language most often heard, a residue from the years before 1919 when the entire eastern Ardennes was a part of Germany. To the south and west, it is French that almost universally greets the visitor, reflecting the area's long and close relationship with France.

For Belgians, the Ardennes vies with the coast as a vacationland par excellence. For the tourist, it is a scenic treat, a gastronomic delight, and a welcome respite from sightseeing centered around ceaseless museum-hopping. That is not to say that the Ardennes is without worthwhile museums—only that with the change in landscape comes a shift of emphasis, from treasures hoarded indoors to outdoor treasures of bracing air, scenic winding mountain roads, sparkling streams, and tranquil lakes. Add a sprinkling of pretty resort towns and the sheer joy of nights lodged in quaint old country inns that provide the ultimate in comfort without losing one whit of their unique character, and you pretty much have the essence of a tour through the Ardennes.

For the sports lover, the Ardennes is a cornucopia of possibilities: canoeing, fishing, hunting, golf, tennis, horseback riding, and swimming. Tourist offices can point the way to any necessary rental equipment, and always there will be contingents of local enthusiasts to share the fun.

It's fair to say "the best way to explore the Ardennes is by car," yet it would be unfair to say it's the only way. A good railway and bus network reaches most points. Biking is a marvelous way to get around this corner of Belgium, and in many places it's possible to rent a bicycle at one train station and return it at another. Camping is very popular with young hikers and bikers, and hundreds of them flock here during summer months.

This is the home of that delicately smoked Ardennes ham so proudly served all over Belgium, and other regional specialties are trout and pike fresh from mountain streams and the game that is so plentiful in this hunter's paradise.

It's difficult to recommend an itinerary for the Ardennes: This is *rambling* country, yet so compact an area that it's equally suited to returning to the same "home away from home" each night or to booking into a different superb country hostelry each night as you move through the region. My personal preference is a night or two in the Dinant-Bouillon district followed by the same in the vicinity of Durbuy-Spa.

The Ardennes is famed for its wealth of gourmet restaurants, and most are part of the country inns in which the innkeeper is very often a fine chef.

1   Dinant, Bouillon, and Orval

Dinant

Dinant has never escaped any of the conflicts that raged in the Meuse Valley over the centuries, and it has gone head-on with the Liègeois, the Burgundians, the French, and the Germans. It was the Duke of Burgundy who demolished the town completely in the 1400s and drowned more than 800 of its residents in the Meuse. In World

What's Special About the Ardennes

Natural Attractions

- Ardennes Forest, the wildest, most forested, least populated region of Belgium.
- A cornucopia of sports possibilities: canoeing, fishing, hunting, hiking, golf, horseback riding, and swimming.
- Natural gastronomic delights—delicately smoked Ardennes ham, fresh trout and pike, plentiful game.
- Spa treatments at the Termes de Spa, in Spa.

Churches

- Abbey of Orval, an impressive complex of religious buildings in a forest setting, tended by a handful of months.

Castles and Fortresses

- Citadel, above Dinant, with two military museums and breathtaking views over the town and river.
- Castle of Bouillon, massive fortifications dating from the 10th century.

Memorials

- American Memorial, at Bastogne, a place of pilgrimage for World War II veterans.

War I the Germans—in a chilling replay of that 15th-century tragedy—executed nearly 700 citizens in reprisal for their stubborn resistance. A reminder of its military background is never out of sight in Dinant, for the 1530 Citadel that crowns a 100-yard bluff dominates the skyline.

Despite all the wars, the town developed such skill in working hammered copper that its engravings were sought after as early as the 13th century. Charles the Bold put a stop to such artistry when he razed the town, but in recent years it is once more coming to life, and you will see fine examples in town shops.

INFORMATION   The **Tourist Office** is at rue Grande 37 (☎ **082/22-28-70**; fax 082/22-77-88), and is open April through November, Monday through Friday from 9am to 7pm.

WHAT TO SEE & DO

The ✪ **Citadel,** Le Prieure, 5500 Anseremme-Dinant (☎ **082/22-36-70**), built in 1530 and perched high above the town and river, can be reached by car or cable car (my personal recommendation)—of course, if you're feeling particularly energetic or can't turn down the challenge, there are 400 steep steps leading to the bluff top. The **weapons museum** and **war museum** at the Citadel are interesting, and there's an audiovisual historical presentation in three languages (including English). But when all is said and done, it's the spectacular view that takes your breath away. Open Saturday through Thursday from 10am to 6pm in summer, from 10am to 4pm other months. Admission of BF 170 ($4.85) for adults and BF 130 ($3.70) for children includes the cable car.

The intriguing **Adolphe Sax Museum** (next door to Tourist Office; ☎ **082/22-28-70**) is near the home of this native son who invented the saxophone. Admission is free.

WHERE TO STAY

 L'Auberge de Bouvignes, rue Fétis 112, route de Namur, 5500 Dinant.
☎ **082/61-16-00.** 6 rms. TV TEL

Rates (including breakfast): BF 1,950 ($56) single; BF 3,000 ($86) double. AE, DC, MC, V.

Two miles from Dinant on route de Namur, this lovely soft-rose brick inn on the banks of the Meuse has one of the best kitchens around, and its six charming guest rooms, beautifully decorated and furnished, are perfect retreats after a day of busy sightseeing. Try to book well in advance.

 Auberge les Falizes, rue de France 70, 5580 Rochefort. ☎ **084/21-12-82.**
6 rms. TV TEL

Rates (including breakfast): BF 1,550 ($44) single; BF 1,850 ($53) double. AE, DC, MC, V.

If there is such a style as "rustic formal," it best describes this lovely little inn that sets velvet-covered chairs in a beamed-ceiling dining room whose plain white walls are as comfortable with gilt-framed paintings as with shelves of country china. That dining room enjoys the highest of reputations around the country, and the guest rooms combine comfort with country charm. One of the best of the small Ardennes inns, it's 20 miles from Dinant, 30 miles from Bouillon. Advance reservations are advised.

Hostellerie de la Poste, av. de Criel, 5370 Havelange. ☎ **083/63-30-90.**
9 rms (7 with bath). TV TEL

Rates (including breakfast): BF 1,500 ($43) single, without bath, BF 1,800 ($51) single with bath; BF 1,500 ($43) double without bath, BF 2,200 ($62) double with bath. AE, DC, MC, V. **Closed:** Jan and mid-Sept to mid-Oct.

Eighteen miles from Dinant, this 200-year-old roadside stone hostelry began life as a coach stop. There's a slightly sophisticated look to the decor, rather than the rustic ambience you might expect. The rooms are especially attractive and comfortable. The restaurant is of gourmet quality.

$ Hôtel de la Citadelle, place Reine-Astrid 5, 5500 Dinant. ☎ **082/22-35-43.**
20 rms (7 with bath). TV TEL

Rates (including breakfast): BF 1,600 ($45) single without bath, BF 1,800 ($51) single with bath; BF 1,700 ($48) double without bath, BF 2,300 ($65) double with bath. No credit cards. **Closed:** Dec–Feb.

This well-kept hotel, centrally located in Dinant, has comfortable rooms, a nice bar, and a reasonably priced restaurant.

 Hôtel de la Couronne, rue Adolphe-Sax 1, 5500 Dinant. ☎ **082/22-24-41** or
22-27-31. 22 rms (some with bath), 2 suites. TV TEL

Rates: BF 1,100 ($31) single without bath, BF 1,850 ($53) single with bath; BF 2,200 ($67) double with bath; BF 3,000 ($85) suite. AE, MC.

In the center of town, this pleasant hotel, which has a good, moderately priced restaurant and tavern, has comfortable and attractive rooms. There's a homey feeling about the place, which features traditional decor and furnishings.

WHERE TO DINE

Restaurant Thermidor, rue de la Station 3. ☎ **22-31-35.**

Cuisine: SEAFOOD. **Reservations:** Recommended.
Prices: Average meal BF 2,000–2,500 ($57–$71). AE, MC, V.
Open: Lunch Wed–Mon noon–2:30pm; dinner Wed–Sun 6–10pm.

Widely considered the best Dinant restaurant, the Thermidor specializes in such delicacies as crayfish dinantaise, and their country-style pâté is terrific. It's located in the town center.

★ **Les Ramiers,** rue Basse 32, Crupet. ☎ **083/69-90-70.**
$

Cuisine: CONTINENTAL. **Reservations:** Recommended.
Prices: Appetizers BF 400–900 ($11–$25); main courses BF 1,000–2,000 ($28–$56); fixed-price meal BF 1,600–2,600 ($45–$74). AE, DC, MC, V.
Open: Lunch Wed–Mon noon–2:30pm; dinner Wed–Mon 6–10pm.

Ten miles from Dinant, this country-style restaurant in a romantic little village is known for its gourmet creations. Try, for instance, the excellent salade tiède de saumon et langoustine au Noilly (salmon and shrimp) or grilled herbed lamb. In cool weather, eat in the simple beamed dining room; have dinner outside on the terrace when it's warm.

Bouillon

A little more than 38 miles southeast of Dinant, the little town of Bouillon sits at a strategic bend of the Semois River. For centuries it guarded the major route from Eifel to Champagne, and the awesome 10th-century feudal castle of Godefroy de Bouillon, leader of the First Crusade to the Holy Land, still stands guard over the town today. It's a stirring sight to see it floodlit, as it is every night during summer months. The **Tourist Office** is in the Bouillon Castle (☎ **061/46-62-57**), open daily from 10am to 5pm.

WHAT TO SEE & DO

Bouillon stretches along the banks of the Semois looking for all the world like a fairytale book illustration, with the massive, sprawling, fortified ⚔ **castle** that was home to Godefroy de Bouillon. That worthy gentleman actually put the castle in hock in order to raise funds for his venture, the First Crusade; and, sadly, he died in a foreign land, far from this pile of stone. That was back in 1096, and the mortgaged castle passed by default into the hands of the prince-bishops of Liège, who continued to hold it for six centuries. Since that time it has been conquered and reconquered as rulers and invading rulers fought over this strategic spot. Life within its thick walls during those turbulent years will come to vivid life as you walk through the ruins and see the old prisons and gallows and so-called Hall of Justice. Open every day, March to November, from 10am to 5pm; closed Monday and Thursday in December. Admission is BF 140 ($4) for adults, BF 70 ($2) for children.

The interesting **Godfrey of Bouillon Museum,** on the grounds, holds souvenirs of the Crusades as well as exhibits on the history and folklore of Bouillon and its ironworks. Admission is BF 120 ($3.40) for adults, BF 60 ($1.70) for children, which includes admission to the Ducal Museum (see below).

The **Ducal Museum,** rue du Petit 1, located in a house from the 18th century, holds exhibits on the region's archeology and folklore. Open daily (changing hours, but usually closed from noon to 2pm).

WHERE TO STAY

★ **Auberge du Moulin Hideux,** route de Dohan 1, 6831 Noirefontaine.
☎ **061/46-70-15.** Fax 061/46-72-81. 10 rms, 3 suites. MINIBAR TV TEL

$ **Rates** (including breakfast): BF 6,500 ($185) single or double; BF 7,500 ($214) suite. AE, DC, MC, V.

About 2¹/₂ miles from Bouillon, this is one of Belgium's prettiest country inns, set beside an old water mill, with wooded hills almost at its doorstep. Inside there's a warm, subdued sophistication to the decor, and a focal point is the crackling log fire, with luxurious leather furniture and touches of brass to complete the lounge scene. The glassed-in bar features plants, and the dining room gets top rating (see "Where to Dine," below). The 10 guest rooms are done with the same sense of style, and facilities include tennis and fishing on the grounds. Forest walks and horse riding are nearby.

★ **Aux Armes de Bouillon,** rue de la Station 9–15, 6830 Bouillon.
☎ **061/46-60-79.** Fax 061/46-60-84. 60 rms, 10 suites. TV TEL

Rates: BF 1,600–2,800 ($45–$78) single; BF 2,200–3,600 ($62–$101) double; BF 3,500 ($98) suite. AE, DC, MC, V.

This large hotel in the town center has nicely appointed guest rooms; and in addition to the indoor heated swimming pool, there's a sauna, whirlpool, Jacuzzi, and sun lamp. Guests have the use of a private garden, and there is a bar as well as a moderately priced restaurant.

★ **Hostellerie du Pieure des Conques,** route de Florenville 179, 6820 St. Cécile.
☎ **061/41-14-17.** Fax 061/41-27-03. 18 rms. MINIBAR TV TEL **Directions:** Take N884 about 14 miles from Bouillon.

Rates (including breakfast): BF 3,500 ($100) single; BF 4,000–5,200 ($114–$148) double. AE, DC, MC, V.

Set in what was a 7th-century convent (although the oldest surviving remains only go back as far as the 12th century), a dependency of the great abbey at nearby Orval, this hotel overlooks green lawns, rose gardens, and the Semois River. Charming guest rooms all have individual shapes and character—some with alcoves, some peeking from under eaves—and their comfort rates just as high as their charm (seating arrangements include easy chairs). The vaulted main dining room is warmed by an open fire, and any overflow of diners spills into a bevy of smaller rooms, also vaulted. This is a spot to enjoy the perfect tranquillity on the edge of an Ardennes forest.

WHERE TO DINE

★ **Auberge du Moulin Hideux,** route de Dohan 1, Noirefontaine. ☎ **46-70-15.**

$ **Cuisine:** CONTINENTAL. **Reservations:** Required.
Prices: Fixed-price meal BF 2,200 ($62). AE, DC, MC, V.
Open: Mid-Mar to July, lunch Fri–Tues noon–2pm; dinner daily 7:30–9pm. Aug–Nov, lunch daily noon–2pm; dinner daily 7:30–9pm. **Closed:** Dec to mid-Mar.

In a beautiful setting 2¹/₂ miles from Bouillon (see "Where to Stay," above), one of Belgium's top restaurants serves gourmet meals featuring baby lamb, saddles of pork, game, and fish delicacies such as the baby lobsters kept in a tank out in the garden until retrieved for each order. Everything is cooked to order, so be prepared to give the fine dinner that will arrive at your table the time it deserves. The wine list here is excellent and a good selection really should be indulged in to do the food justice.

Hostellerie du Pieure des Conques, route de Florenville 179. ☎ **41-14-17.**

Cuisine: CONTINENTAL. **Reservations:** Recommended.
Prices: Fixed-price meals BF 1,300–2,200 ($37–$63). AE, DC, MC, V.
Open: Lunch Thurs–Mon 12:45–2pm; dinner Wed–Mon 7:30–9pm. **Closed:** Dec 26 to mid-Mar.

Try to plan at least one meal in this atmospheric inn on the banks of the Semois, 14 miles from Bouillon, where fresh produce, fish, and meats are presented in simple but elegant combinations. Rack of lamb comes with potatoes and a fluffy turnip purée and is a favorite with patrons. There's a very good wine list at moderate prices.

Orval

From Bouillon, it's only 17 miles to the ✪ **Abbey of Orval** (☎ **061/31-10-60**). In its setting of green forests, the impressive complex of religious buildings is adminis-tered by a handful of monks, who carefully tend reminders of its history from the coming of the first Cistercians in 1110. The ruins left after the French destruction in 1793 are cared for as tenderly as the present church, its gardens, and the brewery that produces one of Belgium's finest beers.

A visit to the abbey is an exercise in serenity these days, with little to suggest the enormous power its Cistercian monks wielded in past centuries. Ruins of the old ab-bey are fascinating, and legend has it that somewhere in the web of underground pas-sages that connected it to seven nearby lakes, a vast treasure lies hidden. It's a tribute to the caretaking monks of this order that ruins are not all there is to see today, for it wasn't until 1926 that they began to rebuild after the devastating pillage of the Napoleonic period.

2 Bastogne

For most Americans, Bastogne is a place of pilgrimage. During World War II it was the town that did more to familiarize the world with the Ardennes than had any other single occurrence in history. It was here, during the fierce and near-fatal Battle of the Bulge in the bitter winter of 1944, that American troops under the command of Brig. Gen. Anthony MacAuliffe held overpowering numbers of German troops at bay un-til weather conditions improved and Allied reinforcements could be flown in. It was a near thing—but for that valiant 101st Airborne Division and their heroic leader, Hitler could have turned the tide and perhaps come out the winner in World War II. Outnumbered and seemingly cut off from any support, the American commander answered German demands for surrender with a single word that has come to stand for raw courage: "Nuts!"

Since the end of the war, Bastogne has been the appointed keeper of memorials to that near disaster and the men who prevented it. Mardasson Hill is a well-signposted mile outside the town, and this is where you'll find both the ✪ **American Memorial** and the **Bastogne Historical Center** (☎ **061/21-14-13**). A visit to the museum first will lay the groundwork for a better appreciation of films of the actual battle you'll see in the gigantic star-shaped gallery that is the memorial. Those interested in retracing the course of the battle will find battlefields clearly posted to identify key points.

Bastogne is a nice day trip from almost any point in the Ardennes and a little out of the way to use as a base for exploring. For more information, call the tourist office in Bastogne (☎ **061/21-27-11**).

3 Durbuy and Spa

Either of these resort towns makes an ideal touring base for the Ardennes. Completely different in character, they each have strong individual appeal. The tourist offices in both towns can furnish maps for scenic woodland walks, a pastime that should not be overlooked even if you're not an avid walker.

Durbuy

Durbuy is every image that the word *quaint* evokes. It's a tiny medieval town on a bend of a picturesque river, with narrow, twisting streets lined with pretty, flower-trimmed stone houses, and with an 11th-century castle to complete the scene.

Wandering the streets of the little town itself is a walk back in time, and if you're armed with the ▣ **"Walk Through the Past of Durbuy"** booklet available from the **Tourist Office,** Halle aux Blés (☎ **086/21-14-28**), virtually every building will reveal its past as you stroll by.

WHERE TO STAY

 Le Clos des Récollets, rue de la Prévoté, 6940 Durbuy. ☎ **086/21-12-71** or **21-29-69.** 10 rms. TV

Rates (including breakfast): BF 2,000 ($57) single; BF 2,600 ($74) double. AE, DC, MC, V.

The guest rooms in this attractive small hotel in the old town are rather plainly furnished, but quite comfortable. There's a good, moderately priced restaurant, with umbrella tables on a terrace for outdoor dining in good weather.

Hostellerie le Sanglier des Ardennes, Grand' Rue 99, 6940 Durbuy. ☎ **086/21-32-62.** Fax 086/21-24-65. 34 rms. MINIBAR TV TEL

Rates: BF 4,250–6,900 ($121–$197) single or double. One- to three-day package rates (including some meals) available. AE, DC, MC, V.

Located in the town center, the comfortable rooms above the internationally known restaurant downstairs are replete with old-fashioned charm. Those on the back overlook the River Ourthe, while those on the front face the old town with mountains in the background.

★ **Hôtel Cardinal,** rue des Récollectines 66, 6940 Durbuy. ☎ **086/21-32-62.** Fax 086/21-24-65. 6 apartments. MINIBAR TV TEL

$ Rates: BF 6,900 ($197) apartment for two to four. AE, DC, MC, V.

Top recommendation could go to the Cardinal for either its accommodations or its setting—the combination is irresistible! The owner Maurice Caerdinael (the award-winning chef of Le Sanglier des Ardennes) has created seven pretty apartments in a stone building that once was part of an ancient convent. Set at the end of a street in the old town, behind 14th-century walls that enclose a small and peaceful garden shaded by fine old trees, the house has a square tower at one side. Inside, the apartments are beautifully furnished and come with private baths in which even the towels and soap have been selected with care to provide the very best. Each refrigerator holds a supply of gourmet goodies—pâté, cheese, beverages, etc.—that reinforces the notion that this is truly your "home away from home."

★ **Hôtel la Falize,** rue A-Eloi 59, 6940 Durbuy. ☎ **086/21-26-66.**
12 rms. MINIBAR TV
$ **Rates** (including breakfast): BF 1,400 ($40) single; BF 1,800 ($61) double. AE, DC, MC, V.

Old-fashioned, comfortable, cozy—all apply to this small hotel, its doorway flanked by colorful potted plants, on a quiet, narrow street in the old town. Its parlor, with a cast-iron stove in one corner, is reminiscent of those homey living rooms of several generations back, as is the warm friendliness of the owners. The rooms are simply furnished.

★ **Le Vieux Durbuy,** rue Jean-de-Bohème, 6940 Durbuy. ☎ **086/21-32-62.**
Telex 42-240. 12 rms. MINIBAR TV TEL
$ **Rates** (including breakfast): BF 3,450 ($98) single; BF 3,900 ($111) double. AE, DC, EU, MC, V.

Owned by the same Maurice Caerdinael (see above), this is another fine old building, once a private home, on a narrow street in the heart of the old town. Its rooms are outfitted with period pieces quite in keeping with their setting, and the same loving care has been taken in supplying baths with luxury supplies. Breakfast is taken in the superb restaurant Le Sanglier des Ardennes, just a short walk away.

WHERE TO DINE

★ **Le Sanglier des Ardennes,** Grand' Rue 99. ☎ **21-32-62.**
Cuisine: CONTINENTAL. **Reservations:** Recommended.
$ **Prices:** Fixed-price meal BF 2,200–3,800 ($62–$108). AE, DC, MC, V.
Open: Lunch Fri–Wed noon–2pm; dinner Fri–Wed 7–9pm. **Closed:** Jan.

In a nest of cozy dining rooms and a covered terrace overlooking the River Ourthe on the main street in the town center, master chef Maurice Caerdinael creates internationally acclaimed classic dishes. Fish straight from the river outside come to table full-flavored, with subtle sauces or seasonings that only add to their delicacy. Game from the Ardennes, the famed smoked jambon (ham), and other regional specialties take on extra dimension after passing through this talented kitchen. The extraordinary wine cellar also reflects the chef's expertise in selecting more than 500 bottles, which are stored with care and sold at surprisingly moderate prices.

Spa

From the start, Spa has been a busy, bustling resort that owes its existence to the curative powers of its mineral waters. Since a medieval blacksmith from other parts bought up the land holding these wondrous springs, the town that grew up around them has catered to the likes of Charles II of England, Montaigne, the queen of Sweden, and Tsar Peter the Great of Russia (probably its most illustrious visitor). So universally was its name equated with the miracles of thermal springs and mineral waters that *spa* is now applied to health and fitness centers of every description.

Belgians and tourists alike continue to gather here both for the healing treatments and for its lively casino action. The turn-of-the-century **Grand Casino** is at rue Royale 4 (☎ **77-20-52**), in the center of town. If you come for the "cures," head for the ornate ☒ **Thermes de Spa,** place Royale 2 (☎ **77-25-60**). There, they can tell you everything you'll need to know about thermal cures, walking cures, drinking cures (*not* the alcoholic kind!), and probably a few other categories.

The **tourist office** is in the Pavillon des Petits Jeux, place Royale 41 (☎ 087/77-17-00).

WHERE TO STAY

★ **L'Auberge Spa,** place du Monument 4, 4900 Spa. ☎ **087/77-44-10.** Fax 087/77-21-79. 20 rms, 12 suites.

$ **Rates** (including breakfast): BF 2,750 ($78) single; BF 4,200 ($120) double; BF 6,950 ($198) suite. AE, DC, MC, V.

This attractive hotel in the town center opens onto a small square, and its ground floor houses a good restaurant. Older rooms are comfortable and homey and look out through casement windows to the town outside. There are also luxury suites, with bedroom, large living room, fully equipped kitchen, and bath. Tastefully furnished, each suite can accommodate up to four people.

Dorint Hotel, route de Balmoral 33, 4900 Spa. ☎ **087/77-25-81.** Fax 087/77-41-74. 97 rms. MINIBAR TV TEL

Rates (including breakfast): BF 2,750–4,000 ($78–$114) single; BF 3,800–4,650 ($108–$132) double. AE, DC, MC, V.

Also on the outskirts of town, this 97-room hotel is a study in modernity, with its gleaming glass front a surprising accent among the pines that surround it. All the guest rooms are spacious and sunny, and all have balconies as well as all the luxury touches you'd expect in a hotel of this quality. Other amenities include an indoor swimming pool and sauna, solarium, table tennis, bars (with periodic entertainment), and a restaurant.

★ **Hôtel la Heid des Pairs,** av. Professor-Henrijean 143, 4880 Spa. ☎ **087/77-43-46.** Fax 087/77-06-44. 11 rms. TV TEL

$ **Rates** (including breakfast): BF 2,700–5,200 ($77–$148) single or double. AE, DC, MC, V.

Out from the center of town, surrounded by lawns dotted with ancient trees, this villa was built for Baron Nagelmackers, whose family founded the *Orient Express.* And the ambience is still that of a private home, with a comfortable drawing room and homey rooms comfortably furnished with a mixture of period and functional pieces. The "at home" touch begins with the fruit and sweets in your room on arrival. Three of the rooms have private balconies, and you may elect to have your breakfast served there or on the terrace downstairs.

WHERE TO DINE

Your best meals will probably be taken in the hotels recommended above. There are also a number of good restaurants in or near Spa, and the following are only a sample.

La Brasserie du Grand Maur, rue Xhrouet 41. ☎ **77-36-16.**

Cuisine: FRENCH/BELGIAN. **Reservations:** Recommended.
Prices: Fixed-price meal BF 1,450 ($41). AE, DC, MC, V.
Open: Lunch Tues–Sun noon–2pm; dinner Tues–Sat 7–9pm. **Closed:** Jan.

This elegant restaurant in the town center, set in a two-centuries-old building, presents gourmet meals, specializing in regional dishes prepared with the very best of local produce.

$ Eurotaverne, in the Casino, rue Royale 4. ☎ **77-39-26.**

Cuisine: REGIONAL/CASUAL MEALS. **Reservations:** Not required.
Prices: Average meal up to BF 1,000 ($28). AE, MC, V.
Open: Lunch Tues–Wed and Fri–Sun noon–2:30pm; Tues–Wed and Fri–Sun 6–9pm.

This place is always packed, and for good reason—at least one meal in the casino's restaurant is virtually obligatory! Each day's menu is centered on the best available fresh ingredients. Outstanding value, and fun.

★ Hôtel des Bains, Lac de Robertville, Waimes. ☎ **080/67-95-71.**

Cuisine: FRENCH. **Reservations:** Recommended, but not required. **Directions:** Drive a short way from Spa on the E5 highway to Exit A27, signposted Malmédy-Waimes.
Prices: Fixed-price meal BF 1,250–2,600 ($35–$74). AE, DC, MC, V.
Open: Lunch daily noon–3pm; dinner Thurs–Tues 7–10pm.

This beautiful hotel sits on the shores of a lake in the Hautes Fagnes Eifel nature reserve. The basically classic French cuisine is served with a light, delicate touch, and often pike from the lake comes poached and served on lettuce with a white butter sauce—*the* choice when it's available.

★ $ La Retraite de l'Empereur, 4910 La Reid. ☎ **37-62-15.**

Cuisine: FRENCH. **Reservations:** Required.
Prices: A la carte meals BF 995–2,350 ($28–$67). AE, MC, V.
Open: Wed and Fri–Mon noon–2pm; dinner Wed and Fri–Mon 6–9pm. **Closed:** July, last week in Dec.

In a long stone building set right on the main street of a tiny village about 5 miles from Spa, this beautifully rustic restaurant has won several prestigious awards for its classical French cuisine. Specialties include game (in season) and lobster, as well as local fish. House wines are as low as BF 500 ($14). The drive out through tranquil, rolling countryside is a delight.

11

Getting to Know Holland

Fᴵʀˢᵀ ᴏꜰ ᴀʟʟ, ᴛʜᴇʀᴇ ɪˢ ᴛʜᴇ ᴍᴀᴛᴛᴇʀ ᴏꜰ ɪᴛˢ ɴᴀᴍᴇ: Hᴏʟʟᴀɴᴅ ᴏʀ ᴛʜᴇ Nᴇᴛʜᴇʀʟᴀɴᴅˢ? Actually, it's both, and before either of those it was called Batavia. Why all the changes? Listen to one Thomas Coryate, writing in 1611: "The name of Batavia was commonly in use til the yeare of our Lord 860, at what time there hapend such an exceeding inundation as overflowed a great part of the country, and did so scowre and wash the very bowels of the earth that it hath bene ever since . . . hollow and spungie. For which cause the old name of Batavia was afterward changed to Holland, . . . or Hol-land . . . for hol in the Flemish tongue doth signifie as much as our word hole."

Technically in modern times that name applies only to the two western provinces of North and South Holland, and the country itself bears the label the Netherlands, meaning "low lands," a designation that from medieval times until 1830 included Belgium—collectively, they were known far and wide as the Low Countries. That title, however, is seldom used outside officialdom; for both its citizens and its visitors, this amazing little country is usually referred to simply as "Holland."

1 Geography, History, and Politics

Geography

While visiting Holland in 1859, Matthew Arnold was so incredulous at what he saw that he wrote home, "The country has no business to be there at all." Well, maybe so—about 50% of its land is, after all, below sea level and surely meant by the Almighty to stay that way. But the Dutch have a ready answer: "God made the earth," they'll tell you, "and the Dutch made Holland." That they did, and they made a fine job of it. Of the 16,000 square miles that make up Holland today, almost 1,000 square miles were under water just 100 years ago! And they're still at it, working away at Zeeland's huge Delta Project to wrest even more land from the sea with the same dogged determination and patience that over the centuries have created this territory.

Of course there are still 1,100 square miles of water within Holland's boundaries, but even that water, because of Dutch industry and ingenuity, is largely channeled— canals and rerouted rivers and lakes that were once open sea. Indeed it is the rivers that have given Holland its historically strategic position in world shipping and trading, for this is where three of Europe's important waterways empty into the sea. From earliest recorded history the Rhine, the Maas (it's the Meuse until it crosses Holland's border from Belgium), and the Waal have brought the products of the rest of the continent to this point on the North Sea for shipment to markets around the world.

The rivers also draw natural divisions across the terrain. To the north, above the rivers, the land is lowest; below the rivers, in the south, are somewhat higher elevations (Holland's highest mountain is only 1,093 feet high). That modest peak is in the southeast province of Limburg; and except for the forests in the central provinces

IMPRESSIONS

My love for plane geometry prepared me to feel a special affection for Holland. For the Dutch landscape has all the qualities that make geometry so delightful. A tour in Holland is a tour through the first book of Euclid. Over a country that is the ideal plane surface of the geometry books, the roads and the canals trace out the shortest distances between point and point.
—Aldous Huxley, *Along the Road,* 1925

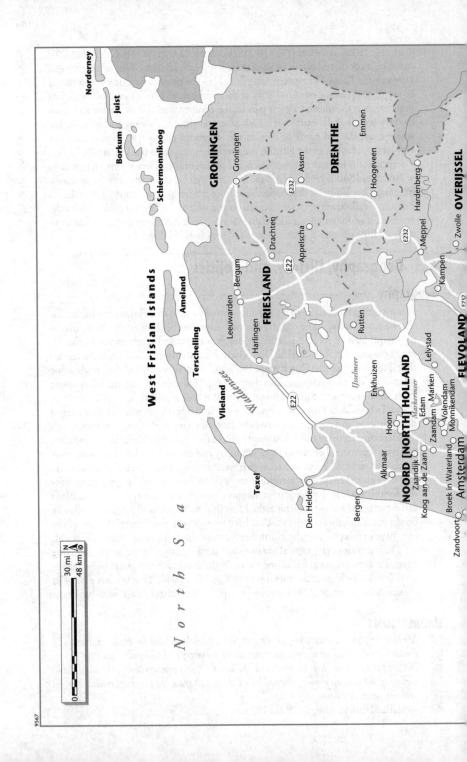

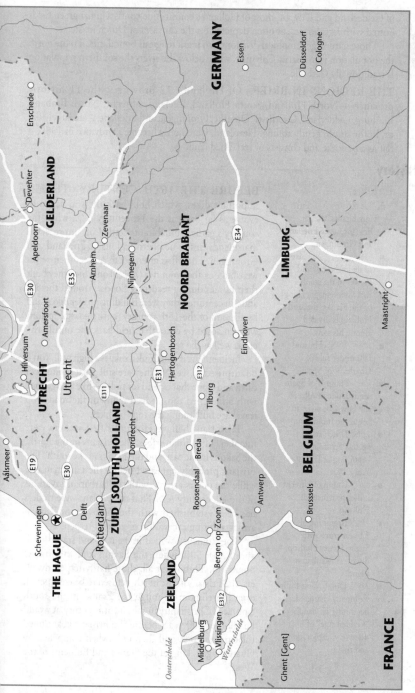

Holland

of Gelderland and Utrecht, most of Holland's countryside consists of flat green fields dotted with farmhouses, as often depicted on the canvases of Dutch masters.

Those natural geographical divisions also mark religious boundaries. To the north the population is primarily Calvinist, while below the rivers the southern population is traditionally Catholic.

THE REGIONS IN BRIEF Of Holland's 12 provinces, the 11 historic provinces—North Holland, South Holland, Zeeland, Utrecht, North Brabant, Limburg, Gelderland, Overijssel, Drenthe, Groningen, and Friesland—are largely flat or, in the south, gently rolling. Flevoland, which only became a province in 1980, is flat as a pancake and consists of reclaimed land.

History

Dateline

- **1st century A.D.** First inhabitants, the Frisians, settle Friesland and Groningen.
- **4th century A.D.** Saxons settle in the east and Franks in the south.
- **814** Charlemagne, king of the Franks, dies and Holland is divided among his sons.
- **Early 1500s** Holland falls under rule of Charles V of Spain.
- **1555** Philip II of Spain sends Duke of Alba to the Low Countries to begin the Inquisition.
- **1568** Dutch rally against Spain in beginning of Eighty Years' War.
- **1579** Union of Utrecht unites provinces of Holland.
- **1609** Beginning of 12-year truce with Spain; Henry Hudson discovers Manhattan island.
- **1621** Dutch West India Company chartered, beginning Holland's "Golden Age" of discovery, exploration, and trade.

➤

BEFORE THE 16TH CENTURY The all-important dikes, which hold back the sea, began to evolve as far back as the 1st century A.D., when the country's earliest inhabitants settled on unprotected marshlands in the northern regions of Friesland and Groningen. Their first attempts to protect themselves were huge earthen mounds (*terpen*) on which they built their homes during recurring floods. Around the 8th and 9th centuries, they were building proper dikes; and by the end of the 13th century, entire coastal regions were enclosed by dikes that held back the unruly rivers as well as the sea.

Incidentally, if you think a dike is a high wall, you'll be surprised to see that they are still great mounds of earth and stone that extend for miles—like a huge rope with a flattened top. Indeed many of the roads you travel are built along the tops of dikes.

Historians believe Holland's first settlers were members of German tribes: the Frisians in the north, the Saxons in the east, and the Franks in the south. The Frisians probably appeared before the Christian era, while the others arrived with the barbarian invasions of the 4th century A.D. That the Frisians were traders has been established with the discovery of Roman artifacts during excavation of ancient terpen.

The Romans invaded in 12 B.C. and stayed until about A.D. 300, when the Saxons and the Franks poured in. Through it all, those hardy terpen dwellers, the Frisians in the north, refused to be conquered, even by religion; although the Franks in the south embraced Christianity in the late 5th century, it would be another 200 years before the Frisians abandoned their pagan gods, and then only when compelled by Charlemagne, king of the Franks and Emperor of the West.

After Charlemagne's death in 814, his vast empire was divided among his sons. Soon Dutch history began to take shape through alliances, marriages, feuds, and outright warfare. By the 13th and 14th centuries the nobility—especially the counts of Holland, the counts of Flanders, and the dukes of Brabant—were busy building most of the castles and fortified manor houses that interest tourists throughout Holland. The Catholic hierarchy grew both powerful and wealthy: The bishoprics of Maastricht and Utrecht played a key role in the politics of the era, as they erected splendid cathedrals, abbeys, and monasteries.

THE 16TH CENTURY   As the 16th century began, political maneuvering brought Holland under the rule of Charles V of Spain. This turn of events coincided with a large-scale Dutch revolt against Catholicism as they rushed to embrace the Protestant church following the conversion of Count William of Orange (the Silent). When Charles relinquished the Spanish throne to his son Philip in 1555, things took a nasty turn for the Dutch since the new king dispatched the infamous Duke of Alba to the Low Countries to carry out the Inquisition's "death to heretics" edict. William of Orange declared: "I cannot approve of princes attempting to use the conscience of their subjects and wanting to rob them of the liberty of faith." Nor, as history has proved time and again in the years since, could his subjects!

Rallying behind William the Silent, the Dutch mounted a fierce resistance even though city after city fell into Spanish hands. The turning point came at Leiden. In a desperate and brilliantly successful move, William flooded the province and sailed his ships to the very walls of the city, catching the Spanish troops at their dinner. The result was a rout—and a new national dish for the Dutch! The stewpot (*hutspot*) left bubbling by the fleeing enemy became a cherished symbol of the triumph of freedom.

With the Union of Utrecht, signed in 1579, the seven provinces of Holland united against their covetous neighbors—France, Spain, and England. However, the struggle with Spain was to continue until 1648, a conflict referred to as the Eighty Years' War. By the early 1600s, however, William's son, Prince Maurice, headed a States-General governing body for the seven Dutch provinces, initiating a new era.

THE 17TH TO THE 19TH CENTURY   Sometimes called Holland's "Golden Age," the newly

Dateline

- **1626** Dutch purchase Manhattan from the Native Americans for $24.
- **1648** End of Eighty Years' War.
- **1652–54** First Anglo-Dutch War.
- **1664** English capture New Amsterdam and rename it New York.
- **1665–67** Second Anglo-Dutch War.
- **1672–74** Third Anglo-Dutch War; Dutch recapture New York.
- **1689** William III and his wife, Mary, become king and queen of England.
- **1780** Fourth Anglo-Dutch War.
- **1782** Dutch first to officially recognize nationhood of the United States; the first to float loans to the U.S.
- **1795** French forces occupy Amsterdam; William V flees to England.
- **1806–10** Holland ruled by Louis Bonaparte as part of the French Empire.
- **1814–31** Holland becomes United Kingdom of the Netherlands, a constitutional monarchy headed by Willem I, first of the House of Orange-Nassau.
- **1917** Holland maintains strict neutrality throughout World War I.

➤

Dateline

- **1932** Enclosing Dike completed, creating freshwater lake IJsselmeer.
- **1940** Holland occupied by Nazi forces; Queen Wilhelmina enters exile in London.
- **1942** Dutch East Indies occupied by Japan.
- **1944–45** Holland liberated by Allied forces.
- **1948** Queen Wilhelmina abdicates in favor of her daughter, Juliana.
- **1949** Holland joins NATO; grants independence to Indonesia.
- **1953** Devastating North Sea storms produce significant coastal flooding. Dutch embark on long-range Delta Project to seal off southwest river estuaries.
- **1962** Dutch relinquish control over western part of New Guinea.
- **1975** Holland grants independence to Surinam.
- **1980** Queen Juliana abdicates throne to her eldest daughter Beatrix.
- **1981** Dutch vigorously oppose any U.S. missiles on their soil.
- **1982** Ruud Lubbers becomes prime minister, replacing Van Agt.

organized Dutch East India and Dutch West India companies engaged in the spice trade: Dutch explorers were trading with Native Americans for "Manhattes" Island and establishing the infant Nieuw Amsterdam; Abel Tasman was sailing around the South Pacific discovering New Zealand, the Fiji Islands, Tonga, and Tasmania; and the Indonesian colonies were established to secure the spice trade. At home, the merchants who financed all those voyages grew richer, built gabled houses, dug canal after canal, and applauded as the young William III married into the English royal family and shared the English throne with his wife.

Holland was also becoming a refuge for persecuted groups. The Pilgrims stopped here for a dozen years before embarking for America; Jews fled the oppressive Spanish and welcomed the tolerance of the Dutch; refugees straggled in from France and Portugal. William of Orange had helped to create a climate of tolerance in Holland. This attracted talented newcomers who contributed to the expanding economic, social, artistic, and intellectual climate of the country.

Conflict arose, however, between Holland and England—in part because of their lively competition on the seas. Needless to say, Dutch support for the new United States of America (Holland was the first to recognize the new struggling nation and extended three substantial loans to the new government) did little to heal the breach with the British. By the time William V—with his mixed Dutch-Anglo background—ascended the Dutch throne, anti-British sentiment was so strong that in 1795 he was exiled to England and a new Batavian Republic was set up, aligning itself with France.

In 1806 Napoléon moved into Holland, declared his brother, Louis Bonaparte, king, and installed him in a palace that had been Amsterdam's Town Hall. Four years later Napoléon returned, drawn by the threat of a British landing in Zeeland.

And then came Waterloo in 1815. With Napoléon finally defeated once and for all, the Dutch recalled the House of Orange and installed yet another William as king—this time as head of a constitutional monarchy. To mark the beginning of their new republic, the Dutch decided that *this* Willem (their native spelling) should become Willem I. Thus began the House of Orange-Nassau, which still continues today.

THE 20TH CENTURY Holland escaped the ravages of World War I by maintaining a staunch neutrality. It was a different story in World War II, when Nazi troops invaded in 1940. The occupation was complete and devastating: Rotterdam sustained heavy bombings and the rest of the country suffered terribly at the hands of its invaders. During the war the Dutch operated one of the most effective underground movements in Europe, which became a decisive factor in the liberation of Holland in 1945.

During World War II the Dutch colonies in the Far East were captured by the Japanese; at war's end the Indonesian colonists took up a determined fight for their independence, which they finally achieved in 1949. In 1963 Holland relinquished control over the western half of New Guinea which became part of Indonesia, and in 1975 it granted independence to Surinam.

The beloved Queen Wilhelmina, having occupied the throne for nearly 60 years, abdicated in 1948 in favor of her daughter, Juliana. The precedent was set, and Queen Juliana stepped aside in 1980 for the present queen, Beatrix, her daughter.

TODAY   In recent decades more land has been reclaimed from the sea; a large part of the new "polder," Flevoland, became dry in 1957, followed by another in 1968. Thus, some 100,000 Dutch citizens now live and work on land that had constituted the Zuiderzee before 1932, when the great Enclosing Dike was completed and that salty arm of the North Sea began the long process of becoming a freshwater lake known as IJsselmeer.

Work proceeds to create more polders since Holland's population has tripled during this century. With a 1994 population exceeding 15 million—due in part to immigration from the former Indonesian colonies—Holland faces problems as one of the most densely populated countries in the world (960 people per square mile).

In 1953 devastating North Sea storms broke through the dikes in many places along the southwest coast, flooding significant areas. There was a substantial loss of life and property. In order to assure greater protection along its coastal areas, Holland embarked upon a long-range Delta Project to seal off the river estuaries in the southwest.

With a scarcity of raw materials and the loss of Indonesia, Holland is making a concerted—and thus far rather successful—effort to develop high-technology industries. Many multinational conglomerates have established their headquarters, branch operations, or plants here. With this influx of new industry and the EU as a market for a significant proportion of its exports, Holland manages to keep its unemployment at about 5%—an enviable record.

For the visitor, Holland today presents much the same face it has over the centuries—a serenely scenic landscape and an industrious population who treasure their age-old tradition of tolerance and who welcome people of all political, religious, and ideological persuasions.

Politics

Holland is a constitutional monarchy headed by Queen Beatrix and her consort Prince Claus. The heir-apparent is their oldest son, Willem-Alexander (born 1967). Parliament consists of two houses—an Upper Chamber and a Lower Chamber. The three major political parties are the Christian Democrats, the Labor party, and the Liberal party.

In 1981 Prime Minister Van Agt supported the deployment of U.S. cruise missiles in Holland; public opposition to this (as well as his controversial economic policy) led to his defeat in the 1982 elections. He was followed by Rudd Lubbers who led a coalition government (Christian Democrats and Labor). Subsequent elections through 1994 have obliged Lubbers to alter the makeup of his coalition.

2 Holland's Famous People

Descartes, René (1596–1650) French mathematician and philosopher who moved to Holland in 1628 and remained for the next 20 years. During this time Descartes undertook scientific research and reflected on philosophical issues. Most of his important works were written during this time. Besides Descartes' contributions in the field of algebra, analytical geometry, and several scientific fields, he is well known for his scrunity of human knowledge. "Cogito ergo sum" ("I think, therefore I am") attempts to determine how human beings can be certain of what exists in the mental and physical world.

Erasmus, Desiderius (1466?–1536) Dutch humanist and scholar. A Roman Catholic priest, he traveled widely and was acquainted with most of the leading scholars of his time. Through his writings, Erasmus deplored many practices of the Catholic Church of that era—clerical abuse and parishioners' ignorance of the bible and church rituals. Although Erasmus urged reform, he did not support Martin Luther's Reformation—believing that it was fostering ill will and intolerance. One of Erasmus's best-known works is *The Praise of Folly* (1509).

Anne Frank (1929–45) The well-known adolescent diarist whose writings came to symbolize the plight of Jewish families who fled the wrath of Hitler during World War II. She escaped with her family to Amsterdam; together with another Jewish family, they were hidden in an attic by a sympathetic Dutch family. Someone betrayed them and they were sent to concentration camps, where Anne died of typhus. Her father first published her diary in 1947.

Anton van Leeuwenhoek (1632–1723) Natural scientist and lens maker. As a draper's apprentice he probably used lenses to examine cloth. He made more than 247 microscopes, some of which magnified objects 200 times, and with their help he provided the first descriptions of bacteria, protozoa, and spermatozoa and made a detailed study of capillary circulation.

Spinoza, Baruch (or Benedict) (1632–77) Philosopher. Born in Amsterdam to Orthodox Sephardic Jewish parents, he was a lens grinder by trade. He received an Orthodox education but also studied such thinkers as René Descartes and Thomas Hobbes; because of his independent thinking, he was excommunicated from the Orthodox community in 1656. He was one of the first philosophers to raise questions about the Bible; because of his pantheism he was distrusted by his contemporaries but his notion of freedom, especially freedom of inquiry, influenced later German idealism. He was offered a professorship at Heidelberg but decided to remain independent. His *A Treatise on Religious and Political Philosophy* published in 1670 is the only work published during his lifetime.

William the Silent, or William of Orange (1533–84) Dutch statesman and prime crafter of Dutch independence. Born in Dillenburg, Germany, he inherited the principality of Orange in 1544 and was later made stadtholder of Holland, Zeeland, and Utrecht. In his early years he served Philip II of Spain as a diplomat, but when the king encroached upon the liberties of the Netherlands and instituted the Inquisition, William led the rebellion against Spain. The struggle was long and the United Provinces, as the Netherlands was then called, did not gain their independence until 1648 at the Treaty of Westphalia, but William the Silent played a crucial role.

3   Art and Architecture

Art

Undisputedly, the 17th century was the Golden Age of Dutch art. During this busy time, the arts thrived as sculptors and stonemasons created lasting monuments to their genius and artists won wealthy patrons whose support allowed them to give free reign to talents that so enrich our 20th-century museums. Art held a cherished place in the hearts of average Dutch citizens too, as Peter Mundy, who traveled to Amsterdam in 1640, observed: "As for the art of painting and the affection of the people to pictures, I think none other goes beyond them, there having been in this country many excellent men in that faculty, some at present, as Rembrandt. All in general striving to adorn their houses, especially the outer or street room, with costly pieces. Butchers and bakers not much inferior in their shops, which are fairly set forth; yea, many times blacksmiths and cobblers will have some picture or other by their forge and in their stall. Such is the general notion, inclination, and delight that these county natives have to paintings." The Dutch were particularly fond of pictures that depicted their world: landscapes, seascapes, domestic scenes, portraits, and still lifes. The art from this Golden Age is among the best ever created in Holland.

One of the greatest landscape painters of all time was **Jacob van Ruisdael** (1628–82), who depicted cornfields, windmills, and forest scenes, along with his famous views of Haarlem. In some of his works the human figure is very small and in others it does not appear at all; instead the artist typically devoted two-thirds of the canvas to the vast skies filled with the moody clouds that float over the flat terrain of Holland.

Dutch realism of this period had its roots in the old Netherlandish tradition of Jan Van Eyck but was also influenced by the new "realism of light and dark." One of the Dutch painters who had studied Caravaggio's style in Rome for years was **Gerrit van Honthorst** (1590–1656). This painter from Utrecht is best known for his lively genre scenes like *The Supper Party* (1620). The people depicted in this informal scene are ordinary and unidealized; typical of his work, they are seen close up and life-size, and strongly outlined against a plain background. Honthorst often used multiple hidden-light sources to heighten the dramatic contrast between light and dark.

Frans Hals (1581–1666), the undisputed leader of the Haarlem school, specialized in portraiture. The relaxed relationship between the portraitist and his subject was a great departure from the formal masks of Renaissance portraits. With the lightness of his brushstrokes, Hals was able to convey an immediacy and intimacy. Hals not only produced perceptive psychological portraits, but had a genius for comic characters; he showed men and women as they are and a little less than they are, such as *Malle Babbe* (1650).

As a stage manager of group portraits such as military companies, Hals's skill is unmatched—except, of course, surpassed by Rembrandt. In baroque fashion, Hals carefully planned and balanced the directions of pose, gesture, and glance, but his *alla prima* brushwork (direct laying down of a pigment) makes these public images— such as *The Archers of St. Aidan* (1633)—appear as spontaneous reportage. It's worth visiting the Frans Hals Museum in Haarlem.

One of the geniuses of Western art is **Rembrandt van Rijn** (1606–69); this highly prolific and influential artist had a dramatic life filled with success and personal tragedy. Rembrandt was a master at showing the soul and inner life of man, in both his portraits and illustrations of biblical stories.

Rembrandt's use of lights and darks was influenced by Caravaggio, like Hals and van Honthorst before him, but was much more refined: The values of light and dark gradually and softly blended together; although some of the drama of chiaroscuro was probably lost, a more truthful appearance was achieved. The light that falls upon a face in a Rembrandt portrait is mysterious yet revealing of character.

Rembrandt's series of religious paintings and prints are highly personal and spiritual; they are expressed in very human terms. Rembrandt depicted Christ as a humble and gentle Nazarene, whose expression is loving and melancholy. There is an overall stillness to Rembrandt's religious paintings that reflects an inner contemplation. Rembrandt achieved much renown with his religious prints (etchings), which were a major source of income during his lifetime.

A spirituality reigns over his self-portraits as well; Rembrandt did about 60 of these during his lifetime. The *Self-Portrait with Saskia* shows the artist with his wife during prosperous times when he was often commissioned by wealthy merchants to do portraits. A transition from youthful optimism to an old man who has been worn down by care and anxiety can be seen in his chronological series of self-renderings. At the Rembrandt House in Amsterdam—which has been restored to much the way it was when he lived and worked there—you can see his self-portraits along with some 250 etchings.

In his group portraits—such as *The Night Watch* (1642), on view at the Rijksmuseum in Amsterdam—each individual portrait is done with care. Although art historians don't know how he proceeded, a long studio sitting may have been required of each man. The unrivaled harmony of light, color, and movement in these works is to be appreciated.

In his later years, while at the height of his artistic powers, Rembrandt's work was judged too personal and eccentric by his contemporaries. Some considered Rembrandt to be a tasteless painter obsessed with the ugly and ignorant of color; this was the prevailing opinion until the 19th century when Rembrandt's genius was reevaluated.

Jan Vermeer (1632–75) of Delft is perhaps the best known of the "little Dutch masters": These painters restricted themselves to one type of painting such as portraiture or genre; although the scope of their painting was narrow, the little Dutch masters rendered their subjects with an exquisite care and faithfulness to their actual appearances.

The subject of Vermeer's work is the activities and pleasures of simple home life. Vermeer placed the figure(s) at the center of his paintings. The background space— with the horizontal and vertical accents of furniture—typically conveys a feeling of stability and serenity. Art historians know that Vermeer made use of mirrors and the *camera obscura,* an early camera, as compositional aids. Vermeer excelled at lighting his interior scenes and rendered his color optically true; these qualities combine to give a wonderful illusion of three-dimensionality. As light—usually afternoon sunshine pouring in through an open window—moves across the picture plane, it caresses and modifies all the colors.

If **Vincent van Gogh** (1853–90) had not failed as a missionary in the mining region of Belgium, he might not have turned to painting and become the greatest Dutch artist of the 19th century. *The Potato Eaters* (1885) was van Gogh's first masterpiece. Dark and crudely painted, it shows the rough life of peasants gathered around the table for their evening meal after a long day of manual labor—gone is the traditional beauty and serenity in Dutch genre painting.

After the death of his father, Vincent traveled first to Antwerp and then to Paris to join his favorite brother, Theo. In Paris, Vincent discovered and adopted the brilliant and rich color palette of the impressionists. Through Theo, an art dealer, Vincent met Gauguin; the two had many conversations on the expressive power of pure color. Van Gogh developed a thick brushwork—with a textilelike texture—that corresponded to his intense color schemes.

In 1888 van Gogh traveled to Arles in Provence, where he was dazzled by the Mediterranean sun and where his favorite color, yellow, which signified love to him, dominated his landscapes such as *Wheatfield with a Reaper* (1889). For the next two years until his death, van Gogh remained in the south of France; here he painted at a frenetic pace in between bouts of madness. In *The Night Café* (1888), van Gogh plays up the complementary colors of red walls and green ceiling to give an oppressive air to this billiard-hall scene. (With red and green, Vincent wrote, he tried to represent "those terrible things, men's passions.") We see the halos around the lights swirl as if we, like some of the patrons slumped over at their tables, have had too much to drink. Perhaps van Gogh's best-known nightscape is *The Starry Night* (1889); with its whirling starlight, Vincent's turbulent universe is filled with personal anxiety and fear.

The Vincent van Gogh Museum in Amsterdam has more than 200 of his paintings—including *The Sunflowers*—presented to Holland by Theo's wife and son with the provision that they not leave Vincent's native land.

Did you know that before **Piet Mondrian** (1872–1944) became a master/originator of De Stijl (also called neoplasticism) he painted windmills, cows, and prairies? One of his expressionistic masterpieces, *The Red Tree*—which looks as though it's exploding on fire against a background of blue (1909), and done at age 41—marked a turning point in his career as a contemporary painter: The artist had always said he would drop one of the two a's in his last name when he had found his true personality; this canvas he signed as Mondrian.

With his friend Theo van Doesburg, Mondrian began a magazine in 1917 entitled *De Stijl* (The Style) in which he expounded the principles of neoplasticism: a simplification of forms, reducing what is represented to a limited number of signs, or in other words, purified abstraction. In large part, this movement was an outgrowth of and reaction against the cubist work of Picasso and Braque, which Mondrian had seen while he lived in Paris from 1912 to 1914.

To Mondrian and the poets, sculptors, and architects associated with De Stijl, abstraction was a moral necessity, simplifying vision would simplify life, and a universal plastic language would bring about a better world. For these reasons, the geometric painters of the De Stijl school attempted a "controllable precision." Their basic form was the rectangle—with horizontal and vertical accents at right angles. Their basic colors were the primaries—red, blue, and yellow—along with black and white. In works like *Composition in Blue, Yellow, and Black* (1936), no part of the picture plane is more important than any other; with its design, Mondrian achieves an equilibrium but does not succumb to a mechanical uniformity.

Mondrian suppressed the use of curves and the color green in his later work because, he said, these reminded him of nature. But it's ironic to note that to support himself Mondrian had to paint flowers on porcelain for much of his life. In 1940 Mondrian moved to New York, which he loved, to escape the war in Europe. In the evenings he would take walks around the art deco Rockefeller Center; the geometry of the lighted windows reminded him of his paintings. Mondrian's last paintings were lively abstract representations of New York: *Broadway Boogie Woogie* (1942) and *Victory Boogie Woogie* (1943).

Architecture

Few examples of early Dutch architecture remain. Chief among the Romanesque examples are the Basilica of Our Lady and St. Servaasbasiliek, both in Maastricht.

In the medieval period Holland was influenced by Germany and the Baltic countries and its Gothic architecture is plainer than the French and Belgian. Utrecht and Haarlem Cathedrals are two examples, along with the church of St. Peter in Leiden.

In the 16th and 17th centuries **De Keyser** (1565–1621) developed the Renaissance-style house. Today the Herengracht, Keizersgracht, and Prinsengracht canals of Amsterdam are lined with these terraced homes, many of which were built by two architect brothers, Philip and Justus Vingboons. Here the medieval stepped gable gave way to a more ornate one with scrolled sides, decorative finials, and other features. He also built the city's Zuiderkerk, the Westerkerk, and the Noorderkerk as well as the Amsterdam Exchange, and the landmark Mint Tower.

Later in the 17th century, Dutch Palladianism developed in The Hague. The most famous example is the city's Mauritshuis, which was designed by Pieter Post and Jacob van Campen. The Renaissance and Palladian styles of architecture remained popular until the advent of neoclassicism and the design of such Second Empire Renaissance buildings as Amsterdam's Amstel hotel by Cornelis Outshoorn. The best-known practitioner of Neo-Gothic, though, is **P. J. Cuypers,** who designed both the Rijksmuseum and the Centraal Station in Amsterdam, with their gables and steep roofs and dormers. He also designed the Vondelkerk and the Maria Magdalenkerk both of brick with polychrome decoration and a wealth of turrets, spires, and arches.

At the end of the century this heavily ornamented look was simplified by, among others, Willem Kromhout, who designed the American Hotel, which is worth visiting. Hendrik Berlage followed, and his Amsterdam Stock Exchange and the Diamond Workers' Trade Union building are two examples of more refined Dutch style.

Holland showed little inclination to dabble in art nouveau, although J. M. Van der Meij approached it with his Scheepvaarthuis or Dock offices on the Prins Hendrik quay in Amsterdam. Among the more modern functionalists, J. P. Oud and Willem Dudok are the best known.

4 Sports and Recreation

Water sports, as you might expect, predominate in Holland. There is hardly anything that can be done on or in the water that isn't done in this water-minded country, including sailing, yachting, windsurfing, and waterskiing. VVV offices can tell you where equipment can be rented, and you'll find the Dutch eager to assist any water-sports enthusiast. Holland's beaches afford good swimming except those where currents are strong and treacherous—it is best to stick to resort areas where waters are safe and lifeguards present. There are also many public swimming pools, both indoor and outdoor.

Fishing is another popular sport, and the VVV can guide you to rental equipment for trying your luck in inland lakes and rivers as well as charter boats for deep-sea fishing. No license is needed for fishing either out at sea or on the shore, and there are no seasonal restrictions. You must have a license for inland fishing, however, available at any post office. Consult the tourist board pamphlet "Fishing" for complete details on regulations and a guide to good fishing locations.

Tennis and golf facilities are fairly spotty in Holland, although local VVV offices can usually point you to tennis clubs and private golf clubs, many of which welcome visitors. Only five public golf courses exist in the country, however: at Rotterdam, Rhoon, Oostvoorne, Velsen/IJmuiden, and Wowse Plantage.

Equestrians will want to obtain a copy of the tourist board's "Horseriding" publication that gives the addresses of stables and horseback-riding schools, along with names of pony camps for children where they are given instruction at all levels.

5 Food and Drink

Food

"Simple, hearty, top-notch ingredients"—that description most accurately fits native Dutch cuisine. "Dull" does not. Unless, that is, you personally consider beautifully fresh fish, fowl, vegetables, and fruits prepared without overembellishment dull. Add to those high-quality ingredients a wide variety of other meats, butter used more lavishly than you might expect, and the world's best cheeses, and you have a choice of stick-to-your-ribs meals that are interesting and always served in ample quantities.

That, briefly, is the Dutch cuisine—which is *not* to say that it's the only cuisine available in Holland. Far from it! Far-ranging Dutch explorers and traders brought back recipes and exotic spices, and the popular Indonesian *rijsttafel* (rice table) has been a national favorite ever since it arrived in the 17th century. If you've never experienced this mini-feast, it should definitely be on your "must eat" list for Holland. If you part company with the Dutch and their love of Indonesian food, you'll find the cuisines of France, China, Italy, Greece, Turkey, Yugoslavia, and several other nationalities well represented.

THE RESTAURANTS

At the top of the restaurant scale are those posh dining rooms that are affiliated with the prestigious Alliance Gastronomique Néerlandaise or the Relais du Centre. They're likely to be elegant and sophisticated or atmospherically Old World or quaint. They will certainly be expensive.

For authentic Dutch dishes, look for the NEERLANDS DIS sign in restaurant windows. There are about 500 restaurants that specialize in the native cuisine, and tourist offices in the United States as well as Holland can supply a leaflet with the addresses of many.

Then there are the numerous moderately priced restaurants and little brown cafés. Dutch families gravitate to the restaurants, while the brown cafés are cozy social centers with simple but tasty food, often served outside on sidewalk tables. Sidewalk vendors, with fresh herring and the ubiquitous *broodjes* (sandwiches) or other light specialty, are as popular as the brown cafés.

A real bargain is the Dutch Tourist Menu served in more than 500 restaurants around the country, especially in Amsterdam and other large cities. Representing the single best dining value, it consists of a three-course fixed-price menu, usually chosen from the restaurant's own specialties. Pick up a directory from any VVV office or from the Netherlands Board of Tourism before you leave home.

Two things you should know about all restaurants: Dutch menus list appetizers, *not main courses,* under "entrée"; and a 15% service charge plus VAT is included in almost all prices.

Note: Most restaurants are open from noon to 2:30pm for lunch, and from 7 to 10pm for dinner seven days a week. However, these hours may be flexible.

THE CUISINE

Broodjes   Sandwiches made of small rolls filled with beef, ham, cheese, or other stuffings.

Croquetten   Delicious fried croquettes with soft innards, usually of cheese or meat and served with mustard.

Erwtensoep   A thick pea soup (usually available only in winter) frequently served with sausage and brown bread—traditionally, it should be thick enough to hold a spoon upright!

Hutspot   The thick stew of potatoes, carrots, onions, and lean meat that is said to have been left behind by Spanish soldiers as they fled the Dutch who broke the siege of Leiden in 1574.

Nieuwe Haring   Fresh-caught herring straight from the North Sea and eaten raw or with onion, available only in summer months; pickled herring is eaten year-round.

Pannekoeken (Poffertjes)   Wonderfully thin, plate-size pancakes served flat, with a choice of such toppings as syrup, jam, cooked apples, hot ginger sauce, or confectioner's sugar.

Rijsttafel   An Indonesian "rice table" with as many as two dozen different small dishes served, along with plenty of rice to buffer the spicy vegetables and fruits; best accompanied by beer, mineral water, or similar cold drink—not with milk or wine.

Saucijzenbrood   A spicy Dutch sausage wrapped in flaky pastry (looks much like a hot dog).

Tostis   Grilled cheese-and-ham sandwiches.

Drink

What to drink? The Dutch favor one of their own excellent beers or the marvelous—and potent!—native gin known as *jenever.* The latter is a fiery, colorless liquid served ice cold to be drunk "neat"—it's not a mixer. *Jonge* (young) jenever is less sweet and creamy than the *oude* (old) variety, but both are known for their delayed-action effectiveness. There are also very good Dutch liqueurs, such as Curaçao and Triple Sec. Wines from all over the world are readily available.

Coffee lovers may agree with my personal opinion that Dutch coffee is the best in the world. Hot chocolate is also a delicious and popular beverage.

6   Recommended Books

ART

Brown, Christopher. *Images of a Golden Past: Dutch Genre Painting of the 17th Century.* Abbeville, 1984.

Fuchs, R. H. *Dutch Painting.* Oxford University Press, 1978.

Sutton, Peter C., and Brown, Christopher. *Masters of Seventeenth Century Dutch Landscape Painting.* University of Pennsylvania Press, 1987.

HISTORY

Attitudes of the Dutch Population on Alternative Life Styles and Environmental Deterioration. UNIPUB, 1980.

Blok, Petrus J. *History of the People of the Netherlands* (5 vol.). Putnam, 1970 reprint of 1912 edition.

Burnchurch R. *An Outline of Dutch History.* Heinman, 1982.

Clark, G. N. *The Birth of the Dutch Republic.* Longwood Pub. Group, 1975.

Hopkins, Adam. *Holland: Its History, Paintings and People.* Faber and Faber, 1988.

Huizinga, John. *The Waning of the Middle Ages: Study of the Forms of Life, Thought and Art in France and the Netherlands.* Doubleday, 1954.

Rogers, James E. *The Story of Holland.* Gordon Press, 1977.

Schama, Simon. *The Embarrassment of Riches: An Interpretation of Dutch Culture in the Golden Age.* Knopf, 1987.

NAZI OCCUPATION

Frank, Anne. *Anne Frank: The Diary of a Young Girl.* Doubleday, 1967.

Hillesum, Etty. *An Interrupted Life.* Pocket Books, 1984.

Janssen, Pierre, trans. by William R. Tyler. *A Moment of Silence.* Macmillan, 1970.

Warmbrunn, Werner. *The Dutch Under German Occupation, 1940–1945.* Stanford University Press, 1963.

12

Planning a Trip to Holland

THIS CHAPTER DEALS WITH THE PRACTICALITIES OF A VISIT TO HOLLAND—AND ABOVE all else, Holland is a practical country. Rail and bus connections to other European destinations are excellent, as they are within the country itself. And whether you choose to drive or use the excellent Dutch public transport system, getting around is a simple matter.

---

1 Currency and Costs

CURRENCY   Holland's basic monetary unit is the **guilder,** yet you'll see it written as Dutch florins (abbreviated "f.," "fl.," or "Dfl."); since this is a holdover from the past, just ignore the written symbol and read all prices as guilders. There are 100 Dutch cents to a guilder, and prices are expressed in the familiar decimal system.

The Dutch Guilder

For American Readers   At this writing $1 = approximately Dfl. 1.90 (or Dfl. 1 = 53¢), and this was the rate of exchange used to calculate the dollar values given in this book (rounded off).

For British Readers   At this writing £1 = approximately Dfl. 2.80 (or Dfl. 1 = 36p), and this was the rate of exchange used to calculate the pound values in the table below.

Note   The rates given here fluctuate from time to time and may not be the same when you travel to Holland. Therefore this table should be used only as a general guide:

Dfl.	U.S.$	U.K.£	Dfl.	U.S.$	U.K.£
.05	.03	.02	15	7.89	5.36
.10	.05	.04	20	10.53	7.14
.25	.13	.09	25	13.16	8.93
1	.53	.36	30	15.79	10.71
2	1.05	.71	40	21.05	14.29
2.50	1.32	.89	50	26.32	17.86
3	1.58	1.07	75	39.47	26.79
4	2.11	1.43	100	52.63	35.71
5	2.63	1.79	125	65.79	44.64
6	3.16	2.14	150	78.95	53.57
7	3.68	2.50	175	92.11	62.50
8	4.21	2.86	200	105.26	71.43
9	4.74	3.21	250	131.58	89.29
10	5.26	3.57	300	157.89	107.14

What Things Cost in Amsterdam	U.S.$
Taxi from the airport to the city center	30.00
Tram from Centraal Station to Waterlooplein	1.57
Local telephone call	.13
Double room at the Amsterdam Renaissance (deluxe)	332.00
Double room at the Canal House Hotel (moderate)	110.00
Double room at the Bridge Hotel (budget)	79.00
Lunch for one at Haesje Claes (moderate)	19.00
Lunch for one at Broodje van Kootje (budget)	6.00
Dinner for one, without wine, at De Kelderhof (deluxe)	35.00
Dinner for one, without wine, at Casa Tobio (moderate)	29.00
Dinner for one, without wine, at the Café de Passage (budget)	19.00
Glass of beer	1.85
Coca-Cola	1.55
Cup of coffee	1.55
Roll of ASA 100 color film, 36 exposures	7.50
Admission to the Rijksmuseum	5.25
Movie ticket	10.50
Concert ticket to the Concertgebouw	18.00

There are six Dutch **coins** currently in circulation: Dfl. .05 (called a "stuiver"), Dfl. .10 ("dubbeitie"), Dfl. .25 ("kwartie"), Dfl. 1 ("guilder"), Dfl. 2.50 ("rijksdaaier"), and Dfl. 5 ("beatrix"). The six Dutch **banknotes** come in different colors: Dfl. 5 (green), Dfl. 10 (blue), Dfl. 25 (red), Dfl. 50 (yellow), Dfl. 100 (brown), and Dfl. 1,000 (green). Each note has a little rough patch in one corner indicating its value in braille.

CURRENCY EXCHANGE   In Holland it's possible to change your traveler's checks or foreign currency outside banking hours at some 65 GWK Bureau de Change offices: 30 of them in railway stations and others at border checkpoints. They have extended evening and weekend hours and can also provide cash advances for holders of American Express, Diners Club, MasterCard, and Visa credit and charge cards. For each cash, traveler's check, or credit/charge-card cash-advance transaction up to Dfl. 50 ($26.30), GWK charges Dfl. 2.50 ($1.30); for Dfl. 50.05 ($26.35) up to Dfl. 150 ($78.95), the charge is Dfl. 4.50 ($2.35); for amounts over Dfl. 150, the charge is 3% up to a maximum charge of Dfl. 25 ($13.15). GWK also does money transfers via Western Union.

Some international trains provide currency exchange, as do many tourist offices in coastal resorts. American Express offices also operate currency exchanges, and there are numerous other commercial bureau de change companies, which invariably charge higher fees.

When to Go—Climate, Holidays, and Events

"In-season" in Holland means mid-April through mid-October. The peak of the tourist season is July and August, and in all honesty, that's when the weather is at its finest. Weather, however, is never really extreme at any time of year; and if you're one of the growing numbers who favor shoulder- or off-season travel, you'll find Holland every bit as attractive during those months. Not only are airlines, hotels, and restaurants cheaper and less crowded during this time (with more relaxed service that means you get more personal attention), but there are also some very appealing things going on in these seasons.

Holland's bulb fields are bursting with color from mid-April to mid-May; its concert and theater season blossoms in January; and on the third Tuesday in September, Queen Beatrix boards a golden coach drawn by eight magnificent horses to ride to the Knights' Hall in The Hague to formally open Parliament amid a burst of old-world pageantry.

CLIMATE   Holland has a maritime climate, which means that there are few extremes in temperature in summer or winter. Summer temperatures average about 67°F; the winter average is 35°F. Expect more than a little rain, however (it's driest from February through May). One Amsterdam hotel, in fact, has done a land-office business with tourists from the Middle East by promising free lodging for every day it doesn't rain during any two-week stay—they don't give away many days, and their rain-parched guests go home happily drenched! The accompanying chart shows both the hours of sunshine and amount of rain for each month of the year, along with average high temperatures.

Holland's Average Temperature, Rainfall, and Sunshine

	Jan	Feb	Mar	Apr	May	June	July	Aug	Sept	Oct	Nov	Dec
Temp. (°F)	40	41	47	53	61	66	69	69	65	57	48	42
Rain (in.)	2.5	1.9	1.9	1.9	2	2.4	3.2	3.3	2.7	2.7	3	2.9
Sunshine (hrs.)	46	66	112	160	205	210	190	185	142	102	53	40

HOLIDAYS   Public holidays in Holland are January 1 (New Year's Day), Good Friday, Easter Sunday and Monday, April 30 (Queen's Day), Ascension Day, Whitsunday and Whitmonday, December 25 (Christmas), and December 26 (Boxing Day).

In addition, there are two "Remembrance Days" related to World War II, neither of which is an official holiday, although you may find some shops closed: May 4 honors all those who died in that war and May 5 celebrates Liberation Day.

Holland Calendar of Events

January

- **Concert and theater season,** in full sway in The Hague and Rotterdam, as well as Amsterdam. Concerts by the Philharmonic Orchestra in The Hague, and theatrical productions by local and touring companies in The Hague and Rotterdam. Jan–Apr.

- **International Film Festival,** Rotterdam. Mid-Jan.
- **Jazz Week,** The Hague. Third week.

February

- **Carnivals,** southern (Catholic) provinces. Seven weeks before Easter.
- **West Frisian Flora,** Bovenkarspel, North Holland. Bulb and household furnishings trade show. Late Feb.

March

- **Spring Fair,** Utrecht. Eight-day celebration. Early to mid-Mar.
- **Opening of Keukenhof flower gardens,** Lisse. Spectacular showing of hyacinths, narcissi, and tulips. Late Mar to May.

April

- **Flower parade,** from Haarlem to Noordwijk. Floats keyed to a different theme each year. Early to mid-Apr.
- **Weekly antiques markets,** The Hague and Breda. Early Apr to Sept.
- **Queen's Day.** Countrywide celebration honoring the House of Orange, with parades, street fairs, and street entertainments. Apr 30.

May

- **World War II Memorial Day.** Countrywide observance, principally marked by two minutes of silence at 8pm. May 4.
- **Liberation Day.** Commemorating the end of World War II and Holland's liberation from Nazi forces. May 5.
- **National Cycling and Windmill Day.** Working windmills around the country open to the public. Second Sat.
- **Flag Day.** The ports of Scheveningen, IJmuiden, and Vlaardingen open herring season, with a highly competitive race to bring the first herring back for Queen Beatrix. Mid-May.
- **Frisian Eleven Cities Tourist Cycle Race,** Bolsward, Friesland. Mid-May.

June

- **Poetry International,** Rotterdam. Worldwide poetry competition, which attracts top talent. Early to mid-June.
- **Equestrian Show,** The Hague. Annual showing with international competitors. Early to mid-June.
- **International Yachting Race,** Harlingen to Terschelling. Mid-June.
- **International Rose-Growing Competition,** Westbroek Park, The Hague. Mid-June to Sept.

July

- **Folklore Market,** Hoorn. Colorful crafts collections held every Wed. July to mid-Aug.
- **North Sea Jazz Festival,** The Hague. One of the world's leading gatherings of top international jazz musicians. Mid-July.

August

- **Flower Parade,** Rijnsburg–Leiden–Noordwijk. First Sat.
- **Flower Parade,** Leersum, Utrecht. Third Sat (date varies; check with the VVV).
- **Festival of Old Music,** Utrecht. Marvelous concerts of music from the Middle Ages through the Romantic era. Mid to late Aug.

- **International Firework Festival,** The Hague. Highlighted by a four-day cycle race. Late Aug.
- **Windmill Day,** Zaanse. All mills are open to the public. Entire month.

September

- **Flower processions,** Aalsmeer, Breda. First two weeks.
- **Holland Dance Festival,** The Hague. Dance, from classical to folk, celebrated by dance troupes from around the world. Early Sept to early Oct.
- **Opening of Parliament,** The Hague. Queen Beatrix rides in a splendid gold coach to the Knights' Hall to open the legislative session. Third Tues.

October

- **Herfstflora,** Laren, North Holland. Splendid display of autumn flowers. Early Oct.
- **Classical Art and Antique Fair,** Delft. Three-week showing in the Prinsenhof Museum. Mid-Oct (dates are flexible, so check with the VVV).

November

- **International Flower Show,** Aalsmeer, Breda. Largest exhibit of autumn-blooming flowers. Early Nov.

December

- **Saint Nicholas's Eve.** Traditional day in Holland for exchanging Christmas gifts. Dec 5.

Amsterdam Calendar of Events

January

- **Concert and theater season,** most active during this month. The Concertgebouw Orchestra stars, with many concerts and recitals of smaller musical groups and performing artists. Theater productions include local and visiting companies. Jan–Apr.

February

- **Auto Rail.** The newest car models from around the world are on display. Second week.

March

- **Hiswa.** Annual water-sports exhibition. First week.
- **Lighting of Bridges.** From sundown to midnight, arched bridges and some gabled buildings are illuminated, giving the canals a fairyland appearance. Mar–Oct.
- **Spui Art Market.** Outdoor exhibition of work by local artists on the Spui. Mar–Dec.

April

- **The Gein Run.** Runners race through the southeast section of the city. Mid-Apr.
- **National Museum Weekend.** Most museums are open to the public without charge; others offer reduced admission fees. Mid-Apr.

May

- **Blue/White Junior Football Tournament,** in the Olympic stadium. Exciting contest for young football players. Mid-May.
- **Floating Amsterdam.** The Amstel River is the setting for musical and theatrical productions near the Muziektheater (opera house). Last two weeks.

June

- **Holland Festival.** Month-long concentration of musical and theatrical performances in the city's theaters. Entire month.
- **Echo Canal Run.** Running race on the pathways by the canals. Second week.
- **Books Along the Amstel River.** Great place to pick up book bargains on the banks of the Amstel near the Muziektheater. Sun in late June.

July

- **Drum International Jazz Festival.** Four days of swinging music in the city's musical venues. First week.
- **Holland Cup.** International junior football (soccer) tournament. Late July to early Aug.

August

- **Prinsengracht concert.** This city-center canal is the setting for musical entertainment from flat-bottomed boats. Date varies, check with the VVV.
- **Folk Dances on the Dam.** Dancers from around the world perform their native dances. Late Aug.

September

- **International Football Tournament.** There's great excitement among sports fans as team gather from around the globe. Date varies; check with the VVV.
- **Hiswa.** Yacht show on the East dock. First week.
- **Floral Parade.** From the flower market at Aalsmeer to Amsterdam. First or second week.

October

- **National Pictura Antiquairs.** Week-long antiques fair. Usually early Oct, but can vary.
- **Jumping Amsterdam.** Prestigious horse show. Late Oct to early Nov.

November

- **Amsterdam Marathon.** Runners take to the city streets. Variable date, usually in early Nov.

December

- **Saint Nicholas's Eve.** Traditional day in Holland for exchanging Christmas gifts. Dec 5.

3 | Getting Around

Like Belgium, Holland is so compact it makes for easy sightseeing. Roads and express motorways are excellent, and nondrivers have one of Europe's best railway systems to take them to virtually any point in the country.

BY PLANE Because Holland is so small, you'll need to fly from one city to another only if you're extremely pressed for time. If so, then the KLM subsidiary, **NLM City Hopper,** can fly you to Rotterdam, Eindhoven, and Maastricht. They also fly to London, Birmingham, Belfast, the Channel Islands, Antwerp, Brussels, Stuttgart, Bremen, Hamburg, and Dusseldorf. If you're only going for the day, they offer attractive discounts on one-day round-trips, as well as weekend discounts. Call local KLM reservations offices for schedules and fares. City Hopper timetables are also on display at most KLM ticket counters.

BY TRAIN All major tourist destinations in Holland are within 2 to 2¹/₂ hours of Amsterdam via **Nederlandse Spoorwagen,** Holland's national rail system. Spotlessly clean and always on time, the trains are a delightful way to travel with the Dutch, who use them even for short journeys to the next town up the line. The trains run so often that you can probably just go to the station and wait for the next train to your destination, knowing that your wait will be short. At even the smallest stations, there is half-hour service in both directions, and major destination points have between four and eight trains an hour in both directions, so you'll never get stuck. Service begins as early as 5am (7am on Sunday and holidays), running until around 1am. A complete rail timetable (*spoorboekje*) is available at railway stations for a small charge, as well as a free intercity timetable (sufficient for most tourist needs).

If all or most of your travel will be by rail, your best investment is one of the **NS special programs,** like Domino Holland, Summer Tour, Benelux Tourrail, and Multi Rover. For example, Summer Tour—valid only in June, July, and August—entitles you to 3 days of travel in Holland within 10 consecutive days and costs Dfl. 79 ($41) in second class, Dfl. 104 ($55) in first class, with a supplement of only Dfl. 40 ($21) for a second person. For more details, call the Netherlands Board of Tourism in Chicago (☎ **312/819-0300**), Toronto (☎ **416/363-1577**), or Holland (☎ **06/9292**).

There are also several very attractive bargain day fares to specific destinations, a train-and-bicycle fare, and family excursion fares. The "Touring Holland by Rail" booklet published by NS gives full details—it's available from tourist offices or major railway stations.

If you're going to travel in all three Benelux countries, the five-day **Benelux Tourrail Ticket** is a good buy, and for rail travel throughout Europe the best value is the **Eurailpass** (see "Getting There" in Chapter 1).

BY BUS A superb bus system connects most Dutch towns, and service details are included in the railway timetable (*spoorboekje*), mentioned above and available at railway stations. For schedule and fare information, contact **Streekvervoer ESO,** Postbus 19222, 3501 Utrecht, or check with local bus stations, which are usually adjacent to or very near railway stations.

BY TAXI Taxis must either be engaged at taxi ranks at hotels, railway stations, and shopping areas or called by telephone. Tip and taxes are included in the meter price, and you need not add another tip unless there has been exceptional service (help with heavy luggage, etc.).

BY CAR   Driving is easy in Holland except, as in most countries, in the larger cities where traffic congestion can be positively ulcer-causing. Outside the cities, however, both major motorways and local roads are excellent; they're well planned (as you'd expect from the efficient Dutch), well maintained, and well signposted, and many are lighted at night.

Rentals   Rental cars with U.S. specifications are available from rental desks at Schiphol Airport and the following Amsterdam addresses (airport pickup and drop-off is also available in most cases): **Hertz,** Overtoom 333 (☎ **020/612-2441**); **Avis,** Nassaukade 380 (☎ **020/683-6061**); and **Europcar,** Wibautstraat 224A (☎ **020/666-8211**). Expect to pay Dfl. 50 to 155 ($26–$81) per day, depending on the type (stick shift or automatic) and model you choose. On a daily basis, you'll pay an additional per-kilometer charge, plus insurance, and a 20% tax. Weekly rates, with unlimited mileage, represent a much better buy, with rates of Dfl. 550 to 3,400 ($290 to $1,790), the latter for a luxury Mercedes.

Gasoline   You'll pay between Dfl. 1.70 and 1.93 (90¢ and $1.01) per liter (0.26 gal.) for gasoline (petrol, or *benzine*) as we go to press, but remember that these prices are among the most likely to fluctuate.

Driving Rules   To drive in Holland, U.S. citizens need only a valid passport, a U.S. driver's license, and a registration for the car you drive. Minimum age for drivers is 18. On motorways, the speed limit is 100kmph (60 m.p.h.); in all cities and urban areas, 50kmph (30 m.p.h.); and in the outskirts of towns and cities, 80kmph (48 m.p.h.). Traffic approaching from the right has the right of way, and pedestrians on the wide strips at crossings *always* have the right of way.

Road Maps   Perfectly adequate road maps for Holland, as well as street maps for major cities, are available from local VVV offices or in advance from Netherlands Board of Tourism offices. Excellent road maps are also published by the KNAC or the ANWB motoring organizations and available from bookshops and some newsagents.

Breakdowns and Assistance   If you're a member of a national automobile club, such as the American Automobile Association, you are automatically entitled to the services of **ANWB Royal Dutch Touring Club.** They sponsor the fleet of yellow *wegenwacht,* a sort of repair shop on wheels that you'll see patrolling the highways, and there are special yellow call boxes on all major roads to bring them to your assistance. Emergency call boxes marked POLITIE will bring the police on the double.

HITCHHIKING   Hitchhiking is illegal on major motorways (which lead to just about every sightseeing destination). You can, however, hitch on entrance and exit roadways, and the Dutch are generally quite amenable to giving a lift.

Suggested Itineraries

If you can spend only one week in Holland, I strongly recommend that you base yourself in Amsterdam and make day trips to nearby cities and towns—none more than an hour away by train and some even closer. Or join the excellent narrated coach tours that fan out from Amsterdam each day covering important nearby destinations in only half a day. By returning each evening to Amsterdam, you'll not only develop a real feeling for that intriguing and fascinating city, but also save a lot of the wear and tear that comes with shifting accommodations every day or so. Of course, should one of those day trips trigger an instant love affair with a special spot, that's the place to plant yourself—you can always let Amsterdam be the day trip.

CITY HIGHLIGHTS

Amsterdam could hold you for the entire length of your stay because of its many enticements. You won't want to miss the great Rijksmuseum, whose most treasured jewel is Rembrandt's *The Night Watch;* you really shouldn't miss the van Gogh Museum; and you can top off your museum tripping with a visit to the Stedelijk Museum, with its contemporary art collection. But it's the fascinating old narrow streets, meandering canals, inviting "brown cafés" and pubs, gabled canal houses, floating flower market, and a hundred other details of this beautiful old city that will hold you enthralled.

The Hague, one of Europe's prettiest capitals, is the seat of the government, the home of Queen Beatrix, and the next-door neighbor of Scheveningen, beach resort par excellence.

Rotterdam has emerged from the total devastation it suffered during World War II with a totally modern face, its life centered around a tremendously efficient and busy harbor, the Europoort.

Delft, whose name has become synonymous with the unique earthenware created here, is a charming and pretty little city, the home of the painter Jan Vermeer.

Leiden clutches a windmill to its heart, right in the middle of town, and relishes memories of the 11-year sojourn of the Pilgrims before they left to sail on to America.

Leeuwarden dates back to the 15th century, and parts of it are built on earthen mounds constructed by Holland's earliest settlers.

Apeldoorn sits in Holland's central forest, one of the most scenic locations in the country. The splendid palace that Queen Wilhelmina loved has been restored and is open to the public, as is an art museum.

Utrecht, capital of that province, is primarily an industrial city, albeit a picturesque one. It is Holland's medieval monument with wonderful old buildings from the 16th century, when this was one of the leading religious centers of Europe—medieval churches, high-gabled houses, and winding canals.

Maastricht is Holland's oldest fortified city, tracing its history all the way back to the Romans, and filled with great medieval buildings.

The **Middelburg** town center is a wonder of Gothic and Renaissance buildings, tiny twisting streets, and a serene abbey.

PLANNING YOUR ITINERARY

If You Have One Week

Days 1 and 2   You'll need at least the first two days to explore Amsterdam and highlights of its outstanding cultural attractions, perhaps including the three-hour sightseeing tour that includes stops at an important museum and a diamond-cutting exhibition.

Day 3   Take a four-hour morning tour to Marken beside the IJsselmeer, visiting a wooden-shoe workshop en route; use the afternoon to visit another of Amsterdam's museums; save this evening for the candlelight cruise of Amsterdam's canals.

Day 4   Spend this day with a city-packed, eight-hour tour that visits The Hague, Scheveningen, Rotterdam, and Delft, returning to Amsterdam for a dinner of traditional Dutch specialties at one of the "Neerlands Dis" restaurants.

Day 5 If your visit falls between March and May when the tulips are at their peak, spend this day visiting the famous flower auction at Aalsmeer, then drive to the beautiful Keukenhof Gardens, passing through acres of bulb fields that lie between Haarlem and Leiden. The gardens are lovely at any time of the year, since different species bloom in different months. If flowers have no appeal, the Haarlem–Leiden drive is worthwhile solely for sightseeing. Nondrivers can take a sightseeing coach tour. Return to Amsterdam for the evening, perhaps at one of the city's prolific jazz clubs.

Day 6 If this is a Friday, be sure to visit Alkmaar and its colorful morning cheese market, where giant wheels of cheese are auctioned in the town square (there's a coach tour every week), returning to Amsterdam by a circular route for stops at Edam and Volendam through windmill-studded countryside. Nondrivers can join an afternoon tour from Amsterdam to Edam and Volendam. Evening in Amsterdam.

Day 7 Save this day for your last Amsterdam sightseeing (have you been to the Anne Frank House yet?) and last-minute preparations for departure. Or use most of the day to travel up to the great Enclosing Dike that made a freshwater lake, IJsselmeer, from an arm of the salty Zuiderzee; return to Amsterdam by way of a dam over the IJsselmeer and the new town of Lelystad in the newest polder, Flevoland—it's a day that ends with respect for all that the Dutch have accomplished in taming the sea.

If You Have Two Weeks

The above pretty much limits you to sightseeing highlights, but if you have two weeks to spend, add the following. A car is not essential for this part of your visit, since every destination is easily reached by train or bus. Mind you, this itinerary will keep you hopping, and you may wish to be selective and save parts of Holland for your next visit. You may also want to juggle the suggested order, but bear in mind that travel will be easier if you save Zeeland for last if you're flying out of Amsterdam, Maastricht if you're traveling on in Europe.

Days 8–10 Drive from Amsterdam north through Hoorn and on across the Enclosing Dike and through the picturesque harbor town of Harlingen to Leeuwarden, in the province of Friesland. With Leeuwarden as a base, explore the countryside, site of Holland's earliest earthen mounds that preceded dikes; visit nearby Groningen, the tile-and-ceramic factory at Makkum, the pottery town of Workum, and Hindeloopen with its furniture painters. Nondrivers can make use of the good rail service from Amsterdam and local bus service within the Friesland region.

Day 11 Travel leisurely southward to the wooded Veluwe region of Gelderland and stay overnight in Apeldoorn (it has a royal palace and a noteworthy museum of modern art).

Day 12 Drive through Arnhem to Maastricht, historic—and surprisingly sophisticated—city in the province of Limburg. Spend the afternoon visiting the awesome Caves of St. Pietersberg, the evening dining in one of the excellent restaurants in the city, followed by a pub crawl through its interesting drinking spots. Stay overnight in Maastricht.

Day 13 Get an early start and drive across the country to Middelburg, in the province of Zeeland. Use the afternoon to explore this quaint city. Stay overnight in Middelburg.

Day 14 Make an early-morning visit to the incredibly massive Delta Project that's building another controlling "gate" to the sea, before driving back to Amsterdam.

SOME SIGHTSEEING TIPS

WINDMILLS   No, they haven't disappeared from Holland's landscape, but their numbers have decreased from some 10,000 to a mere 1,000—only about 200 of which are in use these days. The VVV (or the Netherlands Board of Tourism before you come) can furnish a list of those windmills officially open to the public, but you should know that the hospitable Dutch millers welcome visitors to private mills any time they hoist a flag outside to signify that they're inside and the mill is working.

FLOWERS   Of course you want to see Holland's famous bulb fields! And you will if you come between late March and mid-May. If you don't make it then, not to worry—there are gorgeous flowers in bloom right up to September, but not tulips. What you'll see other months are hyacinths, daffodils, roses, carnations, freesias, rhododendrons, hydrangeas, and even (in nurseries) Dutch orchids. The bulb fields are concentrated in the Leiden–Haarlem–Den Helder area and around Enkhuizen. To see the most lavish display of Dutch blooms, visit Keukenhof, the world's largest flower garden, near Lisse. For cut flowers, don't miss the floating flower market on Amsterdam's Singel Canal and the Aalsmeer flower auction just outside the city.

Fast Facts: Holland

American Express   See "Fast Facts: Amsterdam" in Chapter 13.

Business Hours   Banks are open Monday through Friday from 9am to 4pm (some stay open until 5pm). Some banks also open on late-hour shopping nights. Shops generally stay open weekdays from 8:30 or 9am to 5 or 6pm, on Saturday until 4 or 5pm. Some shops close for lunch, and nearly all have one full closing day or one morning or afternoon when they are closed—signs are prominently posted announcing those closing times. Many shops, especially in Amsterdam, have late hours on Thursday and/or Friday evening.

Climate   See "When to Go," earlier in this chapter.

Clothing   You'll certainly want to bring along a raincoat. Although the rain is not usually a heavy, splashing downpour, showers are frequent and often unexpected; a light jacket or sweater is a good idea to ward off the accompanying chill. In winter you'll need heavy outerwear for the occasional drop in temperature that so gladdens Dutch hearts if it's severe enough for the canals to freeze over. Otherwise, bring casual clothes for daytime activities, comfortable walking shoes (sturdy enough to stand up to cobblestones), and at least one semidressy outfit for after-dark Amsterdam.

Crime   See "Safety," below.

Currency   See "Currency and Costs," earlier in this chapter.

Customs   Before leaving home, be sure to register with Customs (at the airport) any camera, typewriter, etc., you plan to carry with you that could have been purchased abroad; otherwise you may very well have to pay duty on these items when you return home if you cannot prove they were not bought on your trip.

   When reentering the United States, citizens (regardless of age) are allowed up to a $400 exemption for goods bought overseas if they have been away for more than two days and have not had the same duty exemption within one month. Within that amount, those over 21 are allowed 1 liter of alcohol, 100 cigars (no Cuban cigars, however), 200 cigarettes, and one bottle of perfume with a U.S. trademark. Works of art and antiques more than 100 years old may be brought in duty-free (be sure to have its verification of age to present to Customs). No agricultural products or meats from overseas may be brought into the United States and will be confiscated if they're in your luggage. With the exception of alcohol, tobacco, and perfumes valued at more than $5, gifts worth up to $50 may be mailed to the United States as gifts, but only one per day to the same addressee.

Documents Required　See "Information, Entry Requirements, and Money" in Chapter 1.

Driving Rules　See "Getting Around," earlier in this chapter.

Drug Laws　Holland allows possession of up to 28 grams (0.9 oz.) of cannabis for your own consumption. You should, however, exercise a wide degree of discretion in actually smoking it in public in all parts of the country except Amsterdam, which is one of world's most liberal-minded cities when it comes to drug use. Needless to say, you should *not* be caught actually peddling drugs to others.

Electricity　Holland runs on 220 volts, so if you plan to bring a hairdryer, radio (unless it's battery-operated), travel iron, or any other small appliance, pack a European-style adapter plug and a transformer.

Embassies/Consulates　Most countries have embassies in The Hague, and a few also have consulates in Amsterdam. The Embassy of **Australia** is located at Carnegielaan 12, 2517 KH The Hague (☎ **070/310-8200**); the Embassy of **Canada** is at Parkstraat 25, 2514 GD The Hague (☎ **070/364-4825**); the Embassy of the **Republic of Ireland** is located at Dr Kuyperstraat 9, 2514 BA The Hague (☎ **070/363-0993**); and the Embassy of **New Zealand** is at Mauritskade 25, 2514 HD The Hague (☎ **070/346-9324**). The Embassy of the **United Kingdom** is located at Lange Voorhourt 10, 2514 ED The Hague (☎ **070/364-5800**), and there's a consulate in Amsterdam at Koningslaan 44 (☎ **020/676-4343**). Finally, the Embassy of the **United States** is at Lange Voorhourt 102, 2514 AG The Hague (☎ **070/362-4911**), and there's a consulate in Amsterdam at Museumplein 19 (☎ **020/664-5661**).

Emergencies　In case of accident, dial **900.** See Chapter 13 for individual medical, police, and other emergency numbers in Amsterdam.

Flowers　One look at Amsterdam's floating flower market and something in your soul is likely to prod you to buy one of the nicest of all souvenirs. That's fine, but you must know that Dutch flower bulbs can only be exported if they have been awarded an official health certificate. The wise thing to do is not to stick a few in your luggage—which may well be confiscated by Customs when you return home—but place an order with one of the many authorized mail-order companies.

Gasoline　See "Getting Around," earlier in this chapter.

Hitchhiking　See "Getting Around," earlier in this chapter.

Holidays　See "When to Go," earlier in this chapter.

Information　The U.S. addresses for the Netherlands Board of Tourism are given in Chapter 1, "Sources of Information." In Holland, you'll find one of the most efficient, best-organized tourist organizations you're likely to meet up with anywhere. The **Vereniging Voor Vreemdelingenverkeer** (Association for Tourist Traffic) is known by all and sundry as simply the **VVV,** and they operate more than 400 offices in cities, towns, and villages around the country. They can book accommodations for you, help with travel arrangements, tell you what's on where, and . . . well, if there's anything they can't do, I have yet to discover it! Look for a blue-and-white sign (many times triangular in shape) bearing the letters "VVV."

Language No problem here—almost everyone in the major cities speaks English. If you run into someone who speaks only Dutch, you may be sure they'll quickly round up someone who can speak to you in your own language.

Passports U.S. and Canadian citizens who plan to be in the country 90 days or less need bring only a valid passport—no visa is required. Citizens of other countries should consult the nearest Netherlands consulate.

Safety Whenever you're traveling in an unfamiliar city or country, stay alert. Be aware of your immediate surroundings. Wear a moneybelt and keep a close eye on your possessions. Be particularly careful with cameras, purses, and wallets—all favorite targets of thieves and pickpockets. Every society has its criminals. It's your responsibility to be aware and alert even in the most heavily touristed areas.

Telephone/Telex/Fax Telephones in Holland are similar to those in the United States (perhaps a little more efficient). Coin telephones accept the Dfl. 0.25 coin (*kwartie*); it doesn't drop until your call is answered. Direct dialing for other European countries as well as overseas (including the United States and Canada) is available in most hotel rooms in Amsterdam and other large cities. If your hotel is not equipped to handle international calls, they can be placed through most post offices. To avoid hotel surcharges and for the most economical international rates, dial the USA Direct operator (☎ **06/022-9111**). For directory assistance in finding a telephone number anywhere in Holland, call **008**; for numbers outside the country, dial **0018**.

Main post offices in major cities can furnish telex and fax services.

Time Holland is in the central European time zone, six hours ahead of eastern standard time in the United States (9am in New York is 3pm in Holland). Clocks are moved ahead one hour each year at the end of March and back one hour at the end of September.

Tipping Restaurants and hotels almost always include a 15% service charge and the 19% value added tax (VAT). Of course, the Dutch have a rather nice practice you may also want to follow: They invariably round off any bill (in a restaurant, café, taxi, etc.) to the nearest guilder and leave it as an extra sort of "thank you"—not really a tip, just leaving the change. Of course, if you've had exceptional service and want to add a little more, that's perfectly acceptable; it's just not obligatory. Taxis, as noted above, include the tip in the meter reading.

Visas See "Passports," above.

13

Amsterdam

AMSTERDAM HAS BEEN CALLED, AMONG OTHER THINGS, "THE VENICE OF HOLLAND," "the City of Pleasures," "Surprising Amsterdam," and "Amazing Amsterdam." All those titles, however, fall far short of encapsulating this city's essence. Its 160 canals outnumber those of Venice, and Amsterdam's ambience has none of the static "museum city" flavor that characterizes Venice. As for pleasures, it has been written that Amsterdam is "a city of simple pleasures, sophisticated pleasures, wicked pleasures, sacred pleasures"—I certainly wouldn't quarrel with any of those, yet a "pleasure" tag ignores the thriving port and the commercial face of Amsterdam. "Surprising" it most assuredly is, no matter how many times you come, and "amazing" fits too, but both are much too vague.

Many of your most treasured memories of Amsterdam will come from its streets: brightly painted barrel organs, the sound of carillons ringing out over the city every 15 minutes, flowers everywhere, herring stands, sidewalk cafés lining busy squares, and crowds ambling leisurely down pedestrian shopping streets.

BY WAY OF BACKGROUND

Amsterdam began as just a camp set up by two fishermen who recognized the advantages of settling on the River Amstel where it met the IJ (it's pronounced "eye" and means "water" in ancient Dutch), the spot now occupied by Dam Square in the heart of the central city. That was nearly 1,000 years ago, and until the 12th century it remained a simple little fishing settlement. By that time a dam had been constructed across the Amstel and the village called itself Amstelledamme. For a time in the 13th century Count Floris V tried to add it to his extensive holdings, even going so far as to grant special tax and beer-brewing privileges to its citizens. Finally the count bowed to the inevitable and granted "Amsterdam" a city charter in 1275.

From that time on the city thrived, sending its ships farther and farther across the seas to bring back goods from around the world to stock Amsterdam warehouses. Merchants grew wealthy, a banking industry sprang up to serve them, and the port was expanded. In the 17th century, the last three of the main curved canals (the Herengracht, Keizersgracht, and Prinsengracht) were added around the Singel (originally built as a moat to defend the city), which completed the watery crescents that now encircle the oldest part of the city.

Along the canals, merchants and bankers built elegant patrician homes, often with the upper floors used as storage warehouses for goods that could be unloaded from ships sailing up the Zuiderzee, then by canal to their front doors. The distinctive hooks you see today extended from almost every gable were used to pull merchandise to those upper floors, since the narrow inside stairways would not accommodate its bulk. That was the 17th century—Holland's Golden Age.

Because Amsterdam had early on established itself as a surrogate custodian of individual rights, almost every wave of European oppressors sent a wave of the oppressed pouring into the city. And with each wave came new talents, new cultures, and yet another ingredient in the city's *hutspot*. For example, Jews fleeing Antwerp came to Amsterdam and adopted the only trade not governed by a restrictive guild: diamond cutting, an important field in the modern city's economy.

The canal system that worked so well for trade was equally effective as a defense measure, and the forces of both William II and Louis XIV were turned back when the locks were opened to flood them out. Napoléon, however, arrived in the bitterly cold January of 1795, and when the same tactics were tried he sent his horse troops

What's Special About Amsterdam

Canals

- Prinsengracht, Herengracht, and Keizersgracht, lined by stunning canal houses topped by step, bell, and other decorative gables.
- Smaller canals with colorful houseboats anchored along their banks.

Museums

- The Vincent van Gogh Museum, where you can trace the artistic and psychological development of this great impressionist.
- The Stedelijk Museum, with its cache of works by modern artists.
- The Rijksmuseum, 150 rooms of incredible Dutch and other European masters, plus superb decorative-arts and Asian art collections.
- The Anne Frankhuis, a moving and eerily real experience of the World War II hideaway in which the famous diary was written.

After Dark

- The Concertgebouw, offering world-class performances in a hall with superb acoustics.
- The Red Light District, testament to the city's tolerance and pragmatism—not for everyone, though.
- Jazz clubs, brown cafés, tasting houses, coffeehouses, and more—all offering a genial, authentic experience.

Monuments

- *Homomonument*, fashioned out of three pink granite triangles—in memory of those gays and lesbians killed during World War II.
- *The Dockworker*, a moving memorial to the February Strike against the deportation of Jews in World War II.

Neighborhoods

- Jordaans, a lively former working-class area now filled with clubs, coffeehouses, and vibrant life.

Shopping

- Kalverstraat, Amsterdam's main shopping street.
- Nieuwe Spiegelstraat, hunting ground for fine antiques.
- Waterlooplein and Albert Cuypstraat, for the stuff of fleamarkets.

Architectural Highlights

- Bridges—more than 1,200 of them spanning the canals.
- The American Hotel, with its extraordinary art nouveau interior.
- The striking buildings designed by Hendrik Berlage and the Amsterdam School, for example, the Amsterdam Stock Exchange.

Other Highlights

- Diamonds, cheeses, herring, beer, and, of course, flowers, which you'll find at the floating flower market on the Singel Canal.

Festivals

- The Holland Festival—theater, music, opera, and dance—during June.

Historic Homes

- Rembrandthuis, home of the city's greatest portrait painter.

galloping across ice that had quickly formed on the flood waters. It was he who turned the Town Hall on Dam Square into a royal palace, installing his brother as king of Holland, a reign that lasted only five years.

With Napoléon's defeat in 1815 and the return of House of Orange rulers, Amsterdam resumed the business of meeting stiff trade competition on the high seas, primarily from the English, whose huge ships could no longer reach the city because of the silting-up Zuiderzee. That competition and the city's declining access to the sea made a big dent in Amsterdam's prosperity, but with their customary ingenuity the industrious Dutch simply dug a new canal to the sea, the North Sea Canal, with depths that could accommodate large, oceangoing vessels.

In May 1940 Nazi troops swept into the city initiating one of its darkest—and most heroic—periods. In February 1941 the Nazis experienced their first taste of Dutch resistance when all Amsterdam staged a strike protesting the wholesale exportation of Jews. In the end, the strike failed, and there were massive reprisals. The resistance movement worked underground throughout the war years, however, maintaining constant communication with the British government and performing feats of sabotage and prisoner escape that will probably never be fully documented.

By the winter of 1944–45, food supplies in Amsterdam were being confiscated for shipment to a Germany nearing defeat and Amsterdammers were literally starving, some eating tulip bulbs just to stay alive. With no electricity, gas, or coal, centuries-old floorboards were torn up and burned. Some 5,000 premises were simply demolished for their building materials or for lack of repair materials. Known as the "hunger winter," 1944–45 was an endless struggle for the people of Amsterdam, yet its underground organization never once wavered and was in fact a key factor in Holland's liberation by Allied troops in May 1945.

Since then Amsterdam has expanded its port by digging another canal, the Amsterdam-Rhine Canal, this one linking it to Europe's inland industries in 1952. It has waged a highly successful campaign to attract new industries, and it continues to welcome the oppressed, the rebellious, and just plain tourists like you and me with an exuberant, zestful personality that makes "unique" truly an Amsterdam label.

1   Orientation

Arriving

BY PLANE   For details on air travel to Holland, see Chapter 1. Opened in 1968, **Schiphol Airport** (☎ 601-0966) is extremely well organized, with signs in English and an automated baggage system that usually manages to have your luggage waiting by the time you've deplaned and made your way through a streamlined Customs desk and a well-planned escalator/moving-sidewalk network. There are free luggage trolleys. There's good bus service and a fast rail link into Amsterdam, as well as a taxi rank just outside the terminal. A one-way rail ticket to or from Schiphol Airport costs Dfl. 6 ($3.15); the taxi fare averages Dfl. 60 ($31). When it comes to duty-free shops, Schiphol excels; there are more than 50 shops filled with more than 40,000 different items.

There is excellent, frequent train service from the arrivals lounge at Schiphol to Amsterdam, Rotterdam, and The Hague. Motorists will find the airport conveniently located on the A4 motorway running between Amsterdam, The Hague, and Rotterdam.

BY TRAIN   International trains arrive at **Centraal Station.** Call **06/9292** Monday through Friday from 8am to 10pm, on Saturday and Sunday from 9am to 10pm, for rail information for Holland and other European destinations, or consult ticket windows at Centraal Station.

BY BUS   International coaches arrive at the main bus terminal opposite Centraal Station.

BY CAR   Amsterdam is reached via the A4 motorway, which also runs to The Hague and Rotterdam.

Tourist Information

The **main VVV office** is across from Centraal Station at Stationsplein 10 (☎ **06/340-34-066;** fax 020/625-2869), open daily in summer from 9am to 11pm; shorter hours other months. A **subsidiary VVV office** is located at Leidsestraat 106, with daily summer hours of 9am to 10pm.

City Layout

You will be the exception if you don't—at least once—get lost in the maze of Amsterdam's streets. Although the city map (see "Street Maps," below) looks straightforward, the problem is with the "necklace" of canals around the city center, or **Centrum.** It's amazingly easy to find yourself following a curving canal in exactly the opposite direction from the one you intended. Because of that, I strongly suggest you arm yourself with a city map. One consolation, however: This is one city where it may be fun to get lost—no matter where you wind up, it won't be dull, and it gives you a chance to ask passersby for directions, which may open up a friendly, helpful conversation.

Before scanning your map, you should know that *gracht,* when tacked onto a name, means canal (unless, of course, it applies to a street that once was a canal and is now filled in); *kade* usually means the quay (or small street) running down the side of a canal; *straat* simply means street; *plein* is a square; *laan* is a boulevard, usually lined with trees; and *steeg* is an alley.

MAIN ARTERIES & STREETS   Map in hand, look first at the four semicircular canals (Prinsengracht, Keizersgracht, Herengracht, and Singel) that form a half moon at the heart of the city and the smaller canals that cross them much like the spokes of a wheel. Many of the places you will want to go are along these waterways. Next, look for the main focal point of Amsterdam orientation, **Dam Square.** The important street,

IMPRESSIONS

In Amsterdam the foundation costs more than the superstructure, for the ground being soft, they are constrained to ram in huge stakes of timber (with wool about it to preserve it from putrefaction) till they come to a firm basis; so that, as one said. "Whosoever could see Amsterdam under ground should see a huge winter-forest."
—James Howell, 1622

Every building in this magnificent city stands upon enormous piles, and it was in allusion to this forest foundation, that Erasmus, when he first visited Amsterdam, observed, "that he had reached a city, the inhabitants of which lived like crows upon the tops of trees."
—Charles Tennant, *A Tour, etc.,* 1824

Damrak, leads from Dam Square directly to the **Centraal Station,** which is built on an artificial island and is an ornate architectural wonder in itself. This is where you'll go to purchase railway tickets, change money, and perhaps have a good, inexpensive meal in its fine restaurant. It's also the place where most city trams begin and is across the canal from a main departure point for canal-boat tours. Across the square out front is the main office of the **VVV,** with a delightful Koffiehuis whose terrace overlooks the canal, and an inexpensive restaurant inside.

SQUARES & NEIGHBORHOODS   The other important squares to mark on your map are:

Muntplein (Mint Square) is reached from Dam Square by way of the **Rokin** (where there's another canal-tour dock), named for the tall, wonderfully decorated tower whose carillon rings out every half hour. Across the Singel Canal is the famous **floating flower market,** also a busy tram intersection crossed by a large number of tram lines.

Rembrandtsplein, another major landmark, is reached via Reguliersbreestraat from Muntplein, the home of lots of restaurants, bars, sidewalk cafés, cabarets, discotheques, and cinemas. People-watching is terrific in this rather hectic square.

Leidseplein is at the end of Leidsestraat and home of the Stadsschouwburg (Municipal Theater for ballet, opera, and concert performances), the landmark American Hotel with its fanciful art nouveau restaurant/café, plus restaurants, outdoor cafés, and nightspots.

Museumplein, just beyond Leidseplein, is the very heart of Amsterdam's cultural life, holding the Rijksmuseum, the Vincent van Gogh, and Stedelijk museums, with the Concertgebouw concert hall.

Other Amsterdam sections you should know by name are: the **Jordaan,** a residential area west of the Centrum between Rozengracht and Haarlemmerdijk, settled by Jewish refugees who named area streets for flowers, and lately becoming quite gentrified and fashionable; **Amsterdam South,** a fashionable residential neighborhood with several leading hotels along the Apollolaan; and **Amsterdam East,** on the far side of the Amstel River, a residential area that also holds the zoo (Artis), the Netherlands Maritime Museum, and the Tropenmuseum.

STREET MAPS   An excellent street map is published by Falk and is available from newsagents and VVV offices. Many hotels will hand you a complimentary city map along with your room key.

FINDING AN ADDRESS   With the aid of that trusty city street map, you'll be ahead of the game locating a specific address if you know that numbers run from low (left) to high (right). On streets radiating from Centraal Station to the Dam, numbers run from low (top) to high (bottom).

---

2 | Getting Around

BY BUS & TRAM   Trams are the most efficient way to move around, and they're fun to ride. The VVV provides a city map showing all bus and tram routes, and additional information on Amsterdam's public transport is available by phoning **06/9292.**

On your first ride, go in the front door and buy a ticket from the driver (see "Fares," below); after that, you can board at any door along the side and validate your ticket in the machines at the rear or middle of the car—it's an honor system, but periodic checks are made and there's a fine if you don't have a ticket.

Doors at the rear of the tram do not open automatically—you must push the button marked DEUR OPEN, both on the outside of the car to get in and on the inside when you want to get out. Be ready to alight quickly—those doors close in seconds.

Fares   Both bus and tram routes are zoned, with different fares for each zone. Most sightseeing travel will be within Zone 1. You can buy a **day ticket** (*dagkaart Amsterdam*), good for unlimited rides only on the day and night of purchase, from bus or tram drivers for Dfl. 12 ($6.30). A **strip card** (*strippenkaart*), good for 10 Amsterdam Tram & Bus Routerides, costs Dfl. 11 ($5.80). Tickets with longer validity must be purchased at the **GVB/Amsterdam Municipal Transport** ticket booths in front of Centraal Station at Stationsplein, with charges of Dfl. 16 ($8.40) for two days, Dfl. 18.50 ($9.75) for three days, and Dfl. 21.50 ($1.30) for four days.

BY TAXI   You cannot hail a taxi on the street, but taxi ranks are located at major hotels, squares, and shopping areas, as well as at Centraal Station. Or you can call **Taxicentrale** (☎ 677-7777). Tip and taxes are included in the meter price, and you don't need to add another tip unless you've exceptional service (help with heavy luggage, etc.) or unless you want to follow the Dutch custom (not obligatory) of rounding off the charge to the next highest guilder. The basic charge when the flag falls is Dfl. 5.80 ($3.05), with an additional Dfl. 2.80 ($1.45) per kilometer during the day, and Dfl. 3.80 ($2) from midnight to 6am.

BY CAR   The best advice for drivers in Amsterdam is: Don't drive. Traffic is scary enough when you're a pedestrian, and when you're behind the wheel and unfamiliar with narrow, one-way streets just a hair's breadth away from the open edge of a canal, it can be downright terrifying. Public transportation is inexpensive and frequent— and a lot quicker than driving. Save the rental car for excursions out of town. Many hotels provide parking facilities, and the VVV can furnish addresses of public parking areas convenient to your accommodation.

For day trips outside the city or for the remainder of your rambles through Holland, **car rentals** are available through **Avis,** Kiokkenbergweg 15 (☎ 564-1511), and **Budget Rent a Car,** Overtoom 121 (☎ 612-6066).

BY BICYCLE   Amsterdam is full of cyclists, and you may want to climb behind the handlebars yourself. However, that's advisable only on weekends, when traffic is not so heavy. Those bikers you see zipping merrily among trams and cars are doing so with long experience behind them. What *is* a good idea any day of the week is a bike trip outside town. In fact the VVV can provide several good bike routes for touring Amsterdam's environs, and it's a fun way to see things close up. (See also "Sports and Recreation," later in this chapter.)

BY FOOT   While Amsterdam can be foot wearying if you take it all of a piece, the Centrum and individual neighborhoods are ideal walking territory taken one at a time, with bus or tram transport from one to the other.

Fast Facts: Amsterdam

American Express   The offices in Amsterdam are at Damrak 66 (☎ **520-7777**) and van Baerlestraat 38 (☎ **671-4141**).

Area Code   Amsterdam's telephone area code is **020**.

Babysitters   If you need a babysitter, ask your hotel manager or desk clerk.

Business Hours   See "Fast Facts: Holland" in Chapter 12.

Car Rentals   See "Getting Around," earlier in this chapter.

Climate   See "When to Go" in Chapter 12.

Currency   See "Currency and Costs" in Chapter 12.

Currency Exchange   See "Currency and Costs" in Chapter 12. In Amsterdam, you can change your traveler's checks and U.S. dollars outside banking hours at the **GWK Bureau de Change** (DeGrenswisselkantoren N.V.) in the Main Hall, Centraal Station (☎ **622-1324**), open from 7am to 10:45pm (from 8am on Sunday). American Express also operates a currency exchange for cardholders.

Dentist/Doctor   Referrals to English-speaking dentists and doctors are available through the 24-hour Central Doctors and Dental Service (☎ **664-2111** or **679-1821**).

Drugstores   You must be very specific when asking for a drugstore location in Amsterdam. There are two types: Go to an *apotheek* for prescriptions and over-the-counter medications, to a *drogerijen* for toiletries and other sundries. Your hotel can give you the addresses of those close by.

Electricity   See "Fast Facts: Holland" in Chapter 12.

Embassies/Consulates   See "Fast Facts: Holland" in Chapter 12.

Emergencies   In case of an accident, dial **900**.

Holidays   See "When to Go" in Chapter 12.

Hospitals   Major hospitals are Boerhaave Kliniek, at Tenierstraat 1 (☎ **679-3535**) in Museumplein; Valerius Kliniek, at Valeriusplein 9 (☎ **673-6666**) in the Amsterdam South area; and Onze Lieve Vrouwe Gasthuis at Oosterparkstraat 179 (☎ **599-9111**) in Amsterdam East.

Information   See "Fast Facts: Holland" in Chapter 12.

Photographic Needs   All types of film are readily available in Amsterdam, as is one-day service. Shops all along Damrak and Kalverstraat have convenient drop-off points for quick developing.

Police   The police emergency telephone number is **622-2222;** the main police station is at Elandsgracht 117 (☎ **555-1111**).

Post Office   The main post office (☎ **555-8911**) is located at Singel 250, at the corner of Raadhuisstraat and the Singel Canal, in the vicinity of the Royal Palace. It's open Monday through Wednesday and on Friday from 8:30am to 6pm, on Thursday from 8:30am to 8:30pm, and on Saturday from 9am to noon.

Radio   There is regular English news service every day at 7pm at 24/1250 AM (medium wave) and 23 (93.8 MHz) VHF, with supplementary bulletins on what's on in Amsterdam and the immediate weather forecast. BBC World News is broadcast on medium-wave radio several times a day, with varying wavelengths and times of broadcast—inquire at your hotel or consult local newspaper listings.

Religious Services   Amsterdam is a city of churches and synagogues, and the VVV can furnish names and addresses of those holding services in English.

Safety   Whenever you're traveling in an unfamiliar city or country, stay alert. Be aware of your immediate surroundings. Wear a moneybelt and don't sling your camera or purse over your shoulder. This will minimize the possibility of your becoming a victim of crime. Every society has its criminals. It's your responsibility to be aware and alert even in the most heavily touristed areas.

Taxis   See "Getting Around," earlier in this chapter.

Telephones/Telegrams/Telex   Direct dialing to other European countries as well as overseas (including the United States and Canada) is available in most hotel rooms in Amsterdam and at the main post office (see "Post Office," above). For calls within Holland, coin telephones accept Dfl. .25 (13¢), Dfl. 1 (53¢), and Dfl. 2.50 ($1.32) coins.

Television   Dutch, German, Belgian, and French television channels are received in Amsterdam, but most are broadcast in native languages. Broadcasts in English are available on BBC1 and BBC2, both received in Amsterdam.

Transit Information   Call **06/9292** for public transportation information.

---

3 Accommodations

Is your preference old-world charm combined with luxurious quarters? Glitzy international-standards modernity with every conceivable amenity? Small family-run hotels where there may not be an elevator, but you become a part of the family circle? A historic canal house that reflects the lifestyle of centuries past? A modern, medium-size hotel on the fringe of inner-city hustle and bustle? A bare-bones room in a dormitory, which frees up scarce dollars for other purposes? Amsterdam has them all, including some lovely combinations—and it has them in large quantities and many price ranges.

There are more than 25,000 beds available in Amsterdam (the majority in moderately priced hotels).

Because price can sometimes be the determining factor in choice of accommodations, the listings below are in price groupings, although—as is true in many cities—some categories overlap, as when expensive prices are reduced to moderate either by forgoing some amenities or by taking advantage of special package rates. So if a particular hotel strikes your fancy but is out of your price range, it can pay to inquire if special off-season, weekend, specific weekdays, or other restrictive packages will bring prices down to your purse level.

For a complete list of hotels in Amsterdam and the rest of Holland, contact the Netherlands Board of Tourism for their "Hotels" booklet.

Note: Unless otherwise indicated, all the accommodations recommended below come with bath.

RESERVATIONS You may, of course, make reservations directly with any of the hotels below, but be sure you do so in ample time for them to reply before you leave home. Especially during summer months and tulip season, it's advisable to go through a travel agent; through the **Netherlands Reservations Centre,** P.O. Box 404, 2360 AK Leidschendam (☎ **070/20-25-00**), which can also book apartments and theater tickets; or if you're booking from within Holland, through a VVV office.

For the past few years certain Amsterdam hotels have offered significant rate reductions between November 1 and March 31 under a program called **The Amsterdam Way.** Amsterdam, incidentally, is as much a delight then as in the tourist-packed summer months, with a calendar full of cultural events, the full blossoming of many traditional Dutch dishes (such as the hearty, soul- and body-warming *hutspot*) not offered in warm weather, and streets, cafés, restaurants, and museums filled more with locals than with visitors.

There are participating hotels in every class and price range from deluxe to budget, and basic stays can be for one night or three, with lowered rates for each additional night you might wish to tack on. In the moderate and budget categories savings are just as dramatic, and the three days are not restricted to weekends. Along with reductions in hotel rates come discounts on several sightseeing attractions, restaurant meals, entertainments, and—something you'd never get in the summer—free ice skates and admission to the Leidseplein ice rink!

The Netherlands Board of Tourism can provide a brochure outlining current Amsterdam Way prices and what they cover.

Note: For a long list of quite nice budget hotels in virtually every area of Amsterdam, ask the VVV for their list of "Plain but Comfortable" hotels and hostel accommodations. In connection with the latter, you should know that although the idea of staying in one of the houseboat hostels you'll see advertised may be very appealing, there are safety factors involved in some—best consult the VVV before checking in.

At Schiphol Airport

 Golden Tulip Barbizon Schiphol, Kruisweg 495, 2132 NA Hoofddorp. ☎ **020/655-0550,** or toll free **800/344-1212** in the U.S. Fax 020/653-4999. Telex 74546. 242 rms, 2 suites. MINIBAR TV TEL **Bus:** Airport shuttle bus.

Rates: Dfl. 350 ($184) single; Dfl. 395 ($207) double; Dfl. 600 ($315) suites. AE, DC, MC, V.

Those who prefer a more tranquil setting than inner-city accommodations will find a semirural refuge at the Barbizon Schiphol, just 1 mile from the Schiphol Airport. Surrounded by flower-bulb fields, with the Keukenhof Gardens and the flower auctions at Aalsmeer nearby, the hotel is an ideal base for exploring both the city and its environs. Convenience is matched by high standards at this member of the Golden Tulip chain, with free shuttle-bus transportation to the airport and its excellent train and bus service into the city, wheelchair access, and soundproof rooms that shut out aircraft noises. Guest rooms are spacious and beautifully furnished, with a table and chairs creating an attractive seating area. Hairdryers are provided.

Dining/Entertainment: The light, airy Café Barbizon, open daily from 6am to midnight, serves meals buffet style at moderate prices, while stylish De Meerlanden is an intimate gourmet restaurant featuring first-class French and Dutch culinary specialties at lunch and dinner. The Point cocktail bar is a cozy gathering spot, with gourmet snacks in addition to international cocktails, and there's entertainment on Friday evenings.

Services: 24-hour room service, babysitting, car rental, doctor/dentist on call, one-day laundry/valet service, secretarial services, safety-deposit boxes.

Facilities: Pool (with whirlpool and sauna), gift shop, newsstand, conference rooms, fitness center, jogging facilities.

In the City

EXPENSIVE

American Hotel, Leidsekade 97, 1017 PN Amsterdam. ☎ **020/624-5322.**
Fax 020/625-3236. Telex 12545 cbo nl. 188 rms. MINIBAR TV TEL
Tram: 1, 2, 5, 6, 7, or 10. **Bus:** 63; the KLM Schiphol bus stops at the hotel.
Rates: Dfl. 355 ($186) single; Dfl. 425 ($223) double. AE, DC, MC, V.

This marvelous century-old hotel is as European as its name suggests it isn't, with a turreted exterior and art nouveau café so special they've been declared a national monument. Some of the guest rooms (most of which are quite spacious) have balconies overlooking a canal, and all have modern furnishings and decor. The American has become a traditional meeting place for Amsterdammers when they're in the Leidseplein area, and every tourist should take at least one look inside the splendid old building.

Dining/Entertainment: The famous Café Américain, an art deco marvel, is a mecca for writers and artists, and is more casual than the rather formal dining room.

Services: Conferences, dinner parties, wedding receptions arranged.

Facilities: Fitness center with sauna and gym.

★ $ **Amsterdam Ascot Hotel,** Damrak 95–98, NL 1012 LP Amsterdam.
☎ **020/626-0066.** Fax 020/627-0983. Telex 16620. 109 rms, 15 suites.
MINIBAR TV TEL **Tram:** All city-center trams.
Rates: Dfl. 295–395 ($156-$209) single; Dfl. 500 ($265) double; Dfl. 395–500 ($209–$265) suite. AE, DC, MC, V.

This smart little hotel right in the heart of the inner city, just off Dam Square, has all the charm of one of Amsterdam's older buildings combined with all the modern efficiency and bright looks typical of its Swissotel owners. The guest rooms are decorated in light, muted pastels and have marble bathrooms, as well as attractive seating groupings. The suites are so well designed you could settle in as a permanent resident. Le Bistro (see "Dining," later in this chapter) serves excellent French cuisine and casual meals at modest prices. Other facilities include an international newsstand, souvenir boutique, and jewelry shop. The hotel is wheelchair-accessible.

Amsterdam Hilton, Apollolaan 138, 1077 BG Amsterdam. ☎ **020/678-0780,**
or toll free **800/HILTONS** in the U.S. Fax 020/662-6688. Telex 11025 HILA.
271 rms, 12 suites. MINIBAR TV TEL **Tram:** 3, 5, 12, or 16. **Bus:** 63.
Rates: Dfl. 390–480 ($205–$252) single; Dfl. 460–550 ($242–$289) double; Dfl. 945 ($497) suite. Weekend rates available. AE, DC, MC, V.

This international chain hotel injects a lot of graciousness into its posh residential location not far from the Concertgebouw. Its tasteful lobby has an open fire, and the hotel sits in its own lawns. There are 11 floors of spacious guest rooms, with in-house movies on the TV, as well as all the other trappings you'd expect from this luxury chain.

Dining/Entertainment: There's a good restaurant, Roberto's, and the bar overlooks a canal.

Facilities: Amsterdam Casino (free to guests), Juliana's discotheque (free to guests), wheelchair access.

Amsterdam Marriott Hotel, Stadhouderskade 19–21, 1054 ES Amsterdam.
☎ **020/607-5555,** or toll free **800/228-7014** in the U.S. Fax 020/607-5511.
Telex 15087. 392 rms. MINIBAR TV TEL **Tram:** 1, 2, 5, 6, 7, or 10. **Bus:** 63.
Rates: Dfl. 375–425 ($197–$223) single or double. AE, DC, MC, V.

Ultramodern both inside and out, this American-style luxury hostelry faces the busy Leidseplein and is a short walk from major museums, theaters, elegant shops, cafés, and the city's largest park. Guests have a choice of regular double-bedded rooms or a bed-sitter equipped with a Murphy bed.

Dining/Entertainment: The Brasserie is a delightful, airy terrace eatery overlooking Leidseplein, while the more formal Port O'Amsterdam restaurant serves an international cuisine in elegant surroundings.

Services: Secretarial service.

Facilities: Health club, wheelchair access.

★ **Amsterdam Renaissance Hotel,** Kattengat 1, 1012 SZ Amsterdam.
☎ **020/621-2223,** or toll free **800/SONESTA** in the U.S. Fax 020/627-5245.
425 rms. MINIBAR TV TEL **Tram:** 1, 2, 5, 13, or 17.
Rates: Dfl. 332–395 ($174–$207) single or double. AE, DC, MC, V.

This centrally located hotel has arranged its exterior to fit into the ancient heart of Amsterdam without a ripple. It has pulled together a group of 17th-century houses and a circular church (long since deconsecrated and used for such secular purposes as a warehouse) to preserve an undisturbed streetside facade, yet its off-street entrance, public rooms, and guest rooms are as slickly luxurious as you'd find in any glass-walled international chain. The guest rooms are spacious (the baths have huge bathtubs) and have trouser presses and TVs that have a feature-films channel, among other amenities.

Dining/Entertainment: There's an informal sidewalk café, a 300-year-old pub, and a fine restaurant. Frequent open-air performances are held in the little square in front of its entrance, and concerts are held regularly in the old church, many utilizing the massive old pipe organ.

Services: Airport shuttle, airline ticket office.

Facilities: Shopping arcade, movie theater, health club, wheelchair access.

★ **Grand Hotel Krasnapolsky,** Dam 9, 1012 JS Amsterdam. ☎ **020/554-9111.**
Fax 020/622-8607. 420 rms, 5 suites. MINIBAR TV TEL **Tram:** All city-center trams.
Rates (including breakfast): Dfl. 410 ($215) single; Dfl. 485 ($255) double; Dfl. 575–1,150 ($305–$610) suite. AE, DC, MC, V.

Facing Dam Square, opposite the Royal Palace, for more than a century this has been simply "the Kras" to generations of Amsterdammers and guests. Over the years it has evolved into a curious mixture of old-world elegance and streamlined modern additions. Its palm-studded Wintergarden, designed by the founder back in 1880, is stamped with the charm of yesteryear, yet the guest rooms (especially in the Court Wing) are definitely of today—they come with all the extras of a deluxe hotel and are equipped with coffee and tea makers.

American Hotel 13
AMS Hotel Beethoven 26
AMS Hotel Holland 20
AMS Hotel Terdam 12
Amstel Botel 30
Amsterdam
  Ascot Hotel 31
Amsterdam Hilton 24
Amsterdam
  Marriott Hotel 15
Amsterdam
  Renaissance 29
Arena Budget Hotel 38
Bob's Youth Hostel 5
Bridge Hotel 36
Cok City 4
Golden Tulip Schiphol 1
Grand Hotel
  Krasnapolsky 27
Het Canal House 2
Hotel Ambassade 8
Hotel Agora 9
Hotel Appollofirst 22
Hotel Asterisk 37
Hotel de l'Europe 7
Hotel de la Haye 10
Hotel Delphi 23
Hotel Dikker & Thijs 11
Hotel Doelen Karena 34
Hotel Jan Luyken 18
Hotel New York 3
Hotel Piet Hein 19
Hotel Pulitzer 6
Hotel Toro 21
Hotel Trianon 25
Hotel Vondel 14
Jolly Hotel Carlton 35
Museum Hotel 17
Owl Hotel 16
De Poort van Cleve 33
RHO Hotel 32
Victoria Hotel 28

9568

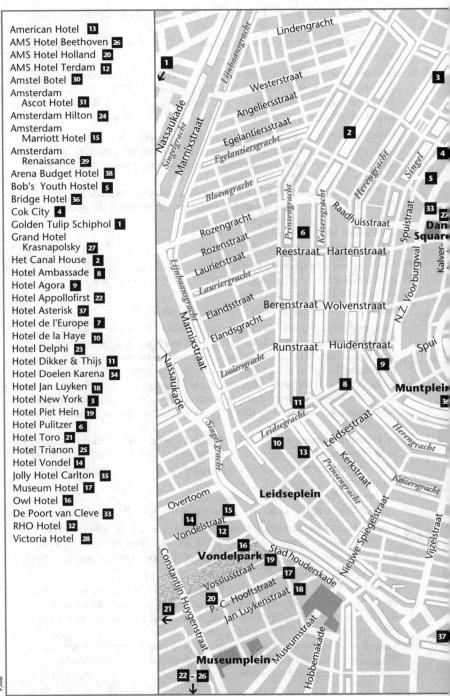

Accommodations in Central Amsterdam

Het IJ

IJ-Tunnel

0 ___ 100 m
___ 110 y
N

Openhaven Front

de Ruijterkade

29

CITY CENTER

Zeedijk

28

Damrak

31

Nieuwendijk

Damrak

Rokin

Oudekerksplein

Geldersekade

Kromme Waal

Oude Waal

Waals Eilandsgracht

30

O o s t e r d o k

32

Oudezijds Voorburgwal

Nieuwe Markt

Prins Hendrikkade

Oude   Schans

Nieuwe Uilenburgerstraat

Uilenburgergracht

Valkenburgerstraat

Kloveniersburgwal

34

Rapenburgerstraat

Hoogtekadijk

Groenburgwal

Entrepotdok

7

Waterlooplein

Herengracht

Plantage Kerklaan

Plantage Doklaan

Rembrandts-plein

Nieuwe

Artispark

Plantage Middenlaan

Nieuwe Keizersgracht

Plantage Muidergracht

Plantage Muidergracht

Utrechtsestraat

Nieuwe Kerkstraat

Nieuwe Prinsengracht

Amstel River

Nieuwe   Achtergracht

Nieuwe Weesperstraat

Sarphatistraat

Falckstraat

Frederiksplein   Sarphatistraat

Mauritskade

38

Ooster-park

ingelgracht

adhouderskade

Ruyschstraat

Blasiusstraat

Dining/Entertainment: The Golden Palm Bar is popular with locals as well as guests; the Krasserie is a pleasant lobby coffee shop looking out to Dam Square; Le Reflet d'Or is an elegant belle époque restaurant specializing in French cuisine; and Edo is an outstanding Japanese eatery.

Services: 24-hour room service.

Facilities: Fitness center, sauna, business center, beauty parlor, wheelchair access.

Hotel de l'Europe, Nieuwe Doelenstraat 2–8, 1012 CP Amsterdam. ☎ **020/623-4836.** Fax 020/624-2962. Telex 12081. 100 rms, 21 suites. MINIBAR TV TEL **Tram:** 4, 9, 14, 16, 24, or 25.

Rates: Dfl. 395–495 ($208–$260) single; Dfl. 495–710 ($260–$373) double; Dfl. 845–1,370 ($444–$721) suite. AE, DC, MC, V.

This marvelous old 1895 hotel has a prime city-center location right on the banks of the Amstel River across from Muntplein. You're within an easy walk of virtually everywhere you'll want to go, and its rooms are fairly dripping with traditional elegance and come with such luxury extras as terrycloth bathrobes. This is a small hotel, and despite its elegance there's nothing stuffy about its friendly, obliging staff.

Dining/Entertainment: There's a small, cozy bar and two of Amsterdam's finest restaurants that overlook the river (see "Dining," later in this chapter).

Services: 24-hour room service.

Facilities: Indoor pool, sauna.

⭐ **Hotel Doelen Karena**, Nieuwe Doelenstraat 24, 1012 CP Amsterdam. ☎ **020/622-0722.** Fax 020/622-1084. 85 rms, 1 suite. MINIBAR TV TEL $ **Tram:** 4, 9, 14, 16, 24, or 25.

Rates: Dfl. 320 ($168) single; Dfl. 385 ($202) double; Dfl. 550 ($289) suite. AE, DC, MC, V.

Right next door to the elegant Hôtel de l'Europe, the Doelen is one of the city's oldest hotels and is, in fact, where Rembrandt's masterful *The Night Watch* was first hung. Its marvelous center staircase spirals up to a dome that tops the high-ceilinged lobby. Guest rooms are nicely done up, and some rooms have good views of the Amstel River, others of the Mint Tower. Amenities include hairdryers and tea and coffee makers. There's a clubby, wood-paneled bar and a good restaurant specializing in French cuisine. Near Museumplein, this is a terrific location, and good value.

⭐ **Hotel Pulitzer**, Prinsengracht 315–331, 1016 GZ Amsterdam. ☎ **020/523-5235.** Fax 020/627-6753. 240 rms, 10 suites. MINIBAR TV TEL **Tram:** 2, 13, 14, or 17.

Rates: Dfl. 395–455 ($207–$239) single; Dfl. 455–525 ($239–$276) double; Dfl. 1,050 ($552) suite. AE, DC, MC, V.

Inside, this popular hotel is as contemporary as can be, with a modern lobby and reception area and glassed-in walkways hung with changing art exhibits. Its exterior, however, has retained the facades of some 24 canal houses dating back 200 to 400 years, and those glass-walled corridors look out over a lovely and peaceful inner garden. No two guest rooms are alike—some feature brick walls and overhead beams in a decidedly rustic decor, while others are done up in more modern dress; some overlook the canal, and others face the garden. All guest rooms are spacious and have TVs with closed-circuit movies and personal safes with a combination you set yourself, among other amenities.

Dining/Entertainment: The handsome bar is a favorite gathering place for locals as well as guests, and the lovely De Goudsbloem restaurant (with sunny, country-style decor) serves gourmet cuisine (see "Dining," later in this chapter).

Services: Airport shuttle.

Facilities: Lobby shop, business facilities.

 Jolly Hotel Carlton, Vijzelstraat 4, 1017 HK Amsterdam. ☎ **020/622-2266.** Fax 020/626-6183. 219 rms. A/C MINIBAR TV TEL **Tram:** 4, 9, 14, 16, 24, or 25.

 Rates (including breakfast): Dfl. 300–400 ($157–$210) single; Dfl. 400–500 ($210–$263) double. Children under 12 stay free in parents' room. AE, DC, MC, V.

Located just off the Singel Canal near Muntplein, with some rooms overlooking the floating flower market and the Mint Tower, this venerable hotel has been a fixture on the Amsterdam hotel scene for years. Built in the days when rooms were individual in both shape and size, the Carlton had pretty much passed its heyday until the Jolly hotel firm from Italy took it over and embarked on a dedicated campaign to upgrade the place. Not only is there a gleaming marble lobby, with the inviting Carlton Corner bar and lounge and popular café (see "Dining," later in this chapter), but on upper floors renovations have made the most of spacious corridors (each floor has a small lobby space from which corridors branch off) and nonstandardized rooms. Jolly standards are high, and the Carlton once more provides accommodations befitting its fantastic central location. Some guest rooms have sitting alcoves; others are irregularly shaped. Trouser presses are among the in-room amenities. The second-floor Caruso restaurant serves outstanding international cuisine at moderate prices, with a limited number of specialties available for room service. Add to all this a friendly, helpful staff and you come up with convenience personified and a very good value.

★ **Victoria Hotel**, Damrak 1–6, 1012 LG Amsterdam. ☎ **020/623-4255.** Fax 020/625-2997. 321 rms. MINIBAR TEL TV **Tram:** Stationsplein, terminus for most tram lines.

Rates: Dfl. 325–355 ($171–$187) single; Dfl. 395–425 ($207–$223) double. AE, DC, MC, V.

Set almost directly across from Centraal Station, this delightful old building is a marvel of old Amsterdam architecture, an ivory-colored mass with a domed turret at its entrance and an interesting carved-stone facade. It's convenient to canal-boat departure points, the main tram terminus, the VVV office, and railway connections to anywhere in Holland or the rest of Europe. The public rooms have a warm sort of jazzy elegance, and just off the lobby there's the popular Tasman Piano Bar, made cozy by an open fireplace. Many of the staff have been with the hotel for years, which leads to a very personalized brand of service. The guest rooms are spacious and very nearly luxurious after an extensive facelift and all new furnishings. In addition to the Seasons garden restaurant, there are shopping facilities, a business center, a hairdresser, and the Scandic Active Club health club, with sauna, Turkish bath, and swimming pool.

MODERATE

AMS Hotel Beethoven, Beethovenstraat 43, 1077 HN Amsterdam. ☎ **020/664-4816,** or toll free **800/528-1234** in the U.S. Fax 020/662-1240. 60 rms. MINIBAR TV TEL **Tram:** 5.

Rates (including breakfast): Dfl. 240 ($126) single; Dfl. 310 ($163) double. Rate reductions available mid-Nov to mid-Mar. AE, DC, MC, V.

Located on a beautiful shopping street near the RAI Congress and Exhibition Center, the Beethoven is a member of the Best Western chain. Its hairdryer-equipped guest rooms are attractive and comfortable, and it has a good restaurant with a cozy bar and a glassed-in sidewalk café that's heated in winter.

AMS Hotel Terdam, Tesselschadestraat 23, 1054 ET Amsterdam. ☎ **020/612-6876.** Fax 020/683-8313. 95 rms. TV TEL **Tram:** 1, 2, 5, 6, 7, or 10.

Rates (including breakfast): Dfl. 180 ($94) single; Dfl. 260 ($136) double. Discounts available off-season. AE, DC, MC, V.

With all the entertainment and nightlife brashness of the Leidseplein just around the corner, the Terdam is a quiet refuge on a tree-lined street, with its own sophisticated bar. The rooms are attractive, and there are also small apartments with kitchenettes (slightly higher rates).

Cok City Hotel, Nieuwe Zijds Voorburgwal 50, 1012 SC Amsterdam. ☎ **020/422-0011.** Fax 020/422-0357. 106 rms. TV **Tram:** 1, 2, 5, 13, or 17 (one stop from Centraal Station).

Rates (including breakfast): Dfl. 170 ($90) single; Dfl. 220 ($116) double; Dfl. 260 ($137) triple. AE, MC, V.

This brand-new hotel occupying six floors is well located only a five-minute walk from Centraal Station and Dam Square. The modern rooms are brightly decorated in different colors and come equipped with full bath, color TV, trouser press, hairdryer, and safe. Added conveniences include food, beverage, and ice dispensers on every floor, as well as rooms equipped for ironing. Several shops that stay open 24 hours are also located on the ground floor. The buffet breakfast features eggs, cereals, and fruit. Here you'll find reasonably priced comfortable accommodations.

★ **Het Canal House,** Keizersgracht 148, 1015 CX Amsterdam. ☎ **020/622-5182.** Fax 020/624-1317. 26 rms. TEL **Tram:** 13, 14, or 17.

$ **Rates** (including breakfast): Dfl. 190 ($100) single; Dfl. 210 ($110) double. AE, DC, MC, V.

This charming canalside hostelry, which now includes the building next door, has proved a great favorite with our readers. Behind a 1630 facade, the salon is a cozy collection of Victoriana overlooking a lovely small back garden, which is softly illuminated at night. The rooms are furnished and decorated in antique style, with canopy beds and other period pieces. There's a Victorian bar and a lovely chandeliered breakfast room, and the friendly staff is a decided plus.

Hotel Agora, Singel 462, 1017 AW Amsterdam. ☎ **020/627-2200.** Fax 020/627-2202. 15 rms. TV TEL **Tram:** 1, 2, or 5.

Rates (including breakfast): Dfl. 115–170 ($60–$90) single; Dfl. 125–190 ($65–$100) double. AE, DC, MC, V.

This small and comfortable hotel—another old canal house that has been thoroughly modernized inside—is right in the middle of things. The rooms are nicely furnished, and each comes with a big easy chair in addition to standard fixtures.

★ **Hotel Ambassade,** Herengracht 341, 1016 AZ Amsterdam. ☎ **020/626-2333.** Fax 020/624-5321. 52 rms. TV TEL **Tram:** 1, 2, or 5.

$ **Rates** (including breakfast): Dfl. 215 ($113) single; Dfl. 265 ($139) double. AE, DC, MC, V.

There's a decidedly homey ambience to the Ambassade, which has been created from eight patrician canal houses. Access to the guest rooms is by way of a narrow, curving staircase or the recently added elevator. Once on the upper floors you'll find very spacious rooms (some of those in front have two large windows overlooking the canal) with comfortable and attractive furnishings, and hairdryers and wall safes, among other amenities. The parlor is all Georgian elegance and the two-level breakfast room gives every table a full canal view.

★ **Hotel Apollofirst,** Apollolaan 123, 1077 AP Amsterdam. ☎ **020/673-0333.** Fax 020/675-0348. 38 rms. TV TEL **Tram:** 3, 5, 12, or 16. Bus: 63.

Rates (including breakfast): Dfl. 215 ($113) single; Dfl. 265 ($139) double. AE, DC, MC, V.

The guest rooms in this small, elegant hotel near Museumplein are roomy, with exceptionally lovely furnishings. Those at the back overlook the hotel's gardens and the terrace on which guests enjoy a snack or drink in summer months. The small Angelina dinner-theater restaurant serves a good international menu at moderate prices, with cabaret performances on Friday and Saturday evenings.

Hotel Delphi, Apollolaan 101–105, 1077 AN Amsterdam. ☎ **020/679-5152.** Fax 020/675-2941. 50 rms. TV TEL **Tram:** 4.

Rates (including breakfast): Dfl. 175–198 ($92–$104) single; Dfl. 240–270 ($126–$143) double. AE, DC, MC, V.

This homey little red-brick hotel shares its residential area location (near the RAI Congress) with the posh Hilton and Apollo hotels. All the guest rooms are done in contemporary decor with standard amenities, and some face a pretty garden out back.

Hotel Dikker & Thijs, Prinsengracht 444, 1017 KE Amsterdam. ☎ **020/626-7721.** Fax 020/625-8986. 25 rms. MINIBAR TV TEL **Tram:** 13, 14, or 17.

Rates: Dfl. 250–280 ($131–$147) single; Dfl. 315–365 ($165–$192) double.

On the corner of Leidsestraat and just two blocks away from the Leidseplein, this small hotel is situated on one of Amsterdam's most famous canals. You enter through a small lobby, and the cozy rooms, grouped around small, individual sitting areas, are quite comfortable. Brasserie Dikker & Thijs is located on Leidsestraat, a terrific place for a coffee or snack to rest weary feet and watch the passing parade. There's also a very good delicatessen.

Hotel New York, Herengracht 13, 1015 BA Amsterdam. ☎ **020/624-3066.** Fax 020/620-3230. 18 rms. TV TEL **Tram:** 1, 2, 5, 11, 13, or 17 from Centraal Station.

Rates (including breakfast): Dfl. 150–175 ($79–$92) single; Dfl. 200–225 ($105–$132) double or twin; Dfl. 275 ($145) triple. AE, DC, MC, V.

This hotel is located on one of the city's most picturesque canals, overlooking the famous Milkmaid's Bridge, a 10-minute walk from Centraal Station. Three historic 17th-century buildings have been joined together to create the hotel, which has a certain charm, partly provided by French manager Philippe. The rooms are spacious and furnished in a modern style. Additional facilities and services include a cocktail lounge, bar, and same-day laundry service. Breakfast consists of cheese, ham, raisin bread, juice, and a boiled egg. If you wish you may have it delivered to your room. Rooms are spread over four floors—but note that there's no elevator.

Hotel Jan Luyken, Jan Luykenstraat 54–58, 1071 CS Amsterdam. ☎ **020/573-0730.**
Fax 020/676-3841. 63 rms. MINIBAR TV TEL **Tram:** 2, 3, 6, 12, or 16.
Rates (including breakfast): Dfl. 250 ($131) single; Dfl. 290 ($152) double. AE, DC, MC, V.

This attractive hotel occupies a corner site in a residential area near the major museums of Amsterdam and offers many of the extras usually found only in larger (and more expensive) hotels. The private baths, for example, come with bidets. There's a charming lounge, and several good restaurants in the area.

Hotel Toro, Koningslaan 64, 1075 AG Amsterdam. ☎ **020/673-7223.**
Fax 020/675-0031. 22 rms. TV TEL **Tram:** 2 from Centraal Station to Emmaplein (about 15 minutes).
Rates (including buffet breakfast): Dfl. 140–170 ($74–$89) single; Dfl. 200 ($105) double; Dfl. 260 ($137) triple. AE, DC, MC, V.

Located on the fringes of Vondelpark in a quiet residential district, this beautiful hotel is one of my top budget choices. The house is furnished and decorated with taste, combining Louis XIV and Liberty styles and featuring stained-glass windows and Murano chandeliers. The rooms are worthy of being featured in *Better Homes and Gardens*. The house also affords guests a private garden and terrace. It's a 10-minute walk through Vondelpark to Leidseplein.

Hotel Vondel, Vondelstraat 28, 1054 GE Amsterdam. ☎ **020/612-0120.**
Fax 020/685-4321. 28 rms. TV TEL MINIBAR **Tram:** 1, 2, 5, or 11 from Centraal Station.
Rates (including breakfast): Dfl. 175 ($92) single; Dfl. 195–300 ($103–$158) double; Dfl. 350 ($184) triple; Dfl. 400 ($211) quad. AE, DC, MC, V.

Named after the famous 17th-century Dutch poet Joost Van den Vondel, this hotel, occupying five floors, opened in late 1993 and has since become one of the leading three-star hotels in Amsterdam. Each room is named after one of Vondel's poems— like Lucifer or Solomon. Three rooms (all with soundproof windows) are on the first floor and are ideal for disabled travelers. The furniture is solid, the rooms spacious, and the service good. The buffet breakfast includes fresh fruit, a choice of cereals, cold meats, and 12 brands of tea. It's a comfortable place, and the location is convenient for the museum area and Leidseplein.

⭐ **Museum Hotel,** P. C. Hooftstraat 2, 1071 BX Amsterdam. ☎ **020/662-1402.**
Fax 020/673-3918. 115 rms. TV TEL **Tram:** 2, 3, 5, 12, or 16.
Rates (including breakfast): Dfl. 180 ($94) single; Dfl. 260 ($136) double. Rates lower off-season. AE, DC, MC, V.

In a corner location on a leading shopping street, just steps away from the Rijksmuseum and its museum neighbors, this attractive hotel features rooms done in contemporary decor. There's a nice restaurant and an inviting lounge-bar.

⭐ **De Poort van Cleve,** Nieuwe Zijds Voorburgwal 178, 1012 SJ Amsterdam.
☎ **020/624-4860.** Fax 020/622-0240. 99 rms, 2 suites. A/C MINIBAR TV TEL
$ **Tram:** 1, 2, 4, 5, 9, 13, 14, 16, 17, 24, or 25.
Rates (including breakfast): Dfl. 182 ($95) single; Dfl. 287 ($151) double; Dfl. 440 ($231) suite.

In a great old building just off Dam Square, this hotel features guest rooms done up in modern furnishings, and a marvelously atmospheric Old Dutch Inn restaurant that's one of the oldest restaurants in Amsterdam and specializes in beefsteak. Great comfort here, and in spite of being in the middle of the busy city center, behind the hotel's facade all is quiet and peaceful.

INEXPENSIVE

AMS Hotel Holland, P. C. Hooftstraat 162, 1071 CH Amsterdam. ☎ **020/676-4253,** or toll free **800/528-1234** in the U.S. Fax 020/683-1811. 62 rms. TV TEL **Tram:** 2, 5, 9, or 13.

Rates (including breakfast): Dfl. 130 ($68) single; Dfl. 180 ($94) double. Discounts available in fall and winter. AE, DC, MC, V.

With all the Centrum attractions within a short walk, this nice modern hotel is on one of Amsterdam's better shopping streets. The guest rooms are contemporary, and there's a nice bar and lounge.

Amstel Botel, Oosterdokskade 2–4 1011 AE Amsterdam. ☎ **020/626-4247.** Fax 020/639-1952. 352 beds. TV TEL **Directions:** Turn left out of Centraal Station, pass the bike rental, and you can't miss it floating in front of you.

Rates (including buffet breakfast): Dfl. 120 ($63.15) single; Dfl. 140 ($73.70) double; Dfl. 190 ($100) triple. AE, MC, V.

This is a boat-hotel, moored 250 yards away from Centraal Station. Aboard you'll find 176 cabins spread out over four decks connected by an elevator. The boat was built in 1993 to serve as a hotel. It has become very popular since it opened because of its central location, adventurous quality, and comfort at reasonable rates.

Bridge Hotel, Amstel 107–111, 1018 EM Amsterdam. ☎ **020/623-7068.** Fax 020/624-1565. 26 rms. TV TEL **Tram:** 6, 7, or 10.

Rates (including breakfast, VAT, and service): Dfl. 130 ($68) single; Dfl. 150 ($79) double. AE, DC, MC, V.

The spacious guest rooms here are nicely appointed, with a bright modern decor and comfortable seating areas that include a sofa, big easy chairs, and a coffee table. There's a sauna, and a good Italian restaurant with moderate prices on the premises. Near the Amstel River.

Hotel Asterisk, Den Texstraat 14–16, 1017 ZA Amsterdam. ☎ **020/626-2396.** Fax 020/638-2790. 25 rms. A/C TV TEL **Tram:** 3, 5, 12, or 16.

Rates (including breakfast): Dfl. 70–85 ($37–$44) single; Dfl. 90–150 ($47–$79) double. MC, V.

This small hotel near the Heineken Brewery and across the canal from Museumplein has surprisingly high standards for its price range. The guest rooms are nicely done up and quite comfortable.

Hotel de la Haye, Leidsegracht 114, 1016 CT Amsterdam. ☎ **020/624-4044.** Fax 020/638-5254. 22 rms. **Tram:** 1, 2, or 5.

Rates (including breakfast): Dfl. 65 ($34) single; Dfl. 100–115 ($52–$60) double. MC, V.

This small, well-run hotel offers rather plain, but quite comfortable rooms at a bargain price. Its convenient location, near Leidseplein, puts you within easy reach of shopping, entertainment, and sightseeing.

Hotel Piet Hein, Vossiusstraat 52, 1071 AK Amsterdam. ☎ **020/662-7205.** Fax 020/662-1526. 40 rms. TV TEL **Tram:** 2 or 5 from Centraal Station.

Rates (including breakfast): Dfl. 95–125 ($50–$66) single; Dfl. 145–175 ($76–$92) double; Dfl. 205–225 ($108–$118) triple. AE, DC, MC, V.

Facing Vondelpark and located near the most important museums, the Hotel Piet Hein is one of the best-kept and most appealing establishments in town. It's located in a dream villa and named after a Dutch folktale hero. The rooms are spacious and well furnished, the staff charming and professional. Half the rooms overlook the park and two of the double rooms on the second floor feature semicircular balconies. The lower-priced rooms are in the annex behind the hotel.

Hotel Trianon, J.W. Brouwersstraat 3-7, 1071 LH Amsterdam. ☎ **020/673-2073.** Fax 020/673-8868. 50 rms. TEL TV **Tram:** 3, 5, 12, or 16.

Rates (including breakfast): Dfl. 130 ($68) single; Dfl. 180 ($94) double. Lower rates mid-Nov to mid-Mar. AE, DC, MC, V.

On a quiet street next to the Concertgebouw and near the museums, this friendly small hotel has nicely appointed rooms. Officially rated as a two-star hotel, it actually offers three-star comfort and value. Situated in a red-brick building, the hotel is just a few minutes' walking distance from the Leidseplein and the major shopping streets. All rooms are spacious, cozily furnished, and equipped with color TV, phone, and hairdryer. The ground-floor bar stays open until midnight.

★ **Owl Hotel,** Roemer Visscherstraat 1, 1054 EV Amsterdam. ☎ **020/618-9484.** Fax 020/618-9441. 34 rms. TV TEL **Tram:** 2, 3, 6, 12, or 16.

Rates (including breakfast): Dfl. 140 ($73) single; Dfl. 190 ($100) double. AE, MC, V.

Originally a private residence in a peaceful neighborhood close to the museums, this family-run hotel now provides bright, average-size rooms. You can opt for breakfast in your room or in the small bar adjoining the garden. The pleasant lounge also overlooks the terrace leading to the garden.

★ **Rho Hotel,** Nes 11–23 (off Dam Sq.), 1012 KC Amsterdam. ☎ **020/620-7371.** Fax 020/620-7826. 105 rms. TV TEL **Tram:** All city-center trams.

Rates (including breakfast): Dfl. 130 ($68) single; Dfl. 190 ($100) double; Dfl. 240 ($126) triple. AE, MC, V.

In a nicely renovated old building just off Dam Square, the Rho is one of the most conveniently located of Amsterdam's inexpensive hotels. Guest rooms are nicely furnished, and breakfast is served in a spacious hall that was originally built as a theater in 1908.

SUPER-BUDGET

Arena Budget Hotel, 's-Gravesandestraat 51, 1092 AA Amsterdam. ☎ **020/625-3230.** Fax 020/663-2649. 600 beds. **Tram:** 6 or 10 to Korte 's-Gravesandestraat, 14 or 9 to Tropenmusem, or 3 to Oosterpark.

Rates: Dfl. 80–90 ($42–$47) double; Dfl. 120–135 ($63–$71) triple; Dfl. 17.50–22.50 ($9.20–$11.85) dorm bed. No credit cards.

Here you'll find eight large dorms with up to 80 beds each, eight smaller dorms with eight bunk beds in each, 34 doubles and four triples (each with shower), and one apartment with six beds. Located in a huge red-brick house built originally in 1890 as a hospital, it serves not only as a dorm but also as a cultural center. It has an information counter, concert hall, TV and video lounge, restaurant, garden, and bikes for rent.

In summer all kinds of concerts, parties, movies, and other happenings enliven the atmosphere.

Bob's Youth Hostel, Nieuwe Zijds Voorburgwal 92, 1012 SG Amsterdam. ☎ **020/623-0063.** 200 beds. **Tram:** 1, 2, 5, 13, or 17 to the second stop from Centraal Station.

Rates (including breakfast): Dfl. 25 ($13.15) per person. No credit cards.

At this very convenient location halfway between Centraal Station and Dam Square, guests are accommodated in dorms containing anywhere from 4 to 16 bunk beds. The atmosphere is very international. Although it attracts primarily a young audience, drinking and drug-taking are definitely banned and there's a 3am curfew. During the summer a dinner for Dfl. 8 ($4.20) is served. In 1994 Bob's opened an annex around the corner at Spui 47 where there are six supermodern apartments with fully equipped kitchenettes accommodating two to four guests and costing a low Dfl. 125 ($66) per unit.

---

4 Dining

It has been estimated that there are between 1,500 and 2,000 places to eat in Amsterdam, and I don't doubt those figures for one minute. What mere numbers don't tell, however, is the sheet variety of places to eat. Not only are there all those different ethnic cuisines mentioned in Chapter 11, but there are even more settings in which to eat them. From elegant 17th-century dining rooms to sophisticated rooms lit by candlelight, to cozy canalside bistros to exuberant taverns with equally exuberant Greek waiters, to exotic Indonesian rooms attended by turbaned waiters, to the *bruine kroegjes* (brown cafés) with their smoke-stained walls and friendly table conversations, the eateries of Amsterdam confront the tourist with the exquisite agony of being able to choose only one or two from their vast numbers each day.

Needless to say, the listings below don't come close to covering Amsterdam's restaurant scene in detail: They simply point out those places that have captured my own heart because of the fare, the ambience, the good-value prices, convenience, or—in more cases than any other one place in my travel experience—a delicious combination of all or most of those factors. You can supplement these recommendations by referring to the VVV's handy restaurant guide with its map reference for instant location of each and a breakdown by type of cuisine. Be sure to pick one up on your first visit to that office.

You should know, however, that there are a few distinctively Dutch foods whose availability is determined by when you visit. Among them: asparagus, beautifully white and tender, in May; "new" herring, fresh from the North Sea and eaten raw, in May or early June (great excitement surrounds the first catch of the season, part of which goes to the queen and the rest to restaurateurs amid spirited competition); Zeeland oysters and mussels (*Zeeuwsoesters* and *Zeeuwsmoselen*), from September to March.

Unless otherwise stated, lunch hours for the restaurants listed are noon to 2:30pm, and dinner hours are 6 to 10 or 10:30pm. The Dutch dine early, and with few exceptions last orders are taken no later than 10pm.

In the top restaurants, it is absolutely necessary to reserve, and for others it's a good idea to phone ahead to avoid disappointment, especially if you have your heart set on dining in a small restaurant. Casual cafés, coffee shops, sandwich shops, etc., are of course exceptions to that rule.

ABOUT PRICES   Those shown below, unless noted to the contrary, are average prices for a three-course meal without wine or other beverages, but including service charge and VAT. Wine by the bottle will add anywhere from Dfl. 22 to 30 ($11 to $15) to your bill; by the glass, about Dfl. 4.50 ($2.30).

In the city's best restaurants you can expect à la carte prices for three courses to total about Dfl. 100 ($52), with fixed-price menus in the Dfl. -60 to -100 ($31 to $52) range.

In the moderately priced restaurants (the majority of those listed here), three courses average Dfl. 40 to 65 ($21 to $34).

Budget prices (listed under "inexpensive") for simple, but tasty and filling, meals will run anywhere from Dfl. 10 to 40 ($5 to $21).

For the absolute best value for the dollar, look for the blue-and-white TOURIST MENU sign that pictures a fork-turned-tourist (complete with hat and camera) displayed on restaurant doors or windows. Wherever you see it, you'll pay only Dfl. 25 ($13) for three courses if you order the set Tourist Menu—no substitutions from the regular menu, but the day's specialties are usually included in the set menu. Dutch specialties offered by restaurants displaying the NEERLANDS DIS soup-tureen sign will average about Dfl. 25 ($13) for three courses, although in some cases they fall into the moderate price range.

Note: A stroll along the little Reguliersdwarsstraat, one block off and parallel to the floating flower market, will give you a choice of moderate meals of the Dutch, French, Mexican, and several other cultures' persuasions. Many of the small restaurants also function as bars, so you can have a drink and "window-shop" before making a decision as to the cuisine of choice.

Expensive

Expensive these most assuredly are, but you'll get your money's worth. Prices average Dfl. 100 ($52) and up for three courses, except for lower fixed-price menus.

Christophe, Leliegracht 46. ☎ **625-0807.**
> **Cuisine:** INTERNATIONAL. **Reservations:** Recommended. **Tram:** 4, 9, 16, 24, or 25 from Centraal Station.
> **Prices:** Main courses Dfl. 50–65 ($26–$34). AE, DC, MC, V.
> **Open:** Dinner only, Mon–Sat 7–11pm.

The chef here uses traditional Mediterranean ingredients—figs, truffles, olives, and saffron—in exciting new ways. Try the pigeon roasted with spices, the lobster with sweet garlic, the quail risotto with truffle juice, or the scallops with orange and saffron. Finish with baked figs with thyme ice cream. A traditional wooden decor prevails with art deco touches.

Excelsior, Nieuwe Doelenstraat 2–8. ☎ **623-4836.**
> **Cuisine:** FRENCH. **Reservations:** Required. **Tram:** 4, 9, 14, 16, 24, or 25.
> **Prices:** Average lunch Dfl. 62 ($32); fixed-price dinner Dfl. 120 ($63). AE, DC, MC, V.
> **Open:** Lunch Sun–Fri noon–2:30pm; dinner daily 6–10:30pm.

One of the finest dining rooms in town, the Excelsior is in the Hôtel de l'Europe near Muntplein, and its wide windows overlook the Amstel River and the Mint Tower. Crystal chandeliers, fresh flowers, candlelight, and soft piano music in the evening—all contribute to the classic elegance here. Veal with leek sauce is only one of the many fine French specialties here, and Dutch traditional dishes such as smoked eel with dill also turn up fairly regularly.

★ **De Goudsbloem,** in the Hotel Pulitzer, Prinsengracht 315–331 (entrance on Reestraat 8). ☎ **523-5283.**

$ **Cuisine:** FRENCH/NOUVELLE CUISINE. **Reservations:** Recommended. **Tram:** 2, 13, 14, or 17.
Prices: Fixed-price meal Dfl. 95 ($50) for four courses, Dfl. 115 ($60) for six courses. AE, DC, MC, V.
Open: Lunch Mon–Fri noon–3pm; dinner daily 6–11pm.

This delightful restaurant in the Hotel Pulitzer (see "Accommodations," earlier in this chapter) has the airy look of a summer garden, and it fairly blooms with gourmet dishes of the nouvelle cuisine variety, such as escalopes de turbot et saumon, cuit sous vide, purée de persil (steamed turbot and salmon with purée of parsley). There's an elegant six-course "menu gourmand" and a four-course "menu gastronomique." The restaurant has a separate entrance on a side street.

★ **D'Vijff Vlieghen (The Five Flies),** Spuistraat 294–302. ☎ **624-8369.**

$ **Cuisine:** DUTCH. **Reservations:** Recommended. **Tram:** 1, 2, or 5.
Prices: Fixed-price meal Dfl. 70 ($37) for three courses, Dfl. 110 ($58) for five courses. AE, DC, MC, V.
Open: Dinner only, daily 5–11pm.

There are seven interesting dining rooms (each of which is a miniature museum) in the five slightly tilting canal houses that date from 1627 and make up this quintessential Amsterdam restaurant—and all seven are always filled. The magic of the place, however, is that each room takes on a cozy, intimate air that banishes any feeling of being in a big, busy restaurant. The menu and specialties are as inherently Dutch as the setting. The traditional waterzoot is terrific here, or you might try veal steak with apple and prunes. Or maybe this is where you decide to try a "royal" dish—roast wild boar (from the Royal Estates) complete with stuffed apple. In the city center.

La Rive, in the Amstel Inter-Continental Hotel, Professor Tulpplein 1. ☎ **622-6060.**

Cuisine: FRENCH. **Reservations:** Recommended. **Tram:** 6 or 7 from Centraal Station.
Prices: Two-course business lunch Dfl. 49.50 ($26); five-course dinner Dfl. 125 ($66). AE, DC, EU, MC, V.
Open: Daily 7am–11pm.

La Rive overlooks the Amstel River and in summer opens onto a grassy terrace along the embankment near Weeserplein. Inside it's as if a small private library had been converted into a private dining room. The walls are paneled in cherry and lined with several display cases filled with books or brass objects. Along one wall is a row of private booths that are particularly romantic and have a view out over the water via some French windows. The cuisine is nouvelle French and the service and wine cellar are in the finest French tradition. In 1994 it was awarded a Michelin star.

Ristorante Mirafiori, Hobbemastraat 2. ☎ **662-3013.**

Cuisine: ITALIAN. **Reservations:** Recommended for dinner. **Tram:** 2 or 5 from Centraal Station.
Prices: Three-course meal with wine Dfl. 90 ($47). AE, DC, MC, V.
Open: Lunch Wed–Mon noon–3pm; dinner Wed–Mon 5pm–midnight.

Founded in 1941 by the same family that runs it today, this typical Italian restaurant between Leidseplein and the Rijksmuseum has welcomed many famous guests to its three intimate dining rooms—the late Sammy Davis, Jr., Liza Minelli, and Eddie Murphy, to name only a few. Soups and 13 pasta dishes introduce the menu, which

9569

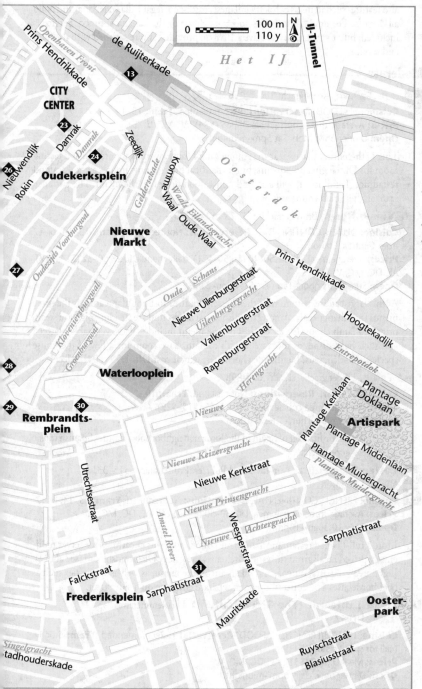

Dining in Central Amsterdam

also features such items as cotoletta milanese, ossobuco, fegato alla veneziana, and pollo all diavolo. For dessert try the luscious zabaglione or the banana al fuoco. Service is included, but it's customary to leave a 10% tip provided you're satisfied with the food and service.

Moderate

★ **Bols Tavern,** Rozengracht 106. ☎ **624-5752.**
Cuisine: SEAFOOD. **Reservations:** Recommended. **Tram:** 13, 14, or 17.
Prices: Average three-course meal Dfl. 65 ($34). AE, MC, V.
Open: Dinner only, Mon–Sat 5pm–midnight.

This 17th-century place, near the Anne Frank House, won its reputation as a tasting room for Dutch gin and liqueurs, but its nautical interior now houses a good seafood restaurant. Landlubbers will also find nonseafood dishes on the menu. The entrance is through a small courtyard.

Cafe Von Puffelen, Prinsengracht 377. ☎ **624-6270.**
Cuisine: DUTCH/CONTINENTAL. **Reservations:** Not required. **Tram:** 13, 14, or 17 from Centraal Station.
Prices: Average meal Dfl. 12.50–40 ($6.50–$21); daily menu Dfl. 27.50–32 ($14–$17). AE, DC, MC, V.
Open: Sun–Thurs noon–1am, Fri–Sat noon–2am.

At this large café/restaurant near the Westerkerk the most popular feature is the three menus that change daily. Among the dishes you might find are suckling pig, veal steak, or grilled lamb chops. Other choices on the menu include salads, vegetable platters, and such light dishes as mozzarella with tomato. Save room for a few of the house specialties—delicious, handmade chocolates, which cost Dfl. 1.50 (80¢) apiece.

Casa Tobio, Lindengracht 31. ☎ **624-8987.**
Cuisine: SPANISH. **Reservations:** Not required. **Tram:** 10.
Prices: Average three-course meal Dfl. 25–55 ($13–$29). AE, V.
Open: Dinner only, Thurs–Tues 6–10pm.

This atmospheric little bit of Spain in the Jordaan neighborhood features Spanish music and a very good paella.

★ **Coffee Shop Pulitzer,** in the Hotel Pulitzer, Prinsengracht 315–331. ☎ **622-8333.**
$ **Cuisine:** FRENCH/CONTINENTAL. **Reservations:** Not required. **Tram:** 13, 14, or 17.
Prices: Average three-course meal Dfl. 30–50 ($15–$26). AE, DC, MC, V.
Open: Daily 10:30am–10pm.

More a full-fledged restaurant than a true coffee shop, this cheerful place serves moderately priced meals from the same kitchen as the pricey De Goudsbloem (see above). Light meals of pasta, quiche, and salads are on the menu, as well as specialties such as beef bordelaise. The coffee shop has a separate entrance on a side street.

De Groene Lanteerne (The Green Lantern), Haarlemmerstraat 43. ☎ **624-1952.**
Cuisine: DUTCH/FRENCH/SEAFOOD. **Reservations:** Recommended. **Tram:** 6 or 16 (call for specific stop).
Prices: Meal Dfl. 60 ($31). AE, DC, MC, V.
Open: Dinner only, daily 6pm–midnight.

You'll wonder how a restaurant could be squeezed into such a narrow space—it claims, in fact, to be the narrowest restaurant in the world—but the 17th-century Old Dutch interior is the setting for some very good Dutch and French dishes, representing good value. They do an excellent quail salad with a crème fraîche and chervil sauce, and I especially like the salmon steak with a white wine and dill sauce. The Lantern is near the Tram Museum.

★ $ **Haesje Claes,** Spuistraat 275. ☎ **624-9998.**

Cuisine: DUTCH. **Reservations:** Recommended. **Tram:** 1, 2, or 5.
Prices: Average three-course meal Dfl. 40 ($21). MC, V.
Open: Mon–Sat noon–10pm, Sun 5–10pm.

It's long and narrow, dark as a brown café, cozy, and named for a 16th-century nun who ran an orphanage across the street. This is also one of the most convivial and comfortable eateries in this part of town, with "Neerlands Dis" awards to attest to the authenticity of its Dutch dishes. A great neighborhood favorite, it features heaping portions of hearty traditional hot and cold dishes, as well as simpler fare (Dover sole, Dutch steaks, omelets, etc.) that falls into the inexpensive category, and the Tourist Menu. Highly recommended. It's in the city center.

Het Stuivertje, Hazenstraat 58. ☎ **623-1349.**

Cuisine: DUTCH/FRENCH. **Reservations:** Required.
Prices: Main courses Dfl. 18–37.50 ($9–$20). AE, DC, MC, V.
Open: Lunch Tues–Sat noon–3pm; dinner Tues–Sun 5:30–11:30pm.

This traditional restaurant is always crowded with people enjoying the seasonal menu of the month or a selection from the menu featuring everything from vegetarian dishes like broccoli soufflé and goat stew with fennel and thyme to more traditional items like salmon with hollandaise or breast of veal stuffed with vegetables.

★ $ **De Kelderhof,** Prinsengracht 494. ☎ **622-0682.**

Cuisine: FRENCH/MEDITERRANEAN. **Reservations:** Not required. **Tram:** 1, 2, 5, 13, 14, or 17.
Prices: Three- and four-course fixed-price meals Dfl. 35–65 ($18–$34). AE, MC, V.
Open: Dinner only, daily 5pm–midnight.

A Mediterranean courtyard has been created in the ground floor of this graceful old canal house, with lots of exposed brick, wicker furniture, and fairy lights in potted trees. Strolling musicians add to the ambience, and there are nine four-course set-menu offerings centered around fish, steak, and pork, as well as an extensive à la carte menu.

De Keyzer Bodega, Van Baerlestraat 96. ☎ **671-1441.**

Cuisine: DUTCH/FRENCH. **Reservations:** Required. **Tram:** 3, 5, 12, or 16.
Prices: Average three-course meal Dfl. 55–70 ($29–$37). AE, MC, V.
Open: Mon–Sat noon–midnight.

Partly because of its proximity to the Concertgebouw, but mostly because of its comfortable tavernlike interior, excellent menu, and good service, this is one of the most popular dining spots in the area. Serving fish and meat, with game dishes in season, it stays open after concerts (another reason for its popularity). There's a not-so-taverny, French-oriented dining room in the back.

Lucius Restaurant, Spuistraat 247. ☎ **624-1831.**

Cuisine: SEAFOOD. **Reservations:** Recommended. **Tram:** 1, 2, 5, 11, 13, or 17 from Centraal Station.

Prices: Main courses Dfl. 30–40 ($16–$21); full meals Dfl. 47.50–95 ($25–$50). AE, DC, MC, V.
Open: Dinner only, Mon–Sat 5pm–midnight.

This restaurant, which opened in 1985, has established a reputation for fine seafood at fairly reasonable prices. Oysters and lobsters imported from Norway and Canada are the specialty. Among the half dozen or so choices featured on the blackboard menu you might find fish soup to start, followed by grilled plaice, Dover sole, bass, or John Dory. The spectacular seafood plate ($50) includes six oysters, 10 mussels, clams, shrimp, and half a lobster. The long, narrow dining room is cooled by ceiling fans and features an aquarium. In summer chairs are placed out on the sidewalk. "Lucius," by the way, means "pike" in Latin.

Oesterbar, Leidseplein 10. ☎ 623-2988.
Cuisine: SEAFOOD. **Reservations:** Recommended. **Tram:** 1, 2, 5, 6, 7, or 10.
Prices: Average three-course meal Dfl. 45–70 ($23–$37). AE, MC, V.
Open: Lunch daily noon–2pm; dinner daily 6–10pm.

Dine casually at the tiled street level, or more formally upstairs in the pretty red-and-white dining room. On Leidseplein, this longtime favorite with locals and visitors alike boasts an extensive menu that includes just about any fish you can name. If you just can't decide, go for the marvelous fish sampler plate.

★ **De Poort van Cleve,** Nieuwe Zijds Voorburgwal 178. ☎ 624-0047.
$ **Cuisine:** STEAKS. **Reservations:** Recommended. **Tram:** All city-center trams.
Prices: Fixed-price lunch Dfl. 35 ($18); average dinner Dfl. 70 ($37). AE, MC, V.
Open: Lunch daily noon–2pm; dinner daily 6–10pm.

This highly regarded vaulted steak house is behind Dam Square in the hotel by the same name (see "Accommodations," earlier in this chapter), and every steak served since 1870 has been numbered—if your steak number should end in 000, it will be complimentary and accompanied by a free bottle of wine. In the smaller Old Dutch Bodega just off the lobby, Delft tiles and magnificent wood paneling create a cozier ambience for a more diversified menu, including such Dutch standbys as the traditional hutspot and zuurkool (sauerkraut with creamed potatoes, bacon, and smoked sausage). This restaurant is scheduled to reopen in the fall of 1995.

★ **Restaurant Adrian,** Reguliersdwarsstraat 21. ☎ 623-9582.
$ **Cuisine:** FRENCH. **Reservations:** Recommended. **Tram:** 16, 24, or 25.
Prices: Appetizers Dfl. 19–36 ($10–$19); main courses Dfl. 25–70 ($13–$37); special menu Dfl. 80 ($42). AE, MC, V.
Open: Dinner only, daily 6pm–midnight.

This gem of a restaurant brings the very essence of French cooking to the heart of Amsterdam. The unpretentious elegance of the small, beamed dining room (seating for 32) comes from soft lighting of shaded wall sconces and candles on each table, creating a warm, cozy intimacy. Table settings are extraordinarily lovely, and service is both professionally polished and friendly. Scallops with red wine and saffron sauce is a standout among starters, while the filets of lamb with thyme come to table with just the right degree of pinkness. Vegetables are beautifully cooked, and desserts are outstanding. The restaurant is one block from the floating flower market.

Restaurant Purnama, Korte Nieuwendjik 33. ☎ **620-5325.**

Cuisine: INDONESIAN.
Prices: Rijsttafel Dfl. 27.50–39.50 ($14–$21); other dishes Dfl. 6.50–19.50 ($3–$10). AE, DC, MC, V.
Open: Daily 1:30–10:30pm.

This small restaurant only five minutes from Centraal Station is always crowded with locals enjoying the good-quality food. Among the favorite dishes are the mini-rijsttafel and the special rijsttafel. The first consists of 11 items, the second of 15 items, that combine sweet and sour tastes and other contrasting spices and flavors. If this is too much for you, try the nasi or bami goreng or choose one of the 8 or 10 meat or fish dishes. For starters, try the sot ayam, a spicey soup.

Sama Sebo, P. C. Hooftstraat 27. ☎ **662-8146.**

Cuisine: INDONESIAN. **Reservations:** Required. **Tram:** 1, 2, 5, or 6.
Prices: Rijsttafel Dfl. 24 ($12) for 8 items, Dfl. 45 ($23) for 20 items; à la carte Dfl. 4–6.50 ($2–$3) per item. AE, MC, V.
Open: Lunch daily noon–2pm; dinner daily 6–10pm.

Acknowledged by all and sundry as Amsterdam's leading Indonesian restaurant, this pretty establishment decorated with Indonesian artifacts is known for its rijsttafels, and there are à la carte combinations that qualify for the "inexpensive" label. The restaurant is at the corner of Hobbemastraat, near Vondelpark.

 Sherry Can Bodega, Spui 30. ☎ **623-2273.**

Cuisine: DUTCH. **Reservations:** Not required. **Tram:** 1, 2, 4, 5, 9, 14, 16, 24, or 25.
Prices: Average three-course meal Dfl. 30–60 ($15–$31). MC, V.
Open: Lunch Tues–Sun noon–2pm; dinner Tues–Sun 6–10pm. (Sidewalk café Tues–Sun 11am–11pm.)

A great favorite of students, businesspeople, and tourists, this is another restaurant of the Singel Canal that has both moderate and inexpensive selections. The attractive sidewalk café (where you need order nothing more than a beer or glass of wine) serves light snacks and an inexpensive lunch menu; while in the cozy upstairs dining room, traditional Dutch cuisine is featured, and the candlelit downstairs dining room has an extensive à la carte dinner menu of steaks, fish, chicken, and pork.

Speciaal, Nieuwe Leliestraat 140. ☎ **624-9706.**

Cuisine: INDONESIAN. **Reservations:** Recommended. **Tram:** 10.
Prices: 15-item rijsttafel Dfl. 50 ($26). AE, MC, V.
Open: Dinner only, daily 5:30–11pm.

You'll have to venture out to the fringes of the central city to the Jordaan area to find this restaurant, but the trip is well worth the effort for this is one of Amsterdam's best rijsttafel restaurants. It's small but cozy, with Javanese decor and a friendly staff.

D'Theeboom, Singel 210. ☎ **623-8420.**

Cuisine: DUTCH. **Reservations:** Not required. **Tram:** 16, 24, or 25.
Prices: Average à la carte meal Dfl. 30–40 ($15–$21). AE, MC, V.
Open: Lunch daily noon–2pm; dinner daily 6–10pm.

This lively café/wine bar on the Singel Canal has a devoted following among the younger Amsterdam set, and its menu features dishes that combine ingredients in fresh, new ways, with very good results. Lunch is usually crowded.

Inexpensive

Le Bistro, in the Amsterdam Ascot Hotel, Damrak 95–98. ☎ **626-0066.**

> **Cuisine:** FRENCH/LIGHT MEALS. **Reservations:** Not required. **Tram:** All city-center trams.
> **Prices:** Sandwiches and pastas Dfl. 15–28 ($8–$15); full meals Dfl. 40–52 ($21–$27). AE, DC, MC, V.
> **Open:** Lunch daily noon–3pm; dinner daily 6–10pm.

This attractive restaurant, convenient to Dam Square shopping and sightseeing, has an exceptionally fine French kitchen. Specialties include asparagus in a mornay sauce and parmesan cheese, salmon with hollandaise sauce, and asparagus with veal tongue antiboise.

Cafe-Restaurant Blincker, St. Barberenstraat 7. ☎ **627-1938.**

> **Cuisine:** CONTINENTAL. **Reservations:** Recommended. **Directions:** Turn onto Nesstreet from Dam Square (which runs parallel to Rokin), then turn left after the Frascati Theater.
> **Prices:** Main courses Dfl. 8.50–26.50 ($4–$14). AE, DC, MC, V.
> **Open:** Dinner only, Mon–Sat 4pm–1am.

This intimate restaurant in the Frascati Theater building on a small side street off Rokin attracts actors, journalists, artists, and other assorted bohemians. At night the place is jammed with people who cluster around the bar.

★
$ **Cafe de Passage,** Nieuwendijk 224. ☎ **624-8439.**

> **Cuisine:** PANCAKES/TRADITIONAL. **Reservations:** Not required. **Tram:** 4, 9, 16, 24, or 25.
> **Prices:** Average meal Dfl. 17–36 ($9–$19). AE, MC, V.
> **Open:** Fri–Wed 11am–8pm, Thurs 11am–10pm.

On one of Amsterdam's busiest pedestrian shopping streets near Dam Square, Sjusi and Ruud Wildbret have created a haven for weary feet and an attractive setting for budget eating. It's a pleasant place, the sidewalk café opening to a cozy interior with lots of dark wood and red plush upholstery. You can just stop in for a beer, indulge in their pancakes with a choice of a dozen or more fillings, order light meals of omelets and salad plates, or go for the excellent dinner menu that includes fish, steak, pork, shish kebab, wienerschnitzel, and several other selections.

Cafe Luxembourg, Spui 24. ☎ **620-6264.**

> **Cuisine:** INTERNATIONAL. **Reservations:** Not required. **Tram:** 1, 2, 5, 11, 13, or 17 from Centraal Station.
> **Prices:** Pastrami sandwich Dfl. 13.50 ($7); coffee Dfl. 3 ($1.55).
> **Open:** Sun–Thurs 10am–1am, Fri–Sat 10am–2am.

This large café opened eight years ago and soon became a favorite hangout for students, journalists, senior citizens, and barflies. Unlike other coffeehouses in Amsterdam, which often draw a distinctive clientele, Cafe Luxembourg attracts all kinds of people because it offers amazingly large portions of food at reasonable prices. Soups, sandwiches, and such dishes as meatloaf are available. It's a relaxing place and people are encouraged to linger and read one of the many international newspapers that are available. In summer there's sidewalk dining.

Cafe 'Tsmalle, Egelantiersgracht 12. ☎ **623-9617.**

Cuisine: SANDWICHES/PASTRIES. **Reservations:** Not required. **Tram:** 10.
Prices: Menu items, Dfl. 10–22 ($5–$11). No credit cards.
Open: Daily 11am–11pm.

This small canalside corner café near the Jordaan section, with its high, beamed ceiling, old geneve pump on the bar, magazines and newspapers on a wall rack, and generous complement of neighborhood regulars, is a delightful place to stop for tostis, sandwiches, quiche, pastries, coffee, beer, and wine. Benches are just outside the door for canal- and people-watching in good weather (although the people-watching inside is terrific). The place dates back to 1780, and its walls are a mini-museum of old beer kegs, bottles, brass, and a tall grandfather clock. For travelers on the canal, there's a platform canalside, a pleasant place to debark for a drink and snack.

Cafe 'Tzwaantje, Berenstraat 12. ☎ **623-2373.**

Cuisine: BARBECUED RIBS/LIGHT MEALS. **Reservations:** Not required.
Prices: Average meal Dfl. 18–26 ($9–$13). No credit cards.
Open: Daily 4:30–11pm. (Bar daily 4pm–1am.)

Delicious spareribs with the chef's special sauce are the specialty at this pretty little neighborhood café, between Prinsengracht and Keizersgracht. The menu also includes hamburgers, salad plates, and omelets for light meals, and full dinners of fish or meat.

★ **Carlton Corner,** in the Hotel Carlton, Vijzelstraat 4. ☎ **622-2266.**

💲 **Cuisine:** CONTINENTAL/SNACKS. **Reservations:** Not required. **Tram:** 4, 9, 14, 16, 24, or 25.
Prices: Lunch, main dishes Dfl. 12.50 ($6.60); supper, main dishes Dfl. 25 ($13.25). AE, DC, MC, V.
Open: Tues–Sun 11am–8pm.

Near Muntplein, this lovely corner café that looks out to the floating flower market has become "the" place to meet for Amsterdammers—whether for a quick drink, a snack of croissant and coffee, a salad plate, a grilled burger or sandwich, pasta, a luscious assortment of fish in puff pastry, or (my personal favorite) eggplant filled with rice, vegetables, and herbs. It's casual elegance and terrific food at budget prices, and in fine weather there are sidewalk tables.

The Old Bell, Rembrandtsplein 46. ☎ **624-7682.**

Cuisine: BEEF/SALADS/BAR FOOD. **Reservations:** Not required. **Tram:** 4, 9, or 14.
Prices: Menu range Dfl. 7.50–21 ($4–$11). AE, MC, V.
Open: Daily noon–8pm.

Set on a corner of lively Rembrandtsplein, the Old Bell is an English-style pub with outstanding food service for its low prices. True to its English orientation, prime ribs, rumpsteak, and sirloin steaks star on the menu, along with pork chops. For a more casual, drop-in meal, there are cold salad plates, omelets, ham and eggs, and fried eggs with cheese, as well as a number of other snack and light-meal items on the extensive menu. From the fully licensed bar comes a steady stream of quite acceptable wines, spirits, and a good selection of beers on draft.

 De Stationsrestauratie, in Centraal Station, Spoor 2A. ☎ **627-3306.**

Cuisine: TRADITIONAL/SNACKS/PASTRIES. **Reservations:** Not required. **Tram:** Most lines to Centraal Station.
Prices: Hot and cold plates Dfl. 10–23 ($5–$12). No credit cards.
Open: Mon–Sat 7am–10pm, Sun 8am–10pm.

One of the most overlooked by all but rail passengers is this large self-service restaurant upstairs at Centraal Station. It's a handsome room, with several divisions to dilute the "barny" feeling, a huge selection of hot and cold plates, and any number of snacks and pastries for much less.

Specialty Dining

PANCAKE HOUSES   Pancakes are the specialty at both the **Bredero Pannekoekenhuysje,** Oude Zijds Voorburgwal 244 (☎ **622-9461**), and **Pancake Bakery,** Prinsengracht 191 (☎ **625-1333**). The latter is a historic building very near the Anne Frank House and is open from noon to 10pm daily.

SANDWICH SHOPS   Some of Amsterdam's best sandwich shops (*broodjeswinkel*) are the three branches of the **Broodje van Kootje** shops sporting bright-yellow signs at Spui, Rembrandtsplein, and Leidseplein.

DINNER AFLOAT   From April to November on Tuesday, Thursday, and Saturday evenings, a marvelous ✪ three-hour cruise through Amsterdam's canals is combined with a very good five-course dinner with before and after drinks and wine with dinner, via Holland International's Amsterdam Dinner Cruise (☎ **622-7788**). The cost is Dfl. 145 ($76).

---

5 Attractions

To be a tourist in Amsterdam is to be thrust into an instant quandary—it's not *what* to see and do that's the problem, it's *how much* of this intriguing city's fascinating sights and activities you'll be able to work into the time you have!

There are miles and miles of canals to float, hundreds of narrow streets to wander, historic buildings to visit, more than 40 museums holding collections of everything from artistic wonders to obscure curiosities, diamond cutters and craftspeople to watch as they practice generations-old skills, and . . . the list is as long as every tourist's individual interests. And these are just a few of Amsterdam's daytime things to see and do. When night falls, another bag of treasures opens up, and we'll get to that in "Evening Entertainment," later in this chapter.

Your very first stop on any sightseeing excursion, of course, should be the **VVV office**—they have information on anything you might want to know and some things you might not have even known you wanted to know.

One way to save money in Amsterdam is to purchase the **Amsterdam Culture Leisure Card,** developed by the Amsterdam Tourist Office. The card contains 25 coupons giving free or discounted admission to the Rijksmuseum, the Stedelijk Museum, and the van Gogh Museum, plus discounts on admission for other attractions, excursions, and restaurants, including reduced rates for the Museum Boat and the Canal Bus. The Leisure Card costs Dfl. 29.90 ($15.75) and can be obtained through the Netherlands Board of Tourism offices in your home country or through the VVV in Amsterdam.

READERS RECOMMEND

Paviljoen de Carrousel, Randwijkplantsoen 1 (Weteringcircuit) (☎ **627-5880**). *"This great place is near the Heineken Brewery and Rijksmuseum and serves great pannekoeken."*—C. Pepkin, Forest Hills, N.Y. [**Author's Note:** The pancakes cost Dfl. 10 to 15 ($5 to $8). The place is open daily from 10am to 6pm.]

The Top Attractions

THE MUSEUMS

While it's impossible to list here all of Amsterdam's museums, the following fall into the "you really shouldn't miss" category. The VVV can furnish a complete list, which could well reveal others with special appeal to you—they cover such diverse subjects as the press (Nederlands Persmuseum), geology (Geologisches Museum Der Amsterdamer Universiteit), and even a money-box museum (Sparbuechsenmuseum), some of which you won't want to miss.

Some of the museums listed here are clustered around Museumplein, but be warned that although they're next-door neighbors, it would be a mistake to take them all in at one whack—these are not places to pass through quickly, and it's a good idea to devote at least half a day to each. If the very thought of museum-hopping makes your feet hurt, there are all those lovely brown cafés down adjacent streets to rest the weary body and quench a mighty thirst.

You should know that you can purchase a **Museum Pass (*Museumkaart*)** for Dfl. 40 ($21.05) for ages 25 and over, Dfl. 25 ($13.15) for ages 25 and under, and Dfl. 20 ($10.50) for senior citizens. The pass covers free admission to some 250 museums throughout the country (16 in Amsterdam). The pass can be bought from the VVV, as well as most museums, and if museums are high on your sightseeing agenda, it's a good investment even if Amsterdam is your only stop in Holland. There's also a Museum Boat Tour (☎ **622-2181**) with six stops and reduced admission fees at 11 museums.

One thing to remember about museum visits: Many are closed on Monday and are open 10am to 5pm Tuesday through Saturday, 1 to 5pm on Sunday and holidays.

 Amstelkring Museum ("Our Lord in the Attic"), Oude Zijds Voorburgwal 40. ☎ **624-6604.**

For some 200 years, beginning in 1578 when Holland fervently embraced Protestantism and forbade the practice of any other religion, Amsterdam's vaunted sense of tolerance had to go underground. With religious bigotry running rampant, Catholics were forced to hold clandestine services, and this moving museum is just one of the 62 hidden chapels that eventually existed in the city. So long as they remained out of public sight, municipal authorities turned a blind eye, and the chapel you climb well-worn steps to see today was used right up to 1887, when Catholics were once more allowed to worship in St. Nicholaaskerk. The chapel occupies the attic space of a canal house and two smaller ones just behind it that were built in 1661 by an Amsterdammer who gave his blessings to the illicit worship in 1663. The long, narrow space is quite plain except for its baroque altar and the swinging pulpit that could be stored out of sight. The 1794 organ is pumped by hand and is used today for concerts, lectures, Christmas Eve mass, and special occasions such as weddings. The residential area of the museum holds very impressive and authentic 17th- and 18th-century period rooms. The *Sael* (drawing room), built in 1663, is the last remaining Dutch classicist living room in Amsterdam, and the unique combination of church and home dating from the city's golden age makes this a very special museum indeed. And, like the Anne Frank House, "Our Lord in the Attic" is a monument to Amsterdam's typical reaction to oppression.

Admission: Dfl. 5 ($2.60) adults, Dfl. 3.50 ($1.85) children 14 and under.

Open: Mon–Sat 10am–5pm, Sun and holidays 1–5pm. **Directions:** Walk from Dam Square via Damstraat to Oude Zijds Voorburgwal, about two minutes.

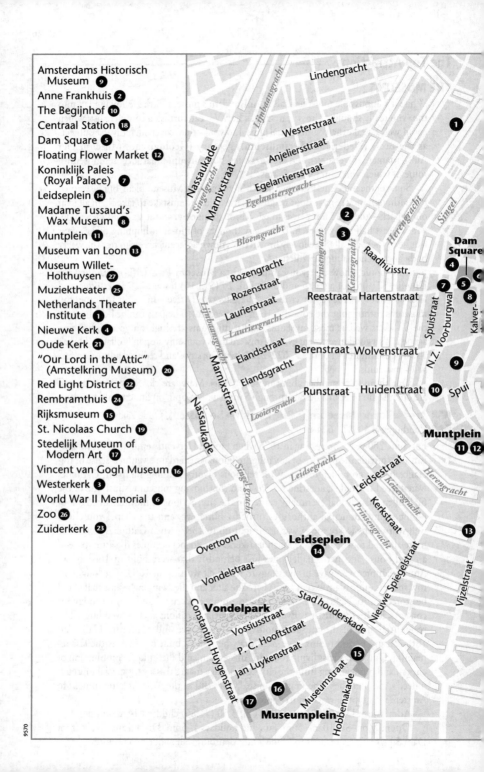

9570

Het IJ

IJ-Tunnel

Openhaven Front

Prins Hendrikkade

de Ruijterkade

18

CITY CENTER

19

Damrak

Nieuwendijk

Damrak

20

Zeedijk

Geldersekade

Rokin

Oudekerksplein

21

Kromme Waal

Waals Eilandsgracht

Oosterdok

22

Oudezijds Voorburgwal

Nieuwe Markt

Oude Waal

Prins Hendrikkade

Kloveniersburgwal

Oude Schans

Nieuwe Uilenburgerstraat

Uilenburgergracht

Hoogtekadijk

23

Valkenburgerstraat

Entrepotdok

Groenburgwal

24

Rapenburgerstraat

25

Waterlooplein

Herengracht

Plantage Kerklaan

Plantage Doklaan

Nieuwe

Artispark

Rembrandts-plein

26

27

Plantage Middenlaan

Nieuwe Keizersgracht

Plantage Muidergracht

Plantage Muidergracht

Utrechtestraat

Nieuwe Kerkstraat

Nieuwe Prinsengracht

Amstel River

Nieuwe Weesperstraat

Achtergracht

Sarphatistraat

Falckstraat

Frederiksplein Sarphatistraat

Ooster-park

Mauritskade

Singelgracht
Stadhouderskade

Ruyschstraat

Blasiusstraat

0   100 m
    110 y

N

Amsterdam Historical Museum, Kalverstraat 92. ☎ **523-1822.**

A tiny setback alleyway leads to a beautiful 1581 gate opening into the courtyard of a 300-year-old complex of classic buildings that served for many years as Amsterdam's orphanage, and before that as a monastery. The children to whom these buildings were home were identified by garb with one red and one black sleeve (the colors of the city's coat-of-arms), and in walls around the courtyard you can still see the set-in lockers that held these uniforms at night. The orphans are gone now, but the old buildings are home to a fascinating record of Amsterdam's history, with room after room of documents, maps, prints, works of art, and artifacts unearthed as recently as the subway excavations. In a unique street gallery, 17th-century historical paintings are hung along the glass-covered passageway leading from the museum into the Begijnhof (see below). This is another loitering place, and the exposed brick walls and beams of the David and Goliath restaurant opening into the courtyard (with service under the great linden tree outside) offer a pleasant respite.

Admission: Dfl. 7.50 ($4) adults, Dfl. 3.75 ($2) children 16 and under.
Open: Daily 11am–5pm. **Closed:** Jan 1. **Tram:** 1, 2, or 5.

★ **Anne Frank House**, Prinsengracht 263. ☎ **556-7100.**

During World War II Amsterdammers went far beyond mere tolerance in finding ways of thwarting Nazi oppression of their Jewish population. As more and more Jews were deported to the infamous "death camps" (some 100,000 Amsterdam Jews never returned), Anne Frank's father hid his family and the family of one of his employees in the attic of an annex to this 1635 canal house, which had been his place of business (the house is along the canal past the Westerkerk). For 25 months the young girl lived in these cramped quarters, passing long days in silence for fear of being overheard. Only 13 years old, she kept a daily record of her innermost thoughts and her family's confined life. In 1944 the family was betrayed, arrested, and sent to separate camps in Germany, where Anne perished at Bergen-Belsen in 1945. Of the family members, only her father, Otto Frank, survived. In 1947 her diary was published, and more than 13 million copies, in 50 languages, have been sold. The rooms you visit are much as they were during those long months of hiding, and downstairs is a small museum, which documents the terrible years of the Holocaust and monitors any current signs of fascism, racism, and anti-Semitism.

Admission: Dfl. 7 ($3.70) adults, Dfl. 3.50 ($1.85) children 10–17, free for children under 10.
Open: Mon–Sat 9am–5pm, Sun and holidays 10am–5pm. **Closed:** Jan 1, Dec 25, and Yom Kippur. **Tram:** 13, 14, or 17 to Westermarkt.

★ **The Begijnhof**, Begijnensteeg, off Kalverstraat.

Although not technically a museum, this serene 14th-century garden surrounded by small houses that date from the 16th and 17th centuries preserves as faithfully as any museum an integral part of Amsterdam's past. It was here that the *begijnes,* a dedicated group of laywomen, devoted their lives to the city's poor and other good works. You can pay homage to these pious women by pausing for a moment at the small flower-planted mound that lies just at the center garden's edge across from the English Reformed church. A simple stone is inscribed "Hier Rust Cornelia Arens, Begijn, Overleden 2 Mei 1654." She is the only one of the begijnes who claimed the right to be buried near the church, a right granted when it was handed over to the Protestant community; all others lie in city cemeteries. Just opposite the front of the church is a secret Catholic chapel built in 1671 and still in use. You're welcomed to the Begijnhof during daylight hours (the city's poor senior citizens now reside in the old homes, and their privacy is respected after sunset).

Admission: Free.

Open: Daily until sunset. **Directions/Transportation:** Back entrance, through the Civic Guard Gallery of the Amsterdam Historical Museum (see above) or through the small alleylike Begijnensteeg off Kalverstraat. Front entrance, take tram no. 1, 2, or 5 to Spui, walk one block east, and turn left on Gedempte Begijnsloot to main gate on the left, halfway down the block.

Heineken Brewery, Stadhouderskade 78. ☎ **653-9239.**

Lovers of Holland's internationally famous beer will want to visit the museum that has been set up in the building in which it was brewed from 1932 until 1988; wheelchair-bound visitors will find a special entrance for easy access. The guided tours take you through the history of the Heineken company and its brewing process, and those age 16 and over will be welcomed with a free glass of beer.

Admission: Dfl. 1 (50¢) donation for local charities.

Open: May–Sept, Mon–Fri six guided tours 9am–2:30pm; Oct–Apr, Mon–Fri three guided tours in morning only (call for exact times). **Tram:** 16, 24, or 25.

★ **Netherlands Maritime Museum,** Kattenburgerplein, just off Prins Hendrikkade. ☎ **523-2222.**

What a bonanza for anyone who loves the sea. In this ancient arsenal of the Amsterdam Admiralty that dates from 1656, exhibits of ship models, charts, instruments, maps, prints, and paintings chronicle Holland's abiding ties to the sea through commerce, fishing, yachting, navigational development, and even war at sea. Brief texts explain each exhibit, and desks with more extensive information are found in every room. Moored at the landing stage are a steam icebreaker, a motor lifeboat, and a sailing lugger, while the historic Royal Barge and two towing barges are lodged indoors. You can reach this museum by taking a 20-minute walk along the historical waterfront, the "Nautisch Kwartier."

Admission: Dfl. 12.50 ($6.60) adults, Dfl. 8 ($4.20) children 17 and under.

Open: Tues–Sat 10am–5pm, Sun 1–5pm. **Closed:** Jan 1. **Bus:** 22 or 28 from Centraal Station.

★ **Rembrandt's House,** Jodenbreestraat 4–6. ☎ **624-9486.**

Rembrandt was bankrupt when he left this house near Waterlooplein in 1660 (purchased in 1639 when he was Amsterdam's most fashionable portrait painter), and it wasn't until 1906 that it was rescued from a succession of subsequent owners and restored as a museum. Because of his insolvency, the artist drew up an inventory for his creditors that proved invaluable in the restoration—could he return to the house today, he would find it very much as it was when he lived and worked here. His self-portraits that preoccupied him hang here, along with some 250 etchings. For the greatest of his masterpieces you must visit the Rijksmuseum, but it is in this house that you'll find a sense of the artist himself, his daily life, his studio, and above all his genius as one of the most important artists in the history of art.

There's an audiovisual program in English, guided tours in English upon request, and a very good museum shop.

Admission: Dfl. 5 ($2.60) adults, Dfl. 3.50 ($1.85) children 10 and over, free for children under 10.

Open: Mon–Sat 10am–5pm, Sun and holidays 1–5pm. **Closed:** Jan 1. **Tram:** 9 to Mr. Visserplein.

★ **Rijksmuseum Amsterdam**, Stadhouderskade 42, on Museumplein.
☎ **673-2121.**

This magnificent structure is the crown jewel of Holland's art treasures and ranks among the greatest in all of Europe. It owes its beginnings to Louis Napoléon, who founded it in 1808 during his brief sojourn as king of Holland; the building itself is the work of Petrus J. Cuypers and was opened in 1885. Its pride and joy is the huge Rembrandt canvas miscalled *The Night Watch,* whose true name is *The Company of Captain Frans Banning Coq and Lieutenant Willem van Ruytenburg.* The misnomer came about because years of accumulated grime and dirt made it appear to be a night scene; it wasn't until a thorough cleaning revealed otherwise that authorities realized the group portrait actually depicted these Amsterdammers in broad daylight.

Rembrandt is only one of the Dutch masters represented in the Rijksmuseum. Works by virtually every Dutch artist of stature from the 16th through the 19th century hang in these galleries—Frans Hals, Johannes Vermeer, Paulus Potter, Jacob van Ruisdael, Jan Steen, de Hooch, Gerard Dou, and Ter Borch among them. Painters from other countries include Goya, Fra Angelico, Van Dyck, and Peter Paul Rubens. The paintings, of course, are the museum's highlights, but there are also marvelous collections of prints (starting with the 15th century), tapestries from France and Belgium and Holland, Dutch and German sculpture, Dresden china and Delft porcelain, laces, ship models, glassware, room after room of furniture, and more.

Admission: Dfl. 10 ($5.25) adults, Dfl. 5 ($2.60) children 6–17, free for children 6 and under.

Open: Tues–Sat 10am–5pm, Sun and holidays 1–5pm. **Tram:** 2 or 5.

Stedelijk Museum, Paulus Potterstraat 13, on Museumplein. ☎ **573-2911.**

Lovers of modern art will revel in this collection that features works by the likes of De Kooning, Mondrian, Appel, Picasso, Chagall, Cézanne, Monet, Manet, Renoir, Calder, Pollock, Dubuffet, Rodin, Andy Warhol, Bruce Nauman, Anselm Kiefer, and Jannis Kounellis. With more than 1,000 exhibits, it is to modern schools of art what the Rijksmuseum is to the Dutch masters.

Admission: Dfl. 7.50 ($4) adults, Dfl. 3.75 ($2) children ages 6–17, free for children under 6 with adults.

Open: Daily 11am–5pm. **Tram:** 2 or 5, or 16 to Museumplein-Concertgebouw.

Theater Institute Nederland, Herengracht 168–170. ☎ **623-5104.**

Housed in five architectural gems on the canal, the theater institute uses two to house—in galleries connected by marble hallways with lavishly decorated ceilings and wall paintings—a wonderfully eclectic collection of theater memorabilia. "Theater" in this case includes opera, cabaret, puppetry, and even the circus. Exhibitions change frequently and include both historical and contemporary items, including puppets, costumes, masks, models, miniature stages, props, drawings, prints, paintings, and a wealth of other informative material. There is also a library of books, films, videos, and records, as well as a theater bookshop. You can enjoy drinks and snacks in the lovely garden out back.

Admission: Dfl. 5 ($2.65).

Open: Tues–Sun 11am–5pm. **Tram:** 13, 14, or 17.

★ **Vincent van Gogh Museum**, Paulus Potterstraat 7–11, on Museumplein.
☎ **570-5200.**

Anyone who has ever responded to van Gogh's vibrant colors and vivid landscapes will find it a moving experience to walk through the rooms of this rather stark contemporary building (1973). It displays in chronological order the more than 200 van Gogh paintings zealously guarded by his brother's wife and her son and presented to the nation with the proviso that they not leave his native land. There are no guided tours (taped tours are available), and you are only required to stand 1 foot back from the paintings, allowing a closer inspection than is usually the case. As you move through the rooms, the canvases reflect his changing environment and much of his inner life, so that gradually the artist himself becomes almost a tangible presence standing at your elbow. Here is the early, brooding *The Potato Eaters, The Yellow House* from his sojourn in Arles, and the painting known around the world simply as *Sunflowers,* although he titled it *Still Life with Fourteen Sunflowers.* By the time you reach the vaguely threatening painting of a flock of black crows rising from a waving cornfield, you can feel as if it were your own, the artist's mounting inner pain that finally he was unable to bear. The enormity of his talent is overwhelming, and even more so in light of the short 10 years in which he painted, selling only one canvas before his 1890 suicide when he was 37.

In addition to the paintings, there are nearly 600 drawings by van Gogh, and a series of paintings by his contemporaries. There's also a wonderful "self-expression" room, where you're invited to take up paintbrush, pencil, or clay, and pour out any pent-up artistic talent of your own. A very good self-service restaurant opens onto a pleasant terrace for sunny-day lunches.

Admission: Dfl. 10 ($5.25) adults, Dfl. 5 ($2.60) children under 18.

Open: Mon–Sat 10am–5pm, Sun and holidays 1–5pm. **Closed:** Jan 1. **Tram:** 2, 5, or 16 to Museumplein-Concertgebouw.

More Attractions

 The Floating Flower Market, along the Singel Canal at Muntplein.

If there is one single image people around the world have of Amsterdam, it's of this stunning mass of flowers strung along the Singel Canal. From permanently moored barges, awnings stretch to cover stall after stall of brightly colored blossoms, bulbs, and potted plants. A stroll down that fragrant line is surely one of Amsterdam's most heart-lifting experiences, and more than one tourist yields to the temptation to buy an armful of color and scent to brighten a hotel room. Prices are incredibly low, so go ahead, yield! Should you be invited to the home of an Amsterdammer, this is where you'll go for flowers to take along with you, a ritual the natives practice themselves.

Koninklijk Paleis (Royal Palace), Dam Sq. ☎ **624-8698.**

Built as a Town Hall to replace the one on this same spot that burned down in 1655, this massive, beautifully proportioned building on Dam Square required a total of 13,659 wooden pilings to support it in the marshy soil underneath. It was only in 1808, when Napoléon Bonaparte's brother, Louis, reigned as king of Holland, that it became a palace, quickly filled with Empire-style furniture courtesy of the French ruler. Today it's the official residence of the royal family (Amsterdam is, after all, capital of the country even though it's not the seat of government), but remains unoccupied since Queen Beatrix and her family prefer living at Huis ten Bosch in The Hague, using this palace only for the occasional state reception. During the summer months, you can visit its high-ceilinged Citizens' Hall, the Burgomasters' Chambers, and the Council Room, as well as the Vierschaar—the marble Tribunal in which death sentences were pronounced during the 17th century.

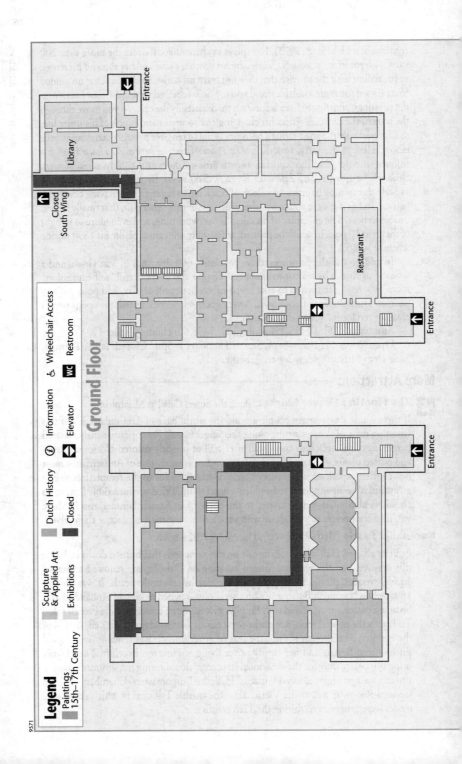

Legend

Paintings
15th–17th Century

Sculpture & Applied Art

Exhibitions

Closed

Dutch History

ⓘ Information

♿ Wheelchair Access

Elevator ↔

Restroom WC

Ground Floor

Entrance

Library

Closed South Wing ←

Entrance ↓

Restaurant

Entrance ←

Entrance ←

9571

Top Floor

The Night Watch

Film Theater

WC

WC

Museum Shop

Museum Shop

Admission: Dfl. 5 ($2.60) adults, Dfl. 1.50 (80¢) children under 12.

Open: Daily 12:30–5pm (last admission at 4pm). **Tram:** All city-center trams to Dam Square.

 Natura Artis Magistra (Amsterdam Zoo), Plantage Kerklaan 38–40. ☎ **523-3400.**

Part of a large complex that includes the Botanical Gardens, Aquarium, and Planetarium, this collection of animals will delight young and old and those in-between. There's an aquarium with rare fish and several animal species that are fast disappearing in the wild, and the Planetarium is the country's largest, with an impressive variety of presentations. It's located just east of the downtown area along Plantage Kerklaan.

Admission: Dfl. 19 ($10) adults, Dfl. 12.50 ($6.60) children under 9.

Open: Daily 9am–5pm. **Tram:** 9 from Centraal Station.

Red Light District (Walletjes)

This warren of streets around Oudezijds Achterburgwal and Oudezijds Voorburgwal by the Oude Kerk is on most people's sightseeing agenda, although, obviously, a visit to this area is not for everyone—and if you do choose to go you need to exercise some caution because the area is a center of crime, vice, and drugs. Stick to the crowded streets. Don't try to take photographs unless you want to lose your camera or have it broken. Still, it's extraordinary to view the prostitutes in leather and lace sitting in their storefronts with their radios and TVs blaring as they do their knitting or adjust their makeup, waiting patiently for customers. It seems to reflect the Dutch pragmatism. If you can't stop the oldest trade in the world, you can at least confine it to a particular area and impose health and other regulations on it.

Vondelpark, close to Museumplein (with an entrance at Zandpad).

The 120 acres that make up this oasis of greenery are a tidy collection of willow-bordered ponds, flower beds, and a bandshell. Named for a famous Dutch poet, it's a lovely place for a picnic. The park is open until 8pm.

World War II Memorial, Dam Sq. at the fish market.

From the beginning, the spot now covered by Dam Square has been the very heart of Amsterdam. At one end, on the site of the ancient Vischmarkt, where fishing boats came up the Amstel to sell the day's catch, a tall, simple spire commemorates Dutch victims of World War II. Holland suffered greatly during the Nazi occupation, and its Dutch East Indies holdings fared no better under Japanese domination. In remembrance of those who did not survive, the urns at the base of the spire hold soil from Holland's 11 provinces and its Indonesian colonies. Somehow, it seems very fitting that Holland should hold their memory to its heart in the heart of its principal city.

CHURCHES & A SYNAGOGUE

Religion has always played an important part in Amsterdam's history, and hundreds of churches are testimony to the great variety of religious beliefs still alive in the city. Most can be visited during regular services (the VVV can furnish a complete list by denomination and hours of service), some have open doors during weekdays so that reverent visitors may have a look around, and the Nieuwe Kerk (see below) has regular visiting hours.

 Nieuwe Kerk, Dam Sq., across from the Royal Palace.

This beautiful church was built in the last years of the 14th century, when the Oude Kerk had become too small to accommodate its congregation. Many of its priceless treasures were removed and colorful frescoes painted over in 1578 when it passed into the hands of Protestants, but since 1814 (when the king first took the oath of office and was inaugurated here—Dutch royalty are not crowned), much of its original grandeur has been restored. Aside from its stately arched nave, elaborately carved altar, great pipe organ that dates from 1645, and several noteworthy stained-glass windows, it holds sepulchral monuments for many of Holland's most revered poets and naval heroes.

Admission: Dfl. 2.50 ($1.30) adults, Dfl. 1 (50¢) children.

Open: Hours vary, but usually Mon–Sat 11am–4pm, Sun noon–2pm. **Closed:** Jan–Feb, and for private events. **Tram:** All city-center trams to Dam Square.

Oude Kerk, at Oudekerksplein on Oude Zijds Voorburgwal. ☎ **624-9183** for information.

Surrounded by small almshouses, this atmospheric old church dates from the 14th century and is used these days for periodic organ recitals.

Open: Daily 11am–4pm. **Tram:** 1, 2, or 5.

Portuguese Synagogue, Mr. Visserplein 3. ☎ **624-5351.**

It was in the early 1600s that Amsterdam opened its arms to an enormous influx of Sephardic Jewish refugees from the Spanish and Portuguese Inquisition. Most settled in the area east of the city center known as the Jewish Quarter, and this beautiful Ionic-style synagogue, facing the square, was built in 1665 as their first place of open worship in more than two centuries. After a 1950s restoration, the synagogue is virtually unchanged from its original state, and more than 1,000 candles are still lit for weekly services.

Admission: Dfl. 5 ($2.60) adults, Dfl. 2.50 ($1.30) children.

Open: Sun–Fri 10am–12:30pm and 1–4pm. **Tram:** 9 or 14 to Mr. Visserplein.

⭐ **St. Nicolaas Church**, Prins Hendrikkade 73. ☎ **624-8749.**

This interesting neobaroque church was built in the late 1800s. There are organ recitals during September, and a traditional crèche and special church tours during the Christmas holidays.

Open: Good Friday–Oct, Tues–Sat 11am–4pm, Christmas holiday tours. In winter one can attend Sun mass at 11am (in Dutch) or 1pm (in Spanish).

Westerkerk, Prinsengracht 281. ☎ **624-7766.**

The Westerkerk holds the remains of Rembrandt and his son, Titus, and this is where Queen Beatrix said her marriage vows in 1966. It was built between 1620 and 1631, and its 275-foot tower, which you can climb during summer months, is the highest in Amsterdam.

Admission: Church, free; tower, Dfl. 2 ($1.05).

Open: May–Sept, daily 10am–4pm; church services, Sun at 10:30am. **Tram:** 13 or 17. **Closed:** Oct–Apr.

Special-Interest Sightseeing

FOR VISITING AMERICANS

There's a strong connection between Amsterdam and America, and you may want to seek out a few places where those links were forged. To begin at the beginning, go by the **Schreierstoren** tower on Prins Hendrikkade (the street directly across from Centraal Station; the tower is a short walk away). Here you'll see a plaque marking the point where Henry Hudson embarked on a voyage in 1609 that would take him to the New World to discover a wide river that would bear his name and an island he

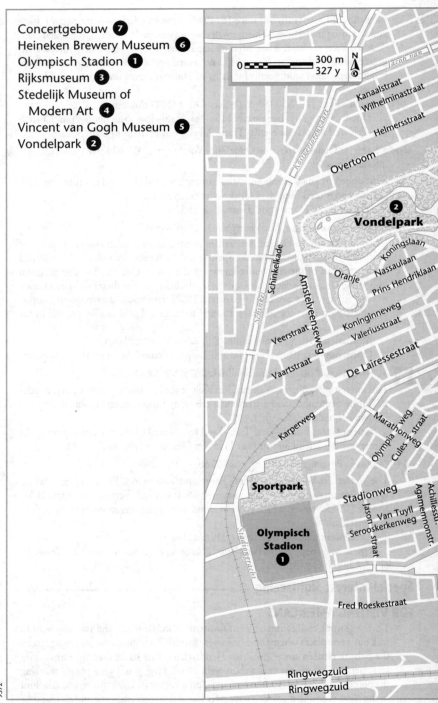

9572

Lennehkanaal

Helmersstraat

Overtoom

Vondelstraat

1e Constantijn Huygensstraat

P. C. Hooftstraat

Jan Luykenstraat

Stad Houderskade

Vondelpark

❷

Paulus Potterstraat

❹ Museumstraat ❺

Museumplein ❸

Horststraat

Hobbemakade

Halsstraat

❻

Vermeerstraat

Quellijnstraat

Daniel Stalpertstraat

Van Eeghenstraat

Willems Parkweg

❼

Pieter de Hoochstraat

Frans

Van Breestraat

Valeriusstraat

Jacob Obrechtstraat

Van Baerlestraat

Ruysdaelkade

Govert Flinckstraat

Johannes Verhulststraat

Nicolaas Maesstraat

Mierisstraat

1e Jan Steenstraat

Emmastraat

De Lairessestraat

Frans van

straat

Ruysdael

Ceintuurbaan

Boerenwetering

Reijner Vinkeleskade

Van Ostadestraat

Jan van Goyenkade

Noorder Amstel Kanaal

Rustenburgerstraat

Hobbemakade

Ferdinand Bolstr.

Apollolaan

Apollolaan

Jozef Israelskade

Titiaanstraat

Jan van Eijckstraat

Amstel Kanaal

Olympiaplein

**Sportpark
Olympiaplein**

Olympiaplein

Gerrit v. d. Veenstraat

Michelangelostraat

Minervalaan

Ruebensstraat

Beethovenstraat

Schubert

straat

Amstelkade

Stadionweg

Richard Wagnerstraat

Churchilllaan

Deurloostraat

Scheldestraat

Stadionweg

Parnassus

weg

Watteaustr.

Diepenbrockstraat

Herman

Heijermansweg

Haringvlietstraat

Oertoom

Stadionkade

Minervalaan

Zuider Amstel Kanaal

Beatrixpark

Prinses Irenestraat

Ringwegzuid

Ringwegzuid

Railroad +++++

would know as "Manhattes." At nearby Haarlemmerstraat, to the right of Centraal Station, read the plaque at no. 75, where the 1623 Dutch West India Company directors planned a settlement to be called Nieuw Amsterdam on the tip of that island, a settlement we know as New York as a result of its seizure by the British in 1664. When you're wandering along the Singel Canal, look for no. 460—in 1782 this building was the premises of the Van Staphorst banking house, where John Adams came to ask for, and received, the first of some $30 million in loans to launch a new and uncertain United States government.

FOR ART ENTHUSIASTS

Vincent van Gogh was 24 years old when he came to Amsterdam in May 1877, where he was to spend only 1 year of his too-short life. During that brief stay, he divided his time between studies in theology, his many relatives living in the city, churches, bookshops, and art galleries, and—his favorite haunt—the Naval Wharf. The VVV has reconstructed a walking tour through the streets and canals that the artist knew well, and their *Amsterdam in the Footsteps of Vincent van Gogh* will take you back in time to view the city through his eyes.

Walking Tours

One of the nicer things about this gracious city is that it has somehow managed to collect its most precious sightseeing jewels in an area compact enough for easy walking from one to the other. The Centrum, or center city, is the old medieval heart of Amsterdam, and all major sightseeing attractions are within the boundaries of its concentric canals, with the exception of the leading museums. And even those are close by—only if you opt for a tram instead of a longish walk to Museumplein will you need transport other than shanks' mare.

There is more to be seen, however, than just sightseeing highlights—every Amsterdam street holds architectural gems and a plethora of memorable street scenes that take on vivid immediacy when you're on foot.

The VVV has put together an excellent collection of walking tours that make for memorable strolls in such areas as Maritime Amsterdam, Jewish Amsterdam, the statues of Amsterdam, the Jordaan neighborhood, and a charming "Voyage of Discovery Through Amsterdam" orientation walk that even points out such things as interesting tea and coffee shops.

When you stroll through the Jordaan, you'll find a hodgepodge of narrow streets and canals, which runs from Rozengracht to Haarlemmerdijk and from Prinsengracht to Lijnbaansgracht. This charming little neighborhood lies west of the Centrum and until recent years was strictly a working-class habitat. Nowadays it has become quite fashionable, with its old houses fast being renovated as chic (and high-priced) apartments. Lots of boutiques and restaurants are sprouting up among the long-established brown cafés, and a stroll through streets and along canals with names like Bloemgracht (Flower Canal) and Leiegracht (Lily Canal) makes for a delightful afternoon, especially on a Sunday when residents are at home, traffic is sparse, and its "neighborhood" character is in full bloom.

Walking Tour
Centraal Station to Muntplein
Start   Centraal Station, Stationsplein.
Finish   Muntplein.

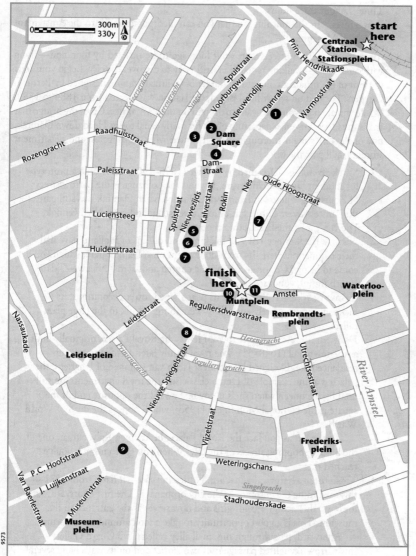

Walking Tour—Central Station to Muntplein

1 Stock Exchange
2 Nieuwe Kerk
3 Former post office
4 Dam Square
5 Amsterdam Historical Museum
6 Begijnhof

7 University of Amsterdam
8 Golden Bend
9 Rijksmuseum
10 Singel Canal Flower Market
11 Muntplein

Time   About three hours.

Best Times   In the morning, so that you can incorporate a visit to the Amsterdam Historical Museum.

Amsterdam's narrow streets were built long ago to be traveled by foot, and—along with canal tours—walking remains a terrific way to discover the city. Begin your tour in front of the ornate architectural wonder of Centraal Station, designed by Petrus J. Cuypers. Located on an artificial island, the station was erected from 1884 to 1889. While you are here you may want to drop in on the VVV office. Cross the bridge that spans the Open Haven, a departure point for many canal tours. Head down Damrak, one of the city's main thoroughfares—it's lined with shops, cafés, and department stores. You'll pass the brick:

1. **Stock Exchange.** Designed by Berlage (1896–1903), it became a prototype for modern Dutch architecture. Beyond the exchange is the narrow street of Zoutsteeg, where salt (*zout*) was unloaded when Damrak was still part of the Amstel River. Turn right onto Gravenstraat and cross Nieuwendijk. You can't miss the late Gothic choir of the:

2. **Nieuwe Kerk.** Since 1815 all the kings and queens of Holland have had their coronations here. Its front door opens onto Dam Square, which you'll come to below. Continue around the church and, across Nieuwe Zijds Voorburgwal, you'll see the:

3. **former post office.** Because of its pear-shaped tower decorations, its nickname appropriately enough is "Perenburg." Walk to the large plaza called:

4. **Dam Square.** As you enter to your left is the Royal Palace, originally built as the town hall (1648–55). The royal family later decided to take up residence here. Designed by architect Jacob van Campen of Haarlem, the palace is a fine example of Dutch classicism; the royal apartments are still used by the queen when she's in town. Toward the opposite end of the square is the National Monument (1956), which honors the dead of World War II.

   To the left as you face the Royal Palace, head down Kalverstraat, one of the busiest shopping streets of the city. When you get to no. 92, you've reached the:

5. **Amsterdam Historical Museum.** Notice the gate—it dates from 1581— this used to be the entrance to the city orphanage. The first courtyard was for boys; the second was for girls and now serves as the entrance to the museum. This is a good opportunity to take a look around the museum.

   Afterward, pass through the small alley called Civil Guard Gallery— this narrow skylighted passage rises two stories and on its walls hang several wonderful regimental paintings. You'll come to the:

6. **Begijnhof.** It was here that the *begijnes* (pious laywomen who devoted their lives to the city's poor) lived. The garden dates back to the 14th century and the houses date from the 16th and 17th centuries. Also on this alleyway at no. 34 is the oldest home in Amsterdam.

   Exit the alley onto Spui; facing you is the main building of the:

7. **University of Amsterdam.** Continue down Spui toward your right. Turn onto the small street next to Café Hoppe and cross the bridges first over Singel Canal and then, via Wijde Heisteeg, over Herengracht canal to one

of the most photographed parts of Amsterdam. The views are of gables and canals. Continue along the Herengracht, crossing over Leidsestraat to the:

8. **Golden Bend,** a residential area filled with grand homes. At this bend is also the entrance to Nieuwe Spiegelstraat, the antiques-shopping street; at the end of which—several blocks away—you'll see the magnificent:

9. **Rijksmuseum,** also designed by Cuypers. This is the crown jewel of Holland's art treasures and contains Rembrandt's masterpiece *The Night Watch.* But Rembrandt is only one of the Dutch masters represented here. Continue along Herengracht and turn left at Vijzelstraat; you'll come to permanently moored barges that hold the:

10. **Singel Canal Flower Market,** where it's always an uplifting treat to browse among the blossoms. Past the market, head to:

11. **Muntplein,** with its 17th century tower, Mint Tower. This square is actually a bridge across the Amstel River. The carillon rings out every half hour. This will conclude your walking tour. Nearby is a busy tram intersection.

Organized Tours

IN THE AIR

A 30-minute bird's-eye view of Amsterdam, the tulip fields, the beaches, and nearby Volendam helps you fix the city firmly in its environs and presents quite graphically its all-important relation to the sea. During summer months, **NLM City Hopper,** KLM's domestic affiliate, flies Saturday- and Sunday-afternoon sightseeing flights from Schiphol Airport. For details, fares, and booking, telephone **649-3252.**

BY BUS

For the quickest overview of the city, take one of several three-hour coach tours. It's a good orientation, and you'll drop in on the Rijksmuseum and visit a diamond factory, for a fare of Dfl. 36 ($19). A four-hour afternoon tour takes you to the Anne Frank House before ending with a canal cruise, with a Dfl. 42.50 ($22.50) fare.

Major tour operators are **Key Tours,** Dam 19 (☎ **624-7304**); **Holland International Excursions,** Damrak 7 (☎ **622-2550**); and **Lindbergh Excursions,** Damrak 26 (☎ **622-2766**). Most depart from Dam Square.

BY BOAT

A ✪ **cruise through the city's canals** should top every visitor's list—even if your time is unlimited, do this first. The fan-shaped canal system dates back to 1609; some 75,000 trees (mostly elms) shade its course, and it holds within its confines more than 7,000 buildings of centuries past. The water-level view of those gabled houses and hundreds of picturesque bridges will lend meaning and color to everything else you do during your stay. Amsterdam's 17th-century golden age becomes a vivid reality as you glide through the waterways that were largely responsible for those years of prosperity. On the one-hour trip aboard glass-topped launches, you'll learn more about the canals and those who have lived along their banks from the informative narrative (delivered in several languages) than you could absorb in hours and hours of study, and photo buffs will be kept busy snapping shots that can only be made from this vantage point.

Your itinerary will take you past such landmarks as the Schreierstoren (Weeping Tower), where sorrowful women bade farewell to their menfolk as they set off across the seas; the narrowest house in Amsterdam; the flood gates that nightly open to cleanse the canals; the official residence of the city's mayor (burgomaster); and before returning to the dock, the dry docks that are so vital to Amsterdam's harbor.

Canal cruises depart from *rondvaart* (canal circuit) docks every 30 minutes from 8:30am to 10pm during summer months (see "Evening Entertainment," later in this chapter, for information on after-dark cruises), every 45 minutes from 10am to 4pm in winter, with a fare of Dfl. 11.50 ($6.05) for adults, Dfl. 8 ($4.20) for children.

Cruise operators and their departure points are: **Holland International** (☎ 622-7788), at Centraal Station; **Smits Koffiehuis B.V.** (☎ 623-3777), at Stationsplein 10; **Rederij Lovers B.V.** (☎ 622-2181), from the Prins Hendrikkade dock opposite no. 25/27; **Rederij P. Kooy B.V.** (☎ 623-3810), from the Rokin near Spui; **Meyers Rondvaarten** (☎ 623-4208), from Damrak jetty no. 4–5; **Rederij Plas C.V.** (☎ 624-5406), from Damrak jetty no. 1–3; and **Rederij Noord-Zuid** (☎ 679-1370), from Stadhouderskade 25, opposite the Parkhotel.

If the launch cruise simply whets your appetite to ramble the canals on your own, there are sturdy **pedal boats** that seat two or four and come with a detailed map, route suggestions, and a bit about the places you'll pedal past. It's great fun in sunny weather, and a different experience when it rains and your boat is covered with a rain shield. You can also rent a "canal bike" for evening rambles, when the canals are illuminated and your bike comes with a Chinese lantern. You'll find moorings at Leidseplein, between the Marriott and American hotels; between the Rijksmuseum and the Heineken Brewery; Prinsengracht at the Westerkerk; and on Keizersgracht near Leidsestraat (a nice feature is that you can rent your canal bike at one of these and return it at another). For two people, the rental is Dfl. 23 ($12) per hour.

6 Special and Free Events

In many ways, the streets of Amsterdam are so filled with the spectacle of a wondrous human mixture that they constitute an ongoing, 24-hour "special event" in themselves. They do, however, come into full bloom at such times as the March through December **Spui Art Market,** when local artists mount outdoor exhibitions along the Spui; April 30, when Amsterdam, along with the rest of the country, holds a gigantic dawn-to-dawn street carnival in celebration of **Queen's Day;** the last two weeks in May, when **Floating Amsterdam** transforms the Amstel River into an outdoor theater, with performances near the Muziektheater; the month of August, when the **Prinsengracht concerts** set the air ringing with music from flat-bottomed boats up and down the canal; late August, when there are **folk dances** on Dam Square with participants from around the world performing their own native dances; and early September, when there's a spectacular **floral parade** from the flower market at Aalsmeer to Amsterdam.

The ✪ **free lunchtime concerts** on Tuesday from 12:15 to 1 pm in the Boekmanzaal (in the Town Hall) and in the Muziektheater, as well as those the same hours on Wednesday in the Concertgebouw, are quite special. The program may be chamber music, symphonic performances, or abbreviated previews of a full concert to be played to paying guests that same evening by local or visiting musical groups.

In mid-April, there's no admission fee at most Amsterdam museums during **National Museum Weekend,** while a few charge greatly discounted fees.

7   Sports and Recreation

SPECTATOR SPORTS

There's an exciting **water-sports exhibition** the first week in March; the **Gein Run** through the streets of southeast Amsterdam in mid-April; the **Blue/White Junior Football Tournament** ("soccer") in the Olympic stadium in mid-May; the **Holland Cup** tournament for junior footballers in late July to early August; the **International Football Tournament** in September; and the prestigious **Amsterdam Horse Show** in late October or early November.

RECREATION

CYCLING   This sport unquestionably takes top billing for recreation in Amsterdam, and there are scores of bike-rental firms around the city, with **Holland Rent a Bike,** Damrak 247 (☎ **622-3207**), one of the most centrally located.

RUNNING   Dedicated joggers can join the **Echo Canal Run** along pathways edging the canals the second week in June or the **Amsterdam Marathon** through city streets in early November.

HEALTH CLUBS   Fitness devotees will find excellent health-and-fitness facilities, including sauna, aerobics, and relaxation rooms at **Sporting Club Leidseplein,** Korte Leidsedwarsstraat 18 (☎ **620-6631**). **Sauna Damrak,** Damrak 54 (☎ **622-6012**), is open to men only, while **Sauna Kylpy,** Marcatorplein 25 (☎ **612-3496**), caters only to women.

GOLFING   For information, contact the **Golf and Conference Centre Amstelborgh,** Borchlandweg 6 (☎ **697-5000**).

8   Savvy Shopping

Amsterdam is a city built on trading, and its modern-day shops uphold the long tradition behind them very well. In flea markets, boutiques, standard shops, large department stores, and diamond centers the trading goes on, offering shoppers goods from around the world as well as the best of Dutch products. Outward-bound airline passengers are treated to an incredible array of duty-free goods that range from luxury extravagances to utilitarian items, at savings of 20% to 40% or more over prices elsewhere.

What a relief—no haggling over prices! For the most part we Americans seem to be fundamentally disinclined to bargain. And when Dutch practicality sets a reasonable price to begin with, then makes it uniform in all shops, it simplifies things all around. Another relief: The prices you see displayed are the prices you'll pay—*all taxes are included.* So when you see what you want, buy it then and there, secure in the knowledge that you won't find it cheaper elsewhere. Of course there are periodic sales, but no discount stores as we know them.

The Shopping Scene

Major shopping streets in Amsterdam, many of which are shut off from vehicular traffic, are: **Kalverstraat,** from Dam Square to Muntplein (inexpensive and moderately priced shops); **Rokin,** parallel to Kalverstraat (quality fashions, art galleries, antiques shops); **Leidsestraat** (upmarket shops for clothing, china, gifts); **P. C. Hooftstraat** and

Van Baerlestraat, near Museumplein (posh fashion, accessories, china, gifts); and **Nieuwe Spiegelstraat,** near the Rijksmuseum (antiques).

SHOPPING HOURS Amsterdam shops are generally open from 1 to 6pm on Monday; from 9am to 6pm on Tuesday, Wednesday, and Friday; to 9pm on Thursday; and to 5pm on Saturday.

Shopping A to Z

Arm yourself with the VVV's excellent booklets "On the Lookout for the Chic and Beautiful," "On the Lookout for Art and Antiques," "On the Lookout in the Jordaan," "On the Lookout for Open-Air Markets," and "On the Lookout Between the Canals" before beginning your shopping safari.

The things that are uniquely Dutch should top your shopping list. True, shops in Amsterdam are filled to bursting with items from around the globe, and you may well run across some especially coveted, hard-to-find bauble. But much of what you see will also be available at home with prices too similar to justify the luggage space. Dutch-made products, on the other hand, will cost far less here and, aside from their practical or aesthetic value, are lasting souvenirs of your visit.

ANTIQUES

Amsterdam's antiques shops rank among the best in Europe, and you'll find the best of them around **Nieuwe Spiegelstraat** and in the **Jordaan** section. The VVV can also furnish a list of antiques **street markets,** which can offer a glorious mix of junk and treasure in some very good selective arrays.

ART

Paintings large and small, originals and reproductions, peer out of every other shop window. You may not pick up the work of a budding Rembrandt for a song, but there's a whole bevy of talented young Dutch artists working away these days, painting the same low landscape under scudding clouds, the same cityscapes, and the same ruddy Dutch faces that their forebears found so fascinating. Exquisite small paintings come with moderate prices, and unless you're a serious art collector, they'll bring you as much pleasure as one of the Dutch masters' paintings. Shop owners are very good about packing paintings for travel, and if the canvas is a large one, they'll take care of shipping it home for you. And who knows, maybe you *will* pick up a budding Rembrandt!

Browse through the large gallery at **Hassel Art** in the shopping arcade of the Grand Hotel Krasnapolsky, Dam 9; or the small **Art Gallery Amsterdam,** Westermarkt 3 (☎ **622-4171**), run by Mr. and Mrs. Kruzmann (open from 10am to 5:30pm). For good-quality reproductions of the masters, **museum shops** are your best bet.

BOOKS

For English-language publications, there's the **American Book Center,** Kalverstraat 185 (☎ **625-5537**), with late openings of 10am to 9pm Monday through Saturday, 11am to 7pm on Sunday, which gives a 10% student discount; **W. H. Smith,** Kalverstraat 152 (☎ **638-3821**), with late hours (to 9pm) on Thursday; **Athenaeum Booksellers,** Spui 14–16 (☎ **622-6248**), which carries one of the city's most comprehensive selections of international magazines and newspapers, as well as books; **Van Gennep,** Nieuwe Zijds Voorburgwal 330, which carries a good selection of quality remaindered hardback English-language books at up to half the original price, as well as English translations of Dutch books; and **A la Carte,** Utrechtsestraat

110–112, which has a wide selection of travel books and maps in many different languages.

For secondhand book bargains, browse through the stalls that often line Spui.

CLOCKS

Dutch clockmakers turn out timepieces in exquisite Old Dutch–style handcrafted cases covered with tiny figures and mottoes, insets of hand-painted porcelain, hand-painted Dutch scenes, and soft-toned chimes. They're hard to resist, and ✪ **B. V. Victoria,** Prins Hendrikkade 47 (☎ **624-7314**), is a happy hunting ground for these treasures. This small shop—also with a good stock of delftware, chocolates, and quality gifts, across from Centraal Station near the Victoria Hotel—has a particularly good selection with reasonable prices and friendly, personal service from Theo, one of the owners, and his staff. You can pay in U.S. dollars if you wish. Open daily from 10am to 6pm.

DELFT

By far the most ubiquitous items you'll see will be those in the familiar blue-and-white "Delft" colors that have almost become synonymous with the world's conception of Holland itself. Souvenir shops, specialty shops, and department stores feature "delftware" earthenware products in the widest variety of forms imaginable. If one has particular appeal, by all means buy it—but be aware that unless it meets certain specifications you are not carting home a piece of the hand-painted earthenware pottery that has made the *Delft* name famous.

First of all, *delftware* is the accurate name for much of what you see displayed, and it can also be red and white or multicolored. If, however, a piece carries the hallmark "Delftware" or "Delft Blue" (with a capital "D"), you may be certain it came from one factory only, in the city of Delft (see Chapter 15). Of equal quality and value are those hallmarked "Makkumware" (again with a capital "M"), fine hand-painted earthenware made only by one firm in the Frisian town of Makkum and often multicolored (see Chapter 16). Technically, copies of each should be called "delftware" and "makkumware" (small "d" and small "m"), and in most cases you'll immediately see the difference. You should learn to recognize the hallmarks of each, however, if you're doing serious shopping. A wide selection of Delftware can be found at ✪ **De Porceleyne Fles,** Prinsengracht 170 (☎ **622-7509**), opposite the Anne Frank House.

DEPARTMENT STORES

De Bijenkorf, at Dam Square, is Amsterdam's largest department store, with a vast array of goods in all price ranges and a very good restaurant. Others are **Vroom & Dreesmann,** on Kalverstraat near Muntplein; **Peek and Cloppenburg,** Dam Square (mainly clothing); and **C & A,** between Damrak and Nieuwendijk (mostly clothing).

DIAMONDS

Amsterdam diamond cutters have an international reputation for high standards, and when you buy from them you'll be given a certificate as to the weight, color, cut, and identifying marks of the gem you purchase. Many open their cutting room (or "factory") to visitors and are happy to give you a quick course in how to recognize the varying types and quality of diamonds. And, happily, there is no pressure to buy, so you can come along for the education and the inevitable test of your willpower. Among those you may visit are: **Rokin Diamonds,** Rokin 12 (☎ **624-7973**); **Van Moppes,**

Albert Cuypstraat 2–6 (☎ 676-1242); and **Palace Diamonds,** Dam Square (☎ 626-0639).

FLEA MARKETS

Nothing is quite as much fun as browsing through the open-air stalls of a European street market, and in Europe, nothing beats the street markets of Amsterdam. There's the famous **Waterlooplein** flea market from 9am to 4pm Monday through Saturday, the marvelous **Oudemanhuispoort** bookstalls between the Oude Zijds Achterburgwal and Kloveniersburgwal canals near Muntplein from 10am to 4pm, several antiques markets, a stamp market, a bird market, and others that defy description. The VVV can give you a complete list, along with addresses and times of operation.

FLOWER BULBS

Gardeners will find it well-nigh impossible to leave Amsterdam without at least one purchase from the ◼ **Floating Flower Market,** on Singel Canal at Muntplein, open daily year-round. Just be certain that the bulbs you buy carry with them the obligatory certificate for entry into the United States.

JEWELRY

Marvelous contemporary designs and materials turn jewelry into an art form at **Galerie Ra,** Vijzelstraat 90 (☎ 626-5100). Owner Paul Derrez specializes in stunning jewelry in the modern mode in gold and silver, and goes a bit farther, turning feathers, rubber, foam, and other materials into pieces that he describes as "playful."

LEATHER

Amazing bargain prices come along with a wide selection of leather clothing for both men and women at ◼ **Topshop,** Nieuwendijk 115 (☎ 623-8128). Designs in jackets, long coats, and women's suits range from conservative to funky.

PIPES, CIGARS & TOBACCO

Amsterdammers treasure ◼ **P. G. C. Hajenius,** Rokin 92–96 (☎ 623-7494), almost as much as they treasure their pipes. Indeed, the elegant and gracious tobacco and pipe shop is the sort that I, for one, thought had long vanished from the face of the earth. Run by the same family since 1826, the warm, wood-paneled store is virtually a museum of antique tobacco humidors (not for sale), and has a beautiful selection of distinctively Dutch styles for sale. Pipes of all description are displayed for your selection, and fine Sumatra and Havana cigars are kept in a room-size glass humidor. Best of all, however, is the courteous interest bestowed on everyone who comes through the door, whether it be for cigarettes, pipe tobacco, or one of their most expensive pipes.

RECORDS

The large ground floor and basement of the **Free Record Shop,** Kalverstraat 230 (☎ 625-7378), stock an incredible number of cassettes, compact discs, and videos at competitive prices. It's open until 9pm on Thursday.

---

9   Evening Entertainment

When the sun goes down, the curtain goes up on a night scene in Amsterdam that can be as highbrow or as lowbrow—or as in-between—as you choose. In this cosmopolitan city, its citizens seem to take it for granted that there are times when nothing will suit as much as a performance of the classical arts, other times when it's jazz or disco music the soul calls for, still other times when good conversation in good company over good drinks is the perfect end of a day—and sometimes something a little less tame than any of those fills the bill (even if it's just to look, not touch!). And with typical Amsterdam respect for individual tastes, they provide it all so you can fit the evening to your mood.

SOME AFTER-DARK TIPS

Because Amsterdammers do take evening "culture"—in whatever form—as just a part of everyday living, dress tends to be more casual than elsewhere, and prices are within an ordinary citizen's reach. That's not to say that nighttime entertainment is cheap or that it's acceptable to show up for a symphony concert in jeans and a T-shirt, but neither do you have to get to the concert hall in a tuxedo and armed with a millionaire's bankroll. Many nightspots charge only for drinks, although others have a nominal cover charge; and there are summer outdoor concerts that are free, where jeans are expected.

Will you be safe moving around Amsterdam after dark? Well, as is true in any large city these days, you'll be safer in some areas than in others. And the cardinal rule of travel safety applies: Don't flash your money around, inviting some nefarious character to take it away from you. The places listed in this section are located in areas where you need exercise only normal caution, and if you're tempted to explore others on your own, just remember that taxis have to be called by phone and Amsterdam street corners don't have telephone booths. If you should find yourself in need of a taxi on the street at night, go into the nearest brown café to call.

Just one more thing: That famous Amsterdam red-light district, the Rosse Buurt, is in the Zeedijk, the so-called sailors' quarter east of the Dam—should you decide to take a look, leave your passport and other valuables in the hotel safe (purse-snatching is common in this area) and be prepared to feel a little sad at the spectacle of rather bored ladies in various states of undress draped over a chair or sofa prominently displayed in picture windows.

Nightlife in Amsterdam is centered mainly around **Leidseplein** and **Rembrandtsplein,** where you'll find a concentration of nightclubs, discos, theaters, cinemas, and restaurants. Most do not require advance reservations, and part of the fun is strolling the streets and "window-shopping" for the night's entertainment. Best of all, there are all those brown cafés where a convivial evening slips by before you know it.

THE ENTERTAINMENT SCENE

Before setting out for the evening, pick up a copy of the VVV publication **What's On in Amsterdam** (from the VVV office or your hotel), check its listings, and when you've made your selections, contact either individual box offices, nightclubs, etc., or head for the VVV office, where they'll book everything for you at a very small fee.

TICKETS   Most upmarket hotels usually have a ticket service, and you can, of course, book through the box office numbers listed below. The VVV will also book cultural and entertainment events for a small fee. Needless to say, you should book as far in advance as possible.

PERFORMANCE HOURS   The Amsterdam concert season is September to mid-June, while other nighttime entertainment goes full tilt year-round. Most music and dance concerts and theater productions begin at 8:15pm. Discos open around

9pm, and close at 4am on weekdays, 5am on weekends, while jazz venues get into full swing about 11pm and some go on to 4 or 5am.

The Performing Arts

OPERA

Opera is performed from September through June by the **Netherlands Opera** at the Muziektheater (opera house), Amstel 3 (☎ **625-5455**). At this splendid modern building, the curtain usually rises at 8pm, and tickets cost Dfl. 10–180 ($5.25–$95).

CLASSICAL MUSIC

One of the world's greatest symphonic orchestras, the ■ **Concertgebouw Orchestra,** Concertgebouwplein 2–6 (☎ **671-8345;** box office open daily 10am to 5pm; 24-hour information line, **573-0573**), attracts audiences from all over Holland and other European countries. So popular are its performances that seats are often placed right on the stage at the sides and rear of the orchestra. The Great Hall of the Concertgebouw, where the orchestra plays is so ideal that every seat offers a clear view of the stage, and the acoustics are world-famous. Recitals are given in the Little Hall, and the **Amsterdam Philharmonic Orchestra** also performs at the Concertgebouw. The concert season is September to mid-June, but periodic concerts are given during summer months, so check when you're there.

    Beurs van Berlage, Damrak 213 (☎ **626-5257** for information; **627-0466** for box office), formerly the Amsterdam Stock Exchange, hosts chamber music concerts, the Netherlands Philharmonic Orchestra, and recitals in the large hall that was once the trading floor of the exchange.

DANCE

Check to see if either of Holland's two important dance companies, the **Dutch National Ballet** and the **Netherlands Dance Theater,** is performing during your visit. Both are excellent and may be seen at the Muziektheater, Amstel 3 (☎ **625-5455**). Most performances begin at 8:15pm, with ticket prices in the Dfl. 15 to 45 ($8 to $24) range.

THEATERS

Homegrown theater productions are almost always in Dutch; but because English is so widely spoken in Amsterdam, it's a favorite venue for road shows from the United States and England. Check *What's On* to see what's doing when you're there. Also, there is now a resident English-language theater company, **English Speaking Theatre Amsterdam** (☎ **624-7248**). Theaters that often host English-language productions are: **Royal Théâtre Carré,** Amstel 115–125 (☎ **622-5225**); **Nieuwe de la**

The Major Concert and Performance Halls

Beurs van Berlage, Damrak 213 (☎ **626-5257** for information; **627-0466** for box office)

Concertgebouw, Concertgebouwplein 2–6 (☎ **573-0573** for information; **671-8345** for box office)

Muziektheater, Amstel 3 (☎ **625-5455**).

Mar, Marnixstraat 404 (☎ **623-3462**); and **De Melkweg,** Lijnbaansgracht 234A (☎ **624-1777** or **624-8492**). Show time is usually 8:15pm, and ticket prices vary widely.

Stitching Studio Anthony, Oude Zijds Voorburgwal 30 (☎ **622-4793**), is a small theater in the middle of old Amsterdam that produces a wide variety of shows, including Yiddish music and cabaret (CHALLE), blues specials, and transvestite shows. Admission is a very low Dfl. 25 ($13).

The Club and Music Scene

JAZZ & BLUES

Amsterdammers love jazz and jazz musicians love Amsterdam—they come from America and all over Europe to play in the city's clubs. When the **North Sea Jazz Festival** is held each July in The Hague, the best of the entire jazz world shows up to put on more than 100 concerts in three days.

In Amsterdam, jazz and blues groups hold forth in bars and the going gets lively around 11pm. You'll find a listing in *What's On* under the heading "Bars/Live Music." At this writing, look for good jazz and blues at the following: **Alto,** Korte Leidsedwarsstraat 115 (☎ **626-3249**); **Joseph Lam Jazz Club,** Diemenstraat 8 (☎ **622-8086**); **Bourbon Street Jazz & Blues Club,** Leidsekruisstraat 6–8 (☎ **623-3440**); and **Bamboo Bar,** Lange Leidsedwarsstraat 64 (☎ **624-3993**).

DISCOS

Amsterdam's disco scene embraces every type of ambience and clientele, from the more sophisticated rooms in large hotels to those that cater to the punk crowd to those favored by the gay community. Most operate on a "members only" basis (except for those in large hotels), but will usually admit tourists if you fit in with the crowd and fork over the entrance fee (around Dfl. 10 $5.25). As in most places, Amsterdam's discos come and go with startling rapidity, so best check the listings in *What's On in Amsterdam* for current addresses when you're there. Three leading discos are: **Boston Club,** Kattengat 1 (☎ **621-2223**); **Juliana's,** Apollolaan 140 (☎ **673-7313**); and **Mazzo,** Rozengracht 114 (☎ **626-7500**).

The Bar Scene

Amsterdam has just about as many bars as it has tulips! Virtually every Amsterdammer has a "local," and all bars welcome visitors. Expect to pay around Dfl. 2.50 to 6.50 ($1.30 to $3.40) for beer, Dfl. 3 to 5 ($1.55 to $2.60) for *jenever,* Dfl. 6.50 ($3.40) for whisky, and up to Dfl. 10 ($5.25) for a mixed cocktail.

BROWN CAFES

You'll see brown cafés everywhere: on street corners, on corners where two canals intersect, down narrow little lanes. They look as if they've been there forever, and they have (rumor has it there's one that hasn't closed its doors since 1574, but I never found it). These are the favorite local haunts and quite likely to become yours as well—they're positively addictive. Typically they will sport lace half-curtains at the front window and ancient Oriental rugs on table tops (to sop up any spills from your beer). Wooden floors, overhead beams, and plastered walls blend into a murky brown background painted by smoke from centuries of Dutch pipes. Frequently there's a wall rack with newspapers and magazines, but they get little attention in the evening when conversations flow as readily as *pils* (beer). If you really want an imported beer, it's usually available at prices considerably higher than the excellent Dutch brews. *Jenever,* the lovely (and potent!) Dutch gin, is on hand in several different flavors, all served ice cold—but never on the rocks.

Your hotel neighborhood is sure to have at least one brown café close at hand, and far be it from me to set any sort of brown-café *kroegentocht* (pub crawl), but you just might want to look into the following: ✪ **Hoppe,** Spui 18–20, on the corner of Spuistraat (☎ **624-0756** or **623-7849**), has been a student and journalist hangout since 1670 and is always packed to the gills, but loads of fun; **Kalkhoven,** at Prinsengracht and Westermarkt (☎ **624-9649**), is an atmospheric old bar that dates back to 1670; ✪ **Cafe 'Tsmalle,** Egelantiersgracht 12 (☎ **623-9617**), in the Jordaan district is a beautifully redone bar in what opened in 1786 as a liqueur distillery and tasting house; **Café Chris,** Bloemstraat 42 (☎ **624-5942**), has been a taphouse since 1624 and construction workers on the nearby Westerkerk came here to receive their wages during the 1630s; and ✪ **Papeneiland,** Prinsengracht 2 (☎ **624-1989**), is a 300-year-old establishment that carries its years lightly and still has a secret tunnel leading under the canal that was used by Catholics in the 17th century.

TASTING HOUSES

As atmospheric and as much fun as the brown cafés are the *proeflokaal,* centuries-old drinking establishments where the favored drink is *jenever* or liquor instead of beer. Do not, however, simply pick up your first drink and swill it down—it's an absolute ritual that you must approach that first drink with your hands behind your back and bend over the bar to drink from a *borreltje* (small drinking glass) that is filled to the brim.

Three tasting houses to look for, all in the Dam area, are: **Bols House of Liqueurs,** Damstraat 36 (☎ **623-1864**); **De Drie Fleschjes,** Gravenstraat 18 (☎ **624-8443**), behind the Nieuwe Kerk; and ✪ **Wynand Fockink,** Pijlsteeg 31, on the tiny street alongside the Grand Hotel Krasnapolsky.

More Entertainment

MOVIES

Amsterdam has more than 50 cinemas, most in the Leidseplein and Rembrandtsplein areas. Since films are always shown in their original language with Dutch subtitles, you can usually find several American and English movies playing in the city. A few that frequently show just-out American films are: **Alhambra 1** and **2,** Weteringschans 134 (☎ **623-3192**), near Frederiksplein; **Alfa 1, 2, 3,** and **4,** Kleine Gartmanplantsoen (☎ **627-8806**), at Leidseplein; and **Tuschinski 1, 2, 3, 4, 5,** and **6,** Reguliersbreestraat 26 (☎ **626-2633**), between Muntplein and Rembrandtsplein.

CANDLELIGHT CANAL CRUISE

No one should leave Amsterdam without memories of a leisurely two-hour ✪ **cruise** through its illuminated canals in a glass-roofed launch. It's one of the city's special treats, with wine and cheese served to make it even better, and there's a stop at one of the canalside brown cafés for a typical Dutch drink. This is an enchanting look at

READERS RECOMMEND

Beerlist Cafe Gollen, Raamsteeg 4 (☎ **626-6645**). *"We highly recommend a visit to this great café, which stocks around 200 kinds of beer."*—J. B. McCarthy, Hawera, New Zealand.

Amsterdam in its sparkling evening attire. The fare is Dfl. 42.50 ($22.50), half that for children under 14, and you can book through **Key Tours,** Dam Square 19 (☎ 624-7304).

GAMBLING CASINOS

There's only one casino in Amsterdam, the brand-new **Casino 2000,** at Max Euweplein 6, near Leidseplein (☎ 620-1006), open daily from 2pm to 2am. Admission is only Dfl. 5 ($2.60), and you can play roulette, baccarat, blackjack, big wheel, and banco. In another part of the building you'll find more than 300 slot machines.

Other casinos in Holland are in Zandvoort (near Haarlem) and Scheveningen (near The Hague).

10 Networks and Resources

FOR STUDENTS   The VVV can supply information on university student organizations to contact, and the monthly publication *Agenda*—which lists current events and information on various services available to students—is generally geared to youthful readers.

FOR GAY MEN & LESBIANS   Information and assistance for gays and lesbians is available through **COC,** Rozenstraat 8 (☎ 626-8600).

The *Best Guide to Amsterdam & the Benelux for Gay Men and Lesbians* lists services, accommodations, bars, and nightclubs, and there's an annual free updating service for the listings. Available in bookshops, or directly from Best Guide (A Division of Eden Cross), Nieuwe Zijds Voorburgwal 66 (Suite 94), 1012 SC Amsterdam, The Netherlands, or P.O. Box 12731, NL-1100 AS Amsterdam.

You'll find most of Amsterdam's gay and lesbian bars in the Kerstraat-Reguliersdwarstraat, Amstel, Amstelstraat, and Warmoesstraat areas.

FOR WOMEN   A central information and organizing center for women's cultural events, as well as other social events, is **Vrouwenhuis,** Nieuwe Herengracht 95 (☎ 625-2066). **Xantippe Bookshop,** Prinsengracht 290 (☎ 623-5854), specializes in feminist titles in English.

FOR SENIORS   The VVV can furnish addresses and telephone numbers for church and social organizations whose activities are slanted toward the upper age brackets. They can also advise you of municipal social agencies that can be of help if you have a specific problem.

11 Easy Excursions

The Holland of your fondest fancies lies just outside Amsterdam—the dikes that have brought into being this improbable country, windmills, wooden shoes, tidy farms, tiny harbors filled with sails, flower fields reaching to the horizon, and sandy beaches looking out to the North Sea.

All are easy day-trips from an Amsterdam base, but don't try to see them all in one day—you'll need at least two days, and preferably three, to get to all the places listed in this section. If you're driving, there are suggested day-long itineraries, with a couple of overnight possibilities in case you should decide to move out of the city and combine any or all of these junkets. One note of caution: You *must* keep headlights on when driving on polder dikes—"polder blindness" can result from a combination of water glare and the unbending, straight-as-an-arrow roads that sometimes bring on a case of semihypnosis for drivers.

If, on the other hand, you take the easy way out and make use of the excellent bus tours available from Amsterdam, may I suggest that you alternate a day of forays into the countryside with one in the city—morning and afternoon schedules make it possible to get in a full day of touring, returning to the city for dinner and an evening out.

Missing from this discussion are the South Holland province cities of The Hague, Delft, and Rotterdam, which will be discussed in more detail in later chapters. All three, however, are well suited for day excursions from Amsterdam.

BUS TOURS

No matter what time of year you come, there's an 8¹/₂-hour **Grand Holland Tour** available that will take you to The Hague, Delft, and Rotterdam, for Dfl. 62.50 ($33); half-day tours to Volendam and Marken, Edam and its windmills, and an afternoon tour of The Hague and Delft costs Dfl. 45 ($24).

During the summer months even more destinations are available, including an eight-hour excursion to the Enclosing Dike and a circle around the IJsselmeer (formerly the Zuiderzee), for Dfl. 66 ($35) the bulb fields and Keukenhof Gardens (March to May only), for Dfl. 45 ($24); and a Friday-morning visit to Alkmaar and its famed cheese market, for Dfl. 42.50 ($22.50).

These major coach-tour companies offer much the same tours at about the same prices: **Key Tours,** Dam 19 (☎ 624-7304); **Holland International,** Dam 6 (☎ 625-3035); and **Lindbergh,** Damrak 26 (☎ 622-2766). Tours depart from the addresses listed, all just off Dam Square, and reservations are usually necessary.

Note: These companies also provide coach tours that go as far afield as Antwerp and Brussels, one way to work in a bit of Belgium if your time is limited.

THE TRAIN

It's also possible to reach virtually every town listed in this section by train—with frequent schedules daily—and with pretty good public transportation once you get there. Your best bet if you plan to visit only one destination is to buy a special one-day round-trip excursion ticket at a discount of about 15%.

Suggested One-Day Itineraries

On your first day of touring, I suggest that you travel from Amsterdam to Zaanse Schans, then continue on to Edam, Volendam, Marken, Monnickendam, and Broek in Waterland (to visit the cheese factory), before returning to Amsterdam.

On your second day of touring, head out from Amsterdam to Hoorn, then continue on to Enkhuizen, the Enclosing Dike (drive to the monument at midpoint), Den Helder, Alkmaar, and Zaanse Schans, before returning to Amsterdam.

On your third day, venture from Amsterdam to Lelystad, Enkhuizen (via the dike road), Hoorn, and Zaanse Schans; then head back to Amsterdam.

On your fourth day, travel from Amsterdam to Aalsmeer, through the bulb fields to Lisse (Keukenhof Gardens), Zandvoort (beach, racetrack, casino), Spaarndam, and back to Amsterdam.

These routes are easily juggled to cover those points you'd most like to see, and an overnight in Volendam will eliminate the return to Amsterdam. Also, if you'll be driving on to Friesland, you can go by way of the Enclosing Dike and do this touring en route.

Nearby Cities and Towns

★ ZAANSE SCHANS

This charming little artificial village sits right in the middle of an industrial area just 10 1/2 miles northwest of Amsterdam, not far from Zaandam. The delightful houses painted the traditional green and white might have disappeared forever in the wake of industrialization had they not been moved to this location to re-create the "dike villages" that once dotted the Zaan region. All but one or two (which have been converted to museums open to the public) are still private residences, set along typical village streets and along a pretty canal. Stop in at the bakery and the old-fashioned grocery store, then stop in at the clog shop to see how the wooden shoes are made. You may be interested to know that they're still a staple in many farming areas, where they're much more effective against wetness and cold than leather shoes or boots. They are also, of course, a tourist staple, and if you plan to buy a pair, this is a good place to do it. Traditionally, those with pointed toes are for women and rounded toes are for men. All must be worn with heavy socks, so when buying, allow the width of one finger when measuring for size. Don't leave without walking over to the four windmills that line the dike. A short tour of one shows you just how these wind machines worked; they're open for visitors at varying hours (check with the VVV in Amsterdam) from late March to October.

At nearby **Koog aan de Zaan** there's a 1751 windmill museum, Het Pink; **Zaandijk** offers the tourist an 18th-century merchant's home furnished in Zaanse style; and at **Zaandam,** a 17th-century shipbuilding center for all of Europe, visit the Het-Peterhuisje, the residence of Peter the Great, tsar of Russia, when he worked in the shipyards here under an assumed name in order to learn skills that would be helpful to his country. You'll see his statue in the marketplace, a gift from Tsar Nicholas II.

BROEK IN WATERLAND

This small village 7 miles from Amsterdam is worth a stop during the summer months to visit the Jakob Wiedermeier & Son farmhouse, where you can see Edam cheeses being made.

MONNICKENDAM

Visit the ★ **Town Hall,** at Noordeinde 5, that began life as a private residence in 1746, and step inside to admire the elaborately decorated ceiling. Then take a walk through streets lined with gabled houses, with a stop to admire the 15th-century late Gothic **Sint Nicolaaskerk,** at Zarken 2.

MARKEN

This tiny fishing village was once an island, but is now reached by a 2-mile-long causeway from Monnickendam. You must leave your car in the parking lot outside before entering the narrow streets lined with green-and-white houses. Occupants of those houses wear traditional dress, although these days it's as much to preserve the custom as for the tourists who pour in daily. There's a typical house open as a sort of museum, a clog maker, and a tiny harbor. You'll be happy to know that taking photos is not frowned upon here, as it is in some other villages that still adhere to the old customs.

Now in case you feel a bit uncomfortable (as I confess I many times do) at seeming to gawk at "the picturesque locals" as they go about their daily routine of hanging out laundry, washing windows, shopping for groceries, etc., it's a comfort to know that in the case of Marken your visit is not crass exploitation. This is a village that lost its livelihood when access to the Zuiderzee was cut off (some of their fishing boats that now sail the IJsselmeer hoist dark-brown sails as a sign of mourning for their lost sea fishing), and tourism has become an alternative industry, with a tax levied on every tour, which goes directly into the village coffers. Gawking quite literally saved Marken's life.

VOLENDAM

Larger than Marken, the town of Volendam is quite obviously geared for tourism in a big way, with lots of souvenir shops, boutiques, gift shops, and restaurants in full swing during summer months. Still, its boat-filled harbor, tiny streets, and traditional houses have an undeniable charm. Its inhabitants, like those in Marken, wear traditional Dutch costumes—although you may see young people of the town clad in the dress of today. If your camera finger develops an itch to preserve all this quaintness on film, feel free—Volendammers will gladly pose. Volendam makes a nice base for exploring this area.

Where to Stay and Dine

⭐ **Hotel Spaander,** Haven 15–19, Volendam. ☎ **02993/63-595.** Fax 02993/69-615. 170 rms. TV TEL

Rates: Dfl. 85–140 ($44–$73) single; Dfl. 130–200 ($68–$105) double. AE, MC, V.

This old-fashioned hotel with its Old Dutch interior offers comfortable and attractive rooms in a waterfront location. If you're here at lunchtime, the hotel's two dining rooms and outside terrace café are excellent restaurant choices, with moderate prices: Dinner averages Dfl. 35 ($18), without wine! It's located in the town center, just off the harbor.

EDAM

About 3 miles north of Volendam, Edam is the town that has given its name to one of Holland's most famous cheeses. Don't expect to find it in the familiar red skin, however—that's for export, and in Holland the skin is yellow. This pretty little town is centered around canals you cross by way of drawbridges, with views on either side of lovely canal houses, complete with beautiful gardens and canalside teahouses.

This was once a port of some prominence, and a visit to the **Captain's House,** just opposite the Town Hall, not only gives you a peek at its history, but also at some of its most illustrious citizens of past centuries (look for the portrait of one Pieter Dirksz, one-time mayor and proud possessor of what is probably the longest beard on record anywhere). Take a look at the lovely "wedding room" in the **Town Hall,** and if you visit during summer months, don't miss the cheese-making display at the **Kaaswaag** (Weigh House). The **Speeltoren** (carillon tower) tilts a bit, and it was very nearly lost when the church to which it belonged was destroyed—no danger now, though, as it is securely shored up. Its carillon dates back to 1561.

ALKMAAR

Try to get to Alkmaar on a summer Friday morning to see the fascinating ■ **cheese market** held in the square adjoining its ancient **Weigh House.** It's a fascinating spectacle, as teams of cheese carriers dressed in white, with straw hats of red, blue, yellow, or green, trot from the ancient auction ring to the Weigh House pulling sleds piled high with cheeses to be weighed. A handclasp seals bids in the ring before the sleds are loaded, and the bill is rallied by each guild's scales. Carriers—members of four sections of their guild, identified by the color of their hats—are so proud of their standards that every week they post on a "shame board" the name of any carrier who has indulged in profanity or has been late arriving at the auction. The square is filled with sightseers, barrel organs, souvenir stalls, and an excitement that's almost tangible.

If you can't make it for the cheese market, Alkmaar is worth a visit for a ramble through its historic 12th-century streets. There's also an excellent porcelain collection in the 1520 **Town Hall.**

HOORN

Hoorn is the home of Willem Cornelis Schouten, who rounded the southernmost tip of South America in 1616 and promptly dubbed it Cape Horn. The **VVV** office, at Statenpoort, Nieuwstraat 23 (☎ **02290/18-342**), can furnish information on Hoorn's many historic buildings and interesting houses, as well as a delightful "Walking in Hoorn" booklet.

Visit the **Westfries Museum,** Rode Steen 1 (☎ **02290/15-783**). The beautiful 1632 building holds 17th-century artifacts brought from Indonesia by the East India Company, armor, weapons, paper cuttings, costumes, toys, naïve paintings, coins, medals, jewels, civic guards' paintings, porcelain, and a second-floor exhibit that details the town's maritime history. There are also tapestries and 17th- and 18th-century period rooms. A collection of Bronze Age relics is exhibited in basement rooms.

During July there's an interesting **craft market** in the marketplace every Wednesday, with demonstrations as well as items for sale; and during most summer months an **antique steam train** takes tourists from Hoorn to Medemblik.

ENKHUIZEN

A great herring fleet of some 400 boats once sailed out of the Enkhuizen harbor, and then came the Enclosing Dike, closing off the North Sea. Now Enkhuizen looks to tourism and pleasure boating for its livelihood, and its population has declined from 30,000 in its 17th-century glory days to a mere 13,000 today.

For the story of this entire region—its lifestyle, furniture, customs, etc.—head for the waterfront ✪ **Zuiderzeemuseum.** It's in a three-centuries-old warehouse once used by the East India Company, and there are amazingly accurate period rooms complete with costumed dummies. Its most fascinating collections, however, are those of the boats from all periods tied up at the pier and those in the huge covered hall that hold relics recovered from the depths of the IJsselmeer, some dating back to Roman times.

From the Enkhuizen/Lelystad dike parking area you can take a ferry over to an **open-air Zuiderzeemuseum,** where old farmhouses, public buildings, shops, and a church from around the Zuiderzee have been brought together to form a cobblestone-street village. The museum is open from mid-April through mid-October, daily from 10am to 5pm, with admissions of Dfl. 12 ($6.30) for adults; Dfl. 6 ($3.15) for senior citizens and children 6 to 18; children under 6 enter free.

Not far away, near the little town of **Medemblik,** the 8th-century **Radboud Castle,** which was fortified in 1288 against possible rebellion from those troublesome Frisians, has been restored to its original state and is well worth a visit. It's open every day from June to August, on Sunday afternoon other months.

★ ENCLOSING DIKE

Its official name is the **Afsluitdijk,** and it's simply impossible to grasp just what a monumental work this is until you've driven its 18-mile length. Dr. Cornelis Lely came up with the plans in 1891, but work was delayed for 25 years as he labored to convince the government to allocate funds for its construction.

The imagination boggles at the thought of what massive effort and backbreaking labor went into this 300-foot-wide dike that stands a full 21 feet above mean water level, keeps back the sea, and through ingenious engineering has converted the salty Zuiderzee into the freshwater IJsselmeer and transformed large areas of its muddy bottom into productive (and dry!) land. It's a heroic achievement.

Midway along its length—at the point where the dike was closed in 1932—there's a beautiful monument to the men who put their backs to the task and a memorial to Dr. Lely. Stop for a light lunch at the café in the monument's base and pick up an illustrated booklet that explains the dike's construction. Nondrivers will find both a biking and a pedestrian path crossing the dike.

When you approach the dike from the town of Wieringerwerf, keep an eye out for the marker about $3^{1}/_{2}$ miles to the east that tells of a Nazi last-ditch tactic in 1945 when the dike was breached only 18 days before the surrender. The indomitable Dutch repaired the dike, pumped the polder dry, and were growing crops in polder fields again by the very next spring!

DEN HELDER

Den Helder is Holland's most important naval base, the site of its **Royal Naval College.** It also has the dubious distinction of being possibly the only port in the world that ever lost a fleet to a company of horsemen! That unique event took place back in January 1794, when the Dutch fleet found itself stuck fast in the frozen waters between Den Helder and Texel Island: French cavalry simply rode out to the ships and captured them all. That was quite a fall from the heights of glory it had known a century earlier when Admirals de Ruyter and Tromp led Dutch ships to victory over a combined English and French fleet just off this very coast in 1673.

Today you can visit the ✪ **Helders Marinemuseum (Maritime Museum),** which holds exhibits illustrating the Dutch Royal Navy's history, and take a look at the state shipyards. During the summer months an even more pleasant idea is to take the 25-minute ferry ride to Texel Island; it's a quiet, family-oriented island resort.

LELYSTAD

This is the new city in Holland's newest polder (see Chapter 17 for more detailed information on Flevoland), and is worth a visit—either as a day-trip from Amsterdam or an en-route stop as you drive to Friesland—to see the ✪ **New Land Information Center,** or **Informatiecentrum Nieuw Land** (☎ **03200/6-07-99**), off the Markerwaard Dike approach road. Its three buildings hold fascinating exhibits explaining in detail the whole Zuiderzee Project, from the construction of the dikes to the pumping operation to the drying-up process. You'll also see shipwrecks recovered from the bottom of the Zuiderzee when this land was drained. Hours are 10am to 5pm daily during the summer, weekdays only in winter, with shorter Sunday hours.

Should you come on a Saturday, be sure to go by the town square to see vendors clad in traditional dress hawking everything from smoked eels to crafts to cheese—a delightful example of a people holding onto tradition in the middle of modern-day progress!

If you have time for the 20-mile drive south to **Harderwijk,** during summer months there's a fascinating **Dolpinarium,** with both a dolphin research station and an entertaining performance by the resident dolphins. Not far away is **Flevohof Park,** with entertainment and water sports for children and a marvelous working exhibition of a typical farm.

AALSMEER

About 3 miles from Schiphol Airport, Aalsmeer is famed for its year-round, daily **flower auction,** the world's largest. From 7:30 to 11:30am, buyers bid with electric buttons on flowers by the lot. The huge clocklike device that keeps track of all the bids is a marvel of efficiency, and it's great fun to watch as about 600 lots change hands every hour.

BULB FIELDS

The largest bulb growers are in the northern corner of the South Holland province and the southern part of North Holland, with the heaviest concentration along the 25-mile ✪ **Haarlem–Leiden** drive. Those organized Dutch make it easy with a signposted *Bolenstreek* (Bulb Route) that covers about 38 ¹/₂ miles, and they suggest that you plan to drive it during weekdays, when stalls along the roads sell flower garlands (do as the natives do and buy one for yourself, another for the car).

LISSE

The 70-acre ✪ **Keukenhof Gardens** here once belonged to one Jacoba van Beieren, who kept a hunting lodge on these grounds in the 15th century. Today they hold breathtakingly beautiful exhibitions of floral beauty, with nearly eight million bulbs in bloom from the end of March right through May. Winding streams pass beneath ancient shade trees, and there's a sculpture garden, as well as a windmill. Hours are 8am to 8pm, and you can reach the famous gardens from Amsterdam by taking a train to Haarlem and a connecting bus to Lisse. Admission is Dfl. 17 ($9) for adults and Dfl. 13 ($7) for students.

ZANDVOORT

This popular North Sea resort was totally demolished by Nazi forces in World War II as they built their Atlantic Wall. Completely rebuilt, it is now the site of international motorcycle and auto races in June and July, and a casino, with the Bloemendaal amphitheater nearby that presents Shakespearean plays during the summer.

✪ HAARLEM

Haarlem is a marvelous mix of medieval buildings, museums, and churches. The buildings around its market square date from the 15th through the 19th century and are a visual mini-course in the development of Dutch architecture. Visit the 14th-century **Town Hall** and 17th-century **Meat Market,** a veritable Renaissance palace. At Groot Heiligland 62, in what was an almshouse back in 1608, you'll find the **Frans Hals Museum,** a wondrous collection of works by this great Dutch master as well as other artists from the 16th and 17th centuries. Stop by the magnificent **Church of St. Bavo;** if you're lucky you'll arrive during one of the periodic concerts on its famous 1738 organ whose keyboard has known the touch of such musical greats as Handel and Mozart.

While you're in the Haarlem area, you might want to visit **Beeckestijn,** a lovely old manor house that dates from the 18th century, at Velsen-Zuid. At **IJmuiden,** take a close look at three great locks of the North Sea Canal, and early risers can go along to the fish auctions at Halkade 4 (from 7am to 11am Monday through Friday).

SPAARNDAM

This little village north of Haarlem is picturesque enough to warrant a visit just for the scenery, but its main claim to fame is a monument to a fictional character who has become an everlasting symbol of Holland and the Dutch people. You remember, of course, Young Pieter (of *Hans Brinker or The Silver Skates* by Mary Maples, 1865), who saved Haarlem from disaster when he plugged a hole in the dike with his finger and steadfastly refused to leave until help came at the end of a long night. His vigil cost him his life, and because that heroic act of this fictional boy so caught the imagination of people around the world, the Dutch government erected a memorial in 1950, dedicating it to the courage of Dutch youth in general.

The Hague, Scheveningen, and Rotterdam

THE HAGUE AND ROTTERDAM ARE ABOUT AS DIFFERENT AS TWO CITIES COULD BE, yet The Hague—stately and dignified—is quite at ease with its brash, modern neighbor.

History, of course, accounts for much of the difference. **The Hague,** with close ties to nobility since the 13th century, has seen the centuries come and go with scarcely a rumble in the foundations of its lofty perch. Technically it's not even a true "city," never having been granted a charter or city rights, but never has a "village" maintained such an imperial disdain for such a triviality. Secure in its regal position, The Hague goes serenely on its way as the seat of Holland's government, even if not its capital, content to be what is undoubtedly the largest "village" in Europe.

Rotterdam, on the other hand, sits on delta land at the junction of the Rhine and Maas Rivers and has been commercial to the core from the very beginning. The legacy of *its* centuries has been somewhat less than elegant, related more to bustling port activity than to nobility, and even its historically significant landmarks literally "bit the dust" when World War II bombings left little but rubble in their wake. Rebuilding has been in a determinedly modern vein, raising a monument to the technology that is responsible for the development of a staggering annual shipping tonnage and the influx of more and more new residents.

1 The Hague

58km (36 miles) SW of Amsterdam

While The Hague is an easy day-trip from an Amsterdam base, it's also ideal if you prefer a quieter, more leisurely paced sightseeing base.

GETTING THERE • By Plane   The Hague is within easy reach of all major Dutch airports. A "Schiphol Line" offers fast rail service (30 min.) to Amsterdam's airport, with a fare of Dfl. 12.50 ($6.60).

• **By Train**   The Hague is an easy train ride from Amsterdam and is on the direct route of many intercontinental trains.

• **By Bus**   There is excellent and frequent bus service from Amsterdam, and most other areas of Holland have good connections through Amsterdam.

• **By Car**   From Amsterdam, take A9, A4, and A44; from Rotterdam, take A13.

• **By Ferry**   The Hook of Holland sea ferries are only 12¹/₂ miles away (35 min. by car, 45 by train); Rotterdam's Europoort is about an hour's drive away, with good bus and train connections.

ESSENTIALS   The **telephone area code** is 070.

Tourist Information   The **VVV office** is at Kon. Julianaplein, near the Central Station (☎ **06/340-3505;** fax 070/361-8888), open April through September, Monday through Saturday from 9am to 9pm and on Sunday from 10am to 5pm; shorter hours other months. Pick up a copy of their publication **"Info,"** which is a good guide to what's on at the moment.

Public Transport   There is good **bus** and **train** transport in The Hague, originating at both the Central Station and Spoor Station. For route, schedule, and fare information, call **06/9292,** or the VVV (see above). **Taxi** ranks are located at both stations and many strategic points around the city. For information, call **390-7722.**

The Hague Accommodations & Attractions

North Sea

SCHEVENINGEN

Promenade
Deynootweg
Oustduinpark
Strandweg Gevers
Zwolsestraat
Nieuwe Schveveningse Bosjes
Voor Haven
Haven
Haven
Nieboerweg Westduinweg Duinstraat
Scheveningseweg
Nieuwe Parklaan
Pompstationsweg
van Alkemadelaan
Klein Zwitserland
Fred. Hendriklaan
Prof. B.M. Teldenweg
Westbroek Park
Landscheidingsweg
Wittlaan
Johan de Witt Zorgvliet
Scheveningse Bosjes
Waaldorperweg
Clingendael
Segbroeklaan
Burg Patijnlaan
Wassenaarseweg
Laan van Meerdervoort
Stadhouderslaan
Javastraat
Raamweg
Zuid Hollandlaan
Benoorden Houtseweg
Weimarstraat
Elandstraat Hogewal-mazie-straat
Park straat
Mauritskade
Haagsche Bos
Kamperfoeliestraat
Valkenboslaan
Loosduinseweg
Waldeck Prymont Kade
Torenstraat
Lange Voorhout
Lange Vijvenberg
Koningskade
Bezuiden Houtseweg
Soestdijksekade
Zuiderparklaan
Prinse Gracht
Grotemarktstraat
Laan van Nieuwe
de la Reyweg
de Heemstraat
Spuizieken
Central Station
Zuiderpark
Amsterdams-veerkade
Prins Bernhard Viaduct
Troelstrakade Moerweg
Fruitweg
Parallelweg
Schenk Viaduct
Schenkkade
Erasmusweg Prinses Beatrixlaan
Station HS
Station van Nieuwe Oost Indie
Oost Indie
Station Voorburg
Mgr. van Steelaan
Binckhorstlaan
Schaapweg
Gouveneurlaan
Rijswijkseweg
Geest-brugweg
Prinses Mariannelaan
Utrechtse Baan
Rijswijk
Gen. Spoorlaan
Haagweg
Sir Winston Churchilllaan

0 — 100 m / 110 y N

ACCOMMODATIONS:
Hotel Aristo 27
Hotel Astoria 28
Carlton Beach Hotel 5
City Hotel 3
Hotel Corona 24
Hotel Intercontinental 18
Hotel/Restaurant Bali 4
Hotel ´t Centrum 19
Hotel Urbis den Haag/Scheveningen 6
Mercure Hotel Central 25
Paleishotel 20
Parkhotel den Haag 21
Promenade Hotel 12
The Seinduin 7
Steigenberger Kurhaus 2

ATTRACTIONS:
The Binnenhof (Parliament) and Hall of Knights 23
Haags Gemeentemuseum (Municipal Museum) 11
Kurhaus (Casino) 1
Madurodam 10
Mauritshuis Royal Cabinet of Paintings 22
Palace Huis ten Bosch 26
Palace Lange Voorhout 17
Palace Noordeinde 16
Panorama Mesdag 14
The Peace Palace 13
Puppet Museum 15
Scheveningen Museum 8
ZeeBiologisch Museum 9

Church Post Office Information

Railway

★ **Madurodam,** Haringkade 175. ☎ **352-0930.**

Called "Holland in a Nutshell," this fantastic display of a miniature "city of Madurodam" sprawls over 28,000 square yards north of the city center. Typical Dutch towns and famous landmarks are here in replica on a scale of 1:25—you'll feel a bit like Gulliver viewing the lilliputian world. The wonder of it all is that this is a *working* miniature city: Trains run, ships move, planes taxi down runways, the barrel organ plays, there's a town fair in progress, and 50,000 tiny lamps light up when darkness falls. Children love it, but surprisingly, 75% of the 1.2 million annual visitors are adults!

Admission: Dfl. 14 ($7.30) adults, Dfl. 11 ($5.80) children.

Open: Daily 9am–10:30pm. **Closed:** Feb. **Tram:** 1 or 9. **Bus:** 22.

★ **Mauritshuis Royal Cabinet of Paintings,** Mauritsbuns. ☎ **346-9244.**

Next to the Binnenhof overlooking the Court Lake, this small, intimate museum in the 17th-century palace of a Dutch count holds golden age art treasures by such artists as Rembrandt (16 paintings), Vermeer, Jan Steen, Frans Hals, Ruisdael, Paulus Potter, Rubens, Van Dyck, Holbein, and Cranach.

Admission: Dfl. 7.50 ($3.95) adults, Dfl. 4.50 ($2.35) children under 18 and senior citizens.

Open: Tues–Sat 10am–5pm, Sun and public holidays 11am–5pm. **Tram:** 1, 2, 3, 7, 8, or 9. **Bus:** 4, 5, 18, 22, or 25.

★ **Palace Huis ten Bosch,** Haagse Bos (Het Bos).

When Queen Juliana abdicated the Dutch throne in 1980, her daughter, Queen Beatrix, moved her family into the Palace Huis ten Bosch (House in the Woods) in the beautiful wooded Haagse Bos, making that the official royal residence. Built in 1645, it was for many years a summer residence for the royal families. Originally it was a small, rather plain palace consisting of several rooms opening from a domed central hall, and it was Prince Willem IV who added the two large side wings in the 1700s. The palace can be viewed only from the park.

Open: Daily daylight hours. **Bus:** 4, 43, or 91.

Palace Lange Voorhout, Lange Voorhout 74. ☎ **338-1111.**

This small, imposing palace—in the heart of the old city—is now used only for receptions and other official functions, but during renovations on the Palace Noordeinde, the queen and her staff had offices here. Not open to the public.

Tram: 1, 9, or 12.

Palace Noordeinde, Prinsessewal.

West of Lange Voorhout and on the elegant shopping street Noordeinde, this palace dates back to 1553 and is the "working palace" for Queen Beatrix and her staff. The splendid neoclassical town palace was quite elegantly furnished when William of Orange's widow was in residence, but had become almost derelict by the beginning of the 19th century. In 1815 restoration brought it back to a state suitable for the residence of Willem I. In 1948 fire damage necessitated extensive renovation, and in the early 1980s further restoration was begun. It is from this palace that Queen Beatrix and Prince Claus, on the third Tuesday of September each year, depart in a golden coach drawn by eight horses, escorted by military corps, bands, local authorities, and a blaze of street pageantry, to proceed to the Binnenhof, where the queen officially opens Parliament with an address to the States General and parliamentary members in the Ridderzaal. No visitors are allowed.

Tram: 3, 7, 8, or 12. **Bus:** 4, 5, or 22.

Panorama Mesdag, Zeestraat 65B. ☎ **310-6665.**

If you have any preconceived notion that all panoramas are alike, forget it! Go just north of the city center and take a look at the world's largest circular painting, with a total circumference of 395 feet. It's the work of Dutch artist Hendrik Willem Mesdag, with the assistance of his wife and two other prominent artists, and it will, quite simply, take your breath away. Walk through a dark passageway, up a stairway, and out onto a circular platform—suddenly you're actually in the 1880 fishing village of Scheveningen! Its dunes, beach, fishing boats, and the village itself are three-dimensional, an illusion enhanced by the artificial dunes that separate you from the realistic paintings.

Admission: Dfl. 4 ($2.10) adults, Dfl. 2 ($1.05) children.

Open: Mon–Sat 10am–5pm, Sun and public holidays noon–5pm. **Closed:** Dec 25. **Tram:** 7 or 8. **Bus:** 4, 5, 13, or 22.

The Peace Palace, Carnegieplein. ☎ **346-9680.**

Just beyond the city center, this imposing building—whose construction between 1907 and 1913 was largely due to donations of Andrew Carnegie—houses the Permanent Court of Arbitration, the International Court of Justice, the International Law Academy, and an extensive library. Its furnishings have been donated by countries around the world. Guided tours are on the hour.

Admission: Dfl. 6 ($3.15) adults, Dfl. 3 ($1.55) children.

Open: Mon–Fri 10am–4pm. **Tram:** 7 or 8. **Bus:** 4 or 13.

Puppet Museum, Nassau Dillenburgstraat 8. ☎ **328-0208.**

A charming collection of more than 1,000 puppets, some more than two centuries old, are housed here just north of the city center, as well as a working theater. Periodically, puppet shows are performed (check with the VVV for current schedules). A great hit with both children and adults.

Admission: Dfl. 1 (50¢).

Open: Sun noon–2pm. **Tram:** 1 or 9. **Bus:** 13 or 18.

ORGANIZED TOURS

An excellent 2^1/2-hour **Royal Tour** by coach focuses on the royal residences and other royal buildings, Scheveningen, and a drive along the North Sea coast. Current fare is Dfl. 19 ($10) for adults, Dfl. 16 ($8.40) for children up to 10 years of age. Call the VVV office for schedule information, departure points, and booking.

Coach tours to the flower fields and Keukenhof Gardens, Delta Expo, Amsterdam, Delft and Rotterdam, Alkmaar cheese market and Zaanse Schans, the windmill district of Kinderdijk, and a Grand Holland tour as well as Antwerp and Brussels are conducted by **Speedwell Travel B.V.,** Valeriusstraat 65 (☎ **070/365-4848**), at prices of Dfl. 60 ($31.55) for adults, Dfl. 30 ($15.80) for children under 10. Tours run in July and August, with destinations scheduled for varying days of the week. Call for schedules and booking.

SHOPPING

Interesting shopping areas in The Hague include **Oude Molstraat,** in the city center, where you'll find a concentration of authentic Dutch shops. Connected to the Central Station, the **Babylon shopping complex** has two floors of over 60 shops, restaurants, and a luxury hotel. Several streets running off the **Groenmarkt** are pedestrian shopping streets.

EVENING ENTERTAINMENT

There's nearly always something going on culturally in The Hague, and nearby Scheveningen has a casino and nightspots. Check **"Info"** and local newspapers for concerts, theater, etc., as well as names and addresses of after-dark entertainment spots.

Where to Stay

You will find hotel accommodations of high standards in every price range, but if you prefer seaside accommodations, see the next section of this chapter.

EXPENSIVE

Hotel Corona, Buitenhof 39–42, 2513 AH The Hague. ☎ **070/336-7930.** Fax 070/361-5785. 26 rms, 3 suites. MINIBAR TV TEL

Rates: Dfl. 300 ($157) single; Dfl. 360 ($189) double; Dfl. 600 ($315) suite. AE, DC, MC, V.

Owned by the Heineken family, this charming small hotel, once a lively coffeehouse, is centrally located opposite the House of Parliament, and between the Binnenhof and the Passage. Public rooms feature contemporary decor, with touches of handsome marble and mahogany in the lobby. The guest rooms are done up in soft pastel colors, with graceful window drapes. The hotel's popularity dates back to the early 1900s, and today's politicians, antiques dealers, and gourmets still congregate here.

Dining/Entertainment: The elegant restaurant, a refuge of French Provincial furnishings, soothing ecrus and brushed blues, has won a Michelin star and is presided over by one of the city's star chefs. In balmy weather, part of the restaurant becomes a sidewalk terrace.

Services: 24-hour room service.

★ **$ Hotel Intercontinental,** Lange Voorhout 54–56, 2514 EG The Hague. ☎ **070/363-2932.** Fax 070/345-1721. 76 rms, 7 suites. MINIBAR TV TEL **Tram:** 1, 3, 7, 8, 9, or 12. **Bus:** 4, 5, or 22.

Rates: Dfl. 390 ($205) single; Dfl. 490 ($258) double; Dfl. 600–1,600 ($315–$842) suite. AE, DC, EU, MC, V.

This elegant old-world hotel right in the center of the oldest part of the city began life as the residence of Baron van Brienen and became a hotel in 1881. Since then it has welcomed royalty, diplomats, celebrities, and tourists, as well as held a prominent place in the social life of The Hague. The guest rooms feature classic decor and furnishings, and are the ultimate in comfort, with telephones in both bedroom and bath, radio, and such extras as bathrobes and hairdryers. Some baths even contain a Jacuzzi whirlpool. Public rooms are breathtakingly beautiful, with lots of marble, polished wood, chandeliers, and velvet upholstery. The gracious lobby lounge is a favorite place with Hagenaars to meet for tea or other refreshments. Highly recommended both for its elegant accommodations and for its location just steps away from good shopping and many of the city's leading attractions.

Dining/Entertainment: The recently restored Le Bar has the ambience of a typical Hague bar, and the fine restaurant, Le Restaurant, is a stylish setting for good eating (see "Where to Dine," below). Both are as popular with locals as with visitors and guests.

Services: 24-hour room service, babysitting.

Facilities: Banquet and conference facilities.

★ **Promenade Hotel,** Van Stolkweg 1, 2585 JL The Hague. ☎ **070/352-5161.**
Fax 070/354-1046. 97 rms, 4 suites. MINIBAR TV TEL
Rates: Dfl. 365 ($192) single; Dfl. 450 ($236) double; Dfl. 875 ($460) suite. AE, DC, MC, V.

This high-rise hotel—a bit out of the city center in a lovely wooded area just a short drive from city sightseeing as well as the beach—features luxury guest rooms with balconies, all with modern and comfortable furnishings, and equipped with hairdryers.

Dining/Entertainment: There's an à la carte restaurant, La Cigogne; a bistro, Flaneur; and an elegant restaurant, the Panorama Room.

Services: 24-hour room service.

Facilities: Gift shop, newsstand, hairdressing salon, conference and banquet facilities, wheelchair access.

MODERATE

Paleishotel, Molenstraat 26, 2513 BL The Hague. ☎ **070/362-4621.**
Fax 070/361-4533. 20 rms. TV TEL
Rates: Dfl. 175 ($92) single; Dfl. 195 ($102) double. AE, DC, MC, V.

This centrally located hotel is convenient for shopping (near the pedestrian shopping promenade) as well as sightseeing, and the guest rooms are both attractive and of a very high standard.

★ **Mercure Hotel Central,** Spui 180, 2511 BW The Hague. ☎ **070/363-6700.**
Fax 070/363-9398. 159 rms. MINIBAR TV TEL
$ **Rates** (including breakfast): Dfl. 260 ($136) single; Dfl. 320 ($168) double. AE, DC, MC, V.

This first-class hotel sits right in the heart of the city, in the immediate vicinity of the Parliament buildings and shopping streets, and no more than a five-minute walk from both rail stations. The public rooms are tastefully furnished, featuring a spacious lounge, two restaurants (Adagio, and the Japanese restaurant Shirasagi), and a gift shop. The guest rooms, outfitted with hairdryers and trouser presses, reflect the same good taste and comfort. The Splash Fitness Club offers a sauna, steambath, and training area.

★ **Parkhotel Den Haag,** Molenstraat 53, 2513 BJ The Hague. ☎ **070/362-4371.**
Fax 070/361-4525. 114 rms. TV TEL
Rates (including breakfast): Dfl. 146–174 ($76–$91) single; Dfl. 225 ($118) double. AE, DC, MC, V.

Close to good shopping streets and many of the city's sightseeing attractions, this pleasant hotel is on a quiet street, and its breakfast room overlooks the gardens of a former royal palace. The guest rooms are comfortable and attractive, having recently been tastefully redecorated.

Dining/Entertainment: No restaurant, but many fine eateries in the vicinity. Cozy, attractive bar.

Facilities: Conference facilities.

INEXPENSIVE

Hotel Aristo, Stationsweg 164, 2515 BS The Hague. ☎ **070/389-0847.**
21 rms (2 with bath).

Rates (including breakfast): Dfl. 55 ($29) single without bath, Dfl. 80 ($42) single with bath; Dfl. 85 ($45) double without bath, Dfl. 105 ($56) double with bath. AE, DC, MC, V.

Only a five-minute walk from the station, this small hotel is nothing to rave about but it has a friendly English-speaking staff and large, adequately furnished rooms.

Hotel Astoria, Stationsweg 135, 2515 BM The Hague. ☎ **070/384-0401.** 16 rms (7 with bath).

Rates (including breakfast): Dfl. 65 ($34) single without bath, Dfl. 75 ($39) single with bath; Dfl. 90 ($47) double without bath, Dfl. 125 ($65) double with bath. AE, MC, V.

The furnishings here are plain but the rooms are clean and the hotel is located a short walk from the station. There's no restaurant in the hotel but plenty of eateries around the corner.

$ **Hotel 'T Centrum**, Veenkade 6, 2513 EE The Hague. ☎ **070/346-3657.** 10 rms. TV

Rates (including breakfast): Dfl. 100 ($52) single; Dfl. 115 ($60) double. No credit cards.

A welcome addition to the accommodations in The Hague is this small, inexpensive family hotel near the queen's palace, Noordeinde. There's a cozy bar, and the guest rooms are nicely decorated and comfortably furnished.

A NEARBY HOTEL

★ **$** **Auberge de Kieviet**, Stoeplaan 27, 2243 CX Wassenaar. ☎ **01751/192-32.** Fax 0175/017-51. 25 rms, 6 suites. A/C TV TEL **Directions:** Take the A44 highway 10 minutes from The Hague and follow the signs; it's 20 minutes from Schiphol Airport, Amsterdam.

Rates: Dfl. 195 ($102) single; Dfl. 250 ($130) double; Dfl. 350 ($185) suite. AE, DC, MC, V.

This luxurious small hotel is well worth the drive from The Hague, Amsterdam, or Scheveningen. The guest rooms are attractive, with 24-hour room service—something not always available in the smaller hostelries. There's a bar and a brasserie, and the excellent gourmet restaurant is a member of the prestigious (and demanding) Alliance Gastronomique Néerlandaise. The hotel is located about $1^1/_2$ miles from the sea, and nearby woods and dunes provide lovely walking or cycling routes; golf, riding, swimming, and tennis are close at hand.

Where to Dine

In both ambience and cuisine, The Hague offers a wide range of places to eat, thanks primarily to its wealth of international visitors. In addition, The Hague has a multitude of casual outdoor cafés, sandwich and coffee shops, and brown cafés, any one of which will serve you good, fresh food for about Dfl. 6 to 15 ($3 to $8). The VVV's booklet "The Hague" (see "What to See and Do," above) contains a comprehensive listing of restaurants by cuisine categories, those with music, and bars—well worth the small cost.

The following selections appear roughly in order of price, from most to least expensive:

EXPENSIVE

Le Bistroquet, Lange Voorhout 98. ☎ **360-1170.**
  Cuisine: FRENCH. **Reservations:** Required.
  Prices: Average three-course menu Dfl. 50 ($26). AE, DC, MC, V.
  Open: Lunch Mon–Sat noon–2pm; dinner Mon–Sat 6–10:30pm.

This small and very popular restaurant in the city center is one of The Hague's best, with lovely table settings in a quietly elegant setting. The menu is mostly French, with lamb, fish, and fresh vegetables featured.

Hotel Corona, Buitenhof 39–42. ☎ **363-7930.**

Cuisine: FRENCH/CONTINENTAL. **Reservations:** Recommended.
Prices: Lunch Dfl. 60 ($31); dinner Dfl. 100–200 ($52–$105). AE, DC, MC, V.
Open: Lunch daily noon–2pm; dinner daily 6–10:30pm.

When the Heineken family acquired this lovely old hotel in the city center opposite the House of Parliament, they set about transforming its restaurant into one of The Hague's top dining spots. That they have succeeded admirably is evident in the beautiful decor, widely spaced tables, and—most of all—when food comes to the table beautifully prepared by chef Robert Kranenborg, who has made this one of the city's most distinguished kitchens and is responsible for the one-star rating awarded by Michelin. Starring on the menu are such creations as braised turbot with bouchots mussels and saffron and roast saddle of lamb with dates and mustard. There's also an outstanding wine cellar.

★ **Le Restaurant,** in the Hotel Intercontinental, Lange Voorhout 54–56.
☎ **363-2932.**
$ **Cuisine:** CONTINENTAL. **Reservations:** Recommended.
Prices: Average three-course menu Dfl. 80 ($42) at lunch, Dfl. 100–150 ($52–$79) at dinner. AE, DC, MC, V.
Open: Lunch daily noon–2pm; dinner daily 6–10:30pm.

In the city center, the Intercontinental's exquisite dining room is a beloved spot for locals, visiting dignitaries, and tourists. Probably the most elegant and refined dining spot in The Hague, Le Restaurant dishes up such delicacies as a starter of smoked breast of duck salad, and main courses might include filet of lamb with a sweet garlic sauce and poached filet of turbot in morel sauce. Outstanding among desserts is the sinfully sweet mosaic of chocolate parfait. Needless to say, there's an extensive and very fine wine list.

READERS RECOMMEND

Other Dining Choices. *"On one of the little side streets off Denneweg is **Pannekoekhuis Oud Haagsch**, Maliestraat 10 (☎ 326-2474), a little Dutch restaurant that specializes in pannekoeken and other old Dutch traditional dishes. The atmosphere is old country, the pancakes are served on huge Delft platters, and some of the best we have eaten—reasonably priced, too. For vegetarians and lovers of great cheese fondue, around the corner from the Pannekoekhuis is **De Dageraad**, Hooikade 4 (☎ 364-5666). It's small and cozy, and the area is beautiful. If you walk straight down Denneweg and cross over the bridge at Javastraat, the street becomes Frederikstraat. At no. 231 is the deli **Toko Frederik** (☎ 360-3125), and they have a very nice selection of Indonesian dishes for eat-in or take-out, with reasonable prices. It's a nice place."*—Mrs. Charles W. Brewer, American Embassy, The Hague. [**Author's Note:** Average pancake meals at Oud Haagsch cost Dfl. 27.50 ($14), De Dageraad charges Dfl. 28.50 ($15) per plate for fondue, and Toko Frederik serves tasty Asian dishes for around Dfl. 16 ($8). All three are open Tuesday through Sunday from 10am to 10pm.]

MODERATE

Adagio, in the Mercure Hotel Central, Spui 180. ☎ **363-6700.**

Cuisine: FRENCH. **Reservations:** Recommended.
Prices: Average lunch Dfl. 40 ($21); average dinner Dfl. 60 ($31). AE, MC, V.
Open: Lunch daily noon–2pm; dinner daily 6–10pm.

The menu in this moderately priced restaurant in the city center is surprisingly extensive, and French specialties of lamb, seafood, and chicken are nicely prepared.

$ Restaurant Garoeda, Kneuterdijk 18A. ☎ **346-5319.**

Cuisine: INDONESIAN. **Reservations:** Recommended for lunch.
Prices: Rijsttafel Dfl. 38–45 ($20–$24). AE, DC, MC, V.
Open: Mon–Sat 11am–11pm, Sun 4–11pm.

If it's rijsttafel you're hankering for, you couldn't find it any better than at this pleasant and very popular Indonesian restaurant in the city center. Crowded at lunch, so reserve or come early or late.

★ Restaurant Saur, Lange Voorhout 47. ☎ **346-2565.**

Cuisine: FRENCH/SEAFOOD. **Reservations:** Required.
Prices: Average three-course menu Dfl. 50 ($26) at lunch, Dfl. 70 ($37) at dinner. AE, DC, MC, V.
Open: Lunch Mon–Sat noon–2pm; dinner Mon–Sat 6–10pm.

Overlooking a beautiful square in the city center, the Saur has been a favorite of Hagenaars for generations. The traditional French cuisine is superb, and the service is impeccable.

INEXPENSIVE

Eatcafé Valerius Inn, Valeriusstraat 18. ☎ **346-1958.**

Cuisine: LIGHT MEALS/SNACKS. **Reservations:** Not required.
Prices: Lunch Dfl. 24–40 ($12–$21); dinner Dfl. 40–50 ($21–$24); snacks Dfl. 8–20 ($4–$10). No credit cards.
Open: Wed–Mon 8am–10:30pm.

Near President Kennedystraat, a few blocks off Scheveningen, this popular brasserie caters mainly to the younger crowd, offering such budget-priced snacks as small pizzas, hamburgers, and ice cream.

★ $ 'T Goude Hooft, Groenmarkt 13. ☎ **346-9713.**

Cuisine: DUTCH/LIGHT MEALS/SNACKS. **Reservations:** Not required.
Prices: Snacks Dfl. 10–25 ($5.25–$13.15); average lunch Dfl. 30 ($16); average dinner Dfl. 50 ($26.30). AE, MC, V.
Open: Daily 10am–midnight.

There's a definite Old Dutch flavor to this large, happy restaurant overlooking the Market Square, yet its 1600s exterior cloaks a 1938 interior installed after a disastrous fire. The wooden beams, brass chandeliers, rustic chairs and tables blend harmoniously with stained-glass windows and here and there a touch of whimsy. There's a large terrace café overlooking the "Green Market" square, pleasant on sunny days, and the long menu covers everything from snacks to light lunches to full dinners, as well as the budget-priced Tourist Menu. It's also a good place to drop by for nothing more than a beer or coffee. Highly recommended (I love this place!).

Rhodos, Buitenhof 36. ☎ **365-2731.**

Cuisine: GREEK. **Reservations:** Recommended at dinner.
Prices: One plate dishes, wine included, Dfl. 30–45 ($16–$24). AE, DC, MC, V.
Open: Lunch Thurs–Tues 11:30am–3pm; dinner Thurs–Tues 6:30–11:30pm.

One of five Greek restaurants in town, located near the station, this large restaurant serves most of the traditional Greek specialties, such as moussaka, grilled veal, rabbit, souvlaki, mussels, and Greek salad. The dining rooms are decorated with traditional pictures of the Acropolis and Rhodes, and colorful wood paneling.

WORTH THE SHORT DRIVE

★
$ **Auberge de Kieviet,** Stoeplaan 27, Wassenaar. ☎ **01751/192-32.**

Cuisine: CONTINENTAL. **Reservations:** Required. **Directions:** Take A44 and follow the signs, about a 10-minute drive.
Prices: Fixed-price meal Dfl. 55 ($29) at lunch, Dfl. 90 ($47) at dinner. AE, DC, MC, V.
Open: Lunch daily noon–3pm; dinner daily 6–10pm.

A gourmet meal in this brasserie-style restaurant is more than worth the short drive from The Hague. Indeed, such is its reputation that Amsterdammers often make the slightly longer drive to eat here. Not surprising, with such specialties as filet of hare with green pepper and mango, leg of lamb with mushrooms, and salmon with strips of pumpkin and truffle featured on the menu.

2 Scheveningen

4km (2¹⁄₂ miles) NW of the city center of The Hague

GETTING THERE° By Tram There is frequent service from The Hague via tram no. 1, 7, 8, or 9.

° **By Car** From The Hague, take A44 and follow the signs.

ESSENTIALS The **VVV office** is on Gevers Deyjnootweg opposite the Europe Hotel (☎ **06/340-3551;** fax 07/361-5459).

SPECIAL EVENTS Each year, usually in late June or early July, jazz greats from around the world gather in Scheveningen for the North Sea Jazz Festival, three days of nonstop music. It's an exciting, energizing experience, and a delight to meet some of those "greats" mingling with audiences to hear some of their favorites.

First of all, there's its name—just try to pronounce it! It's so difficult to do that correctly, in fact, that during World War II the Dutch underground used it as a code name for identification—not even the Germans, whose language is similar, could get it right!

Until about 1813 Scheveningen was a sleepy little fishing village. It wasn't until its beaches began to attract holiday crowds that it began to evolve as an internationally known seaside resort, with accommodations in all price ranges, restaurants with international cuisines, shops that run the gamut from exclusive to budget, and nighttime entertainment. The magnificent Kurhaus Hotel draws Europe's crowned heads and celebrities from around the globe, and gamblers flock to the casino nightly. Businesspeople and diplomats stay here, making the 10-minute drive into The Hague to conduct their affairs. The little harbor is still crowded with fishing boats and lined with restaurants that feature fish right off the boats. This is where the Dutch herring fleet is launched each year in May with a colorful Flag Day celebration and returns with the first herring catch amid just as much fanfare, sending the first batch off to the queen and conducting a lively auction with leading restaurateurs for the rest.

Because so many of its attractions are now enclosed against the elements, Scheveningen has become a year-round resort.

What to See and Do

ATTRACTIONS

In addition to its wide, sandy beach bordered by the 2-mile-long promenade, Scheveningen has the **Kurhaus casino** (open 2pm to 2am daily); the **400-yard Pier** with four entertainment "islands," one of which holds a replica of Jules Verne's submarine *Nautilus* of *20,000 Leagues Under the Sea* fame; a glassed-in **Sealife Center;** the seashore **Promenade** and the **Palace Promenade,** both with scores of interesting year-round shops that are open seven days a week; the historical **Scheveningen Museum** at Neptunusstraat 92; and the **ZeeBiologisch Museum,** at Dr. Lelykade 39.

Scheveningen's neighbor, **Kijkduin,** is a quieter, family-oriented beach resort, where the main attractions are the sea and dunes. There's a covered **shopping complex** with 50 interesting shops open seven days a week, year-round.

EVENING ENTERTAINMENT

After dark, look for nightclubs in Gevers Deynootplein in front of the Kurhaus and theater productions at the Circustheatre, which may include opera and ballet as well as musical theater.

Where to Stay

Budget bed-and-breakfast hotels, family hotels with kitchenettes, modern high-rise hotels with moderate rates, and the incomparable Kurhaus that provides ultimate luxury, all make up the accommodation scene in Scheveningen.

EXPENSIVE

Hotel Kurhaus, Gevers Deynootplein 30, 2586 CK Scheveningen. ☎ **070/416-2636,** or toll free **800/777-5848** in the U.S. Fax 070/416-2646. 241 rms. MINIBAR TV TEL

Rates (including breakfast, service, and VAT): Dfl. 365 ($192) single; Dfl. 425 ($223) double. Children 3–12 in their parents' room are charged Dfl. 30 ($21); no charge for children 2 years and under. Rates include admission to the casino and enclosed wave pool. AE, DC, MC, V.

Undisputed grande dame of the North Sea coast, the five-star Kurhaus began life in 1818 as a four-room wooden bathing pavilion in which bathtubs were filled daily with warm or cold sea water and guests were transported to the sea in enclosed "bathing coaches" so they would not shock the public by their daring! In the years since, it has survived fires, several rebuildings, two world wars, a depression that left it bankrupt, plans to demolish it and build apartments, designation as a national monument, and in the late 1970s a 110-million-guilder renovation. Its Kurzaal concert hall has seen performances by leading musical artists as disparate as violinist Yehudi Menuhin and the Rolling Stones, and its casino rivals any in the world. Its leather-bound guest register, which opens with the signature of the 13-year-old Queen Wilhelmina, is filled with the names of the world's great and illustrated by leading artists who embellished their signatures with original drawings. Actually, all that just *hints* at the rich history of this lovely place that, in the words of one writer, goes beyond fantasy.

The luxury guest rooms, many with balconies facing the sea, are spacious and feature luxurious decor and furnishings, plus safes, hairdryers, and trouser presses. Highly recommended—one of the great hotel experiences.

Dining/Entertainment: The Kurzaal Restaurant and Kurzaal Café are both popular eateries, and the splendid Kandinsky has earned an international reputation (see "Where to Dine," below).

Services: 24-hour room service, babysitting.

Facilities: Direct access to recreation center with indoor and outdoor swimming pools, sauna, and solarium. For the large business clientele, there are 14 conference and banqueting rooms.

MODERATE

Carlton Beach Hotel, Gevers Deynootweg 201, 2586 HZ Scheveningen.
☎ **070/354-1414.** Fax 070/352-0020. 185 rms. TV TEL

Rates (including breakfast): Dfl. 267 ($140) single; Dfl. 330 ($173) double. AE, DC, MC, V.

This modern seaside hotel, on the northern edge of the Promenade, has recently been renovated to move it into the four-star category. The guest rooms are well planned, attractive and comfortable; hairdryers are provided. There's a cozy bar, two restaurants, and a Health Centre with sauna, solaria, and swimming pool.

 Hotel Ibis Den Haag/Scheveningen, Gevers Deynootweg 63, 2586 BJ Scheveningen. ☎ **070/354-3300.** Fax 070/352-3916. 87 rms. TV TEL

Rates (including breakfast): Dfl. 115 ($60) single; Dfl. 189 ($99) double. AE, MC, V.

Just one block from the sea, this bright, attractive hotel has recently undergone a complete renovation, with its guest rooms redecorated. The decor is bright, the furnishings are comfortable, most rooms have a balcony, and many rooms have sea views. There's a terrace bar and a cozy lounge.

INEXPENSIVE

City Hotel, Renbaanstraat 1, 2586 EW Scheveningen. ☎ **070/355-7966.**
Fax 070/354-0503. 35 rms (20 with bath). TV

Rates (including breakfast): Dfl. 70 ($37) single without bath, Dfl. 85 ($45) single with bath; Dfl. 120 ($63) double without bath, Dfl. 165 ($87) double with bath. AE, MC, V.

The guest rooms in this small, family-type hotel are pleasant and comfortable. The food is good, there's a cozy bar, and the sea is only a short walk (three minutes) away.

 Hotel Bali, Badhuisweg 1, 2587 CA Scheveningen. ☎ **070/350-2434.**
Fax 070/354-0363. 34 rms (28 with bath). A/C TV TEL

Rates (including breakfast): Dfl. 75 ($39) single without bath, Dfl. 95 ($50) single with bath; Dfl. 150 ($79) double without bath, Dfl. 175 ($92) double with bath. AE, DC, MC, V.

"Exotic" is the word for the Bali, whose Indonesian motif is carried throughout this delightful budget-priced hotel. The guest rooms are plainly furnished, but very bright and comfortable, with wicker chairs and greenery (in some rooms) adding the Balinese touch. The small bar is inviting, and its restaurant is widely famed for its rice table (see "Where to Dine," below). It's a short walk to the sea.

The Seinduin, Seinpostduin 15, 2587 CA Scheveningen. ☎ **070/355-1971.**
Fax 070/355-7891. 18 rms. MINIBAR TV TEL
Rates (including breakfast): Dfl. 90 ($47) single; Dfl. 130 ($68) double. AE, MC, V.

This rather plain small hotel has guest rooms that are quite comfortable, with rates that make it a very good value for dollar. It's near the beach.

Where to Dine

Scheveningen is filled with restaurants of all price ranges, cuisines, and ambience. The square in front of the Kurhaus (the Gevers Deynootplein) holds a nest of international restaurants, the wharf is lined with good seafood eateries on a street called Dr. Lelykade, and the Promenade and Strandweg have a variety of very good eating places.

⭐ **La Galleria,** Gevers Deynootplein 120. ☎ **352-1156.**
Cuisine: ITALIAN. **Reservations:** Recommended.
Prices: Average three-course dinner Dfl. 45 ($23). AE, MC, V.
Open: Dinner only, daily 6–10pm.

La Galleria, on the square in front of the Kurhaus, is one of my personal favorites in Scheveningen. The warm, intimate room is the perfect setting for a relaxing dinner, and the menu offers everything Italian from pizza to full dinners, at moderate prices. The staff is friendly and welcoming, and the service is good.

⭐ **Kandinsky Restaurant,** in the Hotel Kurhaus, Gevers Deynootplein 30.
☎ **416-2636.**
$ **Cuisine:** FRENCH. **Reservations:** Required.
Prices: Five-course meals Dfl. 90–150 ($47–$79). AE, DC, MC, V.
Open: Lunch daily noon–2pm; dinner daily 6–10:30pm.

Save your most special Scheveningen meal for this small exquisite restaurant, officially opened by Mme Claude Pompidou, widow of the late French president. Located on the beach, the dining room overlooks the sea and its decor features signed lithographs by abstract artist Wassily Kandinsky. The cuisine here is classic French; and thanks to new technical facilities, you can order vintage wines by the glass.

The Kurhaus also serves a lavish buffet daily at Dfl. 55 ($29) for lunch, Dfl. 65 ($34) for dinner, both spread in the gorgeous Kurzaal area, where dancing is added to dinner on Friday and Saturday nights at only slightly elevated prices.

⭐ **Restaurant Bali,** Badhuisweg 1. ☎ **350-2434.**
Cuisine: INDONESIAN. **Reservations:** Required.
$ **Prices:** Lunch Dfl. 40 ($21); dinner Dfl. 60 ($31). AE, MC, V.
Open: Lunch daily noon–2pm; dinner daily 6–11pm.

Since 1946, the Bali has been serving a superb "rice table"—a selection of spicy dishes, beautifully prepared, and served by an Indonesian staff in native dress—and over the years, it has become widely recognized as the best in the region. In the adjoining Bali

READERS RECOMMEND

Harbor Area Restaurants. "*Over in the harbor area are a couple of goodies:* **Bistro Aan,** *Dr. Lelykade 15 (☎ 355-5358), where you should ask for a table overlooking the harbor; and* **Haven Restaurant,** *Treilerdweg 2A (☎ 354-5783), a favorite with almost everyone—a very plain seafood restaurant that looks like a dump on the outside, but the food is wonderful!*"
—Mykell J. Brewer, American Embassy, The Hague.

bar, international cocktails are served with expertise (try the Bali Mystery after dinner—and don't ask *me* its ingredients, all I know is that it's great). It's a short walk from the sea.

Visrestaurant Ducdalf, Dr. Lelykade 5. ☎ **355-7692.**
Cuisine: SEAFOOD. **Reservations:** Recommended.
Prices: Lunch Dfl. 40 ($21); dinner Dfl. 55 ($29). AE, MC, V.
Open: Daily noon–10pm.

This pleasant place on a street along the wharf reflects its nautical setting, and you can rest assured that the fish you order is not long out of local waters. The beautifully presented menu lists an amazingly varied selection of main courses, with steak, veal, and chicken for non-seafood lovers. There's a very good mixed grill, and filet of sole appearing in no fewer than 11 different guises.

---

3 Rotterdam

71km (44 miles) SW of Amsterdam, 23km (14 miles) S of The Hague

GETTING THERE • By Plane   Rotterdam's airport is located at Heathrowbaan 4 (☎ **446-3455**); bus no. 33 will take you into the city center.

• **By Train**   There is frequent rail service to Rotterdam from all around Holland, Brussels, and Paris, arriving at the Central Station, Stationsplein. From Amsterdam, there are two trains each hour around the clock; the trip takes 50 minutes. For information on train schedules, call **06/9292.**

• **By Bus**   Buses from Amsterdam and other major centers around Holland arrive at the Central Station (see above).

• **By Car**   From Amsterdam, take A2 to Utrecht, then A12 to Gouda, then A20 to Rotterdam; from The Hague, you'll take A13.

ESSENTIALS   The **telephone area code** is 010.

Information   The **VVV office** is at Coolsingel 67, on the corner of Stadhuisplein (☎ **06/3403-4065;** fax 010/413-0124), reached by tram no. 1, Stadhuis stop of Metro. April through September, it's open Monday through Thursday from 9am to 5:30pm, on Friday from 9am to 9pm, on Saturday from 9am to 5pm, and on Sunday from 10am to 4pm; October through March, Monday through Thursday from 9am to 5:30pm, on Friday from 9am to 9pm, and on Saturday from 9am to 5pm; closed Sunday and major holidays.

There's also a VVV office in the Central Station (tram no. 1, 3, 4, 5, or 7; bus no. 33, 38, 45, or 49) open Monday through Saturday from 9am to 10pm and on Sunday from 10am to 10pm; closed major holidays.

At either office, pick up a copy of their publication **"Deze Maand"** (This Month) for listings of current happenings. They can also arrange accommodations and furnish a city map that shows major attractions.

GETTING AROUND • By Public Transport   Rotterdam has an extensive public transport network of bus, tram, and underground (Metro). The VVV can furnish a map of routes for all.

• **By Taxi**   Taxis are expensive, but are a time-saving way to get around the city. Ranks are sprinkled throughout the city, or you can call the Rotterdam Taxi Base (☎ **462-6060**).

• **By Foot**   Its sprawling size makes Rotterdam a city to be explored on foot one area at a time, using public transport or taxis to move from one area to another.

ORGANIZED TOURS • **By Tram**   A one-hour tram tour of the city beginning and ending at Central Station is organized by the VVV during summer months. Tickets are available at VVV offices. This tour can be combined with a short boat ride in the harbor, extending the tour time to 2¹/₂ hours.

• **By Boat**   Actually, a boat tour of the harbor is practically obligatory for every visitor, and it certainly gives the most graphic insight as to how and why Rotterdam has developed into the world's leading port. ◪ **Spido Havenrondvaarten** (tours of the port), Willemsplein (☎ **413-5400**), provides one-hour cruises with fascinating and informative narrations, costing Dfl. 12 ($6.30).

Rotterdam is only a half hour from The Hague and an hour from Amsterdam, but it's centuries away from both in appearance and personality.

Founded in 1228 as a small fishing village much like Amsterdam, it developed as a major port (again like Amsterdam), but unlike Amsterdam and The Hague, in only one tiny section of modern-day Rotterdam—Oude Haven (Old Harbor)—will you see any trace of its ancient history. World War II takes the blame for that. The city center was totally burned out by incendiary bombs in 1940, and in 1944 Nazi occupation forces sent demolition squads to finish off the entire harbor, including every one of its ancillary installations. By the end of the war Rotterdam was utterly devastated.

With incredible efficiency and fortitude, *within four days* Rotterdam's city fathers set in motion plans to rebuild their city, and they were determined that it should adhere to modern standards, with no attempt to raise ancient styles from the still-smouldering ruins. Although the task was to consume several years, the wonder is that it did not require decades.

Today Rotterdam is a bustling metropolis with the world's largest port, created when its several harbors were opened directly to the sea (some 20 miles away) by the dredging of a deep-water channel that will accommodate even the largest oil tankers, as well as cargo vessels representing more than 400 international concerns. Its population numbers over one million, and more arrive annually. Indeed it's expanding at such a rate that many Dutch believe a few more decades will see it reach the outskirts of The Hague, swallowing up Delft on its way. What a megalopolis *that* would be!

What to See and Do

Before setting out to experience Rotterdam, stop by the VVV for their helpful brochure "Welcome to Rotterdam," which includes an excellent city map keyed to major attractions.

To see the only corner of Old Rotterdam that's left, take tram no. 6 or 9 to **Delfshaven,** what many years ago was the harbor of Delft. Of special interest to Americans is the old **Pilgrim Fathers Church** in which the Pilgrims said their last prayers before boarding the *Speedwell* for the New World in 1620. They are remembered each Thanksgiving Day by special services. Look also for the two quayside warehouses that have been restored as the city of Rotterdam's official **historical museum, de Dubbelde Palmboom** (treat yourself to a stop in the atmospheric coffee shop upstairs). **Craftspeople** are at work in the old Grain Sack Carriers Guild House (*zakkendragershuisje*), and many of their products are ideal gift items.

Space limitations make this a necessarily abbreviated listing of Rotterdam attractions. The VVV can furnish a more comprehensive listing (see "Information," above).

MUSEUMS

African Cultural Center, Eendrachtsweg 41. ☎ **433-2400.**

Art, objects of art, and old utensils fill this interesting collection from Africa.

Admission: Dfl. 1 (50¢).
Open: Wed and Fri–Sun noon–5pm. **Tram:** 5.

⭐ **Boymans Van-Beuningen Museum,** Museumpark 20. ☎ **441-9400.**

Art lovers will find a collection of works by Dutch and Flemish artists of the 16th and 17th centuries, among them masterpieces by Rubens, Hals, Rembrandt, and Steen. Other galleries hold international modern art, applied arts, ceramics, sculpture, prints, and drawings.

Admission: Dfl. 6 ($3.15).
Open: Tues–Sat 10am–5pm, Sun and holidays 11am–5pm. **Metro:** Eendrachtsplein. **Tram:** 5.

National Schools Museum, Nieuwe Markt 1A. ☎ **404-5425.**

The history of education in Holland from the Charlemagne era right up to today is traced through six marvelous fully furnished classrooms populated by lifelike figures of teachers and pupils, pictures, prints, and documents.

Admission: Dfl. 3.50 ($1.85) adults, free for children under 17 and for everyone on Wed.
Open: Tues–Fri 10am–5pm, Sat–Sun 11am–5pm. **Metro:** Blaak. **Tram:** 3 or 7.

⭐ **Prins Hendrik Maritime Museum,** Leuvehaven 1. ☎ **413-2680.**

There's a marvelous collection of nautical lore and technical references in this remarkable museum that is devoted entirely to harbor activities past and present. Located in the harbor area, it consists of two sections: the main building, and *De Buffel,* a beautifully restored 1868 warship. The constantly changing exhibits will give you new insight into the close relationship between the Dutch and the sea. In the museum harbor basin, some 20 vessels dating from 1850 to 1950 are moored. There's also a bookshop and a coffee shop.

Admission: Dfl. 6 ($3.15), adults, free for children under 17 and for everyone on Wed.
Open: Tues–Sat 10am–5pm, Sun 11am–5pm. **Metro:** Beurs/Churchillplein. **Tram:** 3, 6, or 7. **Bus:** 32 or 49.

Prof. van der Poël Belastingmuseum, Parklaan 14. ☎ **436-5629.**

You may well want to skip this one, but I thought you should know it's there—it's a *tax museum,* with historic collections on taxation and smuggling down through the centuries.

Admission: Free.
Open: Tues–Fri 9am–5pm. **Tram:** 5.

IMPRESSIONS

Rotterdam is remarkedly clean: the Dutch even wash the outside brick-work of their houses.
—Mary Shelley, 1817

HOLLAND

Rotterdam

ACCOMMODATIONS:
Bienvenue **3**
Commerce **5**
Golden Tulip Barbizon Capelle **1**
Hotel Breitner **8**
Parkhotel **15**
Savoy **12**

DINING:
De Pijp **6**
La Vilette **16**
Le Coq d'Or **19**
Restaurant Engels **4**
The Old Dutch **7**

ATTRACTIONS:
African Cultural Center **18**
Blijdorp Zoo **2**
Boymans–van Beuningen Museum **17**
Euromast & Spacetower **10**
Holland Casino Rotterdam **11**
National Schools Museum **13**
Prins Hendrik Maritime Museum **9**
Prof. van der Poël Belastingmuseum **20**
Tropicana **14**

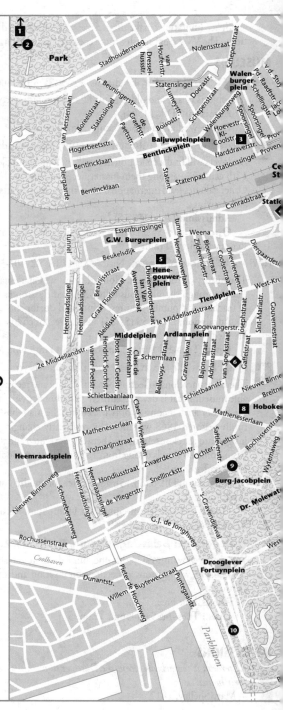

9575

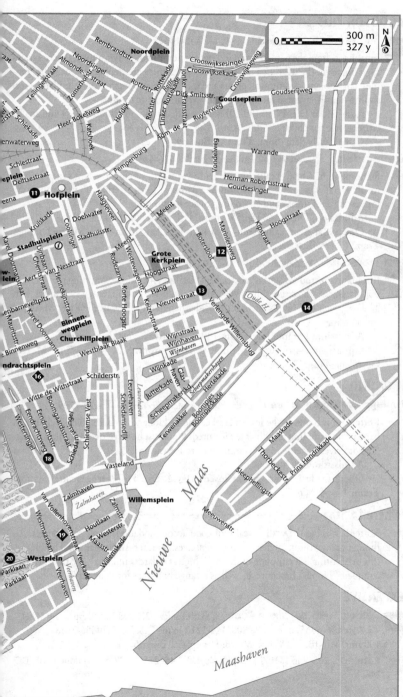

Rotterdam Accommodations, Dining & Attractions

Information ⓘ   Railroad ┼┼┼┼┼

COOL FOR KIDS

 Blijdorp Zoo, Van Aerssenlaan 49. ☎ **443-1431.**

Inhabitants from the natural world feel right at home in this environment that re-creates their homes in the wild. In a large enclosed plaza there are elephants, crocodiles, reptiles, amphibians, and tropical plants and birds. An Asian section that simulates a real swamp houses Javanese monkeys, a bat cave, and exotic birds.

Admission: Dfl. 17.50 ($9.20) adults, Dfl. 12 ($6.30) children 4–9 and senior citizens, free for children under 4.

Open: Daily 9am–5pm. **Tram:** 3. **Bus:** 39.

Euromast and Spacetower, Parkhaven 20. ☎ **436-4811.**

Standing some 611 feet tall, this slender tower is indisputably the best vantage point for an overall view of Rotterdam and its environs. More than that, however, there are interesting exhibitions and an exciting Space Cabin ride.

Admission: Dfl. 12.50 ($6.55) adults, Dfl. 8 ($4.20) children 4–12.

Open: Mar–Sept, daily 10am–7pm; Oct–Feb, daily 10am–6pm. **Metro:** Dijkzigt. **Tram:** 6 or 9. **Bus:** 39.

 Tropicana, Maasboulevard 100. ☎ **402-0700.**

In a luxuriant tropical setting, recreational facilities include a swimming pool, a wave pool, a sauna, water slides, hot whirlpools, a wild-water strip, and a swimmers' bar. The revolving La Meuse restaurant provides panoramic views of the River Maas and surroundings.

Admission: For four hours, Dfl. 13 ($6.85), free for children under 5.

Open: Mon–Fri 10am–11pm, Sat 10am–6pm, Sun 10am–7pm. **Metro:** Oostplein. **Tram:** 3 or 6.

A CASINO

Holland Casino Rotterdam, in the Hilton Hotel, Weena 10. ☎ **414-7799.**

Rotterdam is home to the fourth legal casino in Holland; roulette, blackjack, punto banco, and gambling machines are featured. You must be 18 or over and show a passport or driver's license to gain admittance to the casino.

Admission: Dfl. 5 ($2.60).

Open: Daily 1:30pm–2am. **Closed:** May 4, Dec 31. **Metro:** Central Station. **Tram:** 1, 3, 4, 5, or 7.

Where to Stay

Rotterdam is blessed with a wealth of good accommodations in all price ranges. Although many visitors prefer to base themselves in either Amsterdam or The Hague, this brief listing is a sampling of the city's high standards, and the VVV can furnish a complete "Hotels" brochure, as well as arrange bookings for your stay.

EXPENSIVE

 Golden Tulip Barbizon Capelle, Barbizonlaan 2, 2908 MA Cappele a/d IJssel. ☎ **010/456-4455,** or toll free **800/344-1212** in the U.S. Fax 010/456-7858.

100 rms. MINIBAR TV TEL **Metro:** Hesseplaats. **Bus:** 35.

Rates: Dfl. 205–245 ($107–$129) single; Dfl. 245–275 ($129–$144) double. AE, DC, MC, V.

This spectacularly modern high-rise in a suburb of Rotterdam is the perfect getaway from city chaos—and only a 10-minute drive to the city center and airport. The guest rooms, equipped with hairdryers and trouser presses, are superbly furnished, with a pleasing decor, and public rooms exude graciousness as well as functional expertise. CNN News and in-house movies are available, and guests enjoy complimentary fruit and daily newspapers.

Dining/Entertainment: There's the convivial Luigi's Bar, and fine dining in the Rousseau restaurant.

Services: 24-hour room service, valet service, laundry service.

Facilities: Gift shop, conference rooms, wheelchair access.

Parkhotel, Westersingel 70, 3015 LB Rotterdam. ☎ **010/436-3611.** Fax 010/436-4212. 157 rms. MINIBAR TV TEL **Metro:** Eendrachtsplein. **Tram:** 5.

Rates (including breakfast): Dfl. 160 ($84) single; Dfl. 295 ($155) double. AE, DC, MC, V.

For city-center convenience, you can't do better than this modern high-rise. The guest rooms are the ultimate in luxury, and many sightseeing attractions are within walking distance.

Dining: There's a good dining room serving all three meals.

Services: 24-hour room service.

Facilities: Sauna, gym, wheelchair access.

MODERATE

Commerce, Henegouwerplein 56–62, 3021 BA Rotterdam. ☎ **010/477-4800.** Fax 010/425-7829. 39 rms (32 with bath). TV TEL **Bus:** 38 or 45.

Rates (including breakfast): Dfl. 75 ($39) single without bath, Dfl. 100 ($52) single with bath; Dfl. 95 ($50) double without bath, Dfl. 130 ($68) double with bath. AE, MC, V.

There's good bus transport to other parts of the city from this small, friendly hotel near Central Station. The guest rooms are nicely done up and quite comfortable.

Savoy, Hoogstraat 81, 3011 PJ Rotterdam. ☎ **010/413-9280.** Fax 010/404-5712. 94 rms. TV TEL **Metro:** Blaak. **Tram:** 3 or 7.

Rates: Dfl. 160 ($84) single; Dfl. 175 ($92) double. AE, MC, V.

Guest rooms in this modern hotel are of very high standard, and although there's no restaurant, several eateries are nearby.

INEXPENSIVE

Bienvenue, Spoorsingel 24, 3033 GL Rotterdam. ☎ **010/466-9394.** Fax 010/467-7475. 10 rms (8 with bath). TV **Tram:** 3, 5, or 9.

Rates (including breakfast): Dfl. 55 ($29) single without bath, Dfl. 65 ($34) single with bath; Dfl. 75 ($39) double without bath, Dfl. 95 ($50) double with bath. MC, V.

This small, budget-priced hotel on the canal has exceptionally comfortable rooms for the cost. It's one of the best hotels in its price range, with some rooms overlooking the canal.

$ **Hotel Breitner**, Breitnerstraat 23, 3015 XA Rotterdam. ☎ **010/436-0262.** Fax 010/436-4091. 30 rms (19 with bath). TV TEL **Bus:** 38 or 45.

Rates: Dfl. 63 ($33) single without bath, Dfl. 95 ($50) single with bath; Dfl. 90 ($47) double without bath, Dfl. 125 ($65) double with bath. AE, MC, V.

Located quite near the picturesque Delfshaven historic area as well as the ultramodern Euromast and Central Station, the Breitner is a friendly hostelry with attractive, no-frills guest rooms. There's a good-size lounge and a garden with a terrace.

Where to Dine

EXPENSIVE

Brasserie La Vilette, Westblaak 160. ☎ **414-8692.**

Cuisine: FRENCH. **Reservations:** Recommended.
Prices: Average lunch Dfl. 55 ($29); average dinner from Dfl. 80 ($42). AE, DC, MC, V.
Open: Lunch Mon–Sat noon–2pm; dinner Mon–Sat 6–9:30pm.

Without doubt the most elegant restaurant in town, La Vilette is a plant- and flower-filled oasis in the city center, with soft rose-colored walls and starched white table linen. The cuisine is classic French (awarded one star by Michelin) and the service is both polished and friendly. This member of the Alliance Gastronomique is much favored by leading business executives.

★ **Le Coq d'Or,** Van Vollenhovenstraat 25. ☎ **436-6405** or **436-5906.**

$ **Cuisine:** FRENCH. **Reservations:** Recommended.
Prices: Average meal Dfl. 50–120 ($26–$63). AE, DC, MC, V.
Open: Lunch Mon–Fri noon–2pm; dinner Mon–Fri 6–10pm.

Close to the harbor by the river, this fine restaurant has a spacious secluded garden for outdoor dining in the summer months. Indoors it has a classic rustic decor with open hearth and exposed beams, with paintings by van Meegeren and other artists hung about. Prices are a bit higher in the more formal upstairs dining room. Specialties change with the seasons. The wine cellar here is excellent.

★ **The Old Dutch,** Rochussenstraat 20. ☎ **436-0344.**

Cuisine: DUTCH/FRENCH. **Reservations:** Recommended.
Prices: Average lunch Dfl. 35–40 ($18–$21); average dinner 60–130 ($31–$68). AE, DC, MC, V.
Open: Lunch Mon–Fri noon–2pm; dinner Mon–Fri 6–10pm.

This atmospheric restaurant in the city center is housed in what was once a traditional-style home. One of Rotterdam's leading restaurants, it offers a menu as traditional Dutch as its decor, which is not to gainsay the appearance of many fine dishes representing the best in French cuisine.

MODERATE

De Pijp, Gaffelstraat 90. ☎ **436-6896.**

Cuisine: INTERNATIONAL. **Reservations:** Recommended.
Prices: Average meal Dfl. 30–55 ($15–$29). AE, MC, V.
Open: Lunch Mon–Sat noon–2pm; dinner Mon–Sat 6–10pm.

Steaks and a number of international dishes are prepared right in the middle of this delightful restaurant that attracts a mixed bag of regulars—students, bankers, business executives, blue-collar workers—a real "Rotterdam" ambience. It's located in the city center.

Restaurant Engels, Stationsplein 45. ☎ **411-9551** or **411-9550.**
Cuisine: INTERNATIONAL/LIGHT MEALS. **Reservations:** Recommended if you want a particular room.
Prices: Average meals in ethnic rooms Dfl. 30–50 ($15–$26); Viking Room seafood buffet Dfl. 29 ($15); light meals in the New Yorker Counter Restaurant Dfl. 20–40 ($10–$21); sandwiches and burgers Dfl. 6–14 ($3–$7). AE, DC, MC, V.
Open: Daily 8am–midnight.

Located next to the Central Station in the huge Engels Groothandelsgebouw (Business Center), this marvelous restaurant is actually a complex of seven dining rooms, each dedicated to a different international cuisine: Viking (Scandinavian), Don Quijote (Spanish), Tokaj (Hungarian), Bistro Chez François (French), Beefeater and Pub Old John (British), New Yorker (American), and 't Oude Engels (Old Dutch). There's live music in Tokaj and Don Quijote. In addition there's an à la carte menu (full dinners, light meals, sandwiches, omelets, snacks, etc.), the Tourist Menu, and a Vegetarian Menu.

15

South Holland's Historic Towns

THE TRIANGLE FORMED BY HISTORIC GOUDA, DELFT, AND LEIDEN MAKES FOR leisurely sightseeing, with distances short enough to allow you to visit all three from a base in Rotterdam, The Hague, or Amsterdam while rambling instead of rushing. The roads you travel will take you through a landscape straight out of a Dutch master painting, with flat, green fields ribboned by canals, distant church spires piercing a wide sky—and, from time to time a clump of industrial smokestacks representing a 20th-century intrusion. Still, for the most part, this is the Holland of your imagination, the Holland you came to see.

1 Gouda

25km (15¹/₂ miles) NE of Rotterdam, 25km (15¹/₂ miles) E of The Hague, 32km (20 miles) SE of Leiden, 25km (16 miles) E of Delft

GETTING THERE • **By Train/Bus**   There are rail and bus connections to Gouda from The Hague, Amsterdam, Rotterdam, and Utrecht. The rail and bus stations are north of the town center. For rail information, call **06-9292.**

• **By Car**   Gouda is reached by A12 and A20.

ESSENTIALS   The **telephone area code** for Gouda is 0182. The **VVV office** is at Markt 27 (☎ **0182/513-666;** fax 0182/8320).

You know about its cheeses, of course, but do you know that in Holland its name is pronounced *"Howdah"*? Try to come on a Thursday morning (9am to noon) during July and August—that's when the lively cheese market brings farmers in their everyday work clothes to town driving farm wagons painted with bright designs and piled high with round cheeses in their orange skins. It's an altogether different scene from the market in Alkmaar. Gouda received its charter in 1272.

What to See and Do

If you arrive on ⊠ **cheese market** day, walk to the back of the Town Hall, where you'll be given a sample of the famous Gouda cheese and treated to a video explaining how it's made. The gray stone **Town Hall** with its stepped gables and red shutters is reputed to be the oldest in Holland, and parts of its Gothic facade go back to 1449. Gouda has been the center of a thriving **clay pipe** industry since the 17th century. One style of pipe that was made here has a pattern on the bowl that's invisible when the pipe is new and only appears as the pipe is smoked and darkens—it's called a "mystery pipe" because the designs vary and the buyer never knows what the design will be until he smokes the pipe.

ATTRACTIONS

Adrie Moerings Pottenbakkerij & Pijpenmakerij, Peperstraat 76. ☎ **512-842.**

This interesting factory presents fascinating demonstrations of the craftsmanship demanded in producing beautiful pottery, as well as clay pipes, many made in centuries-old shapes. You can see the work going on at the moment and visit their pottery exposition and viewing room. A good place to pick up one of those uniquely Dutch mementos of your visit, it's a five-minute walk from Markt.

Admission: Free.

Open: Mon–Sat 11am–5pm.

What's Special About South Holland's Historic Towns

Gouda
- The cheese market on Thursday mornings.
- Factories where you can see demonstrations of pottery making and painting and pick up some mementos.
- The Red Lion Windmill, completely renovated and grinding away.
- Sint Janskerk, Holland's largest church, with some of Europe's most beautiful stained-glass windows.

Delft
- Perhaps the prettiest little town in all of Holland.
- Nieuwe Kerk, with the magnificent tomb of William the Silent.
- De Porceleyne Fles, where you can see Delft Blue being hand-painted.

Leiden
- Walk in the footsteps of the Pilgrim Fathers, who sought refuge here before sailing to the New World.
- The Molenmuseum de Valk, with exhibits dedicated to windmills and located in a monumental one.

★ **De Roode Leeuw (The Red Lion) Windmill,** Vest 65.
This 1727 grain mill, known as "The Red Lion," has been completely renovated and is now grinding away happily. It's located west of Markt.
Admission: Dfl. 2.50 ($1.30).
Open: Mon and Wed–Sat 9am–3pm.

★ **Sint Janskerk (Church of St. John),** South Markt.
This majestic 15th-century church just south of Markt is Holland's largest, and it holds some of Europe's most beautiful stained-glass windows—64 in all, with a total of 2,412 panels. Some date back to the mid-1500s, and they represent a craft that in the 16th century had been elevated to an art. To see the contrast between that long-vanished art and the work being done today, take a look at the most recent window, no. 28A, commemorating the World War II years in Holland.
Admission: Dfl. 2.50 ($1.30).
Open: Mon–Sat 9am–5pm.

Stedelijk Museum Het Catharina Gasthuis, Oosthaven 10. ☎ **513-800.**
This 1665 mansion near Sint Janskerk houses Gouda's municipal museum. The jewel of its collections is a gold chalice that Countess Jacqueline of Bavaria presented to the Society of Archers in 1465. Its whereabouts was unknown for over a century before it was recovered in the Town Hall's attic and brought here. There are also colorful guild relics, antique furniture, and a terra-cotta plaque whose Latin inscription proclaims that the humanist Erasmus may have been born in Rotterdam, but he was *conceived* in Gouda. There's limited access for wheelchairs.
Admission: Dfl. 3.50 ($1.85).
Open: Mon–Sat 10am–5pm, Sun noon–5pm.

Stedelijk Museum de Moriaan, Westhaven 29. ☎ **88-440.**
During the 17th century, this was the home of a Gouda merchant. Today it holds a large and interesting pipe collection, as well as many beautiful ceramics.

Admission: Dfl. 3.50 ($1.85).

Open: Mon–Fri 10am–5pm, Sat 10am–12:30pm and 1:30–5pm, Sun and holidays noon–5pm.

EASY EXCURSIONS FROM GOUDA

There are several places of interest within easy driving distance of Gouda that can be worked into a day's excursion.

★ **KINDERDIJK**   If you're into windmills, this is where you'll find the largest concentration (19) in Holland today. Most are in full operation on summer Saturday afternoons, and there's a mill open to the public Monday through Saturday in summer.

★ **OUDEWATER**   Only about 8 miles from Gouda is a charming little village that looks anything but sinister. Yet back in the 1500s this was the scene of some of Europe's most horrifying witch trials. The situation got so bad that the town's reputation of having the most honest merchants with the most accurate scales on the Continent was in danger of being ruined forever. To remedy that bad press, the town fathers devised a system of judging accused witches by having them stand on scales clad in nothing but a paper costume and paper broom. Present for this "trial" were the mayor, the alderman, the weighmaster, and the local midwife. When the weighmaster had finished juggling his weights and balancing the scales, he then could honestly proclaim that the accused witch weighed far too much to fly through the air supported only by a broomstick, thus could not possibly be a witch, and a certificate was issued stating just that. You can believe that Europe's accused witches flocked here in droves! Now, if you have some doubt about anyone in your party (or yourself!), between May and September you can step on the Oudewater Weigh House scales and—provided you're not too skinny—walk away with your very own certificate.

As you walk through the quaint streets of this village, take a look at the storks' nests on the Town Hall roof—the big birds have been nesting here for over three centuries.

SCHOONHOVEN   This little town is where they make most of the **silver** objects and souvenirs you see around the country. The small workshops welcome visitors, and it's fascinating to see the skill required to produce the delicate work. The place to see it demonstrated is the **Edelambachtshuis,** on the main canal. When you're walking past the lovely old **Town Hall** (1452), give a thought to the poor "witch" who never made it to those scales in Oudewater and was burned to death at the spot marked now by a circle of stones on the bridge near the Town Hall.

Also in Schoonhoven, the **Nederlands Goud, Zilver en Klokkenmuseum,** Kazerneplein 4 (☎ **0182/385-612**), holds a wonderful collection of old clocks, as well as gold and silver objects of great beauty. Open from noon to 5pm Tuesday through Sunday; admission is Dfl. 4 ($2.10).

Where to Dine

Mallemolen, Oosthaven 72. ☎ **15-430.**

Cuisine: FRENCH/DUTCH. **Reservations:** Recommended.

Prices: Fixed-price meal Dfl. 75 ($39). MC, V.

Open: Dinner only, Tues–Sun 5pm "until the last guest departs."

Gouda's excellent traditional restaurant is located on what is known as "Rembrandt's corner," and there's even an ancient windmill in the street. The setting sets the tone of the restaurant, which is Old Dutch, although the cuisine is chiefly French.

2 Delft

10km (6 miles) SE of The Hague, 14km (9 miles) NW of Rotterdam,
35km (22 miles) W of Gouda, 30km (19 miles) SW of Leiden

GETTING THERE • By Train/Bus   There are rail and bus connections to Delft from Amsterdam, Rotterdam, and The Hague.

• **By Car**   Delft is just off A13, the main The Hague–Rotterdam motorway.

ESSENTIALS   The **telephone area code** for Delft is 015. You'll find the **VVV office** at Markt 85 (☎ **015/126-100;** fax 015/158-695).

Perhaps the prettiest little town in all of Holland, Delft presents without pretension streets lined with houses whose Renaissance and Gothic facades reflect age-old beauty, and tree-lined canals that enhance the sense of tranquillity that pervades the very air. Around every corner and down every street you'll walk into a scene that might have been composed solely for the canvas of a great artist. Indeed, it's easy to understand why Vermeer chose to spend most of his life surrounded by Delft's soft beauty.

Royalty lies buried in Delft—William the Silent was assassinated in the Prinsenhof and now rests in a magnificent tomb in the Nieuwe Kerk. Every member of the House of Orange-Nassau since King Willem I has been brought to Delft for burial, and it's the final resting place of someone named as Karl Naudorff, but who is suspected of being Louis XVII, dauphin of France. Two of Holland's greatest naval figures, Admirals Tromp and Heyn, are entombed in the Oude Kerk. A good part of Holland's history, it would seem, is preserved in the tombs of Delft.

Of course, to many tourists Delft means just one thing—the distinctive blue-and-white earthenware still produced by the tedious methods of old, with every piece still painted by hand.

What to See and Do

The first thing to do is park the car and walk! Although the town's layout allows easy driving, it's by strolling its streets that you absorb its special ambience. Walking can be supplemented, of course, by a leisurely tour of its canals via the numerous water taxis that operate during the summer.

The 14th-century ✪ **Nieuwe Kerk,** at the market is well worth a visit on its own, but you won't want to miss the magnificent tomb of William the Silent, surrounded by 22 columns and embellished with figures representing Liberty, Justice, Valor, and Religion. The royal dead of the House of Orange-Nassau lie in a crypt beneath the remains of the founder of their line. There's a marvelous panoramic view of the town from the church tower. The church is open daily April through October from 9am to 6pm, and November through March 11am to 4pm. Admission is Dfl. 2.50 ($1.30) for adults and Dfl 1 (50¢) for children.

Museum Lambert van Meerten, Oude Delft 199. ☎ **602-358.**

If you came to Delft to see its famous earthenware, you'll find the most fascinating collection, including lovely tiles, in this 19th-century mansion north of the market, near Prinsenhof.

Admission: Dfl. 3.50 ($1.85).
Open: Tues–Sat 10am–5pm, Sun 1–5pm.

Museum Paul Tetar van Elven, Koornmarkt 67. ☎ **124-206.**

The 19th-century artist van Elven lived and worked here, south of the market, and his furnishings are just as he left them. The 17th-century-style studio stands ready for the artist to enter and pick up his brushes.

Admission: Dfl. 3.50 ($1.85) adults; Dfl. 1.50 (80¢) children.

Open: May–Oct, Tues–Sat 11am–5pm. **Closed:** Nov–Apr.

★ **De Porceleyne Fles**, Rotterdamseweg 196. ☎ **560-234.**

The Delft Blue you came to town to find is made by a traditional painstaking method at De Porceleyne Fles, where you can watch the hand-painting of each item and see an audio-slide show that explains the entire process. Delft potters have been at it since they met the competition of Chinese porcelain imported by the East India Company. And if you thought the trademark blue-and-white colors were the only Delft, here is where you will see exquisite multicolored patterns. Your purchases can be packed carefully and shipped home directly from this factory.

Admission: Free.

Open: Mon–Sat 9am–5pm, Sun 10am–4pm. **Closed:** Sun Nov–Mar.

★ **The Prinsenhof**, entrance at St. Agathaplein 1. ☎ **602-358.**

On the banks of Delft's oldest canal, the Prinsenhof dates from the late 1400s and was originally a convent. This is where William the Silent elected to stay when in Delft, and where an assassin's bullets ended his life in 1584 (you can still see the bullet holes near the bottom of a staircase). Its restoration has re-created the interior William would have known, and a museum preserves the record of Dutch struggles to throw off the yoke of Spanish occupation between 1568 and 1648. There are impressive tapestries and paintings. It's a short walk north of the market, near the Oude Kerk, a five-minute walk from the train station.

Admission: Dfl. 3.50 ($1.85).

Open: Tues–Sat 10am–5pm, Sun 1–5pm.

Where to Dine

★ **Spijshuis de Dis**, Beestenmarkt 36. ☎ **131-782.**

Cuisine: DUTCH. Reservations: Recommended.

Prices: Fixed-price three-course menu Dfl. 22–30 ($12–$16); Dutch specialties Dfl. 28–36 ($15–$19). AE, MC, V.

Open: Thurs–Tues 4:30–10pm.

Some of the best Dutch cooking in Delft is dished up in this atmospheric restaurant east of the market. Try their waterzooi, one of the best versions of this beloved dish I've come across. They also do a great lamb filet, and if you're feeling especially sinful, opt for the luscious dessert of vanilla ice cream with hot cherries, whipped cream, and cherry brandy.

OTHER RECOMMENDATIONS

Space does not permit full writeups of the following, most of which have hours of noon to 2pm and 6 to 10pm, and some are closed on Monday or Wednesday. Food

IMPRESSIONS

> *It is a most sweet town with bridges and a river in every street.*
> —Samuel Pepys, 1660

is served at moderate prices and in the medieval manner at **Stadsherberg De Mol,** Molslaan 104 (☎ **121-343**), and there's live music and dancing. There's good food at moderate prices, with friendly, professional service at **Prinsenkelder,** Schoolstraat 11 (☎ **121-860**), in the Prinsenhof. **La Fontanella,** Voldersgracht 8 (☎ **135-929**), is a snazzy Italian café with inexpensive crêpes, omelets, and the like, as well as excellent coffee.

3 Leiden

20km (12 miles) NE of The Hague, 44km (27 miles) N of Rotterdam, 32km (20 miles) NW of Gouda, 30km (19 miles) NE of Delft

GETTING THERE • By Train/Bus   Rail and bus connections to Leiden from points around Holland are frequent. Both stations are located to the northwest of the town center (about a 10-minute walk).

• **By Car**   Leiden is reached via A4 and E19.

ESSENTIALS   The **telephone area code** for Leiden is 071. The **VVV office** is at Stationsplein 210 (☎ **071/146-846;** fax 071/125-318). Ask about their guided tours during the summer months, as well as their self-guided walking-tour brochure.

A visit to Leiden is in the nature of a pilgrimage (you should pardon the pun) for Americans, for it was here that the Pilgrim Fathers found refuge during the long years they waited to sail to a fresh beginning in the New World. Their sojourn was, however, but one small incident in Leiden's long history.

The high point in that history is surely the heroism with which it met a five-month siege by the Spanish in 1574. Thousands of its residents perished, and the food situation became so intolerable that the mayor offered his own body to be used as nourishment for the starving population—talk about heroism! His offer was not accepted, but his memory is honored by a town park in which his statue stands.

The Dutch fleet finally rescued Leiden on October 3 after a dramatic advance over fields flooded as dikes were broken to open up a watery route to the beleaguered citizens. From that terrible siege came one of Holland's most beloved national dishes, *hutspot* (hotpot), so named for the bubbling kettle of stew left behind by fleeing Spaniards—a kettle now ensconced in the Lakenhal Museum (see below). If you should be in Leiden on any October 3, you'll see that anniversary observed as *haren en witte brood* (herring and loaves of white bread) are distributed just as they were in 1574.

William the Silent, in recognition of Leiden's courage, rewarded the city with a choice between freedom from taxation and the founding of a university in the town. Perhaps to the consternation of some present-day residents, those 16th-century residents chose the university, Holland's first, which today is a leader in the fields of medicine and law.

Leiden is also known in artistic circles as the birthplace of Rembrandt, Jan Steen, and Lucas van Leyden.

What to See and Do

To touch base with the courageous spirit of those humble Pilgrim Fathers, pick up the VVV brochure **"A Pilgrimage Through Leiden: A Walk in the Footsteps of the Pilgrim Fathers."** When you set out, be sure to stop by the tiny ◼ **Documentatie**

Centrum (Leiden Pilgrim Collection), Boisotkade 2 (entrance at Vliet 45), near the Vliet River, to view a comprehensive slide show in English and a model kitchen of the period. Then walk past the **house on Herensteg** (marked by a plaque) where William Brewster's Pilgrim Press published the religious views that so angered the Church of England. Plaques at **Sint Pieterskerk** (in a small square off Kloksteeg) also remember the Pilgrim Fathers, especially the Rev. Jon Robinson, who was forced to stay behind because of illness and is buried in this church (an almshouse, the Jean Pesijnhofje, now occupies the house in which he died). Special Thanksgiving Day services are held each year in honor of the little band of refugees who worshiped here. There is also an exhibit of Pilgrim documents in the Lakenhal (see below).

The **University of Leiden** is located near the Rapenburg Canal, and the small street on which Rembrandt was born is Weddesteeg, on the north side of Noordeinde.

The ■ **Stedelijk Museum de Lakenhal,** at Oude Singel 28 (☎ 254-620), a 17th-century guildhall, is Leiden's municipal museum. Its fine collections of paintings by Dutch artists of the 16th and 17th centuries include works by Lucas van Leyden, Rembrandt, Steen, and Dou, and temporary modern art exhibitions are organized regularly. The cloth merchants guild (original occupants of the building) is represented in historical exhibits, and there are maps and other documents relating to this town of the Pilgrim Fathers.

Among the fascinating scientific exhibits housed in the **Museum Boerhaave (National Science Museum),** at Lange Sint Agnietenstraat 10 (☎ 214-224), are thermometers made by Fahrenheit, globes that once belonged to the cartographer Blaeu, and microscopes made by van Leeuwenhoek. Astronomy, chemistry, biology, and other scientific subjects are also represented. The museum is open from 10am to 5pm Tuesday through Friday and noon to 5pm on Saturday and Sunday; closed January 1 and October 3.

The small ■ **Molenmuseum de Valk,** located in a monumental windmill at 2 Binnenvestgracht 1, has exhibits dedicated to various types of windmills. The focus is on the history of grinding grain and the construction and working of a corn mill in particular. Open Tuesday through Saturday from 10am to 5pm and on Sunday from 1 to 5pm. Admission is Dfl. 3.50 ($1.85).

Where to Dine

★ **Rotisserie Oudt Leyden**, Steenstraat 51. ☎ 133-144.

Cuisine: DUTCH. **Reservations:** Recommended.
Prices: Fixed-price menu Dfl. 45 ($23) for three courses, Dfl. 55 ($29) for four courses. AE, DC, MC, V.
Open: Tues–Sat noon–9:30pm, Sun 2–10pm.

The traditional decor and cuisine here sustain Leiden's historical atmosphere. In the Rotisserie room, specialties are seafood and roast meats, while in the 't Pannekoekeuhuysje it's Holland's tasty pancakes in a large variety. The restaurant is located north of the town center, near Lakenhal.

READERS RECOMMEND

Where to Stay. *"For those who want to stay in Leiden, we highly recommend the bed-and-breakfast operated by **Mrs. Bik,** Witte Singel 92 (☎ 071/122-602). This outgoing, friendly woman, with a good command of English, helped us out in many extra ways, as did her husband."*—Anthony Glavin, Amherst, Mass. [**Author's Note:** Including breakfast, singles cost Dfl. 40 ($21) and doubles are Dfl. 70 ($37).]

16

Holland's Northern Provinces

HOME TO HOLLAND'S EARLIEST SETTLERS, HOLLAND'S NORTHERN PROVINCES compress an astounding geographic and historical encyclopedia into an amazingly compact area. Friesland, so ancient as to be almost another world, complete with customs and a language all its own, is a landscape of charming little villages and 11 cities surrounded by miles of flat farmlands. It is dotted by huge earthen mounds (terps) that were the forerunners of Holland's dikes, and has some 30 lakes and two large islands off its coast. From its farms have come the world-renowned Frisian cattle and the lovely black Frisian horses that are so responsive to music that they are favorites with circuses around the globe.

Groningen, the Province of Groningen's capital city, is the north's most important commercial and industrial center and university city, in striking contrast to the medieval monastery in the southeastern corner of the province.

Drenthe, as old as Friesland, hides 20th-century oil wells behind stands of trees to lessen their impact on the natural scenic beauty of lakes, forests, moors, and picturesque villages.

1   Friesland

You can tour the Friesland province by car, bicycle, boat, and during the winter on skates. Its 11 cities are arranged in such a way that you can make the circuit with ease, stopping overnight in good, moderately priced hotels or selecting as a home base the beautiful château that is now a luxury inn in centrally located Beetsterzwaag. You can, of course, plot your own way from a map, but a much better idea is to go directly to the VVV office in Leeuwarden and pick up one of their carefully **routed tour guides.** They can even arrange do-it-yourself auto or **bicycle tours** with prebooked accommodations each night.

Road signs along Frisian roads are in two languages, one of which you have not seen elsewhere—the ancient Frisian language that broke off from the Germanic tongue long before the Dutch language followed suit, which is spoken daily by some 70% of the Frisian population. These fiercely independent people also have their own flag, their own coat-of-arms, and their own national anthem! Which is not to say they're not Dutch: they are, but *first* they are Frisian.

That independent spirit has stood the United States in good stead, for it was here, in the capital city of Leeuwarden, that documents were signed making Holland the first nation to officially recognize the new nation.

Leeuwarden, the Provincial Capital

Leeuwarden, about 105 miles northeast of Amsterdam, is the capital city of Friesland. There are good rail and bus connections to Leeuwarden from around the country, and the rail and bus stations adjoin each other at Stationsplein. By car, you can get to Leeuwarden by A31, N353, N355, and N359.

The **VVV office** for both the city of Leeuwarden and the Province of Friesland is next door to the railway station at Stationsplein 1 (☎ **06/3202-4060;** fax 058/ 136-555), open Monday through Friday from 9am to 6pm and on Saturday at 9am to 2pm. The staff is exceptionally helpful, and can provide directions for several interesting **day trips from Leeuwarden,** among them the terpen tour to see the earthen mounds built to escape flood waters, the wouden tour through Friesland's beautiful woodlands, and lakes tour, and the "Forefathers Heritage Route."

The **telephone area code** for Leeuwarden is 058.

What's Special About Holland's Northern Provinces

Friesland
- Fries Museum, with prehistoric artifacts dating back to the Ice Age, one of Rembrandt's portraits of Saskia, and a replica of a tobacco shop.
- Friesland Resistance Museum, a very moving experience documenting the heroism during Nazi occupation.
- The sandbar islands of Terschelling and Vlieland, with their wide strands and bird sanctuaries.
- Planetarium of Eise Eisinga, remarkably accurate even today.

Groningen
- Groninger Museum, devoted to antiquities relating to the history of the province.
- The Bell Casting Museum, depicting the history of bell casting, with demonstrations.

Drenthe
- The fascinating Provinciaal Museum van Drenthe, exhibiting artifacts from the Stone Age and Roman sarcophagi.
- Noorder Dierenpark/Zoo, where animals roam in habitats as close to their natural homes as possible.
- 't Aole Compas, a reconstructed peatcutters' village.

WHAT TO SEE & DO

Before setting off to explore the rest of Friesland, take time to look around its capital city. Like most Dutch cities, Leeuwarden is best seen on foot. The VVV has an excellent walking-tour guide, **"A Walk Through the Town of Leeuwarden,"** that will take you to major points of interest.

 Fries Museum, Turfmarkt 24. ☎ **123-001.**

This fine museum houses prehistoric artifacts dating back to the Ice Age, medieval and Renaissance treasures, colorful painted furniture from Hindeloopen, Rembrandt's painting of his Frisian wife, Saskia (they were married in the village of St. Anna Parochie in 1634), a replica of a tobacco shop, costumes, and a multitude of other items that will give you a better understanding of these hardy, resourceful people. It's located in the town center.

    Admission: Dfl. 1 (50¢).

    Open: Tues–Sat 10am–5pm, Sun 1–5pm.

 Frisian Resistance Museum, Turfmarkt 24. ☎ **133-335.**

A very human, moving experience is in store when you visit this museum in the town center. It documents the heroism of the Frisian people during Nazi occupation in World War II with photos, personal mementos, and a taped radio message that actually went out over Radio Oranje plays as you view a diorama depicting a Frisian farmer listening intently. There's detailed information available in English, as well as a Walkman-taped commentary in English, to explain the exhibits and tell the story of the Dutch resistance movement. It's a certainty that you will look at the Frisian farmer in his fields through different eyes after a visit to this museum.

Admission: 2.50 ($1.30).

Open: Tues–Sat 10am–5pm, Sun 1–5pm.

Het Princessehof Museum, Grote Kerkstraat 9–15.

In the 18th century, this beautiful building in the town center was the home of Princess Maria Louise of Hessen-Kassel, William IV's mother; one of her rooms is preserved just as it was in her time. The museum also holds the largest collection of Dutch tiles in the world, as well as a marvelous collection of Chinese porcelain and ceramics from China and Holland.

Admission: Dfl. 3 ($1.55 adults, Dfl. 2 ($1.05) children.

Open: Mon–Sat 10am–5pm, Sun 2–5pm.

Provincial House, Tweebaksmarkt 52. ☎ **925-524.**

There's a bit of New York State here in the form of a bronze plaque that the DeWitt Historical Society of Tompkins County in Ithaca presented to the people of Leeuwarden in 1909 in gratitude for their having been the first to vote for Holland's recognition of the infant United States in 1782. There's also a letter written by John Adams in 1783 expressing that same gratitude. Another document of interest to Americans is that relating to one Petrus Stuiffsandt—the same Peter Stuyvesant who had such an important role in America's beginnings and who was born in Scherpenzeel, a Friesland town. The house is located in the town center.

Admission: Free.

Open: Inquire at the VVV for varying days and hours.

WHERE TO STAY

In Town

$ Hotel de Pauw, Stationsweg 10, 8911 AH Leeuwarden. ☎ **058/123-651.** 30 rms (none with bath).

Rates: Dfl. 43.50 ($23) single; Dfl. 77.50 ($40) double. AE, MC, V.

This old-fashioned budget hotel, with its Old Dutch lobby furnishings and wood-paneled bar, has rooms with and without private shower (all toilets are down the hall). The guest rooms are all quite adequate, but of varying standards. There's a good restaurant on the premises that serves lunch and dinner at moderate prices. The hotel is located across the street from the railway station.

★ Oranje Hotel, Stationsweg 4, 8901 BL Leeuwarden. ☎ **058/126-241.** Fax 058/121-441. 78 rms. A/C TV TEL

$ Rates (including breakfast, service, and VAT): Dfl. 165 ($87) single; Dfl. 210 ($110) double. AE, DC, MC, V.

You'd never suspect that this beautiful hotel is actually over a century old, so successful has its modernization been. Its location is convenient to the railway station, yet within an easy walk of everything you'll want to see in Leeuwarden. The nice thing is that the management failed to modernize its old-fashioned hospitality, liberally laced with genuine friendliness. The staff goes out of its way to make you feel at home, and you'll find yourself among lots of local residents in the bright, moderately priced restaurant and cozy bar. There's also a formal gourmet restaurant (see "Where to Dine," below) where I had perhaps my best meal in Holland. The guest rooms are luxuriously done up, with a table-and-armchairs grouping in one corner. Recommended.

A Luxury Château Nearby

 Hotel Lauswolt, van Harinxmaweg 10, 9244 CJ Beetsterzwaag.
☎ **05123/812-45.** Fax 05123/814-96. 58 rms. TV TEL

 Rates: From Dfl. 190 ($100) single; from Dfl. 270 ($142) double. Weekday and weekend packages available. AE, DC, MC, V.

Located on the edge of the typical Frisian village of Beetsterzwaag, 28 miles from Leeuwarden, this gracious three-story château is surrounded by green lawns and huge shade trees. There's an 18-hole golf course on the grounds, tennis courts, and any number of beautiful forest walks. The restaurant enjoys a top reputation throughout this part of Holland and is a member of the prestigious Alliance Gastronomique Néerlandaise. The decor throughout the château, in both public rooms and guest rooms, is one of quiet elegance, and the spacious guest rooms are luxuriously furnished. The hotel offers wheelchair access. The high level of service, swimming pool, and sauna add to the attractions of this lovely place. Highly recommended.

Bed-and-Breakfasts

The VVV, Stationsplein 1, Leeuwarden (☎ **06/3202-4060**), can also furnish names of town and country homes that welcome bed-and-breakfast guests. Rates, whether in a small town or a rural area, are standardized at Dfl. 35 ($18) per person.

WHERE TO DINE

Leeuwarden has several very good restaurants, and you'll find outdoor cafés and small local eateries serving good food at low prices in almost every village. You might also wander along the Nieuwestad canal, where there are several interesting choices.

In Town

In addition to the two establishments recommended below, you'll find Frisian specialties at moderate prices at **Onder de Luifel**, Stationsweg 6 (☎ **129-013**), open Monday through Saturday from 9am to 8pm. **De Stadthouder,** Nieuwestad 75 (☎ **121-568**), has a good Dutch/French menu at moderate prices; it's open daily from 10am to 9pm. In the old 16th-century Weigh House, the bistro **Herberg de Waag,** Nieuwestad 148B (☎ **137-250**), is the top-floor occupant, specializing in beef. It's open Monday through Saturday from 10am to 9:30pm.

$ The Oranje Tavern, Stationsweg 4. ☎ **126-241.**
Cuisine: DUTCH/LIGHT MEALS. **Reservations:** Not required.
Prices: Average meal Dfl. 15–30 ($8–$16), snacks and light meals Dfl. 10–15 ($5.25–$8). AE, DC, MC, V.
Open: Daily 10am–9:30pm.

This is the pleasant informal restaurant of the Oranje Hotel, with moderate prices and typical Dutch dishes available, as well as a wide range of other selections, sandwiches, and salads.

★ Restaurant l'Orangerie, Stationsweg 4. ☎ **126-241.**
Cuisine: FRENCH. **Reservations:** Required.
Prices: A la carte meals Dfl. 33–45 ($17–$24); fixed-price meal Dfl. 45 ($23) for three courses, Dfl. 55 ($29) for four courses, Dfl. 83 ($44) for five courses. AE, DC, MC, V.
Open: Dinner only, daily 6–10pm.

This gourmet restaurant of the Oranje Hotel is surprisingly sophisticated in both ambience and service. The menu is mostly French, and dishes are beautifully prepared with fresh, fresh ingredients. Their presentation, and the professional, yet friendly, manner of the staff matched the high standards of the food, and as I said above, the dinner I had here ranked with the best I experienced in Holland.

Worth the Drive

⭐ **Hotel Lauswolt,** van Harinxmaweg 10. ☎ **05126/12-45.**

Cuisine: FRENCH. **Reservations:** Required.
Prices: Fixed-price meal Dfl. 30–50 ($16–$26) at lunch, Dfl. 75–115 ($39–$60) at dinner. AE, DC, MC, V.
Open: Lunch daily noon–2pm; dinner daily 6:30–9:30pm.

Dine by candlelight in the gracious paneled dining room overlooking the garden in this lovely château. Fresh ingredients go into the menu's classic French dishes, and there's an exceptionally good wine cellar.

Around the Province

SUGGESTED CIRCULAR TOUR   From a Leeuwarden base, it's easy to make a circular swing around the province's most interesting towns and villages, beginning and ending in the capital. The suggested route is: Leeuwarden, Franeker, Harlingen, Makkum, Hindeloopen, Bolsward and the Aldfaers Erf Route (Forefathers Heritage Route), Sneek, Leeuwarden (see the descriptions below). Actually, it's at Sneek that you must choose to return to Leeuwarden or continue on to Groningen (for that routing, see below).

WHERE TO STAY & DINE EN ROUTE

Should you fall "victim" to the delights of Friesland rambling and decide to overnight it along the way, the following accommodations can be recommended.

In Harlingen

 Hotel Anna Casparii, Noorderhaven 67–71, 8861 AL Harlingen.
☎ **05178/120-65.** Fax 05178/145-40. 15 rms (10 with bath). TV

Rates: Dfl. 65 ($34) single without bath, Dfl. 95 ($50) single with bath or shower; Dfl. 95 ($50) double without bath, Dfl. 125 ($66) double with bath or shower. AE, MC, V.

This charming little canal-house hotel in the town center has comfortable and attractive guest rooms. Ask for one with a view of the sea. There's also a very good restaurant with moderate prices, specializing in seafood fresh from the boats that come into this fishing village.

In Bolsward

Hotel de Wijnberg, Marktplein 5, 8701 KG Bolsward. ☎ **05157/2220.**
Fax 05157/2665. 37 rms. TV TEL

Rates: Dfl. 50 ($26) single; Dfl. 90–106 ($47–$56) double. AE, MC, V.

The guest rooms in this modern hotel on the town square are nicely decorated and quite comfortably furnished. There's a good restaurant and open-air terrace with an extensive menu—both à la carte and fixed price, as well as a Tourist Menu at Dfl. 25 ($13.15).

FRIESLAND'S TOWNS

FRANEKER   In this enchanting little town, 10¹/₂ miles west of Leeuwarden, stop to visit the ❏ **Planetarium of Eise Eisinga,** Eise Eisingastraat 3. This simple house was the home of a woolcomber who in the late 1700s spent seven years building a replica of the planetary system in his evening leisure hours. Guides are on hand to explain the works, amazingly accurate even today, which are in an attic room. Admission is Dfl. 7.50 ($4), and from May through September it's open Monday through Saturday from 10am to 12:30pm and 1:30 to 5pm and on Sunday from 1 to 5pm; closed Sunday and Monday other months.

HARLINGEN   This picture-postcard-pretty little harbor town 18 miles west of Leeuwarden sits by the Wadden Sea, which separates the mainland from the offshore sandbar islands of ⊠ **Terschelling** and ⊠ **Vlieland.** The wide strands of these islands draw vacationers every summer and **bird sanctuaries** attract a host of feathered visitors.

Harlingen itself is a maze of tiny canals filled with fishing boats and lined with gabled canal houses. Visit the **Hannemahuis Museum,** Voorstraat 56 (open April to June, Tuesday through Saturday from 2 to 5pm; July through mid-September, daily from 10am to 5pm), to see its seafaring exhibits, and stop in to see the **tile-painting workshop,** Harlinger Tegelfabriek at Voorstraat 75.

If you have the time and can't resist the temptation, you can take a 1¹/₂-hour ⊠ **ferry ride** out to Terschelling or Vlieland island for about Dfl. 40 ($21), plus another Dfl. 20 ($10.50) for your car, round-trip. A Hovercraft crossing (subject to the weather) costs an additional Dfl. 20 ($10.50).

MAKKUM   There have been **tile makers** and **ceramics craftspeople** in Makkum, 10 miles south of Harlingen, since the 1500s, and the craft is carried on today at the ⊠ **Tichelaar** workshop, where you are taken through the entire process and see the exquisite designs being painted by hand. This interesting firm has been in operation for over 300 years, and in 1960 the "royal" designation was conferred on their work. This is the only Dutch ornamental earthenware made from Dutch clay, and the factory has used the same procedures since the 17th century. The salesroom is a bonanza for buying anything from a simple tile to a larger piece with an elaborate design.

In the old ⊠ **Weigh House** there's a fascinating museum of five rooms filled with examples of Makkum earthenware from the 17th through the 19th century. The building itself is worth the stop.

HINDELOOPEN   In this tiny little town 10 miles south of Makkum on the shores of the IJsselmeer, talented craftspeople have for centuries adorned their homes, their furniture, their built-in cupboard beds, and even their wooden coat hangers with the vivid colors and intricately entwined vines and flowers that we associate with the Pennsylvania Dutch in America. It is thought that originally the designs were brought from Scandinavia by Hindeloopen sailors who sailed the North Sea in the days when the IJsselmeer was the Zuiderzee. Wherever it originated, this colorful decoration has reached its highest development in this little village, and a good place to view it is at **Stallmann's,** Nieuwstad 22 (☎ 05142/2637). Every wooden surface in the house, which dates from 1650, is covered with delightful designs.

BOLSWARD   From Hindeloopen, turn north again and retrace your steps to the town of Workum, then continue north on the signposted road to the little town of Bolsward. This is the starting point of one Friesland's most intriguing attractions, the ⊠ **Aldfaers Erf Route (Forefathers Heritage Route).** Not one town, but an entire small area of restored buildings grouped into three country villages, the Aldfaers Erf leads you to **Exmorra,** with its 19th-century grocer's and schoolhouse; to **Allingawier,**

where a bakery serves Frisian pastries and snacks and a slide presentation is given in an old church; and to **Piaam,** with its bird museum. The buildings are open every day from 9am to 6pm during the summer months.

SNEEK From Bolsward, drive 10 miles southeast to this little town whose lakes, canals, and waterways have made it a **yachting center.** Both the **Town Hall** and the **Frisian Shipping Museum** are worth a visit; and take note of the beautiful old (1613) **Watergate,** the only remains of the town's old defense works.

This is where you must decide whether to return to Leeuwarden via the signposted road north (about 18 miles) or head for Groningen.

Friesland to Groningen

From Sneek, take A7 for the approximately 50-mile drive to Groningen. If you've been on the move all day, Drachten is an ideal place to break this stretch of driving. From Leeuwarden, it's about 58 miles to Groningen via N355.

WHERE TO STAY & DINE EN ROUTE

 Hotel Drachten, Zonnedauw 1, 9202 PE Drachten. ☎ **05120/207-05.** Fax 05120/232-32. 48 rms. TV

Rates: Dfl. 125 ($55) single; Dfl. 190 ($100) double. Lower rates on weekends. AE, DC, MC, V.

This four-star modern motel sits at the junction of two major motorways (the A1 and A7). Its guest rooms are nicely appointed, and there's a coffee shop, bar, and an excellent restaurant—with fondues a specialty and many gourmet dishes on the menu.

2 Groningen

The Province of Groningen is one of Holland's most commercial and industrial, and at the same time one of its most historic. The busy capital city of Groningen is an important port with oceangoing vessels sailing up the 15-mile-long Eems Canal from Delfzijl, the province's largest port. Slochteren is the source of the world's largest-known natural-gas deposit (discovered in 1959) and supplies over one-third of Holland's power and heat requirements, and also has some very attractive old buildings. Heiligerlee is an agricultural industry center, and has famous bell factories producing the smallest dinner bells as well as massive carillons.

The province's long history, stretching back beyond the 12th century, is reflected in the architecture of many buildings in the capital city, in numerous terp (mound) villages, in a 15th-century castle, in a 14th-century monastery, and in any number of picturesque villages. Among historical figures it can claim as its own is Abel Tasman, one of the greatest of Dutch navigators, who was born in 1603 in the town of Lutjegast.

Most visitors base themselves in the city of Groningen, but there are one or two optional choices worthy of note.

Groningen, the Provincial Capital

Groningen, capital of the province of the same name, is 184km (114 miles) northeast of Amsterdam and 57km (35 miles) east of Leeuwarden. There are good rail and bus connections to Groningen from around the country, and the rail and bus stations adjoin each other south of the city center. If you're driving, you can reach Groningen by A7, A28, and N355.

The **VVV office,** Kattendiep 6 (☎ **06/3202-3050;** fax 050/136-358), can furnish information on both the city and the remainder of the province, as well as book accommodations. They also provide a free booklet, "Rekreatiekrant," which lists current entertainment and cultural events.

The **telephone area code** for Groningen is 050.

WHAT TO SEE & DO

You'll want to spend some time in the city of Groningen with its two beautifully designed central squares, the 15th-century **St. Martenkerk** (St. Martin is Groningen's patron saint and the patron saint of tourists!), and the Renaissance **Goudkantoor** (gold office) near the Town Hall.

The ✪ **Groninger Museum,** across from the train station (☎ **183-343**), open Tuesday through Saturday from 10am to 5pm and on Sunday from 1 to 5pm, is devoted to antiquities relating to the history of the city and the province, with a collection of Eastern ceramics, paintings, and prints, and sculpture from the 16th century to present-day modern art. There's an admission fee of Dfl. 6 ($3.15).

The interesting **Nordelijk Scheepvaart en Tabacologisch Museum,** Brugstraat 24–26 (☎ **122-202**), traces the history of shipping in the northern provinces and the history of Holland's long involvement with the tobacco trade. Admission is Dfl. 5 ($2.60), and hours are 10am to 5pm Tuesday through Saturday, from 1 to 5pm on Sunday.

More than 250 years of topiary gardening have produced the breathtaking 250-acre **Prinsenhof Gardens** in the Prinsenhof (entrance on Turfsingel), open April to mid-October, daily from 10am to sundown, which has been the seat of the bishops of Groningen since 1568. There's no admission fee.

ORGANIZED TOURS   During June, July, and August, there are regular ✪ **Canals of Groningen cruises.** Contact the VVV or call **128-379** or **122-713** for schedules, fares, and departure points.

WHERE TO STAY

In Town

Hotels in a wide price range are available in Groningen, and the VVV can also furnish a list of a limited number of private homes near the city that take paying guests at about Dfl. 35 ($18.50) per person per night.

$ **De Doelen,** Grote Markt 36, 9711 VL Groningen. ☎ **050/127-041.** Fax 050/146-112. 49 rms. TV TEL

Rates: Dfl. 150 ($79) single; Dfl. 195 ($102) double. AE, MC, V.

De Doelen is about as centrally located as you can get. It has nice guest rooms with attractive decor and comfortable furnishings, and a steakhouse restaurant with moderate prices.

★ **Mercure Hotel Groningen,** Expositielaan 7, 9727 AK Groningen. ☎ **050/258-400.** Fax 050/271-828. 156 rms. A/C MINIBAR TV TEL

Rates: Dfl. 140 ($73) single; Dfl. 190 ($100) double. AE, DC, MC, V.

This modern four-star motel is convenient to downtown, the city park, and the university. There's a good restaurant (see "Where to Dine," below), a cocktail bar, indoor swimming pool, solarium, and sauna. Among the extras in its well-appointed guest rooms are satellite TVs, videos, and trouser press.

A Nearby Hotel

 Family Hotel Groningen, Groningerweg 19, 9765 TA Paterswolde,
☎ **05907/954-00.** Fax 05907/1157. Telex 77157. 72 rms. MINIBAR TV TEL
Rates: Dfl. 150 ($79) single; Dfl. 250 ($131) double. AE, DC, MC, V.

Set on 30 wooded acres, this lovely hotel has spacious guest rooms, wheelchair access,
24-hour world news on CNN, a gift shop, a hairdresser, a sauna, a solarium, a swimming pool, tennis courts, and bikes for hire. There's a nice bar and good restaurant.
A restful respite from the city center—a 10-minute drive.

WHERE TO DINE

In Groningen, hotel restaurants offer the best top-level dining. The **Mercure Restaurant,** Expositielaan 7 (☎ **258-400**), in the hotel listed above, offers excellent Dutch
and French menus at moderate prices; **Café De Stadlander,** Poelestraat 35
(☎ **127-191**), features the Tourist Menu and an inexpensive à la carte menu; and
the **Croissanterie Cave du Patron,** Grote Markt 36 (☎ **127-041**), in De Doelen
hotel (see "Where to Stay," above), is a convenient, quite good drop-in spot for inexpensive sandwiches, salads, light meals, and snacks at Dfl. 9 ($4.50) and under.

Around the Province

While one circular tour of provincial towns is not convenient in Groningen, the
listings below are arranged by geographic areas so that all under one heading may
be visited in easy day trips.

TOWNS NORTH & WEST OF GRONINGEN

WARFFUM   About 16 miles north of Groningen, Warffum is typical of the "mound
villages" that were built above flood level in past centuries. ★ **Het Hogeland (High-
land Museum)** holds fascinating relics from the mounds, as well as medieval costumes
and other artifacts. It's open April through September, Tuesday through Saturday from
10am to 5pm and on Sunday from 1 to 5pm, with an admission of Dfl. 6 ($3.15).

UITHUIZEN   Some 20 miles north of Groningen in Uithuizen, the **Castle of
Menkemaborg,** a double-moated fortified manor house, dates from the 14th century,
with 17th- and 18th-century wings. It's beautifully furnished in the style of its past
and is noted for its 18th-century formal gardens. There's a restaurant serving lunch
from 11am to 2pm in the old carriage house. Open Tuesday through Saturday from
10am to 5pm and on Sunday from 1 to 5pm in summer; shorter hours in winter.
Admission is Dfl. 6 ($3.15). Closed the month of January.

DELFZIJL   This port city, 20 miles east of Groningen, is also a shipbuilding city
and important industrial city. Aside from Delfzijl's busy, colorful harbor, there's
an ★ **aquarium and shell exhibition** at Zeebadweg 7 (☎ **05960/123-18**), open
Monday through Saturday from 10am to 5pm; admission is Dfl. 6 ($3.15).

SLOCHTEREN   This little town, about 15 miles west of Groningen, is the source
of the world's largest-known natural gas deposit (discovered in 1959) and supplies
over one-third of Holland's power and heat requirements. There are several picturesque old buildings, and at the 16th-century **Fraeylemaborg,** Hoofdweg 32
(☎ **05982/1568**), there are lovely woods and gardens. Fraeylemaborg is open Tuesday through Sunday from 10am to noon and 1 to 5pm; admission is Dfl. 4 ($2.10).

HEILIGERLEE   This agricultural industry center, 21 miles east of Groningen, is most famous for its bell factories that produce sizes from the smallest dinner bells right up to massive carillons. The ◼ **Bell Casting Museum,** Provincialeweg 46 (☎ **05970/ 217-99**), is set in the restored Van Bergen bell-casting works, and its exhibits depict the history of bell casting. There are also casting demonstrations. It's open Tuesday through Friday from 10am to 5pm and on Saturday from 5pm; admission is Dfl. 6 ($3.15).

Where to Stay and Dine in Delfzijl

Du Bastion, Waterstraat 78, 9934 AX Delfzijl. ☎ **05960/18-771.** Fax 05960/17-147. 40 rms. TV TEL

Rates (including breakfast): Dfl. 90 ($47) single; Dfl. 110 ($58) double. AE, MC, V.

This small hotel in the town center has comfortable rooms at moderate rates. There's a good moderately priced restaurant that features traditional Dutch dishes as well as the Tourist Menu.

TOWNS SOUTH OF GRONINGEN

LEEK   The **Rijtuigmuseum (National Carriage Museum)** in Leek, about 14 miles southwest of Groningen, has a wonderful collection of antique horse-drawn carriages, sleighs, and the uniforms and accessories of their drivers. Open Easter through September, Monday through Saturday from 9am to 5pm and on Sunday from 1 to 5pm; admission is Dfl. 6 ($3.15).

HAREN   Exotic flowers and plants of all climates, from alpine to tropical, are collected in the **Botanical Garden and Tropical Paradise** (an adjunct to Groningen University), located in Haren, about 3 miles south of Groningen.

TER APEL   Hidden away in a peaceful forest of beech trees near the little village of Ter Apel (not far from Stadskanaal, about 24 miles southeast of Groningen) is a tranquil ◼ **monastery** whose cloister dates from the 1300s. Plan time for walking into the surrounding woods.

---

3   Drenthe

Mooi Drenthe, the Dutch call it, meaning "beautiful Drenthe." And with good reason, for this is a land of deep forests, broad moors and peat bogs, small lakes, and picturesque villages. Its beauty and the traditional life of its peasant farmers and peatcutters drew Vincent van Gogh for a three-month sojourn early in his career, painting his moody, moving canvases *The Potato Eaters* and *Weavers* during that period.

Drenthe is also a land of prehistoric mysteries in the form of *hunebedden* (giants' beds), huge boulders that must have served as burial mounds. It is believed that these gigantic smooth stones were transported here from Scandinavia by Ice Age glaciers, and legend has it that they were the home of a race of giants. Be that as it may, Holland's earliest inhabitants obviously used them to mark tombs since they have yielded stone axes, wooden vessels, and other relics. Drenthe has also been the site of large deposits of oil, providing roughly one-third of the country's total production from wells that are carefully landscaped to prevent their marring the lovely countryside.

Assen, the Provincial Capital

Some 42km (25 miles) south of Groningen, Assen is the capital of Drenthe. The best rail and bus connections are from Groningen, and the rail and bus station is on Stationsstraat, a short walk from the town center. If you're driving, you can reach Assen by A28.

The **VVV office** is at Brink 42 (☎ **05920/143-24;** fax 05920/173-06). Although easily toured from an Amsterdam, Leeuwarden, or Groningen base, Drenthe is idyllic holiday country, with a wealth of small hotels, cottages, and campgrounds. Since both Friesland and Groningen provinces can be toured from a Drenthe base, this may be the place to combine a relaxing holiday with sightseeing. The VVV can help you set up a stay in the province in accommodations that appeal to you most and in your price range. Refer to the VVV Tourist Menu and "Neerlands Dis" booklets for small local restaurants, the best source of meals.

Assen's **telephone area code** is 05920.

Situated in the former Provinciehuis (Provincial Hall), the fascinating ✪ **Provinciaal Museum van Drenthe,** Brink 5, exhibits the Stone Age artifacts that have come from Drenthe's *hunebedden,* as well as weapons, pottery, and jewelry of Celtic and Merovingian origin. There are also Roman sarcophagi and other well-preserved items that have turned up in the peat bogs of Drenthe. These silent relics of the past are captivating to anyone with the tiniest interest in history. It's open Tuesday through Sunday from 10am to 5pm. Admission is Dfl. 5 ($2.60).

What to See and Do Around the Province

There are more than 50 *hunebedden* in the province, found primarily around Borger, Rolde, Anlo, Emmen, Sleen, Vries, and Havelte. In Havelte, residents have had to restore their "giants' beds" to where they lay for centuries, since during World War II Nazi occupying troops dislodged the huge boulders to clear an airstrip and dumped them all into a large hole.

EMMEN   Located 23 miles southwest of Assen, Drenthe's largest town is a delightful mix of old buildings left from its village beginnings and modern edifices reflecting its prosperity in recent years. Emmen's most appealing tourist attraction is the gigantic ✪ **Noorder Dierenpark/Zoo,** Hoofdstraat 18. Here animals roam freely in habitats as close to their natural homes as possible. There's also a magnificent butterfly garden, and "Biochron," an impressive depiction of the history of life on earth. Admission is Dfl. 19 ($10) for adults and Dfl. 15 ($8) for children, and it's open daily from 9am to 6pm year-round.

BARGER-COMPASCUUM   Set squarely in this town's peat moors about 5 miles southeast of Emmen is the open-air museum called ✪ **'t Aole Compas,** at Berkenrode 4. At this reconstructed peatcutters' village, you can see demonstrations of peat cutting, as well as butter churning, weaving, and clog making. It's open mid-March through October, daily from 9am to 5:30pm. Admission is Dfl. 15 ($8) for adults, Dfl. 7.50 ($4) for children.

SCHOONOORD   Here on the grounds of the ✪ **De Zenen Marken Open-Air Museum,** Tramstraat 73 in Schoonoord, 15 miles northeast of Emmen, are sod huts, a smithy, a saw mill, a bee farm, and geological exhibits. It's open March through October, daily from 9am to 6pm. Admission is Dfl. 4.50 ($2.35) for adults and Dfl. 3.50 ($1.85) for children.

THE OIL FIELDS   Near **Coevorden and Schoonebeek** (about 16 miles south of Emmen) is one of Europe's largest oil fields. While it has indisputably brought change to this part of sleepy Drenthe, beauty-conscious natives hurry to surround each pumping installation with a grove of fast-growing trees to cloak these industrial pockmarks in nature's green drapery. Schoonebeek has, in fact, been called "the best-dressed oil field in the world."

THE LAKES   While there are scores of lovely small lakes within Drenthe's borders, it shares its two largest with neighboring Groningen province. ◪ **Lake Paterswolde,** some 12 miles northeast of Assen on the Groningen border, is a sailing and water-sports center with a holiday village on its shores. To the southeast, **Lake Zuidlaren** and its village by the same name also attracts water-sports enthusiasts; in October, this is the setting for one of Holland's largest horse fairs.

Central Holland

17

From the new to the very old, Holland's central provinces spread before you its unique history, incomparable scenic beauties, and incredible engineering feats. The IJsselmeer polders are the country's newest land, reclaimed from the former Zuiderzee. Utrecht is nearly 2,000 years old. Overijssel and Gelderland share a park-like landscape punctuated by historic towns, castles, industrial towns, and villages that can only be described as "quaint."

GETTING AROUND CENTRAL HOLLAND All four provinces have good **rail and bus** connections from Amsterdam and other major centers, with discount tourist tickets frequently available. Check with any VVV office for schedules and special prices. **Drivers** should check with a VVV office for details of several signposted tourist routes. The flatness of the landscape also makes this ideal **cycling** country.

1 Flevoland

For centuries the Dutch have been protecting themselves from an ever-encroaching sea. One of their most formidable opponents has always been the Zuiderzee, a salty incursion of the North Sea that began A.D. 200 to 300 when it washed over Frisian dunes to flood vast inland areas, culminating in the 1200s when a series of storms drove it all the way to the inland lake known as Flevo. Around its shores the sleepy, picturesque villages presented quite a different picture when their harbors were alive with great ships that sailed for the Dutch West and East India Companies, and carried Dutch navigators on explorations to the far reaches of the South Pacific and around Cape Horn, North Sea fishermen returned to Zuiderzee home ports, and Amsterdam flourished as ships from around the world sailed to its front door.

Still, Holland needed to control the waterway, which had earned a reputation as a "graveyard of ships," and as early as the 1600s there was talk of driving back the sea and reclaiming the land it then covered. Parliament—in the manner of governments since time began—finally got around to authorizing such a project in 1918, and in the 1920s work was begun. By 1930 some 50,000 acres had been dried out in the Wieringermeer Polder and four more polders were on the drawing board. In 1932, in an unparalleled feat of engineering, the North Sea was sealed off with the 19-mile Enclosing Dike, and since then the Dutch have been pumping dry thousands of acres, and in the process converting fishing villages into farming villages, joining island villages to the mainland, and transforming North Sea fishermen into IJsselmeer freshwater fishermen.

Periodic storms and floods hindered the ongoing work, but the most devastating blow came in April 1945 during the final days of World War II. Nazi troops, in a desperate effort to hold back Allied forces, bombarded the Enclosing Dike and sent the sea flooding over the entire polder, leaving a seascape 12 to 14 feet in depth, dotted with church spires. The Nazis surrendered just 18 days later and the Dutch lost no time in setting things right again—they pumped the polder dry in 4 months, and in the space of 12 months homes were once more occupied and crops were being sown in the fields. As they have done over the ages, Hollanders had accomplished the seemingly impossible!

Today the 10 villages surrounding Emmerloord township occupy 119,000 acres in the second of the projected polders; the third (East Flevoland Polder) came dry in 1957, adding some 133,000 acres of usable land; the South Flevoland Polder (142,000 acres) fell dry in 1968; and the Markerwaard dike that will make possible completion of the five-polder plan has been completed.

What's Special About Central Holland

Flevoland
- Zuiderzee Project, with exhibits explaining how the dikes were built, the pumping process, and the final drying operation.
- Polder towns, once fishing villages and now farming villages.
- Smoked eels, offered everywhere.

Overijssel
- Beautiful forests.
- Picturesque castles and villages.
- The Venice-like village of Giethoorn.

Gelderland
- The Netherlands Open-Air Museum, a delightful minicourse in Dutch history, customs, dress, and architecture.
- Boat rides on the Rhine.
- De Hoge Veluwe National Park, a wealth of nature's treasures.
- National Museum Kröller-Müller, with a collection of van Goghs and Mondrians, and a sculpture park.

Utrecht
- The magnificent Domkerk in the capital, with one of the best views of the city from the tower.
- The Dutch Rail Museum, for train buffs.
- From musical box to barrel organ, a delightful collection of mechanical music makers.

From time to time in the polders you'll come across groups of men working along-side the road. These are the *polderjongens* (polder men), who travel from place to place, wherever there is a need for their special training. The polder settlers, incidentally, only rent their land from the government, which retains title, and obtaining a lease entails work on the polders for extended periods before an application can even be filed.

Riding along broad, straight roads between flat fields laced with equally straight canals, even the most world-weary traveler must thrill to this awesome accomplishment in defeating the forces of the sea!

The Polder Towns of Flevoland

The polders can be easily visited from a base in Amsterdam or The Hague, as a natural incorporation of one route to the northern provinces, or as part of a one- or two-day circle of the IJsselmeer (see Chapter 16). See also Biddinghuizen/Dronten, below.

LELYSTAD   Take time to walk around this newest of the polder towns (31 miles northeast of Amsterdam), with a population of some 50,000. On Saturday mornings the town square is filled with vendors, many in traditional dress, carrying on the old market-day traditions.

Look for the ◩ **Poldermuseum Nieuw Land** (☎ 03200/607-99) just off the Markerwaard dike approach road and allow plenty of time to ponder the exhibits that explain the Zuiderzee Project in great detail. You'll learn how the dikes were built, all about the pumping process, and the final drying-up operation. There are also relics of ships that went to a watery grave in the Zuiderzee, possibly at the very spot on which you stand. It's a fascinating place that will send you off with a much deeper understanding of what you'll be seeing. It's open Monday through Friday from 10am to 5pm and on Saturday and Sunday from 11:30am to 5pm.

BIDDINGHUIZEN/DRONTEN   Due east of Lelystad, the marvelous recreation center of ✪ **Flevohof,** at Spijkweg 30 (☎ **03211/1524**), centers on the activities of farms that cover some 350 acres. On the livestock farm you can actually spend a day engaged in such rural chores as milking a cow, churning butter, or pitching hay. There are also modern demonstration and exhibition centers, where you can see the Holland Happening audiovisual presentation, the beautiful Gardens of the World, and a great fun park with horse-drawn trains, a Children's Village, and a Red Indian village. Several restaurants take care of any hunger pangs. There are also some 70 very comfortable rental bungalows, ideal for those who prefer a noncity sightseeing base. Open April through October daily from 10am to 6pm. Admission is Dfl. 28 ($15) for adults, Dfl. 25 ($13) for children.

KETELHAVEN   In this little town on the shores of the Ketelmeer (between Lelystad and Urk), the **Museum voor Sheepsarcheologie** (☎ **03210/132-87**) exhibits ships wrecked in the Zuiderzee as far back as Roman times, all revealed as waters were pumped out to make the polder. It's open daily from 10am to 5pm, and admission is Dfl. 3.50 ($1.85) for adults and Dfl. 1.50 (80¢) for children.

URK   This quaint little fishing village 10 miles north of Lelystad was for more than 700 years a Zuiderzee island, its isolation undisturbed until the reclamation project joined it to the mainland in 1942. In 1948 a roadway was constructed to facilitate an overland route to the village, a roadway so unwelcome to residents that they promptly banned all automobiles, requiring them to park on the outskirts. In the end, practicalities (and the Dutch are nothing if not practical), such as getting to market the eels for which their fishing fleet is famous, forced them to reconsider and lift the restriction. So while you will certainly encounter automobiles in the narrow, brick-paved streets of Urk, it's *still* a good idea to park outside and take to your feet.

As you walk past picturesque brick homes lining those tiny streets, notice the decorated wooden doors and elaborate wrought ironwork. At long piers in the harbor, you'll see the sturdy fishing boats that sail in search of eels. A word of caution: Smoked eel is sold everywhere in Urk, and you'll show yourself an expert if you select only the skinny ones (fat ones aren't nearly so nice).

Many of the women of Urk still wear traditional long dresses, light-blue corsets with protective patches of chamois leather for longer wear, and a hand-embroidered *kraplap* (bodice cover), as well as garnet necklaces and bonnets with earflaps. Men sport baggy felt pants held up with silver buttons adorned with scenes from the Bible, and blue knit stockings with their hand-stitched shoes. Many do not speak English, and while they're quite cordial to outsiders like you and me (and provide plenty of souvenirs for sale), they still insist—actually, *require*—that we respect their Sunday customs, when it is forbidden to drive an automobile, sail a boat, or ride a bicycle. If you can walk into town on a Sunday morning just after church services end, you'll see most of Urk's citizens making a ritual walk through the town and down to the harbor.

SCHOKLAND   This town is not much more than a wide spot in the road nowadays, situated on a small mound only 20 feet above the surrounding flatland on the road east of Urk that runs from Nagele to Ens. It now consists of a church, a cannon from the 1500s that once was fired to warn of rising waters, and a few old anchors left from the days when there was an island fishing village here. Unlike Urk, which was left with an IJsselmeer harbor, the polder completely surrounded Schokland and the village faded away.

Keep a sharp eye for this place, however, for the museum in the church is not to be missed. Called the **IJsselmeer Poldersmuseum (Seafloor Museum)** (☎ **03200/ 607-99**), it holds Bronze Age tools, mammoth bones, and other prehistoric relics, as well as stone coffins from the 1100s and pottery dating as far back as 900. All were discovered on the sea bottom when the polder was drained. It's open 10am to 5pm Monday through Saturday and 1 to 5pm on Sunday, with an admission of Dfl. 7.50 ($4) for adults and Dfl. 4 ($2.10) for children 4 to 15.

2   Overijssel

The Province of Overijssel is all too often a pass-through part of Holland for tourists. And that's really a shame, because within its boundaries lie beautiful forests, lakes, and parks; steep-roofed, half-timbered farmhouses; the medieval town of Ootmarsum; the Venice-like village of Giethoorn, where everyone gets around on canals instead of streets; picturesque castles and villages where your camera will be welcomed; and the strict Calvinist village of Staphorst where it won't. Its capital is Zwolle, whose fortified walls have been demolished and replaced by the greenery of parks and landscaped lawns, the moat transformed into a tree-lined canal.

You'll find the **regional VVV office** at Grote Kerkplein 14, Zwolle (☎ **038/ 213-900;** fax 038/222-679).

The Provincial Towns of Overijssel

This province extends from the young Noordoostpolder in the northwest to Twente in the east with its history rooted in antiquity to the Salland district bordered by the Vecht and IJssel Rivers where historic towns have found prosperity through 20th-century industry.

ZWOLLE   The provincial capital of Zwolle is ringed by canals and fortified gates that remind us of its long history. Look for the **Sassenpoort** gateway that dates from 1408 and sports four octagonal towers.

The **Provincial Overijssels Museum (Provinciaal Overijssel Museum),** Melkmarkt 14 (☎ **038/214-650**), features exhibits relating to Zwolle's history, including an authentically restored 16th-century kitchen, and an interesting collection of French furniture. Open Tuesday through Saturday from 10am to 5pm and on Sunday from 2 to 5pm; admission is Dfl. 2.50 ($1.30).

St. Michaelskerk dates from the early 1400s and is interesting for its triangular hall, for its famous 4,000-pipe Schnitger organ, and as the burial place of the renowned religious writer Thomas à Kempis, who spent over 70 years here.

STAPHORST   North of Zwolle on the Meppel road, this is the Dutch village of your imagination, with colorfully dressed residents living as their ancestors did. This is no tourist act, and you'll seldom get an enthusiastic welcome from these devout Calvinists. That especially applies on Sunday, when the entire population observes a regimen that dates back centuries: With downcast eyes, separate lines of men and women form a silent procession to the churches. No automobiles are allowed into the village on the Sabbath, nor is there anything so frivolous as bicycle riding. Whenever you come to Staphorst—on Sunday or a weekday—be sure to respect their conservative ways and keep the cameras out of sight.

GIETHOORN   Northwest of Staphorst, you wouldn't want to miss this town with no streets, only canals. Leave the car and follow a path to the ★ **main canal,** where motorboats and punts wait to take you past enchanting canalside cottages.

Other charming villages to seek out are **Ommen** (look for the Eerde castle) and **Dalfsen.**

KAMPEN   Some 10 miles west of Zwolle, oceangoing vessels tie up at Kampen wharves on the River IJssel, continuing a tradition of trade that goes back to the Middle Ages.

Stop in at the **Town Hall (Oude Raadhuis)** for a look at the Aldermen's Room (Schepenzaal), with its rich paneling and great carved fireplace that date from the 1540s. Open 9am to 5pm Monday through Friday.

DEVENTER   About 16 miles south of Zwolle, this town had its beginnings in the 11th century, but has kept up with the march of time in its economic life. Among the products manufactured here are Smyrna carpets and metal goods, and its own Deventer Koek (a delicious spicy gingerbread) has outgrown the cottage-industry stage. With all that, you'll see some fine medieval houses along its streets.

The **Municipal Museum** holds artifacts relating to the area and a marvelous collection of costumes (open 10am to 4pm, Monday through Friday; small admission charge), and the large library of **medieval books and manuscripts** in the Town Hall is well worth a look (open Monday through Friday from 10am to 4pm; free).

A few miles west of Deventer, **Rijssen** and **Holten** are lovely little villages whose residents tenderly care for the graves in a Canadian war cemetery.

Where to Stay

Because Overijssel is so easily reached from major centers like Amsterdam, few tourists seek accommodations within the province itself. There is, however, one very special inn in Ootmarsum (listed below) that will tempt you to move in for a few days as you explore the contrasting faces of Overijssel.

★ **Hotel de Wiemsel,** Winhoffin 2, 7631 HX Ootmarsum. ☎ **05419/921-55.** Fax 05419/932-95. 49 rms. MINIBAR TV TEL

Rates (including service and VAT): Dfl. 225–330 ($118–$173) single; Dfl. 295–400 ($155–$210) double. AE, DC, MC, V.

This country inn (about 35 miles from Zwolle) has the look of a traditional farmhouse, with timber-and-brick construction topped by a steeply sloping roof. Inside, all is graciousness, from the antique-filled lobby and lounges to the attractive dining room. Each of the spacious guest rooms has a terrace, with dividers separating a living room area from sleeping quarters. The rooms feature baths with heated towel racks, refrigerators, and radios, among other amenities.

The setting, in a beautiful area not far from the German border, lends itself to peaceful days of outdoor rambling, and the hotel can send you off via bicycle or on horseback (from its own stables) with a picnic lunch. On the grounds there are lighted tennis courts, an indoor swimming pool, a solarium, and a sauna. Aside from nature's beauties, there is also the lovely village of Ootmarsum and other nearby sights to fill your days. Gourmet meals are served in the restaurant, costing Dfl. 70 to 120 ($36–$63), without wine.

Where to Dine

In addition to the following restaurant in Blokzijl (north of Zwolle, about 8 miles from Emmeloord), the Hotel de Wiemsel (see "Where to Stay," above) offers gourmet meals.

⭐ **Kaatje Bij de Sluis,** Brouwerstraat 20, Blokzijl. ☎ **05272/1833.**
Cuisine: SEAFOOD/CONTINENTAL. **Reservations:** Recommended.
Prices: Fixed-price meals Dfl. 55–135 ($29–$71). AE, DC, MC, V.
Open: Lunch Wed–Fri and Sun noon–3pm; dinner Wed–Sun 6–9:30pm.

Its name means "Kate's by the Sluice," appropriate enough in this small fishing village that has become forever landlocked—losing its port to the Zuidezee project. The kitchen here has earned a fine reputation that lures Amsterdammers to make the 60-mile drive across the polder just to have dinner. The freshest ingredients are used and the menu changes daily—sometimes twice in the course of a day—according to what's available. Seafood, as you might expect, is high on the list of specialties, along with beef and wild duck. There are also eight comfortable double rooms if you decide to stop overnight.

3 Gelderland

Gelderland is the province of the Rhine, and its large parks, nature reserves, and recreation centers are favorite holiday venues for Hollanders from around the country. North of the Rhine, stretching to sandy beaches along the Veluwemeer that separate it from the Flevoland polder—the region known as "The Veluwe" is the largest nature reserve in Holland, and offers all kinds of camping facilities as well as bungalow and other holiday accommodations.

The Veluwe, however, is just one face of this large province. Its cities beckon with attractions like the royal palace museum in Apeldoorn and Arnhem's Netherlands Open-Air Folklore Museum. For centuries an independent duchy ruled by the dukes of Gelderland, the province has castles all over the place, some of which can be visited.

Arnhem, the Provincial Capital

Arnhem, 73 miles south of Zwolle, is Gelderland's capital city. Its name became a household word during World War II when it sustained massive Allied air attacks against its Nazi occupiers, and today thousands make pilgrimages to its battlefields each year. On a less grim note, however, Arnhem is a city of parks, a marvelous open-air museum, and the departure point for boat trips on the Rhine.

The **VVV office** is at Stationsplein 45 (☎ **085/420-330;** fax 085/422-644).

WHAT TO SEE & DO

In the City

Right in the heart of Arnhem, the 100 acres of the ◼ **Netherlands Open-Air Folklore Museum,** Schelmseweg 89 (☎ **576-111**), hold a delightful mini-course in Dutch history, customs, dress, and architecture. Gathered from all around the country, farmhouses, step-gabled town houses, windmills, colorful costumes of the past, and even ancient means of transport bring together in one place much of the Holland of years gone by. If you see nothing else in Arnhem, don't miss this. Open Monday through Friday from 9:30am to 5pm and on Saturday and Sunday from 10am to 5pm. Admission is Dfl. 12.50 ($6.55) for adults, Dfl. 8 ($4.20) for children.

In the **Arnhem Municipal Museum,** Utrechtseweg 87, are archeological relics found in the province, an interesting topographical map of Holland, and contemporary and classic artworks, with an emphasis on contemporary Dutch painting and sculpture. There's also a sculpture garden, and a coffee room and open-air café. It's open from 10am to 5pm Tuesday through Saturday and 11am to 5pm on Sunday and holidays; admission is free except for major exhibitions, for which there's a small charge.

For ✪ **boat rides** on the Rhine, only in July and August, there are cruises each day from Arnhem into the Rhine region, which include a short incursion into Germany. For schedules, fares, and booking, contact the VVV or Rederij Heymen (☎ 51-51-81).

Nearby

Located in the former Hotel Hartenstein (the British Command Center during World War II) in Oosterbeek, which adjoins Arnhem, the **Airborne Museum,** Utrechtseweg 232 (☎ 337-710), has exhibits detailing the 1944 Battle of Arnhem. Open Monday through Saturday from 11am to 5pm and on Sunday and holidays from noon to 5pm. Admission is Dfl. 4 ($2.10) for adults, Dfl. 2.50 ($1.30) for children.

Also, while in Oosterbeek (which traces its history back to the Roman era), stop in its old Catholic church to see Jan Toorop's famous *Fourteen Stations of the Cross.*

In Doorwerth (just beyond Oosterbeek), the former residence of a Rhine baron was rebuilt after heavy damage in World War II in its original architectural style. Today, as the **Museum for Game and Game Management,** Doorwerth Castle, Fonteinalee, Doorwerth (☎ 335-375), it holds interesting exhibits on game animals and antique weapons. Open weekdays (except Tuesday) from 10am to 5pm and on Saturday and Sunday and holidays from 1 to 5pm. Admission is Dfl. 6 ($3.15) for adults, Dfl. 3.75 ($2) for children.

The beautiful ✪ **De Hoge Veluwe National Park,** Apeldoornseweg 250 (☎ 08382/1627), covering some 22 square miles in a setting flanked by Arnhem, Apeldoorn, and Ede, shelters a wealth of nature's treasures, and also has a statue park within its boundaries as well as the art museum listed below. The park is open daily from 8am to sunset; admission is Dfl. 7.50 ($4) for adults, Dfl. 3.75 ($2) for children up to 12 years of age.

Located in De Hoge Veluwe National Park, the ✪ **National Museum Kröller-Müller,** Houtkampweg 6 (☎ 08382/1041), is where you'll find most of the Vincent van Gogh paintings not in the Amsterdam museum. Also included in this major art collection are paintings by Mondrian, Braque, and Picasso. A sculpture park holds works by Rodin, Moore, and Lipchitz, among others, and there are exhibitions of Chinese porcelain and Delft. Open 10am to 5pm Tuesday through Saturday and 1 to 5pm on Sunday and holidays. Admission is Dfl. 7.50 ($4) for adults, Dfl. 3.75 ($2) for children.

The 90-acre **Burgers' Zoo and Safaripark,** Schelmseweg 85 (☎ 424-534), allows you to drive slowly through its grounds as more than 300 animals roam freely behind protective fencing. Its chimpanzee and gorilla enclosures are internationally acclaimed, and there's a three-acre tropical rain forest. Hours are 9am to 7pm daily. Admission is Dfl. 20 ($10.50).

Rhenen is a short distance out from Arnhem (past Oosterbeek, Doorwerth, and Renkum), and **Ouwehand's Zoo,** Grebbeweg 109, Rhenen (☎ **08376/191-10**), makes the trip well worthwhile. In addition to royal Bengal tigers, lions, elephants, reindeer, polar bears, and many other animals and birds, there's an aquarium and a dolphinarium with daily performances. There's also a playground for children and a terrace café. Open daily from 9am to 6pm; admission is 20 ($10.50) for adults, Dfl. 15 ($8) for children, free for tots 3 and under.

The ancient town of **Wageningen,** a little over 10 miles west of Arnheim, holds the famous **agricultural university,** where experiments vital to Holland's agro-economy are carried out. It was also the setting (in De Wereld restaurant) of the **German surrender** in May of 1945. Models of new ship designs are tested in ship basins in Wageningen, where they are put through simulated weather conditions that their full-scale counterparts will have to face on the open seas.

Apeldoorn

"Royal Apeldoorn" is a title often bestowed on this city, as well it might be, since it has played host to the likes of Willem III in 1685, Louis Napoléon in 1809, Queen Wilhelmina from 1948 until her death in 1962, and Princess Margriet from 1962 to 1975. It's also a city of many parks and gardens.

The **VVV office** is at Stationsplein 28, (☎ **055/788-421;** fax 055/211-290).

WHAT TO SEE & DO

In the City

A 1685 palace has sheltered all that royalty, and since 1984 it has served as the magnificent home for the ✪ **Het Loo Palace National Museum,** Koninklijk Park 1 (☎ **212-244**), celebrating the history of the House of Orange. The splendid palace is an ideal setting for paintings, furniture, silver, glassware, and ceramics, as well as memorabilia of the royal family. The vintage car and carriage collection is also fascinating, and the formal gardens are truly worthy of royalty. Hours are 10am to 5pm Tuesday through Sunday. Admission is Dfl. 11 ($5.75) for adults, Dfl. 9 ($4.75) for children.

Nearby

A few miles southeast of Apeldoorn, in the old town of **Zutphen** on the banks of the Ijssel River—and in a magnificent structure that also houses important works of art— the ✪ **Walburgiskerk Library** of medieval books and manuscripts is still in use, its rare publications all chained to reading desks. Hours are 10am to 5pm Tuesday through Friday.

The ✪ **Eight Castles Tour** (by bicycle) actually begins in Vorden, some 6 miles southeast of Zutphen, and you can pick up a booklet detailing the route from the Zutphen VVV office at Wijnhuis/Markt (☎ **05750/193-55**). Not all the castles are open to the public, but the scenery is terrific and even from the outside the castles are worth seeing. The fee is Dfl. 1.50 (80¢), plus Dfl. 25 ($13.15) for bike rental.

WHERE TO STAY

Although most tourists prefer to visit Gelderland from an Amsterdam base, you may want to move to a central location in Apeldoorn—and if you succumb to all that scenic beauty and decide to follow the Dutch example of making this your holiday home, the listing below gives you several options for accommodations, and the VVV in

Amsterdam or the Netherlands Board of Tourism in Chicago can provide a list of many more similar facilities.

Hotel Bloemink, Loolaan 56, Apeldoorn. ☎ **055/214-141.** 80 rms, 2 suites. TV TEL

Rates: Dfl. 195 ($102) single; Dfl. 210 ($110) double; Dfl. 250 ($131) suite. AE, MC, V.

In the Het Loo palace vicinity on the edge of town, this hostelry offers spacious and nicely furnished rooms (some with terraces). Suites come with kitchenettes, and there's an indoor heated swimming pool.

★ **Hotel de Keizerskroon,** Koingstraat 7, 7315 HR Apeldoorn. ☎ **055/217-744.** Fax 055/214-737. 100 rms, 6 suites. TV TEL

$ **Rates:** Dfl. 275 ($144) single; Dfl. 295 ($155) double; Dfl. 510 ($268) suite. AE, DC, MC, V.

In a setting on the edge of town and adjacent to Het Loo Royal Palace, this attractive hotel has spacious rooms whose furnishings include a writing desk in each room. Some have balconies overlooking the landscaped grounds. Le Petit Prince is their classic gourmet restaurant and more casual meals are served in De Keizersgrill. Other amenities include a rooftop swimming pool, sauna, solarium, and fitness center.

$ **Hotel-Pension Berg en Bos,** Aquamarijnstraat 58, 7314 HZ Apeldoorn. ☎ **055/552-352.** Fax 055/731-412. 17 rms. TV

Rates (including breakfast): Dfl. 49 ($26) single; Dfl. 98 ($52) double. Dinner Dfl. 27.50 ($14.50). MC, V.

This inexpensive little hotel in the city center has a quiet, peaceful setting and provides comfortable rooms. There's a bar and lounge.

WHERE TO DINE

★ **Restaurant de Echoput,** Amersfoortseweg 86, Hoog Soeren/Apeldoorn. ☎ **05769/1248.**

$ **Cuisine:** CONTINENTAL. **Reservations:** Recommended.
Prices: Average lunch Dfl. 60 ($31); average dinner Dfl. 85 ($45) MC, V.
Open: Lunch Tues–Fri noon–2pm; dinner Tues–Sat 6–9:30pm, Sun 1–9:30pm.

This lovely—and widely acclaimed—place is named for the old well at which travelers once watered their horses (its name means "echoing well"). It's located on the edge of the Royal Wood, about 10 miles west of Apeldoorn. From the outside it has the look of a luxury hunting lodge, and the surprise comes when you enter an ultrasophisticated lounge and dining room done up in shades of chocolate and pewter. Windows look out to pools and fountains and forest greenery. The specialty here is game in season (fall and winter), and summer specialties include lamb, beef, and poultry. No matter what the season, you may be sure your meal will be both superb and memorable.

Nijmegen

One of Holland's two oldest cities (Maastricht is the other), Nijmegen dates back to A.D. 105. Its strategic position is clearly visible from the **Valkhof,** where there are magnificent views of the surrounding region. Here you will also find the ruins of 12th-century **St. Martin's Chapel** and another little 1030 chapel that has been called the **Carolingian Chapel** because of the long-held belief that it was built by Charlemagne (Nijmegen was a favorite residence for the emperor), although it was actually built by Conraad II. More excellent views are visible at the 15th-century **Belvedere** watchtower. Around the picturesque **Grote Markt,** look for the 1612 **Weigh House (Waag),** and the **Kerkboog** vaulted passageway that dates from 1545.

The **VVV office** is at St. Jorisstraat 72 (☎ **080/225-440;** fax 080/601-429).

WHAT TO SEE & DO

Biblical Open-Air Museum, Profetenlaan 2, Heilig Landstichting. ☎ **229-829.**

A little to the southeast of town on the road to Groesbeek, this 120-acre museum holds life-size replicas of biblical scenes depicting the life of Christ.

Admission: Dfl. 10 ($5.25) adults, Dfl. 5 ($2.60) children under 14.

Open: Daily 9am–5:30pm.

Liberation Museum 1944, Wylerbaan 4, Groesbeek. ☎ **744-04.**

In nearby Groesbeek, about 5 miles from Nijmegen, through the use of a model of the area as it was during World War II, photographs, films, and a slide show, this museum tells the story of the airborne operation that liberated Nijmegen from Nazi forces in 1944. It was the largest airborne operation in history, and the museum has been maintained as a token of local gratitude.

Admission: Dfl. 6 ($3.15) adults, Dfl. 5 ($2.60) children under 15.

Open: Mon–Sat 10am–5pm, Sun and holidays noon–5pm.

⭐ **Provincial Museum G. M. Kam,** Museum Kamstraat 45. ☎ **220-619.**

Relics of the prehistoric, Roman, and Frankish eras in this region form the bulk of the exhibitions here in the town center.

Admission: Dfl. 3 ($1.55) adults, Dfl. 1.50 (80¢) children under 18.

Open: Tues–Sat 10am–5pm, Sun 1–5pm.

Stedelijk Museum (Municipal Museum), Franse Plaats 3. ☎ **229-193.**

This interesting reconstruction of a 1600 Knights of St. John hospital holds contemporary exhibits as well as artifacts tracing regional history. It's located in the town center.

Admission: Dfl. 2.50 ($1.30) adults, free for children under 19.

Open: Mon–Sat 10am–5pm, Sun 1–5pm.

4   Utrecht

The smallest of Holland's provinces, Utrecht would come in a very close second to Gelderland if there were ever a contest for the *official* title of "royal." This is where Queen Juliana chose to live when she abdicated in favor of her daughter, Beatrix, and castles of one sort or another literally dot the landscape. The provincial capital, also named Utrecht, is at least 2,000 years old, yet is one of Holland's most progressive industrial centers. New Yorkers will want to look up the tiny village of Breukelen (it's on the River Vecht north of Utrecht) and drive across the *original* Brooklyn Bridge— exactly 20 feet long and one car wide (and I'm sure it's not for sale!). Medieval centuries are recalled in Amersfoort and Oudewater, and Doorn was the home in exile of Kaiser Wilhelm II, of World War I fame. The interesting "witch city" of Oudewater, which lies in the province of Utrecht, has been described in Chapter 15.

Like most of central Holland, Utrecht is usually toured from a base in Amsterdam or The Hague. Special lodgings you may want to consider are included in this chapter.

Utrecht, the Provincial Capital

The capital city of Utrecht (only 26 miles southeast of Amsterdam) is a good starting point for exploring the province. A prestigious bishopric since the earliest establishment of Christianity in Holland, the city played an active role in Dutch politics. Its religious heritage accounts for the many church buildings, many of them dating back to medieval times.

The **VVV office,** located at Vredenburg 90, in the Music Centre (☎ **06/ 340-340-85;** fax 030/331-417), is open from 9am to 6pm Monday through Friday and 9am to 4pm on Saturday.

Every Sunday, **Bus Line M (Museum and Green Line)** departs from Central Station and Rhijnauwen every hour on the hour from 9am to 5pm. Stops are at many museums, some of which offer varying discount admissions to M Line passengers.

WHAT TO SEE & DO

Every Sunday from mid-May to mid-September, the VVV organizes ✪ **walking tours** of the city with different themes. Check with them for exact times and booking. If you prefer a do-it-yourself walking tour they can supply an excellent Walkman tour.

Sightseeing **coach tours** through Utrecht and its environs are conducted by the VVV during summer months. Check for schedules, itineraries, and booking.

One-hour ✪ **boat tours** through the Utrecht canals are also available in summer for about Dfl. 10 ($5.25) for adults and Dfl. 7.50 ($4) for children under 14. There are also trips by boat on the River Vecht to Loenen, with a stop to visit the Terra Nova estate, and a boat trip on the Kromme Rijn to the Rhijnauwen estate. Check with the VVV for schedules and booking.

VVV Utrecht can also organize **day trips, city walks, coach tours,** and **social events** for private groups upon advance request.

Attractions in the City

★ **Domkerk (Cathedral) and Domtoren (Dom Tower),** Domplein.
☎ **919-540** or **310-403.**

This magnificent cathedral in the city center was built between 1254 and 1517, with a 365-foot tower that until recently dominated Utrecht's skyline (modern buildings now surpass its height, though they don't come close to its beauty). That tower now stands across a square from its mother building, a circumstance that came about in rebuilding after the church collapsed during a storm, leaving the tower unharmed. One of the best views of Utrecht is from the top of the Domkerk tower, a climb of some 465 steps (don't faint—about halfway up there's the 14th-century St. Michael's Chapel where you can stop and ease the panting!). The climb goes past the 50 massive church bells you'll hear all through your stay in Utrecht. The cathedral cloisters are connected to the former Hall of the Chapter, where the signing of the 1579 Union of Utrecht took place.

Admission: Cathedral, free; tower, Dfl. 6 ($3.15) adults, Dfl. 2.50 ($1.30) children under 12.

Open: Cathedral and tower, May–Sept, daily 10am–5pm; Oct–Apr, Mon–Sat 11am–4pm, Sun 2–4pm.

Museum Catharijneconvent (St. Catherine's Convent),
Nieuwe Gracht 63. ☎ 313-835.

The extensive collections of paintings, religious relics, carvings, and church robes trace
the development of Christian religions in Holland from the 8th through the 20th
century.

Admission: Dfl. 8 ($4) adults, Dfl. 6.50 ($3.40) children 6–12, free for children
under 6.

Open: Tues–Fri 10am–5pm, Sat–Sun and holidays 11am–5pm. **Bus:** 2, 22,
or M.

★ **National Museum van Speelklok tot Pierement (From Musical Box
to Barrel Organ),** Buurkerkhof 10. ☎ 312-789.

This delightful collection consists of mechanical music makers of all descriptions from
the 18th century to the present, including those street organs you see on Dutch streets.

Admission: Dfl. 7.50 ($4) adults, Dfl. 4 ($2.10) children under 13.

Open: Tues–Sat 10am–5pm, Sun and holidays 1–5pm; guided tours on the hour.
Bus: 2, 22, or M to Domplein/Lijnmarkt.

★ **Nederlands Spoorwegmuseum (Dutch Rail Museum),**
Johan van Maliebaanstation. ☎ 306-206.

Rail buffs will find it difficult to tear themselves away from this former railway station
and its marvelous collection of more than 60 steam engines, carriages, and wagons.
There are also moving models, paintings, and films relating to rail travel. Fascinating.

Admission: Dfl. 10 ($5.25) adults, Dfl. 5 ($2.60) children.

Open: Tues–Sat 10am–5pm, Sun 1–5pm. **Bus:** 3 to Maliebaan.

Castles Nearby

As I said before, Utrecht is a treasure trove of castles, and the following is only a small
sampling.

If you have time for only one castle jaunt, make it to ★ **De Haar** at Kasteellaan 1,
Haarzuilens (☎ **03407/1275**), about 3 miles west of Maarssen, which lies 3 miles
north of Utrecht. The imposing 15th-century castle suffered a disastrous fire in the
1800s, but it has now been restored to its former glory and its owners use it as their
primary residence. You can, however, take a look at the gorgeous furnishings and
priceless paintings between March and mid-August and from mid-October to
mid-November. Go to see the formal gardens, if nothing else—they're magnificent.
Hours are 11am to 4pm Monday through Friday and 1 to 4pm on Saturday and
Sunday. Admission is Dfl. 6 ($3.15).

Slot Zuylen, on Zuilenselaan, in Maarssen (3 miles north of Utrecht), is one of
Holland's best examples of medieval castles. It was built in the 1200s and was lived in
until the early part of this century. Since 1952 it has been a museum, with rooms left
just as they were when the family was in residence. Open during the summer, Tuesday through Saturday from 10am to 4pm and on Sunday from 2 to 4pm for Dfl. 6
($3.15) admission.

Kasteel Sypesteyn—Nieuw Loosdrechtsedijk 150, Nieuw Loosdrecht (☎ **02158/
3208**), a few miles northeast of Maarssen—is a castle turned art gallery and museum.
Rebuilt in the early 1900s on the foundations of a late-medieval manor house that

was destroyed about 1580, it now holds some 80 paintings from the 16th, 17th, and 18th centuries, with artists such as Moreelse, Maes, and Mierevelt represented. There are also collections of old weapons, glassware, silverware, pottery, porcelain, and furnishings. The parklike grounds hold a lovely rose garden. From May 1 to September 15, there are tours Tuesday through Friday at 10:15 and 11:15am and 2 and 3pm. Admission is free.

Savvy Shopping

The vast covered **shopping mall** of Hoog Catherine, Central Station, is a six-block, multitiered shopper's paradise, and is so large it encompasses a 40-room exhibition hall. Along the Oude Gracht (canal), Utrecht has transformed the area with a unique ✪ **bilevel wharf** filled with shops, restaurants, and sidewalk cafés.

Evening Entertainment

The **Music Centre Vredenburg** (☎ **030/314-544**) presents more than 450 concerts each year—call ahead to find out what's on when you're there and to book.

WHERE TO STAY

Accommodations can be a problem in Utrecht, possibly because of its proximity to Amsterdam, and my best advice is to book as far in advance as possible if you plan to stay in the city.

★ **Hôtel des Pays-Bas,** Janskerkhof 10, 3512 BL Utrecht. ☎ **030/333-321.** Fax 030/313-169. 47 rms. MINIBAR TV TEL **Bus:** 3.

Rates: Dfl. 115 ($60) single; Dfl. 195 ($102) double. AE, MC, V.

Literally in the shadow of the Dom (cathedral), this excellent hotel is also within a two-minute walk of the canal with its bilevel wharf, restaurants, and shops. The guest rooms are nicely appointed and quite comfortable.

★ **Malie Hotel,** Maliestraat 204, 3581 SL Utrecht. ☎ **030/316-424.** Fax 030/340-661. 29 rms. TV TEL **Bus:** 4 or 11.

Rates (including breakfast): Dfl. 140–170 ($73–$89) single; Dfl. 170–200 ($89–$105) double. MC, V.

Two 19th-century mansions in a quiet neighborhood near the university "Uithof" complex are the setting for this lovely small hotel. The guest rooms are tastefully decorated and comfortably furnished, and both the breakfast room and bar overlook the garden.

★ **Scandic Crown Hotel,** Westplein 50, 3531 BL Utrecht. ☎ **030/925-200.** Fax 030/925-199. 120 rms. A/C TV TEL

Rates: Dfl. 285 ($150) single; Dfl. 325 ($171) double. AE, DC, MC, V.

This centrally located hotel is as modern as tomorrow, with a bright, attractive Scandinavian decor and luxurious guest rooms. The Rhapsody restaurant specializes in Swedish cuisine, and other amenities include a sauna, whirlpool, and fitness center. It's within walking distance of Central Station and Industries Fair.

IMPRESSIONS

At Utrecht you begin to have a sniff of dry, wholesome air, and the trees look as if they stood in real ground, and the grass as if it was not growing in the water.
—Matthew Arnold, 1859

WHERE TO DINE

⭐ **Het Draeckie,** Oude Gracht 114–118. ☎ **321-999.**
Cuisine: DUTCH. **Reservations:** Recommended.
Prices: Average meal Dfl. 30 ($16). MC, V.
Open: Daily noon–2am.

Set in a canalside vaulted cellar, Het Draeckje could well provide one of your most memorable Utrecht meals. Dutch specialties change with the seasons, the grills are always excellent, and for cheese lovers, there's the terrific fondue. It's located in the city center.

⭐ **Restaurant de Hoefslag,** Vossenlaan 28, Bosch en Duin. ☎ **784-395.**
💲 **Cuisine:** SEAFOOD/GAME/CONTINENTAL. **Reservations:** Recommended.
Prices: Average meal Dfl. 90 ($47). MC, V.
Open: Dinner only, Tues–Sat 6–9:30pm.

Considered by many to be Holland's top restaurant, this beautiful dining spot is in wooded grounds just a little northeast of the city of Utrecht. Amsterdammers think nothing of driving the 30 miles down here for dinner. There's a sort of Victorian-garden feel to the lounge, while the dining room is reminiscent of a rather upscale hunting lodge, with lots of dark wood, an open hearth, and ceiling-to-floor doors opening to the terrace. Originally a coaching inn, the de Hoefslag changes its menu daily, setting specialties after the chef has done the marketing. Seafoods are superb, as are pork, lamb, and other meats, and venison and other game dishes are served in season.

The Provincial Towns of Utrecht

AMERSFOORT This lovely old medieval city 14 miles east of Utrecht has held onto its ancient character despite its industrial development. Indeed, its medieval heart is guarded by a double ring of canals—the only city in Europe to have this feature. Stop by the **VVV office,** at Stationsplein 28 (☎ **033/635-151;** fax 033/650-108), before you set out to see the town.

Look for the tall 15th-century **Gothic Tower of Our Lady,** and if you're here on a Friday, listen for its **carillon concert** between 10 and 11am. If you should be here on a summer Saturday, you may be lucky enough to encounter the colorful **trumpeters** who show up from time to time in the city center.

At the **Museum Flehite,** Westingel 50, the history of Amersfoort is the subject of the large collection of artifacts. It's open Tuesday through Friday from 10am to 5pm and on Saturday and Sunday from 2 to 5pm; admission is Dfl. 6 ($3.15).

SOESTDUK The beautiful **Palace of the Queen Mother** (sometimes called the "white palace") is located in this town near Baarn (between Utrecht and Amersfoort). It can be admired only on the outside.

HEUSDEN The tiny village of Heusden has a tiny harbor, a tiny white balance bridge, and two not-so-tiny windmills atop earthen ramparts. It's 25 miles almost due south of the city of Utrecht, and "charm" is the first word that comes to mind.

WHERE TO STAY & DINE IN HEUSDEN

⭐ **Hotel in den Verdwaalde Koogel,** Vismarkt 1, 5256 BC Heusden.
☎ **041/621-933.** Fax 041/621-295. 12 rms. TV TEL
Rates: Dfl. 115 ($60) single; Dfl. 145 ($76) double. MC, V.

Charming—that overworked word also applies to this 17th-century town house in the town center that has been converted into an inn whose name means "The Stray Bullet." The rooms here are small and the furnishings are not luxurious, although those on the upper floors are quite charming, with exposed beams or rafters. The largest room is the "honeymoon suite," which is furnished with antiques and has nice views (only slightly more expensive than other rooms).

The restaurant, decorated in Vermeer colors, with antique-gray beams overhead and antique clocks among its decorations, is a cozy setting for superior meals such as Texel Island lamb or salmon smoked over oak by the chef. Prices are moderate, the service is friendly, and the restaurant alone is sufficient reason for a detour through this picturesque little village.

Holland's Southernmost Provinces

ALL TOO OFTEN, THE SOUTHERNMOST PROVINCES OF HOLLAND ARE MERELY entrance or exit routes for tourists who rush through on their way to or from Belgium, Luxembourg, and other European destinations. Yet from the watery islands of Zeeland to the forests and moors of Noord Brabant to Limburg's wooded hill country, there is a rich vein of tourist experience waiting to be mined, and no visit to Holland is complete without a foray into these interesting provinces. History, recreational activities, and some of Holland's most beautiful scenery are in this southern region.

1 Zeeland

This "Sea Land" on Holland's western coast has often been likened to three fingers of land pointing out into the North Sea, and Napoléon declared in 1810 that it was little more than "the silt thrown up by French rivers" (and in truth, much of the province is formed by alluvial deposits at the mouth of the Scheldt, the river that controls access to Antwerp). Zeelanders, however, cling to the firm Dutch belief that "who cannot master the sea is not worthy of the land," and century after century they have cherished their precious group of islands and former islands, rescuing them each time the sea roared in to claim them as its own.

In 1421 the St. Elizabeth Flood came close to tipping the balance in favor of the North Sea, in 1944 it was bombs from Allied planes that loosed flood waters to flush out Nazi troops entrenched in bunkers along the coast, and in 1953 a fierce hurricane sent sea water crashing through the province and as far inland as Rotterdam. In between those disasters were numerous "little floods" that swamped only a few islands. Always, Zeelanders have pushed back the angry sea and reinforced protective measures in this ongoing, uncompromising battle. Today, with the completion of an ingenious system of dikes, storm-surge barriers, and sluice gates known as the Delta Project, it's more likely to be the North Sea that will finally have to concede defeat, acknowledging for all time Zeeland's firm grasp on its cluster of islands.

At the center of Zeeland, Walcheren (still called Walcheren Island even though polders have long connected it to South Beveland and the mainland) holds the provincial capital of Middelburg, a medieval city that has resolutely rebuilt its historic landmarks, so steadfastly holding to their original designs that, seeing them today, it's difficult to believe they have not stood undisturbed through the centuries. To the north lie North Beveland and the islands of Schouwen-Duiveland, St. Philipsland (now a peninsula), and Tholen. To the south of Walcheren, and separated from it by the River Schelde, Zeeuwsch-Vlaanderen (Zeeland Flanders) reaches to the Belgian border.

The western part of Walcheren (often called the Zeeland Riviera), from Westkapelle to Domburg, is a string of delightful small seaside villages, with all sorts of recreational facilities. About the only somber note along the coast at this point is struck by bunkers and other mementos of World War II.

As you explore Zeeland, keep an eye out for the **national costume,** still worn here in Walcheren and South Beveland (in the latter, the women wearing bonnets shaped like conch shells are Protestant, those whose bonnets form a trapezium with a light-blue underbonnet showing through are Catholic). Incidentally, the gold-and-silver ornaments you see worn by both men and women with the national costume can be bought as souvenirs. Also, if you're lucky you'll happen on the traditional game of tilting at the ring from bare horseback—it's called *krulbollen,* and the VVV can tell you if, when, and where you can see it during your visit.

What's Special About Holland's Southernmost Provinces

Zeeland
- Middelburg Abbey, an astonishing restoration of the original 13th-century abbey.
- Zeeland Museum, with a wonderful collection of antiquities including a Roman altar.
- The Zeeland Riviera, with its long stretches of white-sand beaches.
- Delta Project, a massive system of dikes, sluice gates, and storm-surge barriers.

Noord Brabant
- Eurobird Park, a unique collection of tropical and other foreign birds.
- De Efteling Family Leisure Park, with all sorts of amusements, boating facilities, and a miniature city.

Limburg
- Boat tours on the River Meuse.
- Basilica of Our Beloved Lady, with its statue of Lady Stella Mare, which is credited with miracles.
- Caves of St. Pietersberg, unique underground chambers that have served as a refuge for people and masterpieces of art.
- Basilica of St. Servatius, with a large reliquary of the saint and Grandmère, the largest bell in Holland.

Because it's so vital to the future of Zeeland, and because it's one of the most exciting engineering feats of the modern world, no visitor should miss the **Delta Expo** (see below).

INFORMATION   Scattered about the province are some 40 local **VVV** offices, so keep a lookout for the blue-and-white triangular sign that identifies them.

The **Provincial VVV Office,** at Markt 65, Middelburg (☎ **01180/330-00;** fax 01180-407-64), is open Monday through Saturday from 9am to 5pm. They can help you with bike rentals (Zeeland is wonderful biking country—park the car and hit the pedals if the spirit moves you!), special events during your visit, market days in the various villages, where to find 17th- and 18th-century windmills, accommodations along your travel route, and a host of other matters.

GETTING AROUND   Nondrivers will find a network of **bus** connections covering the province, and there is **rail** transportation from around the country to Middelburg, Vlissingen, and Goes.

A Driving Tour   If you're driving, virtually any of the provincial destinations is an easy day trip from Middelburg. Alternatively, begin from a Middelburg base (with a day-trip to Veere), then head south to Vlissingen and plan to stay over at one of the many lovely accommodations along the Zeeland Riviera (Westkapelle to Domburg) northwest of Vlissingen. The following day, drive to Stellendam, allowing plenty of time to tour the Delta Project, with a possible overnight at Zierikzee, a few miles to the south.

CHOOSING A BASE   Take your pick: a base in charming, historic Middelburg, the little harbor town of Veere that's virtually an open-air museum, the bustling port of Vlissingen (Flushing), the medieval village of Zierikzee, or holiday digs at small beach villages such as Westkapelle, Oostkapelle, and Domburg. In this small province, you're never far from any of its attractions.

DINING   Your best meals in Zeeland will be in hotel dining rooms, but inquiry of the locals or in local VVV offices will often unearth good small restaurants that are beginning to open with more frequency than in past years. Needless to say, any seafood you order in this watery province will be fresher than fresh—right off local boats.

Special sweet-tooth note: A Zeeland specialty is called "bolus," and when I asked my Zeelander friends to define it exactly for me, the only explanation they could come up with was "they're these round things with sugar and. . . . " Well, actually, I think its base is bread, but no matter what the ingredients, stop by a pastry shop or bakery and try them.

Middelburg, the Provincial Capital

Middelburg began as a 9th-century fortress, erected as a defense against Norman attacks. The fortifications expanded into a real settlement about A.D. 1150, when the abbey was established (see below). Today the abbey is just one of the city's more than 1,000 historic buildings. Middelburg's colorful **market day** is Thursday, when you can mingle in the Market Square with Zeelanders, some of whom are in native dress.

WHAT TO SEE & DO

Make your first stop the **VVV Office,** Markt 65A (☎ **01180/330-00**). Among the mass of information and helpful literature, they furnish an excellent walking-tour brochure. They also conduct ✪ **guided walking tours.**

Middelburg sights not to miss are the **picturesque streets** of Kuiperspoort and Bellinkstraat; the **Vismarkt,** which dates from 1559, with Doric columns and little auctioneers' houses, where summer Thursdays are days for an **art and craft market;** the **Blauw (Blue) Gateway;** and the **Koepoort (Cow Gate).**

Town Hall, Markt.

The Town Hall, another of Middelburg's miraculous reconstructions, consists of two distinct sections. The side facing the Markt is Gothic and dates from the 15th century, while the Noordstraat side, from the 17th and 18th centuries, is classic in style. Inside are such treasures as Belgian tapestries from the 1600s, a brass model of de Ruyter's flagship, 17th-century Makkum tiles, and the Middelburg coat-of-arms, originally located on the eastern facade of the building. The old tribunal hall is now known as the "wedding hall," and several ceremonies are held there each week. The banquet hall, originally the first cloth market in the Netherlands, is now used for official receptions, "welcome" evenings for new residents of Middelburg, and periodic concerts.

Admission: Dfl. 3.50 ($1.85) adults, Dfl. 2.50 ($1.30) children.

Open: Tours, Apr–Oct, Mon–Sat 1:30–3pm. **Closed:** Nov–Mar.

The Middelburg Abbey Complex

Middelburg Abbey, Abdijplein at Onder de Toren.

The sprawling 13th-century abbey in the center of town had a life of traumatic ups and downs over the centuries, as it went from Catholic to Protestant to secular headquarters for governmental agencies and suffered the devastation of fires and careless

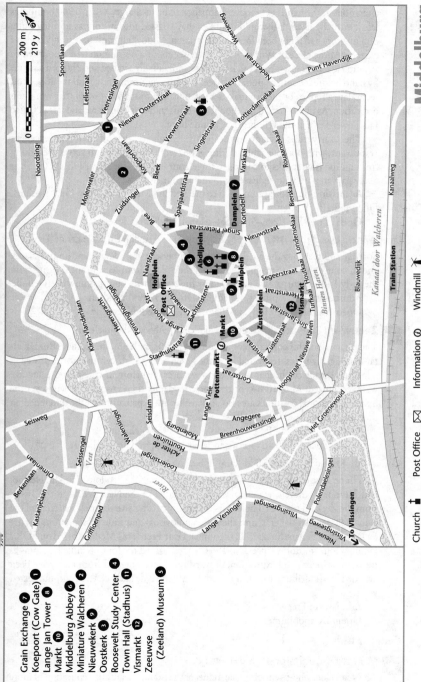

Middelburg

Grain Exchange **7**
Koepoort (Cow Gate) **1**
Lange Jan Tower **8**
Markt **10**
Middelburg Abbey **6**
Miniature Walcheren **2**
Nieuwekerk **9**
Oostkerk **3**
Roosevelt Study Center **4**
Town Hall (Stadhuis) **11**
Vismarkt **12**
Zeeuwse (Zeeland) Museum **5**

Church ✝ ▪   Post Office ⊠   Information ❶   Windmill ⚒

Train Station

0   200 m
0   219 y

Spoortlaan
Noordsingel
Seisweg
Berkenlaan
Kastanjelaan
Olmenlaan
Seissingel
Vest River
Griffioenpad
Klein-Vlandelaan
Herengracht
Penninghoekssingel
Molenwater
Zuidsingel
Bree
Koepoortlaan
Veersesingel
Nieuwe Oosterstraat
Leliestraat
Veersesingel
Bleek
Spanjaardstraat
Naarstraat
Hofplein
Abdijplein
Singel Pieterstraat
Venverustraat
Singelstraat
Breestraat
Nederstraat
Weeresweg
Kortedelft
Varskaai
Rotterdamsekaai
Rouaansekaai
Bierskaai
Londensekaai
Turfkaai
Houtkaai
Nieuwstraat
Dampein
Walplein
Segeerstraat
Herenstraat
Sint-Janstraat
Zusterstraat
Zusterplein
Vismarkt
Binnen Haven
Hoogstraat Nieuwe Haven
Gravenstraat
Corstraat
Lange Viele
Markt
Pottenmarkt
VVV
Stadhuisstraat
Lange Noord Str.
Lange Delft
Bathenstene
Lombaadse
Post Office
Seisdam
Molenburg
Houtunien
Achter de
Looperssingel
Lange Versingel
Walensingel
Seissingel
Lange Versingel
Vlissingsesingel
Angegere
Breenhouwerssingel
Het Groenewoud
Polendaelsingel
Nieuwe
Vlissingseweg
To Vlissingen
Blauwedijk
Kanaal door Walcheren
Kanaalweg
Punt Havendijk

alterations at the hands of whoever happened to be in charge. When 1940 bombings left it virtually leveled, it would doubtless have passed into history as nothing but a dim memory had it not been for the dedication of Middelburg authorities and Zeeland citizens. At the close of World War II, they set about a restoration that amounted to a complete rebuilding—each brick had to be individually scraped and chipped smooth by hand before it could be put into place. It was an enormous task, and the abbey you see today, a replica of the original, is an astonishing monument to all that work and dedication. As in medieval days, the abbey, its magnificent courtyard, and its tall Lange Jan Tower serve as the very heart of Middelburg.

The courtyard is a shady rest stop during sightseeing, and there's an excellent **restaurant,** with outdoor tables during good weather, for lunch. It serves everything from inexpensive snacks to complete three-course menus for about Dfl. 28 ($15). It really pays to plan your sightseeing to include lunch at the abbey.

Admission (including admission to the Zeeland Museum): Dfl. 6 ($3.15) adults, Dfl. 4 ($2.10) children.

Open: Tues–Fri 10am–5pm; Sat–Mon 1:30–5pm. **Closed:** Jan 1.

Lange Jan (Long John) Tower, Middelburg Abbey, Abdijplein at Onder de Toren.

Soaring 289 feet into the air, Long John can be seen from any point on the island, and of course there are magnificent panoramic views from its summit. Dating from the early 14th century it was destroyed by fire several times but has now been rebuilt.

Admission: Dfl. 2.50 ($1.30) adults, Dfl. 1.75 (90¢) children.

Open: Easter–Oct, Mon–Sat 10am–5pm. **Closed:** Nov–Mar.

★ **Zeeuwse (Zeeland) Museum,** Middelburg Abbey, Abdijplein 3.

There's a wonderful collection of antiquities in this museum, including a Roman altar to a pagan goddess recovered from the beach after a 17th-century storm, as well as a medieval stone coffin that was used to water cattle before its true purpose and age were recognized. Also, 16th-century tapestries depict the victory of Zeeland over the Spanish. National costumes are also displayed, with explanations of the differences in dress from one island or one village to another.

Admission: Dfl. 4.50 ($2.35) adults, Dfl. 1 (50¢) children.

Open: Tues–Fri 10am–5pm, Sat–Mon 1:30–5pm. **Closed:** Jan 1, Dec 25.

Roosevelt Study Center, Middelburg Abbey, Abdijplein 9. ☎ **315-90.**

This impressive research center was established in honor of Theodore, Franklin Delano, and Eleanor Roosevelt, whose ancestors emigrated to the New World in the 1640s from the Zeeland town of Tholen. Its library holds extensive research material on the Roosevelt presidential eras, and there are audiovisual and slide presentations for use by European scholars. Since 1982 the annual **Four Freedoms Medals** (based on FDR's famous "four freedoms" speech in 1941, which named the four essential freedoms as freedom of speech and expression, of worship, from want, and from fear) have been awarded in Middelburg in even-numbered years; in Hyde Park, N.Y., in odd-numbered years.

Admission: Free.

Open: By appointment.

Cool for Kids

 Miniature Walcheren, Molenwater Park.

This marvelous one-twentieth-scale model of the island is a faithful replication of more than 200 buildings, moving trains and ships, and windmills. It's a delight for both young and old, and a good place to visit before you leave Middelburg to explore the rest of Walcheren, where you'll see the origins of these models. It's located near Middleburg Abbey.

Admission: Dfl. 6 ($3.15) adults, Dfl. 4 ($2.10) children.

Open: Easter–June and Sept–Oct, daily 9:30am–5pm; July–Aug, daily 9:30am–6pm. **Closed:** Nov–Easter.

WHERE TO STAY

⭐ **Hotel de Huifkar,** Markt 19, 4331 LJ Middelburg. ☎ **01180/129-98** or **243-59.** Fax 01180/123-86. 5 rms. TV TEL

Rates: Dfl. 90 ($47) single; Dfl. 135 ($71) double. AE, MC, V.

This pleasant little hotel overlooks the Market Square, right in the heart of the city. While not luxurious, the guest rooms are nicely furnished and quite comfortable. Downstairs is a very good restaurant with moderate prices and Tourist Menu meals.

Hotel de Nieuwe Doelen, Loskade 3–7, 4331 HV Middelburg. ☎ **01180/121-21.** Fax 01180/366-99. 24 rms. TV TEL

Rates: Dfl. 95 ($50) single; Dfl. 125 ($66) double. AE, MC, V.

Conveniently located, just a short walk from the central Markt, this small hotel facing a canal has comfortable rooms.

⭐ **Hotel du Commerce,** Loskade 1, 4331 HV Middelburg. ☎ **01180/360-51.** Fax 01180/264-00. 48 rms. MINIBAR TV TEL

Rates (including breakfast): Dfl. 90–100 ($47–$52) single; Dfl. 125–155 ($65–$81) double. AE, MC, V.

This small canalside hotel is just opposite the railway and bus terminal and an easy walk from the town center, in one of the most convenient locations in town. The guest rooms are comfortably furnished, and there is also a good restaurant serving French and Spanish specialties at moderate prices.

WHERE TO DINE

⭐ **Den Gespleten Arent,** Vlasmarkt 25. ☎ **361-22.**

Cuisine: SEAFOOD. **Reservations:** Recommended.

Prices: Average lunch Dfl. 25 ($13); average dinner Dfl. 50 ($26). AE, DC, MC, V.

Open: Lunch Wed–Mon noon–2pm; dinner Wed–Mon 5:30–9pm.

Priced a bit above most local restaurants, but very good value for money, meals in this patrician-house setting are exceptionally good. Fish specialties are the order of the day, with the freshness of local waters. It's located near the old Fish Market in the town center.

READERS RECOMMEND

Le Beau Rivage, Loskade 19, 4331 HW Middelburg (☎ **01180/380-60**). "*This very nice, quiet hotel on the large ring canal has a large parking lot across the street (free) and serves a good breakfast. There is also an old ramming ship, now a museum, docked in front of the hotel on the canal. It's across the canal from the train station and just a few minutes' walk from downtown.*"—Mykell J. Brewer, American Embassy, The Hague. [**Author's Note:** The nine rooms here rent for Dfl. 135 ($71) single and Dfl. 155 ($81) double, breakfast included.]

$ De Kabouterhut, Oostkerkplein 8. ☎ 122-76.

Cuisine: DUTCH/PANCAKES. **Reservations:** Not required.
Prices: Average meal under Dfl. 25 ($13).
Open: Lunch Mon–Sat noon–2pm; dinner Mon–Sat 6–9pm.

There are more than 60 kinds of Dutch pancakes on the menu here, and many other Dutch specialties are served as well. There's also a money-stretching Tourist Menu. It's located in the town center.

★ Visrestaurant Bij Het Stadhuis, Lange Noordstraat 8. ☎ 270-58.

Cuisine: SEAFOOD. **Reservations:** Recommended.
Prices: Appetizers Dfl. 5–15.50 ($2.60–$8.15); main courses Dfl. 17–39.50 ($9–$21). No credit cards.
Open: Lunch Wed–Sun noon–2:30pm; dinner Wed–Sun 5:30–10pm.

Almost every variety of fish and shellfish you can name is offered on the extensive and moderately priced menu at this restaurant across from the Town Hall.

A Seafood Restaurant in Nearby Yerseke

★ Restaurant Nolet Het Reymerswale, Jachthaven 5. ☎ 01131/16-42.

$

Cuisine: SEAFOOD. **Reservations:** Recommended.
Prices: Average meal Dfl. 75–95 ($39–$50). AE, MC, V.
Open: Dinner only, Thurs–Mon 6–10pm.

About a 25-mile drive from Middelburg, this very special fish restaurant is worth the trip to the busy little port town of Yerseke, which you might otherwise overlook. This cozy upstairs room is right at the waterfront and, under the watchful eye of owner Theo Nolet and his wife, Gerda, has become one of the country's best seafood restaurants. Theo is also the chef, with extensive training and experience behind him, and you may be sure that whatever lands on your plate has just come from fishing boats in the harbor below.

The Port Towns of Zeeland

VEERE   This charming little village is just 4 miles northeast of Middelburg and was an important port for Scottish wool from the 14th to the 18th century. The original fortifications are still intact, their ancient tower now housing an excellent restaurant (see "Where to Dine," below), and streets are lined with houses and buildings straight out of the past.

Stop by the VVV office, at Oudestraat 28 (☎ 01181/1365), and pick up their ✪ "Historical Walk Through Veere" booklet.

You shouldn't miss the **Stadhuis,** Markt 5, which dates from 1474—look for the *kaak* outside, an iron brace that locked around a wrongdoer's neck in olden times to hold him or her in disgrace as townspeople pelted him/her with refuse and spittle; over it hangs the "stones of the law" which an offender was forced to drag through the town in penance. The Stadhuis is open June to mid-September, Monday through Saturday from 10am to 5pm.

The so-called **Scotch Houses (De Schotse Huizen),** Kade 25–27, are two mansions of 16th- and 17th-century Scottish wool merchants, serving also as their warehouses and offices. The small folklore museum inside is well worth a visit; it's open during the summer, Tuesday through Saturday from 10am to noon and 1:30 to 5pm.

Other Veere "don't miss" sights include the ✪ **Campveerse Toren (Tower of Campveer),** which sits at the entrance to the harbor and dates from 1500; and the

Grote Kerk, whose construction took more than a century (1405–1560), and which Napoléon turned into a stable, barracks, and hospital.

VLISSINGEN The port city of Vlissingen (with ferry service to England and river pilots who guide Antwerp-bound ships down the Scheldt River) is also a popular seaside resort. New Yorkers are sure to feel at home, since Vlissingen's name translates to Flushing.

Go by the **VVV office,** located at Nieuwendijk 15 (☎ **01184/123-45;** fax 01184/174-26), for information on the town's long and interesting history, and visit the ✪ **Stedelijk Museum** for an overview of the region's maritime history, interesting ship models, and archeological relics. Other interesting sites are the **Oude Markt,** the **Grote Kerk** (dating from the 14th century), and **St. Jacobskerk.** Whatever you do, don't leave the city without at least one stroll down the seafront **promenade** that's named variously de Ruyter, Bankert, and Evertsen in honor of those Dutch naval heroes.

WHERE TO STAY

 De Campveerse Toren, Kade 2, 4351 AA Veere. ☎ **01181/12-91.** Fax 01181/16-95. 14 rms, 2 suites. TEL

Rates: Dfl. 100 ($52) single; Dfl. 125 ($65) double; Dfl. 200–275 ($105–$144) suite. AE, MC, V.

This delightful hotel (with the same ownership as the adjoining restaurant, one of the best in Zeeland) consists of rather plain but comfortable rooms. You couldn't ask for a more romantic location than the 16th-century waterfront fortress of which it is a part. Just steps away are the equally ancient and historic buildings that make of Veere a charming open-air museum.

WHERE TO DINE

De Campveerse Toren, Kade 2. ☎ **01181/12-91.**
Cuisine: SEAFOOD. **Reservations:** Recommended.
Prices: Average meal Dfl. 50–95 ($26–$50). AE, MC, V.
Open: Lunch daily noon–2pm; dinner daily 6–10pm.

If you don't bust the budget anywhere else in Zeeland, do it here in this wonderfully atmospheric restaurant. It perches in a 16th-century tower room overlooking the Veersemeer, a lake busy with the comings and goings of sailboats, yachts, and swans. The tower has an interesting history and is filled with brass and copper antiques; the restaurant was a great favorite of Grace Kelly's when she was a special guest here (ask about the "parfait d'amour" created just for her). The menu is extensive, seafood dishes are specialties, and the atmosphere is not only gracious but also a lot of fun.

The Zeeland Riviera

A few miles northwest of Vlissingen, there's the delightful little village of **Koudekerke,** starting point for a tour of what is often called the Zeeland Riviera because of its long stretches of wide, white-sand beaches. Not so much sightseeing territory, this is holiday country, much loved by Hollanders around the country. Beaches are pollution free and safe for **swimming.** Several small villages along the route from Westkapelle to Domburg offer a variety of recreational facilities, from **boating** to **golf and tennis** facilities, to **squash** (in Domburg) to **fishing** (inland or sea angling), to **walks** in wooded areas near the beaches. Westkapelle and Domburg are both family-oriented resorts, with activities aplenty for the younger set as well as their parents.

WHERE TO STAY & DINE EN ROUTE

The area abounds with accommodations, including upscale hotels, bungalows, rustic cabins, and camping facilities. The listings below are only a small sample; any VVV office in this area or in Middleburg can help you find the hostelry of your choice.

In Westkapelle

★ **Hotel Zuiderduin,** De Bucksweg 2, 4361 SM Westkapelle. ☎ **01186/1810.** Fax 01186/22-61. 67 rms. MINIBAR TV TEL

$ **Rates:** Dfl. 151 ($79) single; Dfl. 230 ($121) double. AE, MC, V. **Closed:** Last week in Dec to first week in Jan.

A variety of accommodations is offered at this modern hotel set just behind the dunes. There are spacious rooms with private baths and kitchenettes, each with either a private balcony or a terrace, as well as complete apartments that can sleep up to five people. On the premises are a heated swimming pool, sauna, solarium, and an all-weather tennis court. The restaurant attracts natives as well as tourists, with seafood and continental specialties at remarkably moderate prices.

In Domburg

Hotel de Burg, Ooststraat 5, 4357 BE Domburg. ☎ **01188/1337.** Telex 34004. 22 rms. TV TEL

Rates: Dfl. 67.50 ($35.50) single; Dfl. 130 ($68) double. AE, MC, V.

Guest rooms in this modern hotel set on Domburg's main street are attractive and comfortable, and the beach is just a short walk away.

★ The Delta Expo

Located on the island of Neeltje Jans several miles northeast of Middelburg in the Eastern Scheldt near Burghsluis and Schouwen-Duiveland, the Delta Expo tops my personal list of Zeeland sightseeing. The whole of Holland is, of course, awe-inspiring because of the way in which land has been snatched from the very bottom of the sea, but nothing within Holland is quite so breathtakingly impressive as the massive system of dikes, sluice gates, and storm-surge barriers known collectively as the Delta Project. It was begun as a protective measure for Zeeland, but in the course of its development revolutionary ideas about sea management have surfaced and been implemented. As a result, rather than simply a system of dams to hold the sea back, there is in place a gigantic network of barriers that can be opened and closed as storms and tidal variations demand.

It took a good 15 years of, as the Delta people told me, "dredging, dumping, towing, and building" to create the component parts of this network, and when I remarked on the dedication of the hardworking men who never flagged during all those years of effort, the reply was simply, "The water is in these men—they know it well and what it can do and they know it must be managed."

READERS RECOMMEND

The Wigwam, Herenstraat 12, 4357 AL Domburg (☎ **01188/1275**). "*We thoroughly enjoyed our stay at this small, family-style hotel. There's a nice bar and a good restaurant, and our children loved being near the beach. It was a nice break in our sightseeing schedule.*"—Selma Larkin, Buffalo, N.Y. [**Author's Note:** The Wigwam has 31 rooms costing Dfl. 78 ($41) for a single without bath and Dfl. 114 ($60) for a double without bath; add $15 per person for a room with bath. No credit cards.]

To give visitors an overall view of the massive undertaking and an easily understood explanation of how everything works, the Delta people have built a huge scale model of the complex, as well as a map of the entire country on which tiny lights switch on and off to show how the Delta Project also plays a vital role in freshwater management of virtually the whole of Holland. Conducted tours come with or without a boat trip around the storm-surge barrier, which is well worth the Dfl.-12 ($6.30) fare. Then there's a film history and map demonstration, after which you descend into the very innards of one of the 36 sluice-gate engine rooms. Allow yourself no less than 1 1/2 hours at this intriguing place, even if you don't think you have any interest in dams and engine rooms, etc. At the end of your tour there's a cozy coffee shop whose terrace affords panoramic views that would be worth the trip on their own.

The Delta Expo is open from April 1 through mid-November, daily from 10am to 5pm, with an admission fee of Dfl. 8 ($4) per person.

Getting There   Drivers can purchase a special **Delta Expo Route Map** from the VVV for Dfl. 2.50 ($1.30). The VVV can also furnish details of special **coach tours** from Middelburg, and do-it-yourselfers can take bus no. 104 from Middelburg.

Zierikzee

This 11-centuries-old little town on the Oosterschelde (south of the Delta Expo, northeast of Middelburg) lives within its medieval town walls, still guarded by fortifications built during the Middle Ages. Strolling its narrow, cobblestone streets, it's easy to imagine everyday life of its citizens in those ancient times, especially if you're there for a colorful Thursday ⊠ **market day.** Founded in 849, this is reputedly the best-preserved town in Holland, and the **Stadhuismuseum** in the Town Hall traces its history through archeological finds and other relics. It's open May through September, Monday through Friday from 10am to 5pm. Look for the **Sint Lievens Monstertoren** (great tower) on the cathedral. Standing 199 feet tall, the tower is actually incomplete, since townspeople lacked the funds to take it to its planned 680-foot height.

The **VVV office,** at Havenpark 29 (☎ 01110/124-50), can provide **walking-tour** information, as well as details and booking on **cruises** on the Oosterschelde during summer months.

WHERE TO STAY

$ **Mondragon,** Havenpark 21, 4301 JG Zierikzee. ☎ **01110/130-51.** 8 rms. TV TEL

Rates: Dfl. 100 ($52) single; Dfl. 145 ($76) double. AE, MC, V.

This canalside hotel offers nicely appointed, comfortable guest rooms, as well as a moderately priced restaurant. It's located in the town center.

WHERE TO DINE

$ **Auberge Maritime,** Nieuwe Haven 21. ☎ **121-56.**
Cuisine: SEAFOOD/SNACKS. **Reservations:** Not required.
Prices: Average meal under Dfl. 30 ($15). AE, MC, V.
Open: Daily 11am–9pm.

This informal bar-café-restaurant in the town center makes a pleasant stop for just a drink, snacks, or full meals (especially their seafood specialties) at moderate prices.

2 Noord Brabant

Brabant is one of Holland's most scenically beautiful provinces, forestland alternating with neat farmsteads and parkland edging its moors. The people who live in this part of the country, "below" the Rivers Rhine and Meuse, sometimes seem as much Belgian as Dutch, with a more relaxed view of the world and great emphasis on the joys of eating well and life's other pleasures—a bit different from the Dutch who live "above" the rivers. Brabant is a province of blurred cultural distinctions, and there is one town where even the national border itself becomes blurred, with homes on one side of a street inside Holland, those across the street in Belgium!

For the visitor, this is a restful, interesting area filled with historic towns, castles, and important centers of industry dotted about the lovely countryside.

While there is sightseeing aplenty in the province of Noord Brabant, it's the scenery that will enthrall you most of all. There are the waterways and polders in the north and west; the sand drifts, fir and deciduous woods in the south and east; and everywhere picturesque villages and ancient towns.

Accommodation standards are quite high and hotels numerous in Brabant, yet during July and August they tend to be especially tightly booked, making it highly advisable to make your reservations in advance if you plan to stay the night.

GETTING AROUND   There is **rail** service to 's Hertogenbosch, Tilburg, Breda, and Eindhoven, with good **bus** connections from around the country. Drivers will find the destinations in this section listed in a logical driving itinerary. Better still, explore the province from a 's Hertogenbosch or Breda base, making day trips to other points of interest.

's Hertogenbosch (Den Bosch), the Provincial Capital

The capital city, 's Hertogenbosch, is affectionately known simply as Den Bosch (The Woods)—maybe they, too, have given up on the pronunciation of the longer version! Located 51 miles southeast of Amsterdam and more than 800 years old, it's a cathedral town and seat of a bishop, and was once a heavily fortified city.

The **VVV office** is at Markt 77 (☎ **073/123-071;** fax 073/128-930).

WHAT TO SEE & DO

In the City

★ **Sint Janskathedraal** is a magnificent Gothic cathedral whose origins date back to the 1100s, although the present church was rebuilt over the course of a century when the earlier structure burned in 1240. Notice the little stone mannikins on the flying buttresses and up the copings—miniature copies of these delightful figures are on sale in local gift shops and make marvelous souvenirs to take home.

Het Zwanenbroedershuis Lieve Vrouwebroederschap (Illustrious Brotherhood of Our Lady), Hinthamerstraat 94, is an interesting small museum depicting monastic life during the Middle Ages. It's closed the month of August but open other months on Friday from 11am to 3pm, and there's no admission. The **Noordbrabants Museum,** Bethaniestraat 4, holds manuscripts, maps, weapons, coins, and archeological finds from this region. Hours are 10am to 5pm Tuesday through Friday, and noon to 5pm on Saturday, Sunday, and holidays; admission is Dfl. 7.50 ($4).

Nearby Attractions

Birdlovers will want to head for **Oisterwijk** (9 miles southwest of 's Hertogenbosch), sometimes called the "Pearl of Brabant," to visit the unique ★ **Eurobird Park,** with a large collection of tropical and other foreign birds, as well as European species. Open April through October, daily from 9am to 6pm, with an admission of Dfl. 7.50 ($4).

Some 14 miles southwest of Den Bosch, **Tilburg** is interesting for its **Town Hall,** a palace that once housed Willem II. At nearby Hilvarenbeek there's the **Beekse Bergen Safari Park,** where some 40 different species live together.

A few miles north of Tilburg at **Kaatsheuvel,** there's the ★ **De Efteling Family Leisure Park** (☎ 01031/4167/881-11). Just outside town, this 700-acre recreational park has amusements, restaurants, and facilities for boating. Most remarkable, however, is the miniature city, with towers and castles for just about every fairytale character who ever stirred childhood's imagination. It's open mid-March to mid-October, daily from 10am to 6pm, with an admission of Dfl.25 ($13); free for children up to age 3.

In and around **Overloon,** a little village some 35 miles southeast of Den Bosch, tank corps of opposing forces met in fierce combat during September and October of 1944, toward the end of World War II, leaving some 300 tanks wrecked in the area. Today the 35-acre **Oorlogsmuseum (War Museum)** commemorates that battle in this park holding a vast collection of mechanized war vehicles, as well as an incredible display of antitank devices. There are also moving exhibits documenting the Nazi occupation of Holland during World War II. Open daily from 10am to 6pm June through August, 9:30am to 5pm in other months, with an admission fee of Dfl. 7.50 ($4).

WHERE TO STAY

Eurohotel, Hinthamerstraat 63, 5211 MG 's Hertogenbosch. ☎ **073/137-777.** Fax 073/128-795. 46 rms. TV TEL

Rates (including breakfast): Dfl. 90 ($47) single; Dfl. 120 ($63) double. AE, MC, V.

This small hotel in the city center offers comfortable guest rooms and a restaurant with moderate prices.

★ **Golden Tulip Central,** Burg Loeffplein 98, 5211 RX 's Hertogenbosch. ☎ **073/125-151.** Fax 073/145-699. 125 rms, 3 suites. MINIBAR TV TEL

$ **Rates:** Dfl. 175 ($92) single; Dfl. 225 ($118) double; Dfl. 385 ($202) suite. AE, DC, MC, V.

You couldn't ask for a more romantic location than at this large hotel on the city's medieval market square. The Central somehow manages to be both modern and cozy. The guest rooms are nicely appointed, and even include a room safe for valuables, as well as hairdryers. There's a coffee shop, a bar, an à la carte restaurant, and a 14th-century cellar eatery (De Hoofdwacht).

★ **Hotel-Restaurant de Swaen,** De Lind 47, 5061 HT Oisterwijk. ☎ **04242/190-06.** Fax 04242/858-60. 18 rms. A/C TV TEL

$ **Rates:** Dfl. 225 ($118) single; Dfl. 275 ($144) double. AE, MC, V. **Closed:** Two weeks in July.

Here in this quiet little village of Oisterwijk (9 miles southwest of 's Hertogenbosch), de Swaen follows a three-centuries-old tradition of innkeeping. Indeed, the exterior of the neat white two-story hotel on the market square, with its long veranda across the front and neat, blue-trimmed windows, calls to mind the coaching inn that preceded it in this same location. Since its complete renovation, however, it has become one of Holland's most popular hostelries, and its dining room has earned international renown (see "Where to Dine," below). The plush guest rooms feature baths done up in Italian marble, with such luxurious touches as gold-plated faucets. Tiny chocolates decorated with white swans appear on your pillow each evening, just one more example of the qualities that make this place so special. Highly recommended.

WHERE TO DINE

De Pettelaar, Pettelaarseschans 1. ☎ **137-351.**
  Cuisine: CONTINENTAL/NOUVELLE CUISINE. **Reservations:** Recommended.
  Prices: Average lunch Dfl. 35–50 ($18–$26); average dinner Dfl. 50–80 ($26–$42). MC, V.
  Open: Mon–Fri noon–midnight, Sat–Sun 3pm–midnight.

This pretty restaurant in the town center specializes in beef, veal, and pork dishes.

★ **De Raadskelder**, Markt 1A, ☎ **136-919.**
  Cuisine: REGIONAL. **Reservations:** Not required.
  Prices: Average meal Dfl. 35–80 ($18–$42). AE, MC, V.
  Open: Lunch Tues–Sat noon–2pm; dinner Tues–Sat 6–9:30pm.

This atmospheric cellar restaurant in the Gothic Town Hall serves excellent meals at moderate prices.

★ **De Swaen**, De Lind 47, Oisterwijk. ☎ **04242/190-06.**
[$] **Cuisine:** CONTINENTAL/REGIONAL. **Reservations:** Recommended.
  Prices: Five-course meal Dfl. 135 ($71). AE, MC, V.
  Open: Dinner only, Tues–Sun 6–10pm. **Closed:** Two weeks in July.

Located in the Hotel-Restaurant de Swaen (see "Where to Stay," above), this is the most widely recognized restaurant in Noord Brabant. Its chef, Cas Spijkers, was born in this region and trained in leading kitchens throughout Europe before coming back to lead De Swaen to its prestigious position. A firm believer in freshness, he asserts that "the choice of your products determines the quality of your kitchen," and he selects the best of local products, travels to Brussels twice a month to the excellent markets there, smokes his own fish, meat, and game, and bakes all breads and pastries right on the premises. The result is meals that have earned De Swaen a Michelin star and a devoted following. In the elegant cream-and-gilt dining room you'll be thrown into an agony of indecision as you study the tantalizing menu, but let me suggest that you simply order his five-course menu of the day—rest assured it will be the best of the day's ingredients and prepared to perfection.

The Provincial Towns of Noord Brabant

BREDA

Historic Breda, on the main Rotterdam–Antwerp motorway and some 25 miles southwest of 's Hertogenbosch, was granted its charter back in 1252. In 1625 the town withstood a nine-month siege before surrendering to superior Spanish forces. In 1660 England's exiled Charles II took refuge here, and in 1667 the Treaty of Breda (between England, France, the United Provinces, and Denmark) awarded the colonies of New Amsterdam and New Jersey to the English. Today, life centers around the rectangular Grote Markt and the town's many fine parks.

What to See and Do

Check with the **VVV office,** located at Willemstraat 17 (☎ **076/222-444;** fax 076/218-530), for details on their conducted ■ **"Historical Kilometer"** walking tour that takes you to the **Castle of Breda** (from 1536, now a military academy), the **Great Church of Our Lady** (with its striking tomb of Count Engelbert II and his wife), and other historical points of the town.

For an in-depth view of the town's long history, visit the ■ **Stedelijk en Bisschoppelikj Museum,** 19 Grote Markt, which also holds a good collection of religious art.

Parks that offer open-air relief from city sightseeing include Valkenburg Park, Brabant Park, Sonsbeek Park, and Trekpot. Breda is also surrounded by beautiful **rural estates,** many of which open their grounds to the public, and great **public forests** such as the Mastbosch and Liesbosch, whose ancient trees form peaceful retreats. Check with the VVV for directions and details.

Art lovers will want to stop by the village of **Zundert,** just south of Breda. This is the birthplace of Vincent van Gogh, and there's a touching statue of the painter and his devoted brother, Theo, commissioned by the townspeople and sculpted by Zadkine.

Where to Stay and Dine

Hotel Breda, Roskam 20, 4813 GZ Breda. ☎ **076/222-177.** Fax 076/223-125. 50 rms. TV TEL **Directions:** Drive just southwest of Breda (exit at Rijsbergen from Hwy. E19).

Rates: Dfl. 115 ($50) single; Dfl. 130 ($68) double. AE, DC, MC, V.

This large modern hotel has well-equipped guest rooms. Its cozy bar and lounge features an open fireplace, and there's an excellent à la carte restaurant. Other amenities include an indoor pool, sauna, and solarium.

 Hotel Mastbosch, Burg Kerstenslaan 20, 4837 BM Breda. ☎ **076/565-00-50.** Fax 076/560-0040. Telex 54406. 51 rms. MINIBAR TV TEL

Rates: Dfl. 148 ($78) single; Dfl. 250 ($131) double. AE, DC, MC, V.

In a wooded site near the Mastbosch woods on the outskirts of town, this first-class hotel offers a relaxing atmosphere, modern comfortable rooms, a sun terrace, and a good restaurant.

BAARLE-NASSAU/BAARLE HERTOG

This is the town that literally can't make up its mind whether to be in Belgium or in Holland, so exists in both. The line wavers so that houses use colored number plates to identify their citizenship—if the figures are blue, the occupants are Dutch; if they're black on a white plate with a black, yellow, and red vertical stripe, the occupants are Belgian. Must get confusing!

EINDHOVEN

Eindhoven's charter dates from 1232, and for centuries it limped along as not much more than a small village, 22 miles south of 's Hertogenbosch. Yet today it ranks as Holland's fifth-largest town with all the attributes of a modern industrial city. That transformation is due almost entirely to the Philips electronics company, which has headquartered here for over 100 years, expanding into neighboring villages and making them a part of Eindhoven. Not only is this a manufacturing center, but much important research is conducted by the company.

What to See and Do

The **VVV office** is at Stationsplein 17 (☎ **040/2449-231;** fax 040/243-3435). Despite its industrialized face, Eindhoven has two fine museums. **Stedelijk van Abbe Museum,** Bilderdiiklaan 10, exhibits such giants of modern art as Picasso, Mondrian, and De Stijl. It's open Tuesday through Sunday from 11am to 5pm, with a Dfl. 5 ($2.60) admission. ◪ **Kempeland Museum,** Antoniusstraat 5–7, features exhibits depicting the history of this region, and is open Tuesday through Sunday from 1pm to 5pm, with an admission of Dfl. 4 ($2.10).

On the southern edge of Eindhoven, the ◪ **Recreatiecentrum De Tongelreep,** Antoon Coolenlaan (☎ **123-125**), is the perfect place for a time-out from sightseeing. There's a subtropical wave pool, chute-the-chute, bubble pools, paddling pool, whirlpools, a 165-foot indoor swimming pool, and an outdoor pool with a sunbathing area. There's a large parking space, and bus no. 7 takes you to the main entrance. It's open May to August, Monday through Friday from 10am to 6pm and 7 to 10pm, and on Saturday and Sunday from 10am to 5:30pm; other months, 2 to 10pm Monday through Friday, and 10am to 1pm and 2 to 5:30pm on Saturday and Sunday. Admission is Dfl. 6.25 ($3.30) per person, free for children under 4.

Where to Stay

★ **Dorint Hotel,** Vestdijk 47, 5611 CA Eindhoven. ☎ **040/326-111.**
Fax 040/440-148. 203 rms, 6 suites. A/C MINIBAR TV TEL

Rates: Dfl. 277 ($145) single; Dfl. 324 ($170) double; Dfl. 440 ($231) suite. AE, DC, MC, V.

This large modern hotel is located in the city center, not far from the central railway station. The guest rooms are spacious, with bright, attractive decor and come with such extras as a safe and in-house movies. There's the Bruegel Brasserie as well.

★ **Golden Tulip Geldrop,** Bogardeind 219, 5664 EG Geldrop. ☎ **040/867-510.**
Fax 040/855-762. 139 rms. A/C MINIBAR TV TEL

Rates (including breakfast): Dfl. 225 ($118) single; Dfl. 280 ($147) double. AE, DC, MC, V.

At the outskirts of Eindhoven on the A3 highway, this modern hotel sits at the edge of the Strabrechtse heath, a restful retreat away from the bustle of city streets. The large, nicely furnished guest rooms have in-house movies, and other amenities include a good restaurant, an indoor swimming pool, tennis courts, a solarium, a keep-fit track, hairdryers, and a sauna.

★ **Hostellerie du Château,** Kapelstraat 48, 5591 HE Heeze. ☎ **04907/635-15.**
Fax 04907/638-76. 14 rms, 1 suite. MINIBAR TV TEL

$ **Rates:** Dfl. 150 ($79) single; Dfl. 200 ($105) double; Dfl. 260 ($136) suite. AE, MC, V.

Situated in the little village of Heeze (about a 20-minute drive from Eindhoven) and directly across from a 17th-century château, this old 18th-century coaching inn has been redone in a fashion that disavows its somewhat rustic heritage. Its guest rooms feature opulent furnishings and tasteful decor, and its restaurant is considered one of Holland's best (see "Where to Dine," below).

$ Motel Eindhoven, Aalsterweg 322, 5644 RL Eindhoven. ☎ **040/123-435.**
Fax 040/120-774. 175 rms, 2 suites. TV TEL
Rates: Dfl. 104 ($54) single or double; Dfl. 140 ($73) suite. AE, MC.

The guest rooms are comfortable and nicely furnished at this moderately priced
motel on the A67 motorway, and there's a pool as well as a good restaurant (see
"Where to Dine," below).

Where to Dine

★ Bruegel Brasserie, in the Dorint Hotel, Vestdijk 47. ☎ **326-111.**
Cuisine: DUTCH. **Reservations:** Recommended.
Prices: Lunch Dfl. 40 ($21); dinner Dfl. 70 ($36). AE, DC, MC, V.
Open: Lunch Mon–Fri noon–2:30pm; dinner Mon–Sat 6–9:30pm.

The Bruegel (in the Dorint Hotel; see "Where to Stay," above) serves the "Neerlands
Dis" Old Dutch menu, as well as lunch and dinner buffets and snacks. With good
food, good atmosphere, and good value for money it's a good, centrally located stopping place for almost any kind of meal you're in the mood for.

★ Hostellerie du Château, Kapelstraat 48, Heeze. ☎ **04907/635-15.**
$ Cuisine: FRENCH. **Reservations:** Recommended.
Prices: Average lunch Dfl. 57 ($30); average dinner Dfl. 100 ($52). AE, DC, MC, V.
Open: Lunch Sun–Fri noon–2:30pm; dinner daily 6–9:30pm.

Even if you're staying in Eindhoven, it's worth the 20-minute drive to this inn in Heeze
(see "Where to Stay," above) for a meal by owner/chef Hans Huisman. The cuisine is
basically classic French, and gourmet regulars often come from Belgium and Germany
when the season is right for asparagus from his own fields. The wine cellar is one of
the best in Holland.

★ De Karpendonkse Hoeve, Sumatralaan 3. ☎ **813-663.**
Cuisine: INTERNATIONAL. **Reservations:** Required.
Prices: Average lunch Dfl. 65 ($34); average dinner Dfl. 95 ($50). AE, MC, V.
Open: Lunch Mon–Fri noon–2pm; dinner Mon–Sat 6–10pm.

This first-class restaurant, a member of the prestigious Alliance Gastronomique
Néerlandaise, specializes in game in season and always the best of local products in a
pretty setting with terrace dining in good weather. It's located on the outskirts of town.

$ Motel Eindhoven, Aalsterweg 322. ☎ **123-435.**
Cuisine: REGIONAL. **Reservations:** Not required.
Prices: Fixed-price menu Dfl. 30–55 ($15–$29). AE, MC, V.
Open: Daily 7am–11:30pm.

There are three-, four-, and five-course fixed-price menus in this attractive motel
dining room (see "Where to Stay," above). Regional specialties such as schnitzel and
pork chops with mushrooms are featured. It's located on the A67 motorway.

3 Limburg

Of all Holland's provinces, Limburg is the least likely to fit any "Dutch" image you
bring with you. Missing are the flat fields interlaced with canals, the windmills (although there are a few), and most of the other traditions we associate with Holland.
It is, however, one of the most beautiful of the provinces, and it's such marvelous
holiday country that the Dutch themselves flock there in droves.

Limburg is surrounded on three sides by Germany and Belgium, and since Roman times it has been a well-trod pathway for invaders, defenders, refugees, and just plain travelers. Its own cities draw liberally from the richness of other European cultures and cities that are close at hand. For those of a gambling nature, it provides the casino at Valkenburg, near Maastricht.

Northern Limburg shelters holiday parks and villages in a landscape of wooded hills and broad heaths that extend across central Limburg; southern Limburg occupies the highest ground in Holland, with its capital city, Maastricht, an exuberant, joyful center of history, higher education, and inborn hospitality extended at the drop of a smile.

SEEING THE PROVINCE There's a wealth of sightseeing—numerous castles and mansions, historic churches, picturesque villages, and mysterious caverns that tunnel into the heart of high cliffs. To all that, add the attractions of cities like Liège, Antwerp, Brussels, Cologne, Aachen, Düsseldorf, Bonn, and Luxembourg, all just a hop, skip, and a jump away. By no means, however, would I want to imply that Limburg is simply a province to pass through on your way elsewhere in Europe—this is a province so rich in holiday attractions that I urge you to make your base here and let day-trips take care of all those adjacent destinations.

You can reach Maastricht by **air** from Amsterdam via **NLM City Hopper,** which offers frequent daily flights. **Drivers** should take A2 or A25 to reach the provincial capital. The Province of Limburg is easily toured by car, of course, but nondrivers will also find it easy to get around by either **train** or **bus.** The scenic countryside also lends itself to **hiking** or **cycling.** While most of your sightseeing is likely to be from a Maastricht base in the south of the province, a trip north to Thorn and Venlo is well worthwhile.

WHERE TO STAY Accommodations come in all shapes, sizes, locations, and price ranges in Limburg. There are castle hotels, posh luxury establishments, homey small hotels with moderate rates, and bed-and-breakfast accommodations in private homes.

WHERE TO DINE Maastricht, the capital of Limburg, is filled with good places to eat—it's not uncommon for people to drive from nearby Liège or Aachen just to have dinner there. Spotted around the province are several outstanding restaurants, and many others that serve excellent meals at moderate prices. And, of course, there are those castles.

Maastricht, the Provincial Capital

Maastricht, 131 miles southeast of Amsterdam, is Holland's oldest fortified city, tracing its roots back to a Roman settlement in 50 B.C. here on the Rivers Meuse and Jeker at the foot of Mount St. Peter. From Mount St. Peter, the Romans and all those who came after them took great chunks of marlstone, a type of limestone that is as soft to carve and chisel as soap until it hits the air, when it quickly becomes as hard as any stone. Many of Maastricht's buildings are constructed of marlstone, and as more and more was extracted, Mount St. Peter became honeycombed with great caverns, some 20,000 passages boring into the cliff.

The Romans stayed four centuries, and with their departure, Maastricht was, for nearly another 400 years, the seat of bishops (Saint Servatius was the first, about 380, and Saint Hubert was the last, in 722), and from the early 1200s until the late 1700s it was under the feudal rule of the dukes of Brabant. The city was also the last earthly sight for the hero of Alexandre Dumas's *The Three Musketeers:* It was here that d'Artagnan lost his life during King Louis XIV's seige of Maastricht in 1673. It was French forces who, in 1795, occupied the city and declared it capital of a French province.

That changed with Napoléon's defeat at Waterloo, and when Belgium gained its separation from Holland in 1830, this little province stayed Dutch, with Maastricht its capital. Over the years Maastricht sustained 21 sieges as one ruler after another sought to control its strategic position. Today the city is a charming mixture of historic buildings and monuments (more than 1,450), university students, cultural activities, a lighthearted carnival famous throughout Europe, and some of the finest restaurants to be found in any Dutch city its size.

WHAT TO SEE & DO

INFORMATION   You'll find the Maastricht **VVV** tourist office at Het Dinghuis, Kleine Straat 1, 6211 ED Maastricht (☎ **043/252-121;** fax 043/213-746). One of the best equipped, most helpful, and friendliest in Holland, it is open 9am to 6pm Monday through Saturday, and in July and August also from 11am to 3pm on Sunday.

WALKING TOURS   To begin your tour of this lovely and lively city, go by the VVV office and pick up their **"Historic Walking Tour of Maastricht"** brochure. It guides you from their office, located in the busy shopping district, through city streets to a number of historic buildings and monuments. If you fall under Maastricht's spell as completely as I have done, you'll keep the brochure with you and ramble, finally completing the entire 1 1/2-hour route in two or three days! Keep your eye out for the little square called **Op de Thermen,** where you can still see the outline in its cobblestones of a Roman bath; the **Markt,** where vendors gather on Wednesday and Friday mornings to open colorful stalls (some from as far away as Belgium and Germany); the statue of the cheerful little *'t Mooswief (Vegetable Woman)* in the Markt square; the small, impish *Mestreechter Geis* statue in a tiny square at Kleine Stokstraat (he embodies the joie de vivre of Maastrichters, and his name means "Spirit of Maastrichters"); and the **Vrijthof Square** at the heart of the old city. The **St. Servatius Bridge** dates from 1280 and is one of the oldest in Holland. And as you walk around the city, look for the 250 or so **17th- and 18th-century houses** with sculpted gable stones showing the name of the house and the year it was built. Some of the prettiest are on Hoogbrugstraat, Rechtstraat, Markt square, Boschstraat, Stokstraat Quartier, Platielstraat, and Achter het Vleeshuis.

The VVV also conducts ✪ **guided walking tours** from late June through August that cost Dfl. 6 ($3.15) for adults, Dfl. 3.50 ($1.85) for children. Included is a fascinating **Maastricht Fortifications Walk** past the remains of the medieval city and buildings with a military history, relics of the second half of the 19th century when Maastricht was still a fortified city with heavy walls and outworks.

BOAT TOURS   ✪ **Rederij Stiphout River Cruises,** Maaspromenade 27 (☎ **043/ 25-41-51**), provide one of the nicest ways to see Maastricht from the River Meuse. Year-round every hour on the hour one of these river boats leaves the landing stage between the St. Servatius and Wilhelmina Bridges for a 55-minute cruise past Mount St. Peter (you can leave the boat, tour the caves, and catch the next boat to continue the cruise) and on to the sluices at the Belgian border. The fare is Dfl. 8 ($4) for adults, Dfl. 5 ($2.60) for children, and you should book a day ahead on these popular cruises.

There are also delightful day-long cruises to Liège and a romantic sunset cruise that includes dancing and dinner—call for schedules, fares, and booking.

The Sights

 Basilica of Our Lady, Vrouweplein. ☎ **251-851.**

The west wing and crypts of this medieval Romanesque cruciform structure date from the 12th century, and there is evidence of an even earlier Christian church, as well as a pagan place of worship, on this same site in the city center. But it is the side chapel sheltering the pilgrim's statue of Our Beloved Lady Stella Mare (dating from 1500) that most people come to see. The richly robed statue is credited with many miracles, even during long years when it had to be hidden away because of religious persecution. It is said that in the early 1600s, when the Catholic religion was once more recognized, as many as 20,000 pilgrims came to worship at her shrine every Easter Monday. When the Calvinists came into power in 1632 the statue once more went into hiding, and in 1699 legend says that Our Lady herself established the "prayer route" by which she was returned to her proper place by stepping down from her pedestal and leading a devout parishioner through the muddy streets. It is recorded that the morning after the miraculous walk there was indeed mud on the hem of Our Lady's robe! The church treasury contains a rich collection of tapestries, reliquaries, church silver, etc.

Admission: Dfl. 4 ($2.10) adults, Dfl. 1.50 (80¢) children.

Open: Treasury, Mon–Sat 11am–5pm, Sun 1–5pm. Basilica, July–Aug daily 10am–4pm; Sept–June 10am–5pm.

Bonnefanten Museum of Art and Archeology, avenue Ceramique 250. ☎ **290-190.**

Don't miss this intriguing collection. The archeological finds date from 250,000 B.C. to the Middle Ages and the art includes works from the medieval to the modern. It's housed in a modern E-shaped building near the River Meuse that was opened in early 1995.

Admission: Dfl. 10 ($5.25) adults, Dfl. 5 ($2.60) children 13–18 and senior citizens.

Open: Tues–Sun 11am–5pm.

 Caves of St. Pietersberg.

If you do no other sightseeing during your Maastricht visit, you shouldn't miss these unique underground chambers. From the days of the Romans to the long days of several sieges to the months and years of enemy occupation during two world wars, these 20,000 passages have served as a place of refuge to people who have left behind interesting drawings and signatures on the marlstone walls. During World War II they also served as a refuge for such Dutch masterpieces as Rembrandt's *Night Watch* and other treasures that were hidden away from the Nazis. You'll follow your guide's lantern through about 2 miles of what some say are the nearly 200 miles (others say only 6 miles) of 20- to 40-foot-high tunnels. Stay close to that lantern—there are tales told in Maastricht of those who entered here and were never seen again (ask about the four monks). Look closely at the signatures you pass and you'll see many names straight from the history books.

Admission: Dfl. 6 ($3.15) adults, Dfl. 3 ($1.55) children.

Open/Directions: Check with the VVV office for exact hours (tours leave from two entrances at different hours), and directions to reach the caves by city bus or boat.

★ **Natuur Historisch Museum,** De Bosquetplein 6–7. ☎ **293-064.**
You really should visit this museum *after* you've seen the Caves of St. Pietersberg, for then you can more fully appreciate the fossils that have come from the walls of those caverns. In addition, there are other rocks and minerals and a traditional garden of local lore and flora. It's located in the city center, near the Music Conservatory.
Admission: Dfl. 4 ($2.10) adults, Dfl. 3 ($1.55) children.
Open: Mon–Fri 10am–12:30pm and 1:30–5pm, Sun 2–5pm. **Closed:** Holidays.

★ **St. Servaasbasiliek (Basilica of Saint Servatius),** Keizer Karl.
This majestic medieval cruciform church in the city center dates its oldest parts back to the year 1000, and it was considerably enlarged in the 14th and 15th centuries. Saint Servatius, Maastricht's first bishop, is buried in its crypt, and its treasury holds a large reliquary of the saint and several of his religious items (staff, pectoral cross, drinking beaker, etc.), as well as a rich collection of religious vestments and other objects. The southern tower of the cathedral's west wall holds Grand-mère (Grandmother), the largest bell in Holland and a beloved symbol of the city.
Admission: Dfl. 4 ($2.10) adults, Dfl. 1.50 (80¢) children under 13.
Open: Treasury and basilica, Tues–Sun 10am–5pm. **Closed:** Mon.

Shopping

At Kesselskade 55, ✦ **Olivier Bonbons b.v.** (☎ **215-526**) is a small shop that has been turning out chocolates and other sweets for more than 30 years, and one of their specialties is a porcelain reproduction of the much-loved Bell of Grand-mère (Grandmother) filled with luscious chocolates, a lovely gift to take home for friends or family (or yourself?).

There are **souvenir shops** all through the shopping streets of Maastricht, but one with an exceptionally good selection at reasonable prices is **H. Corsius,** Brugstraat 34 (☎ **214-226**). It's a small shop, crammed with gifts and souvenirs in just about all price ranges.

Evening Entertainment

During the winter months there are frequent performances of **theater, ballet, operettas, musicals, cabaret,** etc. Check with the VVV for current happenings. Year-round, there's plenty going on after dark in Maastricht, not the least of which goes on in more than 500 cozy **bars** and **cafés.** To get you started in the right direction, the VVV issues a **"Pub Crawl"** booklet, but you'll undoubtedly find your own favorite route.

Easy Excursions from Maastricht

Limburg sometimes calls itself the "Land Without Frontiers," and it would certainly seem so when you learn that it's possible to plan day trips by coach to Belgium (Liège, Antwerp, Brussels, Ardennes), Germany (Moselle, Tuddern, Eifel, Aachen), Luxembourg (both the capital city and the small towns around the Grand Duchy), and France (Givet and Paris). The VVV can give you details of the many options and arrange bookings.

Dutch Railways also offers attractive routes and rates across borders as well as within Limburg itself, and there is good bus service around the province. Inquire at the railway station in Maastricht for schedules and fares.

WHERE TO STAY

Although accommodations are plentiful in Maastricht, they can also be booked up in the peak summer months, so reserve ahead if possible and turn to the VVV office for help if you arrive without a place to rest your head. Also, if you'd like to stay in a private home, the VVV can arrange that for you.

★ **Golden Tulip Barbizon Maastricht,** Forum 110, 6229 GV Maastricht.
☎ **043/838-281,** or toll free **800/344-1212** in the U.S. Fax 043/615-62. 79 rms. A/C MINIBAR TV TEL.

Rates: Dfl. 260 ($136) single; Dfl 380 ($200) double. Special rates for sports package holidays. AE, DC, MC, V.

This luxurious modern hotel at the Maastricht Exposition and Congress Center, about a three-minute walk from a secondary railway station, offers deluxe rooms with luxury bathrooms. Amenities include a hairdryer and trouser press. There's a gourmet restaurant specializing in French cuisine, an English-style pub that also serves Italian specialties at modest prices, and a sauna/fitness center. The hotel also offers wheelchair access.

$ **Grand Hôtel de l'Empereur,** Stationstraat 2, 6221 BP Maastricht.
☎ **043/213-838.** Fax 043/216-890. 61 rms. A/C TV TEL

Rates (including breakfast): Dfl. 205 ($108) single; Dfl. 235 ($123) double. AE, DC, MC, V.

Set on a corner across from the railway station, this lovely old turreted hotel has comfortable, attractive guest rooms, as well as apartments that can sleep up to four people. Some rooms feature trouser presses. There's a cozy lounge bar that draws a local clientele and a restaurant. Other amenities include a sauna and whirlpool.

Holiday Inn Maastricht, De Ruiterij 1, 6221 EW Maastricht. ☎ **043/509-191.** Fax 043/509-192. Telex 56822. 111 rms, 23 suites. A/C MINIBAR TV TEL

Rates: Dfl. 265 ($139) single; Dfl. 345 ($181) double; Dfl. 600 ($315) suite. AE, DC, MC, V.

Stretched along the riverfront, this modern deluxe (five-star) hotel is elegant from top to bottom. Some of the spacious guest rooms come with balconies or terraces, and all have in-house movies and hairdryers. There's a lively bar and lounge overlooking the river, a coffee shop, and a good restaurant.

★ **Hotel Beaumont,** Wijekerbrugstraat 40, 6221 BP Maastricht. ☎ **043/254-433.** Fax 043/210-747. 82 rms, 2 suites. TV TEL

Rates (including breakfast): Dfl. 160 ($84) single; Dfl. 190 ($100) double; Dfl. 175–240 ($93–$127) suite. AE, DC, MC, V.

Run by the third generation of one family, this well-established hotel is located between the railway station and the river, just a short walk from the town center. The Beaumont's decor is warmly classical, and the guest rooms are comfortable and attractive. There's the Restaurant Alsacien, a cozy but stylish restaurant serving very good, moderately priced meals.

$ **Hotel-Cafe de Poshoorn,** Stationstraat 47, 6221 BN Maastricht.
☎ **043/217-334.** 14 rms. TV TEL

Rates (including breakfast): Dfl. 95 ($50) single; Dfl. 135 ($71) double. MC, V.

You register with the friendly owner in the ground-floor café at this small corner hotel, where comfortable guest rooms are above the eatery. It's near the railway station.

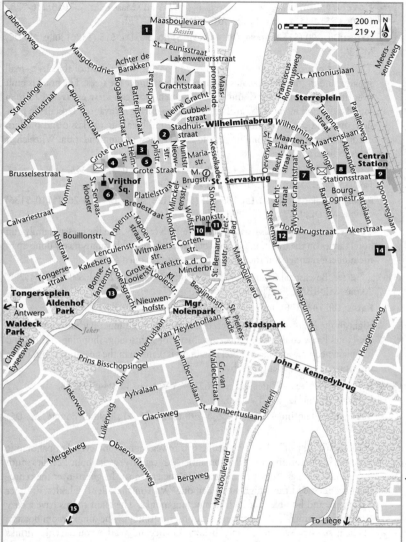

Maastricht

Church   ✝■   Post Office ⊠   Information ⓘ

ACCOMMODATIONS:

Golden Tulip Barbizon
   Maastricht **14**
Grand Hotel de l'Empereur **9**
Holiday Inn Maastricht **12**
Hotel Beaumont **7**
Hotel du Casque **3**
Hotel-Cafe de Poshoorn **8**
Hotel Derlon **10**
Hotel Pauw **1**

ATTRACTIONS:

Basilica of Our Lady **11**
Bonnefanten Museum
   of Art and Archeology **5**
Caves of St. Pietersberg **15**
Cultural Center **4**
Natuur Historisch Museum **13**
Stadhuis **2**
St. Servaasbasiliek
   (Basilica of St. Servatius) **6**

★ **Hotel Derlon,** Onze Lieve Vrouweplein 6, 6211 HD Maastricht. ☎ **043/216-770.**
Fax 043/251-933. 41 rms, 1 suite. A/C MINIBAR TV TEL

$ **Rates:** Dfl. 290 ($152) single; Dfl. 410 ($215) double; Dfl. 615 ($326) suite. AE, DC,
MC, V.

This jewel of a deluxe, four-star hotel sits on one of the loveliest of the city's small
squares, and in summer operates a terrace café out under the trees. The hotel is built
over ancient Roman ruins, and in its basement you can view excavated Roman
foundations and many of the artifacts uncovered during excavation. Upstairs in public rooms and the guest rooms there is a beautiful blending of classic and modern
decor, and each guest room is bright and airy. Highest recommendation. Wheelchair
accessibility.

Hotel du Casque, Helmstraat 14, 6211 TA Maastricht. ☎ **043/214-343.**
Fax 043/255-155. 38 rms. MINIBAR TV TEL

Rates (including breakfast): Dfl. 185–235 ($97–$123) single; Dfl. 210–260 ($110–$136)
double. AE, DC, MC, V.

There's been an inn at this location since the 15th century, and the present family-run
hotel carries on the tradition in good style, with comfortable rooms nicely done up in
the modern manner and friendliness of the old-fashioned sort.

Hotel Pauw, Boschstraat 27, 6211 AS Maastricht. ☎ **043/212-222.** Fax 043/213-432.
70 rms. MINIBAR TV TEL

Rates: Dfl. 148 ($78) single; Dfl. 190 ($100) double. AE, DC, MC, V.

Right in the heart of the city center, overlooking the old inner harbor called Bassin,
the Hotel Pauw couldn't be more convenient for sightseeing, shopping, dining, and
just plain people-watching. A hotel restaurant is planned in the near future, but in the
meantime there are plenty nearby.

★ **Kasteel Wittem,** Wittemerallee 3, 6286 AA Wittem. ☎ **04450/1208.**
Fax 04450/1260. 12 rms. TV TEL

Rates (including breakfast): Dfl. 230–290 ($121–$152) single or double. AE, DC,
MC, V.

If you're lucky, you'll draw one of the two tower rooms (one even has panoramic
windows in the bathroom!) in this romantic 12th-century castle about 12 miles south
of Maastricht, where stately swans adorn an ancient moat. Its guests over the centuries have included the Knights of Julemont, William the Silent, Charles V, other
noblemen, and humble folk such as traveling monks. The guest rooms have a cozy
charm with country-style decor and beautiful furnishings. The dining room boasts a
Michelin star (see "Where to Dine," below), and in good weather you can enjoy drinks
on the garden terrace.

★ **Ons Krjtland Hotel,** Julianastraat 22, 6285 AH Epen. ☎ **04455/1557.**
Fax 04455/24-15. 32 apartments. MINIBAR TV TEL

$ **Rates:** Dfl. 190–250 ($100–$131) apartment. AE, DC, MC, V.

Set among beautiful wooded hills in the Geul river valley (15 miles southeast of
Maastricht), this comfortable first-class apartment hotel provides easy access to the
main roads to Maastricht, Belgium, and Germany. The nicely furnished and appointed
apartments sleep two to four people, all with kitchenettes and a terrace. There's an

indoor swimming pool, a sauna/fitness center, a bar, and a lovely restaurant with valley views—all the services of a hotel and all the comfort of your own apartment, which makes a nice change.

WHERE TO DINE

★ **Au Coin des Bons Enfants**, Ezelmarkt 4. ☎ **212-359.**
Cuisine: FRENCH/BELGIAN. **Reservations:** Recommended.
Prices: Average lunch Dfl. 50 ($26); dinner Dfl. 65–100 ($34–$52). MC, V.
Open: Lunch Mon–Fri noon–2pm; dinner Mon–Sat 6:30–10pm.

Beauty and sophistication plus an open log fire create an elegant ambience at this restaurant in the city center. In fine weather there's outdoor dining in a rustic courtyard. There's an exceptionally good wine cellar here to complement fine French specialties (lovely asparagus and ham dishes in season).

Au Premier, Brusselsestraat 13. ☎ **219-761.**
Cuisine: DUTCH/FRENCH. **Reservations:** Recommended.
Prices: Average meal Dfl. 30–60 ($15–$31). MC, V.
Open: Lunch Tues–Fri noon–3pm; dinner daily 6–10pm.

Also in the moderate-to-expensive range, Au Premier is a stylish, intimate restaurant. In summer, you can dine on the pretty garden patio. The cuisine features regional specialties utilizing fresh local produce, as well as provincial French dishes. It's located in the city center.

★ **Chateau Neercanne**, Cannerweg 800. ☎ **251-359.**
Cuisine: FRENCH. **Reservations:** Recommended.
$ **Prices:** Fixed-price meal Dfl. 90 ($47). AE, DC, MC, V.
Open: Lunch Mon–Sat noon–2pm; dinner Mon–Sat 6–9:15pm.

Set into a high hill 2 miles south of Maastricht above the River Jeker and the Belgian border, this gracious château was built in 1698 for a Dutch nobleman. Its wide stone terrace, where you can dine or have drinks in fine weather, affords views of the beautiful Jeker valley. Inside, tasteful renovations have created a classic, romantic ambience with baroque wallpaper, shades of beige and burgundy, and Venetian glass chandeliers. Marlstone caves extending back into the hillside serve as wine cellars, with an arched-roof, candlelit room made for cozy before- or after-dinner drinks. Fresh herbs and vegetables straight from its own gardens and the best of local ingredients assure top quality. The menu changes almost daily, depending on what's available. A member of Alliance Gastronomique Néerlandaise.

★ **In Mestreechter Geis**, Hoenderstraat 16. ☎ **250-923.**
Cuisine: SEAFOOD/GAME. **Reservations:** Required.
$ **Prices:** Average meal Dfl. 35–70 ($18–$36). AE, MC, V.
Open: Lunch Tues–Fri noon–3pm; dinner Tues–Sun 6–10pm.

This lovely little restaurant, located in a former mussels shop in the city center, is now an intimate oasis of white walls, dark exposed beams, and open fireplace. It's a warm, friendly, family-owned and -operated place specializing in excellent fish dishes, with a talented chef (son of the owners) using fresh, seasonal catches to create memorable meals. In the fall, they often serve wild boar, hare, and other game specialties, and spring brings delicate new asparagus and other seasonal delights to table. Highly recommended.

★ **In den Ouden Vogelstruys,** Vrijthof 15. ☎ **214-888.**

Cuisine: BAR FOOD/DUTCH. **Reservations:** Not required.
💲 **Prices:** Average meal Dfl. 15 ($8). No credit cards.
Open: Daily 9:30am–2am.

This traditional café-bar in the city center is wonderfully atmospheric (there's a cannonball in its wall that lodged there in 1653—ask about the story), and it sits diagonally across from a white house that over the centuries has guested both Charlemagne and Napoléon. The bar's rustic interior and faithful local clientele make it a great place to stop for a light lunch or just for a drink.

★ **Kasteel Wittem,** Wittemerallee 3, Wittem. ☎ **04450/12-08.**

Cuisine: FRENCH. **Reservations:** Required.
Prices: Average meal Dfl. 80–140 ($42–$73). AE, DC, MC, V.
Open: Dinner only, daily 6–9pm.

The beautiful dining room in this lovely castle about 12 miles south of Maastricht (see "Where to Stay," above) is paneled in French oak and has a warm, clubby atmosphere. Its cuisine is of such high quality that it has long boasted a coveted Michelin star.

Sagittarius, Bredestraat 7. ☎ **211-492.**

Cuisine: SEAFOOD/DUTCH/FRENCH. **Reservations:** Recommended.
Prices: Average dinner Dfl. 55 ($30). MC, V.
Open: Dinner only, Tues–Sat 6–10pm.

This light, airy, two-level restaurant is on one of Maastricht's prettiest streets, in the city center across from the Stadsschouwburg theater. Chef Jan van Werven prepares modern and classic variations of local and French cuisine as you watch in his open kitchen. The menu changes daily to feature the freshest ingredients, and among my personal favorites is the excellent bouillabaisse et sa rouille. In summer there's pleasant garden dining.

💲 **Stap In,** Kesselskade 61. ☎ **219-710.**

Cuisine: DUTCH. **Reservations:** Not required.
Prices: Average meal Dfl. 15–20 ($8–$10). AE, DC, MC, V.
Open: Daily 10am–9pm. (Sidewalk café open later in summer.)

The extensive menu at this bright, popular spot in the city center features Dutch traditional specialties, hamburgers, omelets, spaghetti, sandwiches, and who knows what else. The food is excellent, and best of all it comes at budget prices. Tables are set outside in fine weather.

'T Plenkske, Plankstraat 6. ☎ **218-456.**

Cuisine: DUTCH/FRENCH. **Reservations:** Recommended.
Prices: Average meal Dfl. 45–65 ($23–$34). MC, V.
Open: Lunch Mon–Sat noon–2:30pm; dinner Mon–Sat 6–10:30pm.

In the moderate-to-expensive range, 'T Plenkske, located in the beautifully renovated Stokstraat quarter in the city center, features regional specialties from Maastricht and Liège, with a goodly number of French classics thrown in for good measure. This lovely restaurant, with its light, airy decor and outdoor patio overlooking the Thermen (site of ancient Roman baths), is a great local favorite.

The Provincial Towns of Limburg

VALKENBURG

Valkenburg is some 7 miles east of Maastricht, and you'll find the Limburg provincial **VVV office** in Den Halder Castle, Valkenburg (☎ **04406/133-64; fax 04406/167-25).

What to See and Do

In an art deco setting, the **Holland Casino Valkenburg,** Odapark, Valkenburg (☎ **04406/155-50**), operates French and American roulette, blackjack, and mini punto banco. There is also a jackpot Club, a separate area with jackpot machines of all shapes and sizes, plus a restaurant, bar, and lounge. You should know that a dress code is observed (jacket and tie—or turtleneck—for men, dress or dressy pants suit for the ladies), and you'll need your passport to show you're over 18 years of age. The management tells me that "if you're at least 18, carry a valid ID, and are correctly dressed, you'll be most welcome." The good times roll seven days a week from 2pm to 2am. Admission is Dfl. 10 ($5.25) per day. Good luck!

About 3 miles south of Valkenburg, the **Margraten Military Cemetery,** on the Maastricht–Aachen highway, the final resting place for all American troops who died in Holland in World War II, is a place much revered by the Dutch, who tend the graves and many times leave wreaths and flowers behind as symbols of gratitude for the sacrifices that liberated them from Nazi oppressors.

Where to Stay and Dine

Prinses Juliana, Broekhem 11, 6301 HD Valkenburg. ☎ **04406/122-44.** Fax 04406/144-05. 19 rms, 6 suites. MINIBAR TV TEL

Rates: Dfl. 200 ($105) single; Dfl. 250 ($131) double; Dfl. 350 ($184) suite. AE, DC, MC, V.

Only about a 10-minute drive (7 miles) east of Maastricht, this pleasant small hotel houses one of Holland's most respected restaurants, with a gourmet menu. The cheerful garden restaurant is a pleasant setting for light meals and the famed Sunday buffet lunch. The guest rooms are truly luxurious, all tastefully decorated and furnished, and the exquisite suites are the ultimate in luxury.

HEERLEN

Back when Heerlen (14 miles northeast of Maastricht) was a major point on Roman roads, the *sudatorium* (sauna), *natatio* (swimming pool), and gymnasium that were such a part of life in Rome traveled with Romans all across Europe, and the remains of one such are preserved in the modern **Museum Thermen,** Coriovalumstraat 9. Open from 10am to 5pm Tuesday through Friday, from 2 to 5pm on Saturday and Sunday; closed most holidays.

An interesting collection of fossils, rocks, minerals, geological models, and maps tells the story of Limburg's landscape history at the **Geologisch Museum Heerlen,** Voskuilenweg 131. It's open Monday through Friday from 9am to noon and 2 to 5pm; closed holidays.

Where to Stay and Dine

Baron Hotel Heerlen, Wilhelminaplein 17, 6411 KW Heerlen. ☎ **045/713-333.** Fax 045/715-491. 62 rms, 2 suites. MINIBAR TV TEL

Rates (including breakfast): Dfl. 120 ($63) single; Dfl. 130 ($68) double; Dfl. 150 ($79) suite. AE, DC, MC, V.

Not far from the Aambos park, this member of the Baron hotel chain has deluxe rooms and suites. It has a very good, attractive restaurant, a coffee shop, and a nice bar/lounge with an open fire.

 Hotel Winseler Hof, Tunnelweg 99, 6372 XH Landgraff. ☎ **045/464-343.** Fax 045/352-711. 49 rms. TV TEL

 Rates: Dfl. 155 ($81) single; Dfl. 190 ($100) double. AE, MC, V.

This lovely deluxe hotel a mile from Kerkade occupies what was once a gentleman farmer's estate, built in 1500. The guest rooms are in two wings surrounding a large cobbled courtyard, and on the third side there's a spectacular ballroom in what used to be a barn. The remaining side holds a candlelit cocktail lounge, with a gourmet Italian restaurant upstairs. While the guest rooms are equipped with the very latest comforts, there are such historical touches as exposed brick walls and original ceiling beams.

 Kasteel Erenstein, Oud Erensteinerweg 6, 6468 PC Kerkrade. ☎ **045/461-333.** Fax 045/460-748. 44 rms, 16 suites. MINIBAR TV TEL

Rates: Dfl. 180 ($94) single; Dfl. 195 ($103) double; Dfl. 220–350 ($116–$185) suite. AE, DC, MC, V.

This splendid Renaissance castle 7 miles southeast of Heerlen is actually used now only for its renowned restaurant. Accommodations are across the road in a remodeled 270-year-old *boerderij* (a two-story, fortified farmhouse built around a central court-yard) that is a national monument. The guest rooms are beautifully furnished in a contemporary style, and the 10 suites, some with private terraces, are spacious. There's also a health club with a whirlpool, sauna, steambath, and hot tub for a very small fee. Breakfast is extra, but the additional charge is minimal and a real bargain when you consider that your morning repast can be served in your room, in the winter garden/ terrace, or in the castle's grand hall.

In a beautiful natural park and surrounded by a moat, the marvelous 14th-century castle across the road serves gourmet meals in its elegant grand hall. The cuisine is mainly French, and specialties change daily according to what's available locally to ensure freshness of every ingredient. The fixed-price meal is Dfl. 85 ($44), and *advance reservations* are absolutely essential.

THORN

In this lovely little medieval townlet (often called the "White Village" because all the houses are painted white), about halfway between Maastricht and Venlo (27 miles northeast of Maastricht, 22 miles southwest of Venlo), virtually all public buildings are painted white, and its huge **Abdijkerk** stone church has a stunning baroque inte-rior and high altar, as well as a small museum well worth a visit. There's also a **Radio and Gramophone Museum** and a **Doll Museum.**

Where to Stay and Dine

 Hotel la Ville Blanche, Hoogstraat 2, 6017 AR Thorn. ☎ **04756/2341.** Fax 04756/7328. Telex 30526. 23 rms. MINIBAR TV TEL

Rates (including breakfast): Dfl. 110 ($58) single; Dfl. 160 ($84) double. AE, MC, V.

Right in the center of the village, this small hotel offers nicely done-up guest rooms. Amenities include the Cellar Bar and the attractive La Ville Blanche restaurant, with excellent food and moderate prices.

VENLO

The fortified town of Venlo, 27 miles northeast of Maastricht, received its city rights as far back as 1343, and although it is now a thriving industrial and commercial center, its history is apparent in the Renaissance 16th-century **Town Hall,** where the walls in its council room are covered with Cordovan leather. The **VVV office** is at Koninginnen Square 2 (☎ **077/543-800;** fax 077/540-633).

The beautiful period rooms in the **Goltzius Museum,** Goltziusstraat 21, bring to life the history of Venlo and North Limburg, and there are also interesting arts and crafts collections. Hours are 10am to 4:30pm Tuesday through Friday, from 2 to 5pm on Saturday, Sunday, and holidays. Admission is Dfl. 6 ($3.15).

Where to Stay and Dine

Hotel Venlo, Nijmeegseweg 90, 5916 Venlo. ☎ **077/544-141.** Fax 077/543-133. 88 rms. MINIBAR TV TEL

Rates: Dfl. 85 ($44) single; Dfl. 95 ($50) double. AE, DC, MC, V.

Rooms are modern, attractive, and well furnished in this large motel on E34/A67, with such extras as in-house movies. Three rooms are also fitted for the handicapped. The excellent restaurant is open daily from 6am to midnight, with regional specialties featured on fixed-price menus for Dfl. 30–40 ($15–$21), lower for breakfast and lunch.

19

Getting to Know Luxembourg

THE GRAND DUCHY OF LUXEMBOURG IS SUCH A TINY LITTLE COUNTRY (ONLY 999 square miles) it hardly seems possible that its borders could embrace a treasure trove of travel delights worthy of a nation many times its size. Yet within those borders are the remnants of a rich history and a landscape whose scenic beauties vary from wild highlands to peaceful river valleys to southern plains dotted with picturesque villages and farmlands. Its people have emerged from a turbulent past to forge a prosperous present and build the framework for an optimistic future not only for their own country, but for the entire European Union.

This is a land that captures the imagination and begs the traveler to tarry—a unique, colorful bazaar of travel memories.

1 Geography, History, and Politics

Geography

Geographically, the Grand Duchy consists of two very distinct regions. The Ardennes hills, richly forested, lie in the northern half, while to the south are rolling farmlands, woods, and the valley of the Moselle with its famous vineyards. The mining district is tucked away in the extreme south.

Luxembourg City sits in the center of the southern region and is a marvelously contrasting mix of the old and the new. The older city runs along a deep valley beneath the brooding casements that have lent themselves so readily to defense in times of war, while the more modern part of town crowns steep cliffs overlooking the old.

In the northern Ardennes region, handsome castles are found around virtually every bend, with especially interesting ones at Clervaux and Esch-sur-Sûre. Medieval Vianden, surrounded by beautiful forests and proud site of a huge restored fortress, is a pretty Ardennes holiday town.

For Americans, the Ardennes hold another fascination, for it was here, in places like Berdorf and Clervaux and Ettelbruck, that U.S. forces engaged Nazi troops in the fierce Battle of the Bulge. Memorials to those who fell during those closing days of World War II mark the route that finally led to Luxembourg's total liberation on February 12, 1945.

Along the valley of the Moselle, vacationers camp and hike and fish, and tourists come by the busload to visit world-famous wineries.

History

BEFORE THE 12TH CENTURY Long before recorded history, the Grand Duchy was home to Magdalenian, Neolithic, and Celtic tribes. It was the Celts, those fiercely loyal people who resisted invaders to the death, whose Treviri tribe finally fell to Roman legions intent on bringing all of Europe under Caesar's rule. Their defeat came in the 1st century A.D., and for almost 500 years afterward one Roman emperor after another put down numerous uprisings as their independent-minded subjects stubbornly refused to give up their strong Druidism worship for the paganism of Rome.

Christianity succeeded where paganism failed, however, and by the 5th century the only reminders of the

Dateline

■ 963 Count Sigefroi, founder of the House of Luxembourg, exchanges some of his lands for a Roman fortress called Lucilinburhuc and builds a small castle on a rocky outcrop called the Bock, laying the foundation for the future city of Luxembourg.

➤

Dateline

- **1244** Countess Ermesinde grants town of Luxembourg personal freedom for its citizens and autonomy to its administration.

- **1288** Luxembourg suffers a crushing defeat in the Battle of Worringen, putting an end to its acquisition of land in Limburg and Brabant.

- **1354** John of Luxembourg, king of Bohemia, raises Luxembourg to a duchy.

- **1364** Luxembourg reaches the peak of its political power as it gains more lands and two members of the House of Luxembourg become emperors.

- **1388** Wenzel II gives the duchy to his nephew, Jost von Mahren, as a fiefdom, with disastrous effects on Luxembourg.

- **1443** Philip the Good of Burgundy captures the fortress of Luxembourg and establishes French rule.

- **1506** Beginning of Spanish rule, which was to last until 1684.

- **1684** The fortress is recaptured and the country is once more under French rule.

- **1697** Start of the second period of Spanish rule, when France returns the duchy to Spain under the "Treaty of Ryswick."

Romans in Luxembourg were the bits and pieces of their urban civilization, a network of bridges that marked their progress across the land, and place names such as Ettelbruck (Attila's Bridge). Luxembourg was by then quite firmly in the Frankish camp.

Along with the monasteries that sprang up and flourished (with the support of the people) came educational and cultural influences that helped form the foundation of today's Luxembourg. The great Frankish leader Charlemagne brought in Saxons to settle in the Ardennes and added another ethnic imprint to the face of the region.

It was the youngest of the counts of Ardennes, Sigefroi, who obtained a large land grant from the Abbey of Saint Maximin (the deed, dated April 12, 963, is still kept in the Pescatore Museum in Luxembourg). He built his castle on the ruins of Castellum Lucilinburhuc, an ancient Roman fort that had guarded the crossing of the Paris–Trier road with that connecting Metz with Aix-la-Chapelle. From that strategic spot there grew a town and eventually a country that went by the name of Lützelburg.

THE 12TH & 13TH CENTURIES   By the 12th century, the counts of Luxembourg were at the helm, and they enlarged their territory by wars with other noblemen, fortunate marriages, and various diplomatic shenanigans until they began to absent themselves for long periods, joining the forces of Godfrey of Bouillon to travel to the Holy City during the Crusades. Some never returned (having fallen in battle), and those who did return found that much of their land had been confiscated by other overlords during their absence.

When Henry IV the Blind's daughter, the Countess Ermesinde, reached adulthood in the early 1200s, things were in disarray. Through a couple of marriages, Ermesinde was able to restore some of Luxembourg's lost territory, and when her last husband died in 1225 she boldly took charge of the affairs of state. By bringing together in a central governing body noblemen who had always been at each other's throats, she achieved such revolutionary reforms as establishment of a court of justice and limited judicial rights for ordinary citizens. Many individual rights were granted to lessen the tight rein of feudal lords over their burghers. Countess Ermesinde also began to establish convents and monasteries to provide education and culture for her people. Her legacy to her people was a united nation with enlightened social standards.

➤

Dateline

- **1713** Beginning of the Golden Age of Luxembourg, when Philippe V forfeits his rule in favor of Charles VI and Maria Theresa of Austria.
- **1794** French lay siege to Luxembourg, gaining control when Austrian garrison is starved out.
- **1814** The French garrison leaves the fortress.
- **1815** Treaty of Vienna partitions Luxembourg; its lands east of the Moselle, Sûre, and Our are ceded to Prussia, and the remainder go to Holland's William of Orange.
- **1839** Under the Treaty of London, Luxembourg's Walloon districts are returned to Belgium; although still allied to Holland, the duchy's independence is acknowledged in its first constitution.
- **1867** The Treaty of London guarantees Luxembourg's neutrality under the protection of the great powers; all fortifications are razed.
- **1914** German troops occupy the country.
- **1922** Agreement on economic union with Belgium signed in Brussels.
- **1940** German army invades Luxembourg on May 10 and royal family and government go into exile.
- **1944** American troops liberate Luxembourg.

➤

THE 14TH THROUGH 18TH CENTURIES In 1308 Henry VII of the House of Luxembourg became emperor of the Holy Roman Empire, and he spent the rest of his life trying to unite all of Europe under his rule. His son, John the Blind, was a valiant warrior who perished at Crécy fighting the forces of Edward III of England, after ordering his men to lead him into the thickest battle. Today he is revered as Luxembourg's national hero. His son, Charles IV, favored extending his domain through treaty and marriage; by the time his son, Wenceslas, gained the throne, the House of Luxembourg ruled a territory some 500 times the size of today's Luxembourg.

The glory days did not last long, however, King Wenceslas's son, Sigismund, proved to be far less capable than his ancestors; by the mid-1400s Luxembourg had been reduced to the status of a province ruled over by the dukes of Burgundy. During the next 400 years that rule shifted among Spain, France, Austria, and Burgundy. One would have thought that this might crush forever the Luxembourgers' strong spirit of independence that began with their Celtic forebears and was rekindled when Countess Ermesinde started granting individual rights.

THE 19TH CENTURY Yet that stubborn sense of individual worth refused to be crushed, no matter who sat on the throne; in self-defense, each successive ruler found it necessary to strengthen even more a capital city that was already one of Europe's strongest. Luxembourg, then, became a problem to the rest of Europe: Its position was too strategic and its fortifications too strong to allow it to be self-governing—or even to be controlled by any one nation. The answer seemed to be to divide the country among several nations; therefore, the Congress of Vienna handed over most of the country to Holland's William of Orange-Nassau and the remainder to Prussia. Then with the Treaty of London in 1839, more than half of Holland's Luxembourg was given to Belgium (that Belgian province still bears the name Luxembourg).

Since its boundaries were becoming smaller and smaller, the Grand Duchy of Luxembourg posed no real threat to anyone. Still, there were a great many fortifications. So in 1867 the European powers convened in London and decided that freedom would be granted the Grand Duchy on condition that its fortifications be dismantled. Luxembourgers were overjoyed, and in October 1868 they affirmed a constitution that boldly proclaimed "The Grand Duchy of Luxembourg forms a free state, independent and indivisible." Today there are green parks throughout the capital city to make the sites of those mighty fortifications, and tiny Luxembourg has led the way toward peaceful economic unification of Europe's separate nations.

THE 20TH CENTURY Since that momentous announcement of independence, Luxembourg has seen periods of prosperity (largely due to its important steel industry) and periods of decline that have prompted thousands to emigrate in search of suitable work. Twice—in World Wars I and II—the country has suffered the agonies of military occupation. Some 3,000 Luxembourgers perished fighting with the Allies between 1914 and 1918, and the heroism of the Luxembourg underground resistance movement during World War II is legendary. Many of the younger men made their way to Allied countries to fight in their ranks, while those at home actually went out on strike when the Nazis imposed compulsory service in the Wehrmacht—a move that brought swift retribution from the Nazis—thereby adding to Luxembourg's severe suffering. By the close of World War II in 1945, more than 60,000 homes and 160 bridges and tunnels had been destroyed. Once more, determined Luxembourgers set about to rebuild their homeland, and within a remarkably short time, fields were once again being plowed, highways and railways restored, and homes rebuilt.

Since the beginning of the Benelux Customs Union in 1948 (which became an economic union in 1958), Luxembourg has been actively involved in the affairs of its neighbors.

TODAY In 1994 the Grand Duchy of Luxembourg, a constitutional monarchy, has a population of about 400,000. Economically it has a strong iron and steel industry and a growing number of light industries. The strength of its banking and financial institutions has attracted more than 219 foreign banks (which employ one out of every 23 Luxembourgers), and it has been chosen as headquarters of the European Investment Bank. Its economic strength attracts European immigrants, and some 25% of the total population (65% of the work force) is comprised of foreigners. Furthermore, about 30,000 commute daily to the Grand Duchy from neighboring countries; thus, Luxembourg has one of the highest concentrations of foreigners.

Dateline

- **1944–45** Battle of the Bulge brings mass destruction of much of the Grand Duchy.
- **1948** Customs Union with Belgium and the Netherlands takes effect (it becomes an economic union in 1958). Luxembourg's constitutional revision provides for the right to work, social security, and recognition of trade unions.
- **1949** Luxembourg joins NATO.
- **1952** As a founding member of the European Coal and Steel Community, Luxembourg is chosen as the seat of important European institutions.
- **1958** Luxembourg joins the European Economic Community.
- **1964** Head of State Grand Duchess Charlotte abdicates in favor of her son, Grand Duke Jean.
- **1966** Opening of the European Centre in Kirchberg, and Luxembourg's financial market and stock exchange gain outstanding reputation worldwide.
- **1992** The Chamber of Deputies ratifies the Treaty on European Union by an overwhelming majority vote.
- **1993** Luxembourg opposes efforts of other EU members to impose withholding tax on savings and investments in the Grand Duchy.

Luxembourg   Geography, History, and Politics

Agriculture, once the major industry, is still important, as are the vineyards of the Moselle Valley. The enchanting Luxembourg countryside has become a favorite holiday destination for many Europeans, making tourism an important industry.

Politics

Grand Duke Jean of the House of Nassau succeeded his mother, Grand Duchess Charlotte, as head of state in 1964. Luxembourg has a one-house legislature, the Chamber of Deputies, which is made up of 60 members who are elected for 5-year terms.

In addition to its membership in the Benelux economic union, Luxembourg belongs to the UN, the Council of Europe, NATO, and the EU.

2 Luxembourg's Famous People

Grand Duchess Charlotte (1896–1985) Charlotte, who began her reign as grand duchess in 1919, was already well loved by Luxembourgers when the country was overrun by Nazi troops in 1940, but she won a permanent place in the hearts of her people when she fled to England and established a government in exile. Throughout the years of occupation, she made regular broadcasts on Radio Free Europe and was a source of inspiration and courage to those back home. In 1964 she abdicated in favor of her son, Grand Duke Jean, and lived on to the age of 89. Her statue, financed by public subscription, was unveiled at Clairefontaine Square in 1990 as a lasting monument to this much revered lady.

Countess Ermesinde (1196–1247) Daughter of Henry IV the Blind, Ermesinde made two fortuitous marriage alliances that restored the previously lost counties of Durbuy and Laroche to her holdings. When her last husband, Waleran of Limburg, died in 1225 she established a central governing body of noblemen who had previously been enemies. Her most lasting achievement was the establishment of reforms including a court of justice and limited judicial rights for citizens. She also established convents and monasteries to provide education and culture for her people.

Robert Schuman (1886–1963) Born in Luxembourg, Schuman became a leading statesman in France, was a member of the Resistance during World War II, and served as prime minister in 1947–48. His Schuman Plan of 1950 led to creation of the European Coal and Steel Community and laid the groundwork for the eventual European Union.

Edward Steichen (1879–1973) World-famous photographer often called the Patriarch of Photography, Steichen and his family emigrated to America in 1881. His photographic career included portraits of prominent figures for *Vanity Fair* and *Vogue;* management of the photography department of the U.S. Marines in World War II; and director of the photography department of the Museum of Modern Art in New York. His most lasting memorial is the gigantic *Family of Man* exhibition he assembled from around the globe, which was donated (at his urging) to the government of Luxembourg in 1966.

3 Art, Architecture, and Literature

ART   Luxembourg's most outstanding art is to be found in its churches. Carved wooden altarpieces, altar paintings, and frescoes—many dating back to medieval times—adorn religious edifices throughout the Grand Duchy. On the contemporary art scene, Luxembourg claims the widely praised expressionist painter Joseph Kutter.

ARCHITECTURE   Architectural patterns of the neighboring countries that played such a vital part in Luxembourg's history are reflected in harmonious combination throughout the Grand Duchy. Private homes vary in size and style from simple farm cottages to palatial town houses, from plain, smoke-blackened beams to ornate plasterwork. The most striking architecture, however, is evident in the plethora of medieval fortresses and castles, while the architecture of its many churches ranges from Roman to Renaissance style. Of special interest are the Gallo-Roman complex at Echternach and Gallo-Roman baths near Mamer.

LITERATURE   Although literature has experienced something of an upsurge since the 1970s, most writing is in German, and no single Luxembourg author has achieved world stature. The literary scene, however, is an active one, with frequent readings sponsored by the Writers' Federation.

4 Religion and Folklore

RELIGION   The vast majority (some 95%) of Luxembourgers are Roman Catholic, although a significant percentage of those hasten to make it clear that they are *nonpracticing* Catholics. It is, however, rare to meet one who does not observe the customs, traditions, and mores of the church.

Although Catholic through and through, Luxembourg also follows a staunch policy of religious freedom, and along with Catholic priests, the state supports the Chief Rabbi and Official Protestant Pastor. There are also small clusters of other Christian and non-Christian faiths. While religious instruction is a part of the school curriculum, upper levels can choose instead an ethics-and-morality course.

FOLKLORE   Legend says that within Luxembourg City's tremendous rocky fortress a beautiful maiden named Mélusine sits knitting, but she manages only one stitch each year—and that's a very good thing. You see, should she finish her knitting before she is released from the rock, all of Luxembourg and its people will vanish into the rock with her! How did she come to be there, and how can her release be won? Well she got there when Siegfroi married her in ignorance that she was really a mermaid, a secret she managed to keep by reverting to her natural state only on Saturday, on which day of every week she had pledged her husband to observe her personal privacy. When his curiosity got the better of him and he peeked, she vanished into the rock. Once every seven years Mélusine returns, either as a serpent with a golden key in its mouth or as a beautiful woman. All it will take to win her freedom is for some brave soul to kiss the womanly vision or take the key from the serpent's mouth. That brave soul has yet to appear, and in the meantime all of Luxembourg (or at least that part of Luxembourg that credits the legend) prays she will drop a stitch or two or else that whatever it is she's knitting will take a *very* long time to complete!

5 Cultural and Social Life

LUXEMBOURG'S PEOPLE "We are very much a combination of what surrounds us," Prince Jean de Luxembourg (second son of Grand Duke Jean) is quoted as saying. That is undeniably true—in such a small country it could hardly be otherwise. But it's a strange sort of combination, one that results in a distinctive individuality that even extends to their language that is vaguely related to both French and German, yet quite different from both.

A combination they and their language may be, but that combination has produced a people who are very much their own, with a personality and inborn traits that are hard to pin down in mere words. And while those unique traits may elude description, Luxembourgers seem content to leave it simply at *"Mir woelle bleiwe wat mir sin"* ("We want to remain what we are") with no need to spell out "what we are" in detail. You'll see that national motto inscribed over old door frames, hear it echoed in songs, and recognize its essence in everyone you meet in the Grand Duchy.

Among the things they are is hardworking. Foreign firms that open branches in Luxembourg will tell you that productivity is far higher than in other locations. One look at well-tended farms or shops will reveal the industry of their owners. Go into a Luxembourg home and the cleanliness and order will speak more loudly than words of the homemaker's pride in the work. And, of course, the swiftness with which Luxembourgers repaired World War II devastation in their country is ample testimony to their collective abilities.

Above all else, Luxembourgers are patriotic. Despite centuries of domination by first one ruler then another, there is a collective memory of independence and individual liberties they have always claimed as their own even as they endured those who would deny them.

Spend a little time in Luxembourg with these proud and charming people and you may well find yourself silently echoing their motto, with the slight addition, "We want you to remain what you are!"

CULTURE In the cultural area, Luxembourg has produced the contemporary expressionist painter Joseph Kutter, the internationally acclaimed photographer Edward Steichen, and many lesser-known artists whose works are displayed in galleries throughout the Grand Duchy.

SOCIAL CUSTOMS The people of Luxembourg are also quite cosmopolitan. From their cuisine (a combination of the best from surrounding countries) to their culture to their dress, they are at home in the world, eager to travel, and secure enough in their own uniqueness to appreciate the special qualities of others.

To say that Luxembourgers are fond of eating is an understatement. Cafés are everywhere, and if there's an important matter to discuss, decision to be made, or social crisis to resolve, Luxembourgers repair to the nearest café or pastry shop. It goes without saying, then, that they are also fond of cooking—don't go away without indulging in their luscious pastries, and forget the calories!

THE LANGUAGE *Luxembourgish,* the national language, has a vague Germanic base with overtones of French, yet is as distinct from either language as Luxembourgers are different from either nationality. They learn and use their native tongue from earliest childhood, study German in their first school years, and add French to their curriculum early on.

As for anyone who isn't native born learning *Letzebuergesch,* forget it—it's a tongue twister, and as any Luxembourger will tell you, one must be born to it. Not to worry, however—for while the native tongue is widely used among Luxembourgers, and although French is most often used in official and cultural activities, and German is heard frequently—*everyone* speaks English. In other words, you'll encounter few, if any, language difficulties in the Grand Duchy.

6 Performing Arts and Evening Entertainment

Music is the first love of most Luxembourgers, and wherever you travel you'll encounter local bands, choral groups, and musical theater groups—in the capital city hardly a summer evening passes without open-air concerts in place d'Armes. The vitality of Luxembourg City's music scene is evident in an active Folk Club, Jazz Club, and Society for New Music, as well as the Spring Music Festival.

Outside the city a few hotels offer after-dark entertainment, but most evening activity is centered in local cafés.

The country's only casino is at Mondorf-les-Bains, where there's also an excellent spa and a host of concerts and sporting activities.

THEATER   Outstanding young, dynamic theater groups such as the Théâtre des Capucins, Theatre of Centaure, and Théâtre Ouvert de Luxembourg are an important part of the capital city's cultural life and in summer, the Casemates Theatre presents modern plays in the historic Bock casemates. In Esch-sur-Alzette, the Schluechthaus is the center of theatrical activity.

FILMS   Luxembourg has inaugurated an incentive program for filmmakers with costs averaging 30% below those in other countries. As this is written, the program is still in its infancy, but keep an eye out for Luxembourg-based films in the near future. At the moment, cinemas show foreign films in their original version, with subtitles in French and Dutch, with a fair smattering of top American films on offer.

7 Sports and Recreation

Golfers will want to try their luck on the course maintained by the Grand-Ducal Golf Club in Luxembourg City, a course known throughout Europe for its difficult, narrow fairways. Arrangements can be made for visitors to play by contacting Golf Club Grand-Ducal, Senningerberg/Luxembourg (☎ **34-00-90**). The Hotel Association of Clervaux also offers attractive golf holiday packages at country hotels (contact the Clervaux Tourist Office, 97110 Clervaux, Luxembourg; ☎ **9-20-72**).

Walkers will find marked walking paths throughout the Grand Duchy, and during the summer, organized walking tours of 6 to 25 miles are run from Luxembourg City. Contact the Fédération Luxembourgeoise des Marches Populaires, rue de Rollingergrund 176, Luxembourg (☎ **44-93-02**).

Many of the resort areas offer tennis facilities, and there are squash courts in Luxembourg. Contact the Institute National des Sports (☎ **478-34-34**) for details on where to find them and how to arrange to play.

Horseback riding is a favorite sport in Luxembourg, with several very good stables offering mounts at about LF 350 ($10) per hour. For a full list of stables and riding schools, contact Sports et Loisirs de la Fédération Luxembourgeoise des Sports Equestres, rue du Fort Elisabeth 9, Luxembourg. The organization also puts together horseback tours of Luxembourg City and of the Valley of the Seven Castles.

The rivers of the Grand Duchy are a fisherperson's paradise, and licenses are issued by the district commissioners in Luxembourg City, Diekirch, and Grevenmacher, and by a few communal administrations like those in Ettelbruck, Vianden, and Wiltz. If you're suddenly bitten by the fishing bug, just ask locally where you can obtain a license—there's sure to be a source close by. A license to fish from the banks of eastern-border rivers and lakes costs LF 400 ($11) for a month. Fishing from boats requires a special license for LF 400 ($11) per week, LF 1,000 ($28) per month. There are several rather complex and often-changing regulations governing fishing in frontier waters. For complete details on all types of fishing, contact the Administration des Eaux et Forêts, B.P. 411, 2014 Luxembourg.

8 Food and Drink

Food

RESTAURANTS   Luxembourg City, because of its large number of international diplomatic and business visitors, has many fine restaurants with international cuisine. There are, however, just as many small cafés and bistros featuring traditional dishes. In towns and villages around the Grand Duchy, hotel restaurants are often quite good, and there's excellent eating in small local cafés.

Note: Most restaurants are open for lunch from noon to 2:30pm and for dinner from 7 to 10pm. The hours, however, may be flexible. Some are closed one day a week.

THE CUISINE   The subtleties of French cuisine star on many a Luxembourg menu, and German influence expresses itself in the wide range of cheeses that are enormously popular with natives of the Grand Duchy. As for Luxembourg cuisine, among the national favorites are some of the best pastries you're ever likely to eat; Luxembourg cheese (delicious); trout, crayfish, and pike from local rivers; hare (during the hunting season); and in September, lovely small plum tarts called *quetsch*. Other taste treats include *quenelles* of calf's liver dumplings with sauerkraut and boiled potatoes, black pudding (*treipen*) and sausages with mashed potatoes and horseradish, and smoked pork with broad beans.

Drink

WATER & SOFT DRINKS   You need have no concerns about Luxembourg's water—it's clear, pure, and safe. As for soft drinks, they go by the name of "minerals," and most leading European brands are available, along with some from the United States.

BEER & WINE   Although you'll be able to order almost any of the fine beers you've come to appreciate in Belgium and Holland, Luxembourg has its own that take a backseat to none—look for such brand names as Mousel (pronounced "*Mooz*-ell"), Bofferding, and Henri Funck. And of course the Moselle wines (mostly white) will top any list—look for the National Mark, which certifies that they are true Luxembourg wines.

In 1993 it was reported that Luxembourg had the highest worldwide per capita consumption of alcohol—the equivalent of about three beers a day for every man, woman, and child.

Planning a Trip to Luxembourg

20

AS IS TRUE OF THE OTHER TWO BENELUX COUNTRIES, LUXEMBOURG IS AN EASY country in which to travel, and whether you plan to go top-drawer or pinch pennies all the way, you'll find that the Grand Duchy has smoothed the way.

1 Currency and Costs

Luxembourg's currency is tied to the Belgian franc, and Belgian currency is freely accepted throughout the Grand Duchy. The **Luxembourg franc** is made up of 100 centimes, and notes are issued in 50-, 100-, 500-, 1,000-, and 5,000-franc denominations. Coins come in 1, 5, and 20 francs, and it's a good idea to keep a small supply of these on hand for small tips, telephone calls, and the like.

The Luxembourg Franc

For American Readers At this writing $1 = approximately 35 francs (or 1 franc = 2.8¢), and this was the rate of exchange used to calculate the dollar values given in this book (rounded off).

For British Readers At this writing £1 = approximately 53 francs (or 1 franc = 1.9p), and this was the rate of exchange used to calculate the pound values in the table below.

Note The Luxembourg franc has the same exchange rate as the Belgian franc, which is accepted as the second currency in Luxembourg.

The rates given here fluctuate from time to time and may not be the same when you travel to Luxembourg. Therefore this table should be used only as a guide:

LF	U.S.$	U.K.£	LF	U.S.$	U.K.£
1	.03	.02	500	14.29	9.43
5	.14	.09	750	21.43	14.15
10	.29	.19	1,000	28.57	18.87
20	.57	.38	1,250	35.71	23.58
25	.71	.47	1,500	42.86	28.30
30	.86	.57	1,750	50.00	33.02
40	1.14	.75	2,000	57.14	37.74
50	1.43	.94	2,500	71.43	47.17
75	2.14	1.42	3,000	85.71	56.60
100	2.86	1.89	3,500	100.00	66.04
125	3.57	2.36	4,000	114.29	75.47
150	4.29	2.83	4,500	128.57	84.91
200	5.71	3.77	5,000	142.86	94.34
250	7.14	4.72	6,000	171.43	113.21

What Things Cost in Luxembourg City*	U.S.$
Taxi from the airport to the city center	20.00
Bus from the airport to the city center (with luggage)	3.42
Local telephone call	.28
Double room at the Grand Hôtel Cravat (deluxe)	177.00
Double room at the Hôtel Italia (moderate)	80.00
Double room at the Hôtel Carlton (budget)	45.00
Lunch for one at Restaurant Châtelet (moderate)	21.00
Lunch for one at Roma (budget)	13.00
Dinner for one, without wine, at La Lorraine (deluxe)	85.00
Dinner for one, without wine, at Sorbas the Greek (moderate)	40.00
Dinner for one, without wine, at the Brasserie Chimay (budget)	21.00
Glass of beer	1.50
Coca-Cola	1.00
Cup of coffee	1.50
Roll of ASA 100 color film, 36 exposures	5.00
Admission to the National Museum	Free
Movie ticket	5.70
Concert ticket	11.50

*Costs outside Luxembourg City vary only slightly.

2   When to Go—Climate, Holidays, and Events

"In-season" in Luxembourg means mid-April through mid-October. The peak of the tourist season is July and August, and in all honesty, that's when the weather is at its finest. The weather, however, is never really extreme at any time of year, and if you're one of the growing numbers who favor shoulder- or off-season travel, you'll find the Grand Duchy every bit as attractive during those months. Not only are airlines, hotels, and restaurants cheaper and less crowded during this time (with more relaxed service that means you get more personal attention), but there are also some very appealing things going on in all three of the Benelux countries.

Theater is most active during winter months in Luxembourg, and outside the city, on the second weekend in September, Grevenmacher celebrates its Wine and Grape Festival with a splendid folklore procession.

CLIMATE   The Grand Duchy is blessed with a moderate climate, with less annual rainfall than either Belgium or Holland, since North Sea winds have usually wept their tears before they get this far inland. May to about mid-October are the most agreeable months to visit, with highest temperatures—around 60°F (16°C)—in July and August and winter temperatures averaging about 37°F (3°C).

HOLIDAYS Public holidays in Luxembourg are: January 1 (New Year's Day), Shrove Monday, Easter Monday, May 1 (Labor Day), Ascension Day, Whitmonday, June 23 (Luxembourg National Holiday, the grand duke's birthday), Assumption Day, November 1 (All Saints' Day), December 25 (Christmas Day), and December 26 (Boxing Day).

Luxembourg Calendar of Events

March

- **Carnival Parade,** Pétange. Mid-Lent. Late Mar.

April

- **Easter Exhibition,** Grevenmacher. Agricultural and handicrafts. Easter Sat through the Thurs after Easter.
- **Eimaischen,** Nospelt. Popular traditional festival and sale of pottery. Easter Mon.
- **Wine Fair,** Grevenmacher. Thurs after Easter.
- **Dancing Procession,** Echternach. 1,200-year-old colorful procession in honor of St. Willibrord. Whittues.

May

- **Grand Wine Tasting Day,** Remerschen. In the Cooperative Cellars. May 1.
- **Octave of Our Lady of Luxembourg,** Diekirch. Fifth Sun after Easter.

June

- **International Music Festival,** Echternach. All month.
- **National Day,** Esch/Alzette. Gala celebration with fireworks. June 22–23.
- **Wine Festivals,** Remich. Open-air celebrations. End of June through Aug.

July

- **Remembrance Day,** Ettelbruck. Celebration to honor Gen. George S. Patton, World War II American hero. Second weekend.
- **Folkloric and Gymnastic Shows, Ballet, and Exhibitions,** Diekirch, Mersch, Echternach, Wiltz, Mondorf-les-Bains, Vianden, Larochette. Series of events spread among small towns. July–Aug.
- **Old Diekirch Festival,** Diekirch. Second weekend.
- **International Open-Air Theater Festival,** Wiltz. Mid-July.
- **WorldFolklore Festival,** Ettelbruck, Mersch. Mid-July.
- **Beer Festival,** Diekirch. Third Sun.
- **Folklore Festival,** Wellenstein. End of July.

August

- **Day of the Riesling,** Wormeldange. In Cooperative Cellars. First Sat in Aug (held July 31 when Aug 1 is a Sun).
- **Agricultural Fair,** Ettelbruck. First weekend.
- **Jumping CSI,** Mondorf-les-Bains. International riding tournament. Mid-Aug.
- **Procession of the Holy Virgin,** Girsterklaus. Pilgrimage dating back to 1328. Sun after Aug 15.

September
- **Grand Wine Festival,** Schwebsingen. First Sun.
- **Remembrance Day of the Liberation,** Pétange. Ceremony in front of American soldier monument. Sept 9.
- **Wine and Grape Festival,** Greiveidange. Third weekend.

Luxembourg City Calendar of Events

March
- **Musical Spring.** Festival of musical events in various venues around the city. End of Mar through the end of May.

April
- **Eimaischen.** Popular traditional festival. Easter Mon.

May
- **Octave of Our Lady of Luxembourg.** Fifth Sun after Easter.
- **International Trade Fair.** Last 9 days.

June
- **Luxembourg National Day.** Gala celebration, festival activities, grand duke reviews his troops, and fireworks. June 23.

July
- **Open-air concerts.** Nightly concerts in place d'Armes. July–Aug.

August
- **Schobermesse.** Amusement fair and market. Two weeks beginning next-to-last Sun.

October
- **Theatrical Season Opens.** Beginning of winter-long theatrical productions.

3 Getting Around

BY TRAIN & BUS Luxembourg National Railways (Chemins de Fer Luxembourgeois) operates fast and frequent schedules throughout the Grand Duchy, with good connecting bus service to those points it doesn't reach. Travelers over the age of 65 are eligible for a 50% reduction in both first and second class except to or from a frontier point. In addition, special half-fare weekend and holiday round-trip tickets are offered throughout the system except from frontier points. A **one-day network ticket,** good for unlimited travel by rail and bus, costs LF 140 ($4); for five days, the cost is LF 540 ($15.40), and travel may be for any five days within a one-month period; for one month (valid from the first day of travel to same date of following month), it's LF 1,300 ($37).

Porters (available only at Luxembourg City station) charge a flat fee of LF 50 ($1.40) per bag. For **rail and bus information,** telephone **49-24-24** any day from 7am to 8pm.

In addition to frequent bus service to all points in the Grand Duchy, there are several well-planned motorcoach tours from Luxembourg City that cover the most scenic countryside locations (see Chapter 21).

BY TAXI   During the day, taxis charge LF 90 ($2.55) when the meter starts and LF 30 (85¢) per kilometer, with a 10% surcharge after 10pm, and on weekends and holidays. Waiting time is charged at the rate of LF 10 (30¢) per minute.

BY CAR   Roads within the Grand Duchy are kept in very good repair and are well signposted, although some roadways are narrow, with many curves, especially in the Ardennes region.

Parking discs (available in stores and banks at no charge) are required in "blue zones" in Luxembourg City, Esch-sur-Alzette, Dudelange, Remich, and Wiltz, and in many other places there are parking meters or half-hour parking-ticket dispensers.

The **Automobile Club du Grand Duché de Luxembourg** is at route de Longwy 54, Luxembourg-Helfenterbruck (☎ **450-04-51**).

Rentals   If you plan to rent a car after your arrival in the Grand Duchy, you'll need a driver's license valid in your own country, and you'll be required to purchase insurance when you book the car. Car-rental rates begin at about LF 900 ($26) a day, and leading car-rental firms in Luxembourg City are: **Budget Rent a Car,** Luxembourg airport (☎ **44-19-38**); **Avis,** place de la Gare 2 (☎ **48-95-95**); and **Hertz,** 20 rue Wessange (☎ **48-54-85**) and at the airport (☎ **43-46-45**).

Gasoline   Gas ("petrol" in these parts) will run about LF 25 (70¢) per liter; diesel fuel LF 20 (56¢) per liter.

Driving Rules   Speed limits are set at 50kmph (31 m.p.h.) in built-up areas, 90kmph (57 m.p.h.) on rural roadways, and 120kmph (75 m.p.h.) on motorways. The use of seatbelts is compulsory, and horn blowing is permitted only in case of imminent danger.

Road Maps   An excellent road map of the Grand Duchy, which shows camping grounds, swimming pools, and tourist attractions as well as main roads, is available at no cost from the Luxembourg National Tourist Office in Luxembourg City. Other good road maps include the Ordnance Survey maps (two sheets) and Michelin map no. 215.

Breakdowns/Assistance   The Automobile Club du Grand Duché de Luxembourg, route de Longwy 54, Luxembourg-Helfenterbruck (☎ **450-04-51**), affords a 24-hour emergency road service.

HITCHHIKING   Hitchhiking is generally quite safe but, as in most countries, it pays to have a companion along.

BY BICYCLE   The Luxembourg countryside lends itself to cycling, and while you're free to ramble down any road that strikes your fancy, there are several cycling tracks leading through some of the most scenic regions. Local tourist offices can furnish suggestions for cycling tours on these tracks or less-traveled roadways. Also, tourist offices in Luxembourg City, Diekirch, Echternach, Mondorf-les-Bains, Reisdorf, and Vianden can arrange **bike rentals.** Bicycles are transported by train for a very small set fee, regardless of distance traveled, but this is subject to space availability (not usually a problem).

ON FOOT   If ever the Almighty planned a country especially for the walkers of the world, it must have been the Grand Duchy of Luxembourg! Shanks' mare, in fact, is perhaps the best way of all to travel through this beautiful land. Great walkers themselves, Luxembourgers have set out some 20 walking paths (one of the densest networks of any country in the world), most of them signposted. All youth hostels are linked by walking paths designated by white triangular signs, and bookshops carry maps of some 142 walking routes. Many local tourist offices have brochures of walking tours, and the Luxembourg Youth Hostels Association, place d'Armes, Luxembourg (☎ 22-55-88), issues Ordnance Survey maps on which walking paths are marked in red.

Suggested Itineraries

If You Have One Week

With only one week in this lovely country, your first day should be devoted to arriving and settling into the capital city. On the second day, start the morning with a visit to the tourist office, then take a leisurely stroll around that immediate area. In the afternoon, there's an excellent city and countryside tour that will give you an overview of the entire area. On the third and fourth days, plan to visit those attractions that have sparked your interest during the above tour. Explore Luxembourg City's unique network of cliffside casements, impressive cathedral, Grand Ducal Palace, fortress remains, and European Center. Then it's time to head outside the environs of Luxembourg City, either behind the wheel or by way of the full-day and/or half-day coach tours. Your next three days can be divided among the Ardennes and Wiltz (site of World War II's Battle of the Bulge); the lake of the upper Sûre; feudal castles at Esch-sur-Sûre, Clervaux, Vianden, and the Sûre Valley; Echternach; Grevenmacher, to visit one of the leading wineries; and the Moselle Valley.

If You Have Two Weeks

See above for Week 1. For your second week, from your day-trip overview of the Grand Duchy's lovely countryside select a favorite rural town or village and hie yourself off for a serene night or two in two or three of the many quaint, comfortable inns that abound outside the city.

If You Have Three Weeks

Your third week may well be the icing on the cake of your visit to Luxembourg. Athletic types can spend the entire week walking or cycling around the Grand Duchy, following the terrific trails outlined in a series of tourist office brochures. Or you may prefer a week of angling and/or boating on the rivers and lakes that draw sports enthusiasts from all over Europe. It's the perfect end to your Benelux holiday, and an even better *beginning* if you arrive suffering from the stresses and strains of modern-day civilization.

Themed Choices

Luxembourg's tourist office can help you plan your holiday around several special interests: historical and religious sites, hiking, fishing, and cycling, to mention just a few.

Fast Facts: Luxembourg

American Express The American Express office is located at av. de la Porte-Neuve 34, Luxembourg (☎ **22-85-55**).

Business Hours Banks are open Monday through Friday from 8:30am to noon and 1 to 4:30pm. Currency-exchange offices are open daily at the airport and the central station in Luxembourg City. Shops generally stay open from 10am to 6pm Monday through Saturday, and many also open on Sunday for shorter hours.

Climate See "When to Go," earlier in this chapter.

Crime See "Safety," below.

Currency See "Currency and Costs," earlier in this chapter.

Customs Before leaving home, be sure to register with Customs (at the airport) any camera, typewriter, etc., you plan to carry with you that could have been purchased abroad; otherwise you may very well have to pay duty on these items when you return home if you cannot prove they were not bought on your trip. When reentering the United States, citizens (regardless of age) are allowed up to a $400 exemption for goods bought overseas if they have been away for more than two days and have not had the same duty exemption within one month. Those over 21 are allowed, within that amount, 1 liter of alcohol, 100 cigars (no Cuban cigars, however), 200 cigarettes, and one bottle of perfume with a U.S. trademark. Works of art and antiques more than 100 years old may be brought in duty-free (be sure to have verification of age to present to Customs). No agricultural products or meats from overseas may be brought into the United States, and will be confiscated if they're in your luggage. With the exception of alcohol, tobacco, and perfumes valued at more than $5, gifts worth up to $50 may be mailed to home as gifts, but only one per day to the same addressee.

Documents Required See "Information, Entry Requirements, and Money" in Chapter 1.

Driving Rules See "Getting Around," earlier in this chapter.

Drugs Possession and/or use of drugs is illegal in Luxembourg, with severe penalties imposed for offenders.

Electricity If you plan to bring a hairdryer, radio (other than battery-operated), travel iron, or any other small appliance with you, pack a European-style transformer, adapter, and several different styles of plugs, since the electricity in Luxembourg is almost always 220 or 130 volts AC, 50 cycles, and outlets come in various sizes and shapes.

Embassies/Consulates Australia, Canada, and New Zealand do not have embassies in Luxembourg. The closest embassies for these countries are located in Brussels (see "Fast Facts: Belgium" in Chapter 3). The Embassy of the **Republic of Ireland** is located at route d'Arlon 28, 1140 Luxembourg (☎ **45-06-10**); the Embassy of the **United Kingdom** is located at bd. Roosevelt 14, 2450 Luxembourg (☎ **22-98-64**); and the Embassy of the **United States** is at bd. Emmanuel-Servais 22, 2535 Luxembourg (☎ **46-01-23**).

Emergencies In case of emergency, dial **113.**

Gasoline See "Getting Around," earlier in this chapter.

Hitchhiking   See "Getting Around," earlier in this chapter.

Holidays   See "When to Go," earlier in this chapter.

Information   In the United States, the Luxembourg National Tourist Office is at 17 Beekman Place, New York, NY 10022 (☎ 212/935-8888). In Luxembourg, the Grand Duchy of Luxembourg Office du Tourisme is in place de la Gare (☎ 352/48-11-99) by the Central Station, open daily from 9am to noon and 2 to 6:30pm (9am to 7pm July 1 to mid-September), with another office at the airport (☎ 352/40-08-08), open daily from 10am to 6:30pm. The local Tourist Information Office for Luxembourg City is in place d'Armes (☎ 22-28-09 or 22-75-65), open July to mid-September Monday through Saturday 9am to 7pm, Sunday 9am to noon; rest of year Monday through Saturday 9am to noon, 2 to 6:30pm, closed Sunday. Throughout the Grand Duchy, there are some 20 local Tourist Information Services in small villages and towns.

Mail/Post Office   The post office at place de la Gare 1 in Luxembourg City is open daily for letters from 6am to 10pm, but packages are not accepted for mailing after 5pm. At the airport post office, hours are 7am to 8pm daily. Postage charges are LF 14 (40¢) for postcards or letters under 20 grams (.7 oz.) mailed to European addresses, LF 32 (90¢) outside Europe.

Maps   See "Getting Around," earlier in this chapter.

Passports   U.S. and Canadian citizens who plan to be in the country 90 days or less need bring only a valid passport—no visa is required. Citizens of other countries should consult the nearest Luxembourg consulate.

Safety   Whenever you're traveling in an unfamiliar city or country, stay alert. Be aware of your immediate surroundings. Wear a moneybelt and keep a close eye on your possessions. Be particularly careful with cameras, purses, and wallets, all favorite targets of thieves and pickpockets. Every society has its criminals. It's your responsibility to be aware and alert even in the most heavily touristed areas.

Telephone/Telex/Fax   The entire country of Luxembourg is in the same local dialing area so no **telephone** area codes are necessary. To phone Luxembourg from within Europe, dial **09** (which gets you into the European long-distance network), **352** (the country code for Luxembourg), and then the five- or six-digit local number; from North America, dial **011** (for AT&T international service, or the access code for your long-distance company), **352** (the country code for Luxembourg), and then the local number. Direct dialing to other European countries as well as overseas (including North America) is available in most hotels. To avoid hotel surcharges on calls placed from your room, use a pay phone. You'll save money on calls to the United States if you request AT&T's USA Direct service, but you must call collect or use an AT&T credit card. Coin telephone boxes that display stickers showing flags of different countries can also be used to place international calls with operator assistance. Coin telephones accept LF-5 (15¢) and LF-20 (55¢) coins, and it's advisable to have a good supply of these coins when you place a call. However, most coin phones also accept plastic phone cards; these cost LF 250 ($7) or LF 500 ($14), and are sold at post offices and newsstands.

If your hotel has no machines available for guests, you'll find **telex** and **fax** facilities at the downtown branch of the post office, rue Aldringen 25, open Monday through Saturday from 7am to 7pm.

Time   Luxembourg is six hours ahead of eastern standard time in the United States (when it's 3pm in Luxembourg, it's 9am in New York, 8am in Chicago, 7am in Denver, and 6am in San Francisco). Clocks are moved ahead one hour each year at the end of March and back one hour at the end of September.

Tipping   Restaurants and hotels will almost always include a 16% service charge and the 15% value-added tax (VAT). If you've had really exceptional service you may want to add a little more, but it isn't necessary. Porters at Luxembourg's Central Station charge a fixed LF 30 (85¢) per bag.

Tourist Offices   See "Information," above.

Visas   See "Passports," above.

The City of Luxembourg

21

OFTEN CALLED THE "GIBRALTAR OF THE NORTH," LUXEMBOURG CITY IS AN attractive mixture of the remnants of Europe's unceasing battles for power in the past, Luxembourger's equally unceasing determination to create a comfortable lifestyle, and modern Europe's search for peaceful cooperation between nations.

The city of Luxembourg grew up around Count Sigefroi's fortifications on the Bock promontory. It was an astute choice of location for the count, since the 156-foot-high cliffs overlooking the Pétrusse and Alzette Valleys were natural obstacles to invading forces. In time there came to be three rings of battlements around the city, including the cliff bastions, some 15 forts surrounding them, and an exterior wall around those that was interspersed with nine more forts, three of them cut right into the rocks. Even more impressive than those above-ground fortifications were the more than 15¹/₂ miles of underground tunnels that sheltered troops by the thousands, their equipment, horses, workshops, artillery, arms, kitchens, bakeries, and even slaughterhouses! Legend says that within those tremendous rocky walls of the fortress sits a beautiful maiden named Mélusine whose knitting needles hold the fate of Luxembourg (see "Religion and Folklore" in Chapter 19).

Over the centuries, Burgundians, French, Spanish, Austrian, and Germanic Confederation forces managed to take control of the strategic Luxembourg fortifications, each in turn adding to its already-formidable defenses. Eventually its strength so frightened the rest of Europe that those fears stood in the way of Luxembourg's very freedom and independence. Finally, in 1867 the Treaty of London mandated the dismantling of all those battlements, and what you see today represents only about 10% of the original fortifications. Beautiful parks, that so distinguish the face of today's city of Luxembourg, now cover ground once occupied by strong forts.

Today it seems fitting indeed that the EEC Council of Ministers meets here, since it was Luxembourg City that gave Europe Robert Schuman, often called the "Father of Europe" because of his role in bringing together the European Economic Community.

1 Orientation

Arriving

BY PLANE Luxembourg's modern **Findel** airport (☎ 4-79-81) is 3¹/₂ miles outside Luxembourg City, with regular flights from all major European countries, the U.K., Ireland, and North America. There is also an **air taxi** (☎ 47-98-22-85; telex 2247).

A Luxair bus service from the airport into the central station costs LF 150 ($4.25). City bus service to or from the city center, the youth hostel, and the central station costs LF 35 ($1) plus LF 35 ($1) per piece of luggage, but you should know that this service can be refused during peak hours (around noon) to those carrying a mountain of luggage. Taxi fare from the airport into the city is LF 700 ($20).

BY TRAIN Luxembourg is linked by rail to most major European countries. The city **railway station,** in the southern part of town, is also the terminus for all city bus lines, and has a **national tourist information center,** currency exchange, and luggage-storage facilities. For rail or bus information, telephone **49-24-24** daily from 7am to 8pm.

What's Special About Luxembourg City

- Beautiful parks, that cover ground once occupied by strong forts.
- Restaurants with more stars per capita than any other European country.
- Place de la Constitution, with a marvelous view of the Pétrusse Valley.
- The National Museum, with the exquisite Bentinek-Thyssen Collection of works by Rubens, Van Dyck, Brueghel, Rembrandt, and others.
- Market Day, when place Guillaume is awash with the color and exuberance of country folk.
- National Day (June 23), when the grand duke reviews his troops, plus spectacular fireworks at night.

BY BUS   Luxembourg is well connected by bus to the rest of Europe, with connections to virtually every corner of the Grand Duchy. The main **bus station** is in the railway station (see above).

BY CAR   Highways A31/E25, E44, N6, and N4 provide direct motor access to Luxembourg City.

Tourist Information

The **Luxembourg City Tourist Information Office,** place d'Armes (☎ **22-28-09** or **22-75-65**), is open July to mid-September Monday through Saturday 9am to 7pm, Sunday 9am to noon; rest of year Monday through Saturday 9am to noon, 2 to 6:30pm, closed Sunday.

City Layout

MAIN SQUARES, ARTERIES, AND STREETS   The heart of Luxembourg City revolves around two main squares in the old city center. The smaller, **place d'Armes,** was once a parade ground, and this is where you'll find the tourist office, scads of outdoor cafés, and marvelous band concerts during summer months. The much larger **place Guillaume** is the setting for morning markets on Wednesday and Saturday during summer months, as well as the **town hall** and statues of William II and Luxembourg poet Michel Rodange.

Main arteries ringing the old city center are **boulevard Grande-Duchesse Charlotte** to the north, and **boulevard Franklin D. Roosevelt** to the south. The principal shopping street is **Grand Rue.** The **promenade de la Corniche** is a pleasant walkway connecting the Bock casemates to the Citadelle du St-Esprit fortifications, and there are steps, as well as an elevator, from place St-Esprit down to the **Grund** neighborhood in the valley below.

STREET MAPS   The tourist office on place d'Armes provides a free, detailed city map that lists outstanding attractions.

NEIGHBORHOODS IN BRIEF

The **old city center,** north of the Pétrusse Valley, occupies a small plateau whose squares and narrow, winding streets hold many of Luxembourg's main sightseeing attractions. A vital part of the old city is the **fish market,** an area adjacent to rue du Marché-aux-Herbes that is laced with tiny, winding streets and ancient buildings.

Across on the southern side of the valley lies the **new city center,** often called the **station area,** since it's the site of the railway and bus station, as well as masses of modern office buildings and shops. Both the pont Adolphe and Passerelle (bridges high above the valley) connect it to the old city. This is also where you'll find many of the city's most inexpensive accommodations.

One of the most attractive city areas is the **Pétrusse Valley,** a long, rambling, naturally landscaped city park. This oasis of greenery presents a unique perspective of the massive fortifications high above, a vivid reminder of their importance to the old city.

Just east of the Passerelle is the area known as **Grund,** the old working-class section of the city, and just east of the Bock is the more affluent **Clausen** neighborhood.

Pfaffenthal lies to the north, and the impressive pont Grande-Duchesse Charlotte (known to Luxembourgers as the "Red Bridge") across the Alzette Valley joins the Centre Européen, which can only be visited by special arrangement, and its **Kirchberg plateau** site to the old city.

2 Getting Around

BY BUS Because of the city's compactness, you may have little need to use the **public bus** network, which is pretty extensive but can mean a lengthy wait between buses. Bus fare (valid for one hour) is a standard LF 35 ($1), and there's a moneysaving **day ticket** at LF 140 ($4), as well as a **10-ride ticket** for LF 270 ($7.70).

BY TAXI During the day taxis charge LF 90 ($2.55) when the meter starts and LF 30 (85¢) per kilometer, with a 10% surcharge after 10pm and on weekends and holidays. Waiting time is charged at the rate of LF 10 (30¢) per minute. For 24-hour taxi service, call Benelux Taxis, rue d'Orchimont 32 (☎ **40-38-41**).

BY CAR Driving in Luxembourg is not difficult, but my best advice is to park your car and save it for day trips outside the city. You'll find that most attractions are within easy walking distance, with little real need for a car within the city.

Rentals See "Getting Around" in Chapter 20.

Parking Although street parking can present a problem in Luxembourg, there are so many parking garages sprinkled around the city that you'll seldom be far from a safe haven for your car. The detailed street map supplied by the tourist office (see above) has parking areas clearly marked, and the three most centrally located underground car parks are just off boulevard Royal near the post office, just off rue Notre-Dame, and at place du Théâtre.

Driving Rules See "Getting Around" in Chapter 20.

BY BICYCLE Luxembourg's deep valleys and high cliffs don't lend themselves to easy cycling. However, if you plan to make day trips around the city's environs, the bike is a delightful mode of transport. **Bike rental** runs about LF 400 ($11.40) per day, and if you bike out, then return by train, your bike travels for just LF 35 ($1) from anywhere in the Grand Duchy. The tourist office can supply addresses of bike-rental agencies, as well as well-planned cycling routes.

BY FOOT   Luxembourg is truly a city just *made* for walking—that's really the only way to do it justice. Few attractions will be farther apart than an easy walk through picturesque streets, and the many green spaces and parks invite either a soul-refreshing sit-down or a leisurely stroll to slow your sightseeing pace.

Fast Facts: Luxembourg City

American Express   American Express International, Inc., is located at av. de la Porte-Neuve 34, Luxembourg (☎ **22-85-55;** fax 22-85-50).

Area Code   Luxembourg's national area code (applicable to all parts of the country) is **352;** to dial to Luxembourg from within Europe, you must dial **09-352.**

Babysitters   Most hotels can recommend reliable babysitters.

Bookstores   The best source of English-language publications is Librairie Ernster, rue du Fosse 27 (☎ **22-50-77**), open from 9am to 6pm Monday through Wednesday, and 9am to 8pm Thursday through Saturday. Some English titles are also stocked at Interpress, av. de la Porte-Neuve 16, a tobacco, newspaper, paperbacks, and magazine shop that also carries a good variety of Luxembourg and European road maps; it's open from 8am to 8pm daily.

Business Hours   See "Fast Facts: Luxembourg" in Chapter 20.

Car Rentals   See "Getting Around" in Chapter 20.

Climate   See "When to Go" in Chapter 20.

Currency   See "Currency and Costs" in Chapter 20.

Dentist/Doctor   Dial **112** for referrals to English-speaking dentists and doctors.

Emergencies   Call **113.**

Holidays   See "When to Go" in Chapter 20.

Hospitals   The most centrally located hospital is the Clinique Ste-Elisabeth, av. Emile-Reuter 19 (☎ **45-11-12,** ext. 1).

Information   See "Tourist Information" in "Orientation," earlier in this chapter.

Newspapers/Magazines   The English-language *News Digest* is published weekly in Luxembourg, and English newspapers are often available at the newsstand in the railway station.

Police   Central police headquarters is at rue Glesener 58–60 (☎ **40-94-01**).

Post Office   The main post office, rue Aldringen 25, is open Monday through Friday from 7am to 8pm and on Saturday from 7am to 1pm. The branch just opposite the railway station on Station Square, place de la Gare 28, is open daily from 6am to 8pm.

Safety   See "Fast Facts: Luxembourg" in Chapter 20.

Taxis   See "Getting Around," earlier in this chapter.

Telephone/Telex/Fax   See "Fast Facts: Luxembourg" in Chapter 20.

3 Accommodations

Luxembourg's top hotels are designed to answer the needs of some of Europe's most discriminating diplomats and businesspeople, and they rank with the best luxury hostelries anywhere in the world. The city provides many small hotels in the more moderate price ranges, some with rooms above excellent ground-floor restaurants, with comfortable and attractive accommodations. One note of caution: If you plan a late arrival, *be sure to notify your hotel*—otherwise your booking may be canceled. Unless otherwise stated, all my recommended accommodations come with bath, and service and tax are both included in the price.

Expensive

IN TOWN

⭐ **Grand Hôtel Cravat**, bd. Roosevelt 29, 2450 Luxembourg. ☎ **22-19-75.** Fax 22-67-11. 60 rms, 2 suites. A/C MINIBAR TV TEL

💲 **Rates** (including buffet breakfast): LF 5,400–5,900 ($154–$168) single; LF 6,200–7,200 ($177–$205) double; LF 18,000 ($514) suite. AE, DC, MC, V.

For almost a century there's been a Hôtel Grand Cravat at this central location overlooking the Pétrusse Valley and place de la Constitution. Under third-generation management of the same family, the luxury hotel retains much of its old-world charm and maintains high standards and friendly hospitality. The guest rooms are beautifully furnished and have hairdryers and courtesy terry bathrobes, among other amenities, and some come with balconies. The hotel also offers babysitting service. Its elegant Restaurant Le Normandy is noted for fine French and seafood cuisine—the average dinner price without wine is LF 2,000 ($57) and there's a fixed-price menu for LF 1,400 ($40). Just off the lobby is the gracious Le Trianon Bar, where you'll often see Luxembourg's leading businesspeople gathered at the end of the day. Inexpensive meals are served in the traditional restaurant La Taverne (see "Dining," later in this chapter).

Hôtel le Royal, bd. Royal 12, 2449 Luxembourg. ☎ **4-16-16.** Fax 2-59-48. 150 rms, 20 suites. A/C MINIBAR TV TEL

Rates (including breakfast): LF 7,900–11,500 ($214–$328) single; LF 8,900–12,500 ($254–$357) double; LF 16,900–44,000 ($482–$1,257) suite. AE, DC, MC, V.

This pretty luxury hotel is located across from a park in the old city center. The guest rooms are beautifully decorated, and there are two good restaurants, the gourmet Le Relais Royal and Le Jardin, with terrace dining in summer. Its piano bar features live music after 6pm, and other amenities include a hairdresser, boutiques, a sauna, a solarium, massage, bodybuilding, a swimming pool, 24-hour TV news from the States, and 24-hour Reuters information service. There's also a free shuttle service to and from the airport.

NEARBY

Hôtel Inter-Continental, rue Jean-Engling 12, 1466 Luxembourg-Dommeldange. ☎ **4-37-81.** Fax 43-60-95. 240 rms. A/C MINIBAR TV TEL

Rates (including breakfast): LF 6,350–7,950 ($181–$227) single; LF 7,350–8,950 ($210–$255) double. AE, DC, MC, V.

A little out from the city center in a wooded setting to the northwest, the Inter-Continental is the epitome of luxury in its guest rooms and its public facilities. Catering to a business and EU clientele, its decor is smartly sophisticated, and there's an elegant restaurant. Other amenities include an indoor swimming pool, tennis court, and health club.

Moderate

IN TOWN

  Auberge du Châtelet, bd. de la Pétrusse 2, 2320 Luxembourg. ☎ **48-88-47.** Fax 40-36-66. 39 rms. TV TEL

Rates (including breakfast): LF 2,800–3,500 ($80–$100) single; LF 2,500–3,100 ($71–$88) double. AE, DC, MC, V.

This small hotel, owned and operated by the friendly and gracious Mr. and Mrs. Ferd Lorang-Rieck, is a longtime favorite of visiting academics and businesspeople. Its rooms are divided between two lovely old Luxembourg homes, and all have modern, comfortable, and attractive furnishings. The rustic restaurant, a local favorite, serves traditional Luxembourg specialties and a nice variety of fish and meat dishes at very moderate prices. It's near the Pétrusse Valley on the edge of the new city center.

Cheminée de Paris, rue Michel-Rodange 38, 1130 Luxembourg. ☎ **49-29-31.** Fax 40-54-44. 35 rms. TV TEL

Rates (including breakfast): LF 1,800–2,100 ($51–$60) single; LF 2,400–2,600 ($66–$74) double. AE, MC, V.

A small hotel on a quiet street south of the Pétrusse Valley in the new city center near the railway station, the Cheminée de Paris features comfortable guest rooms. Its reasonably priced restaurant (see "Dining," later in this chapter) specializes in regional favorites.

Hôtel Alfa, place de la Gare, 2561 Luxembourg. ☎ **49-00-11.** Fax 49-00-09. 100 rms. TV TEL

Rates (including breakfast): LF 2,000 ($57) single; LF 2,800 ($80) double; LF 4,000 ($114) triple. AE, DC, MC, V.

This hotel is located directly across from the main entrance of the station in a building easily identified by its cast-iron balconies and rooftop turrets. The rooms, spread over six floors, are unusually large and the bathrooms are equipped with bidet and either tub or shower. Hairdryers and irons can be borrowed at the front desk. The hotel has a brasserie named after General Patton, who set up his headquarters here in this hotel during the Battle of the Bulge. A fixed-price menu with wine is available for LF 600 ($17), and à la carte meals for around LF 2,000 ($57).

Hôtel Central Molitor, av. de la Liberté 28, 1930 Luxembourg. ☎ **48-99-11.** Fax 48-33-82. 36 rms. A/C TV TEL

Rates (including breakfast): LF 3,400 ($97) single; LF 4,400 ($125) double. AE, DC, V.

This traditional hotel is located in a handsome corner building not far from the central railway station and is very handy to good shopping, restaurants, and nightspots. Its guest rooms come with private wall safes, among other amenities, and all are nicely furnished. There's a cocktail lounge, as well as a good, moderately priced restaurant.

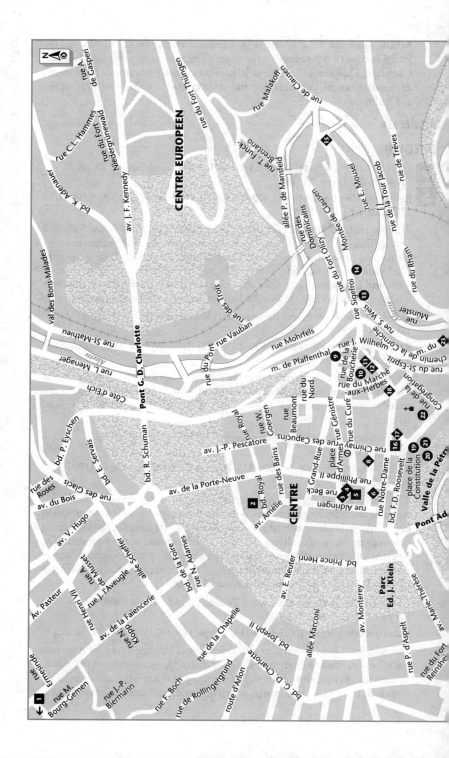

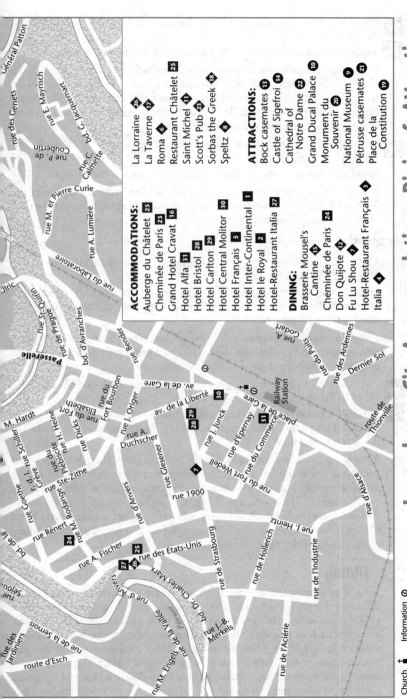

ACCOMMODATIONS:

Auberge du Châtelet **25**
Cheminée de Paris **23**
Grand Hotel Cravat **16**
Hotel Alfa **31**
Hotel Bristol **28**
Hotel Carlton **29**
Hotel Central Molitor **30**
Hotel Français **5**
Hotel Inter-Continental **1**
Hotel le Royal **2**
Hotel-Restaurant Italia **27**

DINING:

Brasserie Mousel's
    Cantine **15**
Cheminée de Paris **24**
Don Quijote **12**
Fu Lu Shou **7**
Hotel-Restaurant Français **3**
Italia **4**

La Lorraine **26**
La Taverne **17**
Roma **6**
Restaurant Châtelet **25**
Saint Michel **11**
Scott's Pub **23**
Sorbas the Greek **18**
Speltz **8**

ATTRACTIONS:

Bock casemates **13**
Castle of Sigefroi **14**
Cathedral of
    Notre Dame **22**
Grand Ducal Palace **10**
Monument du
    Souvenir **20**
National Museum **9**
Pétrusse casemates **21**
Place de la
    Constitution **19**

Church **✝■**   Information **ⓘ**

Luxembourg City Accommodations, Dining & Attractions

★ **Hôtel Français,** place d'Armes 14, 2014 Luxembourg. ☎ **47-45-34.** Fax 46-42-74. 26 rms. TV TEL

$ **Rates** (including breakfast): LF 3,000 ($85) single; LF 3,900 ($112) double. AE, MC, V.

In about as convenient a location as you could hope to find, the Hôtel Français is one of the nicer moderately priced hotels ringing place d'Armes in the heart of the old city center. The guest rooms in the small hotel are above a popular French/Italian restaurant (see "Dining," later in this chapter), and some are on the small side. All, however, have bright, modern, and comfortable furnishings.

★ **Hôtel-Restaurant Italia,** rue d'Anvers 15–17, 1130 Luxembourg. ☎ **48-66-26.** Fax 48-08-07. 20 rms. TV TEL

Rates (including breakfast): LF 2,400–2,800 ($68–$80) single or double. AE, DC, MC, V.

Not far from the central railway station in a quiet location in the new city center, this lovely small hotel has attractive and quite comfortable guest rooms upstairs over one of the city's best Italian restaurants.

Inexpensive

Hôtel Bristol, rue de Strasbourg 11, 2561 Luxembourg. ☎ **48-58-29.** Fax 48-64-80. 30 rms (22 with bath). TV TEL

Rates: LF 900–1,200 ($25–$34) single without bath, LF 1,200–2,100 ($34–$60) single with bath; LF 1,400 ($40) double without bath, LF 2,400 ($68) double with bath. Breakfast LF 200 ($5.70) extra. MC, V.

The guest rooms in this conveniently located hotel (near financial and shopping centers) are attractive and comfortable, and it's great value for the dollar for those who don't mind a short trip down the hall to the bathrooms.

★ **Hôtel Carlton,** rue de Strasbourg 9, 2561 Luxembourg. ☎ **48-48-02** or **48-17-45.** Fax 48-64-80. 45 rms (35 with bath).

$ **Rates:** LF 550–950 ($16–$27) single without bath, LF 1,300 ($37) single with bath; LF 1,300 ($37) double without bath, LF 1,600 ($45) double with bath. Breakfast LF 150 ($4.30) extra. AE, MC, V.

A real budget stretcher, this bright, friendly hotel has rather plain guest rooms, but none are lacking in comfort. Loads of good shopping and eateries are nearby, and the main bus terminal is a short walk away for good transportation to other areas of the city. Managed by Mr. Gianni, a multilingual young man who will bring the *Herald Tribune* to your breakfast table and treat you like a person, not as a number, the Hôtel Carlton is one of the best deals in its category you can find not only in Luxembourg, but in Europe. Highly recommended.

4 Dining

Some of my greatest dining pleasures in Luxembourg have come on balmy summer evenings as I've enjoyed a meal in almost any of the sidewalk cafés under the trees in place d'Armes while listening to a band concert in the square. Reflected in every face around me has been an obvious appreciation for the food and the ambience—if there's a more relaxing pastime, I have yet to find it. There are, however, many very fine restaurants down quiet little streets, in old and elegant buildings, just waiting for those times when something a little less informal is called for. It is Luxembourg's proud boast that its restaurants have earned more Michelin stars per capita than any other European country—enough said as to the quality of the cuisine! The pocket-size weekly

"City Luxembourg Agenda" booklet, available free at the tourist office, contains extensive restaurant listings.

Expensive

La Lorraine, place d'Armes 6. ☎ 47-46-20.
Cuisine: SEAFOOD/FRENCH. **Reservations:** Recommended.
Prices: Appetizers LF 750–1,100 ($21–$31); main courses LF 2,000–3,000 ($57–$85). AE, DC, MC, V.
Open: Dinner only, daily 6–10pm.

On a prominent corner of place d'Armes, this popular fish restaurant excels in preparation of its many specialties of the sea as well as the friendly efficiency of its staff. Downstairs is a casual, brasserie-style room, while elegance reigns upstairs. The bouillabaisse is a standout among seafood dishes, while there's a deft French touch to the duck with honey-vinegar sauce and the succulent lamb.

 Saint Michel, rue de l'Eau 32. ☎ 22-32-15.
Cuisine: FRENCH. **Reservations:** Required, at least a day in advance.
Prices: Average meal LF 2,500–3,400 ($71–$97). AE, DC, MC, V.
Open: Dinner only, Mon–Fri 7–11pm.

Elegance in setting, service, and classic French cuisine make this one of Luxembourg's most highly esteemed restaurants. Situated in the old part of the city near the Grand Ducal Palace, down a narrow little street, the restaurant more than justifies its high price range, and there's an excellent wine list.

Speltz, rue Chimay 8. ☎ 47-49-50.
Cuisine: LUXEMBOURG/SEAFOOD. **Reservations:** Recommended.
Prices: Appetizers LF 300–450 ($8–$12); main courses LF 800–1,200 ($23–$34); fixed-price dinner LF 1,800 ($51). AE, DC, MC, V.
Open: Lunch Tues–Sun noon–2pm; dinner Tues–Sat 6–10pm.

Set in an atmospheric old town house in the old city center, this fine restaurant serves traditional Luxembourg favorites as well as superb fish dishes (try the turbotin with hollandaise sauce). The desserts are excellent and there's a good wine list.

Moderate

Brasserie Mousel's Cantine, Montée de Clausen 46. ☎ 47-01-98.
Cuisine: LUXEMBOURG. **Reservations:** Recommended.
Prices: Appetizers LF 200–450 ($5–$13); main courses LF 480–650 ($13–$18); children's plate LF 250 ($7). AE, MC, V.
Open: Lunch Mon–Sat noon–2pm; dinner Mon–Sat 7–10pm.

Next door to the Mousel Brewery, the Cantine is an excellent place to sample regional taste treats. Rather rustic in decor, its front room overlooks the rather quaint street outside, while the back room is hung with oil paintings. Luxembourg favorites such as sauerkraut with sausage, potatoes, and ham come in large portions, served by an efficient, friendly staff.

Cheminée de Paris, rue Michel-Rodange 38. ☎ 49-29-31.
Cuisine: LUXEMBOURG/GRILLS/PIZZA. **Reservations:** Not required.
Prices: Average meal LF 1,000 ($28); plat du jour LF 280 ($8); pizza LF 250–300 ($7–$8.50). AE, MC, V.
Open: Lunch daily noon–2:30pm; dinner daily 6–9:30pm.

This attractive restaurant on the ground floor of the small hotel of the same name (see "Accommodations," earlier in this chapter) presents excellent traditional dishes, grills, and pizzas—you can eat well in almost any price range, with the assurance that quality will be high even when the price is low. It's near the railway station.

★ **Don Quijote**, rue de l'Eau 32. ☎ **22-95-38.**

Cuisine: SPANISH/SEAFOOD. **Reservations:** Recommended.
Prices: Average lunch LF 1,000 ($28); average dinner LF 2,200 ($63). AE, DC, MC, V.
Open: Wed–Mon noon–2pm; dinner Wed–Mon 7–11pm.

Steak and other beef specialties have star billing at this colorful Spanish restaurant near the Grand Ducal Palace. While you can't go far wrong with any menu choice, let me recommend especially their paella and their plateau fruits de mer (seafood platter).

★ **Hotel-Restaurant Français**, place d'Armes 14. ☎ **47-45-34.**

Cuisine: FRENCH/ITALIAN. **Reservations:** Not required.
Prices: A la carte dishes LF 470–820 ($13–$23); fixed-price meals, wine included, LF 1,250 ($35). AE, DC, MC, V.
Open: Daily 10am–11pm.

You can dine little or lot, inside or out (in good weather), at this pleasant restaurant, with its extensive à la carte menu. Stop in for light refreshments, a salad plate at lunch, or one of their excellent full-meal fixed-price menus. It's located in the heart of the old city center.

★ **Italia**, rue d'Anvers 15–17. ☎ **48-66-26.**

Cuisine: ITALIAN/CONTINENTAL. **Reservations:** Recommended.
Prices: Appetizers LF 390–580 ($11–$16); main courses LF 590–790 ($17–$22); fixed-price meal LF 900–1,800 ($25–$51). AE, DC, MC, V.
Open: Lunch daily noon–2:30pm; dinner daily 6–10:30pm.

Italian and other continental dishes are featured at this pretty restaurant in the small hotel by the same name (see "Accommodations," earlier in this chapter). There's a long à la carte menu, with outstanding specialties such as scampi al ferri and entrecôte ala peperonata.

★ **La Taverne**, in the Grand Hôtel Cravat, bd. Roosevelt 29. ☎ **22-19-75.**

Cuisine: LUXEMBOURG. **Reservations:** Not required.
$ **Prices:** A la carte dishes LF 500–760 ($14–$21); fixed-price meal LF 950 ($27) for three courses, LF 1,250 ($35) for five courses; breakfast LF 250 ($7). AE, DC, MC, V.
Open: Daily 10am–11pm.

This casual ground-floor restaurant in a leading hotel in the old city (see "Accommodations," earlier in this chapter) serves marvelous traditional dishes, a wide range of fish, meat, and chicken selections, and light salads and snacks such as herring, smoked salad, shrimp cocktail, and escargots. A personal menu favorite is the luscious chicken pie in light-as-a-feather pastry and a cream-and-mushroom sauce—at only LF 400 ($11.50). This is a great lunchtime favorite with local businesspeople, but since it has continuous service you can plan lunch early or late to avoid a possible wait. It's less crowded at dinner. They also have a very good late-breakfast menu in case you missed out at your hotel.

★ **Restaurant Châtelet**, bd. de la Pétrusse 2. ☎ **48-88-47.**

Cuisine: LUXEMBOURG. **Reservations:** Not required.
$ **Prices:** Average lunch LF 750 ($21); average dinner LF 1,200 ($34). AE, MC, V.
Open: Lunch Mon–Fri noon–2:30pm; dinner Mon–Sat 6–9pm.

This friendly little neighborhood restaurant (some 80% of the daily clientele are people who live nearby) serves an excellent lunch menu for LF 500 ($14) with main courses featuring steak, pork chops, ham, fish, and smoked fish. A sample evening meal could be entrecôte, french fries, and salad. It's located near the Pétrusse Valley on the edge of the new city center.

Sorbas the Greek, rue de la Loge 8B. ☎ **22-39-90.**

Cuisine: GREEK. **Reservations:** Recommended at dinner.
Prices: Main courses LF 390–650 ($11–$19); average meal LF 1,400 ($40). AE, DC, MC, V.
Open: Lunch Tues–Sun noon–2pm; dinner Tues–Sun 7–11pm.

To reach this lively Greek restaurant located in catacomblike premises near the Grand Ducal Palace, turn off rue de l'Eau through a stone-arched passageway and walk down a short flight of steps. Among the 28 dishes served you might choose scampi with a lemon sauce, deviled chicken, lamb chops, or pepper steak.

Inexpensive

Fu Lu Shou, rue de Strasbourg 56. ☎ **48-57-20.**

Cuisine: ORIENTAL. **Reservations:** Not required.
Prices: Main dishes LF 340–480 ($9.50–$13.50); light meals LF 130–300 ($3.60–$8.40). AE, DC, MC, V.
Open: Lunch daily noon–2pm; dinner Sun–Fri 5:30–11pm. **Closed:** Sat evening.

This is the only restaurant in Luxembourg City that serves five different types of Far-eastern food: Chinese, Thai, Vietnamese, Japanese, and Malaysian. It is located just a few minutes' walk form the Central Station. The dining room, which accommodates 60 people, is decorated with red dragons, colored lamps, and bamboo curtains. The menu du jour is a popular choice among patrons; it costs LF 315 ($8.80) and may be eaten in the restaurant or requested for take-out. Appetizers include deep-fried chicken wings, garlic prawns, bean curd (tofu), fish-ball soup, dumplings stuffed with vegetables or meat, and shredded pork, and cashew chicken —all good choices costing around LF 150 ($4.20) each.

★ **Roma,** rue Louvigny 5. ☎ **22-36-92.**
💲
Cuisine: ITALIAN. **Reservations:** Recommended.
Prices: Appetizers LF 180–250 ($5–$7); main courses LF 570–730 ($16–$21); pasta LF 300–450 ($8.50–$13). AE, DC, MC, V.
Open: Lunch Tues–Sun noon–2:30pm; dinner Tues–Sat 7–10:30pm.

In the center of the old city, this cheerful, attractive restaurant has an amazingly extensive menu. There are, for example, more than 20 homemade pasta dishes from which to choose, which includes no less than seven kinds of spaghetti! Then there's veal escalope with either white wine or marsala wine sauce and a terrific veal piccata (with lemon sauce).

Scott's Pub, Bisserweg 4. ☎ **22-64-74.**

Cuisine: ENGLISH/FRENCH. **Reservations:** Not required.
Prices: Snacks LF 75–100 ($2.15–$2.85); drinks LF 60–130 ($1.70–$3.70).
Open: Daily noon–1am.

A typical English pub, Scott's is more a place to drink and chat than to eat. The outdoor terrace is always crowded in the evenings with a jovial crowd. If you want some company, this is one place to hang.

Late-Night Eateries

The **Café Um Bock,** rue de la Loge 4–8 (☎ **46-17-15**); the **Hôtel Walsheim restaurant,** place de la Gare 28 (☎ **48-47-98**); and **L'Académie,** place d'Armes 11 (☎ **22-71-31**), stay open until midnight seven days a week.

5 Attractions

Luxembourg City is a delight for the sightseer. Most of its attractions are in a compact, easily walked area, and there are inexpensive coach tours to take you to those farther afield. My best advice, in fact, is to stash the car in a garage and take it out only when you head out to see the rest of the Grand Duchy.

The Top Attractions

The ✪ **place de la Constitution,** across from rue Chimay on boulevard Roosevelt, affords a marvelous view of the Pétrusse Valley and the impressive Adolphe Bridge that spans it. The tall **Monument du Souvenir** in the center of the square is in memory of those who have perished in Luxembourg's wars—take time to read the bronze plaque at its base that declares in four languages: "This is to remind us of the brutal act of the Nazi occupant who, in destroying this monument on October 21, 1940, turned it into a symbol of our freedom, thus sparking off the desperate resistance of a deeply humiliated nation whose only weapon was its bravery." The monument, known affectionately as "Gelle Fra," was erected in 1923. In 1958 it was partly rebuilt, but it wasn't until 1985 that it was finally restored to its original form, with funds raised by national subscription. Luxembourgers who remember those bitter years give an involuntary shudder when they pass the villa at boulevard de la Pérusse 57; it now houses the Ministry of Public Health, but from 1940 to 1944 it was the dreaded Gestapo headquarters.

The ✪ **Luxembourg casemates** may be entered from two points: The place de la Constitution entrance is to the Pétrusse casemates and the Montée de Clausen entry leads to the Bock casemates. These vast, hand-hewn fortifications are extremely moving when you realize the numbers they sheltered over the centuries. They're open from 10am to 5pm daily, March to October only, and there's an admission charge of LF 70 ($2) for adults, LF 50 ($1.40) for children.

The **Cathedral of Notre Dame,** with an entrance on boulevard Roosevelt, is a magnificent structure built between 1613 and 1621. Gothic in design, it has a Renaissance entrance on rue Notre-Dame. It holds the royal family vault and the huge sarcophagus of John the Blind, as well as a remarkable treasury (seen only on request, made to the sacristan, whose office is on the right as you enter). This is also the scene of a lovely ceremony every year on the fifth Sunday following Easter, **Octave of Our Lady of Luxembourg,** when thousands of pilgrims arrive to pray for protection by the miraculous statue of the Holy Virgin before forming a procession to carry the statue from the cathedral through the streets to altars covered with flowers. There is no charge to visit the cathedral.

Located in the oldest part of the city, the ✪ **National Museum of Art and History,** Marché-aux-Poissons (Fish Market), holds fascinating archeological, geological, and historical exhibits, as well as the exquisite Bentinek-Thyssen Collection of works of art by 15th- to 18th-century Flemish artists Rubens, Van Dyck, Breughel, Rembrandt, and others. There's no charge to visit, and hours are 10am to 4:45pm Tuesday through Saturday, and 10am to noon and 2 to 6pm on Sunday.

At the **Grand Ducal Palace,** rue du Marché-aux-Herbes, the oldest part of this interesting building, newly renovated, dates back to 1572 (its "new" right wing was built in 1741 and renovated in the 1890s). Next door is the Chamber of Deputies. The palace is normally open Monday, Tuesday, and Thursday through Saturday during the summer months at varying hours (ask for a current schedule at the Tourist Information Office), with an admission fee of LF 100 ($2.85) for adults, LF 50 ($1.40) for children. Note, however, that the palace is closed for restoration until late 1995.

The ruin of the **Castle of Sigefroi,** Montée de Clausen, is all that's left of the original fortification built in 963 by the city's founder. It's always open, and there's no charge.

The **United States Military Cemetery** is 3 miles east of Luxembourg City, where some 5,076 of the 10,000 American troops who fell in Luxembourg during World War II lie in a peaceful setting surrounded by pinewoods. There are 101 graves of unknown soldiers and airmen, and 22 sets of brothers buried side by side. The graves are arranged with no distinction by rank, religion, race, or state of origin, the only exception being the grave of Gen. George Patton because of the many visitors to his final resting place. Over the doorway of the nondenominational chapel is the moving inscription "Here is enshrined the memory of valor and sacrifice." About a mile away is the German Military Cemetery, which holds 11,000 graves.

More Attractions

The suburban areas of ✪ **Clausen, Grund,** and **Pfaffenthal,** south of the Pétrusse Valley, are among the oldest, most picturesque sections of Luxembourg, and each merits at least an hour's stroll, although be warned—you'll probably want to loiter at least half a day.

Greenbelts of dense forests ring the city of Luxembourg, giving the visitor an easy, close-at-hand escape from the rigors of city sightseeing. None is more than 4 miles from the city, and there are park and recreation areas aplenty. Take your pick: **Bambesch,** to the northwest, whose more than 8,000 acres hold play areas for children, tennis courts, and footpaths through its *Grengewald* forest; or **Kockelscheuer,** to the south, which holds a campsite, ice rink, tennis courts, and a pond for fishing. The tourist office can supply detailed information on both.

Tours

WALKING TOURS The Tourist Information Office has an excellent brochure titled **"A Walk Through the Green Heart of Europe"** to guide you through the heart of Luxembourg City. The tour can be covered in an hour, 1¹/₂ hours, or 2¹/₂ hours.

ORGANIZED TOURS One of the nicest tours is the brightly painted **miniature train** on tires that leaves twice each hour between 9:30am and sundown from Constitution Square to travel paved pathways through the Pétrusse and Alzette Valleys, and on through some of the oldest sections of town to one of the original city gates. It's called the ✪ **Luxembourg Live Pétrusse Express,** and you can simply sit back and enjoy the passing scenery, or don earphones and listen to a historical commentary (given in English, French, German, Dutch, and Luxembourgish). The 45-minute ride costs LF 220 ($6.30) for adults, half that for children (under 4, free).

There are **coach tours** of the city every morning during the summer months that run from 10 to 11:30am and visit the cathedral, the Grand Duke's Palace, the remains of the fortress, the European Center, the U.S. and German cemeteries, Radio

Television Luxembourg, and some of the most important of Luxembourg's avenues. Adults pay LF 350 ($10); children, LF 230 ($6.50). Book at the tourist office or through Segatos Tours, Bisserwee 9 (☎ 46-16-17), the day before. There are several pickup points, and the tourist office can tell you which is closest to your hotel.

A three-hour ✪ **afternoon coach tour** covers much of the same territory as the city tour above, and adds a foray to several outlying destinations, including a restored castle, the Grengewald forest, and the airport. Cost is LF 380 ($11) for adults, LF 250 ($7) for children. Book at the tourist office.

6 Special and Free Events

Saturday is ✪ **market day** in Luxembourg City, when place Guillaume is awash with the color and exuberance of country folk manning stalls filled with brilliant blooms, fresh vegetables, and a vast assortment of other goods.

If you're lucky enough to hit town during Lent, there are enough **street carnivals** and general festivity to keep you entertained without spending a farthing! A more solemn—but colorful and free—seasonal celebration is the **Octave of Our Lady of Luxembourg** procession the fifth Sunday after Easter (see "Attractions," earlier in this chapter).

On Luxembourg's ✪ **National Day,** June 23, it's great fun to watch as the grand duke reviews his troops and city streets ring with festive sounds until well after dark, when spectacular fireworks over the Pétrusse Valley ring down the curtain.

7 Sports and Recreation

There's an excellent **golf course** about 4 miles northeast of Luxembourg City. Visiting members of other clubs are welcomed, and arrangements to play should be made through the Gold Club Grand-Ducal de Luxembourg, Senningerberg (☎ 3-40-90).

For addresses and hours of play at the numerous **tennis courts** in Luxembourg, contact the Sports Ministry (☎ 43-10-14). **Squash** players should contact the Squash Club Luxembourgeois, route de Trèves 7, or the Squash d'Or club (☎ 48-01-40).

Horseback riding is popular, and visitors can arrange riding time through the Hohenhof Riding School, in Findel (☎ 34-84-56), about 4 miles outside the city.

8 Savvy Shopping

A very comprehensive guide to shopping in Luxembourg City and around the Grand Duchy is *Les Rues de la Mode et du Shopping au Luxembourg,* a glossy publication available from bookshops and some newsagents.

In the old city, upmarket shops are clustered around the **Grand Rue** and adjacent streets and **rue de la Poste.** Many of Europe's leading designers are represented in boutiques in this area, and there are good art galleries as well. In the station area, **avenue de la Gare,** which joins the Passerelle (bridge) to the new city, is lined with shops, most in the moderate price range.

Luxembourg City is filled with souvenir shops selling attractive **handcrafted items, clocks, pottery,** and miscellaneous objects. **Paintings** by artists from the Grand Duchy, as well as the rest of Europe, are featured at many fine galleries in the city of Luxembourg. **Porcelain plates,** decorated with painted landscapes of the Grand Duchy, and **cast-iron wall plaques** produced by Fonderie de Mersch, depicting castles, coats-of-arms, and local scenes, are excellent mementos of a Luxembourg visit.

9   Evening Entertainment

Luxembourg City stays up late, and there are numerous nightspots, jazz clubs, theater performances, concerts, etc. It's as true here as in any other city, however, that clubs come and go rather frequently, so your best bet is to stop by the Tourist Information Office on place d'Armes and pick up a copy of **"La Semaine à Luxembourg"** ("The Week in Luxembourg") to see what's doing during your visit. Also, pick up a copy of the *Luxembourg News*, an English-language newspaper (published every Friday), which carries listings of current happenings. **City Luxembourg Agenda** also lists leading entertainment venues in addition to restaurants.

THE PERFORMING ARTS

CONCERTS, MUSIC & DANCE   The **Municipal Théâtre,** rond-point Robert Schuman (☎ **47-08-95**), has two principal halls and from May through October presents major concert artists from around the world, as well as concerts by the local Orchestre Symphonique RTL. Year-round, there are dance (ballet and modern) performances and musical revues by visiting artists. Admission varies according to what's on, averaging around LF 650 ($18.50).

THEATER   The ◘ **Round Tower Players** presents high-caliber productions at **Théâtre des Capucins,** place du Théâtre 9 (☎ **22-06-45**). Founded by Irish expatriates Gilbert and Claire Johnston, the company tends to favor the work of Irish playwrights, and they have won universal accolades for production and acting quality. Admission runs around LF 450 ($13).

LOCAL CULTURAL ENTERTAINMENTS   May through September there are excellent open-air **band concerts** in place d'Armes, with the program varying from classical to light classics to showtunes performed by the Grand Ducal Big Band for Military Music or bands from other towns around the Grand Duchy. There are also periodic performances by local **dance** and **jazz** school students at Théâtre des Capucins (see above).

THE CLUB & MUSIC SCENE

Many of Luxembourg's deluxe hotels (such as the Royal and Inter-Continental) offer nighttime entertainment in lounges. It is, however, in the city's convivial bars and discos that nighttime musical entertainment thrives.

DISCOS   The numerous establishments concentrated in the station area tend to be a bit—and sometimes a *big* bit—sleazy, and you'll have to use your own judgment about exploring them. The leading discos in other areas at this writing (with no guarantee they'll survive until you get there) are: **Casablanca,** bd. d'Avranches 36 (☎ **49-69-40**), just south of the Pétrusse Valley, which also serves food from 8pm to 1am, with jazz featured in its basement bar and disco going on until 3am on the weekend; and **Melusina,** rue de la Tour Jacob 145 (☎ **43-59-22**), in Clausen, which alternates rock and jazz groups, who play until 3am. Both have cover charges running LF 200 to 300 ($5.70–$8.50); opening hours and days of the week vary—call ahead.

THE BAR SCENE

Two lively, interesting pubs in the old city with largely a young clientele are **Um Piquet,** rue de la Poste 30, and **Interview,** rue Aldringen 21 (☎ **46-36-65**); **Club 5,** rue Chimay 5, is a trendy bar with a good upstairs eatery. Down in the valley, Clausen is blessed with several good pubs: **Scott's,** Bisserweg 4 (☎ **22-64-74**), serves Guinness and English ale to a mostly expatriate crowd; ✪ **Am Haffchen,** Bisserweg 9, a popular watering hole across the street from Scott's, is in an atmospheric old building; **Pygmalion,** rue de la Tour Jacob 19, is a typical Irish pub; and ✪ **Malou,** rue de la Tour Jacob 57, is a favored hangout with locals as well as visitors.

MORE ENTERTAINMENT

FILMS Luxembourg cinemas show films in their original languages, sometimes with subtitles in French or Dutch. However, American and other English-language first-run movies are usually showing at any given time. Leading cinemas are: **Cinémathèque Municipale,** place du Théâtre 17 (☎ 47-96-26-44), which sometimes shows avant-garde films as well as a series of film classics; **Ciné-Club 80** and **Ciné Utopia,** both at av. de la Faïencerie 16 (☎ 47-21-09), with five screens; and **Ciné Cité,** rue Genistre 3 (☎ 4-19-70), also with five screens. Admission is LF 200 ($5.70), LF 140 ($4) on Monday.

10 Networks and Resources

FOR STUDENTS/WOMEN/SENIORS While Luxembourg has no organizations specifically focused on students, women, or seniors, the tourist office is very helpful in putting you in contact with locals in these categories.

FOR GAY MEN & LESBIANS At this writing, the only gay and lesbian organization in Luxembourg is called **Big Moon,** at rue Vauban 14 (☎ 43-17-46).

11 Easy Excursions

Day trips from Luxembourg City to virtually any Grand Duchy destination are an easy matter. Browse through Chapter 22 and let your fancy dictate your itinerary. Having said that, let me add that if Vianden, Clervaux, or other points north of Echternach have special appeal, you'll be well advised to plan an overnight at the least, two days or more at the best.

Around the Grand Duchy

22

ONCE OUTSIDE LUXEMBOURG CITY YOU FIND YOURSELF IN A MAGICAL FAIRYLAND countryside. It's as though Mother Nature drew together her most sparkling scenic beauties—high hills, rushing rivers, and broad plains—and plunked them down in this tiny corner of Europe. Mankind then came along and sprinkled her stunning landscape liberally with lovely little medieval villages, picture-book castles, wineries, and idyllic holiday retreats. If it's *romantic* Europe you're looking for, you'll find it right here inside the borders of the Grand Duchy.

SEEING THE GRAND DUCHY

Any one of the regions detailed in this chapter can be covered in day trips from a Luxembourg City base. However, a circular tour of the Grand Duchy is also an easy matter, and spending a few days in the process provides more leisurely sightseeing, as well as soul-restoring memories of relaxed travel through all that natural splendor. Good train and bus connections, as well as a wealth of walking and cycling paths, make it easy for the nondriver to ramble around all parts of the Grand Duchy. Drivers will find good roads and more-than-adequate signposting.

If time is limited, however, or your own interests dictate more time in Luxembourg City itself, there are excellent **full- and half-day motorcoach trips** to provide tantalizing glimpses of the Grand Duchy. For example, one 9:30am-to-5pm tour takes you to the Valley of the Seven Castles, the Ardennes, Vianden, and a good part of the Moselle Valley; another visits the Ardennes, the Upper Sûre Valley, Clervaux, and Vianden; and still another covers Little Switzerland, Echternach, and the Moselle Valley. Full details and booking are available at the Tourist Information Office in place d'Armes in Luxembourg, most hotels, and Voyages Henri Sales, rue du Curé 26 (☎ 46-18-18), in Luxembourg.

Do-it-yourselfers can head northwest from Luxembourg City via the **Valley of the Seven Castles** route (see Section 1 below), turn north from **Mersch** for the **Ardennes Region** (see Section 2 below) via **Ettelbruck** (with a side trip to nearby **Diekirch**), **Wiltz**, and **Clervaux.** Turning south, pass through **Vianden** en route to the **Moselle Valley** (see Section 3 below). Each of these districts can be toured from a Luxembourg City base, and mileages from the capital are listed in the routes below.

1 Valley of the Seven Castles

It's really the Valley of the Eisch River, but somehow that just doesn't have the same panache as "Valley of the Seven Castles"! And if any country in the world deserves a region designated by castles, the Grand Duchy has to be it—this little triangular area holds one of Europe's most spectacular concentrations of those grand edifices and the name is well taken.

Seeing the Valley

To explore the valley, one of the most scenically beautiful in the country, leave Luxembourg City on Highway E9 west to Steinfort (about 20km/12½ miles), the location of the first castle. The route to follow thereafter (with distances seldom more than 10km/6 miles apart) is: **Steinfort** through **Koerich** to **Septfontaines** to **Ansembourg** (with a castle high on a hill and another in the valley) to **Hollenfels** (stop at this castle, now a youth hostel, to see the beautiful carving in the Knights' Hall) to **Mersch,** the geographical center of the Grand Duchy, with a feudal castle and an interesting Roman Museum on rue des Romains that exhibits mosaics, sculpture, and wall paintings, then head north for the Ardennes Region (see Section 2, below).

What's Special Around the Grand Duchy

- A magical countryside with high hills, rushing rivers, and broad plains.
- Picture-book castles, wineries, and idyllic holiday retreats.
- Patton Square, with a nine-foot statue of the general, and the Patton Museum in Ettelbruck.
- The Museum of the Battle of the Bulge, with life-size dioramas.
- Mondorf-les-Bain, a health resort renowned throughout Europe.

TOURIST INFORMATION   There's a **Tourist Information Office** in the Town Hall at Mersch (☎ **3-25-23**), open Monday through Friday from 8:30am to noon and 2 to 5pm. In July and August, there's also an office in St. Michael's Tower (☎ **32-96-18**) with the same hours.

WHAT TO SEE & DO   The **landscape** and numerous small, picturesque **villages** will keep you enthralled as you ramble through the valley from castle to castle. Most of the **castles** you see along this route are in ruins and not open to the public. Nevertheless, perched on rocky hilltops or nestled in foothills, they are an impressive sight and by the end of the day you're sure to feel something of what life was like when those majestic piles housed powerful men and their families.

WHERE TO STAY & DINE   If possible, you should try to have lunch at one of the outstanding hotels listed below, even if you plan to return to a Luxembourg base. Failing that, if it's fine weather, take along a **picnic** (or stop and buy the makings in one of the villages you pass through) at Hunnebour, a beautiful picnic spot between Hollenfels and Mersch (its name means "Huns' Spring," and the story is that Attila's army pitched camp here).

GAICHEL/EISCHEN

The exceptional accommodations listed below make the few miles' detour west of the Steinfort/Septfontaines road well worth while.

La Bonne Auberge, 8469 Gaichel/Eischen. ☎ **3-91-40.** Fax 39-71-13. 18 rms. TV TEL

> **Rates:** LF 2,450 ($70) single or double. AE, MC, V.

This delightful small hotel on the edge of town offers attractive and comfortable guest rooms, most with good views. In the excellent restaurant, wild boar in wine sauce is a specialty in season, while fish and local meats star other times. Menu prices run LF 1,600 ($45) and up.

 Hôtel de la Gaichel, 8469 Gaichel/Eischen. ☎ **3-91-29.** Fax 3-90-37. 13 rms. TV TEL

> **Rates:** LF 3,750 ($107) single; LF 4,250 ($121) double. AE, DC, MC, V.

This small hotel is a gracious old home in the town center surrounded by green lawns and luxurious shade trees. There's a terrace for outdoor dining in good weather, and the guest rooms are attractively done up, some with good views of the surrounding countryside. Other amenities include golf and tennis facilities and a sauna. The lovely restaurant specializes in seafood, as well as expert use of meats, such as veal with rhubarb, and you can expect dinner without wine to be about LF 2,600 ($74).

2 The Ardennes Region

Spilling over from the Belgian Ardennes, this region is a treat for the nature lover and a haven for those in search of a quiet holiday. It also bears more visible scars of World War II than any other Luxembourg region because of the fierce fighting that took place here as Allied troops valiantly pushed back von Rundstedt's forces during the Battle of the Bulge.

While easily explored from a Luxembourg City base, it begs more time of travelers and provides country inns and small hotels of all price ranges and amenities for stopovers.

Seeing the Ardennes

From **Mersch** (12¹/₂ miles north of Luxembourg City), drive 31¹/₂ miles north to **Ettelbruck** and plan a short side trip east to **Diekirch** before continuing northwest 16 miles to **Wiltz** and another 10¹/₂ miles north to **Clervaux,** before heading south for 18 miles to reach **Vianden** and another 21 miles for **Echternach.** To the south lies the Moselle Valley (see Section 3, below).

REGIONAL ACCOMMODATIONS & DINING Accommodation bookings are advised as far in advance as possible because of the popularity of the Luxembourg Ardennes as a summer holiday spot.

Restaurants in the hotels listed (indeed, in most hotels in the Ardennes) reach high standards in the preparation of meals, and you'll find prices a bit lower than in Luxembourg City.

ETTELBRUCK

The most interesting thing to Americans about this crossroads of tourist routes is **Patton Square,** on the edge of town in Patton Park. The park holds a nine-foot statue of the general, and close by is a Sherman M4-A1 tank similar to the ones that arrived to liberate Ettelbruck in 1944. The **Patton Museum** in town is open daily during the summer from 10am to noon and 2 to 4:45pm; admission is LF 50 ($1.40).

DIEKIRCH

Diekirch, a 23¹/₂-mile day trip east of Ettelbruck, was a Celtic stronghold in the days before recorded history, and a relic from those long-ago ages is the **dolmen** called "Devil's Altar."

Be sure to see the ancient **church** here—it dates back to the 7th and 9th centuries and is open at no charge from 10am to noon and 3 to 5pm daily. There are Roman mosaics from as far back as the 4th century in the **Municipal Museum,** open Wednesday through Sunday from 10am to noon and 2 to 6pm, with an admission of LF 50 ($1.40). Of special interest to Americans is the **National Museum of Military History,** commonly known as the **Museum of the Battle of the Bulge,** Bamertal 10 (☎ **80-89-08** or **80-87-80**). Situated in an old brewery that's part of a 130-year-old complex, the museum presents a series of life-size dioramas depicting American and German military forces, as well as civilians in the area. There's also a diorama of the crossing of the Sauer River near Diekirch in January 1945, an event that marked the turning point in the Battle of the Bulge. All in all, it's an incredibly realistic and moving display, augmented by artifacts such as military equipment, uniforms, weapons, maps, and several large items such as a tank, artillery guns, tracked vehicles, etc. The week preceding and following Easter, and from April through October, the museum is open daily from 10am to noon and 2 to 6pm, with an admission of LF 150 ($4.20).

Where to Dine

 Hiertz, Clairefontaine 1, 9201 Diekirch. ☎ **80-35-62.**
Cuisine: REGIONAL. **Reservations:** Not required.
Prices: Average meal LF 1,500–2,000 ($42–$57). AE, MC, V.
Open: Lunch daily noon–2pm; dinner daily 7–9:30pm.

This small hotel in the town center has won wide recognition for the excellence of its kitchen, which has won it a coveted chef's toque in the Gault-Millau ratings. Local produce is featured in creative Luxembourg specialties. There are also seven recently renovated guest rooms, costing LF 2,200 ($67) single and LF 2,700 ($77) double, breakfast included.

WILTZ

You might call Wiltz schizophrenic! It's split right down the middle, with a 500-foot difference in height between "uptown" and "downtown." Wiltz is a popular holiday town, with beautiful walks in its heavily wooded setting and many sports facilities.

What to See and Do

Almost as wide a chasm in time as that 500-foot difference in height between uptown and downtown separates the 1502 stone cross at whose feet the powerful lords of Wiltz once meted out justice and the 1944 armored tank that sits at the bend of the approach road. The 12th-century **castle** ("modernized" in the 1600s) perhaps best telescopes the town's history, since its ancient left wing houses a museum commemorating the 1944–45 fighting. There is also in the town a memorial to those who died following a general strike protesting military conscription during Nazi occupation. The **Niederwiltz Church,** a Romanesque and Renaissance marvel, holds richly ornamented tombs of the counts of Wiltz, and there's a beautiful 1743 Renaissance altar made by a local artist in the Oberwiltz church.

ESCH-SUR-SURE   Twelve miles south of Wiltz, this town, a popular angling center on the River Sûre, has a picturesque ruined medieval castle, floodlit on summer evenings. But it's fishing, boating, hiking, and other outdoor sports, however, that bring tourists in such hordes.

There's a **Tourist Information Office,** rue de l'Eglise 6 (☎ **8-93-67**), open July to mid-September, Tuesday through Sunday from 10am to noon and 2 to 6pm.

CLERVAUX

The 12th-century castle at Clervaux dominates this little town, and although it was heavily damaged during World War II fighting, it has now been restored. It houses scale models of several other medieval fortresses, uniforms and arms from World War II, and Edward Steichen's moving *Family of Man* photographic essay. From July 1 to mid-September, you can visit from 10am to 5pm, and there's an admission fee of LF 150 ($4.30). Other months, hours are 1 to 5pm.

The **Tourist Information Office** is in the castle (☎ **9-20-72;** fax 92-93-12) and is open from 10am to noon and 2 to 6pm weekdays during the summer months.

Where to Stay

 Grand Hôtel du Parc, rue du Parc 2, 9701 Clervaux. ☎ or fax **9-10-68.**
8 rms. TV TEL
Rates: LF 1,350 ($38) single; LF 2,600 ($74) double. MC, V.

Located on the outskirts of town and surrounded by a beautiful wooded park, this lovely old manor house has been completely modernized inside to offer attractive and comfortable guest rooms. Public rooms have an old-world charm, and outside terraces overlook the picturesque little township of Clervaux. There's an excellent chef in the kitchen here, as well as a good wine list, and other amenities include a sauna and solarium.

$ **Hôtel Koener,** Grand-Rue 14, 9701 Clervaux. ☎ **9-10-02.** Fax 9-28-26. 48 rms. TV TEL

Rates: LF 1,700 ($48) single; LF 2,500 ($71) double. MC, V.

This century-old hotel right in the center of Clervaux faces the town square. The guest rooms are comfortable and attractive and there's a good restaurant on the ground floor. It's in one of the most convenient locations in town.

Hôtel Le Commerce, rue de Marnach 2, 9709 Clervaux. ☎ **9-10-32.** Fax 92-91-08. 54 rms. TV TEL

Rates: LF 1,800 ($51) single; LF 2,600 ($74) double.

This attractive hotel sits at the foot of the castle, and its public facilities include two good restaurants, a warm, friendly bar, and a television room. Some of the guest rooms have balconies.

VIANDEN

In 1871 an exiled writer-resident of Vianden—Victor Hugo by name—wrote of the town as a "jewel set in its splendid scenery, characterized by two both comforting and magnificent elements: the sinister ruins of its fortress and its cheerful breed of men."

What to See and Do

The **Tourist Information Office** is in the **Victor Hugo House,** rue de la Gare 37 (☎ **8-42-57**), open during the summer months, Thursday through Tuesday from 9:30am to noon and 2 to 6pm. You can tour the house for a small admission fee.

It is the mighty 9th-century **Château de Vianden,** a fortress castle perched on a hill above the town, however, that draws most visitors to Vianden. Restored to its original plans, you can now see the 11th-, 12th-, and 15th-century additions that are even more impressive than the earlier sections. The castle is open daily during the summer months from 9am to 7pm, with shorter hours other times of the year, and an admission fee of LF 110 ($3.10).

For the best view of Vianden's narrow, winding streets, the castle, and the river valley, take the **chair lift** that operates daily from 11am to 6pm for a charge of LF 140 ($4).

Vianden also has a charming folklore museum, the ✪ **Musée d'Art Rustique,** Grand-Rue 98, open daily from 9am to noon and 2 to 6pm, with an admission charge of LF 70 ($2).

Where to Stay

Hôtel Heintz, Grand-Rue 55, 9410 Vianden. ☎ **8-41-55.** Fax 8-45-59. 30 rms. TV TEL

Rates: LF 2,000 ($57) single; LF 2,800 ($80) double. MC, V.

Set in a former monastery, one of the Grand Duchy's oldest buildings, this lovely hotel has thoroughly modernized guest rooms. Rooms facing south have large balconies, and there's a cozy bar and a good restaurant.

ECHTERNACH

This little town is a living open-air museum. From its picturesque market square to its medieval walls and towers to its beautiful Town Hall (1444) to its 18th-century abbey and basilica to its patrician houses, it is the repository of the ages since St. Willibrord arrived from Northumberland as a missionary in 658 and established the abbey to make this one of the Continent's earliest centers of Christianity. If you arrive on Whit Tuesday, there's religious solemnity mixed with a liberal dose of native gaiety in the world-famous dancing parade of pilgrims from all over Europe who march and chant, sing, and dance to an ancient tune performed by bands, violinists, and other musicians in the procession. Allow yourself enough time in this enchanting town to soak up the medieval atmosphere that permeates the very air you breathe.

The **Tourist Office** is at St. Willibrord Basilica (☎ **7-22-30**; fax 72-75-24), open Monday through Friday from 9am to noon and 2 to 5pm, with Saturday and Sunday hours only in July and August.

Where to Stay and Dine

All the following hotels can be personally recommended as places to eat as well as stay.

 A la Petite Marquise, place du Marché 18, 6460 Echternach. ☎ **7-23-82.** Fax 7-23-22. 33 rms (25 with bath). TV TEL

 Rates: LF 1,200 ($34) single without bath, LF 1,500 ($42) single with bath; LF 2,200 ($62) double without bath, LF 2,500 ($71) double with bath. MC, V.

This small, homey hotel on the town square has a very good restaurant, as well as comfortable, nicely done-up rooms. Bath and toilet facilities are conveniently located to those rooms without private baths. The higher double rate is for rooms with a view of the square. Its restaurant is excellent, and there's an open-air terrace for meals in fine weather.

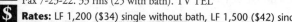 **Hôtel Bel-Air,** route de Berdorf 1, 6409 Echternach. ☎ **72-93-83.** Fax 72-86-94. 32 rms. TV TEL

Rates: LF 2,700–4,250 ($77–$121) single; LF 3,630–5,800 ($103–$165) double. AE, DC, MC, V.

About half a mile out of town, this luxury hotel (a member of Relais & Châteaux) sits in its own park overlooking the Sûre Valley, with lovely terraces, glass-walled gourmet restaurants, attractive lounges, tennis, and serene wooded walks just outside the door. Friends in other European countries have extolled the excellence of this hotel, and personal inspection bore out all their raves.

Le Petit Poète, place du Marché 13, 6460 Echternach. ☎ **7-20-72.** Fax 7-23-22. 17 rms (13 with bath). TV TEL

Rates: LF 1,200 ($34) single without or with bath; LF 1,600 ($45) double without bath, LF 1,800 ($51) double with bath. MC, V.

This is a companion hotel to A la Petite Marquise, with the same owner management and also on the town square but with a slightly different view of it. It too has a very good restaurant with outdoor dining in good weather and attractive rooms.

Where to Dine Nearby

 Melickshaff, on the Luxembourg road, Echternach. ☎ **7-22-05.** **Cuisine:** LUXEMBOURG. **Reservations:** Recommended. **Rates:** Average meals LF 400–900 ($11–$25). No credit cards.

Open: Lunch Mon–Fri noon–2pm; dinner Mon–Fri 6–9pm.

The talented chef in this attractive farmhouse restaurant half a mile from town is owner Paul Weber, whose culinary expertise turns out excellent local specialties with good-value prices.

3 The Moselle Valley and Southern Luxembourg

This vineyard and winery region of Luxembourg is set in a landscape quite different from that of the Ardennes. Your drive will take you along the flat banks of the broad Moselle River, with the gentle slope of low hills rising on both sides of the river. For miles those slopes are covered with vineyards and the riverbanks are alive with campers, boaters, and fisherpeople. Several wineries open their doors to visitors, and they'll take you on a guided tour, explain just how still wine or the sparkling varieties are made, and top off your visit with a glass of what comes out of their vats.

At the southern end of the wine district, Luxembourg's only casino and a widely recognized health spa are located at Mondorf-les-Bains. To its west, almost on the French border are Bettembourg, the mining towns of Dudelange, Kayl, and Rumelange, as well as Esch-sur-Alzette, a major trade and industrial center and Luxembourg's second-largest city.

Seeing the Regions

To explore the Moselle Valley, begin at Echternach (about 19 miles northeast of Luxembourg City), and follow the well-marked Route du Vin (Wine Route) south through Wasserbillig, Grevenmacher, Machtum, Wormeldange, Ehnen, Remich, Wellenstein, to Mondorf-les-Bains.

Exploration of the southern Luxembourg industrial and mining district is a matter of easy driving via this suggested route: Mondorf-les-Bains (about 11 miles southeast of Luxembourg City) west to Bettembourg, south to Rumelange, north to Kayl, west to Esch-sur-Alzette.

REGIONAL ACCOMMODATIONS & DINING Most tourists make the Moselle Valley tour a day trip from Luxembourg City. If you're beguiled by this peaceful part of the country, however, there are accommodations aplenty along the route. As elsewhere in the Grand Duchy, your best meals will probably be in hotels, although small local restaurants almost always take pride in the excellence of their kitchens.

WASSERBILLIG

The delightful ★ **aquarium** (☎ 7-40-40) here in this town is open daily from 10 to 11:30am and 2:30 to 6pm during the summer months (weekends and holidays only in other months), with an admission charge of LF 40 ($1.15).

GREVENMACHER

You'll find the **Caves Coopératives des Vignerons** (Cooperative Wine Cellars), rue des Caves 12 (☎ 7-51-75), open to the public May through August, daily from 9am to 5pm (by appointment other months). Cost of the tour is LF 80 ($2.30).

Interesting tours of the sparkling wine cellars of ★ **Bernard-Massard,** rue du Pont 8 (☎ 7-55-45), are given April through October, daily from 9am to noon and 2 to 6pm, with a charge of LF 100 ($2.85).

Where to Stay

 Le Roi Dagobert, rue de Trèves, 6793 Grevenmacher. ☎ **7-57-17.** Fax 75-97-92. 18 rms. TV TEL

Rates: LF 1,900 ($54) single; LF 2,600 ($74) double. AE, DC, MC, V.

This picturesque old-style hotel (a turn-of-the-century manor house) so centrally located to several leading wineries is ideal as a touring base. The guest rooms are nicely done up and there's an attractive bar as well as a very good restaurant. An outdoor swimming pool is a minutes-away walk from the hotel—a refreshing thought at the end of a sightseeing day.

Where to Dine Nearby

Chalet de la Moselle, route du Vin 35, 6841 Machtum. ☎ **7-50-46.**

Cuisine: SEAFOOD. **Reservations:** Recommended.
Prices: Average meal LF 1,100–2,600 ($31–$74). AE, DC, MC, V.
Open: Lunch Fri–Tues noon–3pm; dinner Thurs–Tues 6–11pm.

This charming chalet restaurant on the Wine Route between Grevenmacher and Ahn specializes in fish and seafood dishes—and of course it prides itself on its wine list! From the extensive seafood menu, select moules au Riesling (mussels in Riesling), sole meunière, or the wonderful cassolette de crustaces et de fruits de mer (seafood casserole) for two. There are also two lovely upstairs guest rooms that go for modest rates.

WORMELDANGE

The **Caves Coopératives des Vignerons** (Cooperative Wine Cellars), route du Vin 115 (☎ **76-82-11**), at Wormeldange are open April through October, Monday through Friday from 8am to noon and 1 to 5pm. There's a fee of LF 80 ($2.30) for the conducted tours.

EHNEN

In Ehnen, you can visit the ◼ **Maison et Musée du Vin,** route du Vin 115 (☎ **7-60-26**). Set in a beautiful old winegrower's mansion that has been lovingly restored, the museum serves as an information center for the wineries of this region, and a comprehensive exhibit explaining viniculture processes now occupies what was once the fermenting cellar. Open April through October, Tuesday through Sunday from 9:30 to 11:30am and 2 to 5pm; admission is LF 80 ($2.30).

Where to Stay and Dine

 Bamberg's Hôtel-Restaurant, route du Vin 131, 5416 Ehnen. ☎ **7-60-22.**
 Fax 7-60-56. 15 rms. TV TEL

Rates: LF 2,200 ($62) single; LF 2,900 ($82) double. AE, MC, V.

This lovely small traditional hotel (in town, overlooking the river) is also known for its very good restaurant. The guest rooms are beautifully decorated and nicely furnished, and the public rooms have a relaxed, homey feel. That restaurant, which draws locals as well as visitors, has an old-world atmosphere, with a fireplace, dark wainscoting, and exposed rafters. The cuisine is French, supplemented by Luxembourg specialties, and prices are in the moderate range. A good place to stop for lunch (noon to 2pm) or dinner (6 to 9pm) even if you're not staying in the hotel.

REMICH

The **Tourist Information Office** (☎ 69-84-88) is located at Esplanade (in the bus station) and is open in July and August, daily from 10:30am to noon and 3 to 7pm.

The **St-Martin Wine Cellars,** route du Vin 21 (☎ 69-90-91), are open April through October, daily from 9 to 11:30am and 1:30 to 5:30pm. The admission fee of LF 80 ($2.30) covers an interesting, informative tour.

Where to Stay

Hôtel Saint-Nicolas, Esplanade 31, 5533 Remich. ☎ 69-83-33 or 69-88-88. Fax 69-90-69. 40 rms. TV TEL

Rates: LF 2,550 ($72) single; LF 3,200 ($91) double. AE, DC, MC, V.

Overlooking the Moselle, on a broad promenade along the river, this large hotel has attractive, comfortable guest rooms. Other amenities include a thermal bath, whirlpool, and Turkish bath. There's a good restaurant with fixed-price menus for LF 1,000–1,800 ($28–$51), a nice bar and lounge, and a solarium.

WELLENSTEIN

The **Caves Coopératives des Vignerons** (Cooperative Wine Cellars), rue des Caves 13 (☎ 6-93-21), are open to the public with daily hours of 9 to 11am and 1 to 4pm. There's a LF-60 ($1.70) charge for the tour.

MONDORF-LES-BAINS

The ❚ **health resort** of Mondorf-les-Bains is renowned throughout Europe for its idyllic location, with vineyards and woods to the east and the Lorraine hills to the west. Its thermal baths, health center, fitness center, and recreation facilities (tennis, golf, squash, fencing, archery, horseback riding, and outdoor pool) are all excellent, and there are frequent concerts by the health-center orchestra.

For those whose preference runs to *indoor* activities, there's Luxembourg's only casino. In fact, dedicated gamblers may well want to begin their Grand Duchy tour here. The ❚ **Casino 2000** (Casino de Jeux) at Mondorf-les-Bains is open year-round (except December 23–24) from 7pm until the wee hours (they simply put it, "from 7pm on . . . "—which usually means 3am). A dress code requires jacket and tie (or turtleneck) for men and suitable dress for women, and you must have your passport to prove you're over 18. Admission is LF 100 ($2.85) per day. There's the lively **Vis-à-Vis Bar,** and the gourmet **Sulky** restaurant, which stays open until 3am and often has dinner/entertainment specials featuring first-class musical revues and leading musical artists.

The **Tourist Information Office** is located at av. Fr. Clement 31 (☎ 6-75-75), and is open from Easter to September, 9am to noon and 2 to 6pm Monday through Friday and 2 to 6pm on Saturday and Sunday.

READERS RECOMMEND

Hôtel des Vignes, route de Mondorf 29, 5552 Remich (☎ 69-91-48; fax 69-84-63). *"We really liked this hotel, which overlooks a vineyard and the Moselle. It's a quiet, scenic location, the hotel is well maintained, and the restaurant is excellent."*—Nancy Hughes, Damascus, Md. [**Author's Note:** Rates for 1995, including breakfast, are LF 2,400 ($68) single, LF 3,000 ($85) double, and LF 3,600 ($102) triple. Pets are welcome, for a weekly charge of LF 200 ($5.70). Most credit cards are accepted.]

Where to Stay and Dine

★ **Hôtel Casino 2000,** rue Th.-Flammang, 5618 Mondorf-les-Bains.
☎ **66-10-10.** Fax 66-10-10-229. 34 rms. A/C TV TEL
Rates: LF 3,200 ($91) single; LF 4,100 ($117) double. AE, DC, MC, V.

If gambling's your main interest in this little town, you just couldn't be closer to the action than this four-star, first-class hotel at the northern end of town. Guest rooms and suites are elegantly furnished; there's a gourmet French restaurant; there's ballroom dancing every Saturday and Sunday; and, of course, the casino itself is right at hand.

Hôtel du Grand Chef, av. des Bains 36, 5601 Mondorf-les-Bains. ☎ **6-81-22.**
Fax 66-15-10. 38 rms. TV TEL
Rates: LF 2,500 ($71) single; LF 3,500 ($100) double. AE, MC, V.

Set in its own private park facing the spa center, within walking distance of the casino, this gracious hotel occupies the 1852 home of a French nobleman. Although completely modernized, it has lost none of the charm and elegance of its beginnings. If it's peace and quiet you're after, take note that this hotel is a member of the Relais du Silence. There are heated terraces, and there's a good restaurant and attractive bar.

BETTEMBOURG

Originally an agricultural center, Bettembourg is today a major rail and highway junction. Its **baroque castle,** right in the middle of town, now houses a cultural center.

Children young and old will enjoy a day or half day at the ★ **Parc Merveilleux,** route de Mondorf (☎ **51-10-48**), in Bettembourg, a wonderfully fanciful entertainment park alive with fairytale characters, games, a mini-train, pony rides, miniature golf, mini-boats, a luna park, and outdoor concerts. It's open April 1 to October 15, daily from 9:30am to 7pm, and admission is LF 240 ($6.85) for adults, LF 180 ($5.15) for children.

The **Tourist Information Office,** Town Hall (☎ **51-80-80**), is open Monday through Friday from 9:30am to noon and 2:30 to 4:30pm.

RUMELANGE

If mining interests you, the **Mining Museum** in this town (☎ **56-31-21-1**) gives you a chance to experience exactly what the miners feel as they head underground, for this unusual museum is located right inside a mine—you get to ride the mine cars and see the works firsthand. Open only during summer months, daily from 2 to 5pm, with an admission charge of LF 120 ($3.40).

ESCH-SUR-ALZETTE

It's claimed that the history of this trade and industrial center can be traced back some 5,000 years. Before it evolved into a quiet rural village during medieval times, it was a Celtic settlement—that's a past totally at odds with its modern incarnation. It was not, in fact, until the mid-19th century that the discovery of a rich iron-ore seam brought prosperity and growth at such phenomenal speed. Recent years have seen a decline in the town's steel industry, and attention is once more being directed to the past, with significant renovations going on in the "old city"—*Nei Wunnen an Al Esch* (It's worth living in old Esch).

For up-to-date sightseeing information, make your first stop the **Tourist Information Office,** Town Hall (☎ **54-73-83-245**).

A highlight of your visit is almost certain to be the ⭐ **Musée National de la Résistance,** place de la Résistance (☎ **54-73-83-3**). You'll recognize it by the impressive monument at the entrance—it commemorates the courage of Luxembourgers during the World War II occupation. Exhibits inside cover the period from just before war broke out right up to the country's liberation. It's open only on Tuesday from 3 to 6pm, but an advance phone call will arrange a visit at other times.

Where to Stay and Dine

Hôtel Renaissance, place Boltgen 2, 4044 Esch-sur-Alzette. ☎ **54-19-91.**
Fax 54-19-90. 41 rms. A/C MINIBAR TV TEL

Rates: LF 2,750–3,600 ($78–$102) single; LF 3,600–4,700 ($102–$134) double. AE, DC, MC, V.

The Renaissance is as modern as Esch/Alzette is old. Housed in a traditional-style building, the hotel's interior is sleek and bright. The guest rooms are nicely appointed, and there's an informal brasserie, Le Bistroquet, as well as a very good restaurant, Le Sabayon.

Appendix

A Basic Phrases and Vocabulary

General

ENGLISH	FRENCH	DUTCH/FLEMISH
Please	S'il vous plaît	Alstublieft
Thank you very much	Merci beaucoup	Dank U zeer
Good morning	Bonjour	Dag
Good evening	Bonsoir	Goeden avond
Good night	Bonne nuit	Goede nacht
Good-bye	Au revoir	Tot ziens
Sir (or Mr.)	Monsieur	Mijnheer
Miss	Mademoiselle	Juffrouw
Mrs.	Madame	Mevrouw
Gentlemen	Messieurs	Heren
Ladies	Dames	Dames
Excuse me	Excusez-moi	Pardon
I understand	Je comprends	Dat begrijp ik
I don't understand	Je ne comprends pas	Dat begrijp ik niet
I would like a single room	Je voudrais avoir un chambre à un lit	Ik zou willen hebben een eenpersoonskamer
I would like a double room with twin beds	Je voudrais avoir un chambre à deux lits	Ik zou willen hebben een kamer met twee bedden
... with bath	... avec salle de bain	... met bad
round-trip ticket	billet aller-retour	en en weer rit
one-way ticket	billet aller	enkele reis
fare	prix du billet	prijs van het reiskaartje

ENGLISH	FRENCH	DUTCH/FLEMISH
No smoking	Défense de fumer	Verboden te roken
All aboard!	En voiture!	Instappen!
How much?	Combien?	Hoeveel?
expensive	cher	duur
cheap	bon marché	goedkoop
Where is?...	Où est?...	Waar is?...
Is this the right way to?...	Est-ce bien la route de?...	Is dit de goed weg naar?...
Town Hall	Hôtel de Ville	Raadhuis (or Stadhuis)
art gallery	musée d'art	schilderijenmuseum
airmail	par avion	Luchtpost
ordinary mail	comme lettre ordinaire	Gewone post
special delivery	comme exprès	Express
stamp	timbre	Postzegel
Monday	Lundi	Maandag
Tuesday	Mardi	Dinsdag
Wednesday	Mercredi	Woensdag
Thursday	Jeudi	Donderdag
Friday	Vendredi	Vrijdag
Saturday	Samedi	Zaterdag
Sunday	Dimanche	Zondag
one (1)	un, une	een
two (2)	deux	twee
three (3)	trois	drie
four (4)	quatre	vier
five (5)	cinq	vijf
six (6)	six	zes
seven (7)	sept	zeven
eight (8)	neuf	acht
nine (9)	neuf	negen
ten (10)	dix	tien
fifty (50)	cinquante	vijftig
one hundred (100)	cent	honderd
two hundred (200)	deux cent	tweehonderd
one thousand (1,000)	mille	duizend

Dining

Waiter!	Garçon!	Garcon!
Waitress!	Mam'selle!	Juffrouw!
Please give us the menu	Donnez-nous la carte, s'il vous plaît	Mag ik het menu zien?
Please give me the check	L'addition, s'il vous plaît	Mag ik de rekening, alstublieft
Have you included the tip?	Est-ce que le service est compris?	Service inclusief?
Please give us some ...	Servez-nous, s'il vous plaît ...	Geeft U ons wat ...

ENGLISH	FRENCH	DUTCH/FLEMISH
fried	frit	gebakken
roasted	rôti	gebraden
smoked	fumé	gerookt
stewed	en ragoût (or étuvé)	gestoofd
rare	saignant	bleu
medium	a point	half gaar
well done	bien cuit	goed gaar
pork chop	côtelette de porc	varkenskotelet
roast beef	rosbif	rosbief
chicken	poulet	kip
duck	canard	eend
goose	oie	gans
rabbit	lapin	konijn
flounder	limande	bot
herring	hareng	haring
salmon	saumon	zalm
trout	truite	forel
lobster	homard	kreeft
oysters	huîtres	oesters
shrimp	crevettes	garnalen
asparagus	asperges	asperges
beans	fèves	bonen
cabbage	chou	kool
carrots	carottes	wortelen
mushrooms	champignons	champignons
onions	oignons	uien
peas	petit pois	erwten
potatoes	pommes de terre	aardapplen
tomatoes	tomates	tomate
water	eau	water
milk	lait	melk
coffee	café	koffie
tea	thé	thee
beer	bière	bier
wine	vin	wijn
red	rouge	rode
white	blanc	witte

B   Metric Measures

Length

1 millimeter (mm)	=	.04 inches (or less than $1/16$ in.)
1 centimeter (cm)	=	.39 inches (or just under $1/2$ in.)
1 meter (m)	=	39 inches (or about 1.1 yards)
1 kilometer (km)	=	.62 miles (or about $2/3$ of a mile)

To convert kilometers to miles, multiply the number of kilometers by .62 (for example: 25km × .62 = 15.5 mi.). Also use to convert speeds from kilometers per hour (kmph) to miles per hours (m.p.h.).

To convert miles to kilometers, multiply the number of miles by 1.61 (for example: 50 mi. × 1.61 = 80.5km). Also use to convert speeds from m.p.h. to kmph.

Capacity

1 liter (l)	= 33.92 fluid ounces = 2.1 pints = 1.06 quarts = .26 U.S. gallons
1 Imperial gallon	= 1.2 U.S. gallons

To convert liters to U.S. gallons, multiply the number of liters by .26 (for example: 50 liters × .26 = 13 U.S. gallons).

To convert U.S. gallons to liters, multiply the number of gallons by 3.79 (for example: 12 gallons × 3.79 = 45.48 liters).

To convert Imperial gallons to U.S. gallons, multiply the number of Imperial gallons by 1.2 (for example: 8 Imperial gallons × 1.2 = 9.6 U.S. gallons).

To convert U.S. gallons to Imperial gallons, multiply the number of U.S. gallons by .83 (for example: 12 U.S. gallons × .83 = 9.95 Imperial gallons).

Weight

1 gram (g)	= .035 ounces (or about a paperclip's weight)
1 kilogram (kg)	= 35.2 ounces = 2.2 pounds
1 metric ton	= 2,205 pounds = 1.1 short ton

To convert kilograms to pounds, multiply the number of kilograms by 2.2 (for example: 75 kg × 2.2 = 165 lb.).

To convert pounds to kilograms, multiply the number of pounds by .45 (for example: 90 lb. × .45 = 40.5kg).

Area

1 hectare (ha)	= 2.47 acres
1 square kilometer (km²)	= 247 acres = .39 square miles

To convert hectares to acres, multiply the number of hectares by 2.47 (for example: 20ha × 2.47 = 49.4 acres).

To convert acres to hectares, multiply the number of acres by .41 (for example: 40 acres × .41 = 16.4ha).

To convert square kilometers to square miles, multiply the number of square kilometers by .39 (for example: 150km² × .39 = 58.5 square miles).

To convert square miles to square kilometers, multiply the number of square miles by 2.6 (for example: 80 square miles × 2.6 = 208km²).

Temperature

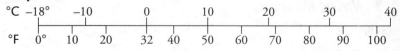

To convert degrees Fahrenheit to degrees Celsius, subtract 32 from °F, multiply by 5, then divide by 9 (example: 85°F −32 × 5 ÷ 9 = 29.4°C).

To convert degrees Celsius to degrees Fahrenheit, multiply °C by 9, divide by 5, and add 32 (example: 20°C × 9 ÷ 5 + 32 = 68°F).

Index

HOLLAND

LUXEMBOURG

Now Save Money On All Your Travels By Joining
FROMMER'S™ TRAVEL BOOK CLUB
The World's Best Travel Guides
At Membership Prices!

Frommer's Travel Book Club is your ticket to successful travel! Open up a world of travel information and simplify your travel planning when you join ranks with thousands of value-conscious travelers who are members of the Frommer's *Travel Book Club*. Join today and you'll be entitled to all the privileges that come from belonging to the club that offers you travel guides for less to more than 100 destinations worldwide. **Annual membership is only $25.00 (U.S.) or $35.00 (Canada/Foreign).**

The Advantages of Membership:

1. Your choice of **three free** books (any **two** Frommer's Comprehensive Guides, Frommer's $-A-Day Guides, Frommer's Walking Tours or Frommer's Family Guides—plus **one** Frommer's City Guide, Frommer's City $-A-Day Guide or Frommer's Touring Guide).

2. Your own subscription to the **TRIPS & TRAVEL** quarterly newsletter.

3. You're entitled to a **30% discount** on your order of any additional books offered by the club.

4. You're offered (at a small additional fee) our **Domestic Trip-Routing Kits.**

Our **Trips & Travel** quarterly newsletter offers practical information on the best buys in travel, the "hottest" vacation spots, the latest travel trends, world-class events and much, much more.

Our **Domestic Trip-Routing Kits** are available for any North American destination. We'll send you a detailed map highlighting the best route to take to your destination—you can request direct or scenic routes.

Here's all you have to do to join:
Send in your membership fee of $25.00 ($35.00 Canada/Foreign) with your name and address on the form below along with your selections as part of your membership package to the address listed below. Remember to check off your three free books.

If you would like to order additional books, please select the books you would like and send a check for the total amount (please add sales tax in the states noted below), plus $2.00 per book for shipping and handling ($3.00 Canada/Foreign) to the address listed below.

FROMMER'S TRAVEL BOOK CLUB
P.O. Box 473
Mt. Morris, IL 61054-0473
(815) 734-1104

[ ] **YES!** I want to take advantage of this opportunity to join Frommer's Travel Book Club.

[ ] My check is enclosed. Dollar amount enclosed_____*
(all payments in U.S. funds only)

Name _____

Address _____

City _____ State _____ Zip _____

Phone (   ) _____ (In case we have a question regarding your order).

All orders must be prepaid.

To ensure that all orders are processed efficiently, please apply sales tax in the following areas: CA, CT, FL, IL, IN, NJ, NY, PA, TN, WA and CANADA.

*With membership, shipping & handling will be paid by Frommer's Travel Book Club for the three FREE books you elect as part of your membership. Please add $2.00 per book for shipping & handling for any additional books purchased $3.00 Canada/Foreign).

Allow 4-6 weeks for delivery for all items. Prices of books, membership fee, and publication dates are subject to change without notice. All orders are subject to acceptance and availability.

Please send me the books checked below:

FROMMER'S COMPREHENSIVE GUIDES

*(Guides listing facilities from budget to deluxe,
with emphasis on the medium-priced)*

	Retail Price	Code		Retail Price	Code
☐ Acapulco/Ixtapa/Taxco, 2nd Edition	$13.95	C157	☐ Jamaica/Barbados, 2nd Edition	$15.00	C149
☐ Alaska '94-'95	$17.00	C131	☐ Japan '94-'95	$19.00	C144
☐ Arizona '95 (Avail. 3/95)	$14.95	C166	☐ Maui, 1st Edition	$14.00	C153
☐ Australia '94-'95	$18.00	C147	☐ Nepal, 2nd Edition	$18.00	C126
☐ Austria, 6th Edition	$16.95	C162	☐ New England '95	$16.95	C165
☐ Bahamas '94-'95	$17.00	C121	☐ New Mexico, 3rd Edition (Avail. 3/95)	$14.95	C167
☐ Belgium/Holland/ Luxembourg '93-'94	$18.00	C106	☐ New York State '94-'95	$19.00	C133
☐ Bermuda '94-'95	$15.00	C122	☐ Northwest, 5th Edition	$17.00	C140
☐ Brazil, 3rd Edition	$20.00	C111	☐ Portugal '94-'95	$17.00	C141
☐ California '95	$16.95	C164	☐ Puerto Rico '95-'96	$14.00	C151
☐ Canada '94-'95	$19.00	C145	☐ Puerto Vallarta/ Manzanillo/Guadalajara '94-'95	$14.00	C135
☐ Caribbean '95	$18.00	C148			
☐ Carolinas/Georgia, 2nd Edition	$17.00	C128	☐ Scandinavia, 16th Edition (Avail. 3/95)	$19.95	C169
☐ Colorado, 2nd Edition	$16.00	C143	☐ Scotland '94-'95	$17.00	C146
☐ Costa Rica '95	$13.95	C161	☐ South Pacific '94-'95	$20.00	C138
☐ Cruises '95-'96	$19.00	C150	☐ Spain, 16th Edition	$16.95	C163
☐ Delaware/Maryland '94-'95	$15.00	C136	☐ Switzerland/ Liechtenstein '94-'95	$19.00	C139
☐ England '95	$17.95	C159	☐ Thailand, 2nd Edition	$17.95	C154
☐ Florida '95	$18.00	C152	☐ U.S.A., 4th Edition	$18.95	C156
☐ France '94-'95	$20.00	C132	☐ Virgin Islands '94-'95	$13.00	C127
☐ Germany '95	$18.95	C158	☐ Virginia '94-'95	$14.00	C142
☐ Ireland, 1st Edition (Avail. 3/95)	$16.95	C168	☐ Yucatan, 2nd Edition	$13.95	C155
☐ Italy '95	$18.95	C160			

FROMMER'S $-A-DAY GUIDES

(Guides to low-cost tourist accommodations and facilities)

	Retail Price	Code		Retail Price	Code
☐ Australia on $45 '95-'96	$18.00	D122	☐ Israel on $45, 15th Edition	$16.95	D130
☐ Costa Rica/Guatemala/ Belize on $35, 3rd Edition	$15.95	D126	☐ Mexico on $45 '95	$16.95	D125
☐ Eastern Europe on $30, 5th Edition	$16.95	D129	☐ New York on $70 '94-'95	$16.00	D121
☐ England on $60 '95	$17.95	D128	☐ New Zealand on $45 '93-'94	$18.00	D103
☐ Europe on $50 '95	$17.95	D127	☐ South America on $40, 16th Edition	$18.95	D123
☐ Greece on $45 '93-'94	$19.00	D100			
☐ Hawaii on $75 '95	$16.95	D124	☐ Washington, D.C. on $50 '94-'95	$17.00	D120
☐ Ireland on $45 '94-'95	$17.00	D118			

FROMMER'S CITY $-A-DAY GUIDES

	Retail Price	Code		Retail Price	Code
☐ Berlin on $40 '94-'95	$12.00	D111	☐ Madrid on $50 '94-'95	$13.00	D119
☐ London on $45 '94-'95	$12.00	D114	☐ Paris on $50 '94-'95	$12.00	D117

FROMMER'S FAMILY GUIDES
*(Guides listing information on kid-friendly
hotels, restaurants, activities and attractions)*

	Retail Price	Code		Retail Price	Code
☐ California with Kids	$18.00	F100	☐ San Francisco with Kids	$17.00	F104
☐ Los Angeles with Kids	$17.00	F103	☐ Washington, D.C. with Kids	$17.00	F102
☐ New York City with Kids	$18.00	F101			

FROMMER'S CITY GUIDES
*(Pocket-size guides to sightseeing and tourist
accommodations and facilities in all price ranges)*

	Retail Price	Code		Retail Price	Code
☐ Amsterdam '93-'94	$13.00	S110	☐ Montreal/Quebec City '95	$11.95	S166
☐ Athens, 10th Edition (Avail. 3/95)	$12.95	S174	☐ Nashville/Memphis, 1st Edition	$13.00	S141
☐ Atlanta '95	$12.95	S161	☐ New Orleans '95	$12.95	S148
☐ Atlantic City/Cape May, 5th Edition	$13.00	S130	☐ New York '95	$12.95	S152
☐ Bangkok, 2nd Edition	$12.95	S147	☐ Orlando '95	$13.00	S145
☐ Barcelona '93-'94	$13.00	S115	☐ Paris '95	$12.95	S150
☐ Berlin, 3rd Edition	$12.95	S162	☐ Philadelphia, 8th Edition	$12.95	S167
☐ Boston '95	$12.95	S160	☐ Prague '94-'95	$13.00	S143
☐ Budapest, 1st Edition	$13.00	S139	☐ Rome, 10th Edition	$12.95	S168
☐ Chicago '95	$12.95	S169	☐ St. Louis/Kansas City, 2nd Edition	$13.00	S127
☐ Denver/Boulder/Colorado Springs, 3rd Edition	$12.95	S154	☐ San Diego '95	$12.95	S158
☐ Dublin, 2nd Edition	$12.95	S157	☐ San Francisco '95	$12.95	S155
☐ Hong Kong '94-'95	$13.00	S140	☐ Santa Fe/Taos/ Albuquerque '95 (Avail. 2/95)	$12.95	S172
☐ Honolulu/Oahu '95	$12.95	S151			
☐ Las Vegas '95	$12.95	S163	☐ Seattle/Portland '94-'95	$13.00	S137
☐ London '95	$12.95	S156	☐ Sydney, 4th Edition	$12.95	S171
☐ Los Angeles '95	$12.95	S164	☐ Tampa/St. Petersburg, 3rd Edition	$13.00	S146
☐ Madrid/Costa del Sol, 2nd Edition	$12.95	S165	☐ Tokyo '94-'95	$13.00	S144
☐ Mexico City, 1st Edition	$12.95	S170	☐ Toronto '95 (Avail. 3/95)	$12.95	S173
☐ Miami '95-'96	$12.95	S149	☐ Vancouver/Victoria '94-'95	$13.00	S142
☐ Minneapolis/St. Paul, 4th Edition	$12.95	S159	☐ Washington, D.C. '95	$12.95	S153

FROMMER'S WALKING TOURS

(Companion guides that point out the places
and pleasures that make a city unique)

	Retail Price	Code		Retail Price	Code
☐ Berlin	$12.00	W100	☐ New York	$12.00	W102
☐ Chicago	$12.00	W107	☐ Paris	$12.00	W103
☐ England's Favorite Cities	$12.00	W108	☐ San Francisco	$12.00	W104
☐ London	$12.00	W101	☐ Washington, D.C.	$12.00	W105
☐ Montreal/Quebec City	$12.00	W106			

SPECIAL EDITIONS

	Retail Price	Code		Retail Price	Code
☐ Bed & Breakfast Southwest	$16.00	P100	☐ National Park Guide, 29th Edition	$17.00	P106
☐ Bed & Breakfast Great American Cities	$16.00	P104	☐ Where to Stay U.S.A., 11th Edition	$15.00	P102
☐ Caribbean Hideaways	$16.00	P103			

FROMMER'S TOURING GUIDES

(Color-illustrated guides that include walking tours,
cultural and historic sites, and practical information)

	Retail Price	Code		Retail Price	Code
☐ Amsterdam	$11.00	T001	☐ New York	$11.00	T008
☐ Barcelona	$14.00	T015	☐ Rome	$11.00	T010
☐ Brazil	$11.00	T003	☐ Tokyo	$15.00	T016
☐ Hong Kong/Singapore/ Macau	$11.00	T006	☐ Turkey	$11.00	T013
☐ London	$13.00	T007	☐ Venice	$ 9.00	T014

Please note: If the availability of a book is several months away, we may
have back issues of guides to that particular destination.
Call customer service at (815) 734-1104.